THE ART OF INTERPRETATIVE SPEECH

THE ART OF INTERPRETATIVE SPEECH

Principles and Practices of Effective Reading

Fourth Edition

CHARLES H. WOOLBERT

Late of the University of Iowa

and

SEVERINA E. NELSON

University of Illinois

New York

APPLETON-CENTURY-CROFTS, INC.

Editor's Foreword to Fourth Edition

Of making textbooks there is no end, but their average life span is brief indeed. Some flare into meteoric popularity only to fall back suddenly into the limbo of the forgotten. Others grow steadily in the esteem of teachers as the decades come and go. *The Art of Interpretative Speech* has established itself in this second group. When a textbook has retained its vitality for a period of thirty years, its longevity raises the presumption that it has unusual intrinsic merit and that it has been making a substantial contribution to its field. So it is with this book.

My service as editor of this fourth edition has been a labor of love. For many years, Charles Woolbert was my close professional associate and my dear personal friend. His name long since has been indelibly inscribed on the shining scroll of the few truly great scholars and teachers who have brought dignity and distinction to speech as an academic discipline. Much of our clearest light and most profound understanding have flowed from what he wrote and taught. His original thinking and his brilliant dialectic have become the priceless heritage of all teachers of speech everywhere. His writings constitute a part of his enduring monument. To have played even a minor role in maintaining this memorial in good repair gives me sincere satisfaction.

In my judgment no one is better qualified than Severina Nelson to keep this text abreast of the times, while preserving the spirit and the essence of the original. Her years of association with Woolbert provide her with a sure sense of what her collaborator would wish to have done in fitting the book to changing conditions and needs in the field of literary interpretation. I believe that she has done a remarkably effective job in this latest revision which is permeated with the genuine Woolbertian philosophy of speech education in general and interpretative speech in particular and yet is as modern as next year's automobile. The best features of previous editions have been reactivated and enriched with fresh and interesting materials, including many new literary selections for study and practice.

I am happy to give this work my enthusiastic endorsement. I bespeak and predict for it a continuation of the widespread favor and patronage which preceding editions have enjoyed.

Andrew Thomas Weaver

PREFACE

One cannot lightly revise the work of a man who is generally regarded as one of the most original and challenging writers in the field of speech. These pages, packed with Woolbertian philosophy, seem to enjoy an unbelievably enduring and ever increasing popularity as they approach their thirtieth year. This fact reinforces the solidity of Woolbert's theory that if students come into contact with the finest literature and assimilate it into their own experience, they will derive the pleasure of communicating it to someone else, *provided that they master the use of their vocal tools.* Woolbert's basic belief that the printed page has no single invariable meaning but is meaningful to each person according to his own experiential background is reiterated in some form in every chapter. This point of view no doubt has contributed to the long life of the book; it gives students an opportunity to express and communicate their innermost thoughts and reactions about literature—an experience which is always stimulating and enriching. The techniques involved in the interpretation of worthwhile literature are designed to assist in developing good taste and judgment.

In the current revision, the former chapters "Emotional Setting" and "Logical Details" have been expanded and retitled "The Author" and "The Author's Meaning," respectively. Interest has been centered on the personality and philosophy of authors by short discussions of well-known writers. In many instances, possible meanings have been *suggested* to provide the student with cues for further study. The four chapters on vocal quality, force, tempo, and pitch now contain fuller explanation of these elements and have been enriched by numerous new selections from contemporary writers.

Excerpts from critical evaluations of literature should prove stimulating to the student in the analysis of meaning. There are new literary selections in the chapters on choral interpretation and radio interpretation, and the latter includes some discussion of the differences in radio and television techniques. The mechanical drills and exercises for vocal and articulatory improvement have been amplified and brought together in an appendix for the greater convenience of those who need to work on particular vocal and articulatory deficiencies.

Each of the exercises throughout the text is preceded by an explanation of the selections included in it; in many cases, interpretative high points are suggested. Listening projects have been added to increase the student's sensitivity in evaluating voices and, indirectly, in establishing criteria of good taste. There is no better way for the student to study emotional values in the voice than to listen, not once but many times, to the voices of interpretative artists. We call this procedure "auditory training," but perhaps T. S. Eliot's phrase "auditory imagination" may be more motivating to both the student and the teacher.

Above all, this revision, like the previous ones, preserves Woolbert's original objectives of unleashing the student's innate abilities and then helping him establish control over his powers of interpretation through the development of understanding and appreciation.

S. E. N.

CONTENTS

Part I
FUNDAMENTAL PRINCIPLES
OF INTERPRETATION

CHAPTER 1

Interpretation as an Art

THE NATURE OF INTERPRETATION

Interpretation and Reading

The terms *interpretation* and *reading* have been used so interchangeably that many people consider them synonymous. Although this usage is thoroughly acceptable and in good standing, for textbook purposes it is necessary to differentiate the two terms. Reading is too frequently thought of as no more than the distinct and accurate pronunciation of words, phrases, and sentences so that everyone may hear and understand them, as, for example, the droning of the minutes by the secretary of the meeting or of the bill by the clerk of the legislature. Other situations could be mentioned in which intelligent reading from the page has been called for, but in which, instead, there has been the same lifeless, unimpressive mumbling of words without sense or feeling.

Dull speakers are often dull readers. Surprisingly enough, however, lively speakers also are often dull readers. We have all seen an excellent speaker of fine carriage, with effective voice, with impressive command of ideas and language, in full swing before his audience. Everyone listens intently to what he has to say. In the progress of his discourse, he finds it necessary to read a passage from a pamphlet, a document, or a book. In many cases, his reading is unintelligible; after the speaker has mumbled two or three sentences, no one knows what he is trying to get over, and, after a few more sentences, no one cares. Time and time again in a deliberative body, an interesting man who is also an interesting speaker suddenly becomes dull because he reads from a paper like a frightened schoolboy.

In the pulpit, this experience is also common. At every service, the preacher has a chance to deliver two impressive sermons; at least one can be superlatively good, because it is from a superlatively good source—the Scriptures. Any preacher who can read the Scriptures with intelligent and vivacious interpretation can preach a sermon that will probably outlive anything he has to say in his own sermon. The regular Sunday morning reading of a passage from the Bible by some men is a tremendously impressive ceremony. We have heard ministers whose effectiveness in interpreting the Bible furnishes the best part of the service. Yet too many times, when we go to church, we hear a man in the pulpit mouthing and mutilating the beauty of the literature that the prophets and teachers of old have given us.

Very often, too, college professors read extensively in the course of their lectures, and not always well! Many men who are charming conversationalists and even interesting public speakers are painfully adept in putting their classes to sleep when trying to convey meaning from the printed page. They call off words, and words only, and they give their students nothing that savors of an interesting interpretation of the thoughts and attitudes which constitute the essential meanings.

The reader should interpret the full meaning of what he reads and should also make his reading satisfactory and pleasurable to his audience. Unfortunately, as we have noted, this is frequently not done. Consequently, although many of us can remember certain "readers" whom we have enjoyed immensely, we can also remember others whose reading was far from effective.

When you *interpret,* however, you are attempting to re-create for your audience, as nearly as you can, real experience as revealed by the author. You are interested in making the meaning impressive and in thus moving your audience not only to understand but to feel. Therefore, in order to avoid confusion about the kind of reading expected of the interpreter, we intend to use the term *interpretation* rather than *reading.* In this way, we can discard all lifeless and unintelligent reading as not belonging to our study and talk in terms of re-creating the full, rich meaning for the audience, which must always be the paramount purpose of the interpreter.

The Standard of Interpretation

The study of interpretative speech should make the student realize the constant need for the kind of communicativeness that is produced by effective projection of the voice and body. *Projection* should be understood as the integration of voice and bodily movement to meet the expectations of the audience. The interpreter's aim should be to stir up the meaning of the literature for the audience through vital expression. This is the *standard* of the interpreter.

Yet some might ask, "Do you wish to advocate elaborate and fancy elocution in the mere reading of a report or a scientific paper or an essay on commonplace things?" Lest we get into misconceptions here, let us make clear our terminology and our intentions. Of course, no one is advising that a senator in reading a statement of a governmental policy should try to be a Charles Laughton or a Tyrone Power; we can plead for a vital interpretation of what is written without asking for something nonsensical. By the term *interpretation,* we mean a presentation that is eminently sensible. Again, we emphasize that interpretation should stir up richness of meaning for the listeners. Manifestly, the ideas a writer intended to put on the printed page meant something to him; he thought them important enough to write them down. The man interpreting them also thinks them important enough to pass on to others. It is sensible to say, therefore, that the performer must find some way to integrate his voice and his body action to show his auditors what the ideas are and to prove that they are as important as he and the writer consider them.

Accomplishment of these ends does not usually demand great histrionic display, vocal gymnastics, or rare impersonative technique; but the reader of any matter-of-fact statement should at least give the impression that he is interested in what he is reading and believes it worthy of the attention of his audience. He should be as active and energetic and urgent as when he is pressing his own ideas upon his hearers. If there are ideas to convey, and if they are worth presenting, they must be re-created as vital truth—they must be interpreted.

By the constant use of the term *interpretation* then, we assume an obligation: we must hold ourselves to an artistic standard of effectiveness. He who genuinely interprets must re-present the thought and feeling that he believes the author wished to present. Anything less than a *full charge of meaning*, rich and varied, does not measure up to the standard of *effectiveness* implied in the term *interpretation*.

Technique Involved in Interpretation, Impersonation, Acting

Before launching into the actual study and practice of interpretation, we should determine the ways in which interpretation, impersonation, and acting differ from each other. These three sister arts are easily differentiated on the basis of the amount of activity and projection each requires. The interpreter does not seek as much "audience-contact"—or, if you will, as much "directness"—as the public speaker; but the interpreter recognizes his audience in a more direct manner than either the impersonator or the actor. Consequently, in interpretation, there is a balance of direct communicativeness and projection—an interplay of the two. Impersonation is more indirect and involves a more complete characterization; that is, the impersonator uses more facial expression and bodily gesture and exercises greater liberty in moving about the platform. The impersonator is trying always to imitate a *person*. We never speak of the impersonation of a poem. Acting is the least direct of these three arts. Artistic acting calls for "esthetic distance" between the performer and the audience. Seldom does the modern actor try to establish direct contact with the audience. Acting involves complete identification with the character; it uses the whole man—voice, arms, body, face—integrated into a meaningful and convincing character. In addition, acting employs a blending of costuming, lighting, stage settings, properties, stage movement, rhythm, and adaptation to a group of people on the stage to produce a unified mood or scene. It is the most complete form of expression dealing with the interpretation of "lines."

Any attempt to make the audience believe they see and hear somebody not yourself is impersonation, whether it is an old man with a weak back, a tittering schoolgirl, a sophisticated playboy, or a person of foreign or provincial speech. If you hope to make your audience think you are a rheumatic farmer who is angry because someone has cheated him, your impersonation is ineffective unless you go through the visible actions—postures, gestures, and voice—that such a man would use. If you are acting such a character in a play, you will be dressed appropriately and you will move about the stage to take your part in the ensemble. If, on the other hand, you are only *interpreting* such a person, with no intention of making the audience feel that they both hear and see the man, you confine yourself chiefly to effective vocal intonations and quality, with mere suggestions of body set, gesture, and facial expression.

There are, in fact, no hard and fast lines of demarcation among these three arts, for the problem of how much projection and amplification of the voice and body are necessary is solved always in terms of the audience and the intention of the performer. In a pulpit on a Sunday morning, you would not set a stage and act on it, and you would be—or should be—hesitant about indulging in impersonation. You would be more disposed to confine your message to the meaning you could carry through the voice, aided by an adequate projection from the rest of the body. In open places and very large auditoriums, however, before thousands of people, you would be strongly tempted to exaggerate your facial expressions and bodily movements or to impersonate in order to hold the visual attention of the audience. On the other hand, a teacher of English, bringing out the meaning of a poem by Tennyson or a passage from Shakespeare, will use no acting, no impersonation, but will interpret with a maximum of vocal skill plus suggestions of emotional reactions through the facial muscles. A vaudeville artist will impersonate and come very close to acting. A chairman of a committee in a conference or deliberative body will confine himself wholly to vocal emphasis and alacrity in making clear and unambiguous the documentary matter he is presenting.

And what of the participant in reading contests? He should *interpret,* unless everyone concerned has agreed that the contestants are to impersonate. He should *not* act. His interpretation should reflect sincerity instead of studied imitation. The exhibitionism of the typical contest reader certainly originates with the teacher who has not been trained in purposeful interpretation and, consequently, does not know what constitutes good taste, not only in interpretation but also in impersonation. The difference between the sincere artistic interpreter and the wildly gesticulating contestant can be likened to the difference between professional acting and the exaggeration seen in variety shows. The vaudeville artist, however, is honest about his efforts. He admits by his broad actions and his byplay that he is not pretending to be an actor; he shares his secret with his audience. The contestant who insists on galloping all over the stage trying to assume the positions of five men and two women certainly should be rewarded for his unusual acrobatic feat but should not expect a share in the admiration of interpreters who prefer sincerity and purposeful meaning to gymnastics, contortions, and slapstick maneuvers. The day is passing, we hope, for the costumed interpreter, the musically minded interpreter who improvises at the piano as he pours out a "reading" of "Trees," or the co-ed who waltzes all over the stage as she gasps out Dorothy Parker's "The Waltz." Most thoughtful audiences are embarrassed by the histrionics of this type of "reader" or contestant. On the other hand, too many contestants look askance at the interpreter who reads with meaning and good taste and avoids mimicry and display.

Many strange and wonderful things have been heard from interpreters who have tried Shakespeare's famous dagger scene from *Macbeth.* True, the scene does lend itself to imaginative flights; there are so many things that can be done with the hands and eyes. Perhaps it is an injustice to Shakespeare to do anything but *act* the lines, because he wrote them for an actor. It will be difficult to stay within the confines of interpretation; it will be easy to use impersonation. But even here, you will find the necessity—because the lines are so written—to act out every gesture or movement before refining for interpretation.

IS THIS A DAGGER?

MACBETH
 Is this a dagger which I see before me,
 The handle toward my hand? Come, let me clutch thee.
 I have thee not, and yet I see thee still.
 Art thou not, fatal vision, sensible
 To feeling as to sight? or art thou but
 A dagger of the mind, a false creation,
 Proceeding from the heat-oppressèd brain?
 I see thee yet, in form as palpable
 As this which now I draw.
 Thou marshall'st me the way that I was going,
 And such an instrument I was to use.
 Mine eyes are made the fools o' the other senses,
 Or else worth all the rest. I see thee still,
 And on thy blade and dudgeon gouts of blood,
 Which was not so before. There's no such thing.
 It is the bloody business which informs
 Thus to mine eyes.
                          WILLIAM SHAKESPEARE, *Macbeth*

The following passage from Shakespeare will be simpler for
the interpreter because he can keep most of his visible activity
confined to the facial expression; the impersonator, again, will
find it effective to assume a particular posture, to hunch the
shoulders, to use the hands in dramatic tension, to glance askance
at the "fawning publican," perhaps even to spit upon his enemy
or in his direction. We hope the interpreter can demonstrate more
control as he expresses the hatred Shylock feels:

IF I CAN CATCH HIM

SHYLOCK
 How like a fawning publican he looks!
 I hate him for he is a Christian;
 But more for that in low simplicity
 He lends out money gratis, and brings down
 The rate of usance here with us in Venice.
 If I can catch him once upon the hip,
 I will feed fat the ancient grudge I bear him.
 He hates our sacred nation; and he rails,

Even there where merchants most do congregate,
On me, my bargains, and my well-won thrift,
Which he calls interest. Cursed be my tribe,
If I forgive him!
                    William Shakespeare, *The Merchant of Venice*

Problems Involved in Interpretation

If we are to follow the above standard of effectiveness in interpretation, we must not use the hit-or-miss, trial-and-error method. Our method must consist of a sure technique. We must know how to start, what tools to use, and how to use them; we must know the deviations, the turns and twists, the danger signs on the road we are to follow. We must keep in mind always the final test before an audience—whether it is an audience of a few people, of the street, of the business world, of the drawing room, or of the auditorium.

A principle to be remembered is that richness of meaning is synonymous with fullness of understanding or appreciation and fullness of oral expression. To interpret literature to other people, you must first have a complete impression, then you must use the technique of good speech, and, finally, you must employ your impression and your technique in such a way as to suit your audience—always considering their tastes, their age, and their number. In turn, your own tastes and your own speech technique determine for you your ability to place your own construction upon what you find on the printed page. A person who has cultivated a speech technique will carry over a richer meaning than the novice. That is why the college sophomore cannot get as much out of Shakespeare either for himself or for others as can Lawrence Olivier or Maurice Evans. The student will grasp the skeleton sense, but he usually misses the deeper, inner meanings which can be derived and expressed only by a carefully developed speech technique. We must remember, though, that our task is distinctly an attempt by one human being to interest another human being in what he finds on the printed page, to get an impression of the author's ideas, and then to re-create that impression by the correct expression of the body and voice. So the problems of the interpreter are:

1. How can I, the interpreter, find the meaning of the printed page?
2. How can I, the interpreter, give expression to this meaning and thereby induce someone else to appreciate my interpretation?

The first problem will be discussed in Part II of this book, "The Technique of Impression"; the second one will be dealt with in Part III, "The Technique of Expression."

The Nature of the Printed Page

Before we discuss the technique of interpretation, we must understand the essential nature of the printed page. There is actually nothing on the printed page but black marks. There are not even words; words do not exist on a printed page. They do not even live in the air between one person and another while spoken; only sound waves travel through the air. Words are solely and everlastingly and inevitably within a human being. The marks on the printed page are symbols only.

But these black marks on the printed page are not just ordinary smudges. They are marks that possess a sort of magic. They have power; they do things to us. They fly up and strike us in the face, and we are never the same again. They lift us to heights of joy or depress us to depths of sadness; they relax us in comfort or tense us in anxiety; they make us blush or smile or weep or groan or laugh. As a matter of closer analysis, they really make us *talk to ourselves*. Silent reading, or "reading to ourselves," is nothing more than talking to ourselves, or more technically, *inner speech*.

This description of silent reading follows the psychology of speaking which teaches that "thinking" is the outgrowth or off-spring of our overt or open speech. All thinking and all reading and writing begin in the child's early attempts to talk. When a baby first has some slight grip on the instrument of speech, it does most of its thinking openly. On learning to talk, and so on dis-covering the possibilities of thinking, it likes to indulge in think-ing, but tends to do all its thinking aloud. But the child probably gets checked by its parents and friends in its delight in too much open talk and soon learns that it does not pay to think everything so that others can hear. Accordingly, by some hard lessons, the child learns to go through these same motions of talking without letting anybody else hear. This is what is meant by *inner speech;* it is the basis of all those complex processes which we later designate as thought. While thinking, we can catch ourselves talking to ourselves with practically the same mechanism that we use when we talk to other people. The chief difference is that we do not use the "out-loud" machinery—the sound-making mechanism; and for the same reason that we are not thus projecting sounds to other people, we use mechanisms with less degree of intensity than when we are talking aloud: tongue, lips, and larynx especially.

Thus the marks on the printed page make us talk to ourselves in silent reading. Words come into existence only when these symbols stir in us a *meaning,* and this meaning we call a *word.* Symbols that mean nothing do not startle us into doing anything meaningful; symbols that represent an unknown tongue or nonsense language mean nothing to us because they do not start us talking to ourselves. Try the following combination of black marks, *oiaio.* Now it happens that these marks are a symbol that might be called a word, but not to a user of the English language; they constitute the Hawaiian word for "truth." On the other hand, marks that tell us that a member of our family is in great distress or that announce some good fortune are rich in meaning—rich in the extent of things they do to us. They make us say to ourselves something clear and unmistakable. The only possible way of getting meaning into written symbols is by means of a human being who can look at them and then so react through his inner speech that he interprets the symbols. Otherwise they are meaningless. Printed page symbols have no effect on dummies or automatons.

It follows, then, that completeness of interpretation is dependent in turn upon the richness of the life and experience of the interpreter. We read with delight, either to ourselves or to others, only those things for which our experience has fitted us. There is practically no delight in the new experience from a piece of literature which we do not understand, for the meaning of every word, phrase, or thought is conditioned by a blend of our experiences, not only social but psychological, educational, and physical. If the poem or composition makes us do things to our-selves that cause us no particular joy or that are altogether too new, we find the printed page uninteresting and any attempt to interpret it futile. Many there are who cannot enjoy Shakespeare because their lives have been too dull or because their experience with the Shakespearean language is deficient; the black marks that represent Shakespeare's thoughts do nothing to such inter-preters to tickle their fancy or to stir their pleasure in life. Those who have lived rather simply and have not done much thinking get an easy thrill out of Robert Service, Edgar A. Guest, and Ella Wheeler Wilcox. But it takes a person skilled in language and accustomed to some of the complexities of living and thinking to get much delight out of Tennyson's "In Memoriam" or Browning's "Rabbi Ben Ezra." Some black marks on the printed page are for people who enjoy only the most simple experiences; other black marks are for those who have gone into some of the byways of life and have moved from the mountains to the valleys and changed from summer to winter.

For instance, the following passage needs an understanding of many aspects of life and a knowledge of word meanings and English grammar. We can give you a start which may induce you to study the passage line by line for further meaning. Here is old age talking to youth and saying, "Grow old along with me," for he has learned that an apparent failure can be a success; that this life is but a preparation for another; that youth may fail to recog-nize these truths because youth has high ambitions:

> Not that, admiring stars,
> It yearned, "Nor Jove, nor Mars;
> Mine be some figured flame which blends, transcends them all!"

Youth is not to be blamed for these aspirations, however, but should learn to "welcome each rebuff," "each sting that bids nor sit nor stand but go!" and will probably learn, as time goes on, the "paradox which comforts while it mocks" that life can be successful through its failures.

RABBI BEN EZRA

Grow old along with me!
The best is yet to be,

The last of life, for which the first was made:
Our times are in his hand
Who saith, "A whole I planned,
Youth shows but half; trust God: see all, nor be afraid!"

Not that, amassing flowers,
Youth sighed, "Which rose make ours,
Which lily leave and then as best recall?"
Not that, admiring stars,
It yearned, "Nor Jove, nor Mars;
Mine be some figured flame which blends, transcends them all!"

Not for such hopes and fears
Annulling youth's brief years,
Do I remonstrate: folly wide the mark!
Rather I prize the doubt
Low kinds exist without.
Finished and finite clods, untroubled by a spark.

Poor vaunt of life indeed,
Were man but formed to feed
On joy, to solely seek and find and feast;
Such feasting ended, then
As sure an end to men;
Irks care the crop full bird? Frets doubt the maw-crammed beast?

Rejoice we are allied
To that which doth provide
And not partake, effect and not receive!
A spark disturbs our clod;
Nearer we hold of God
Who gives, than of his tribes that take, I must believe.

Then, welcome each rebuff
That turns earth's smoothness rough,
Each sting that bids nor sit nor stand but go!
Be our joys three-parts pain!
Strive, and hold cheap the strain;
Learn, nor account the pang; dare, never grudge the throe!

For thence,—a paradox
Which comforts while it mocks,—
Shall life succeed in that it seems to fail:
What I aspired to be,
And was not, comforts me:
A brute I might have been, but would not sink i' the scale.
                                        ROBERT BROWNING

Pleasure in Reading Is Egocentric

As long as you read to yourself, your interpretation is all engrossing to you and belongs to you. Your likes and your dislikes are your own. When you like a good poem, the word symbols have done something to you that pleases you; when you do not like a poem, the words have done something unpleasant to you or have not affected you at all. The meanings that come to you are your meanings, and the rest of the world has nothing to say about what you like *while you are reading to yourself*. When you try to interpret for others, it is quite another matter.

In addition to the printed-page composition doing things to you that you like, it will also make you do queer things. The same principle is true with song notes: a printed page with song notations on it makes a skilled singer do certain things and an unskilled singer, quite different things. Each may find enjoyment in what he is doing because he is doing it his own way and for himself; but when he starts singing for someone else, the un-skilled singer will be most unfortunate. In interpreting "Crossing the Bar" to yourself, you use inner speech in such a way as to please yourself with your own secret way of reading it—and so you like the poem. But when you interpret it for someone else, you have to have some knowledge of how to present that meaning for your listeners.

Consequently, the printed page symbols mean what *you* make them mean. There is no *absolute* meaning. Take these black marks, "Yes, I like her," and notice some of the potential meanings:

1. Yes, I like her. (She is probably all right, but I am not eager for her friendship. *Or,* I'd better say I like her, but don't believe it.)
2. *Yes,* I like her. (I'm sure of it.)
3. Yes, *I* like her. (Whatever others think, she suits me. *Or,* I like her, though my friend does not.)
4. Yes, I *like* her. (I like her, but no more than that.)
5. Yes, I like *her.* (I like her but not the other girl, her family, etc.)
6. *Yes,* I *like* her. (Who said I did not?)
7. *Yes, I like her.* (I think she is a fine girl.)
8. Yes, I like her. (She's wonderful!)

From this demonstration of what black marks can mean, the only reasonable conclusion about the author's meaning is that within you, the interpreter, a feeling always exists that says, "Ah, I have it; this is what he means!" But is it? May not another interpreter have another meaning? You may be a Macbeth who has just left the murder scene. You may back into the room away from the murder scene. You may be so tortured and yet so fascinated by your murderous act that you whisper, "This is a sorry sight." Or you may be a Macbeth who staggers into the room with your hands over your eyes; you may feel the blood trickle down, and thrusting your hands out of sight, you may blurt out, "This is a sorry sight." Or you may be a Macbeth who is so horrified that your eyes may be fixed on your hands, and your speech may be broken and tense, "This—is a—sorry—sight." Or you may be a Macbeth who has lost all control and is on the verge of hysterics, and, increasing your attack, you may say, "This is a *sorry* sight." Why not? One can hear these various interpretations on the stage from actors who have gained the reputation of being true artists. Discuss various possible interpretations:

DUNCAN MURDERED

LADY MACBETH. Alack, I am afraid they have awak'd,
And 'tis not done. The attempt and not the deed
Confounds us. Hark! I laid their daggers ready;
He could not miss 'em. Had he not resembled
My father as he slept, I had done 't.
                    Enter MACBETH
                              —My husband!
MACBETH. I have done the deed. Didst thou not hear a noise?
LADY M. I heard the owl scream and the crickets cry.
    Did not you speak?
MACBETH.   When?
LADY M.   Now.
MACBETH.   As I descended?
LADY M. Ay.
MACBETH. Hark!
    Who lies i' the second chamber?
LADY M.   Donalbain.
MACBETH. This is a sorry sight.
                    WILLIAM SHAKESPEARE, *Macbeth*

Study the following speech of Marullus to the mob. Be sure that you can defend your interpretation of it. Are you going to say, "*Wherefore* rejoice? What *conquest* brings he home?" Or will you try, "Wherefore *rejoice?* What conquest brings *he* home?" Are you going to shout and build to a climax, or are you going to be gently persuasive and forgiving on the lines:

> You blocks, you stones, you worse than senseless things!
> O you hard hearts, you cruel men of Rome,
> Knew you not Pompey?

Will you soften your tones, will you be sarcastic, or will you be very emphatic on the *now*'s as you say:

> And do you now put on your best attire?
> And do you now cull out a holiday?
> And do you now strew flowers in his way,
> That comes in triumph over Pompey's blood?

It is a fascinating game, but you must be able to defend your interpretation. Try it:

WHEREFORE REJOICE?

MARULLUS
  Wherefore rejoice? What conquest brings he home?
  What tributaries follow him to Rome
  To grace in captive bonds his chariot-wheels?
  You blocks, you stones, you worse than senseless things!
  O you hard hearts, you cruel men of Rome,
  Knew you not Pompey? Many a time and oft
  Have you climb'd up to walls and battlements,
  To towers and windows, yea, to chimney-tops,
  Your infants in your arms, and there have sat
  The live-long day, with patient expectation,
  To see great Pompey pass the streets of Rome;
  And when you saw his chariot but appear
  Have you not made an universal shout,
  That Tiber trembled underneath her banks,
  To hear the replication of your sounds
  Made in her concave shores?
  And do you now put on your best attire?
  And do you now cull out a holiday?

And do you now strew flowers in his way
That comes in triumph over Pompey's blood?
Be gone!
Run to your houses, fall upon your knees,
Pray to the gods to intermit the plague
That needs must fall on this ingratitude.
                    WILLIAM SHAKESPEARE, *Julius Caesar*

This interpretative study is an attempt on your part to face
the printed page and make it live. It is a task of transforming the
black marks on a sheet of paper into living, breathing, vital
thought and emotion. It is also a task of changing the dull and
ineffective maker of mere sounds into a lively and interesting
person. Interpretation is essentially an enterprise started by one
imaginative human being who writes and continued by another
imaginative human being who interprets for other people what
he thinks the other person has written. In other words, interpretation is the audible presentation, or re-creation, of what the interpreter thinks the writer meant by the black marks on the printed
page. But unless there is vigor and vitality in both the writer
and the interpreter, there is no such thing as real interpretation.
The printed symbols cause no stir in a dull clod.

Read the next poem to yourself several times and try to
analyze the meaning as carefully as you can:

THE MOCKING FAIRY[1]

"Won't you look out of your window, Mrs. Gill?"
    Quoth the Fairy, nidding, nodding in the garden;
"*Can't* you look out of your window, Mrs. Gill?"
    Quoth the Fairy, laughing softly in the garden;
But the air was still, the cherry boughs were still,
And the ivy-tod 'neath the empty sill,
And never from her window looked out Mrs. Gill
    On the Fairy shrilly mocking in the garden.

"What have they done with you, you poor Mrs. Gill?"
    Quoth the Fairy, brightly glancing in the garden;
"Where have they hidden you, you poor old Mrs. Gill?"
    Quoth the Fairy dancing lightly in the garden;
But night's faint veil now wrapped the hill,

[1] By permission from *Collected Poems.* Copyright, 1920, by Henry Holt
and Company, Inc. Copyright, 1948, by Walter de la Mare.

> Stark 'neath the stars stood the dead-still Mill,
> And out of her cottage never answered Mrs. Gill
> The Fairy mimbling mambling in the garden.
>   WALTER DE LA MARE

When you have decided that you are well aware of the author's meaning and are sure that the black marks have done something to you, read these comments about this poem:[2]

If this sounds, at first, like one more pretty, unpretentious fairy story, designed only for small children, read it again; if necessary, again and again, until you begin almost to be ghostly haunted by it and know that more is here than meets the casual eye. Mrs. Gill, from her name, seems like a harmless, home-loving old body; but the fairy is, as the title tells us, not a good fairy; he is a *mocking* fairy, he has come by night, and his *mimbling mambling* hints that his haunting the garden is to no good purpose. Amused, at first, he laughs softly at Mrs. Gill with his invitation, "Won't you look out of your window?" which is pleasant enough. But his second question, *"Can't you look out of your window, Mrs. Gill?"* with the italics of emphasis for *can't* is a first hint that something is wrong. Mrs. Gill couldn't come out, even if she heard the fairy and wanted to. Then everything is so still: air, cherry boughs, and ivy bush (*tod*); the mill is *dead*-still; only the fairy is in motion. The cottage is *cold*. Now, the meaning should strike home. Mrs. Gill is dead. That is why she never answers, why she *can't* come out. De la Mare does not tell us what the fairy wanted of Mrs. Gill, nor whether he was anything more sinister than a *mocking* fairy. But if we know the ways of fairies with mortals, if we have read at all in the lore of witchcraft, we may well be disturbed about Mrs. Gill's fate. No, this isn't a child's poem. No slight part of its magic is in what is unsaid, in De la Mare's refusal to resolve all problems, answer all questions. Suggestion as a stimulus to imagination is more powerful than direct statement.

Another part of the magic is in the simplicity and surface naturalness which make the supernatural more supernatural. The scene is a domestic cottage garden—the kind of garden the speaker in Frost's poem [Daniels is referring to Frost's poem, *Stopping By Woods On A Snowy Evening*] might conceivably have had at home—on a quiet night with stars. There is a hill, and somewhere, not definitely located —the indefiniteness is part of the poet's intention—a mill, closed after the day's work. We are not very much disposed to quarrel with the fairy when he makes his appearance, for his *nidding, nodding* seems to tell of friendliness. But the details, held up for analysis, transform domesticity into gooseflesh, goblin terror as we watch. In addition to

[2] Earl R. Daniels, *The Art of Reading Poetry* (New York, Rinehart and Company, Inc., 1952), pp. 58-59.

those already pointed out, observe how the fairy's voice becomes *shrill* at the end of the first stanza; how the night's *veil* is *faint*, barely wrapping the hill, so that the mill stands out *stark*. Stillness becomes stiller by the emphasis of repetition. Consider too the added force, once the meaning of the poem begins to strike home, of the contrasting, pleasant words like *laughing softly, brightly glancing, dancing lightly*. With all its ghostliness the poem maintains an easy, almost conversational tone. The poet does not raise his voice, does not become rhetorical. The real and the unreal are combined with telling effectiveness.

Compare your interpretation of the following conversation with the interpretations of other students in your class. Is the German soldier desperate, sarcastic, reminiscent, hateful, nonchalant? Or is he a composite of all these moods, and perhaps others? Sentence by sentence will have to be studied for emotional meanings underlying his attitude. For instance, several meanings can be drawn from the first sentence, "And where have we to go?" And in the second line, the sentence, "There is no place," could be interpreted as if the soldier were explaining very quietly to an unbeliever, or as if he were desperately acknowledging the hopelessness of the situation, or as a calm statement of fact. Seventeen lines down, there is a question which appears to be quite obvious in meaning, "What can we do?" Is it obvious? Notice how this paragraph gains in momentum as he talks about those who will profit from the war experiences of the soldiers, until he comes to the sentence, "He will destroy us." The last paragraph is not so difficult because the author has given cues: "chuckling, confused sound"; "groping for some explanation of an emotional crisis"; "smiling in a bitter, despairing fashion"; "he whistled softly." These are potent black marks; make them mean something real.

WHAT CAN WE DO?[3]

The German soldier has come upon Lily Shane unexpectedly in a deserted French village.

"And where have we to go? If we sought to escape where have we to go? There is no place. Because the monkeys . . . the fools have

[3] From Louis Bromfield, *The Green Bay Tree*, pp. 301-303. Copyright, 1924, by Frederick A. Stokes Company. Reprinted by permission of the publishers.

civilized all the world, so that they might sell their cheap cotton and
tin trays. They have created a monster which is destroying them.
There is no longer any peace . . . any solitude. They have even
wrenched the peasant from his plow . . . the shepherd from his hillside. They have driven them out upon the plains where the cauldrons
have overflowed across all Europe. It is the monsters, Madame, who
are at the bottom of all this. Ah, commerce, industry, wealth, power.
When this is over, who do you think will have gained? Not the
peasant, Madame. Not the shepherd, not the poet. Ah, no! They will
be shovelled under the earth . . . whole bodies and pieces of bodies
because they are no longer any use. Not the worker, Madame, whom
the monster devours. Ah, no. It is the monster who will have gained
. . . the monster and the men whose pockets he fills with gold . . .
the monster of material, of industry. He will destroy us. He will devour
us. What can we do? You see, I know. I have lived in France. I have
lived in England. I would prefer to live in England. But, no! I was
in England three weeks ago. And suddenly I must go home to join
my regiment, to set out on an expedition that has brought me here to
this trampled garden. What for? Who can say? Why? Who knows?
Not surely because it gives me pleasure. Not surely because I care a
fig whether the German empire lives or dies. That is merely an excuse
to drag us into battle. You see, this is why I cannot sleep. I have been
thinking of these things. They are not the sort to lull a man to sleep.
There is blood on my hands. I killed today . . . by shooting and
stabbing. I assure you it gave me no pleasure. I should doubtless have
loved the men I killed. I am helpless. I cannot fight against it. No,
there is only one thing to be done. I must kill as many men as possible.
I must destroy all that is possible to because if we destroy enough the
monster will have nothing to feed upon. He too, will die . . . and
with him this civilization . . . banal, ugly, materialistic, unchristian
. . . this greed-ridden world."

The Uhlan fell forward upon the table, burying his face in his
arms. At the sight, Lily raised herself gently and watched her strange
companion in a wondering silence. At last she said softly, "Why do
you tell me this? Is it because you are afraid?"

The man made a chuckling, confused sound and sat up once more.
"Ah, no! Madame. You fancy I am hysterical. Well, so I am. I don't
deny it. You see it is not easy for me to be a warrior. I am a little
mad. No, I talk like this because. . . ." For a moment he hesitated
as if groping for some explanation of an emotional crisis which in a
soldier was not logical at all. "Because . . . well, there is a time when
fear does not matter, when terror does not exist, when one is enveloped by a despair so great that what happened to one's body is of
no concern. You understand that. You have answered it yourself a
little time before, when you said there came a time when it was useless
to be afraid. It does not matter." In the faint light from the lower
windows of the chateau it was plain that he was smiling in a bitter,

despairing fashion. "No, I shall go on killing until I am killed. It will not be a long affair. It is absurd to hope that I shall live many more days." He whistled softly. "I might even be killed to-night . . . after I have left you. I shall kill as many men as possible. I can only submit. There is nothing I can do. I am not a boy full of playing soldier."

"Invictus" has been interpreted as the belligerent defiance of a disappointed youth, and it has been interpreted as the proud confidence of undefeated old age. What do *you* think the author intended?

INVICTUS

Out of the night that covers me,
    Black as the pit from pole to pole,
I thank whatever gods may be
    For my unconquerable soul.

In the fell clutch of circumstance
    I have not winced nor cried aloud.
Under the bludgeonings of chance
    My head is bloody, but unbowed.

Beyond this place of wrath and tears
    Looms but the horror of the shade,
And yet the menace of the years
    Finds and shall find me unafraid.

It matters not how strait the gate,
    How charged with punishments the scroll,
I am the master of my fate;
    I am the captain of my soul.

               WILLIAM E. HENLEY

Is there wonder or is there poignant sadness in this next poem?

THE WAY OF A STAR[4]

A strange thing in a star to be putting a sorrow on me,
And I sitting quiet with no dark heart at all,
But a wonder on me for the simple things,
Like the way of the day to come and the night to fall,
And the wind that is blind to the eye and a sting to the flesh,
And is leaping over the bog to howl on the sea;

[4] Reprinted from *Poetry* (October 2, 1926), p. 36, by permission of the publishers.

Or just the glad way of the gorse to be smelling sweet . . .
And a little star to be putting a sorrow on me.

CHARLOTTE ARTHUR

In Untermeyer's lines you may find bitterness or resignation or
an appealing persuasiveness or an incredible numbness or defiance or wistful hopefulness. If the black marks stir a certain
meaning in you, believe in *your* interpretation:

CALIBAN IN THE COAL MINES[5]

God, we don't like to complain—
  We know that the mine is no lark—
But—there's the pools from the rain;
  But—there's the cold and the dark.

God, You don't know what it is—
  You, in Your well-lighted sky—
Watching the meteors whizz;
  Warm, with the sun always by.

God, if You had but the moon
  Stuck in Your cap for a lamp,
Even You'd tire of it soon,
  Down in the dark and the damp.

Nothing but blackness above
  And nothing that moves but the cars . . .
God, if You wish for our love,
  Fling us a handful of stars.

LOUIS UNTERMEYER

Hagedorn is doing more than just talking about the closing of
a door in his poem below. If your interpretation is merely casual,
you can be sure that you have failed to find the complete meaning suggested in these haunting lines:

DOORS[6]

Like a young child who to his mother's door
  Runs eager for the welcoming embrace,

[5] From *Challenge*, p. 104. Copyright, 1914, by Harcourt, Brace and Company, Inc. Reprinted by permission of the publishers.
[6] From *Poems and Ballads*, p. 26. Copyright, 1912, by Houghton Mifflin
Company. Reprinted by permission of the publishers.

And finds the door shut, and with troubled face
Calls and through sobbing calls, and o'er and o'er
Calling, storms at the panel—so before
A door that will not open, sick and numb,
I listen for a word that will not come,
And know, at last, I may not enter more.

Silence! And through the silence and the dark
By that closed door, the distant sob of tears
Beats on my spirit, as on fairy shores
The spectral sea; and through the sobbing—hark!
Down the fair-chambered corridor of years,
The quiet shutting, one by one, of doors.

HERMANN HAGEDORN

THE ART OF INTERPRETATION

Interpretation Involves New Experience

As you studied some of the foregoing selections, perhaps the realization that here was an experience you had never had and cared less to have came over you. If you had the desire for correct interpretation, your interest was immediately stimulated; for to the degree that the situation or the language is unusual, compelling, so is your interest aroused in interpreting the meaning. It is true that when we find a bit of prose or poetry that we wish to reveal to others, we discover that the material almost always is new, unique, exciting, even overpowering. All poems, short stories, and dramas deal with sentiments that have been lifted out of everyday experiences and are expressed in language that has been carefully selected for the situation and mood; certainly the language does not have the haphazard carelessness of everyday speech. For this reason, we must not be commonplace when we feel moved to interpret for someone else. Many readers can never be good interpreters because they assume that everything they read aloud should be interpreted as they normally talk. But the interpreter does not really speak with everyday casualness; he creates the illusion of doing so and thus becomes involved in the *art* of interpretation. Just as all activities classified as art are successful only through the skillful use of techniques, so effective interpretation results only from practice with techniques that are so integrated and blended as to create the illusion of reality.

What Is Art?

What do we mean by art? The simplest and most inclusive answer is that art is merely doing something well. Do anything better than mediocre and you *approach* art. We have art of many and diverse kinds: architecture and cooking, painting and dancing, acting and singing, writing and diving, sculpturing and fly-casting. If you are sincere and work with more than average skill, you will experience the feelings and promptings of the artist. As a matter of fact, if you have not the artistic urge toward doing something well, however commonplace or simple it may seem to be, you are doomed to a humdrum existence.

But this does not tell us what is actually involved in producing art. Will it help to say that it is being artistic? Probably not much, because that merely says again that art is based upon doing things in an artistic manner. This constitutes a faulty definition. Will it help to test the meaning of art in terms of certain words that sound very much like it? That sounds hopeful. Let's try it.

First, take the word *artful*. If this means "full of art," then what is art? Something clever? A sly trick? Something to put over? Not exactly, and yet that is about what artful means. The meaning is not difficult to appreciate if you understand that art is, after all, some sort of illusion. Obviously the paint on the canvas is not really a landscape or a man's head, and the piece of marble is not a man throwing a discus, and the acting on the stage is not done by people who are angry or in love or perplexed or saintly or villainous—at least not in just the way they *seem* to be! These are all illusions for the benefit of the observer. But they are —and the artist who made them was—artful.

Next consider the word *artifice*. Again we are dealing with something that is not everything it seems to be. A backdrop is an artifice; so are a steeple on a church, the vertical stripes on a plump woman's dress, the green jacket on a red-headed girl, and the streamline of an automobile body. These are all devices to make something seem to be just a little different from what it actually is. An artifice is always figured out with an intent to gloss over something or to hide what is not to be noticed. An artificer then is one who deals in artfulness; for a true artificer makes bronze into a *Winged Mercury* which is not-bronze, or glass into flowers which are not-glass, or wool into broadcloth which is not-wool. But is an artificer an artist?

This question leads easily to a consideration of the word *artificial*. By definition, the artificial is opposed to the natural, the genuine, the honest-to-goodness reality. What has art to do with the artificial, most especially the art of giving voice to the thoughts of others as found on the printed page? At first glance, the mere suggestion seems scandalous; for interpretation, of all things, must seem to be sincere and real. It must be even more; it must seem to be "natural." At least one hears that interpretation and artificiality have nothing to do with one another. But not so fast. There is a certain artificiality in all art if artists are artful and if all art uses artifices. So if interpretation is to be classed as an art, it cannot be altogether "natural."

Art is never natural; it only seems to be. The very core and heart of artistry is the creating of illusion—making things appear to be different from what they are. This illusion is produced by making a selection of parts to give an impression of reality, and that impression is re-created by working out a harmony, a co-ordination of the principles involved in the technique of that particular kind of art. A *Venus de Milo* in marble never occurred in nature and never will. She had to be made in an artificial way by an artificer who purposely used subtle artifices. A *Hamlet* never happened in real life, and no one ever spoke Hamlet's language naturally. Hamlet had to be made by a master technician. Not even acting and play production are natural; it is all make-believe, illusion. Everything on the stage and around the stage is arranged for building up a mood, a movement, a climax, an actor. The gun must go off at the right time, the light cues must click at the crucial moment, the make-up must be blended in with the lighting—all to create an illusion of reality. Chairs, lamps, doors, windows are used according to the schemes of an artist or artificer intent on producing an artificial situation that *seems* real. The audience is led to believe that true love is always lasting, that virtue is triumphant, and that life amid beautiful furniture and fine clothes is all sparkle and joy. The very lines of

the manuscript are artificial, for to make the story *seem* real they
have to be artificially—and artfully—concise, artificially couched
in the best—or worst—English, and artificially pronounced according to the best standards of stage diction. Yet the drama is
the form of art nearest to that which we call natural.

Art is always in a measure artificial because in good art everything is consciously planned to produce the right effect. A genuine artist knows ahead of time what effects he wants to produce,
and he plans accordingly. Not a thing is left to chance if he is
really an artist and not a mere blunderer or extemporizer. Imagine building a cathedral solely by inspiration and an unpremedi-
tated outpouring of the soul. It simply cannot be done. Nor is it
done in actuality, even in so immediate and spontaneous an art
as improvising on a piano or an organ; for into such performances
goes much of one's past training. Consider the improvisations of
a novice; the result may be perfectly natural—and quite terrible.
So with any art, even the art of talking or speaking in public.
Many speakers are by nature awkward and halting, or else glib,
rambling, and generally not equal to a public performance. If
told to be natural before an audience, they will only exaggerate
every fault they have. No man can be natural before an audience,
because everything about the situation is strange and unnatural,
unless he has grown up before audiences. The only cure, as in
successful interpretation, is the study and practice of the technique of that art. If there is no planning and preparation, no
training and practice, there is, in reality, no art.

Interpretation Involves Artfulness

Interpretation is of necessity an artifice. When you, the interpreter, utter the words in the best way you can in order to give
the meaning of the author, you are really creating an illusion.
You are most successful when you carry the impression that your
interpretation comes genuinely from *you* and is a part of *you*.
The worst of all interpretation is the kind that shows the audience clearly that you, the interpreter, have not assimilated the
meaning yourself and have not made the author's ideas and
intention your own. At best, you are genuine and honest, but
still not entirely what you *seem* to be. Insofar as you present

adequately the ideas and feelings of the author, you are dealing
in the precise kind of illusion on which all other arts are and
must be built.

Yet it must be said that of all the arts interpretation calls for
the most sincere searching of one's thoughts and feelings and
the most thorough use of one's truest and best, for it is the most
face-to-face of all arts, the most intimate, the most direct. In it,
shallowness and dishonesty are quickly disclosed. Architecture
and painting have a certain intangibility. You stand apart and
gaze, and if you feel yourself in touch with the mood of the
artist, you are pleased. Music intimately gathers you to its bosom,
but it is the intimacy of feelings only, almost never of ideas. Interpretation, impersonation, and acting are close, immediate,
heart-to-heart, mind-to-mind, and soul-to-soul.

Interpretation, then, belongs among the arts for the very reason
that it is a form of illusion, the success of which depends upon the
artistry and the artful technique of the interpreter. At the moment that it seems most honest and sincere it is most an illusion,
seeming to be something that it is not.

The Best Art Conceals Its Artistry

Although the existence of any "art for art's sake" is to be
doubted, its twin in the language of artistry, the "art that conceals
art," has much to be said in its defense. The highest art always
seems so easy that as we observe it we feel sure we could accomplish the artistic with a very small amount of practice, and
we wonder why others have not done it before. Sonja Henie
seems not to be exerting herself in her skillful skating performances; Lynn Fontanne works so easily and naturally that she
seems not to be acting; Heifetz never moves a muscle more than
is needed. So it *seems.* They make us wonder whether they ever
had to practice. Yet what the audience receives is the fine fruit
of endeavor of the most exacting and unstinted kind. What they
do, they do so well that it seems effortless. This is what is meant
by the "art that conceals art." In no art is this apparent ease more
needed than in the interpretation of the printed page; for this
particular art demands that the artist *seem* to be what he is not,

and to make thoughts, feelings, and the soul of another live in his own voice and action.

Before we can go forward with this most human of all arts, we must dispel the mistaken notion that good interpretation is possible only for those who are naturally gifted. In this field, as in all others, gifts make a difference; but when one decides to capitalize on gifts, one must spend energy and work on the project. Schiller tells us, "All art is dedicated to joy." This should mean not merely joy in one's native talents but joy in work, joy in the opportunity to drive oneself nearer and nearer to the goal of perfection. Schiller, who worked so intensely, would have been a good example of a doctrine paraphrased from his own dictum: "All art is dedicated to hard work." There is no doubt that good interpretation comes more readily to some than to others, but no good work continues to come from those who rest too early upon their talents or their genius. Probably the worst interpreters on the platform and on the stage are those who thought work unnecessary after reaching a moderate degree of skill. All this means that art never comes by chance or luck or by trusting to a kindly nature. It is always brooded upon, blocked out, planned, sketched, blueprinted, tried, and retried. It takes study, training, patience, and mastery.

The following poem, it so happens, carries one of the most important secrets of art. Can you probe the meaning and find the secret?

A MUSICAL INSTRUMENT

What was he doing, the great god Pan,
   Down in the reeds by the river?
Spreading ruin and scattering ban,
Splashing and paddling with hoofs of a goat,
And breaking the golden lilies afloat
   With the dragon-fly on the river?

He tore out a reed, the great god Pan,
   From the deep cool bed of the river,
The limpid water turbidly ran,
And the broken lilies a-dying lay,
And the dragon-fly had fled away,
   Ere he brought it out of the river.

High on the shore sat the great god Pan,
  While turbidly flowed the river;
And hacked and hewed as a great god can,
With his hard bleak steel at the patient reed,
Till there was not a sign of the leaf indeed
  To prove it fresh from the river.

He cut it short, did the great god Pan,
  (How tall it stood in the river!),
Then drew the pith, like the heart of a man,
Steadily from the outside ring,
And notched the poor dry empty thing
  In holes, as he sat by the river.

"This is the way," laughed the great god Pan,
  (Laughed while he sat by the river),
"The only way, since gods began
To make sweet music, they could succeed."
Then dropping his mouth to a hole in the reed,
  He blew in power by the river.

Sweet, sweet, sweet, O Pan!
  Piercing sweet by the river!
Blinding sweet, O great god Pan!
The sun on the hill forgot to die,
And the lilies revived and the dragon-fly
  Came back to dream on the river.

Yet half a beast is the great god Pan,
  To laugh, as he sits by the river,
Making a poet out of a man:
The true gods sigh for the cost and pain—
For the reed which grows nevermore again
  As a reed with the reeds in the river.

                        ELIZABETH BARRETT BROWNING

CHAPTER 2

Control in Interpretation

Technique

Some artists affect to be greatly frightened by the word *technique,* fearing that it necessarily makes for artificiality. Yet there is no artistry without artifices; and it does not follow at all that artifices and technique lead to dullness, insincerity, banality, or any other form of ineffectiveness. For the fact is that there can be no art without orderly process, which is nothing less than a matter of method and procedure. That is what we mean by *technique:* acting in conformity to certain known procedures which will vary according to the literature, the interpreter, and the situation. Mastery of techniques will give control to the interpreter.

To those who know the word *technique* only as a mechanical procedure embodying rigid rules, let us say that technique correctly employed is not necessarily mechanical. It may become so if the interpreter is unable to reach beyond the technical control to the spirit of the literature. Certainly we are aware of the fact that most successful living involves adjustments which are accomplished because we have mastered techniques that give us assurance, control, and a general *savoir-faire*. Even such a minor technique as achieving tasteful color combinations in dress re mains only an empty procedure if the "how-to-wear-it" element is absent. The correct blend of lipstick with the color of the blouse or hat, the contrasting accessories used in both men's and women's dress are more than just good taste; they are techniques devised to make ourselves attractive to others. As soon as the techniques become too obvious because of lack of taste and judgment—by using too much make-up or repeating a color to the extent of monotony—the desired results are lost. We know, too, that we can be carried away by the illusion of the stage play until some unhappy incident not scheduled by the director reveals procedures instead of mood or meaning. The master pianist knows that the unending drills, the co-ordinating exercises of the two hands, the interminable practice of crescendos and arpeggios are the prerequisites to his final flawless performance. The concert singer, too, spends hours in vocal exercises before he is ready for a public recital. Yet one would not call these artists mechanical or exercise minded.

When does technique in interpretation seem mechanical? Usually when a pattern repeats itself over and over again, never deviating in form or procedure, so that spontaneity is not present. Because the pattern becomes monotonous, the meaning is obscured. There are those who tell a student of interpretation that unless he finds in a piece of literature the one particular meaning that the teacher has found, he does not understand the selection. The student is told how to present his meaning by pausing here and emphasizing there. An instructor who insists that a poem be interpreted in a certain manner, with certain pauses, certain inflections, certain emphasis on certain words by some thirty members of an interpretation class is asking for monotony, is making interpretation drudgery instead of joy, and is encouraging an automatic, imitative technique instead of a living, inspiring experience. Furthermore, he is setting himself up as one who knows the absolute meaning of every piece of literature.

But, someone asks, "Why not be *natural* in interpretation instead of working for skillful control?" You must drop the notion that art comes by nature and is natural—if and when it comes. It will never just *come;* it has to be *achieved.* Art involves control, management, mastery. Control of what? Control of self and, thereby, control of audience and situation. Control your fingers and arms and you can manage a keyboard or a chisel; control your legs and you can dance or skate; control your voice and your visible action and you can speak, sing, interpret. Some who are more skillful in analysis and imaginative thinking become writers, philosophers, critics. But they work for what they achieve. They pay the price, the price of competence, of mastery. It is also true that most people who can control their hands, can control their other bodily parts; or, if they can control their eyes and tongues, they can, by concentration and effort, control their feet and hands. Mastery in any field of endeavor, after all, is mastery of the whole person, of the "all" of you. We all know the promising musician who has been stopped in his career by his natural triumphs with the mouth organ, or the painter who has been lost by too much natural success in drawing cartoons of his teacher, or the singer who has been satisfied by the loud acclaim over her efforts in the Easter cantata. Easy self-confidence, the willingness to be blown up from outside with a divine afflatus and a sweet content in one's inherent superiority, leads directly to mediocrity.

Control of Self

If interpretation is an art, it involves planning, foresight, and execution by a person who is skilled in speaking. This can have no other meaning than that interpretation is dependent upon the mastery, the control, which the interpreter holds over himself.

No art calls for a more severe taskmaster than this art of interpretation. Note with what it deals: the ability to make a successful decision as to what the author meant by his words; an understanding of words and sentences in their finest nuances and intricacies; a command of one's sensibilities and good sense so as to avoid crotchets and snap judgments; a mastery of one's emotion, which means control of the whole body; a mastery of the intricacies of vocal activity, including the problem of vowel making, consonantal accuracy, and interplay of larynx, lips, tongue, palate, and jaw; the ability to keep one's zeal high enough to furnish enthusiasm for those who are cold and inert; and, finally, an appreciation of the esthetic level of the audience before which the interpretation is given. An art that includes these talents and tasks indeed involves control of self. Now let us talk more about what is included in this control.

Control of Meaning

The successful interpreter must be well-informed. The marks on the page mean something to him only in proportion to his ability to be stirred by them. To the ignorant man, they mean little or nothing. To the one who can barely read, some few black marks will have a little meaning; but to one who is wise in the information that life has to give, black marks can stir up many kinds of meaning. A grade-school boy can try to pronounce all the words on a page of *Macbeth* or *Hamlet;* but he will have little chance to carry full and correct meaning to a listener. You have to understand words and people before you can thoroughly understand Falstaff or Iago or Juliet or Malvolio. Think what a hilarious, roaring, roistering, yet tender, tolerant, and gentle soul "Will" Shakespeare must have been to understand the people whose characters he created. Think then how much one interpreting these personages needs the same potentiality in order to understand and appreciate them through the medium of print. If you want to be a true interpreter of literature, you must bring to the task completeness of living—which comes from many sources: daily living, conversations, newspapers, books, addresses, concerts, operas, plays, good fortune, disaster, crises of life, travel. Ordinarily, the person who has had rich experiences will get the deepest meaning from the printed page.

Control of Emotions

On the other hand, not all who understand can interpret well; some cannot master themselves. They have made the world bow to their wishes, but they have not learned how to make themselves bow. To charm and delight other people with speech, one must have mastered one's own feelings. This is best shown on the stage. Actors who have not conquered their own spirit are likely to strut about, reminding us of stage parrots. The actor who interprets his lines best is the one who best strikes a balance between restraining his feelings and letting them go.

Should an interpreter or an actor "live his part" just as the character would in life? True, one is adjured many times to "live the part," to "become wholly absorbed in what one is interpreting," to "lose oneself," to "sink one's identity in that of the author or character." Each of these principles is a valuable ideal for the young and hopeful interpreter; but all of them must be taken with some allowance and understanding. They are helpful only when the interpreter knows what they mean. Complete absorption in one's art is helpful only when one is a skilled technician. All the absorption in the world will not paint a good picture unless the artist knows his colors and how to handle his brush. We all have heard deeply absorbed musicians who have made us shiver and shudder. It is nonsense to believe that in order to act Macbeth well you must be overpowered with ambition to the point of murder, to act Lear you must be "every inch a king," to act Katherine you must, for the time, *be* an uncontrolled shrew. Carry this belief to its logical conclusion and you would find it would be entirely impossible to find an actor to play Richard III and keep out of jail; Hamlet, and stay out of the madhouse; or Caliban, and escape the psychopathic hospital. No, the rule is not so simple as that; yet it is very understandable. In brief, it is that the interpreter or actor must feel the emotion deeply and sincerely enough to interpret or act well, but not enough to be lost in it and to lose control of himself. Sincerity is not a saving grace in itself; the only interpreter whose sincerity helps him to success is the one who knows what he is doing. In the last analysis art rests upon skill. In actual achievement, skill comes first in importance; purpose, absorption, and sincerity follow. You will find that many of the most sincere speakers fail and, every now and then, that an insincere one becomes the hero of his little hour, largely because of his ability to control skillfully.

Let us explain this matter further, for it is the key to the problem of controlling the emotions in interpretation. To be successful, an interpreter of lines must be sensitive to the meaning of the lines; he must be moved by them as the author intended. If he lacks this sensitivity, he might just as well be angry when trying to portray love or be jealous when trying to imitate ambition; it will not make much difference, for he will miss the meaning anyway. If, however, he is capable of experiencing anger, remorse, love, or serenity, he has a chance of interpreting the lines with some success. But because all art requires headwork and planning and foresight, the interpreter must not allow himself to become so absorbed in his emotion that he loses his judgment and his sense of values. No matter how moved he may be or how moved he may seem to be, he must have sufficient control at all times to know exactly what he is doing, to know whether he has gone far enough or too far. Whenever he has not wit enough to tell how near he has come to hitting the mark, he is no artist; he is just a temperamentalist having a pleasant little orgy all by himself.

The psychology of the situation reaffirms this. In the first place, one cannot go through all the motions and tensions of being angry or passionate or frightened without feeling something of anger, passion, or fright, because, after all, emotion itself is a pattern of tensing and relaxing, due to an integration of the motor mechanism, involving especially the activity of the smooth muscles and the endocrine glands. So the interpreter, who, by his skill and control of his bodily parts, can make his body go through the tensions of anger, will be to that extent, angry. This holds true especially the first few times he tries it. For instance, you have had the experience of being so moved to tears by a certain story that you could not read it aloud because it gave you the tensions and postures of weeping. But after several readings, you could interpret it with fewer tears, and, finally, having been thoroughly conditioned to it, you could read it with complete composure.

Herein lies the secret of successful emotional presentation by an actor or an interpreter. His first sweeping emotion goes all through him and ought to be overpowering; at the end, through practice of, and skill in, his art, he has learned control. The interpreter's first problem is to be caught in the emotion on reading the lines to himself; then he must get that emotion controlled so that he can study, calculate, and criticize what he is doing and note what effect it has upon other people. This is the answer to the question, "Must an actor or interpreter live his part?" Yes, he must, up to a certain point; but then he must have the control that all artists need so that he can put his part on and off as he would a cloak. Control will save the interpreter and the actor from exhaustion.

Control Through Personality and Magnetism

There is a widespread and abiding conviction among men that art is something more than mere skill and control. We are agreed that there is always the man behind the pen or the brush, the violin bow, or the voice. In no art is this more pertinent and crucial than in the art which uses man himself as the instrument with which to work—no marble and chisels, no oils and canvas, no bricks and stones and steel. Probably the greatest of all arts is acting; greatest, because, more than any other, it involves mastery of self as the instrument of the artist, and the crucial test of acting is the actor's ability to know what the lines mean and to carry that meaning to the audience. The greatest thing about an actor always is himself, his personality, his character. His "brains" count, his appearance, and his manners; but back and above and through all is himself.

Now what is this "self," this personality? One of the vaguest terms now bandied from lip to lip is *personality*. It is character, of course; it is physical structure; it is manners and habits; it is training, skill, and accomplishment, the result of one's labors and struggles. All these it is surely; whether or not it is more than these, we do not know. One can be sure that what we call personality usually means speech efficiency. Nine times out of ten, when people discourse upon this or that man's personality, they mean his qualities of speech: his bodily control, his emotional balance, his use of words and language, the quality of his voice, his control of the volume of sound, the use of pauses and phrasing, and the modulations of pitch. Listen to people discussing personalities and note how negligible the factors are after the speech characteristics have been analyzed. A screen star has personality; how do we know? By his looks, his actions, his voice. A speaker has personality; how do we detect it? By his voice, his speech manners, his vivacity of thought as shown through his words and sentences. An interpreter has personality—through his voice, his bodily mastery, and his skill in using the organs of speech.

Some people seem magnetic without conscious effort; their bodily structure and co-ordination, aided and abetted by their training and study and travail of practice, have made them attractive to their fellows. Magnetism is merely another way of talking about adaptability in the arts that make up artistic speech or interpretation. It is something you and I read into others when we are caught by their adaptability to a particular situation.

There is more of the practice hour than of the divine afflatus in what we call magnetism. It is largely a problem of finding the kind of work and associations for which one's interests and desires best fit one.

Control of Body

Much of this confusion in popular thought concerning artistic achievement can be resolved if we get the basic concept that whatever we are or do depends upon the physical structure of the body and how we control it. Good interpretation is hardly conceivable in a body that is out of control. No doubt all of us can think of instances of interesting interpretation from people who are not in the best of health or who are in a state of un-controlled ecstasy. Some can interpret best when they are in-ebriated, we will be told. But let us say truthfully that no one ever interpreted well unless he represented, at the moment, a high degree of co-ordination of his bodily parts and activities. He may have been in a delirium, but the effect of the delirium might have been to organize him and integrate him to the very height of his powers. The emotional condition itself can be the body's response to some stimulus that excites ambition, longing, fear, or jealousy; and all of these may help to integrate the body to its best endeavors. Truly some seemingly abnormal conditions of the body can drive us to do our best because of the intensity of the co-ordination and centralization of our powers. The abnormal part shows in the aftermath, when we feel the penalty for whip-ping the body into false enthusiasm and efficiency.

Then how far shall one go in driving one's body? If the state of the body and its parts determines one's success or failure, and if it is easy enough to dislocate the body's workings, then how does one know when one has gone far enough? The answer is found in the quality that every artist has to have: the art of "let-ting go." To be natural, really natural—not the kind of natural-ness that is after all just illusion—but to be naïvely natural, is to show a certain amount of restraint. Not so art; for art calls for a cutting loose from one's moorings. A natural man is full of caution and of craving for quiet and safety. An artist is full of

the desire to get out in front where he knows that he may encounter greater risks. He has to be a great taker of chances, a
volunteer for hazardous commissions. The man who cannot let go
never will be an artist.

The French have the idea for this; it is found in the concept of
abandon. The Frenchman means by *abandon* "cutting one's
cables," "burning one's bridges," "being free from artificial re-
straints," "letting go." The diver on the springboard demonstrates the idea: if he is to make a good dive, he abandons all
hope of hanging on to the board or of keeping anything solid
underneath his feet. He must literally cut himself off from his
foundations. The worst diving comes from an attempt to hang
on to the board while sailing out through the air. It cannot be
done.

Thus it is with all art. Every artist is a plunger. The history of
the world shows that really great writers and painters and sculp-
tors and architects and actors and orators were people who took
the plunge and never openly flinched at the possible consequences. Here is where the principle of projection plays so important a part in speech and in interpretation; you have to be
willing to get out of your everyday self and find a self that is
willing to dash into the limelight and offer itself as a target for
others. The advice "Be yourself" was never intended for interpreters, impersonators, and actors. It is for homebodies. The artist
always gets out of this tame self into one anxious to get somewhere other than its immediate location.

Thus, success in interpretation calls for freedom, an enlarging
of the concept of self, a bursting of the bonds of the everyday
and the commonplace. Burgess Meredith, writing of his portrayal
of Mio in Maxwell Anderson's play *Winterset,* tells how he began
with a broad characterization, which he polished and toned down
to the final characterization. One can understand why the rule of
practice should be: *Begin with overdoing.* The interpreter should
be sure to go far enough at first. Halfway practice and work
leaves him in the air, with one foot still reaching for the springboard. He must work hard enough but also let the thing he prac-
tices, the exercises he sets himself, be freely done. Some few may
well fear the evils of exaggeration and bombast; but the majority

of our American youth will do well, if they wish to delight others
with the spoken word, to practice and cherish the virtues of going two miles when only one is demanded.

Control of Voice

We should consider also man's most powerful instrument on
the stage, on the platform, on the street, in the classroom, in the
home—his voice. The voice is powerful in the sense that it conveys our thoughts and arouses emotional responses in others, so
that they think, feel, believe as we do. But from the structural
standpoint the voice is a delicate instrument. According to the
manner in which it is treated much of the time, one would believe the vocal mechanism to be made of iron and steel. We think
too seldom in terms of control of the voice. We accept the vocal
mechanism too matter-of-factly, and use it to the limit of its
endurance, without any consideration of whether or not we are
using it correctly or wisely. At a football game, we whoop ourselves into a state of hoarseness and "sore throat"; we tense the
delicate vocal muscles; and only when the voice seems to have
disappeared and the tissues of the larynx are inflamed and
nodules appear, do we begin to evaluate the voice as a possession.

The first step involved in vocal control is to learn to listen to
voices, to become conscious of the sound, not only of other
voices but of your own. The startled look on the face of a person
who hears his voice for the first time indicates how little attention
he has given to the sound of his voice.

The next step in the control of voice is to know how the vocal
mechanism operates and how the personality of the interpreter is
reflected in the voice. If the quality is nasal or husky, or the
pitch is too high or monotonous, or the attack is too strong or too
weak, or the rhythm is too slow or too fast, or the sounds are
muffled or too articulate, adjustments must be made for the correct production and control of the voice, or for the personality,
or perhaps for both.

The last step involves the use and control of the voice so that
it may be employed in a variety of ways, depending upon the
literature to be interpreted. The interpreter must learn to control the voice, for it is his main instrument. The judicious and art-

ful use of the voice in its more delicate manipulations will be discussed in later chapters.

Development of Taste in Interpretation

As an interpreter you may have a good voice, you may have a co-ordinated and animated body, you may understand the meaning of your material, but you may lack good taste and judgment in using your talents. What is meant by taste? One answer is that taste is the expression of a man's esthetic judgment. But then we must ask: What is esthetic judgment? It is an expression of your likes and dislikes, what you appreciate and what you reject in the field of art. Tastes differ—always do, always have, always will—because tastes grow out of individual life experiences.

Your likes and your dislikes come from a wide variety of influences: from your general bodily sprightliness or slowness, from an inheritance that is phlegmatic or one that is "fidgety," from a disposition to like people or to live as a recluse, from an inferiority complex or a feeling that you own the earth. Your tastes are influenced by the kind of people with whom you have lived: sociable or individualistic, loving ease or courting struggle, self-centered or philanthropic, "go-getters" or servants of the common good. Early education counts heavily: teachers who have drawn out your talents or teachers who have held back your ambitions; playmates who were willing to see and express beauty or playmates who sneered at any love of fine things; school buildings with statues, pictures, and libraries, or buildings that were bare and depressing; school administrators who believed in music, drama, speech, and the expression of good literature, or administrators who believed in nothing but examinations and grades. Then probably the most potent influence of all is your exposure to things esthetic, to poems, stories, music, pictures, statues, buildings. Along with these, travel is very important in forming your tastes, for through travel you become exposed to the beautiful things men have made in other times and places.

So good taste is governed by your innate feelings, by your training and background. For the interpreter, there are no absolute criteria that can be listed because much depends on the literature, the audience, the situation, as well as the interpreter.

There is no disputing the fact that among the many kinds of people in the world, somebody, somewhere, will like what you dislike and dislike what you like. It is just a bit dangerous to say that you positively must not do this or positively must do that in interpretation; the very thing you might inveigh against most vigorously might be exactly the thing that others would appreciate most. It is legitimate to defer to the taste of one's audience as far as the selection of literature is concerned, but never to the point where the interpreter has to put on a side show rather than a well-balanced interpretation to demonstrate his powers. For instance, a group of university students might enjoy James Thurber, Robert Benchley, or Stephen Leacock; but a group of university professors might care for a more profound type of literature. High comedy might be well received by a woman's club in the city but probably would not be appreciated by the same kind of club in a small town. The interpreter should know whether his audience wants to be informed, educated, or entertained. It is possible to do all three in a carefully prepared program.

Mastery of Technique for the Audience

Interpretation is the art of all arts in which the artist can have a good time by himself. There is no doubt that there is joy in interpreting good thoughts for oneself. The art of extracting delight and instruction and inspiration just for oneself is one of the sure rewards of the artist in interpretation. Who gets greater delight than the man who knows what good poetry is or the man who can imagine the full panoply and procession of a play, or the man who can get the lilt and rhythm and melody of winged and breathing words? To be such an interpreter is, in a way, to provide your art for your audience of one.

However, the test for good oral interpretation is in its objectivity. It must "listen" well to others. The *technique* that you have acquired is primarily for yourself; the expression that follows mastery of technique is for the other person. Whenever the personality or the idiosyncrasies of the interpreter become dominant over the literature and its meaning, then you can be sure that purposeful communication of the literature is not the chief goal.

What the voice and body can do must always be considered as a means to an end—and that means to an end will be most successful and the illusion will be most complete when the techniques are least obvious.

A good interpreter, then, must have a sense of values, He must appreciate, and he must be willing to take the plunge with abandon; but he must also know what he is doing and have control with economy of effort. He is like a good horseman who has learned to ride in rhythm with his horse. It is the inexpert horseman who flaps his arms, bounces, pulls at the bit, and rides wildly. He shows plainly that his technique has not passed the learning stage, has not reached the period when control and mastery begin to show. In like manner, the interpreter must show control of the meaning, of the emotions, of the bodily tensions, of the voice and, thereby, control of the audience.

Techniques Involved in Interpretation

We are confronted now with the need to find the methods by which we may gain control. Before we discuss this problem, we must talk about the foundation on which the principles rest. We must be reminded again that there is no one meaning which the page compels us to take. The elasticity of language and the complications of our own thought processes allow for such tremendous leeway in the interpretation of the symbols on the page that it is rare indeed when any given set of printed letters can have only one meaning. Even though lawyers are extremely careful about the wording of legal contracts, there have been many famous lawsuits which hinged on the position of a word in a sentence or the meaning of a word or phrase. The author has never existed who can put on the paper exactly what he thinks and means. He can only direct readers toward a meaning. As we noted in the previous chapter, the statement, "Yes, I like her" can have at least eight different meanings, each with a corresponding mood. We know that whatever meaning the interpreter gets from a poem or story is the outgrowth of his life's experiences, multifarious and infinitely intricate. In other words, the interpretation of the page is always highly personal. In a way, it is merely a guess; at any rate, it is a hazard or a venture. The interpreter may think he knows exactly what the page means and yet may find that no one else agrees with him. Probably if the author annotated every phrase he wrote, the interpreter would be closer to the meaning that the author intended. But any piece of literature so minutely analyzed would never give the enjoyment and pleasure found by the reader in discovering for himself a corresponding mood and "oneness" with the poetry or prose.

Neither is it true that what one understands one can communicate effectively. Some can—without effort; some cannot—even with effort. Every interpreter would like to read with the full knowledge and experience of the author; but this is not possible. Some of the most intelligent people are the dullest readers of literature. Understanding meaning and expressing meaning to others involve two different capabilities. A professor of Shakespeare may know the meaning of a passage from Shakespeare but be unable to interpret that meaning for his students. Even authors have been known to write literature of great beauty and yet be unable to re-create it for an audience.

The rest of this book discusses these problems: how the interpreter can find the author's meaning and how he can then re-create it for others. The answers are found in the study of two techniques. The first of these is the *technique of impression*, which involves understanding the author's motivation and philosophy and understanding his meanings, both logical and emotional, through the study of words and the interrelationship of ideas which culminate to give us as much of the total meaning as it is possible to get from the printed page. The second is the *technique of expression*, which involves the spoken re-creation of the author's meanings by the proper use of the voice and visible action. Insofar as these are two distinct problems, the techniques are fundamentally different.

Part II

THE TECHNIQUE OF IMPRESSION

CHAPTER 3

The Author

(His Character, Philosophy, and Motivation)

The author is your first concern in gaining an impression of the literature you are to interpret. Who is he? What is his philosophy? What is his motivation? What is his theme? What literary vehicle does he use to convey his purpose and meaning?

We will agree that it is possible to interpret without any knowledge of the author; but it is not possible to interpret well without establishing some kind of relationship with him. If you do not feel an intellectual curiosity about his manner of philosophizing and living with others, then you will tend to be only a superficial interpreter. Of course, you cannot be certain that you will ever know the author as a close friend, but an attempt to understand his character, philosophy, and motivation for writing is surely worthwhile and also interesting. Furthermore, in planning a program of readings from literature, you should be able to recount, in a concise and pertinent manner, some facts about the author and his writings.

Your second concern includes the study of the author's words for meanings, both logical or denotative and emotional or connotative. This includes understanding the arrangement of ideas in the selection, so that you will be able to interpret the total meaning as fully as possible and then re-create that meaning for someone else. If you follow through carefully on the meaning as related to the author's mood and philosophy, you should feel satisfied that your impression embodies his theme or purpose.

47

THE AUTHOR'S CHARACTER AND PHILOSOPHY

The author should be more than a name to the interpreter, if he is worth studying seriously. He should be regarded as a vital person, endowed with flesh, blood, glands, nerves, and brain tissue; as a person who is aware of trends and tendencies among his fellow-men; as one who reacts in his own individual way to the philosophy and thoughts of others, not only of his own generation but of earlier periods.

Because of his way of thinking and living, the author feels the urge to put into written symbols what he has experienced and decides on the form he wishes to use as his means of expression. As he contemplates the impression, the emotion, the characterization, the belief—whatever his purpose is—the author develops and molds his theme into the form which he instinctively, or perhaps consciously, finds most adaptable to his talents and to his philosophy. These two factors—(1) the author's theme, mood, and philosophy, and (2) the author's literary form—are then blended into an effective piece of literature. In order to have a composite picture of what is to be revealed by the author, the interpreter should be keenly aware of the person who has written the literature as well as understanding the media of his expression.

Blended into every author's works are the emotional experiences of his life. The incidents of his childhood and youth, the maturing of his ideas, and his basic attitudes are reflected in his writing. Here, then, is one interpretation of Buffon's statement, "Style is of the man himself." Understanding these attitudes is one of the first keys to the meaning or part of the meaning of what we are to interpret. Let us examine a few well-known poets for their character and philosophy as revealed in their works and as some of the critics see them.

Cavalier Poets

These poets wrote as they lived—lightly, gaily, nonchalantly, as if they were flicking a thread from their coat sleeve. This spirit is expressed by Robert Herrick in "The argument of his book":

I sing of brooks, of blossoms, birds, and bowers,
Of April, May, of June and July flowers.
I sing of may-poles, hock-carts, wassails, wakes,
Of bridegrooms, brides, and of their bridal cakes.
I write of youth, of love, and have access
By these to sing of cleanly wantonness.
I sing of dews, of rains, and piece by piece,
Of balm, of oil, of spice, and ambergris.
I sing of times trans-shifting, and I write
How roses first came red, and lilies white.
I write of groves, of twilights, and I sing
The court of Mab and of the Fairy King.
I write of hell; I sing (and ever shall)
Of heaven, and hope to have it after all.

This typical lightheartedness is found also in the verses of Sir John Suckling:

CONSTANCY

Out upon it, I have loved
   Three whole days together!
And am like to love three more,
   If it prove fair weather.

Time shall moult away his wings,
   Ere he shall discover
In the whole wide world again
   Such a constant lover.

But the spite on't is, no praise
   Is due at all to me:
Love with me had made no stays,
   Had it any been but she.

Had it any been but she,
   And that very face,
There had been at least ere this
   A dozen in her place.

SIR JOHN SUCKLING

Shakespeare

Sometimes authors of the past are difficult to know except through their writings. We have no way of knowing Shakespeare except as we know his Merrie England. He wrote as he and his friends thought, and his humor is often coarse and bawdy. His plays are masterpieces of characterization and have lines of great beauty, but they are also packed with murders, ghosts, revenge, mystery, and swordplay—the Elizabethan equivalent of our present-day gunplay—because his audience was entertained by that kind of excitement. For instance, they would be hilarious over the escapades of that rollicking, hearty, self-excusing, and adipose rogue, Falstaff, when he recounted his adventures of being plunged into a "buck-basket" and then thrown into the Thames by the merry wives:

FALSTAFF
> Nay, you shall hear . . . I suffered the pangs of three several deaths . . . To be stoo'd in, like a strong distillation, with stinking clothes that fretted in their own grease. Think of that,—a man of my kidney,—think of that,—that am as subject to heat as butter; a man of continual dissolution and thaw,—it was a miracle to scape suffocation. And in the height of this bath, when I was more than half stew'd in grease, like a Dutch dish, to be thrown into the Thames, and cool'd, glowing hot, in that surge, like a horse-shoe; think of that,—hissing hot,—think of that, Master Brook.
>
> WILLIAM SHAKESPEARE, *The Merry Wives of Windsor*

They considered *Hamlet* a "thriller" because the Ghost appears and with sonorous tones bids Hamlet, "Revenge his foul and most unnatural murder." This same audience enjoyed the charming pretense of *A Midsummer-Night's Dream,* especially of the Pyramus-Thisbe play as directed by Bottom, whose final instructions are typical of the busy play director:

Get your apparel together, good strings to your beards, new ribbons to your pumps; meet presently at the palace; every man look o'er his part . . . let Thisby have clean linen . . . And most dear actors, eat no onions nor garlic, for we are to utter sweet breath; and I do not doubt but to hear them say, it is a sweet comedy.

And no doubt the Shakespearean audience agreed with Demetrius that the wall, as portrayed by Snout, was "the wittiest partition that ever I heard discourse."

Byron

We know that Shakespeare went his merry way with his companions of the stage, working evidently with prodigious energy and enjoyment. Not so Byron, the nineteenth-century poet of struggle and disillusionment and revolt. Byron's personal experiences form the background of the philosophy found in his poetry, which shows much the same exultation that one finds in Browning but certainly not Browning's optimism. Byron is always defiant, ironic, skeptical, rebellious. Typical are these famous lines from *Childe Harold's Pilgrimage:*

Stanza 97

Could I embody and unbosom now
That which is most within me—could I wreak
My thoughts upon expression, and thus throw
Soul, heart, mind, passions, feelings, strong or weak,
All that I would have sought, and all I seek,
Bear, know, feel—and yet breathe—into *one* word,
And that one word were Lightning, I would speak;
But as it is, I live and die unheard,
With a most voiceless thought, sheathing it as a sword.

Stanza 113

I have not loved the World, nor the World me;
I have not flattered its rank breath, nor bowed
To its idolatries a patient knee,
Nor coined my cheek to smiles, nor cried aloud
In worship of an echo; in the crowd
They could not deem me one of such—I stood
Among them, but not of them—in a shroud
Of thoughts which were not their thoughts, and still could,
Had I not filed my mind, which thus itself subdued.

It is perhaps unfair to say, as we did above, that Byron was *always* rebellious. Two of his lyrics are unexcelled for their serenity:

SHE WALKS IN BEAUTY

She walks in beauty, like the night
    Of cloudless climes and starry skies;
And all that's best of dark and bright

Meet in her aspect and her eyes:
Thus mellow'd to that tender light
  Which heaven to gaudy day denies.

One shade the more, one ray the less,
  Had half impair'd the nameless grace
Which waves in every raven tress
  Or softly lightens o'er her face;
Where thoughts serenely sweet express
  How pure, how dear their dwelling-place.

And on that cheek, and o'er that brow
  So soft, so calm, yet eloquent,
The smiles that win, the tints that glow,
  But tell of days in goodness spent,
A mind at peace with all below,
  A heart whose love is innocent!

NO MORE A ROVING

So, we'll go no more a roving
  So late into the night,
Though the heart be still as loving,
  And the moon be still as bright.

For the sword outwears its sheath,
  And the soul wears out the breast,
And the heart must pause to breathe,
  And love itself have rest.

Though the night was made for loving,
  And the day returns too soon,
Yet we'll go no more a roving
  By the light of the moon.

Browning

The name of Robert Browning brings up the memory of such poems as "My Last Duchess," "Rabbi Ben Ezra," "Andrea del Sarto," "Fra Lippo Lippi"—moments of vivid characterization which are unforgettable. You may have read somewhere, or you may have experienced in reading his poetry, the thought that here is a most alive person, one who lived, loved and wrote intensely. Auslander and Hill point up Browning as you should know him:[1]

[1] Joseph Auslander and Frank E. Hill, *The Winged Horse* (New York, Doubleday & Company, Inc.. 1927). p. 328.

The love of horses, like his inquisitive and tenderly careful love of creeping things too small for a name, was all part of Browning's healthy animal exultation. He loved men and women in precisely the same way. Perhaps it was partly because of his excellent digestion. But it was more than that; certainly, it was because his soul was immensely alive and vigorous as well. He believed fiercely in life. He plunged himself up to the armpits in it. In one form or another, through all his poetry, and in himself, he was life's strenuous champion.

That intense exultation in living and interest in people and surroundings are carried over into his dramatic monologues, which reveal superbly finished delineations of each character caught at a revealing moment of his life.

Virginia Woolf's delightful story *Flush* gives us an opportunity to watch Browning's courtship of Elizabeth Barrett through the jealous eyes of her cocker spaniel.[2] On Browning's first visit to the Barrett home, Flush looked over this strange visitor: 'Twisting his yellow gloves in his hands, blinking his eyes, well-groomed, masterly, abrupt, Mr. Browning strode across the room. He seized Miss Barrett's hand, and sank into the chair at her side. Instantly they began to talk." To Flush, a dog who had lived in the warmth, seclusion, and stillness of Miss Barrett's room for four or five years, this "dark, taut, abrupt, vigorous man, with his black hair, his red cheeks, and his yellow gloves," was an enemy to be attacked. "The very sight of him, so well tailored, so tight, so muscular, set his teeth on edge. Oh! to let them meet sharply, completely in the stuff of his trousers!" So thought Flush as he lay watching his archenemy, the "hooded-man" who had suddenly turned his world with Miss Barrett into turmoil, and more than that, had deprived him of Miss Barrett's undivided affection.

Nowhere in literature will the student find a more dynamic picture of Browning than in the play, *The Barretts of Wimpole Street*. The following scene is a portrayal of the first meeting between Robert Browning and Elizabeth Barrett; in it Browning's love of life, his optimism, and his general well-being are sensitively revealed.

[2] From Virginia Woolf, *Flush*, pp. 37-40. Copyright, 1933, by Harcourt, Brace and Company, Inc. Reprinted by permission of the publishers.

AT LAST! [3]

HENRIETTA. Mr. Robert Browning.

ROBERT BROWNING *enters. He is a dark, handsome man in the middle thirties, faultlessly, perhaps even a trifle foppishly dressed. Over his shoulder he wears a cape fastened with a chain at the throat. He carries his high hat, lemon-coloured gloves, and clouded cane.* BROWNING'S *manner is sincere and ardent; his speech rapid, voluble, and emphasized by free gestures.* HENRIETTA *goes out.*

BROWNING. (*Pausing a few steps beyond the threshold*) Miss Barrett?

ELIZABETH. (*Stretching out her hand*) How-do-you-do, Mr. Browning?

BROWNING. (*Quickly lays aside his hat, cane and gloves, and crossing to the sofa, takes her hand in both of his*) Dear Miss Barrett—at last! (*Raises her hand to his lips*) At last!

ELIZABETH. (*Still all nerves, and rather overcome by the ardour and unconventionality of his manner*) I—I've had to put off the pleasure of meeting you much longer than I wished. . . .

BROWNING. (*Still holding her hand*) Would you ever have received me if I hadn't been so tiresomely insistent?

ELIZABETH. As you know from my letters, I've not been all well during the winter, and I—(*Realizing that her hand is still in his, she gently withdraws it*) But won't you take off your cape?

BROWNING. Thank you.

ELIZABETH. I—I hope you don't find the room very close, Mr. Browning?

BROWNING. No, no. . . .

ELIZABETH. My doctor obliges me to live in what I am afraid must be to you a—a hot-house temperature. . . .

BROWNING. (*Who has thrown a quick glance round the room*) Wonderful! You may think, Miss Barrett, that this is the first time I've been here. You're quite wrong, you know!

ELIZABETH. But—

BROWNING. Quite wrong. I have seen this room more times than I can remember. It's as familiar to me as my own little study at home! Before I came in, I knew just how your books were arranged, just how that tendril of ivy slanted over the window panes—and those busts of Homer and Chaucer are quite old friends, and have looked down on me often before!

ELIZABETH. (*Smilingly protesting*) No, really—!

BROWNING. But I could never make out who the other fellows were on the top of the wardrobe, and—

ELIZABETH. (*Laughing, and now quite at ease*) Oh, come, Mr. Browning! I know that dear Mr. Kenyon is never tired of talking about his

[3] From Rudolf Besier, *The Barretts of Wimpole Street*, pp. 59-66. Copyright, 1930, by Rudolf Besier. Reprinted by permission of Little, Brown & Company.

friends; but I can't believe that he described my poor little room to you in detail!

BROWNING. (*Seating himself beside her*) I dragged all the details I possibly could out of him—and my imagination supplied the rest. Directly after I had read your brave and lovely verses I was greedy for anything and everything I could get about you.

ELIZABETH. (*Smilingly*) You frighten me, Mr. Browning!

BROWNING. Why?

ELIZABETH. Well, you know how Mr. Kenyon's enthusiasms run away with his tongue? He and I are the dearest of friends. What he told you about poor me I quite blush to imagine!

BROWNING. You mean, Miss Barrett, about you—you *yourself?*

ELIZABETH. I feel it would be hopeless for me to try to live up to his description.

BROWNING. He never told me anything about you—personally—which had the slightest interest for me.

ELIZABETH. (*Puzzled*) Oh?

BROWNING. Everything he could give me about your surroundings and the circumstances of your life I snatched at with avidity. But all he said about *you* was quite beside the point, because I knew it already—and better than Mr. Kenyon, old friend of yours though he is!

ELIZABETH. But— Oh, Mr. Browning, do my poor writings give me so hopelessly away?

BROWNING. Hopelessly—utterly—entirely—to *me!* . . . I can't speak for the rest of the world.

ELIZABETH. (*Smilingly*) You frighten me again!

BROWNING. No?

ELIZABETH. But you do! For I'm afraid it would be quite useless my ever trying to play-act with you!

BROWNING. Quite useless!

ELIZABETH. I shall always have to be—just myself?

BROWNING. Always.

ELIZABETH. Oh . . . (*quickly*) And you too, Mr. Browning?

BROWNING. Always—just myself! (*He stretches out his hand; she takes it with a smile. Then, with a sudden laugh*) But really, you know, Miss Barrett, I sha'n't be able to take much credit for that! Being myself comes to me as easily as breathing. It's play-acting I can't manage—and the hot water I've got into in consequence . . . If life's to run smoothly we should all be mummers. Well, I can't mum!

ELIZABETH. Yes, I can believe that now I know you. But isn't it extraordinary? When you are *writing* you never do anything else but —play-act.

BROWNING. I know—

ELIZABETH. You have never been yourself in any one of your poems. It's always somebody else speaking through you.

BROWNING. Yes. And shall I tell you why? I am a very modest man. (*Quickly, after a slight pause*) I am really!

ELIZABETH. (*With suppressed amusement*) I didn't question it, Mr. Browning.

BROWNING. So modest, I fully realize that if I wrote about myself— my hopes and fears, hates and loves, and the rest of it—my poems would be intolerably dull.

ELIZABETH. (*Laughing, vivaciously*) Well—since we are pledged to nothing but the truth, I won't contradict that—until I know you better!

BROWNING. (*With a laugh*) Bravo!

ELIZABETH. (*Ardently*) Oh, but these poems, with their glad and great-hearted acceptance of life—you can't imagine what they mean to me! Here am I shut in by four walls, the view of Wimpole Street my only glimpse of the world. And they troop into the room and round my sofa, these wonderful people of yours out of every age and country, and all so tingling with life! life! life! No, you'll never begin to realize how much I owe you!

BROWNING. You—you really mean that?

ELIZABETH. Why, why Mr. Browning—

BROWNING. But of course you do, or you wouldn't say it! And you'll believe me when I tell you that what you have said makes up to me a thousand times over for all the cold-shouldering I've had from the public?

ELIZABETH. (*Fiercely*) Oh, it infuriates me! Why can we never know an eagle for an eagle until it has spread its wings and flown away from us for good? Sometimes—I detest the British public!

BROWNING. (*Lightly*) Oh, no, no! Dear old British public! At least it gives us generously the jolly pastime of abusing it! And mind you, Miss Barrett, I've an uneasy feeling that my style is largely to blame for my unpopularity.

ELIZABETH. (*A little too eagerly*) Oh, surely not!

BROWNING. Didn't we agree never to play-act with each other?

ELIZABETH. (*With a laugh*) Touché! Well, perhaps, there *are* passages in your work a little invol—I mean a little too—too profound for the general reader.

BROWNING. Oh, no! It's not what I say, but how I say it.

ELIZABETH. Oh, but—

BROWNING. And yet to me it's all simple and easy as the rule of three! And to you?

ELIZABETH. Well . . . not *quite* always. Sometimes there *are* passages. . . . (*She picks up a book*) I have marked one or two in your "Sordello" which rather puzzle me. Here, for instance . . .

BROWNING. (*Taking the book*) Oh, "Sordello!" Somebody once called it "a horror of great darkness!" I've done my best to forget it. However—(*He reads the passage to himself, smiling. The smile fades; he passes his hand over his brow and reads it again. She watches*

him, covertly smiling. He mutters) Extraordinary. . . . But—but
a passage torn from its context. . . .
(*He rises and goes to the window, as though to get more light
on the subject, and reads the passage a third time.* ELIZABETH *has
some difficulty in suppressing her amusement. He turns to her with
an expression of humorous chagrin*)
ELIZABETH. Well? . . .
BROWNING. Well, Miss Barrett—when that passage was written only
God and Robert Browning understood it. Now only God understands it.

Two poems—in a way, companion poems—provide good interpretative possibilities: Mrs. Browning's famous sonnet, "How Do
I Love Thee," [4] and her husband's "Prospice," which he wrote
after her death. You would do well to listen to Basil Rathbone's
interpretation of these poems.[5] The sonnet, which every student
of interpretation should try to interpret, is presented by Rathbone
with its full emotional depth but with fine restraint.

HOW DO I LOVE THEE?

How do I love thee? Let me count the ways.
I love thee to the depth and breadth and height
My soul can reach, when feeling out of sight
For the ends of Being and ideal Grace.
I love thee to the level of every day's
Most quiet need, by sun and candle-light.
I love thee freely, as men strive for Right;
I love thee purely, as men turn from Praise.
I love thee with the passion put to use
In my old griefs, and with my childhood's faith.
I love thee with a love I seemed to lose
With my lost saints,—I love thee with the breath,
Smiles, tears, of all my life!—and, if God choose,
I shall but love thee better after death.
ELIZABETH BARRETT BROWNING

"Prospice" (meaning "to look forward") is presented as Browning
would have given it, for it has Browning's vigorous rhythmic

[4] From *Sonnets from the Portuguese,* which is a collection of original
compositions, not translations.
[5] *Masterpieces of Literature: Great Themes in Poetry* (Columbia, E11-10),
sponsored by the National Council of Teachers of English.

stamp. Note Rathbone's vocal versatility in interpreting these two poems.

PROSPICE

Fear death?—to feel the fog in my throat,
　　The mist in my face,
When the snows begin, and the blasts denote
　　I am nearing the place,
The power of the night, the press of the storm,
　　The post of the foe;
Where he stands, the Arch Fear in a visible form,
　　Yet the strong man must go:
For the journey is done and the summit attained,
　　And the barriers fall,
Though a battle's to fight ere the guerdon be gained,
　　The reward of it all.
I was ever a fighter, so—one fight more,
　　The best and the last!
I would hate that death bandaged my eyes, and forbore,
　　And bade me creep past.
No! let me taste the whole of it, fare like my peers
　　The heroes of old,
Bear the brunt, in a minute pay life's glad arrears
　　Of pain, darkness and cold.
For sudden the worst turns the best to the brave,
　　The black minute's at end,
And the elements' rage, the fiend-voices that rave,
　　Shall dwindle, shall blend,
Shall change, shall become first a peace out of pain,
　　Then a light, then thy breast,
O thou soul of my soul! I shall clasp thee again,
　　And with God be the rest!

ROBERT BROWNING

Whitman

Like Browning, Whitman had exuberant optimism, but the two poets differ entirely in manner, in character, and in choice of themes. Walt Whitman sang lustily, vigorously, expansively of America and democracy. "I sound my barbaric yawp over the roofs of the world," he wrote. His poetry shows none of the subtleties and highlights of Browning's dramatic characterizations. Rather, it swings along in broad movements, without obvious metrical pattern but with a rhythm that surges with life and enthusiasm. He was an American, living in America, hobnobbing with Americans of all classes. Whitman, as a young man, is described in *The Winged Horse*:[6]

In reality the most important thing he was doing in all these years was what people called his loafing. Young Walt Whitman never seemed in a hurry. Something of a Broadway dandy, carrying a cane, wearing a bud in his buttonhole, he stopped on his way to the office to see workmen tinning a roof, or to talk with a policeman. He saw the crowd pour from the ferryboat. He rode on the Broadway omnibuses for hours. He sat there beside Broadway Jack, the driver, or Pop Rice or Old Elephant. Jack and Pop would spin a yarn, or Walt would recite *Julius Caesar*.

These lines, from "Give Me the Splendid Silent Sun," are typical of Whitman, the friend of all:

LIFE IN MANHATTAN[7]

Give me faces and streets—give me these phantoms incessant and
    endless along the trottoirs!
Give me interminable eyes—give me women—give me comrades and
    lovers by the thousand!
Let me see new ones every day—let me hold new ones by the hand
    every day!
Give me such shows—give me the streets of Manhattan!
·   ·   ·   ·   ·   ·   ·   ·   ·   ·   ·   ·   ·
Give me the shores and wharves heavy-fringed with black ships!
Oh, such for me! Oh, an intense life, full to repletion and varied!
The life of the theatre, barroom, huge hotel, for me!
The saloon of the steamer! the crowded excursion for me! the torch-
    light procession!
The dense brigade bound for the war, with high-piled military wagons
    following;
People, endless, streaming, with strong voices, passions, pageants,
Manhattan streets with their powerful throbs, with beating drums as
    now,
The endless and noisy chorus, the rustle and clank of muskets,
Manhattan crowds, with their turbulent musical chorus!
Manhattan faces and eyes forever for me.

[6] Auslander and Hill, *op. cit.*, p. 350.
[7] From *Poems*, introduction by Carl Sandburg, p. 267. Copyright, 1921, by Boni & Liveright Company. Reprinted by permission of the publishers.

When *Leaves of Grass* was first published in 1855, it met with both clamor and furor. Carl Sandburg, one of its stanch defenders, has declared it to be the "most wildly keyed oath that America means something and is going somewhere that has ever been written; it is America's most classic advertisement of itself as having purpose, destiny, banners, and beacon fires." [8] Sandburg relates how Whitman met the criticism at the time of the publishing of the second edition in 1856: [9]

The poet published as a frontispiece a picture of himself in shirtsleeves, knockabout clothes, the left hand in the pants pocket, the right hand on the hip akimbo, the hat tossed at a slant, and the head and the general disposition of the cosmos indicating a statement and an inquiry, "Well, here we are; it looks good to us; and while it isn't important, how do you like us?"

On the cover of the book were the words gilded on a green background: "I greet you at the beginning of a great career—R. W. Emerson." The generally accredited foremost reputable figure of American Letters and philosophy had written those words to Whitman the year before.

And in order to let everybody in and give free speech full play, there was printed as the last thing in the book, a criticism by a reviewer in the Boston Intelligencer of May 3, 1856, closing with this paragraph: "This book should find no place where humanity urges any claim to respect, and the author should be kicked from all decent society as below the level of the brute. There is neither wit nor method in his disjointed babbling, and it seems to me he must be some escaped lunatic, raving in pitiable delirium."

Whitman will live because of *Leaves of Grass,* in which a poet's philosophy has been expressed in such a personal vein that it has been said of the poem, "Who touches this touches man." He will also live for his devoted allegiance to Lincoln. Every student in the grades knows Whitman's memorial poem to Lincoln, "O, Captain, My Captain!" Certainly those interested in interpreting from Whitman will read "When Lilacs Last in the Dooryard Bloomed," which Sandburg calls "the most majestic threnody to death in the English language." [10]

[8] *Ibid.,* p. v.
[9] *Ibid.,* p. v.
[10] *Ibid.,* p. viii.

Like an echo hallooing to us in the dusk are the memorable closing lines of "Song of Myself":[11]

> I bequeath myself to the dirt, to grow from the grass I love;
> If you want me again, look for me under your boot-soles.
>
> You will hardly know who I am, or what I mean,
> But I shall be good health to you nevertheless,—
> And filter and fiber your blood.
>
> Failing to find me at first, keep encouraged;
> Missing me one place, search another;
> I stop somewhere, waiting for you.

But you will always remember his great faith in America:[12]

> I hear America singing, the varied carols I hear
>
> .   .   .   .
>
> Each singing what belongs to him or her and to none else
>
> .   .   .   .
>
> Singing with open mouths, their strong melodious songs.

Kipling

Another poet who was interested in common folk was Rudyard Kipling, the great portrayer of the everyday man. According to the critic, C. E. Carrington:[13]

It is useless to search in Kipling's works for an elaborate scheme of philosophy, because it never occurred to him to attempt one. His talent lay in insight; he splashed his observation like a searchlight, with uncanny accuracy, upon the world around him. He was interested in almost everything his neighbors were interested in, but least perhaps in the theories of highbrow coteries.

If we are to plot his literary pedigree, we might describe him by Whitman out of Emerson. From the latter he inherited the rule of Self-Reliance, the strongest element in his character, and it may be mentioned that verbal echoes from Emerson are common in Kiping's earlier work. From Whitman he derived a deep sense of the poetry of common life, and like Whitman he had no false delicacy. If ordi-

---

[11] *Ibid.*, p. 78.

[12] *Ibid.*, p. 10.

[13] "Maugham's Choice of Kipling's Best," *New York Times Book Review* (August 30, 1953).

nary folk were brutal and vulgar, then brutality and vulgarity would appear in his work. The searchlight of his observation would reveal the bare phenomenon and then, with consummate skill, he would reproduce the sound and the smell and the taste of it. He loved technicalities, and his own technique was the use of words.

Very few of us can forget the lilt of the words in "Mandalay":

> Come you back to Mandalay,
> Where the old Flotilla lay:
> Can't you 'ear their paddles chunkin'
>   from Rangoon to Mandalay?
> On the road to Mandalay,
> Where the flyin'-fishes play,
> An' the dawn comes up like thunder
>   outer China 'crost the Bay!

Nor can we easily duplicate in literature the sensory vividness revealed in lines like these from "Gunga Din":

> I sha'n't forgit the night
> When I dropped be'ind the fight
> With a bullet where my belt-plate should 'a' been.
> I was chokin' mad with thirst,
> An' the man that spied me first
> Was our good old grinnin', gruntin' Gunga Din.
> 'E lifted up my 'ead,
> An' 'e plugged me where I bled,
> An' 'e guv me 'arf-a-pint o' water—green:
> It was crawlin' and it stunk,
> But of all the drinks I've drunk,
> I'm gratefullest to one from Gunga Din.
> It was "Din! Din! Din!
> 'Ere's a beggar with a bullet through 'is spleen;
> 'E's chawin' up the ground,
> An' 'e's kickin' all around:
> For Gawd's sake git the water, Gunga Din!"

Poe

Edgar Allan Poe, aloof, proud, self-willed, never too amiable or too kind, is usually thought of as a technician, as one striving for effects. Instead of the ruggedness of Kipling or the lusty singing of Whitman, there is only an escape into unreality—weird and grotesque.

He wrote with enormous pretense to knowledge, gesticulating angrily in print over unhappy authors whose work displeased him. But all the time he was turning more and more to a realm of imagination in which phantoms made a gorgeous parade. Here he could win a kind of true mastery, marshalling his shadows and incredible lights and sounds into stories or verse that, like a madman's, had a marvellous exactness and made unreality seem real. And, having set his triumph down in words, he could carry it out of dream into print; he could force the practical world to come under the spell he created and admit his mastery. Then he could exult. He cried: "I love fame. I dote upon it. I idolize it. I would drink to the dregs the glorious intoxication; I would have incense arise in my honour from every hamlet." [14]

In his essay, "The Philosophy of Composition," Poe reports how exactly he constructed "The Raven": not by a "species of fine frenzy—an ecstatic intuition," but "step by step, to its completion with the precision and rigid consequence of a mathematical problem." He builds the essay to a dramatic climax—a climax which must have been as studied as the climax in the poem— by quoting the following lines from "The Raven":

And the Raven, never flitting, still is sitting, *still* is sitting
On the pallid bust of Pallas just above my chamber door;
And his eyes have all the seeming of a demon's that is dreaming,
And the lamp-light o'er him streaming throws his shadow on the floor;
And my soul from out that shadow that lies floating on the floor
    Shall be lifted—nevermore!

Sandburg

Unlike Poe, Carl Sandburg, the singing bard of America, rubs shoulders with people in his honest, forthright way. He writes vivid, blunt, sometimes tender, sometimes raucous—but usually in the pattern of American ruggedness—poetic lines because he has lived, like Whitman, in the stream of American activity. Louis Untermeyer gives a bird's-eye view of Sandburg's varied experiences in seeking a livelihood:[15]

Carl Sandburg was born in Galesburg, Illinois, in 1878. Like Frost and Robinson he had to wait until he was almost forty before his

[14] Auslander and Hill, *op. cit.*, p. 342.
[15] *American Poetry Since 1900* (New York, Henry Holt and Company, Inc., 1923), p. 67.

work received recognition; unlike them, he earned his living by his hands, having been, in rapid succession, porter in a barber-shop, scene-shifter in a dingy music-hall, truck-handler in a brickyard, dishwasher in Omaha hotels, harvest-hand in Kansas, soldier in Porto-Rico. These varied activities, strange preparation for a poet, gave him contacts which helped him become the laureate of industrial America. There are, I hasten to add, two Sandburgs; the muscular, heavy-fisted, hard-hitting son of the streets, and his almost unrecognizable twin, the shadow painter, the haunter of mists, the lover of implications and overtones.

We know too that Sandburg during his college days was captain of the basketball team, editor of the college newspaper, and that later he became a newspaper man, held a job as advertising manager, and engaged in politics in Wisconsin.

The virility of these lines from "Upstream," the surging rhythm of the phrases and the vivid imagery, are typical of much of Sandburg's work:[16]

> The strong men keep coming on.
> They go down shot, hanged, sick, broken.
> They live on fighting, singing, lucky as plungers.
> The strong mothers pulling them on . . .
> The strong mothers pulling them
>   from a dark sea, a great prairie,
>   a long mountain.
> Call hallelujah, call amen, call
>   deep thanks.
> The strong men keep coming on.

The following poem is illustrative of Sandburg's lightness of touch and gentleness of manner:

AT A WINDOW[17]

> Give me hunger,
> O you gods that sit and give
> The world its orders.

[16] From *Slabs of the Sunburnt West*, p. 30. Copyright, 1922, by Harcourt, Brace and Company, Inc.; renewed by Carl Sandburg. Reprinted by permission of the publishers.

[17] From *Chicago Poems*, p. 115. Copyright, 1916, by Henry Holt and Company, Inc. Reprinted by permission of the publishers.

Give me hunger, pain and want,
Shut me out with shame and failure
From your doors of gold and fame,
Give me your shabbiest, weariest hunger!—

But leave me a little love,
A voice to speak to me at the day's end,
A hand to touch me in the dark room
Breaking the long loneliness.
In the dusk of day-shapes
Blurring the sunset,

One little wandering, western star
Thrust out from the changing shores of shadow.
Let me go to the window,
Watch there the day-shapes of dusk
And wait and know the coming
Of a little love.

His approach to poetry and fame is different from Poe's. As he expresses it:[18]

People write poetry because they want to. It functions in them as air in the nostrils of an athlete in a sprint. Moods, thoughts, emotions, surge over writers as they do over inventors and politicians. It is a dark stuff of light that comes and goes. . . . Unless we keep on the lookout we write book language and employ the verbiage of dead men instead of using the speech of people alive today.

Frost

One of the best-known American poets today is Robert Frost, about whom much has been written. Many find the flavor and atmosphere of New England in his poetry. Frost would never write a poem like "Annabel Lee"; neither would he produce the ruggedness of "Chicago." His poetry is built from observations, from experiences that many would overlook as insignificant. The setting for most of his poetry is New England country, and his people are the farm folk; his words are those of everyday speech, called by Frost the "unmade words" which must be transformed by the poet's touch into words that "make" poetry. Dorothy Can-

[18] Carl Sandburg, "The Work of Ezra Pound," *Poetry* (February, 1916). Reprinted by permission of the publishers.

field's description of his Shaftesbury house suggests the background from which his "earthiness" comes.[19]

A long time the house has stood there, about a hundred and thirty
years and nothing unusual has happened to it. But it is the kind of
house that can afford to wait, and turn all the riper and sweeter for
it, built as it is of stone from out of its own home ground. To us, his
house looks not at all grim or sombre, but homelike and strong and
cheerful and protecting, when we look up at it as we start to climb
Peleg Cole's hill, and see it at the top, standing wide-roofed and substantial, with its old lilac and syringa bushes, and the lily-of-the-valley
bed, earlier to bloom than in any other of our gardens, because of
the earth's warmth reflected from the grey stone walls against which
it is planted.

Now if we add to the picture of the house a description of the
man the atmosphere for his poetry becomes more interesting:[20]

I see him dressed in a gray suit, a gray cap snatched down over a
finely-shaped head, shaggy, granite-streaked hair straggling out; blue
eyes, twinkling blue eyes with whimsical crinkles playing hide and
seek around the corners, hooded with quizzical eyebrows; below, a
droll, friendly, engaging expression, yet something elusive about it
as though he viewed life with an amused detachment.

John Holmes tells us more about Frost as a person:[21]

The man's talking presence is unforgettable. With one or two present for an evening, he starts all but flat on his back, deep in a big
chair, in his house in Cambridge, or at the cabin near Bread Loaf. He
looks tired; perhaps he is. But you learn never to underestimate the
powerful physique, the durability, the tough-bodied liveliness of this
old Roman. He begins, casting here and there with a question or two.
Then as he warms up to his favorite occupation, he sits up a little,
then more, until he is in full swing, carrying the evening away. He
rumples his hair with a hand now and then. He likes to be easy
when the occasion requires—and he will chuckle at the next thing
he is going to say. The deep-set eyes glint; the full lower lip pushes
out; and some wise or wicked or very funny remark comes forth. He
loves nothing better than to work away at his talking until he sur-

[19] "Robert Frost's Hilltop," *The Bookman* (December, 1926).
[20] Paul Benjamin, "The Poet of Friendliness," *The Survey* (November 27,
1920).
[21] "Robert Frost," *New York Times Book Review* (March 26, 1950).

prises himself into saying a new thing. He keeps this state of readiness of mind always.

Another picture of Robert Frost is given by Wilfred Wilson Gibson:[22]

> . . . In the lamplight
> We talked and laughed; but, for the most part, listened
> While Robert Frost kept on and on and on,
> In his slow New England fashion, for our delight,
> Holding us with shrewd turns and racy quips,
> And the rare twinkle of his grave blue eyes.
>
> We sat there in the lamplight, while the day
> Died from rose-latticed casements, and the plovers
> Called over the low meadows, till the owls
> Answered them from the elms, we sat and talked—
> Now, a quick flash from Abercombie; now,
> A murmured dry half-heard aside from Thomas;
> Now, a clear laughing word from Brooke; and then
> Again Frost's rich and ripe philosophy,
> That had the body and tang of good draught-cider,
> And poured as clear a stream.

One of the best-known poems of Robert Frost, "The Road Not Taken," is discussed briefly by Louis Untermeyer. Perhaps your perspective about the poem will be changed after reading Untermeyer's analysis:[23]

Robert Frost has gone his own way. He could not help it; his destination—and perhaps his destiny—was directed by the spirit behind the man. This inevitable progress is indicated in a much-quoted and much misunderstood poem, "The Road Not Taken." Once while travelling alone, Frost tells us, he stood at a fork in the road, undecided which path to take. Finally, he chose one because it seemed a little less frequented, though actually there was no such difference, for the "passing there had worn them really about the same." Yet, even at the moment of choice, the poet quizzically imagined that the choice

---

[22] From "The Golden Room," *The Golden Room* (New York, The Macmillan Company, 1928), pp. 172-173. Reprinted by permission of The Macmillan Company and the present holders of the copyright, St Martin's Press, Inc.

[23] Louis Untermeyer, ed., *The Road Not Taken: An Introduction to Robert Frost* (New York, Henry Holt and Company, Inc., 1951), pp. 269-270.

was important, that he would some day tell himself he took the less travelled road:

   And that has made all the difference.

 The poet's "difference" is in him from the beginning, long before he sets out on his career. The road that Robert Frost took was not only the "different" road, the right road for him, but the only road he could have taken.

Here is the poem in question:

THE ROAD NOT TAKEN?[24]

Two roads diverged in a yellow wood,
And sorry I could not travel both
And be one traveler, long I stood
And looked down one as far as I could
To where it bent in the undergrowth;

Then took the other, as just as fair,
And having perhaps the better claim,
Because it was grassy and wanted wear;
Though as for that the passing there
Had worn them really about the same,

And both that morning equally lay
In leaves no step had trodden black.
Oh, I kept the first for another day!
Yet knowing how way leads on to way,
I doubted if I should ever come back.

I shall be telling this with a sigh
Somewhere ages and ages hence:
Two roads diverged in a wood, and I—
I took the one less traveled by,
And that has made all the difference.

 It is hoped that these few introductory remarks about Robert Frost will interest the interpreter to investigate further the author's philosophy. Is he one who takes extravagant flights, indulging in fanciful dreams? Is there present the restraint and atmosphere of New England? Is he a realist, as he has sometimes been described? Are his observations on the side of bitter reflection?

---

[24] From *Complete Poems of Robert Frost.* Copyright, 1930–1949, by Henry Holt and Company, Inc. Copyright, 1936, 1948, by Robert Frost. Reprinted by permission of the publishers.

Untermeyer[25] quotes Frost as once saying: "'There are two types of realist. There is one who offers a good deal of dirt with his potato to show that it is a real potato. And there is one who is satisfied with the potato brushed clean. I am inclined to be the second kind. To me, the thing that art does for life is to clean it, to strip it to form.'" Do you agree that he follows this pattern? In the following poem, is he bitter, critical, cynical? Or is his attitude whimsical? Or is he quietly chuckling with tongue-in-cheek?

A CONSIDERABLE SPECK[26]

A speck that would have been beneath my sight
On any but a paper sheet so white
Set off across what I had written there.
And I had idly poised my pen in air
To stop it with a period of ink
When something strange about it made me think.
This was no dust speck by my breathing blown,
But unmistakably a living mite
With inclinations it could call its own.
It paused as with suspicion of my pen,
And then came racing wildly on again
To where my manuscript was not yet dry;
Then paused again and either drank or smelt—
With loathing, for again it turned to fly.
Plainly with an intelligence I dealt.
It seemed too tiny to have room for feet,
Yet must have had a set of them complete
To express how much it didn't want to die.
It ran with terror and with cunning crept.
It faltered; I could see it hesitate;
Then in the middle of the open sheet
Cower down in desperation to accept
Whatever I accorded it of fate.

I have none of the tenderer-than-thou
Collectivistic regimenting love
With which the modern world is being swept.
But this poor microscopic item now!

[25] Untermeyer, *The Road Not Taken*, p. 18.
[26] From *Complete Poems of Robert Frost*. Copyright, 1930–1949, by Henry Holt and Company, Inc. Copyright, 1936, 1948, by Robert Frost. Reprinted by permission of the publishers.

Since it was nothing I knew evil of
I let it lie there till I hope it slept.

I have a mind myself and recognize
Mind when I meet with it in any guise.
No one can know how glad I am to find
On any sheet the least display of mind.

Lowell

Many of you have read Amy Lowell's poetry, but have you ever tried to find out what kind of person she was? She certainly must have been magnetic in personality to have drawn so many friends around her and to have been the leader for years of the poets of her period. Let us see her as Elizabeth S. Sergeant saw her and knew her:[27]

That Amy Lowell's creative spirit occupied a large and unwieldy body is important because triumph lay with the spirit. Her handsome head, unflinching in its carriage, had much to reckon with. First, perhaps a passionate and untrammelled heart. Next, physical illness, disability, and a kind of fleshly discomfort that no woman could bear in youth without suffering self-consciousness, and the sense of a lost paradise. Yet I doubt if I have known a maturity as full-flavoured and wholly sustaining as Amy Lowell's. Every twisted strand, every quirk in her destiny which earlier challenged normality and happiness, became woven into the warp and woof of a noble and dedicated career. There was at last nothing she would have altered if she could, even her mortal shape.

And of her idiosyncrasies while she was at work, Sergeant writes:[28]

Amy Lowell chose to wake and sleep not in the high-ceiled, *piano nobile* part of her house but on that more informal level above, that rookery under the slated eaves where she could more easily perform her conjuring trick of turning midnight to morn and morn to midnight and by another special prescription, accord the most insistent telephone bell with the most abysmal silence. Here, too, kimonas and typewriters, secretaries and—in their time—Scotch sheep-dogs, maids and visitors, breakfasts and lunches, fires and electric fans, manu-

[27] *Fire Under the Andes* (New York, Alfred A. Knopf, Inc., 1927), pp. 11-12. Reprinted by permission of the author.
[28] *Ibid.*, pp. 14-15.

scripts and bandages, keen-pointed pencils and blunt-pointed cigars, could be mingled in that highly organized confusion and bustle which were the spice of a poet's more executive hours.

Her personality, as revealed as a hostess among her literary friends, is dynamic:[29]

When, half-way through the long perfection of the meal, the hostess appeared, now cap-a-pie, dressed in her fine dark-green, full of capricious humor and hearty appetite, she was usually, to be sure, ready to demolish in talk the most distinguished adversary. If necessary, she would, metaphorically speaking, shake him to quiescence, with queer jerks of the head, like a terrier with its prey. She could be ruthless, especially in those earlier days when both she and the movement she was sponsoring were on the defensive. If her tremendous drive encountered an obstacle that drove it back upon itself, she was dangerous as a tidal wave in her destructive force. But by the time she became the most arresting and conspicuous figure among American authors, she brought even to controversy the amenity of assurance. Then that forthright, buccaneering maleness of hers, that eighteenth-century gusto for meeting and defeating others in talk, that fecund interest in books and scholarship and the craft of letters, that hardy curiosity about "Men, Women, and Ghosts" came into its real rights, and made an evening at her house memorable and rich among literary and human adventures.

Amy Lowell's poem, "Patterns," has always been the subject of discussion. Some have taken the meaning literally; others believe she is talking about patterns of living; and still others, that she has attempted to incorporate her stanch belief in free verse into the meaning of the poem. What do *you* think? What is the philosophy revealed?

PATTERNS[30]

I walk down the garden paths,
And all the daffodils
Are blowing, and the bright blue squills.
I walk down the patterned garden-paths
In my stiff, brocaded gown.

[29] *Ibid.*, pp. 22-23.
[30] From *Men, Women, and Ghosts*, p. 3. Copyright, 1916, by Houghton, Mifflin Company. Reprinted by permission of the publishers.

With my powdered hair and jeweled fan,
I too am a rare
Pattern. As I wander down
The garden paths.

My dress is richly figured,
And the train
Makes a pink and silver stain
On the gravel, and the thrift
Of the borders.
Just a plate of current fashion,
Tripping by in high-heeled, ribboned shoes.
Not a softness anywhere about me,
Only whalebone and brocade.
And I sink on a seat in the shade
Of a lime tree. For my passion
Wars against the stiff brocade.
The daffodils and squills
Flutter in the breeze
As they please.
And I weep;
For the lime tree is in blossom
And one small flower has dropped upon my bosom.

And the plashing of waterdrops
In the marble fountain
Comes down the garden-paths.
The dripping never stops.
Underneath my stiffened gown
Is the softness of a woman bathing in a marble basin,
A basin in the midst of hedges grown
So thick, she cannot see her lover hiding,
But she guesses he is near,
And the sliding of the water
Seems the stroking of a dear
Hand upon her.
What is Summer in a fine brocaded gown!
I should like to see it lying in a heap upon the ground.
And the pink and silver crumpled up on the ground.

I would be the pink and silver as I ran along the paths,
And he would stumble after,
Bewildered by my laughter.
I should see the sun flashing from his sword-hilt and the buckles on
    his shoes.
I would choose
To lead him in a maze along the patterned paths,
A bright and laughing maze for my heavy-booted lover,

Till he caught me in the shade,
And the buttons of his waistcoat bruised by body as he clasped me,
Aching, melting, unafraid.
With the shadows of the leaves and the sundrops,
And the plopping of the waterdrops,
All about us in the open afternoon—
I am very like to swoon
With the weight of this brocade,
For the sun sifts through the shade.

Underneath the fallen blossom
In my bosom,
Is a letter I have hid.
It was brought to me this morning by a rider from the Duke.
"Madam, we regret to inform you that Lord Hartwell
Died in action Thursday se'nnight."
As I read it in the white, morning sunlight,
The letters squirmed like snakes.
"Any answer, Madam?" said my footman.
"No," I told him.
"See that the messenger takes some refreshment.
No, no answer."

And I walked into the garden,
Up and down the patterned paths,
In my stiff, correct brocade.
The blue and yellow flowers stood up proudly in the sun,
Each one.
I stood upright too,
Held rigid to the pattern
By the stiffness of my gown.
Up and down I walked,
Up and down.

In a month he would have been my husband.
In a month, here, underneath this lime,
We would have broke the pattern;
He for me, and I for him,
He as Colonel, I as Lady,
On this shady seat.
He had a whim
That sunlight carried blessing.
And I answered, "It shall be as you have said."
Now he is dead.

In Summer and in Winter I shall walk
Up and down
The patterned garden-paths

In my stiff, brocaded gown.
The squills and daffodils
Will give place to pillared roses, and to asters, and to snow.
I shall go
Up and down
In my gown.
Gorgeously arrayed,
Boned and stayed.
And the softness of my body will be guarded from embrace
By each button, hook, and lace.
For the man who should loose me is dead,
Fighting with the Duke in Flanders,
In a pattern called a war.
Christ! What are patterns for?

The foregoing brief comments about poets whose writings you may wish to interpret are by no means definitive but are intended to be suggestive and motivating for further reading. The intent is to focus attention on the spirit and vitality of the person, in the hope that you, the interpreter, will browse further for pertinent background which will give reality to the author and reveal his philosophy and personality. Suppose you find an author whose writing pleases you, one whose work you might wish to interpret for an audience. Before picking any selections, find out what you can about the writer as a person. For instance, do you *know* Archibald MacLeish, who, as William Rose Benét has said, is one of the very few American poets who is trying to get any perspective upon his country? Do you *know* Vachel Lindsay, the robust singer of songs, who in his "Epilogue" states his faith by writing that he would set right the old world's wrong. Do you *know* John Masefield, the writer of salt-water ballads, who began his life on shipboard at the age of sixteen? It is interesting to know that Edwin Arlington Robinson, with a yen for detective stories, once reported that if by chance he had to live on a desert island the rest of his life, he would select three books for company: the Bible, Shakespeare, and the dictionary. Certainly you should know something of Kipling's early life in India, of the disappointments which came later from American publishers, and of the final acceptance in England of his *Barrack Room Ballads,* which tell the story of the common soldier in his everyday rugged living.

Literature is written by people—and people are interesting to know, especially if they appeal to us through their creative writing. The piece of literature may be a masterpiece of form, an abstraction of intellectual activity—called by Untermeyer the work of the "cerebralists"—or it may have been written as a remembered emotion or experience. The cerebralists are those who "speak of the mathematics, the architecture of literature, of mass and planes, of suspensions, dissonances, and modulations of an abstract form"; those who are "preoccupied with verbal craftmanship and deliberate technic." [31] T. S. Eliot's poetry, as far as Untermeyer is concerned,[32] contains an "unearthly light without warmth" and appeals

only to our acquired knowledge. . . . Such poems, for all their intellectual play are not the result of purely cerebral activity. They are not merely thoughtful poems, for poetry that has its inception in the intellect usually remains there. The living poem is something that is felt first and thought out afterwards. "It begins," Frost has said somewhere, "with a lump in the throat; a home-sickness or a love-sickness. It is a reaching-out towards expression; an effort to find fulfilment. A complete poem is one where an emotion has found its thought and the thought has found the words."

Untermeyer continues:[33]

A book whose intelligibility relies on other books, that needs quotations in eight languages, that points to thirty-odd sources for its disjected fragments and the reading of two works of anthropology to elucidate (I quote Eliot) "the difficulties of the poem"—such a work is not so much a creative thing as a piece of literary carpentry, scholarly joiner's work.

This analysis is different from his comments on Sandburg's *Slabs of Sunburnt West*:[34]

This is something carved out of earth, showing dirt and yellow clay; here are great gaps and boulders, steaming ditches and yellow clay, and the deep-chested laughter of workers quarreling, forgetting,

[31] Untermeyer, *American Poetry Since 1900*, p. 41.
[32] *Ibid.*, p. 67.
[33] *Ibid.*, p. 358.
[34] *Ibid.*, p. 97.

building. Here are titanic visions: smoke-belching chimneys, quarries of iron-ribbed rock: the dream of men and machinery. And silence is here—the silence of sleeping tenements, of creeping mist-forms, of sun-soaked cornfields.

Mention has been made only of poets, but it is possible to go on at length and to include many favorite prose writers: James Thurber, who has a special brand of infectious humor, which Fanny Butcher calls "Thurberitis," "a persistent literary virus"; John Mason Brown, the inimitable drama critic who writes so engagingly of his platform and audience reactions; Cornelia Otis Skinner, the sophisticate of *Nuts in May* fame; E. B. White, known for his penetrating but homespun wit as revealed in *One Man's Meat* and *The Second Tree From the Corner*. Incidentally, White writes of the latter book: "Whoever sets pen to paper writes of himself, whether knowingly or not. This then, is a book of revelations: stories, poems, essays, opinions, out of the past, the present, the future, the city, and the country." [35]

THE AUTHOR'S MOTIVATION

The artistic urge is commonly regarded as its own excuse for being: it needs no explanation or defense. Accordingly, most poems, stories, and dramatic episodes justify their right to exist solely by their intrinsic worth, as bits of art interesting enough to be known for their own merits. The poet is supposed to break forth as a lark into song. Story writers presumably write because they cannot help it.

But now and then a certain work needs a footnote. St. Paul's Cathedral is the monument of Sir Christopher Wren who built it; the Rheims Cathedral acquires interest as the place where Jeanne d'Arc brought the Dauphin to be crowned; Whistler's "Study in Black and White" is a portrait of his mother. William Ellery Leonard writes of his first wife in his poem, *Two Lives*. Siegfried Sassoon's poetry vividly describes his experiences in World War I.

[35] E. B. White, *The Second Tree from the Corner* (New York, Harper & Brothers, 1954), Foreword, pp. viii-ix.

EXERCISES

The interpreter's appreciation and understanding of the following selections will increase with a knowledge of the author's motivation. Read these selections carefully. How has a knowledge of motive added to your understanding of each?

I

The following letter was written by a soldier during World War II. The explanation of how the letter originated and how it became a part of guerrilla folklore, and the final information concerning the fate of the mother and child deepen the meaning because of the emotional significance attached to these incidents.

SUCH IS YOUR HERITAGE[36]

In a small town in Yugoslavia there lived a man named Peter. He read many books, dabbled in politics and married a girl named Maria.

When Maria was heavy with child, the Germans occupied Peter's village and took over his home and his business. Peter left to fight in the woods with the Yugoslav Partisans. He was shot several weeks later but before he died he took out a stub of pencil and wrote a letter to his unborn son.

Partisans found Peter's body and the letter. While they waited for a chance to deliver it, the letter was passed from hand to hand and became in time a part of guerrilla folklore. By now it may have been sharpened by the literacy of other men and given added eloquence by the nobility of other men's minds. But what it said was as true when it was scrawled on a scrap of paper in a great whispering forest as it was when it reached London and the outside world:

My child, sleeping now in the dark and gathering strength for the struggle of birth, I wish you well. At present you have no proper shape, and you do not breathe, and you are blind. Yet, when your time comes, your time and the time of your mother, whom I deeply love, there will be something in you that will give you power to fight for air and light. Such is your heritage, such is your destiny as a child born of woman—to fight for light and hold on without knowing why.

May the flame that tempers the bright steel of your youth never die, but burn always; so that when your work is done and your long day ended, you may still be like a watchman's fire at the end of a

[36] *Time* (January 25, 1943), p. 71. Reprinted by permission of the publishers.

lonely road—loved and cherished for your gracious glow by all good wayfarers who need light in their darkness and warmth for their comfort.

The spirit of wonder and adventure, the token of immortality, will be given to you as a child. May you keep it forever, with that in your heart which always seeks the gold beyond the rainbow, the pastures beyond the desert, the dawn beyond the sea, the light beyond the dark.

May you seek always and strive always in good faith and high courage, in this world where men grow so tired.

Keep your capacity for faith and belief, but let your judgment watch what you believe.

Keep your power to receive everything; only learn to select what your instinct tells you is right.

Keep your love of life, but throw away your fear of death. Life must be loved or it is lost; but it should never be loved too well.

Keep your delight in friendship; only learn to know your friends.

Keep your intolerance—only save it for what your heart tells you is bad.

Keep your wonder at great and noble things like sunlight and thunder, the rain and the stars, the wind and the sea, the growth of trees and the return of harvests, and the greatness of heroes.

Keep your heart hungry for new knowledge; keep your hatred of a lie; and keep your power of indignation.

Now I know I must die, and you must be born to stand upon the rubbish heap of my errors. Forgive me for this. I am ashamed to leave you an untidy, uncomfortable world. But so it must be.

In thought, as a last benediction, I kiss your forehead. Good night to you—and good morning and a clear dawn.

The day that the avenging Partisans swept back into Peter's village they found that his widow had been murdered a few days before her child would have been born. The letter that his comrades could not deliver has become instead a letter to all unborn children.

II

Tennyson's *In Memoriam,* a collection of poems, was motivated by the death of his very dear friend, Arthur Henry Hallam. In many of the poems, as in the following, Tennyson expresses his grief; in later poems, he expresses his religious doubts and, finally, his return to his belief and faith:

> Dark house, by which once more I stand
>   Here in the long unlovely street,
>   Doors, where my heart was used to beat
> So quickly, waiting for a hand,

A hand that can be clasped no more—
　Behold me, for I cannot sleep,
　And like a guilty thing I creep
At earliest morning to the door.

He is not here; but far away
　The noise of life begins again,
　And ghastly through the drizzling rain
On the bald street breaks the blank day.

ALFRED TENNYSON

III

"Crossing the Bar," the last poem written by Tennyson, reveals his religious faith. The interpreter must be careful not to read it as if Tennyson felt no hope, for it is written with a hope that he will see his "Pilot face to face":

CROSSING THE BAR

Sunset and evening star,
　And one clear call for me!
And may there be no moaning of the bar,
　When I put out to sea,

But such a tide as moving seems asleep,
　Too full for sound and foam,
When that which drew from out the boundless deep
　Turns again home.

Twilight and evening bell,
　And after that the dark!
And may there be no sadness of farewell,
　When I embark;

For though from out our bourne of Time and Place
　The flood may bear me far,
I hope to see my Pilot face to face
　When I have crossed the bar.

ALFRED TENNYSON

IV

Christina Rossetti wrote the following sonnet to her lover whom she had renounced for a religious life:

Remember me when I am gone away,
　Gone far away into the silent land;

When you can no more hold me by the hand
Nor I half turn to go yet turning stay.
Remember me when no more day by day
You tell me of our future that you planned.
Only remember me; you understand
It will be late to counsel then or pray.
Yet if you should forget me for a while
And afterwards remember, do not grieve:
For if the darkness and corruption leave
A vestige of the thoughts that once I had,
Better by far you should forget and smile
Than that you should remember and be sad.

CHRISTINA ROSSETTI

V

The well-known sonnet of Milton on his blindness is a masterpiece of restraint. One must know the story of his life to appreciate how much has been left untold in his acceptance of his blindness:

When I consider how my light is spent
Ere half my days in this dark world and wide,
And that one Talent which is death to hide
Lodged with me useless, though my soul more bent
To serve therewith my Maker, and present
My true account, lest He returning chide;
"Doth God exact day-labor, light denied?"
I fondly ask. But Patience, to prevent
That murmur, soon replies, "God doth not need
Either man's work or his own gifts. Who best
Bear his mild yoke, they serve him best. His state
Is kingly: thousands at his bidding speed,
And post o'er land and ocean without rest;
They also serve who only stand and wait."

JOHN MILTON

VI

John Mason Brown has evidently allowed himself enough leisure in his busy day of writing and lecturing to read Eleanor Roosevelt's column, "My Day." And so he writes:[37]

[37] From "Seeing the Sights," *Accustomed As I Am*, pp. 138-139. Copyright, 1942, by W. W. Norton & Company, Inc. Reprinted by permission of the publishers.

But those indolent days are no more. Mrs. Roosevelt's example has brought them to an end. In almost every township in the land newspapers can be purchased which carry her Pepys's Diary. Devouring it fills one with shame. Shame and envy. For the First Lady's journal is more than America's Court Circular. It is an alphabet soup of vitamins which the slothful sip at their own peril. Its record of energies untiring and seconds unwasted curdles the conscience of those who have felt fatigue. Worse than that, just when we have surrendered to the need for doing nothing, or been tempted to indulge in a siesta, "My Day" has forced us to jump up guiltily and ask ourselves, "What *would* Mrs. Roosevelt be doing if only she were here?"

The question is sufficiently agitating to drive a bear out of hibernation. Certainly she would not be lolling in the noonday sun. Certainly she would not be napping. Nor would she be tired. The art museum would have taken twenty—at the most twenty-one—minutes of her time. The zoo she would have seen in ten minutes; the arrowheads in four. Her day would have been fuller than the fullest moon. From six in the morning until midnight she would have set us all a model of vitality without ever being victimized by that anemia which drives most of us to rest. For in one respect only does this good and gracious lady resemble Macbeth. She murders sleep, and makes us, who fancy ourselves strong men, feel like worms for ever having slept.

It is she who in her charming person has effected an industrial revolution in the lives of all of us who also lecture. No longer can any of us claim to have seen a town if we have encircled the Civil War monument. An interest in art is not now enough. If we would pattern our day on hers, we, too, must dash from Picasso to the picket lines. We, too, must vary Goya with the garment workers. We, too, must be concerned with the striking of more than chimes. We, too, must go down to the water front again and rejoice that the morning's at seven. We, too, must four-star in our Baedekers the settlement houses, the post-office murals, the clinics, the federal housing projects, and the local handicrafts.

VII

The motivation for Robert G. Ingersoll's *Oration at His Brother's Grave* is evident from the title. Ingersoll has been called an atheist. What do you think? Read the last two paragraphs carefully.

Friends, I am going to do that which the dead often promised me he would do for me.

The loved and loving brother, husband, father, friend, died where manhood's morning almost touched noon, and while the shadows still were falling toward the West.

He had not passed on life's highway the stone that marks the highest point, but, being weary for a moment, he lay down by the wayside, and using his burden for a pillow, fell into the dreamless sleep that kisses down his eyelids still. While yet in love with life and raptured with the world, he passed to silence and pathetic dust.

Yet, after all, it may be best, just in the happiest, sunniest hour of all the voyage, while eager winds are kissing every sail, to dash against the unseen rock, and in an instant hear the rushing billows roar against a sunken ship. For, whether in mid sea or amongst the breakers of the farther shore, a wreck at last must mark the end of each and all. And every life, no matter if its every hour is rich with love and every moment jeweled with a joy will at its close become a tragedy as sad and deep as can be woven of the warp and woof of mystery and death.

This brave and tender man in every storm of life was oak and rock, but in the sunshine he was vine and flower. He was the friend of all heroic souls. He climbed the heights and left all superstitions far below, while on his forehead fell the golden dawning of the grander day.

He loved the beautiful and was with color, form, and music touched to tears. He sided with the weak, the poor, the wronged, and lovingly gave alms. With loyal heart, and with purest hands, he faithfully discharged all public trusts.

He was a worshiper of liberty, a friend of the oppressed. A thousand times I have heard him quote these words: "For justice all place a temple, and all season, summer." He believed that happiness was the only good, reason the only torch, justice the only worship, humanity the only religion, and love the only priest. He added to the sum of human joy; and were every one to whom he did some loving service to bring a blossom to his grave, he would sleep tonight beneath a wilderness of flowers.

Life is a narrow vale between the cold and barren peaks of two eternities. We strive in vain to look beyond the heights. We cry aloud, and the only answer is the echo of our wailing cry. From the voiceless lips of the unreplying dead, there comes no word; but in the night of death, hope sees a star, and listening love can hear the rustle of a wing.

He who sleeps here, when dying, mistaking the approach of death for the return of health, whispered with his latest breath: "I am better now." Let us believe, in spite of doubts and dogmas, of fears and tears, these dear words are true of all the countless dead. And now to you who have been chosen from among the many men he loved, to do the last sad office for the dead, we give his sacred dust.

VIII

The following poem was written after the death of Walt Whitman. Notice how the words and rhythm are reminiscent of Whitman's style.

COME DOWN, WALT WHITMAN[38]

Walt! Walt!
You burly old lover of men and women,
Boisterous shouter of catalogues from the housetops,
Earth's prophet, through whom the Almighty changed His works—
Walt! Walt! Up there! Do you hear us hallooing to you?

Out of stinking alleys,
Out of gutters and dead fields,
Out of the eternal monotony of the factories,
From all abominable glades and places,
Swarms an egregious horde;
Speaking all tongues they come,
Singing new songs, and loving and praying,
And mauling and being mauled;
And pushed down under the slime and bursting out to the heavens.

We do not know them,
We futile men in white collars do not know them.
Walt! Walt!—
You burly old lover of men and women—
Can't you get a furlough?
Stop shouting above the noise of the harps,
Loose your arm from Abe Lincoln's and come down.

Eat with this horde, Walt,
And laugh with them
And weep with them!

Then come forth chanting,
You prophet and diviner,
You lover and seer of men:
Find for us the perfume of their stench,
Shout forth the beauty of their dreams,
Translate their hundred tongues.
Come, Walt! Come!

JOHN R. McCARTHY

IX

Alan Seeger, who served in World War I kept his rendezvous
with death in July, 1917.

[38] Reprinted by permission of James T. White & Company.

I HAVE A RENDEZVOUS WITH DEATH[39]

I have a rendezvous with Death
At some disputed barricade,
When Spring comes back with rustling shade
And apple-blossoms fill the air—
I have a rendezvous with Death
When spring brings back blue days and fair.

It may be he shall take my hand
And lead me into his dark land
And close my eyes and quench my breath—
It may be I shall pass him still.
I have a rendezvous with Death
On some scarred slope of battered hill
When Spring comes round again this year
And the first meadow-flowers appear.

God knows 'twere better to be deep
Pillowed in silk and scented down,
Where Love throbs out in blissful sleep,
Pulse nigh to pulse, and breath to breath,
Where hushed awakenings are dear . . .
But I've a rendezvous with Death
At midnight in some flaming town,
When Spring trips north again this year,
And I to my pledged word am true,
I shall not fail that rendezvous.

ALAN SEEGER

X

Dorothy Wordsworth, in her *Journals*, tells of her experience
crossing Westminster Bridge one clear morning in company with
her brother William:[40] "It was a beautiful morning. The city,
St. Paul's, with the river and a multitude of little boats, made a
most beautiful sight as we crossed Westminster Bridge. The
houses were not overhung by their cloud of smoke, and they were
spread out endlessly, yet the sun shone so brightly, with such a
fierce light, that there was even something like the purity of one

[39] From *Poems*, p. 144. Copyright, 1916, by Charles Scribner's Sons.
Reprinted by permission of the publishers.
[40] From E. de Selincourt, ed., *Journals of Dorothy Wordsworth* (New
York, St Martin's Press, 1941), Vol. 1, pp. 172-173.

of nature's own grand spectacles." Wordsworth, choosing the medium of the sonnet, captured all that his sister saw and felt and added to her images the feeling of quietness, calmness, silence.

WESTMINSTER BRIDGE

Earth has not anything to show more fair:
Dull would he be of soul who could pass by
A sight so touching in its majesty:
This City now doth, like a garment, wear
The beauty of the morning; silent, bare,
Ships, towers, domes, theatres, and temples lie
Open unto the fields, and to the sky;
All bright and glittering in the smokeless air.
Never did sun more beautifully steep
In his first splendor, valley, rock, or hill;
Ne'er saw I, never felt, a calm so deep!
The river glideth at his own sweet will:
Dear God! the very houses seem asleep;
And all that mighty heart is lying still!

WILLIAM WORDSWORTH

XI

Mrs. Hacker wrote to the editor of *The Saturday Evening Post:* "He was only nineteen, and was waist gunner on the Flying Fortress Hellzapoppin. All of the crew but one were killed by an enemy bombardment on one of our airfields—recently captured. The Purple Heart and Citation of Honor certificate have been sent to me since his death."

A WHITE CROSS NEAR ALGIERS[41]

(To my son, Sgt. Larry B. Hagan
Killed in action in Northwest Africa)

White cross, white sand, white silence.
"Somewhere very close to Algiers. . . .
Regret no details can be given."
Mother of God, stay my tears!

[41] *The Saturday Evening Post* (November 20, 1943). Reprinted by permission of the author and the publishers.

Our eyes shall see the glory—
    Freedom's glory through the years.
White peace, white sand, white moonlight,
    White crosses near Algiers.

                                    VERA B. HACKER

XII

The following poem was written after seeing Millet's world-famous painting.

THE MAN WITH THE HOE[42]

*(God made man in his own image,
in the image of God he made him
                —Genesis)*

Bowed by the weight of centuries he leans
Upon his hoe and gazes on the ground,
The emptiness of ages in his face,
And on his back the burden of the world.
Who made him dead to rapture and despair,
A thing that grieves not and that never hopes,
Stolid and stunned, a brother to the ox?
Who loosened and let down this brutal jaw?
Whose was the hand that slanted back this brow?
Whose breath blew out the light within this brain?

Is this the Thing the Lord God made and gave
To have dominion over sea and land;
To trace the stars and search the heavens for power;
To feel the passion of Eternity?
Is this the dream He dreamed who shaped the suns
And markt their ways upon the ancient deep?
Down all the caverns of Hell to their last gulf
There is no shape more terrible than this—
More tongued with censure of the world's blind greed—
More filled with signs and portents for the soul—
More packt with danger to the universe.

What gulfs between him and the seraphim!
Slave of the wheel of labor, what to him
Are Plato and the swing of Pleiades?

[42] From *The Man with the Hoe and Other Poems* (New York, Doubleday & McClure and Company, 1899). Reprinted by permission of Virgil Markham.

What the long reaches of the peaks of song,
The rift of dawn, the reddening of the rose?
Through this dread shape the suffering ages look;
Time's tragedy is in that aching stoop;
Through this dread shape humanity betrayed,
Plundered, profaned, and disinherited,
Cries protest to the Judges of the World,
A protest that is also prophecy.

O masters, lords and rulers in all lands,
Is this the handiwork you give to God,
This monstrous thing distorted and soul-quenched?
How will you ever straighten up this shape;
Touch it again with immortality;
Give back the upward looking and the light;
Rebuild in it the music and the dream;
Make right the immemorial infamies,
Perfidious wrongs, immedicable woes?

O master, lords, and rulers in all lands,
How will the Future reckon with this man?
How answer his brute question in that hour
When whirlwinds of rebellion shake all shores?
How will it be with kingdoms and with kings—
With those who shaped him to the thing he is—
When this dumb terror shall rise to judge the world,
After the silence of the centuries?

EDWIN MARKHAM

THE AUTHOR'S LITERARY FORM

Usually the first observation made of literature is whether it falls within the poetic or prose classification. It should be recognized that this difference has little to do with the meaning but may give you a clue to the presentation of the literature. Care must be taken in analyzing poetry, for the structural pattern may obscure the meaning to less observant readers. Poetry is concentrated in form and distilled in emotional effects; much is left unsaid, except through indirect connotative meanings and allusions. For instance, eight lines of poetry can carry as vivid an impression as eight pages of prose, but the prose may reach more readers because it more easily allows for amplification of ideas; poetry, however, can present only an impression or an idea.

Poetic Forms

Understanding the poetical forms is sometimes considered highly important in interpretation; in fact, some interpretation texts are organized according to the interpretation of these various structural forms. Although knowledge of the structure is essential background information, it is not so vital to your interpretation as knowledge of the meaning. It is assumed, however, that the student of interpretation knows these forms from his course work in literature. The following information will give you a short review and will help you to recall classical examples of each poetical form.

1. Narrative poetry includes the ballad and the epic, as well as romantic tales told in verse.

BALLAD:

Folk Ballad: A simple narrative poem which was sung and added to from generation to generation. The words are simple, the rhythm is marked, repetitions and refrains are numerous, and the style is neither ornate or condensed. The following example has long been a favorite.

LORD RANDAL

"O where hae ye been, Lord Randal, my son?
O where hae ye been, my handsome young man?"
"I hae been to the wild wood; mother, make my bed soon,
For I'm weary wi hunting, and fain wad lie down."

"Where gat ye your dinner, Lord Randal, my son?
Where gat ye your dinner, my handsome young man?"
"I dined wi my true-love; mother, make my bed soon,
For I'm weary wi hunting, and fain wad lie down."

"What gat ye to your dinner, Lord Randal, my son?
What gat ye to your dinner, my handsome young man?"
"I gat eels boiled in broo; mother, make my bed soon,
For I'm weary wi hunting, and fain wad lie down."

"What became of your bloodhounds, Lord Randal, my son?
What became of your bloodhounds, my handsome young man?"
"O they swelled and they died; mother, make my bed soon,
For I'm weary wi hunting, and fain wad lie down."

"O I fear ye are poisoned, Lord Randal, my son!
O I fear ye are poisoned, my handsome young man!"
    "O yes! I am poisoned; mother, make my bed soon,
For I'm sick at the heart, and I fain wad lie down."

Literary Ballad: A poem reminiscent of folk ballad but written by one person. Refrains and repetitions are not so numerous, and the form may be more elaborate. Examples include Kipling's *Barrack Room Ballads,* Coleridge's "The Rime of the Ancient Mariner," Browning's "The Pied Piper of Hamelin," Keats's "La Belle Dame Sans Merci."

from TROOPIN'

Troopin', troopin', give another cheer—
'Ere's to English women an' a quart of English beer.
The Colonel an' the regiment an' all who've got to stay,
Gawd's—mercy strike 'em gentle—Whoop! we're goin' 'ome today.
    We're goin' 'ome, we're goin' 'ome,
        Our ship is at the shore,
    An' you must pack your 'aversack,
        For we won't come back no more.
    Ho, don't you grieve for me,
        My lovely Mary-Ann,
    For I'll marry you yit on a fourp'ny bit
        As a time-expired man.

                RUDYARD KIPLING, *Barrack Room Ballads*

EPIC: A long narrative poem with a central figure—a great hero—struggling through innumerable experiences. The ideals of his country and race are correlated with his adventures, and the characters of the story are courageous. The structure is variable, the rhythm is likely to be stately and ponderous, and the language is dignified and majestic. Some examples are the *Odyssey* and the *Iliad* of Homer, Milton's *Paradise Lost,* Tennyson's *Idylls of the King.*

ROMANTIC TALE: A story of love and adventure, such as Tennyson's *Enoch Arden.*

MONOLOGUE: Insofar as it tells a story, the monologue can be classified as narrative poetry, but it is usually on a highly dramatic level, with many background details suggested rather than narrated. It is, however, a dramatized narrative, having one character speaking under special circumstances which are revealed along with the personality of the speaker. One of the best-known is "My Last Duchess," written by Robert Browning, who was a master of the dramatic dialogue.[43]

[43] See p. 351.

2. Lyrical poems are those expressing the poet's mood or feeling and include the sonnet, ode, elegy, and song.

SONNET: This is the most concentrated of all poetic forms, following a rigid pattern of fourteen lines. The thought is always dignified and concisely expressed.

Italian or Petrarchan Sonnet: This form consists of an octave with a rhyme scheme of *abba, abba,* and a sextet with a rhyme scheme of *cdc, dcd* or *cde, cde.* Examples are Elizabeth Barrett Browning's "How Do I Love Thee?" and Wordsworth's "The World Is Too Much with Us."

THE WORLD IS TOO MUCH WITH US

The world is too much with us; late and soon,
Getting and spending, we lay waste our powers:
Little we see in Nature that is ours;
We have given our hearts away, a sordid boon!
This Sea that bares her bosom to the moon;
The winds that will be howling at all hours,
And are up-gathered now like sleeping flowers;
For this, for everything, we are out of tune;
It moves us not.—Great God! I'd rather be
A Pagan suckled in a creed outworn;
So might I, standing on this pleasant lea,
Have glimpses that would make me less forlorn;
Have sight of Proteus rising from the sea;
Or hear old Triton blow his wreathèd horn.
                 WILLIAM WORDSWORTH

English or Shakespearean Sonnet: This form is made up of three quatrains and a couplet, with a rhyme scheme of *abab, cdcd, efef, gg.* The couplet usually achieves a sudden turn or twist or climax in thought. The finest examples are the sonnets of William Shakespeare, who originated this form.

SONNET LXXIII

That time of year thou mayst in me behold
When yellow leaves, or none, or few, do hang
Upon those boughs which shake against the cold,
Bare ruin'd choirs where late the sweet birds sang.
In me thou see'st the twilight of such day
As after sunset fadeth in the west,
Which by and by black night doth take away,
Death's second self, that seals up all the rest.

In me thou see'st the glowing of such fire
That on the ashes of his youth doth lie,
As the death-bed whereon it must expire,
Consum'd with that which it was nourish'd by.
This thou perceiv'st, which makes thy love more strong,
To love that well which thou must leave ere long.
WILLIAM SHAKESPEARE

ODE: Poems of this form are subjective in theme; they contain noble and elevated sentiment, eulogizing some thing or person. The subject is treated with dignity, the structure is irregular, and the stanza arrangement is complex. Examples include Keats's "Ode to a Nightingale" and Shelley's "Ode to the West Wind."

from ODE TO THE WEST WIND

Make me thy lyre, even as the forest is:
What if my leaves are falling like its own!
The tumult of thy mighty harmonies

Will take from both a deep autumnal tone,
Sweet though in sadness. Be thou, spirit fierce,
My spirit! Be thou me, impetuous one!

Drive my dead thoughts over the universe
Like withered leaves to quicken a new birth!
And, by the incantation of this verse,

Scatter, as from an unextinguished hearth
Ashes and sparks, my words among mankind!
Be through my lips to unawakened earth

The trumpet of a prophecy! O, wind,
If Winter comes, can Spring be far behind?
PERCY BYSSHE SHELLEY

ELEGY: This is subjective in theme, usually lamenting or extolling the dead. The mood is likely to be pensive, solemn, thoughtful. The stanza form varies but is never as complicated as that of the ode or as rigid as that of the sonnet. Some famous elegies are Gray's "Elegy Written in a Country Churchyard," Tennyson's *In Memoriam* and "Crossing the Bar," and Milton's "Lycidas."

from ELEGY WRITTEN IN A COUNTRY CHURCHYARD

The curfew tolls the knell of parting day,
The lowing herd winds slowly o'er the lea,
The ploughman homeward plods his weary way,
And leaves the world to darkness and to me.

Now fades the glimmering landscape on the sight,
And all the air a solemn stillness holds,
Save where the beetle wheels his droning flight,
And drowsy tinklings lull the distant folds:

Save that from yonder ivy-mantled tower
The moping owl does to the moon complain
Of such as, wandering near her secret bower,
Molest her ancient solitary reign.

Beneath those rugged elms, that yew-tree's shade
Where heaves the turf in many a mouldering heap,
Each in his narrow cell forever laid
The rude forefathers of the hamlet sleep.

The breezy call of incense-breathing Morn,
The swallow twittering from the straw-built shed,
The cock's shrill clarion, or the echoing horn,
No more shall rouse them from their lowly bed.
                                        THOMAS GRAY

SONG: This form is noticeably rhythmic in pattern; its verse structure
and subject matter vary. Shakespeare's play *Two Gentlemen of
Verona* contains one of the earliest and most famous English songs:

WHO IS SYLVIA?

Who is Sylvia? what is she,
    That all our swains commend her?
Holy, fair, and wise is she;
    The heaven such grace did lend her,
That she might admiréd be.

Is she kind as she is fair?
    For beauty lives with kindness.
Love doth to her eyes repair
    To help him of his blindness,
And being helped, inhabits there.

Then to Sylvia let us sing,
    That Sylvia is excelling;
She excels each mortal thing
    Upon the dull earth dwelling:
To her let us garlands bring.
                            WILLIAM SHAKESPEARE

EXERCISE

In his analysis of T. S. Eliot's "Rhapsody on a Windy Night," Daniels has demonstrated how to evaluate meaning as revealed through the form of poetry used by the author. Read the poem first for your understanding of the thought; then read Daniels' comment.

RHAPSODY ON A WINDY NIGHT[44]

Twelve o'clock.
Along the reaches of the street
Held in a lunar synthesis,
Whispering lunar incantations
Dissolve the floors of memory
And all its clear relations,
Its divisions and precisions,
Every street lamp that I pass
Beats like a fatalistic drum,
And through the spaces of the dark
Midnight shakes the memory
As a madman shakes a dead geranium.

Half-past one,
The street-lamp sputtered,
The street-lamp muttered,
The street-lamp said, "Regard that woman
Who hesitates toward you in the light of the door
Which opens on her like a grin.
You see the border of her dress
Is torn and stained with sand,
And you see the corner of her eye
Twists like a crooked pin."
The memory throws up high and dry
A crowd of twisted things;
A twisted branch upon the beach
Eaten smooth, and polished
As if the world gave up
The secret of its skeleton,
Stiff and white.
A broken spring in a factory yard,

[44] From *Collected Poems: 1909-1935*, p. 27. Copyright, 1936, by Harcourt, Brace and Company, Inc. Reprinted by permission of the publishers.

Rust that clings to the form that the strength has left
Hard and curled and ready to snap.

Half-past two,
The street-lamp said,
"Remark the cat which flattens itself in the gutter,
Slips out its tongue
And devours a morsel of rancid butter."
So the hand of the child, automatic,
Slipped out and pocketed a toy that was running along the quay.
I could see nothing behind that child's eye.
I have seen eyes in the street
Trying to peer through lighted shutters,
And a crab one afternoon in a pool,
An old crab with barnacles on his back,
Gripped the end of a stick which I held him.

Half-past three,
The lamp sputtered,
The lamp muttered in the dark.
The lamp hummed:
"Regard the moon,
La lune ne garde aucune rancune,
She winks a feeble eye,
She smiles into corners.
She smooths the hair of the grass.
The moon has lost her memory.
A washed-out smallpox cracks her face,
Her hand twists a paper rose,
That smells of dust and eau de Cologne,
She is alone
With all the nocturnal smells
That cross and cross across her brain."
The reminiscence comes
Of sunless dry geraniums
And dust in crevices,
Smells of chestnuts in the streets,
And female smells in shuttered rooms,
And cigarettes in corridors
And cocktail smells in bars.

The lamp said,
"Four o'clock,
Here is the number on the door.
Memory!
You have the key,
The little lamp spreads a ring on the stair.
Mount.

The bed is open; the tooth-brush hangs on the wall,
Put your shoes at the door, sleep, prepare for life."

The last twist of the knife.

T. S. ELIOT

Daniels writes about the poem thus:[45]

First, the title requires attention. A rhapsody is either an ecstatic, highly emotional composition; or, more strictly, it is a portion of an epic, used for public recitation. This second meaning is more suggestive here, for it contains the germ of the poem's basic irony. The central character is an epic hero—a contemporary version of the epic hero—wandering like Odysseus, and like Odysseus finally arriving home. But his wanderings are confined to sordid streets in a modern city, during the early hours of the morning; they are punctuated by the sputterings of uncertain lamps. As there is little which is heroic in his journeyings, there is also little which is heroic about the man himself, a sensitive, morbid kind of individual, alert to beauty, finding only ugliness and meanness. When ancient epic is set against the contemporary scene in this fashion, modern life, at least in the present mood of the poet, appears empty and futile. The heroic has departed. The suggestion, at the end, of sleeping as preparation for living is to give to a stabbing knife one final, unendurable twist in the wound already made in the breast of the too-sensitive hero. . . .

Life has gone out of everything for the protagonist of the poem, just as it has gone out of the twisted branch, thrown up on the beach, out of the twisted, rusted spring in the factory yard. These objects are symbols and put the hero's mood concretely. They reach a kind of climax in the symbol of the crab—an old crab, who gripped the end of a stick poked at him through the water, acting automatically, without intelligence. (Is the hero of the poem very different from this crab?) Branch, spring, crab are, again, in harmony with the sordid human figures, like wraiths, haunting the scene, the woman in the ominous doorway, the empty-eyed child on the wharf. And there is that alley cat, furtively licking at a morsel of rancid butter! Even the moon brings neither brightness nor beauty: she is a worn-out woman, for whom are only paper roses, ugly, faded; she is a moon without enough character to guard a bitterness.

The poem is built around the clocks announcing the four separate hours, and around the speeches the hero imagines addressed to him by four different street lamps, in the course of his walk. Those speeches call up floods of impressions, for night, as we are told in the first section, has dissolved the floor of memory, so that all sorts of things

---

[45] Earl R. Daniels, *The Art of Reading Poetry* (New York, Rinehart and Company, Inc., 1952), pp. 404-405.

seem to come slipping through. Actually, the order is precise, carefully directed to the goal the poet has set for himself, to the conveyance of bitterness and frustration. *It must be noted that this bitterness and frustration are the hero's; there is no warrant, in this poem, for assuming that they represent the poet's own and personal views on life.*

Developmental Forms

Whether he writes in prose or poetry, the author may use various developmental forms or procedures to expand his thought: expository, narrative, descriptive, persuasive, or dramatic. He may blend several of these forms to convey his intent, as the student has already learned in literature courses. Basic to the style is the theme or intent of the author. To the interpreter, the manner of recreating the impression of meaning will depend to a great extent upon the developmental form. Poor taste in interpretation often arises from the fact that the reader thinks there is only one manner to use—the dramatic. Perhaps all the poet intended to do was to create an impression of joy or sorrow.

Decision about the theme of the author will give you the cue for the technique to be employed. If it is to explain—in either factual or humorous manner—then one must be sure of what the author is trying to explain. If it is to tell a story, then the follow-through to the end of the story must be studied to get all the implications. If the author wishes to create an impression without instilling belief, then the interpreter must look to the words that will create the mood. If the author intends to make us believe, his manner of writing will indicate persuasion by a more vivid structure of sentences, by examples, by evidence. If he is dramatizing a story or character, then he will arrange his sentences in dialogue or monologue form, so that the thought of his characters will reveal action and personality. Remember, however, that all these techniques can be patterned through prose and poetry. The forms—expository, narrative, descriptive, persuasive, dramatic—will be discussed separately. The student should acquire the habit of forming a prècis so that he is sure of the author's intent, thereby enabling himself to select the most appropriate manner of interpretation.

Expository. The author is interested mainly in informing when he uses the expository form. Whenever there is explanatory material at the beginning of a dialogue or story, whenever the author tells *about* facts or principles, or states how something is accomplished, or explains *objectively* how someone feels or acts or operates, the interpreter must be ready to state the case simply but effectively. There are times when it is difficult to hold the attention of the audience because of the informative style; therefore, the interpreter must strive for directness. Some have a tendency to hasten over expositions as unimportant; others go too far the other way, thus overemphasizing the importance of the expository portion. Often too, the mannerisms of the interpreter are revealed more plainly in this form of communication than in any other. It requires good taste, without too much talking down to one's audience, without too much display of personality, and yet with the proper amount of appreciation of the author's words. All desire to wave arms and hands, to locate clouds and brooks and the heart must be subordinated to the main purpose of giving information as directly as possible. The person who realizes this point early will be spared the necessity of whining or pleading or chanting or haranguing or waxing dramatic. He will also be spared the embarrassment of being laughed at by intelligent audiences. This does not mean there must be inertia and languor; but it does mean that the interpreter must be sensitive and alert to the meaning of the selection.

EXERCISES

In the following passages, the authors intended to inform. Decide on the theme of each and then note how the author unfolds his theme through this particular form.

I

HOW TO TELL A MAJOR POET FROM A MINOR POET[46]

All poetry falls into two classes: serious verse and light verse. Serious verse is verse written by a major poet; light verse is verse

[46] From *Quo Vadimus?*, p. 68. Copyright, 1930, by E. B. White. Published originally in *The New Yorker* and reprinted here by permission of the author and Harper & Brothers.

written by a minor poet. To distinguish the one from the other, one must have a sensitive ear and a lively imagination. Broadly speaking, a major poet may be told from a minor poet in two ways: (1) by the character of the verse, (2) by the character of the poet. (Note: it is not always advisable to go into the character of the poet.)

As to the verse itself, let me state a few elementary rules. Any poem starting with "And when" is a serious poem written by a major poet. To illustrate—here are the first two lines of a serious poem easily distinguished by the "And when":

> And when, in earth's forgotten moment, I
> Unbound the cord to which the soul was bound . . .

Any poem, on the other hand, ending with "And how" comes under the head of "light verse," written by a minor poet. Following are the last two lines of a "light" poem, instantly identifiable by the terminal phrase:

> Placing his lips against her brow
> He kissed her eyelids shut. And how. . . .

So much for the character of the verse. Here are a few general rules about the poets themselves. All poets who, when reading from their own works, experience a choked feeling, are major. For that matter, all poets who read from their own works are major. All poets who have sold a sonnet for one hundred and twenty-five dollars to a magazine with a paid circulation of four hundred thousand are major. A sonnet is composed of fourteen lines; thus the payment in this case is eight dollars and ninety-three cents a line, which constitutes a poet's majority. (It also indicates that the editor has probably been swept off his feet.) . . .

A poet who, in a roomful of people, is noticeably keeping at a little distance and "seeing into" things is a major poet. This poet commonly writes in unrhymed six-foot and seven-foot verse, beginning something like this:

> When, once, finding myself alone in a gathering of people,
> I stood, a little apart, and through the endless confusion of voices . . .

This is a major poem, and you needn't give it a second thought.

There are many more ways of telling a major poet from a minor poet, but I think I have covered the principal ones. The truth is, it is fairly easy to tell the two types apart; it is only when one sets about trying to decide whether what they write is any good or not that the thing really becomes complicated.

E. B. WHITE

II

YOUR MOVE! [47]

No matter how calm or nervous, conscientious or inspired, a chairman may be, he or she still presents one problem to the speaker to which neither the introducer nor the audience ever gives much thought. That is, what to do, where to look, how to act, while you are being introduced. It seems simple enough from the front.

A chair—one of those chairs—is near the center of the stage. According to the protocol of the platform, the one nearer the entrance is usually yours. Supposedly all you have to do is to walk from the wings to that chair and then sit down on it and wait. But that walk of no more than ten or fifteen feet can seem an eternity. It is apt to be one of the unremembered interludes in the life of any person who has ever taken it. Twenty boards can unite to form a plank. You are in a trance, doing a conscious act unconsciously, driven forward only by the motor of your pounding heart. Matters are not helped by your knowing there is always the chance that the chairman may forget which of the seats he had agreed to occupy and that the two of you may be caught playing "Going to Jerusalem" in public.

When, in some manner unknown to you, you have at last reached your place, graver difficulties arise. The chair may be one of two kinds. Either its high back and its seat, though covered with petit point, may conceal boards so stiff that you are sure the committee must think your sacroiliac needs righting, or it is one of those low-set leather chairs which emits embarrassing noises as you sink down onto its air-filled cushions, and from the depths of which only a derrick can remove you. Once seated, you reach for the arms as if they were the hands of a long-lost friend. After you and the chairman have indulged in those preliminary whisperings, and both you and he have smiled broadly at jokes passed between you that neither of you has heard, the chairman rises to start his introduction.

Then your troubles begin in earnest. Even before he has finished saying "Ladies and gentlemen," you are apt to have crossed, uncrossed, and recrossed your legs so many times that you must look from out front as if you were trying to dance the Highland fling sitting down. Suddenly realizing that poise is desirable, you quiet your shins by wrapping your feet around the far-sprung legs of the chair.

"We have with us tonight—" the chairman goes on. By now you have begun to do strange things with your hands. You have patted them together as if at any moment you were about to applaud yourself. You have surveyed your fingers with a baby's wonder and an

[47] From *Accustomed As I Am*, pp. 35-36. Copyright, 1942, by W. W. Norton & Company, Inc. Reprinted by permission of the publishers.

interest no manicurist has ever shown. You have bitten the knuckle of the right hand's middle finger until it is about to bleed. As the chairman continues, you have started that weird gesture known only to expectant lecturers, that act of public and dry libation in which you seem to wash the face (and every part thereof) with the hands but without benefit of soap and water.

These physical activities, these setting-down exercises, get you so warm before the real gymnastics of the evening have started that while the chairman is still trying to remember your occupation you have reached in despair for your handkerchief and begun waving it as if you were a morris dancer. Strangers in the rear of the auditorium have on occasion been so startled by what they have mistaken for friendly salutations that they have been known to wave back.

These are not the only betrayals of embarrassment which as a lecturer you try clumsily to control. There are others, and their causes are valid, very valid, indeed. When, for example, a frustrated biographer is at work on you, telling your life story in detail, should you appear as bored as the audience is? Or should you look surprised? When the place of your birth is mentioned, should your eyebrows arch with amazement into an "Is *that* so?" formation? When the college you remember slaving at is named, should you shake your head and whisper to yourself, "Well, well, well—do tell? So he went there? How very interesting"? When the introducer insists you are a dramatic critic, and says that you see plays on Broadway, should you make it clear that you are more astounded than anyone else by all this, and mutter audibly, "Fancy that, Hedda. Fancy that"? And if he goes so far as to mention some of your books, should you set a good example by crying, "Well, I'll be!" and whipping out a notebook and a pencil to write down the titles?

On those rare occasions when the chairman gets his circulars mixed and has confused your case history with that of Eve Curie, John Mulholland, or Commander Byrd, is it or is it not forgivable for you to shake your head in gentle protest and indicate regretfully you have one, and only one, life to give to your country's lecture platform, and the introducer is taking it and someone else's in vain? Or should you play dead, exhibiting no more interest in the proceedings than a corpse does in the funeral oration he has provoked? When you are paid a compliment, every word of which drips with jasmine, honeysuckle, and unearned increment, and you feel diabetes sugaring your blood stream, should you show you have not forgotten *Veritas* was printed on your college shield by shouting, "No! No!"? Or should you meet kindness with kindness by crying, "A Daniel come to judgment! Yea, a Daniel!"?

Ought your eyes to be fixed on the footlights, the ceiling, the balcony, your wristwatch, or the introducer? And if upon the introducer, where? If he has struck a forensic attitude, should your eyes trace the outlines of his invisible toga? Or if she has struck a posture suggestive of Venus de' Medici, should your face express gratitude that she is better dressed than the original?

If a giggling friend is winking at you in the fifth row, should you wink back? Or should you try to achieve that faraway look at which certain lecturers excel in their moments of being introduced, when they make it clear that their minds are in the clouds, that they are first cousins to yogis, that the affairs of this world do not interest them, and that—intellectually, at least—they have not as yet made their entrances.

No matter how much being introduced may embarrass you, you miss the introducer at those organizations where he does not appear. He may, by the very nature of his job and yours, develop in you a new sympathy for the criminal who must face the judge while his sentence is being read. But mounting the scaffold alone can be agonizing. Even during the Reign of Terror the people who faced the guillotine did not have to operate it. Confessors were near to hold their hands, and executioners to bow their heads. However awful their deaths may have been, they were not suicides.

It is when you are placed in solitary, and are waiting for the signal to be given, that you become the victim of worse fears than have ever paralyzed a chairman. It is after an experience of this sort that you are most apt to kneel down by your trundle at the hotel in the dark hours of night and thank God you are the kind of speaker who needs an introduction.

JOHN MASON BROWN

III

PERSONALITY IN SMALL BOTTLES[48]

But the vocational experts are also at work, and they administer a test of a beautiful simplicity. You check off on a printed form the things you like to do, read, see and talk about. Answers are counted up by groups, and since the cunning designers have given the same list to five hundred successful persons in each of fifteen professions, by comparing the degree of similitude among answers, it is possible to discover whether you are more like a farmer than a real-estate man of equal eminence. Sometimes the student is allowed to see the list of notables originally taken as a "control group," and the young poet or musician finds that he has been "measured" against syndicated versifiers and tin-pan-alley composers.

Of course no validity is claimed for the test. I have yet to find a

[48] From "Your I.Q. or Your Life," *Teacher in America,* p. 210. Copyright, 1944, 1945, by Jacques Barzun. Reprinted by permission of Little, Brown & Co. and the Atlantic Monthly Press.

test which its maker backs heart and soul as performing what it seems to perform. The usual formula is that the results show high correlation with some other test or with Phi Beta Kappa lists or with *Who's Who.*

But the tests continue to rain down: they measure the depth of information pumped into him, they try to predict medical, legal, engineering aptitude, they delve into emotions, characterize social and other background, classify political "temperament," in short, attempt to decant personality into small bottles.

JACQUES BARZUN

Narrative. In this type of literature a story is being told. The details of the plot must be sensed and appreciated so that a decision can be reached as to the relative importance of events. High lights must be located for emphasis, but, above all, the interpreter must be interested in his story. His manner should not be aloof but friendly and sincere and direct.

EXERCISES

I

Notice how Henry Grady introduces narration in the beginning of his well-known persuasive speech.[49] Why did he choose to tell these stories?

YOUR INDULGENCE, PLEASE!

I bespeak the utmost stretch of your courtesy tonight. I am not troubled about those from whom I come. You remember the man whose wife sent him to a neighbor with a pitcher of milk, and who, tripping on the top step, fell, and with such casual interruptions as the landing afforded, into the basement; and while picking himself up had the pleasure of hearing his wife call out; "John, did you break the pitcher?" "No, I didn't," said John, "but I be dinged if I don't!"

So, while those who call to me from behind may inspire me with energy, if not with courage, I ask an indulgent hearing from you. I beg that you will bring your full faith in American fairness and frankness to judgment upon what I shall say. There was an old preacher once who told some boys of the Bible lesson he was going to read in the morning. The boys finding the place, glued together the connecting pages. The next morning he read on the bottom of one page: "When Noah was one hundred and twenty years old he took unto himself a

---

[49] "The New South," delivered in New York City on December 22, 1886.

wife, who was"—then turning the page—"one hundred and forty
cubits long, forty cubits wide, built of gopher-wood, and covered with
pitch inside and out." He was naturally puzzled at this. He read it
again, verified it, and then said: "My friends, this is the first time I
ever met this in the Bible, but I accept it as evidence of the assertion
that we are fearfully and wonderfully made."

HENRY GRADY

II

Notice how the personality of the narrator is revealed through
the sentence structure of the following selection. State the author's theme.

WHY THE BIRDS ARE OF DIFFERENT COLORS[50]

Whateva you rub aginst in dis worl' some of it's gwine to stick to
you, honey. An' what's mo' when folks looks at you, dey mos' giner'ly
knows what you bin, and who you's bin a'sociatin' wid.

Dat's de way it worked wid de birds, an' it works de same way wid
de res' of us.

When de Good Lawd made de birds in de beginnin' he made 'em
all white, and dey all been white clean up to de time o' de big flood
dat drownded all de critters 'ceptin' de ones dat ole Mr. Noah had
wid him in de ark.

But, La bless you, it took a mighty sight o' water to drown everything in de whole worl', for de folks an' de critters dat wan't in de
ark was a climbin' up on de fences, an' on de stumps an' on de trees
an' on de hills an' on de mountains so dat de Good Lawd's obleege to
have mo' water fo' to finish de business. De rain couldn't rain fast
enough, so the Good Lawd had to bust up all de clouds, an' to bust
holes in de skies, an' to bust up de rivers an' de ponds an' de seas to
git enough water. An' all dis time de lightnin' was a flashin' an' a
slambangin' aroun' an' de thunder was a rollin' an' a rumblin' an' a
bumpin' aroun' in de sky, an' de wilderness was a howlin' fitten to
skeer everybody to death dat wan't already skeered to death or drownded. But atter forty days and forty nights o' water done give clean
out, an' de storm's obleeged to stop cause de wan't no more water, an'
no more thunder an' lightnin' ontil de Good Lawd could fine time to
make some mo'. An' den de water begin to dry up, an' it kep' on a
dryin' up ontil de ark scraped on de bottom an' settled down in de
mud, an' da she was an' da she stayed.

Well, suh, mos' folks would a been powerful glad to git out o' dat
'ar ark, but old Cap'n Noah, he was mighty jubous about de weather.

Atter all o' his troubles he didn't have no confidence in it no mo'. So he jis stick his head out thu' a hole in de side o' de ark an' pass de time o' day wid de Good Lawd, an' ax him how things was a gittin' along, and wedder it look like dey's a gwine to be any mo' rain 'fore mawnin'. An' de Good Lawd respon' dat dey's bin a change o' de moon an' de trouble an' de storm was all over, an' he could open de front do' an' put out de gangplanks an' let all de critters out, an' he could come out hisself an' res' de sole o' his foot. But ole Mr. Noah said he'd hatter 'scuse him 'cause it seem like it 'ud be safer under kiver o' de roof o' de ark in case dey was another shower in de night, an' bein' as he's bin a livin' thar mighty nigh a year, an' bein' he's got de rumatiz powerful bad, it did seem a good deal better for him to stay inside whar it was dry dan to go out dar in all o' dat mud.

Atter a jowerin' an' a ruminatin' back an' fort nearly all day a tryin' to git ole Mr. Noah to open de do' an' come out, de Good Lawd see how de lan' lay. It seem like ole Cap'n Noah was mighty nervous about de rain an' de rumpus dat come along wid it, an' he done mek up his mine he ain't gwine to leave dat ar' ark till he git de promise o' de Good Lawd dat he won't drown 'em no mo'.

So den de Good Lawd scraped all de clouds out'n de whole sky an' pile 'em all up on one side o' de sky whar de sun could shine on 'em an' den he painted on de clouds de biggest an' de purtiest rainbow in de whole worl' wid all de different colors he could think of. An' de two ends o' de rainbow was on de sides o' de worl', an' de top of it retch nearly up to de top o' de sky. An' while he was a makin' of it, ole Mr. Noah an' all his chillen an' his gran'chillen was a peekin' out at de Good Lawd thu' de cracks in de sides o' de ark. But up in de attic o' de ark whar all de birds all roosted nex' to de rafters, de wood- peckers done pecked a lot o' holes all round under de edge o' de roof, an' de birds all had dey haids a stickin' out an' was a listenin' to de confabs, an' a watchin' what was a gwine on. Well, suh, when de Good Lawd got de rainbow all done finished, he wave his han' todes de big rainbow, an' he hollered to ole Mr. Noah, "DAH'S MY PROMISE!" Wid them words he retch over, he did, an' lif off de whole roof o' de ark, an' de birds dat had bin a roostin' in de attic rose all togedder in one big cloud, an' flew todes de big rainbow up in de sky. An' dey was all so glad, dat they crowded up onto de rainbow an' flew right spang through it, while it was all covered wid de colors o' dat fresh paint. An' all de birds dat flew again' de blue color come out blue birds, an' dem dat flew again' de red color come out red birds, and dem dat flew again' de yaller color come out yaller birds. But some of 'em feel so happy dey sort o' wallered aroun' in de rainbow an' dey come out all striped and speckled wid de different kinds of colors. An' de hummin' birds dey flew so fast, an' darted into sich little holes dat dey got all de colors o' de whole rainbow on dey feathers. An' de birds dat flew on de other side o' de ark an' missed de rainbow or was scrouged out by de rest of 'em, dey all stayed white jis like dey was befor' dey come out'n de ark. An' all de birds in de whole worl' from dat time on bin colored des like de ones dat flew into de Good Lawd's big rainbow.

An, dat's what mek me tell you, honey, dat you better be careful what kind o' paint you rub aginst in dis worl', cause it's gwine to stick to you an' it's gwine to stick to your chillen too.

JOHN C. BRANNER

III

A very interesting narrative which an interpreter may arrange for audience approval is Virginia Woolf's story, *Flush*. What is the key sentence below that describes Flush's estimate of himself?

THE PRIVILEGES OF RANK[51]

For the first time he heard his nails click upon the hard paving-stones of London. For the first time the whole battery of a London street on a hot summer's day assaulted his nostrils. He smelt the swooning smells that lie in the gutters; the bitter smells that corrode iron railings; the fuming, heady smells that rise from basements. And also as he trotted up Wimpole Street behind Miss Barrett's chair he was dazed by the passage of human bodies. Petticoats swished at his head; trousers brushed his flanks; sometimes a wheel whizzed an inch from his nose; the wind of destruction roared in his ears and fanned the feathers of his paws as a van passed. Then he plunged in terror. Mercifully the chain tugged at his collar; Miss Barrett held him tight, or he would have rushed to destruction.

At last, with every nerve throbbing and every sense singing, he reached Regent's Park. And then when he saw once more, after years of absence it seemed, grass, flowers and trees, the old hunting cry of the fields hallooed in his ears and he dashed forward to run as he had run in the fields at home. But now a heavy weight jerked at his throat; he was thrown back on his haunches. Were there not trees and grass? he asked. Were these not the signals of freedom? Had he not always leapt forward directly Miss Mitford started on her walk? Why was he a prisoner here? He paused. Here, he observed, the flowers were massed far more thickly than at home; they stood, plant by plant, rigidly in narrow plots. The plots were intersected by hard black paths. Men in shiny top-hats marched ominously up and down the paths. At the sight of them he shuddered closer to the chair. He

[51] From *Flush*, pp. 37-40. Copyright, 1933, by Harcourt, Brace and Company, Inc. Reprinted by permission of the publishers.

gladly accepted the protection of the chain. Thus before many of these walks were over a new conception had entered his brain. Setting one thing beside another, he had arrived at a conclusion. Where there are flower-beds there are asphalt paths; where there are flower-beds and asphalt paths and men in shiny top-hats, dogs must be led on chains. Without being able to decipher a word of the placard at the Gate, he had learnt his lesson—in Regent's Park dogs must be led on chains.

And to this nucleus of knowledge, born from the strange experiences of the summer of 1842, soon adhered another: dogs are not equal, but different. At Three Mile Cross Flush had mixed impartially with tap-room dogs and the Squire's greyhounds; he had known no difference between the tinker's dog and himself. Indeed it is probable that the mother of his child, though by courtesy called Spaniel, was nothing but a mongrel, eared in one way, tailed in another. But the dogs of London, Flush soon discovered, are strictly divided into different classes. Some are chained dogs, some run wild. Some take their airings in carriages and drink from purple jars; others are unkempt and un-collared and pick up a living in the gutter. Dogs, therefore, Flush began to suspect, differ; some are high, others low; and his suspicions were confirmed by snatches of talk held in passing with the dogs of Wimpole Street. "See that scallywag? A mere mongrel! . . . By gad, that's a fine Spaniel. One of the best in Britain! . . . Pity his ears aren't a shade more curly. . . . There's a topknot for you!"

So Flush knew before the summer had passed that there is no equality among dogs: there are high dogs and low dogs. Which then was he? No sooner had Flush got home than he examined himself carefully in the looking-glass. Heaven be praised, he was a dog of birth and breeding! His head was smooth; his eyes were prominent but not gozzled; his feet were feathered; he was the equal of the best-bred cocker in Wimpole Street. He noted with approval the purple jar from which he drank—such are the privileges of rank; he bent his head quietly to have the chain fixed to his collar—such are its penalties. When about this time Miss Barrett observed him staring in the glass, she was mistaken. He was a philosopher, she thought, meditating the difference between appearance and reality. On the contrary, he was an aristocrat considering his points.

VIRGINIA WOOLF

IV

The following poem is a narrative in ballad form. State the theme of the story briefly. If you interpret it, remember to present the narrative as a ballad and not as a dramatic sketch.

THE RAVEN

Once upon a midnight dreary, while I pondered, weak and weary,
Over many a quaint and curious volume of forgotten lore—
While I nodded, nearly napping, suddenly there came a tapping,
As of someone gently rapping, rapping at my chamber door.
" 'Tis some visitor," I muttered, "tapping at my chamber door—
　　Only this and nothing more."

Ah, distinctly I remember it was in the bleak December;
And each separate dying ember wrought its ghost upon the floor.
Eagerly I wished the morrow;—vainly I had sought to borrow
From my books surcease of sorrow—sorrow for the lost Lenore—
For the rare and radiant maiden whom the angels name Lenore—
　　Nameless here for evermore.

And the silken sad uncertain rustling of each purple curtain
Thrilled me—filled me with fantastic terrors never felt before;
So that now, to still the beating of my heart, I stood repeating
" 'Tis some visitor entreating entrance at my chamber door—
Some late visitor entreating entrance at my chamber door;—
　　This it is and nothing more."

Presently my soul grew stronger; hesitating then no longer,
"Sir," said I, "or Madam, truly your forgiveness I implore;
But the fact is I was napping, and so gently you came rapping,
And so faintly you came tapping, tapping at my chamber door,
That I scarce was sure I heard you"—here I opened wide the door;
　　Darkness there and nothing more.

Deep into that darkness peering, long I stood there wondering, fear-
　　ing,
Doubting, dreaming dreams no mortal ever dared to dream before;
But the silence was unbroken, and the stillness gave no token,
And the only word there spoken was the whispered word, "Lenore!"
This I whispered, and an echo murmured back the word, "Lenore!"
　　Merely this and nothing more.

Back into the chamber turning, all my soul within me burning,
Soon again I heard a tapping somewhat louder than before.
"Surely," said I, "surely that is something at my window lattice;
Let me see, then, what thereat is, and this mystery explore—
Let my heart be still a moment and this mystery explore;—
　　'Tis the wind and nothing more!"

Open here I flung the shutter, when, with many a flirt and flutter
In there stepped a stately Raven of the saintly days of yore.

Not the least obeisance made he; not a minute stopped or stayed he;
But, with mien of lord or lady, perched above my chamber door—
Perched upon a bust of Pallas just above my chamber door—
    Perched, and sat, and nothing more.

Then this ebony bird beguiling my sad fancy into smiling
By the grave and stern decorum of the countenance it wore,
"Though thy crest be shorn and shaven, thou," I said, "art sure no
        craven,
Ghastly grim and ancient Raven wandering from the Nightly shore—
Tell me what thy lordly name is on the Night's Plutonian shore!"
    Quoth the Raven, "Nevermore."

Much I marvelled this ungainly fowl to hear discourse so plainly,
Though its answer little meaning—little relevancy bore;
For we cannot help agreeing that no living human being
Ever yet was blessed with seeing bird above his chamber door—
Bird or beast upon the sculptured bust above his chamber door,
    With such a name as "Nevermore."

But the Raven, sitting lonely on the placid bust, spoke only
That one word, as if his soul in that one word he did outpour.
Nothing further then he uttered—not a feather then he fluttered—
Till I scarcely more than muttered "Other friends have flown before—
On the morrow he will leave me, as my hopes have flown before."
    Then the bird said, "Nevermore."

Startled at the stillness broken by reply so aptly spoken,
"Doubtless," said I, "what it utters is its only stock and store
Caught from some unhappy master whom unmerciful Disaster
Followed fast and followed faster till his songs one burden bore—
Till the dirges of his Hope that melancholy burden bore
    Of 'Never—nevermore!' "

But the Raven still beguiling all my fancy into smiling,
Straight I wheeled a cushioned seat in front of bird, and bust and
        door;
Then, upon the velvet sinking, I betook myself to linking
Fancy unto fancy, thinking what this ominous bird of yore—
What this grim, ungainly, ghastly, gaunt, and ominous bird of yore
    Meant in croaking "Nevermore."

This I sat engaged in guessing, but no syllable expressing
To the fowl whose fiery eyes now burned into my bosom's core;
This and more I sat divining, with my head at ease reclining
On the cushion's velvet lining that the lamplight gloated o'er,
But whose velvet violet lining with the lamplight gloating o'er,
    She shall press, ah, nevermore!

Then, methought, the air grew denser, perfumed from an unseen
    censer
Swung by seraphim whose foot-falls tinkled on the tufted floor.
"Wretch," I cried, "thy God hath lent thee—by these angels he hath
    sent thee
Respite—respite and nepenthe from thy memories of Lenore;
Quaff, oh quaff this kind nepenthe, and forget this lost Lenore!"
    Quoth the Raven, "Nevermore."

"Prophet!" said I, "thing of evil! prophet still, if bird or devil!—
Whether Tempter sent, or whether tempest tossed thee here ashore,
Desolate yet all undaunted, on this desert land enchanted—
On this home by Horror haunted—tell me truly, I implore—
Is there—*is* there balm in Gilead?—tell me—tell me, I implore!"
    Quoth the Raven, "Nevermore."

"Prophet!" said I, "thing of evil!—prophet still, if bird or devil!
By that Heaven that bends above us—by that God we both adore—
Tell this soul with sorrow laden if, within the distant Aidenn,
It shall clasp a sainted maiden whom the angels name Lenore—
Clasp a rare and radiant maiden whom the angels name Lenore."
    Quoth the Raven, "Nevermore."

"Be that word our sign of parting, bird or fiend!" I shrieked, upstart-
    ing—
"Get thee back into the tempest and the Night's Plutonian shore!
Leave no black plume as a token of that lie thy soul hath spoken!
Leave my loneliness unbroken!—quit the bust above my door!
Take thy beak from out my heart, and take thy form from off my
    door!"
    Quoth the Raven, "Nevermore."

And the Raven never flitting, still is sitting, *still* is sitting,
On the pallid bust of Pallas just above my chamber door;
And his eyes have all the seeming of a demon's that is dreaming,
And the lamplight o'er him streaming throws his shadow on the floor;
And my soul from out that shadow that lies floating on the floor
    Shall be lifted—nevermore!

Edgar Allan Poe

Descriptive. Description does more than inform, more than
tell a story, although it can be part of a narrative—as you have
noted in the foregoing selections—and can also be part of exposition. One who describes wishes to stir up impressive images,
to connote through suggestive words more than logical meaning ·
will allow. In other words, an impression is to be made on the
reader, an impression that suggests a mood. The interpreter must

be sure to get the image as a whole and then decide which words are most important in creating that impression. "The earth is the Lord's and the fullness thereof" is not, as it is often interpreted, a statement denoting legal possession or economic status. There is a deeper meaning which the interpreter can reproduce by an understanding of "the fullness thereof."

In reading descriptive literature, the interpreter's manner may not be as direct as in reading the narrative or the expository selections, especially if the mood is dominant.

EXERCISES

What is your impression of the following descriptions? What images stand out to give the effect that the author is trying to produce?

I

This poem is like a candid camera shot; the details flash before the eye, emphasizing a figure in silhouette. In his descriptive details, Frost has told us the story of a life that is self-sufficient, aloof from the passing world, but very much a part of his surroundings. The last line completes the picture of complete indifference. What does it tell you?

THE FIGURE IN THE DOORWAY[52]

The grade surmounted, we were riding high
Through level mountains nothing to the eye
But scrub oak, scrub oak and the lack of earth
That kept the oaks from getting any girth.
But as through the monotony we ran,
We came to where there was a living man.
His great gaunt figure filled his cabin door,
And had he fallen inward on the floor,
He must have measured to the further wall.
But we who passed were not to see him fall.
The miles and miles he lived from anywhere
Were evidently something he could bear.

[52] From *Complete Poems of Robert Frost.* Copyright, 1930–1949, by Henry Holt and Company, Inc. Copyright, 1936, 1948, by Robert Frost. Reprinted by permission of the publishers.

He stood unshaken, and if grim and gaunt,
It was not necessarily from want.
He had the oaks for heating and for light.
He had a hen, he had a pig in sight.
He had a well, he had the rain to catch.
He had a ten by twenty garden patch.
Nor did he lack for common entertainment.
That I assume was what our passing train meant.
He could look at us in our diner eating,
And if so moved uncurl a hand in greeting.

ROBERT FROST

II

There is warmth and a personal note in this next description.

HERE IS THE NIGHT[53]

What though the day was full of weariness,
With many a jarring sound and fretful sight,
Here is this night.
Whatever went before, here is an hour
Of pure, clear dark, with peace on wood and hill
And every flower folded honey-cool,
And every quiet pool
Brimful of starlight, and the winds all still.
The day went hard, and with tomorrow's light
May come new care; but by the tender grace
Of God's good thought there falls a little space
Of dusk and dew and dreams.
Here is this night.

NANCY BYRD TURNER

III

The gentleman from "The Round Dozen" is described in a clear-cut manner. We see him as if he were standing in front of us:[54]

The gentleman rose to his feet when the two ladies left, and then resumed his chair. A waiter brought him a glass of heavy port. He smelt it, sipped it, and rolled it round his tongue. I observed him. He was a little man, much shorter than his imposing wife, well-covered

[53] From *Good Housekeeping* (October, 1925), p. 44. Reprinted by permission of the publisher.
[54] From *The Maugham Reader* (New York, Doubleday & Company, Inc., 1950), p. 894.

without being stout, with a fine head of curling grey hair. His face was much wrinkled and it bore a faintly humorous expression. His lips were tight and his chin was square. He was, according to our present notions, somewhat extravagantly dressed. He wore a black velvet jacket, a frilled shirt with a low collar and a large black tie, and very wide evening trousers. It gave you vaguely the effect of costume. Having drunk his port with deliberation, he got up and sauntered out of the room.

W. Somerset Maugham

IV

The words in the next passage have been carefully selected to give you a definite impression. What is it?

NEW ENGLAND SPRING[55]

Perhaps the thing that really makes New England wonderful is this sense of joy, this intuition of brooding and magic fulfillment that hovers like a delicate presence in the air of one of these days. Perhaps the answer is simple: perhaps it is only that this soft and sudden spring, with its darts and flicks of evanescent joy, its sprite-like presence that is only half-believed, its sound that is the sound of something lost and elfin and half-dreamed, half-heard, seems wonderful after the grim, frozen tenacity of the winter, the beautiful and terrible desolation, the assault of the frost and ice on living flesh which resists it finally as it would resist the cruel battering of a brute antagonist, so that the tart, stingy speech, the tight gestures, the withdrawn and suspicious air, the thin lips, red pointed noses and hard prying eyes of these people are really the actions of those who, having to defend themselves harshly against nature, harshly defend themselves against all the world.

Thomas Wolfe

V

Compare the impression of the above selection with that of the following.

NEW ENGLAND ICE-STORM[56]

If we had not our own bewitching autumn foliage, we should still have to credit the weather with one feature which compensates for

---

[55] From *Of Time and the River*, p. 139. Copyright, 1935, by Charles Scribner's Sons. Reprinted by permission of the publishers.

[56] From *Tom Sawyer Abroad* (New York, Harper & Brothers, 1896), pp. 366-367.

all its bullying vagaries, the ice storm—when a leafless tree is clothed with ice from the bottom to the top—ice that is as bright and clear as crystal; every bough and twig is strung with ice-beads, frozen dew-drops, and the whole tree sparkles, cold and white, like the Shah of Persia's diamond plume. Then the wind waves the branches, and the sun comes out and turns all those myriads of beads and drops to prisms, that glow and hum and flash with all manner of colored fires, which change and change again, with inconceivable rapidity, from blue to red, from red to green, and green to gold; the tree becomes a sparkling fountain, a very explosion of dazzling jewels; and it stands there the acme, the climax, the supremest possibility in art or nature of bewildering, intoxicating, intolerable significance.

MARK TWAIN

Persuasive. The author who writes to make people believe has some issue which seems important to him and which he wishes to share with others, in the hope that he may secure belief and acceptance. Persuasive literature, depending on the kind of persuasion used, may show varying degrees of intensity. It may be simple, quiet, and direct, or it may develop into a passionate plea.

EXERCISES

I

Bartolomeo Vanzetti's last speech to the court is persuasive, although it contains no direct plea for his life. You will recall that he and Nicola Sacco were charged on May 5, 1920, with the murder of a paymaster and his guard. They were tried in the spring of 1921 in Dedham, Mass., and found guilty; but their execution did not take place until August 22, 1927. State Vanzetti's theme in this speech.

LAST SPEECH TO THE COURT[57]

I have talk a great deal of myself
but I even forgot to name Sacco.
Sacco too is a worker,
from his boyhood a skilled worker, lover of work,
with a good job and pay,

[57] From *A New Anthology of Modern Poetry*, ed. Selden Rodman (New York, Random House, Inc., 1946), pp. 191-193.

a bank account, a good and lovely wife,
two beautiful children and a neat little home
at the verge of a wood, near a brook.

Sacco is a heart, a faith, a character, a man;
a man, lover of nature, and mankind;
a man who gave all, who sacrifice all
to the cause of liberty and to his love of mankind:
money, rest, mundane ambition,
his own wife, his children, himself
and his own life.

Sacco has never dreamt to steal, never to assassinate.
He and I have never brought a morsel
of bread to our mouths, from our childhood to today
which has not been gained by the sweat of our brows.
Never . . .

Oh, yes, I may be more witful, as some have put it;
I am a better babbler than he is, but many, many times
in hearing his heartful voice ringing a faith sublime,
in considering his supreme sacrifice, remembering his heroism,
I felt small at the presence of his greatness
and found myself compelled to fight back
from my eyes the tears,
and quanch my heart
trobling to my throat to not weep before him:
this man called thief and assassin and doomed.

But Sacco's name will live in the hearts of the people
and in their gratitude when Katzmann's bones
and yours will be dispersed by time;
when your name, his name, your laws, institutions,
and your false god are but a dim rememoring
of a cursed past in which man was wolf
to the man. . . .

If it had not been for these thing
I might have live out my life
talking at street corners to scorning men.
I might have die, unmarked, unknown, a failure.
Now we are not a failure.
This is our career and our triumph. Never
in our full life could we hope to do such work
for tolerance, for justice, for man's understanding
of man, as now we do by accident.
Our words, our lives, our pains—nothing!

The taking of our lives—lives of a good shoemaker and a poor fish-
    peddler—
all! That last moment belongs to us—
that agony is our triumph.

BARTOLOMEO VANZETTI

II

Another kind of persuasiveness is conveyed to us in "Makers
of the Flag." The theme centers around the idea that we are all
makers of the flag through our labors and our dreams. Even
though the essay evaluates the makers of the flag, it achieves an
added impressiveness by means of dialogue and the climaxing
repetitions which, in the end, mount to a belief. You will notice
that the narrative form is used until "a great shout" comes from
the flag. Certainly it is more persuasive than the words spoken by
Woodrow Wilson on June 14, 1915:

The things that the flag stands for were created by the experiences of
a great people. Everything that it stands for was written by their lives.
The flag is the embodiment, not of sentiment, but of history. It represents the experiences made by men and women, the experiences of
those who do and live under that flag.

Compare these lines with the following treatment.

MAKERS OF THE FLAG[58]

This morning, as I passed into the Land Office, The Flag dropped
me a most cordial salutation, and from its rippling folds I heard it say,
"Good-morning, Mr. Flag-Maker."

"I beg your pardon, Old Glory," I said, "aren't you mistaken? I
am not the President of the United States, nor a member of Congress,
nor even a general in the army. I am only a Government clerk."

"I greet you again, Mr. Flag-Maker," replied the gay voice. "I
know you well. You are the man who worked in the swelter of yesterday straightening out the tangle of that farmer's homestead in Idaho,
or perhaps you found the mistake in that Indian contract in Oklahoma,
or helped to clear that patent for the hopeful inventor in New York,
or pushed the opening of that new ditch in Colorado, or made that
mine in Illinois more safe, or brought relief to the old soldier in

[58] From *The American Spirit* (New York, Frederick A. Stokes Company,
1918), p. 128.

Wyoming. No matter; whichever one of these beneficial individuals you happen to be, I give you greeting, Mr. Flag-Maker."

I was about to pass on, when The Flag stopped me with these words:—

"Yesterday the President spoke a word that made happier the future of ten million peons in Mexico; but that act looms no larger on the flag than the struggle which the boy in Georgia is making to win the Corn Club prize this summer.

"Yesterday the Congress spoke a word which will open the door of Alaska; but the mother in Michigan worked from sunrise until far into the night, to give her boy an education. She, too, is making the flag.

"Yesterday we made a new law to prevent financial panics, and yesterday, maybe, a school teacher in Ohio taught his first letters to a boy who will one day write a song that will give cheer to millions of our race. We are all making the flag."

"But," I said impatiently, "these people were only working!"

Then came a great shout from The Flag:—

"The work that we do is the making of the Flag.

"I am not the flag; not at all. I am but its shadow.

"I am whatever you make me, nothing more.

"I am your belief in yourself, your dream of what a people may become.

"I live a changing life, a life of moods and passions, of heartbreaks and tired muscles.

"Sometimes I am strong with pride, when men do an honest work, fitting the rails together truly.

"Sometimes I droop, for then purpose has gone from me, and cynically I play the coward.

"Sometimes I am loud, garish, and full of that ego that blasts judgment.

"But always I am all that you hope to be, and have the courage to try for.

"I am song and fear, struggle and panic, and ennobling hope.

"I am the day's work of the weakest man, and the largest dream of the most daring.

"I am the Constitution and the courts, statutes and the statute-makers, soldier and dreadnaught, drayman and street sweep, cook, counselor, and clerk.

"I am the battle of yesterday, and the mistake of tomorrow.

"I am the mystery of the men who do without knowing why.

"I am the clutch of an idea, and the reasoned purpose of resolution.

"I am no more than you believe me to be and I am all that you believe I can be.

"I am what you make me, nothing more.

"I swing before your eyes as a bright gleam of color, a symbol of yourself, the pictured suggestion of that big thing which makes this nation. My stars and my stripes are your dream and your labors. They are bright with cheer, brilliant with courage, firm with faith, because you have made them so out of your hearts. For you are the makers of the flag and it is well that you glory in the making."

FRANKLIN K. LANE

III

Damon Runyon, in his delightful exhortation on the use of *r* —that "fine, sturdy, upstanding old letter, with the bark on"— has an interesting combination of mock-persuasive appeal and mock-heroic explanation of how he feels about his favorite letter. His lightness of touch must be maintained, even through the "whereasing and thereforing" and even to the punishment for the actor who is discriminating against the *r* in favor of the "sissige sounding" *h*. Another look at the phrase "Round the rugged rock the ragged rascal ran" will indicate that Runyon is persuading lightly, because the therapeutic value of that phrase is not relevant to his complaint, inasmuch as the *r* at the beginning of a word is not the same *r* for which one can substitute the *h* sound.

BETWEEN YOU AND ME[59]

Mister Chairman, and ladies and gentlemen of the convention, I rise at this time to appeal to your sense of fairness, and to ask that some consideration be shown an old and valued friend of mine—the letter "r."

What, I ask you, has the letter "r" done; what crime has it committed that it should be practically ignored in the speech of the day? Why should the letter "r" be, to all intents and purposes, an outcast in our language, when such ignoble letters as "s" and "z" are added to the best society?

Is there no justice?

"R" is a fine, sturdy, upstanding old letter, with the bark on. A good old homespun letter, that gives zest to the tongue, and yet everywhere I find it shunted outside, and sometimes completely eliminated in favor of a letter so sissige sounding as the letter "h."

I go to the theatre, and in three solid acts—well, anyway, acts—I never hear a single "r." I hear actors and actresses lallygagging with the puerile letter "h" until my ears are revolted. They say "heah" and "theah," and "wheah," and "deah," and "feah," and I claim that all

[59] This article was published originally in the *New York American* and is reprinted by permission of the publishers.

this is clearly unconstitutional and opposed to the best interests of the people.

If it keeps on, we will wind up with a nation "h-ing" itself out of breath.

The talkies have recently got the habit. By birth and environment, the good old letter "r" is eminently fitted for use in the talkies, because the normal guttural growl of the dinged machinery is calculated to bring out the "r" in all its hairy-chested manliness.

But, taking their cue from the speaking stage, the talkies are playing the chill for the "r" as completely as—well, let us say, as completely as Mr. Bob Coleman, the clever dramatic critic—which is very completely indeed.

However, in Mr. Coleman's case there are mitigating circumstances. Mr. Coleman comes from south of the Messrs. Mason and Dixon's line, and in those parts an old blue law makes it a misdemeanor to commit "r" in public speech. I believe that down yondah the "r" is the youth of the land, and I am deemed somewhat risqué, if not downright obscene.

It is carefully concealed and I am told that there are persons who were born south of the Messrs. Mason and Dixon's line who did not know there was such a letter as "r" until they were over twenty-one years of age. Mr. Coleman once told me of a bad boy back in his old home town who was arrested for writing the letter "r" on a fence in chalk, having been taught the letter by an evil-minded Yankee who chanced that way.

All right, then, we can excuse persons like Mr. Coleman, who privately admitted to me not so long ago that he has nothing personal against the letter "r" and has occasionally practiced it in secret.

But what about that movie actor I encountered on the screen the other night, who originated in Colorado, and who snubbed the good old "r" and heaved "h's" right in my face?

It is fellows of this ilk that I have a quarrel with. I know this boy was brought up on "r," and there hasn't been an "h" in his family for at least two generations, so how does he get that way?

In Colorado, Mr. Chairman, and ladies and gentlemen, and especially in Pueblo, Colorado, the children are given "r's" to chew from birth, and no one in that state ever heard of "h" as a substitute for the staunch, tongue-filling old "r" until Hume Lewis came back from what he called Hahvahd and started in putting on the "h's" in Mr. Jimmy O'Brien's Opera House bar.

He had remarked "ovah theah" twice hand running, and the citizens put it down to the fact that he was muttering into a mug of beer at the time, which might have muffled his speech, but when he spoke of Denvah, and gratuitously rung in the word Bahtendah, the trouble started. Only the intervention of cooler heads prevented serious difficulty.

Afterwards, Mr. Lewis ran for the State Senate, and his political enemies used the "h's" against him, but Mr. Lewis outwitted them by making a speech every night in which he craftily mentioned Collar-r-radd-der, our true pronunciation, as frequently as possible.

I find it in my heart to forgive the Harvard boys for cutting the "r" in classes, because in nearly every case they revert to normal speech after they return to their homes in Iowa, Indiana, Illinois, Nebraska, and other States where the "r" abounds.

I overlook the Brooklynite's eschewing of the "r" in certain words, such as pearl, which is "poil" to him, because he invents new spots to put in "r's" that no one else ever thought of, as in "erl" for oil, and "ersters" for oysters, and "sawr" for saw. In fact, the "r" is a household letter in Brooklyn, and they wouldn't give you a dime a dozen for "h's" there.

What sense is there to an "h," anyway? It is not handsome. It has no shape. No virility. In my opinion, the English cockneys have the right idea about the "h" in dispensing with it entirely, though the English upper clawsses have picked it up and work it until it aches. I am informed that English actors, hearing the upper clawsses talk, got the "h" idea from them, and brought it to this country.

But I am for Amer-r-iker first, Mister Chairman, and I believe that we should do everything in our power to preserve the purity of our native speech, and it is for that reason that I raise my voice in these halls in an appeal for the good old "r." So, then, I move you, Mister Chairman, that we pass a resolution whereasing and thereforing that any actor hereafter found discriminating against "r" in favor of the "h," be required to write on the blackboard 100,000 times "Round the rugged rock the ragged rascal ran."

Damon Runyon

IV

Persuasion can be found in some of the greatest poetical passages. Antony's oration, for example, is a masterpiece. Read it, remembering that he wishes to persuade a mob. State his theme.

ANTONY'S ORATION

Friends, Romans, countrymen, lend me your ears!
I come to bury Caesar, not to praise him.
The evil that men do lives after them,
The good is oft interred with their bones;
So let it be with Caesar. The noble Brutus
Hath told you Caesar was ambitious:
If it were so, it was a grievous fault,
And grievously hath Caesar answer'd it.
Here, under leave of Brutus and the rest—

For Brutus is an honourable man;
So are they all, all honourable men—
Come I to speak in Caesar's funeral.
He was my friend, faithful and just to me;
But Brutus says he was ambitious,
And Brutus is an honourable man.
He hath brought many captives home to Rome,
Whose ransoms did the general coffers fill;
Did this in Caesar seem ambitious?
When that the poor have cried, Caesar hath wept;
Ambitions should be made of sterner stuff:
Yet Brutus says he was ambitious,
And Brutus is an honourable man.
You all did see that on the Lupercal
I thrice presented him a kingly crown,
Which he did thrice refuse. Was this ambition?
Yet Brutus says he was ambitious,
And, sure, he is an honourable man.
I speak not to disprove what Brutus spoke,
But here I am to speak what I do know.
You all did love him once, not without cause;
What cause withholds you then to mourn for him?
O judgement! thou art fled to brutish beasts,
And men have lost their reason. Bear with me;
My heart is in the coffin there with Caesar,
And I must pause till it come back to me.
                    WILLIAM SHAKESPEARE, *Julius Caesar*

V

The advice of Polonius to his son, Laertes, is a classic for parental counseling. What is his advice?

POLONIUS TO LAERTES

Yet here, Laertes! Aboard, aboard, for shame!
The wind sits in the shoulder of your sail,
And you are stay'd for. There; my blessing with thee!
And these few precepts in thy memory
See thou character. Give thy thoughts no tongue,
Nor any unproportion'd thought his act.
Be thou familiar, but by no means vulgar.
Those friends thou hast, and their adoption tried,
Grapple them to thy soul with hoops of steel;
But do not dull thy palm with entertainment
Of each new-hatch'd, unfledg'd comrade. Beware

Of entrance to a quarrel; but being in,
Bear't that the opposed may beware of thee.
Give every man thy ear, but few thy voice;
Take each man's censure, but reserve thy judgement.
Costly thy habit as thy purse can buy,
But not express'd in fancy; rich, not gaudy;
For the apparel oft proclaims the man,
And they in France of the best rank and station
Are of a most select and generous chief in that.
Neither a borrower nor a lender be;
For loan oft loses both itself and friend,
And borrowing dulls the edge of husbandry.
This above all: to thine own self be true,
And it must follow, as the night the day,
Thou canst not then be false to any man.
Farewell; my blessing season this in thee!

WILLIAM SHAKESPEARE, *Hamlet*

VI

The author is securing belief through the use of rhetorical questions in this next poem. What belief?

"SCUM O' THE EARTH" [60]

At the gate of the West I stand,
On the isle where the nations throng.
We call them "scum o' the earth";
Stay, are we doing you wrong,
Young fellow from Socrates' land?—
You, like a Hermes so lissome and strong
Fresh from the master Praxiteles' hand?
So, you're of Spartan birth?
Descended, perhaps, from one of the band—
Deathless in story and song—
Who combed their long hair at Thermopylæ's pass? . . .
Ah, I forgot the straits (alas!),
More tragic than theirs, more compassion-worth,
Have doomed you to march in our "immigrant class"
Where you're nothing but "scum o' the earth."

You Pole with the child on your knee,
What dower bring you to the land of the free?
Hark! Does she croon
That sad little tune
That Chopin once found on his Polish lea

[60] From *Scum o' the Earth and Other Poems.* Copyright, 1912, by Houghton, Mifflin Company. Reprinted by permission of the publishers.

And mounted in gold for you and for me?
Now a ragged young fiddler answers
In wild Czech melody
That Dvořák took whole from the dancers.
And the heavy faces bloom
In the wonderful Slavic way;
The little, dull eyes, the brows a-gloom,
Suddenly dawn like the day.
While watching these folk and their mystery,
I forget that we,
In our scornful mirth,
Brand them as "polacks"—and "scum o' the earth."

Genoese boy of the level brow,
Lad of the lustrous, dreamy eyes
Agaze at Manhattan's pinnacles now
In the first, sweet shock of a hushed surprise;
Within your far-rapt seer's eyes
I catch the glow of the wild surmise
That played on the Santa Maria's prow
In that still gray dawn,
Four centuries gone,
When a world from the wave began to rise.
Oh, who shall foretell what high emprise
Is the goal that gleams
When Italy's dreams
Spread wing and sweep into the skies?
Caesar dreamed him a world ruled well;
Dante dreamed Heaven out of Hell;
Angelo brought us there to dwell;
And you, are you a different birth?—
You're only a "dago,"—and "scum o' the earth!"

Stay, are we doing you wrong
Calling you "scum o' the earth,"
Man of the sorrow-bowed head,
Of the features tender yet strong,—
Man of the eyes full of wisdom and mystery
Mingled with patience and dread?
Have I not known you in history,
Sorrow-bowed head?
Were you the poet-king, worth
Treasures of Ophir unpriced?
Were you the prophet, perchance, whose art
Foretold how the rabble would mock
That shepherd of spirits, ere long,
Who should gather the lambs to his heart
And tenderly feed his flock?

Man—lift that sorrow-bowed head. . . .
Behold, the face of the Christ!

The vision dies at its birth.
You're merely a butt for our mirth.
You're a "sheeny"—and therefore despised
And rejected as "scum o' the earth."

Countrymen, bend and invoke
Mercy for us blasphemers,
For that we spat on these marvelous folk,
Nations of darers and dreamers,
Scions of singers and seers,
Our peers, and more than our peers.
"Rabble and refuse," we name them.
And "scum o' the earth," to shame them.
Mercy for us of the few, young years,
Of the culture so callow and crude,
Of the hands so grasping and rude,
The lips so ready for sneers
At the sons of our ancient more-than-peers.
Mercy for us who dare despise
Men in whose loins our Homer lies;
Mothers of men who shall bring to us
The glory of Titian, the grandeur of Huss;
Children in whose frail arms shall rest
Prophets and singers and saints of the West.

Newcomers all from the eastern seas,
Help us incarnate dreams like these.
Forget, and forgive, that we did you wrong.
Help us to father a nation strong
In the comradeship of an equal birth,
In the wealth of the richest bloods of earth.

ROBERT HAVEN SCHAUFFLER

VII

This poem, if effectively interpreted, could be more persuasive
than any speech against war and the smugness of citizens during
peace time.

LINES FOR AN INTERMENT[61]

Now it is fifteen years you have lain in the meadow:
The boards at your face have gone through: the earth is

---

[61] From *Collected Poems: 1917-1952*, p. 169. Copyright, 1952, by Houghton, Mifflin Company. Reprinted by permission of the publishers.

Packed down and the sound of the rain is fainter:
The roots of the first grass are dead:

It's a long time to lie in the earth with your honor:
The world Soldier the world has been moving on.

The girls wouldn't look at you twice in the cloth cap:
Six years old they were when it happened:

It bores them even in books: 'Soissons besieged!'
As for the gents they have joined the American Legion:

Belts and a brass band and the ladies' auxiliaries:
The Californians march in the OD silk:

We are all acting like civilized beings:
People mention it at tea . . .

The Facts of Life we have learned are Economic:
You were deceived by the detonations of bombs:

You thought of courage and death when you thought of warfare:
Hadn't they taught you the fine words were unfortunate?

Now that we understand we judge without bias:
We feel of course for those who had to die:

Women have written us novels of great passion
Proving the useless death of the dead was a tragedy:

Nevertheless it is foolish to chew gall:
The foremost writers on both sides have apologized:

The Germans are back in the Midi with cropped hair:
The English are drinking the better beer in Bavaria:

You can rest now in the rain in the Belgian meadow—
Now that it's all explained away and forgotten:
Now that the earth is hard and the wood rots:

Now you are dead . . .

ARCHIBALD MACLEISH

Dramatic. In presenting dialogue and dramatic situations, the author is interested in creating characters in contrasting moods and situations. Stories, monologues, dramatic poetry and plays provide material for this kind of interpretation. Each character must be considered in relationship to others presented in the same scene and, also, to the general rhythm and mood of the entire selection. Not only must the interpreter avoid dramatizing literal statements, but he must avoid using prosy literalness on words that are plainly intended to be dramatic, as in the following passage, in which Othello utters words that are full of anguish. Be sure that you do not slip over lines like "Put out the light, and then put out the light."

In dramatic literature, the interpreter is not as direct in his projection as he is in narration, exposition, and persuasion. Rather, he is conveying meaning indirectly through characterizations in dramatic situations. He begins to create some of the esthetic distance of the impersonator or the actor; but as an interpreter, he should not be completely "lost" to the audience.

EXERCISES

I

This selection contains one of the famous Shakespearean scenes with which every interpreter should be familiar. The setting is dramatic: it is late at night; there is a candle by Desdemona's bedside; Desdemona is sleeping, unaware of any impending disaster. The audience, knowing Othello's jealousy and error in thinking that Desdemona is unfaithful to him, is tense with expectation as Othello looks down on his bride. When she awakens, the tension is increased by the contrast in characterization and becomes almost unbearable until it is broken by the noise of Emilia outside.

Is it the author's intent to create sympathy for Othello or Desdemona? Listen to the recording of Paul Robeson in the role of Othello.[62]

THE DEATH OF DESDEMONA

OTHELLO. It is the cause, it is the cause, my soul,—
Let me not name it to you, you chaste stars!—
It is the cause. Yet I'll not shed her blood,
Nor scar that whiter skin of hers than snow,
And smooth as monumental alabaster.
Yet she must die, else she'll betray more men.
Put out the light, and then put out the light.

[62] *Othello* (Columbia, 5SL-153), with Paul Robeson, Uta Hagen, and José Ferrer.

If I quench thee, thou flaming minister,
I can again thy former light restore,
Should I repent me; but once put out thy light,
Thou cunning'st pattern of excelling nature,
I know not where is that Promethean heat
That can thy light relume. When I have pluck'd the rose
I cannot give it vital growth again,
It needs must wither: I'll smell it on the tree. (*Kisses her*)
Ah, balmy breath, that dost almost persuade
Justice to break her sword! One more, one more.
Be thus when thou art dead, and I will kill thee,
And love thee after. One more, and that's the last;
So sweet was ne'er so fatal. I must weep,
But they are cruel tears. This sorrow's heavenly;
It strikes where it doth love. She wakes.

DESDEMONA. Who's there? Othello?

OTH.   Ay, Desdemona.

DES. Will you come to bed, my lord?

OTH. Have you pray'd to-night, Desdemona?

DES.   Ay, my lord.

OTH. If you bethink yourself of any crime
    Unreconcil'd as yet to Heaven and grace,
    Solicit for it straight.

DES. Alack, my lord, what may you mean by that?

OTH. Well, do it, and be brief; I will walk by.
    I would not kill thy unprepared spirit;
    No; heavens forfend! I would not kill thy soul.

DES. Talk you of killing?

OTH.   Ay, I do.

DES.   Then heaven
    Have mercy on me!

OTH.   Amen, with all my heart!

DES. If you say so, I hope you will not kill me.

OTH. Hum!

DES. And yet I fear you; for you're fatal then
    When your eyes roll so. Why I should fear I know not,
    Such guiltiness I know not; but yet I feel I fear.

OTH. Think on thy sins.

DES.   They are the loves I bear to you.

OTH. Ay, and for that thou diest.

DES. That death's unnatural that kills for loving.
    Alas, why gnaw you so your nether lip?
    Some bloody passion shakes your very frame.
    These are portents; but yet I hope, I hope,
    They do not point on me.

OTH.   Peace, and be still!

DES. I will so. What's the matter?

OTH. That handkerchief which I so lov'd and gave thee
  Thou gav'st to Cassio.
DES.   No, by my life and soul!
  Send for the man, and ask him.
OTH.   Sweet soul, take heed,
  Take heed of perjury; thou art on thy death-bed.
DES. Ay, but not yet to die.
OTH.   Yes, presently:
  Therefore confess thee freely of thy sin;
  For to deny each article with oath
  Cannot remove nor choke the strong conception
  That I do groan withal. Thou art to die.
DES. O, Heaven, have mercy on me!
OTH.   I say, amen.
DES. And have you mercy too! I never did
  Offend you in my life; never lov'd Cassio
  But with such general warranty of heaven
  As I might love; I never gave him token.
OTH. By heaven, I saw my handkerchief in's hand,
  O perjur'd woman! thou dost stone my heart,
  And mak'st me call what I intend to do
  A murder, which I thought a sacrifice.
  I saw the handkerchief.
DES.   He found it then;
  I never gave it him. Send for him hither;
  Let him confess the truth.
OTH.   He hath confess'd.
DES. What, my lord?
OTH. That he hath us'd thee.
DES.   How? unlawfully?
OTH.   Ay.
DES. He will not say so.
OTH.   No, his mouth is stopp'd;
  Honest Iago hath ta'en order for't.
DES. O! my fear interprets. What, is he dead?
OTH. Had all his hairs been lives, my great revenge
  Had stomach for them all.
DES. Alas! he is betray'd and I undone.
OTH. Out, strumpet! weep'st thou for him to my face?
DES. O, banish me, my lord, but kill me not!
OTH. Down, strumpet!
DES. Kill me to-morrow: let me live to-night!
OTH. Nay, if you strive,—
DES. But half an hour!
OTH.   Being done, there is no pause.
DES. But while I say one prayer!
OTH.   It is too late. (*He smothers her*)

EMILIA. (*At the door*) My lord, my lord! What, ho! my lord, my lord!

OTH. What noise is this? Not dead? not yet quite dead?
I that am cruel am yet merciful;
I would not have thee linger in thy pain.
So, so.

EMIL. (*Within*) What, ho! my lord, my lord!

OTH.   Who's there?

EMIL. (*Within*) O, good my lord, I would speak a word with you!

OTH. Yes:—'tis Emilia.—By and by.—She's dead.
'Tis like she comes to speak of Cassio's death,—
The noise was high. Ha! no more moving?
Still as the grave. Shall she come in? Were't good?—
I think she stirs again:—no. What's best to do?
If she come in, she'll sure speak to my wife.
My wife! my wife! what wife? I have no wife.
O, insupportable! O heavy hour!
Methinks it should be now a huge eclipse
Of sun and moon, and that the affrighted globe
Should yawn at alteration.

EMIL. (*Within*)   I do beseech you
That I may speak with you, O good my lord!

OTH. I had forgot thee: O, come in, Emilia.
Soft; by and by.—Let me the curtains draw.—
Where art thou? (*Unlocks the door. Enter Emilia*)
                    What's the matter with thee now?

EMIL. O, good my lord, yonder's foul murder done!

OTH. What, now?

EMIL. But now, my lord.

OTH. It is the very error of the moon;
She comes more nearer earth than she was wont,
And makes men mad.

EMIL. Cassio, my lord, hath kill'd a young Venetian
Call'd Roderigo.

OTH.   Roderigo kill'd!
And Cassio kill'd!

EMIL.   No, Cassio is not kill'd.

OTH. Not Cassio kill'd! Then murder's out of tune,
And sweet revenge grows harsh.

DES. O, falsely, falsely murder'd!

EMIL.   O Lord, what cry is that?

OTH. That! what?

EMIL. Out, and alas! that was my lady's voice.
Help! help! ho! help! O lady, speak again!
Sweet Desdemona! O sweet mistress, speak!

DES. A guiltless death I die.

EMIL. O, who hath done this deed?

Des. Nobody; I myself. Farewell!
   Commend me to my kind lord. O, farewell! (*Dies*)
Oth. Why, how should she be murder'd?
Emil.   Alas, who knows?
Oth. You heard her say herself, it was not I.
Emil. She said so; I must needs report the truth.
Oth. She's, like a liar, gone to burning hell.
   'Twas I that kill'd her.
Emil.   O, the more angel she,
   And you the blacker devil!
Oth. She turn'd to folly, and she was a whore.
Emil. Thou dost belie her, and thou art a devil.
Oth. She was false as water.
Emil.   Thou art rash as fire, to say
   That she was false: O, she was heavenly true!
Oth. Cassio did top her; ask thy husband else.
   O, I were damn'd beneath all depth in hell,
   But that I did proceed upon just grounds
   To this extremity. Thy husband knew it all.
Emil. My husband!
Oth. Thy husband.
Emil. That she was false to wedlock?
Oth. Ay, with Cassio. Nay, had she been true,
   If heaven would make me such another world
   Of one entire and perfect chrysolite,
   I'd not have sold her for it.
Emil.   My husband!
Oth. Ay, 'twas he that told me on her first.
   An honest man he is, and hates the slime
   That sticks on filthy deeds.
Emil.   My husband!
Oth. What needs this iteration, woman? I say thy husband.
Emil. O mistress, villainy hath made mocks with love!
   My husband say that she was false!
Oth.   He, woman;
   I say thy husband: dost understand the word?
   My friend, thy husband, honest, honest Iago.
Emil. If he say so, may his pernicious soul
   Rot half a grain a day! He lies to the heart.
   She was too fond of her most filthy bargain.
Oth. Ha!
Emil. Do thy worst!
   This deed of thine is no more worthy heaven
   Than thou wast worthy her.
Oth.   Peace, you were best.
Emil. Thou hast not half that power to do me harm
   As I have to be hurt. O gull! O dolt!

As ignorant as dirt! Thou hast done a deed—
I care not for thy sword; I'll make thee known,
Though I lost twenty lives.—Help! help, ho! help!
The Moor hath kill'd my mistress! Murder! murder!

WILLIAM SHAKESPEARE, Othello

II

Equally dramatic is this story by Fitzgerald. Notice how tension mounts through the use of short sentences, monosyllabic words, and pauses, which are deliberately created by the author through his particular sentence structure.

COURAGE[63]

When they were youngsters of ten and twelve, the Sprague boys used to walk home alone after Sunday evening services. Peter was the elder, a stocky, unimaginative child, dark-skinned and awkward. Davy had nice features. He was fair like his mother's people.

As they neared the foot of Pride's Hill, Peter would take his brother's hand. Davy was afraid. That was on account of the old Baptist cemetery. The stones gleamed, and there were noises in the underbrush that fringed the road. As they topped the rise, the younger boy would draw away a little, and start chattering again.

Even in those days Peter had understood. Davy was different; things bothered him more.

When the war came, it was inevitable that the Sprague boys should be among the first from Baintree to go.

Davy enlisted in Boston, on his way home from his freshman year at Tufts. Two weeks later, when he left to report for duty, Peter went with him.

It was September. The transport was rocking to the first long swells of the outer harbor. The brothers stood by the rail, watching their convoy nose out ahead. Somewhere in the distance behind them the fog was blurring out the ragged Hoboken water front.

Beneath their feet the great shafts plunged and recoiled—pushing them steadily, relentlessly, toward the unknown.

· · · · · · · · · · · · ·

It was December. The third battalion had halted along the road beyond Menil-la-Tour. At eight that night the division would take over a sector from the French. The men had done twelve muddy miles since noon, and they were profanely tired.

[63] From *The Atlantic Monthly* (November, 1925). Reprinted by permission of the author and the publishers.

The rain had ceased falling and the sky was drawing away, cold and hard. A heavy rumbling came and went among the hills up ahead. A gray-blue camion lumbered by. Its bearded chauffeur dexterously caught a cigarette and grinned his thanks. The poplars dripped. Out of the clumps of O. D., blue shreds of smoke eddied.

Sergeant Sprague, working down the line, reached his brother's squad. Davy was sitting on his unslung pack, a little withdrawn from the others.

"How are the feet, Davy?"

"They're sore, Pete. Got any water?"

"Plenty."

As he took the canteen back, he paused, his fingers on its cover. Out of the distance had come a purring noise—high up. A soft purr with a recurring throb in it. The men grew silent. The noise came louder and louder. Far up in the sky, somewhat off to the right, a tiny black insect was sailing slowly toward them.

Slipping the canteen back in his belt Pete snapped-to the felt covers. The word was passed along to cut out the cigarettes and lie flat.

The Boche plane was droning almost directly overhead. The men lay still. The plane swooped down toward the road. A bomb struck in the field behind them; the explosion beat on them—the Boche had passed over.

A voice came from the next squad, "Missed us, you ——!" A tense suppressed laugh. The Boche came circling back again. The drone of his engine grew louder and louder. It would be close this time. Davy's hand came into Pete's line of vision. It was very still—the hand. Then slowly, spasmodically it twitched. It twitched as a shot rabbit twitches —convulsively. He was aware suddenly of a fear that had been with him from the beginning. Davy couldn't stand it. He was different. He wished to God the war would end—soon.

A flash, and the crash came. On the other side of the road—a bit of iron rang on a helmet.

The plane didn't return. It hummed off toward Menil-la-Tour. The men sat up and followed it with jeering comments. Dave clambered to his feet, laughing unsteadily.

.   .   .   .

Sprague grew leisurely awake. There was a patch of sunlight on the dugout floor. That meant afternoon. Pete had a vague memory of noise, heavy muffled sounds. He had slept since daylight. It was quiet outside. It had been a quiet two weeks. By this time to-morrow they would be back in reserve. The first battalion would be in to relieve them by dawn. He heard someone passing outside; the creak of heavy boots on the duckboards. Fritz had been lying low. It was a bad sign, that. Well—they'd be out to-morrow. He'd speak to the captain then about Davy. It was nothing to be ashamed of. Davy was sick. His nerves were screwed tight—to the breaking-point. They could see for themselves.

He sat up and reached for his shoes, but the image of his brother's white face, the tense look of his eyes, persisted. Only one more day. The bags at the head of the stairs pushed in. It was Sergeant Ferber.

"Sleep through the row?"

"I heard something."

"They threw some Berthas over—knocked in a piece of the support trench."

Ferber stood watching Pete winding on his spirals.

"Your brother's out of luck."

Sprague straightened up and waited—tense.

"He sneaked off post five when the fuss started. They picked him up cryin' like a kid."

It had come.

Sprague drew a quick sharp breath and bent again over his leggings, his back to Ferber. He tucked in the tape ends and turned.

"The kid's all in—he's sick."

"He will be when they get through with him."

Sprague's eyes flamed. Then, without speaking, he went past Ferber to the stairs.

The sky was blue overhead. The guns were quiet, oppressively quiet. There was a soft thud above him. A little sand scattered down. Davy—Davy!

.   .   .   .

The lantern at Captain Doane's elbow flared and smoked. The shadow on the wall behind him bulked grotesquely. He gave no sign. Sprague spoke with an effort, a sense of futility dragging down his words. When he had done, the officer raised his eyes. He looked past Sprague.

"The court can consider his physical condition. That's not up to me."

"Will you recommend clemency, sir?"

"I can't, Sprague. When your brother crawled off his post, he endangered the whole battalion. I can't let any feeling for you—"

There was more; something about justice and Pete's own record. The words blurred together. It didn't matter. Davy would be put under guard in the morning when they started out. They wouldn't shoot him—it would be Leavenworth. The *Concord Times* would have it. Jim Wetherby would bring the paper out to his mother.

The phone stuttered. As Doane reached for the set, Sprague saluted stiffly and turned away.

He was passing out of the orderlies' room when someone grabbed his elbow. "Are you deaf, Sarge? The old man wants you back."

The captain was waiting, drumming nervously on the table. "Price is on number nine. He thinks they've sneaked in and set up a machine gun off to his left."

As Pete listened, his brother's face grew indistinct. The ground sloped off to the left of number nine.

"They could get the support trench from that position, sir."

"If they've got that support trench covered, they've got wind we're going to be relieved. They're going to strafe us when we start out! You know the men. Send someone out to look it over. If the Boches are there, we'll hold up the movement and shell them out in the morning."

A sense of relief—of escape—flashed on him. It would be a way out. Doane was waiting—giving him his chance.

A way out—for him. He stood silent.

"Well? Tell the man who goes, we'll make him if he gets back. That's all, Sergeant."

Sprague wormed his way out through the narrow connecting ditch to number nine post. A fine rain was beginning to fall. The night was black and warm. Price pointed out through the dark. Crouching together, they waited till a flare of light shot up.

"Off to your left," whispered Price, "there's a shell hole. You can't see nothing, but there's a couple of Heinies in there with a machine gun or I'll—"

"All right, Price. I'll send someone out to look it over. Don't open up if you hear us. I'll go part way myself."

Price cursed fervently under his breath. His whisper followed Sprague. "There's a ticket west waiting for the bird that goes."

Sprague knew it.

Davy lay crouched, his face to the wall. At the touch of his brother's hand he shivered and turned to stare up at him hopelessly. He tried to smile. His lips twitched.

Pete's face was granite. "Davy, get your shoes on. The C. O. wants you."

In the trench outside, Pete gripped his shoulder. "You've got to get out and get out quick. They're going to line you up in the morning."

"My God, Pete! They wouldn't do that!"

"They've got to on account of the others." He put his arms around the boy and held him close. Then gently he broke the grasp of his fingers. "You're going over to the Boches, Davy. They will ship you back to a prison camp. After this thing is over, people won't remember."

He was glad of the darkness.

"I can't, Pete."

"It's your only chance. Sure you can. Come."

The boy shrank back.

"It's that or the firing squad, Davy."

A moment later they were on their faces crawling beneath the wire. Out by number nine post. He could hear Davy breathing—quick forced gasps. Groping, he reached and found his hand. They crept on. Out past the vague hump that was number nine post. Five—ten yards beyond. A flare went up, and before the light failed he had aligned the suspected crater.

"I've got to go back now, Dave. Keep straight on till you strike a shell hole, twenty-five yards out. Crawl in there till it starts to get light and then go over."

He drew swiftly back before Davy could hesitate, lest he refuse to go on. He could still get him back. He dug his fingers into the earth. The silence pushed down on him—it was too late now. The seconds hung back.

A roar shattered the night. The waiting Boche had swung his gun on the black smudge that had crept too near. A sharp staccato of shots. The silence settled down again. Sprague crept back under the wire. His lips were bleeding.

Captain Doane looked up anxiously. "Well, Sprague?"

"There's a machine gun there, sir. Thirty yards off post nine." There was a note of exhaustion in his voice. "He opened up and got our man."

Doane fumbled for his pipe. Their eyes met. "Who went, Sergeant?"

Pete lifted a suffering face. "Private Sprague, sir."

"Your lantern's smoking, sir. I'll send Webber in."

He stopped in the orderlies' room, and then went back to his brother's dugout—to gather up Davy's things. They would send them back to his mother.

Brassil Fitzgerald

III

The following poem is dramatic, with no word spoken by the main character. Notice how the action rises to a climax and how the author has managed to portray the powerful emotions of the king.

STAGE DIRECTIONS[64]

Trumpets. Enter a King, in the sunset glare.
He sits in an antique chair. He fingers an antique ring.
The heavy cloak on his back is gold and black.

The hall is tall with gloom. A window stands
Full of scarlet sky. The hands of trees entreat the room,
Plucking and plucking the pane. An oblong stain

[64] From *Golden Fleece*, p. 15. Copyright, 1927, by William Rose Benét. Reprinted by permission of Dodd, Mead & Company.

Of scarlet is flat on the floor. The projected flare
Slants to the foot of the chair. The chamber's farther door
Slowly advances its edge. A smoky wedge

Of thick blue mist, growing wider as the door swings
Noiseless, twitches the king's hands. He is crouched like a spider.
His eyes are green as glass. Shudderings pass

That shrink him deep in his cloak. The door is wide.
The doorway, from side to side, is packed with mist like smoke.
The dreadful scarlet dies from the windowed skies.

Silence crosses the room. Nothing more.
Silence crowds from the door, gathers, gathers in gloom.
His fluttering fingers rise to cover his eyes.

Silence says nothing at all. It is thickly pressed,
Like a multitude obsessed with terror, from wall to wall.
Silence, deep with dread, is the weight of lead

That slowly constricts his breast. Fingers fight
At the throat, in fierce despite of death, as the drowned resist
Green gulfs that roar and ring . . .
Exit the King.
WILLIAM ROSE BENÉT

CHAPTER 4

The Author's Meaning

SECTION ONE: Logical Meaning

The author intends through the structure of his sentences to indicate the logical meaning of the literature he has written. The interpreter must attempt as nearly as he can to approximate that meaning through a study of the sentence structure: what the words mean and how they are related one to the other; how they are formed into phrases; and how the phrases are interrelated. The factors which are most likely to be significant for you, the interpreter, in trying to determine the logical meaning of a passage are these: (1) meaning of words; (2) relationship of words; (3) interrelationship of phrases.

MEANING OF WORDS

Unusual Words

A new word is a discovery; it is a signpost to new paths of experience. To ignore its meaning is to miss the author's message. If any student wishes to bowl merrily and blithely over word after word, the meaning of which he does not understand, then he should not even try to read literature, much less try to interpret it for others. Certainly literature is incorrectly presented more because of lack of understanding than because of any other factor. Unfortunately, the listener can tell usually whether the

136

author's words have stirred up the right meaning in the interpreter, and, occasionally, if the meaning is obscure, he may ask what a certain unusual word means.

EXERCISES

I

In Richard Sheridan's play, *The Rivals*, there is the voluble character, Mrs. Malaprop, who is famous for her misuse of words. You will never appreciate Mrs. Malaprop or be able to interpret her lines with the proper timing and inflection unless you know which words she has misused; and you will never be sure which words she has misused unless you know the meanings of all the words. The first word you should be curious about is the word *malapropism*, which according to Webster's dictionary means "A grotesque misuse of a word."

Underline the words in the following passage that should be checked for meaning. When you are sure that you *know* what words were incorrectly used and have looked for their meaning in the dictionary, then try reading Mrs. Malaprop's lines for hidden laughs.

MRS. MALAPROP

Observe me, Sir Anthony. I would by no means wish a daughter of mine to be a progeny of learning; I don't think so much learning becomes a young woman; for instance, I would never let her meddle with Greek, or Hebrew, or Algebra, or simony, or fluxions, or paradoxes, or such inflammatory branches of learning—neither would it be necessary for her to handle any of your mathematical, astronomical, diabolical instruments.—But Sir Anthony, I would send her, at nine years old, to a boarding school, in order to learn a little ingenuity and artifice. Then, sir, she should have a supercilious knowledge in accounts;—and as she grew up, I would have her instructed in geometry, that she might know something of the contagious countries;—but above all, Sir Anthony, she should be mistress of orthodoxy, that she might not mis-spell, and mis-pronounce words so shamefully as girls usually do; and likewise, that she might reprehend the true meaning of what she is saying. This, Sir Anthony, is what I would have a woman know; —and I don't think there is a superstitious article in it.

RICHARD SHERIDAN, *The Rivals*

II

Many of us have chanted Lewis Carroll's "Jabberwocky" for the fun of uttering the unusual combinations of sounds without too much attention to specific meanings. As the author might say, "Jabberwocky" is a "frabjous" piece of art. You will be unable to find the meaning of the words in a dictionary because Carroll manufactured them for this particular poem. The author explains that two meanings have been packed into one word.

Take the two words "fuming" and "furious." Make up your mind that you will say both words but leave it unsettled which you will say first. Now open your mouth and speak. If your thoughts incline ever so little towards "fuming," you will say "fuming-furious"; if they turn, by even a hair's breadth towards "furious," you will say "furious-fuming"; but if you have that rarest of gifts, a perfectly balanced mind, you will say "frumious."

Today the word *brunch,* a combination of *breakfast* and *lunch,* is used quite acceptably in our language; so are words, like *motel* (*motor* plus *hotel*) and *smog* (*smoke* plus *fog*). The word *chortle* found in this poem has also become a part of our vocabulary. Read the poem and try to solve the meaning of some of the puzzling words before getting help from the list of words, which follows the poem:

JABBERWOCKY

'Twas brillig, and the slithy toves
　　Did gyre and gimble in the wabe;
All mimsy were the borogoves,
　　And the mome raths outgrabe.

"Beware the Jabberwock, my son!
　　The jaws that bite, the claws that catch!
Beware the Jubjub bird, and shun
　　The frumious Bandersnatch!"

He took his vorpal sword in hand:
　　Long time the manxome foe he sought.
So rested he by the Tumtum tree,
　　And stood awhile in thought.

And as in uffish thought he stood,
　　The Jabberwock with eyes of flame,

Came whiffling through the tulgey wood,
 And burbled as it came!

One, two! One, two! And through, and through
 The vorpal blade went snicker-snack!
He left it dead, and with its head
 He went galumphing back.

"And hast thou slain the Jabberwock?
 Come to my arms, my beamish boy!
Oh, frabjous day! Callooh! Callay!"
 He chortled in his joy.

'Twas brillig, and the slithy toves
 Did gyre and gimble in the wabe;
All mimsy were the borogoves
 And the mome raths outgrabe.

LEWIS CARROLL

In his book, *Here, There and Everywhere,* Eric Partridge helps you understand "Jabberwocky" by giving clues to the meaning of words coined by Carroll. Partridge reports that some words are echoic or suggestive of other words, some are blends of several words, and some are "adenoided" (that is, words from which the nasals *m, n,* and *ng* are omitted). Below is a list adapted from Partridge's explanatory remarks.[1]

brillig: an adenoidal, or "cold-in-the-head," word which, according to Humpty Dumpty, means four o'clock in the afternoon, the time when you begin broiling things for dinner. It also may be a blend of *broiling,* as in "a broiling day," and *brilliant,* or the other way around, before the word is adenoided.
slithy: a blend of *slimy* and *lithe;* the *i* is long.
toves: something like badgers, something like lizards, and something like corkscrews; yet there is a clear allusion to *coves,* that is, "fellows."
gyre: to *whirl, revolve, gyrate;* or, as Humpty Dumpty explains it, "to go round and round like a gyroscope."
wabe: wave adenoided.
mimsy: a blend of *miserable* and *flimsy.*
borogrove: a thin, shabby-looking bird with its feathers sticking out all around—something like a live mop.

[1] Adapted from Eric Partridge, *Here, There and Everywhere,* pp. 184-187. Copyright, 1950, by The Macmillan Company. Reprinted by permission of the publishers.

mome: short for *from home;* as Humpty Dumpty says, "meaning that they had lost their way, you know."

rath: a sort of green pig, the word being perhaps apprehended originally as *rat* lisped.

outgrabe: the preterit of *outgribe,* that is, "something between bellowing and whistling with a sort of a sneeze in the middle."

Jabberwock: has nothing in common with *jabber,* "to talk incessantly and incoherently," but probably refers to *jabs,* from its formidable talons. Probably, too, it refers to two echoic terms, *jatter,* "to shatter," and *whacker,* "anything enormous."

Jubjub: may be a pun on *jugjug,* imitative of the note of the euphonious nightingale, and may even blend *jugjug* with *hubbub.*

Bandersnatch: a personification of the animal's proclivities, referring either to *bandog,* a ferocious watchdog, or, less probably, to *bandar,* Hindustani for monkey.

vorpal: a blend of *voracious* and *narwhal* (narwhal is a dolphin-familied cetacean with a long, pointed tusk). Vorpal is now often used to mean *keen-edged.*

manxome: a combination of *maniac* and *Manx* and *fearsome.*

tumtum: a *tumtum* tree is intended to make us, by means of the nursery *tumtum* (tummy, stomach), think of that quite innocuous growth, the bread-fruit tree.

uffish: seems to mean "busy, deep, and fruitful." It may be a combination of *uberous,* "fruitful," and *officious,* in its now rare sense "efficacious," and the adjectival suffix *-ish.*

whiffle: a blend of *whistle* and *puffily.*

tulgey: suggests the presence of *thick, bulgy,* and *bosky,* with something of the sense of each.

burble: an echoic word, either derived from, or at the least, cognate with *bubble.*

snicker-snack: snicker is echoic for *knife,* and *snack* for *share.*

galumphing: galloping in *triumph* or *triumphantly.*

beamish: radiant like the sun's beams, or *beam-reddish.*

frabjous: a blend of *fragrant* and *joyous,* meaning "excellent, pre-eminent, surpassing."

callooh, callay: a variation of *hurroo, hooray.*

chortle: a blend of *chuckle* and *snort.*

III

Semantic differences in word usage among different countries sometimes cause difficulty in the understanding of meanings. Mario Pei comments on these differences as found in British and American usage of words:[2]

[2] From Mario Pei, *The Story of Language,* p. 297. Copyright, 1949, by J. B. Lippincott Company. Reprinted by permission of the publishers.

In Britain, an information bureau is an "inquiry office," a ticket agent is a "booking clerk" (pronounced *clark*); railroad tracks are "metals," a freight car is a "goods-wagon," and a train runs "to time." A "subway" is an "underpass," "underground" being our "subway"; the hood of a car is the "bonnet," while the top of the car is the "hood"; a fender is a "wing," a muffler is a "silencer," and a battery an "accumulator." "Dessert" in Britain means fruit, and you must use "sweet" if you want a dessert, while if you ask for "biscuits" you will get crackers; "scones" (pronounced *scawns*) are the nearest British equivalent of our "biscuits." "Apartment" in Britain means a single room; for the American apartment, one should use "flat" or "rooms," while an apartment house is a "block of flats." To an English bride, a can-opener is a "tin-opener," a pancake turner is an "egg-scoop," and an egg-beater an "egg-whisk." The British equivalent of a cigar-store is a "tobacconist's." An American worker's pay envelope is a British worker's "pay-packet." A "mist" in Britain is a light fog, not a drizzle, as it is in America, and because of this different connotation, American weather stations have given up using the word since 1939. The British "billion" is our trillion, and "milliard" should be used to signify our billion. Bewildering to an American when it comes from a British telephone operator is the expression "You're through!," which means not "You're finished," but "You're connected."

Unless you have some Scotch ancestry, you may not fully understand the following poem, even though you may enjoy the melody and lyrical quality of the lines. A good Scotchman will repeat these lines with happy reminiscence, but an American student will ordinarily push them aside because of the unknown words:

JOHN ANDERSON, MY JO

John Anderson my jo, John,
  When we were first acquent,
Your locks were like the raven,
  Your bonnie brow was brent;
But now your brow is beld, John,
  Your locks are like the snaw,
But blessing on your frosty pow
John Anderson, my jo!

John Anderson my jo, John,
  We clamb the hill thegither
And mony a canty day, John,
  We've had wi' ane anither;

Now we maun totter down, John,
And hand in hand we'll go,
And sleep thegither at the foot,
John Anderson, my jo!

ROBERT BURNS

(*jo,* sweetheart; *acquent,* acquainted; *brent,* smooth; *beld,* bald; *snaw,* snow; *pow,* head; *clamb,* climbed; *thegither,* together; *mony,* many; *canty,* cheerful or happy; *ane,* one; *anither,* another; *maun,* must.)

IV

Be sure of the meaning of words. It is wise not to be caught trying to explain a meaning as Bardolph was in Shakespeare's *King Henry IV, Part II:* "Accommodated; that is, when a man is, as they say, accommodated; or when a man is, being, whereby a' may be thought to be accommodated,—which is an excellent thing."

In the following selections, what do the italicized words mean? [3]

ROASTED CRACKLING

He must be roasted. I am not ignorant that our ancestors ate them *seethed,* or boiled—but what a sacrifice of the exterior *tegument.*

There is no flavour comparable, I will contend, to that of the crisp, *tawny,* well-watched, not over-roasted, *crackling,* as it is well called —the very teeth are invited to their share of the pleasure at this banquet in overcoming the *coy,* brittle resistance—with the *adhesive oleaginous*—O call it not fat—but an indefinable sweetness growing up to it—the tender blossoming of fat—fat cropped in the bud—taken in the shoot—in the first innocence—the cream and *quintessence* of the child-pig's yet pure food—the lean, no lean, but a kind of animal *manna*—or, rather, fat, and lean, (if it must be so) so blended and running into each other, that both together make but one *ambrosian* result, or common substance.

CHARLES LAMB, *A Dissertation upon Roast Pig*

AT OPHELIA'S GRAVE

HAMLET
Dost thou come here to whine?
To *outface* me with leaping in her grave?
Be buried quick with her, and so will I;
And, if thou *prate* of mountains, let them throw
Millions of acres on us, till our ground,

[3] Italics ours.

Singeing his *pate* against the burning zone,
Make Ossa like a wart! Nay, an thou'lt *mouth,*
I'll *rant* as well as thou.

WILLIAM SHAKESPEARE, *Hamlet*

THE DANCE

"Dear Pig, are you willing to sell for one *shilling*
  Your ring?" Said the Piggy, "I will."
So they took it away and were married next day
  By the Turkey who lives on the hill.
They dined on *mince* and slices of *quince,*
  Which they ate with a *runcible* spoon;
And hand in hand, on the edge of the sand,
  They danced by the light of the moon,
      The moon,
      The moon,
  They danced by the light of the moon.

EDWARD LEAR, *The Owl and the Pussy-Cat*

WHALIN'[4]

KEENEY

And d'you s'pose any of 'em would believe that—any o' them
skippers I've beaten voyage after voyage? Can't you hear 'em
laughin' and sneerin'—Tibbots 'n' Harris 'n' Simms and the rest—
and all o' Homeport makin' fun o' me? "Dave Keeney what boasts
he's the best whalin' skipper out o' Homeport comin' back with
a measly four hundred barrel of *ile?*" Hell! I got to git the ile,
I tell you.

EUGENE O'NEILL

A BIRTHDAY

My heart is like a singing bird
  Whose nest is in a water'd *shoot;*
My heart is like an apple-tree
  Whose boughs are bent with thick-set fruit;
My heart is like a rainbow shell
  That paddles in a *halcyon* sea;
My heart is gladder than all these,
  Because my love is come to me.

Raise me a *dais* of silk and down;
  Hang it with *vair* and purple dyes;

[4] From *Ile* in *Plays of Eugene O'Neill,* p. 308. Copyright, 1926, by
Horace Liveright, Inc. Reprinted by permission of the publishers.

Carve it in doves and *pomegranates,*
　And peacocks with a hundred eyes;
Work it in gold and silver grapes,
　In leaves and silver *fleur-de-lys;*
Because the birthday of my life
　Is come, my love is come to me.

Christina Rossetti

THE BLACK VULTURE[5]

Aloof upon the day's *immeasured dome,*
　He holds unshared the silence of the sky.
　Far down his bleak, relentless eyes *descry*
The eagle's empire and the *falcon's* home—
Far down, the *galleons* of sunset roam;
　His hazards on the sea of morning lie;
　Serene, he hears the broken tempest sigh
Where cold *sierras* gleam like scattered foam.

And least of all he holds the human swarm—
　Unwitting now that envious men prepare
　　To make their dream and its fulfillment one,
When, poised above the *caldrons* of the storm,
　Their hearts, contemptuous of death, shall dare
　　His roads between the thunder and the sun.

George Sterling

RANTING

Hamlet
　O, it offends me to the soul to hear a robustious *periwig-pated*
fellow tear a passion to tatters, to very rags, to split the ears of
the *groundlings,* who for the most part are capable of nothing
but *inexplicable dumb-shows* and noise. I could have such a
fellow whipp'd for o'erdoing *Termagant,* It *out-herods* Herod.
Pray you, avoid it.

William Shakespeare, Hamlet

CAPULET

Capulet
　And then to have a wretched *puling* fool,
　A whining *mammet,* in her *fortune's tender,*
　To answer, "I'll not wed; I cannot love."

William Shakespeare, Romeo and Juliet

<hr>

[5] From *Collected Poems,* p. 159. Copyright, 1923, by Henry Holt and
Company, Inc. Reprinted by permission of the publishers.

FALMOUTH

O, there's a wind a-blowing, a-blowing from the west,
And that of all the winds is the one I like the best,
For it blows at our backs, and it shakes our *pennon* free,
And it soon will blow us home to the old countrie.
    For it's home, dearie, home—it's home I want to be.
    Our *topsails* are hoisted, and we'll away to sea.
    O, the oak and the ash and the bonnie *birken* tree
    They're all growing green in the old countrie.
WILLIAM E. HENLEY

VENICE

And round the walls of the porches there are set pillars of *variegated* stones, *jasper* and *porphyry*, and deep-green *serpentine* spotted with flakes of snow, and marbles, that half refuse and half yield to the sunshine, Cleopatra-like, "their bluest veins to kiss"—the shadow, as it steals back from them, revealing line after line of azure *undulation*, as a receding tide leaves the waved sand; their capitals rich with interwoven *tracery*, rooted knots of *herbage*, and drifting leaves of *acanthus* and vine, and mystical signs, all beginning and ending in the Cross; and above them, in the broad *archivolts*, a continuous chain of language and of life—angels, and the signs of heaven and the labours of men, each in its appointed season upon the earth.
JOHN RUSKIN, The Stones of Venice

THE SCHOONER[6]

Just mark that schooner westward far at sea—
    'Tis but an hour ago
When she was lying *boggish* at the *quay*,
    And men ran to and fro,
And tugged and stamped, and shoved, and pushed, and swore,
And ever and anon, with *crapulous* glee,
Grinned homage to *viragoes* on the shore.

So to the *jetty* gradual she was hauled:
    Then one the *tiller* took,
And chewed, and spat upon his hand, and bawled;
    And one the canvas shook

---

[6] From *Collected Poems*, p. 132. Copyright, 1908, by The Macmillan Company. Reprinted by permission of the publishers.

Forth like a moldy bat; and one, with nods
And smiles, lay on the *bowsprit-end*, and called
And cursed the Harbor-master by his gods.

And, rotten from the *gunwhale* to the *keel*,
    Rat-riddled, *bilge-bestank*,
Slime-slobbered, horrible, I saw her reel,
    And drag her oozy *flank*,
And sprawl among the deft young waves, that laughed,
And leapt, and turned in many a sportive wheel,
As she thumped onward with her lumbering *draught*.

And now, behold! a shadow of repose
    Upon the line of gray,
She sleeps, that transverse cuts the evening rose—
    She sleeps, and dreams away,
Soft-blended in a unity of rest
All jars, and strifes *obscene*, and turbulent throes
'Neath the broad benediction of the West—

Sleeps; and methinks she changes as she sleeps,
    And dies, and is a spirit pure.
Lo! on her deck an angel pilot keeps
    His lonely watch secure;
And at the entrance of Heaven's dockyard waits,
Till from Night's *leash* the fine-breath'd morning leaps,
And that strong hand within unbars the gates.

                              THOMAS EDWARD BROWN

V

It is easy to slip over or confuse the meaning of certain words
that are reminiscent of similar-sounding words. Can you distinguish between the meaning of the following paired words?

compliment	respectful	depreciate
complement	respective	deprecate
arduous	healthful	principle
ardent	healthy	principal
illusion	oral	factious
delusion	aural	facetious
ingenious	definite	affect
ingenuous	definitive	effect
antidote	credulous	decorous
anecdote	credible	decorative

Names of People, Places, and Events

Today we are living in a generation that knows the names of people, places, organizations, and world events, mainly because of news commentators. We like to use short cuts made up of initials, such as UNESCO and G.I., or of nicknames, such as one of our favorite presidents, "Ike," or of descriptive terms, like the "Iron Curtain," and the "Atomic Age." The interpreter needs not only to know contemporary names but should become acquainted with the "Churchills" and "MacArthurs" of centuries ago.

The interpretative study of Stephen Vincent Benét's *John Brown's Body* will be superficial unless one knows the historical John Brown. The significance of the following lines is lost to those who are not informed:[7]

> John Brown's body lies a-mouldering in the grave.
> He will not come again with foolish pikes
> And a pack of desperate boys to shadow the sun.
> He has gone back North. The slaves have forgotten his eyes.
> John Brown's body lies a-mouldering in the grave
> John Brown's body lies a-mouldering in the grave.

The same principle of understanding is true also in this prose extract from John Finley's speech on John Brown:

His death made all men either friends or foes of slavery. Between the North and South stood John Brown's gibbet. Henceforth it was slavery or union. Compromise was no longer possible. Had he succeeded, he must have failed. His failure was his success.

Probably every interpreter knows the names of Lincoln, Shakespeare, Mozart, and Burns, but he has to know more than just a name to get the full meaning of a passage like this one from Henry Watterson's *The Secret of Lincoln's Power:*

What was Lincoln's mysterious power, and whence? . . . Inspired he was truly, as Shakespeare was inspired, as Mozart was inspired; as Burns was inspired; each, like him, sprung directly from the people.

[7] From *John Brown's Body* (New York, Rinehart and Company, Inc., 1927), p. 58. Copyright, 1927, 1928, by Stephen Vincent Benét. Reprinted by permission of the Stephen Vincent Benét estate.

Many, many times young orators have spoken with fervor, but perhaps with not too much understanding of the names involved in the final lines of Wendell Phillips' *Toussaint L'Ouverture:*

But fifty years hence, when Truth gets a hearing, the Muse of history will put Phocian for the Greek, Brutus for the Roman, Hampden for England, Fayette for France, choose Washington as the bright consummate flower of our earlier civilization, then dipping her pen in the sunlight, will write in the clear blue, above them all, the name of the soldier, the statesman, the martyr, Toussaint L'Ouverture.

The humor of the following lines certainly cannot be expressed without some appreciation of the vocabulary and the references to people and art and literature. More than that, as has been explained in the preceding chapter, information about John Mason Brown as an individual and an author is important. The author is expressing his dilemma when confronting an audience and while waiting for his introduction to end:

SHOULD YOU PLAY DEAD?[8]

On those rare occasions when the chairman gets his circulars mixed and has confused your case history with that of Eve Curie, John Mulholland, or Commander Byrd, is it or is it not forgivable for you to shake your head in gentle protest and indicate regretfully you have one, and only one, life to give to your country's lecture platform, and the introducer is taking it and someone else's in vain? Or should you play dead, exhibiting no more interest in the proceedings than a corpse does in the funeral oration he has provoked? When you are paid a compliment, every word of which drips with jasmine, honeysuckle, and unearned increment, and you feel diabetes sugaring your blood stream, should you show you have not forgotten *Veritas* was printed on your college shield by shouting, "No! No!"? Or should you meet kindness with kindness by crying, "A Daniel come to judgment! Yea, a Daniel!"?

Ought your eyes to be fixed on the footlights, the ceiling, the balcony, your wristwatch, or the introducer? And if upon the introducer, where? If he has struck a forensic attitude, should your eyes trace the outlines of his invisible toga? Or if she has struck a posture suggestive of Venus de' Medici, should your face express gratitude that she is better dressed than the original?

[8] From "We Have with Us Tonight," *Accustomed As I Am*, p. 35. Copyright, 1942, by W. W. Norton & Company, Inc. Reprinted by permission of the publishers.

Margaret Halsey touches lightly but fondly upon her husband's idiosyncrasies and habits in "Henry's Sartorial Driftwood." [9] The title itself provokes mirth, because "sartorial" is incongruous with "driftwood" and with Henry, an easygoing professor. Throughout, the author makes deft use of contrasting words and phrases, such as her combinations of Silas Marner and Andrew Mellon; or the "pound of flesh" and the "absent-minded 'Ouch!' "; or the "topographical felt hat" which was passed around like a "hot potato"; or the "eight black dinner ties" which had "seen years of service on the town gibbet"; or the "Tuxedos" that make Henry look like a "heron." Why are these phrases humorous? How alike are Silas Marner and Andrew Mellon? Notice how Shakespeare's "pound of flesh" (you will recall Shylock's price of a pound of flesh from Antonio in the *Merchant of Venice*) points up the professor's "absent-minded 'Ouch!' " Be sure you know "topographical," "gibbet," and "heron."

HENRY'S SARTORIAL DRIFTWOOD

October 1st

The day started rainy, but by the time we reached Yeobridge this afternoon, the house and garden were floating in sunlight and looking so snug and pretty and delectable that I said I guessed I would not bother with going back to the womb. I nearly changed my mind, though, when we had had tea and I had to begin unpacking. Stuffing my own rudimentary wardrobe into the nearest drawer is a matter of five minutes, but Henry has a sense of property like Silas Marner and Andrew Mellon combined. You could probably (if he were not so thin) take a pound of flesh from Henry without encountering any more opposition than an absent-minded "Ouch!", but try to separate him from his high school chemistry notes or the scarf his sister made for him when she was eight years old, and you find yourself up against something.

He not only cherishes, but he has brought to Europe with him, such objects as a topographical felt hat, bought in the Tyrol by some distant relative and passed around the family like a hot potato—until it got to Henry. He has brought to Yeobridge with him eight black dinner ties, every one of which has apparently seen years of service on the town gibbet. He has brought two Tuxedos, both so old-fashioned that he looks like a heron in them and people stand still so as not to frighten him away. When I was packing the trunks in New York, I

[9] From *With Malice Toward Some*, pp. 163-164. Copyright, 1938, by Simon and Schuster, Inc. Reprinted by permission of the publishers.

made one last heroic effort to wean him, but he gave me such a look of silent agony and reproach, even at the compromise proposal to leave the things behind in storage, that I was not proof against it.

Phyllis, however, did most of the unpacking. When we first arrived, she was so frightened of us that I thought she was going to cry, but I sent her around to the post office to buy some stamps and regain her composure, and by the time she returned, her natural instinct for running things had come irresistibly to the surface. She weeded out Henry's sartorial driftwood and silently stowed it in the attic; she whisked away part of Mrs. Turney's dark-green and dark-brown library and Mydaughter's French and German grammars to make room for the books we had brought; she catechized me delicately on my ideas about housekeeping and appeared surprised and relieved to discover that I am innocent of any. Finally, after a suitable interim, she produced a dinner with magnificent roast beef and an omelet so light that we had to lay our knives across it and even then it struggled. We haled her in and complimented her fervently on the meal, which made her blush and look pleased, but also a little startled, as if she were not used to praise. It looks as if we have a paragon on our hands.

Dr. Charles Seymour, former president of Yale University, speaking on the topic "Live Magnanimously," described the magnanimous man and then enlarged his meaning by listing a number of historical and literary characters.[10] How do you rank in your knowledge of those he listed?

The word, taken etymologically from the Latin, connotes a large spirit. When Aristotle describes the magnanimous man he finds this spirit so large that he includes no less than twelve virtues that go to make this quality. Three of them deserve special emphasis. First, intelligence, which inspires all the other virtues. Second, self-reliance based on courage. "It is characteristic of the great-souled man never to ask help from others or only with reluctance . . . The great-souled man does not run into danger for trifling reasons; but he will face danger in a great cause and when so doing will be ready to sacrifice his life, since he holds that life is not worth having at every price." And third, generosity. The great-souled man "does not bear a grudge, for it is not a mark of greatness of soul to recall things against people, especially the wrongs they have done you, but rather to overlook them. . . .

It would be illuminating if we should make up a list of magnanimous men of literature and history. These would stand out as objects of our admiration who combine the particular traits that we are con-

[10] *Vital Speeches of the Day,* Vol. 15, No. 20 (June, 1949), pp. 635-637.

sidering: such men as Marcus Aurelius, Chaucer's knight, Francis of Assissi, the Black Prince, St. Louis of France, Henry V, Sir Walter Raleigh, Henry of Navarre, Charles Darwin, and, above all, in modern times—Abraham Lincoln. It would be equally instructive to note the men, no matter how courageous and intelligent, who would have to be excluded from the list: Oliver Cromwell, Louis XIV, the Duke of Marlborough, Frederick the Great, Napoleon Bonaparte.

RELATIONSHIP OF WORDS

No word stands alone in a sentence, even though it may be isolated from other words by punctuation. The essence of knowing what a sentence means is knowing which words relate directly to other words, which words should be emphasized, and which words should be contrasted. Knowledge, then, of the relation between noun and verb, noun and adjective, verb and adverb, adjective and adverb, as well as that of subject and predicate, modifier and modified, become important to you, the interpreter.

Emphasis for Meaning

Emphasis consists solely in making one word or group of words more noticeable or prominent than others so that a clear relationship is obvious. It is a matter of centering attention on words which will reveal the author's meaning. Emphasis on too many words will produce reading that is as monotonous and meaningless as that which comes from emphasis on too few words. Certainly each varying emphasis will bring a slightly different meaning. A sentence like "Every man alone is sincere" can cause difficulty and must be studied. Shall it be "Every man *alone*—is *sincere*" or "*Every man—alone*—is sincere" or "*Every* man *alone* —is *sincere*"?

The italicized words are so marked by Edgar Allan Poe in this passage from his criticism of William Ellery Channing. Why has he italicized them?

It seems that having deduced, from Tennyson and Carlyle, an opinion of the sublimity of everything odd, and of the profundity of everything meaningless, Mr. Channing has conceived the idea of setting up for himself as a poet of *unusual* depth, and *very* remarkable powers of mind. His airs and graces, in consequence, have a highly picturesque effect, and the Boston critics, who have a notion that poets are porpoises, (for they are always talking about their running in "schools") cannot make up their minds as to what particular school he must belong. *We* say the Bobby Button school, by all means. He clearly belongs to that. And should nobody ever have heard of the Bobby Button school, that is a point of no material importance. We will answer for it, as it is one of our own. Bobby Button is a gentleman with whom, for a long time, we have had the honor of an intimate acquaintance. His personal appearance is striking. He has quite a big head. His eyes protrude and have all the air of saucers. His chin retreats. His mouth is depressed at the corners. He wears a perpetual frown of contemplation. His words are slow, emphatic, few, and oracular. His "Thes," and "ands," and "buts," have more meaning than other men's polysyllables. His nods would have put Burleigh's to the blush. His whole aspect, indeed, conveys the idea of a gentleman modest to a fault, and painfully overburdened with intellect. We insist, however, upon calling Mr. Channing's school of poetry the Bobby Button school, rather because Mr. Channing's poetry is strongly suggestive of Bobby Button than because Mr. Button himself ever dallied, to any very great extent, with the Muses. With the exception, indeed, of a *very* fine "Sonnet to a Pig"—or rather the fragment of a sonnet, for he proceeded no farther than the words "*O* piggy wiggy," with the O italicized for emphasis—with the exception of this, we say, we are not aware of his having produced anything worthy of that stupendous genius which is certainly *in* him, and only wants, like the starling of Sterne, "to get out."

Emphasis on Contrasting Ideas

Many times through the study of emphasis, the interpreter will find that the author has used contrasting nouns, adjectives, verbs, and adverbs to point up his meaning. Nouns invite contrast more often than other parts of speech, as in the sentence, "Men have *sight,* women *insight.*" Next are verbs and adverbs, as in "An author *departs,* he does not *die*" or "More men wear *away* than wear *out*" or "Better *deserve* honor and *not* have it than to *have* it and *not* deserve it." The following sentences show how adjectives share emphasis with nouns, and adverbs with verbs; also, they illustrate how an adjective or an adverb gets emphasis from its position in the sentence.

Mr. Tennyson is *quaint only;* he is *never,* as some have *supposed* him, *obscure*—except, indeed, to the *uneducated,* whom he does *not* address. Mr. *Carlyle*, on the other hand, is *obscure* only. He is *seldom*, as *some* have *imagined* him, *quaint*.

Emphasis on New Ideas

When words have been repeated in sentences but new meaning has been added through the use of modifying words, then the word expressing the new idea, not the repeated word, usually receives the emphasis. It is not *"Washington, the immortal Washington"* but *"Washington, the immortal Washington."* The author has thus indicated added meaning by the addition of the word *immortal* to the word being repeated. Notice the emphasis gained through the modifying word in the following verse:

> "This is the *way*," laughed the great god Pan,
> "The *only* way . . ."

Similarly, emphasis is achieved in the sentence, "Every man is *valued* in this world as he shows by his conduct that he *wishes* to be valued.

EXERCISES

I

The meaning of the following sentences is dependent upon your knowledge of the relationship between words. Try to get the proper emphasis to convey your meaning.

1. Life is a foreign language: all men mispronounce it.
2. The more you know, the more you know you ought to know.
3. If people insist on being fooled, someone must do the fooling.
4. He is not only dull himself, but the cause of dullness in others.
5. No matter how thin you slice it, it's still baloney.
6. Never in the field of human conflict was so much owed by so many to so few.
7. What I like in a good author is not what he says but what he whispers.
8. There is no indispensable man.
9. Who faints not achieves.
10. It is hard for an empty sack to stand upright.
11. The Lords of large estates proved in their deaths equality.

12. Wretched are they that hunger and thirst after nothing good for they shall also be filled.
13. Sacrifices are only sweet when needed.
14. What follies are perpetrated in the name of wisdom!
15. A song will outlive all the sermons in the memory.
16. Advertising is not the road to success, but success itself.
17. Handsome is not what is handsome but what pleases.
18. Now this is not the end. It is not even the beginning of the end. But it is, perhaps, the end of the beginning.
19. He who knows how little he knows, knows himself.
20. The reward of a thing well done is to have done it.
21. He who has little silver in his pouch must have more silk on his tongue.
22. He who knows and knows he knows,
     He is wise. Follow him.
  He who knows and knows not he knows,
     He is asleep. Wake him.
  He who knows not and knows not he knows not,
     He is a fool. Shun him.
  He who knows not and knows he knows not,
     He is a child. Teach him.
23.   . . . That we would do
  We should do when we would: for this "would" changes,
  And hath abatements and delays as many
  As there are tongues, are hands, are accidents,
  And then this "should" is like a spendthrift sigh,
  That hurts by easing.
                    WILLIAM SHAKESPEARE, *Hamlet*

II

Find the words contrasted for emphasis in the following sentences.

1. Young men are fitter to invent than to judge, fitter for execution than for counsel, and fitter for new projects than for settled business.
2. No idea is so antiquated that it was not once modern. No idea is so modern that it will not some day be antiquated.
3. Do not let us speak of darker days; let us speak rather of sterner days. These are not dark days: these are great days— the greatest days our country has ever lived.
4. Sentimentally I am disposed to harmony; but organically I am incapable of a tune.
5. There must be, not a balance of power, but a community of power; not organized rivalries, but an organized common peace.

6. I wish to preach, not the doctrine of ignoble ease, but the doctrine of the strenuous life.

7. Girls we love for what they are; young men for what they promise to be.

8. Positive anything is better than negative nothing.

9. The press—right or wrong; when right to be kept right; when wrong to be set right.

10. An acre of performance is worth a whole world of promises.

11. Success depends on backbone, not wishbone.

12. Towers are measured by their shadows and great men by their calumniators.

13. The heart of the fool is in his mouth but the mouth of a wise man is in his heart.

14. A comedy is like a cigar; if good, everyone wants a box; if bad, no amount of puffing will make it draw.

15. 'Tis rather conceit than conscience that makes cowards of us.

16. A graduate is one who is proud of his alma mater. An alumnus is one who is ashamed of her when she loses football games.

17. For I was an hungred, and ye gave me meat; I was thirsty, and ye gave me drink; I was a stranger, and ye took me in.

18. "Praise the Lord, and pass the ammunition," he shouted; but I prayed, "Praise the Lord, the ammunition has passed me."

19. To live content with small means, to seek elegance rather than luxury, and refinement rather than fashion; to be worthy, not respectable; and wealthy, not rich; to study hard, think quietly, talk gently, act frankly; to listen to stars and birds, babes and sages with open heart; to bear all cheerfully, do all bravely, await occasions, hurry never; in a word, to let the spiritual, unbidden and unconscious, grow up through the common. This is to be my symphony.

20. Another summer day, on the banks of the Somme in front of Amiens; again the fearful clash of two armies—one the weapon of Imperial Germany in her bid for world supremacy, the other the shield and symbol of outraged civilization in defense of her liberty.

21. The foolish man seeks happiness in the distance:
The wise grows it under his feet.

22. And the greatest of these?
Understanding—not faith.
Will—not hope.
Service—not charity.

23. BRUTUS. Not that I lov'd Caesar less, but that I lov'd Rome more. Had you rather Caesar were living and die all slaves, than that Caesar were dead, to live all freemen? As Caesar lov'd me, I weep for him; as he was fortunate, I rejoice at it; as he was valiant, I honour him; but, as

he was ambitious, I slew him. There is tears for his love; joy for his fortune; honour for his valour; and death for his ambition.

WILLIAM SHAKESPEARE, *Julius Caesar*

24. BEATRICE. I wonder that you will still be talking, Signior Benedick. Nobody marks you.

BENEDICK. What, my dear Lady Disdain! are you yet living?

BEA. Is it possible disdain should die while she hath such meet food to feed on as Signior Benedick? Courtesy itself must convert to disdain, if you come in her presence.

BEN. Then is courtesy a turncoat. But it is certain I am lov'd of all ladies, only you excepted; and I would I could find in my heart that I had not a hard heart, for truly, I love none.

BEA. A dear happiness to women: they would else have been troubled with a pernicious suitor. I thank God and my cold blood, I am of your humour for that. I had rather hear my dog bark at a crow than a man swear he loves me.

BEN. God keep your ladyship still in that mind! So some gentleman or other shall 'scape a predestinate scratch'd face.

BEA. Scratching could not make it worse, an 'twere such a face as yours were.

BEN. Well, you are a rare parrot-teacher.

BEA. A bird of my tongue is better than a beast of yours.

BEN. I would my horse had the speed of your tongue, and so good a continuer. But keep your way, i' God's name; I have done.

BEA. You always end with a jade's trick: I know you of old.

WILLIAM SHAKESPEARE, *Much Ado about Nothing*

III

How are you going to distribute the emphasis between repeated ideas and new ideas in the following?

1. Has the gentleman done? Has he completely done?
2. Woodrow Wilson! A dreamer of dreams—yes, but great dreams—wonderful dreams! And some day they may all come true.
3. When I was a child, I spake as a child, I understood as a child, I thought as a child: but when I became a man, I put away childish things.

I COR. 13:15

4. It was this fascination that had got hold upon the faculties of the man whom the world was afterward to know, not as a

prince among merchants—for the world forgets merchants, princes—but as a prince among benefactors; for beneficence breeds gratitude, gratitude admiration, admiration fame, and the world remembers its benefactors.

WOODROW WILSON, *When a Man Comes to Himself*

5. Who is this that cometh from Domremy? Who is she in bloody coronation robes from Rheims? Who is she that cometh with blackened flesh from walking the furnaces of Rouen? This is she, the shepherd girl, counselor—that had none for herself, whom I choose, Bishop, for yours. She it is, I engage, that shall take my lord's brief. She it is, Bishop, that would plead for you; yes, Bishop, She—when heaven and earth are silent.

THOMAS DEQUINCEY, *The Martyrdom of Joan of Arc*

6. MACBETH.   If we should fail?
   LADY MACBETH.   We fail.
   But screw your courage to the sticking-place,
   And we'll not fail.

WILLIAM SHAKESPEARE, *Macbeth*

7. TOUCHSTONE. How old are you, friend?
   WILLIAM. Five and twenty, sir.
   TOUCH. A ripe age. Is thy name William?
   WILL. William, sir.
   TOUCH. A fair name. Wast born i' the forest here?
   WILL. Ay, sir, I thank God.
   TOUCH. "Thank God!"—a good answer. Art rich?
   WILL. Faith, sir, so so.
   TOUCH. "So so" is good, very good, very excellent good; and yet it is not; it is but so so.

WILLIAM SHAKESPEARE, *As You Like It*

8. BASSANIO.   Sweet Portia,
   If you did know to whom I gave the ring,
   If you did know for whom I gave the ring,
   And would conceive for what I gave the ring,
   And how unwillingly I left the ring,
   When nought would be accepted but that ring,
   You would abate the strength of your displeasure.

WILLIAM SHAKESPEARE, *Merchant of Venice*

9. CASSIUS. Brutus and Caesar: what should be in that "Caesar"?
   Why should that name be sounded more than yours?
   Write them together, yours is as fair a name;
   Sound them, it doth become the mouth as well;
   Weigh them, it is as heavy; conjure with 'em,
   "Brutus" will start a spirit as soon as "Caesar."

WILLIAM SHAKESPEARE, *Julius Caesar*

10. IAGO.   O grace! O Heaven forgive me!
    Are you a man? Have you a soul or sense?

God be wi' you; take mine office. O wretched fool,
That livest to make thine honesty a vice!
O monstrous world! Take note, take note, O world,
To be direct and honest is not safe.
I thank you for this profit; and from hence
I'll love no friend, sith love breeds such offense.
OTHELLO. Nay, stay. Thou shouldst be honest.
IAGO. I should be wise, for honesty's a fool
 And loses that it works for.
OTHELLO.   By the world,
I think my wife be honest and think she is not;
I think that thou art just and think thou art not.
I'll have some proof. Her name, that was as fresh
As Dian's visage, is now begrim'd and black
As mine own face. If there be cords, or knives,
Poison, or fire, or suffocating streams,
I'll not endure it. Would I were satisfied!
IAGO. I see, sir, you are eaten up with passion;
I do repent me that I put it to you.
You would be satisfied?
OTHELLO.   Would! nay, I will.
IAGO. And may; but, how? How satisfied, my lord?
                    WILLIAM SHAKESPEARE, *Othello*

11. Laughter!
Laughter of streams running red.
Laughter of evil things in the night;
Vultures carousing in the night;
Laughter of ghouls.
Chuckling of idiots, cursed with sight.
Laughter of dark and horrible pools.
Scream of the bullets' rattling mirth,
Sweeping the earth.
Laugh of the cannon's poisonous breath . . .
And over the shouts and the wreckage and crumbling
The raucous and rumbling
Laughter of death.
                    LOUIS UNTERMEYER, *The Laughers*[11]

INTERRELATIONSHIP OF PHRASES

Grouping

You were probably aware, as you worked through the preceding exercises for meaning, that you had to group words by the

[11] From *These Times*, p. 41. Copyright, 1917, by Henry Holt and Company, Inc. Reprinted by permission of the publishers.

use of pauses. Cues sometimes were given to you by means of
punctuation marks; but often *you* had to decide what words belonged together. This interrelationship of phrases is not always
easy to manage. You may have found that you had to control
your breathing pattern to fit the phrasing pattern or that some
phrase had to be emphasized over other phrases, just as an artist
has to secure light and shadow. In the end, all phrases have to
hinge together for the complete meaning, even though you may
for a time feel that subordination of certain phrases is difficult.
This relationship of phrases will become more significant when
you begin to interpret longer selections, or when you have to
follow some idiosyncrasy of style. Cornelia Otis Skinner's hilarious account of attiring her young son in his first formal clothes
will take skill in phrasing; for if you pause too long, or too many
times, the momentum of the action will be lost. Work first for
the meaning, not forgetting the humor of the situation, and then
read aloud to see if you can manage the grouping without seeming to be hurried or breathless. Notice that if you break up the
sentences into too many small groups the humor is lessened.

BUTTON, BUTTON[12]

He slipped on the shirt. Starting ill-advisedly enough with the neckband, I managed, with a good deal of panting, to drill the collar
buttons through the areas in that solid wall of starch and goods
intended to simulate apertures and on into my thumb, where they left
a sizable dent and black mark. My satisfaction over this accomplishment was short-lived for it turned out I'd put the short-stemmed
button where the long-stemmed one belonged and vice versa and it
had to be done all over again, which made for a flurry of rancor on
both sides. The second time, however, was easier, as I had wedged
open the holes with a nail file and enlarged them sufficiently to permit
the collar buttons not only to go on in but, at the least encouragement,
to continue on out.

Punctuation and Grouping

Punctuation marks help us to get the interphrase relationship,
but they are by no means an absolute guide. It is well to remem-

[12] From *Nuts in May*, p. 96. Copyright, 1942, 1944, 1945, 1946, 1948,
1949, 1950, by Cornelia Otis Skinner. Reprinted by permission of Dodd,
Mead & Company, Inc.

ber the oft-quoted statement, "Punctuation is intended for the
eye and not the ear." You will not pause every time you see a
comma. There are times when a comma may confuse the interpreter by requiring a choice between relating the phrase to what
has preceded or to what is to follow. Again a phrase may need to
stand out in reading, yet visual punctuation marks do not so indicate. A period may indicate that the author has completed his
thought, but the period does not necessarily give a note of finality
to the meaning. Often the voice is deliberately raised at the end
of a sentence, even though the author has placed a period there.
In the "Four Little Foxes" by Lew Sarett, the period at the end
of the fourth line is not intended to give a complete, final, determining note; rather, it is a prayerful pause, as if one were uttering "please" under one's breath.[13]

> Speak gently, Spring, and make no sudden sound;
> For in my windy valley, yesterday I found
> New-born foxes squirming on the ground—
>   Speak gently.

Notice in John Mason Brown's description of his inner feelings
while waiting to be introduced as a speaker that the commas are
welcome in deciding certain phrasing, but notice also that you
will have to use other meaningful groupings where no punctuation has been shown.

THE CHAIR[14]

The chair may be of two kinds. Either its high back and its seat,
though covered with petit point, may conceal boards so stiff that you
are sure the committee must think your sacroiliac needs righting, or it
is one of those low-set leather chairs which emits embarrassing noises
as you sink down onto its air-filled cushions, and from the depths of
which only a derrick can remove you. Once seated, you reach for the
arms as if they were the hands of a long-lost friend. After you and
the chairman have indulged in those preliminary whisperings, and
both you and he have smiled broadly at jokes passed between you

[13] By permission from *The Collected Poems of Lew Sarett*, p. 5. Copyright,
1920, 1922, 1925, 1931, 1941, by Henry Holt and Company, Inc.
[14] From "We Have with Us Tonight," *Accustomed As I Am*, p. 35. Copyright, 1942, by W. W. Norton & Company, Inc. Reprinted by permission
of the publishers.

that neither of you has heard, the chairman rises to start his introduction.

Then your troubles begin in earnest. Even before he has finished saying "Ladies and gentlemen," you are apt to have crossed, uncrossed, and recrossed your legs so many times that you must look from out front as if you were trying to dance the Highland fling sitting down. Suddenly realizing that poise is desirable, you quiet your shins by wrapping your feet around the far-flung legs of the chair.

There are instances, however, when certain punctuation marks used by the author and perceived by the interpreter will definitely point up the logical meaning. The following exercises will show you how grouping can be varied through change in punctuation, thereby influencing the intended meaning.

EXERCISES

I

Show the difference in meaning produced by the changes in punctuation:

1. (a) Would you end war?
        Create great Peace . . .
   (b) Would you end war?
        Create great Peace?

2. (a) "But some one digs upon my grave?
        My enemy?—prodding sly?"
   (b) "But some one digs upon my grave!
        My enemy—prodding sly!"

3. (a) Warren returned—too soon, it seemed to her,
        Slipped to her side, caught up her hand and waited.
   (b) Warren returned too soon, it seemed to her,
        Slipped to her side, caught up her hand—and waited.

4. (a) Honest, my lord?
   (b) Honest? My lord?

5. (a) Yet his means are in supposition; he hath an argosy bound to Tripoli; another to the Indies; I understand, moreover, upon the Rialto, he hath a third at Mexico, a fourth for England, and other ventures he hath squandered abroad.
   (b) Yet his means are in supposition; he hath an argosy bound to Tripoli; another to the Indies. I understand, moreover, upon the Rialto, he hath a third at Mexico, a fourth for England, and other ventures he hath, squandered abroad.

6. (a) I want no further information; but if you will remain
with us, and discover the reason for the error, you are
welcome.

(b) I want no further information; but, if you will, remain
with us and discover the reason for the error; you are
welcome.

7. (a) The world is too much with us late and soon;
Getting and spending, we lay waste our powers.

(b) The world is too much with us; late and soon,
Getting and spending, we lay waste our powers.

8. (a) Lay on, Macduff.

(b) Lay on Macduff!

9. (a) What were the results of this conduct? Beggary, dis-
honor, utter ruin, and a broken leg.

(b) What were the results of this conduct? Beggary! Dis-
honor! Utter ruin! And a broken leg!

10. (a) For a dime you can buy two pieces of pie or cake, and
ice cream.

(b) For a dime you can buy two pieces of pie, or cake and
ice cream.

11. (a) Who? Why, absurd!

(b) Who? Why absurd?

II

Notice how the dash is used in various ways: for suspense, for
shifts in meaning, for emphasis, for reinforcement.

1

'Tis a rock—a crag—a cape—
A cape? say rather a peninsula!

EDMOND ROSTAND[15]

2

Why, you might have said—
Oh, a great many things!

EDMOND ROSTAND[16]

3

There is a flower I wish to wear,
But not until first worn by you—
Heart's-ease—of all earth's flowers most rare;
Bring it; and bring enough for two.

WALTER SAVAGE LANDOR, *Heart's-ease*

---

[15] *Cyrano de Bergerac*, trans. Brian Hooker (New York, Henry Holt and
Company, Inc., 1928), p. 40.

[16] *Ibid.*, p. 40.

4

I gazed—and gazed—but little thought
What wealth the show to me had brought . . .
WILLIAM WORDSWORTH, *The Daffodils*

5

All the woods hushed—save for a dripping rose,
All the woods dim—save where a glow-worm glows.
JOHN MASEFIELD[17]

6

And what is a kiss, when all is done?
A promise given under seal—a vow
Taken before the shrine of memory—
A signature acknowledged—a rosy dot
Over the i of loving.
EDMOND ROSTAND[18]

7

A stir, a murmur on the great staircase, a silence spreading up from
the hall beneath and invading the drawing rooms—there was a thrill,
a movement as when a singer ascends the platform and looks about her
in silence before the first crystal note drops into the hush of the waiting audience.
E. BARRINGTON[19]

III

Study the use of punctuation in relation to meaning in the
following passages.

PERHAPS[20]

Perhaps in the Lethal dawn of some far-distant day
I shall breathe the dewy air of forgetfulness
And shall then be able to look with unabated breath
Upon a wild plum-tree, waving its blossomy branches of snow

[17] From "The Watch in the Woods," *Collected Poems*, p. 111. Copyright,
1922, by The Macmillan Company. Reprinted by permission of the publishers.
[18] *Cyrano de Bergerac*, p. 147.
[19] From *Glorious Apollo* (New York, Dodd, Mead & Company, Inc.,
1925), p. 76.
[20] Published originally in *The Lyric West*, a magazine of verse. Reprinted
by permission of the publishers.

Over the new-made grave of winter—
Or behold, unmoved, a moonlit glen brimmed with silver mist—
Or walk unheeding through a field of purple asphodels wet with the
    spring-soft rain.
Perhaps the fragrance of wild thyme will no longer bring a chill of
    heart
When it rises from evening meadows like memorial incense—
Perhaps in that day my soul will not be swathed in robes of memory
Nor haunted by the chime of silver bells in your voice—
Perhaps I shall even forget the subtle song of your white flesh
And the mystic fires under your dewy lashes—
Perhaps. . . .

                              C. H. MARSH

PETS[21]

You take a dog, oncet you get it to love you.
You lose your home, your dough, your grub and all,
The old dog sticks. . . . A cat's a different critter,
More like a slot-machine: put in a meal
You get a purr right back; no meal, no purr—
Claws, prob'ly; then, "So long.". . .

                        I'll take a cur.
                   JOHN V. A. WEAVER

I BENDED UNTO ME[22]

I bended unto me a bough of May,
That I might see and smell:
It bore it in a sort of way,
It bore it very well.
But when I let it backward sway,
Then it were hard to tell
With what a toss, with what a swing,
The dainty thing
Resumed its proper level,
And sent me to the devil.
I know it did—you doubt it?
I turned, and saw them whispering about it.
                THOMAS EDWARD BROWN

[21] From *In American*, p. 23. Copyright, 1923, by Alfred A. Knopf, Inc.
Reprinted by permission of the publishers.
[22] From *Collected Poems*, p. 123. Copyright, 1908, by The Macmillan
Company. Reprinted by permission of the publishers.

EVENING[23]

Far through the dampening air
The frogs' clear serenade trills in the dark.
The distant headlands fade; the woods recede;
The nearer copses cower in the dusk;
The fences stretch away into mere dimness;
And last, the western forest slowly blends
To darkness. Daunted, all the stars terrene
Turn out their feeble lamps; the frogs all hush,
As if to listen to the stillness, and,
Listening, forget to sing, and fall asleep.
. . . . Then night.

EARL HUDELSON

REMORSE

OTHELLO

Now, how dost thou look now? O ill-starr'd wench!
Pale as thy smock! When we shall meet at compt,
This look of thine will hurl my soul from heaven,
And fiends will snatch at it. Cold, cold, my girl!
Even like thy chastity. O cursèd, cursèd slave!
Whip me, ye devils,
From the possession of this heavenly sight!
Blow me about in winds! roast me in sulphur!
Wash me in steep-down gulfs of liquid fire!
O Desdemona! Desdemona! dead!
Oh! Oh! Oh!

WILLIAM SHAKESPEARE, *Othello*

TOUCHSTONE DISPOSES OF A RIVAL

TOUCHSTONE. We shall find a time, Audrey; patience, gentle
 Audrey.
AUDREY. Faith, the priest was good enough, for all the old gentle-
 man's saying.
TOUCH. A most wicked Sir Oliver, Audrey, a most vile Martext.
 But, Audrey, there is a youth here in the forest lays claim to you.
AUD. Ay, I know who 'tis; he hath no interest in me in the world.
 Here comes the man you mean.

Enter WILLIAM

[23] From *Evening near the Campus.* Reprinted by permission of The Stratford Company.

Touch. It is meat and drink to me to see a clown. By my troth, we that have good wits have much to answer for; we shall be flouting; we cannot hold.

William. Good even, Audrey.

Aud. God ye good even, William.

Will. And good even to you, sir.

Touch. Good even, gentle friend. Cover thy head, cover thy head; nay, prithee, be covered. How old are you, friend?

Will. Five and twenty, sir.

Touch. A ripe age. Is thy name William?

Will. William, sir.

Touch. A fair name. Wast born i' the forest here?

Will. Ay, sir, I thank God.

Touch. "Thank God!"—a good answer. Art rich?

Will. Faith, sir, so so.

Touch. "So so" is good, very good, very excellent good; and yet it is not; it is but so so. Art thou wise?

Will. Ay, sir, I have a pretty wit.

Touch. Why, thou say'st well. I do now remember a saying, "The fool doth think he is wise, but the wise man knows himself to be a fool." The heathen philosopher, when he had a desire to eat a grape, would open his lips when he put it into his mouth; meaning thereby that grapes were made to eat and lips to open. You do love this maid?

Will. I do, sir.

Touch. Give me your hand. Art thou learned?

Will. No, sir.

Touch. Then learn this of me; to have, is to have; for it is a figure in rhetoric that drink, being pour'd out of a cup into a glass, by filling the one doth empty the other. For all your writers do consent that *ipse* is he; now, you are not *ipse*, for I am he.

Will. Which he, sir?

Touch. He, sir, that must marry this woman. Therefore, you clown, abandon—which is in the vulgar leave—the society—which in the boorish is company—of this female—which in the common is woman; which together is, abandon the society of this female; or, clown, thou perishest; or, to thy better understanding, diest; or, to wit, I kill thee, make thee away, translate thy life into death, thy liberty into bondage. I will deal in poison with thee, or in bastinado, or in steel. I will bandy with thee in faction; I will o'er-run thee with policy; I will kill thee a hundred and fifty ways; therefore tremble, and depart.

Aud. Do, good William.

Will. God rest you merry, sir.

William Shakespeare, *As You Like It*

ADAM ELHAR[24]

The ACTRESS *and the* POET *are discussing* ADAM ELHAR, *an English financier who has renounced his country and his home.*

THE ACTRESS. He saw in me the embodiment of his childhood dreams; he saw in me the playmates of his childhood, Germany, the eternal Gretchen.

THE POET. And what did you see in him?

THE ACTRESS. A wounded and divided soul, full of generosity, of sadness—a lonely *grand seigneur* and a frightened and confused small boy.

THE POET. Did you never feel that protective mother feeling toward me?

THE ACTRESS. Not so strongly. You have so much—

THE POET. Compared to him?

THE ACTRESS. Yes. He has millions. And with his millions he can't buy what you have unbought and from the beginning: earth, home, speech, inner oneness, inner security.

THE POET. You must have loved him very much.

THE ACTRESS. Why?

THE POET. Because love begets insight. Did he ever ask you to marry him?

THE ACTRESS. We discussed that a hundred times. But so much separated us. I couldn't so easily give up my country in its humiliation, and my art, such as it is, and my friends. And to what end? In England I would always have been a stranger. Even he is in the deeper sense a stranger there. We talked about it until we were both—how shall I put it?

THE POET. A little weary?

THE ACTRESS. Yes, a little weary of the conflicts and abnormalities. We had no way, we two, of building up a life for or with each other—none, none.

LUDWIG LEWISOHN

WHAT'S TOMORROW? [25]

The girl has decided to give up love for wealth and luxury. And then she has this encounter in the park.

At three o'clock in the afternoon few people are in Bryant Park. The shadow of the great library marks velvet lines across the grass. Little, ragged, black-eyed boys with shine kits tumble by the benches,

---

[24] From *Adam*, p. 58. Copyright, 1929, by Ludwig Lewisohn. Reprinted by permission of the author and Harper & Brothers.

[25] Published originally in *Good Housekeeping*. Reprinted by permission of the author and the publishers.

call out to men who pass. Blue-purple pigeons strut along the ground, flutter awkwardly in each other's way, peck at scraps of paper. New York, dense with people, buildings, traffic mobs, piercing little cries of police whistles—a black-steel mesh of elevated tracks—New York moves by.

, A man, neither old nor young, expressionless eyes, blue, gray, mauve perhaps, found a bench and sat down.

A girl came down the walk from the library—a slim, little thing, cream-colored broadcloth, gentle perfume, a touch of scarlet on her lips, a lace handkerchief. She was beautiful! Somehow there came into the man's mind, old-fashioned flowers that had grown in his grandmother's garden—forget-me-nots, a spray of white alyssum.

She didn't see him watching her. She was looking past him across the park. She sat down on the other end of the bench. Against one wrist was a narrow black band, the circle of a gold watch. She held it to her ear—looked at the face of it—then glanced up at the quiet man.

"It's stopped," she said—a young unconsciousness of convention in her face. "Can you tell me if it's three o'clock?"

He told her it was forty-five minutes after two.

She stared down at the pigeons parading along the walk—the sun in bronze copper feathers. The man bought peanuts at a cart, broke the shells, and threw them all around her feet.

All his life this man had been quiet, inside himself, alone, but suddenly now he wanted to put her between himself and a guillotine coming down—between himself and the fact that things had finished.

He took a letter out of his pocket, stamped and addressed to a bank.

"Would you be good enough to mail this for me—to-night or to-morrow?"

She looked up at him quickly. Then, because he was neither old nor young, hair colorless, face expressionless, she answered him.

"I won't be in New York to-night or to-morrow. I'm going away."

"Oh. So am I." He smiled. "Life is too big for me. It's too little for me. I'm going to give it up."

"You mean—give up—*life?*"

"Yes, I haven't anything to keep me."

"Why there must be something. You must hope for something."

"Hope is only bubbles in carbon water. Hope isn't the answer to anything. Ambition—no answer. Striving, waiting, reaching—no answer. Who is there room in the world for? Can any one answer? God made only one answer to every question—only one—that's Love. Love is the house at the end of a long road. It's an open door. It's light in the window—but the ones who know are the ones who haven't got it!"

The girl wanted suddenly to reach for his empty hands, to put something into them—courage, if she could, or pity even! He had forgotten her. She had forgotten herself.

"I've worked for years on an idea that's worth a lot. They don't want it. The struggle isn't worth the chance. I give up."

"But you mustn't!" she told him, with a helpless little gesture. "I'll tell someone, and they'll save you!"

He leaned toward her a little. "Have you ever had the love of somebody?"

"Yes."

"It gave you courage when you didn't have any, didn't it? No matter what you would lose or suffer, you would have love waiting for you—wouldn't you?"

"Yes, oh, yes!"

"If you didn't have it, you'd be going from one thing to another like a blind man, wouldn't you? Questions—questions—eternally questions—what's to-morrow—what's the next day—win or lose—swim or sink—and no answer to any of it! For what should any one save you?"

She shut her fingers over the edge of the bench. "Don't you *want* me to tell someone?" Her voice was an odd, queer, little whisper. "Aren't you—afraid?"

He smiled. "No, I'm not afraid. Next to love comes music—and I shall have music. I know a place where a band is playing. I'll hear music to the very last minute. I won't know I'm dying. I'll only be listening to music. If you told somebody to save me, it would just save me an hour or two longer, and that wouldn't be kind of you, because after an hour or two—the band won't be playing, and—"

He suddenly let go of the words, turned back to his own side of the bench as though he had finished a book and closed the cover.

"It's after three."

Tamara stood up quickly, her lace handkerchief crushed like broken cobweb in her fingers. "Oh, I must go."

She looked through the low trees to Fortieth Street. "Yes, I have to go."

She hesitated a minute. The man was watching the pigeons on the sidewalk. He brought some more peanuts out of his pocket and cracked the shells.

"Good-bye." She didn't know just what to say or do. "Good-bye."

He lifted his hat, his face a mask no one could have guessed behind. "Good-bye."

He watched her going into the crowd of Fortieth Street. He wondered where she was going.

DIXIE WILLSON, *Here Y'Are, Brother*

Breathing Patterns and Phrasing

As an interpreter, you will have to learn how to control and subordinate your breathing patterns to the necessary phrasing patterns. In the following lines from "The Creation," [26] you may break the groups into short phrases as indicated, but the meaning will become distorted to the listener. Try interpreting according to the pause marks.

> Then God reached out/ and took the light/ in His hands,/
> And God rolled the light/ around in His hands/
> Until He made the sun;/
> And He set that sun a-blazing/ in the heavens./
> And the light/ that was left/ from making the sun/
> God/ gathered it up/ in a shining ball/
> And flung it/ against the darkness/
> Spangling the night/ with the moon and stars.
>   JAMES WELDON JOHNSON

What impression have you given? To the experienced ear, you have indicated a lack of control of your breathing pattern, you have distorted the verse rhythm, and you have chopped up the imagery. Since the lines give the impression of expansiveness and completion, anything that you do as an interpreter to make it breathless or incomplete will destroy the author's intent.

EXERCISES

I

Shakespeare often gives the interpreter trouble in phrasing because of the on-rush of words from one line to the next. Try these for control of breathing patterns.

1

MACBETH
> If it were done, when 'tis done, then 'twere well
> It were done quickly. If the assassination
> Could trammel up the consequence, and catch
> With his surcease success; that but this blow
> Might be the be-all and the end-all here,
> But here, upon this bank and shoal of time,
> We'ld jump the life to come.
>   WILLIAM SHAKESPEARE, *Macbeth*

[26] From *God's Trombones*, p. 17. Copyright, 1927, by The Viking Press, Inc. Reprinted by permission of the publishers.

2

IAGO
Who steals my purse steals trash; 'tis something, nothing;
'Twas mine, 'tis his, and has been slave to thousands;
But he that filches from me my good name
Robs me of that which not enriches him
And makes me poor indeed.
WILLIAM SHAKESPEARE, *Othello*

3

HORATIO
Two nights together had these gentlemen,
Marcellus and Bernardo, on their watch,
In the dead waste and middle of the night,
Been thus encount'red. A figure like your father,
Arm'd at all points exactly, cap-a-pie,
Appears before them, and with solemn march
Goes slow and stately by them. Thrice he walk'd
By their oppress'd and fear-surprised eyes,
Within his truncheon's length; whilst they, distill'd
Almost to jelly with the act of fear,
Stand dumb and speak not to him. This to me
In dreadful secrecy impart they did,
And I with them the third night kept the watch;
Where, as they had deliver'd, both in time,
Form of the thing, each word made true and good,
The apparition comes. I knew your father;
These hands are not more like.
WILLIAM SHAKESPEARE, *Hamlet*

II

The following poem will take very careful control as far as breathing is concerned, especially throughout the first twelve lines. One must somehow give the impression of the quickness of destruction which culminates in "all as one/As it falls into the sun."

EARTH[27]

If this little world tonight
Suddenly should fall through space

[27] From *Poems*. Copyright, 1900, by Charles Scribner's Sons. Reprinted by permission of the publishers.

In a hissing, headlong flight,
　　Shrivelling from off its face,
As it falls into the sun,
　　In an instant every trace
Of the little crawling things—
　　Ants, philosophers, and lice,
Cattle, cockroaches, and kings,
　　Beggars, millionaires, and mice,
Men and maggots all as one
　　As it falls into the sun. . . .
Who can say but at the same
　　Instant from some planet far
A child may watch us and exclaim:
　　"See the pretty shooting star!"

OLIVER HERFORD

III

The *Rubáiyát of Omar Khayyám* offers some interesting problems in phrasing for proper meaning. In the verses below, be sure that you examine the following factors before deciding on how and where to pause.

1. Verse 12: A pause after *Thou* in line 2 and also after *me* in line 3 will give a meaning different from the phrase, *Thou beside me.* What is the meaning of *Beside?*
2. Verse 19: How long or how imperceptible should the pause be after *red?*
3. Verse 24: What is the meaning of *sans?* Note that a long final pause just before *sans End* is convincing.
4. Verse 54: The parts of speech of *This* and *That*, and also *endeavor* and *dispute* must be known before pauses can be made effectively. Note that *This* and *That* are capitalized, and that *endeavor* and *dispute* are not. Many students pause to indicate that *This* and *That* modify the words *endeavor* and *dispute*. Is the meaning *this and that endeavor and dispute?* Or are *endeavor* and *dispute* verbs? If they are verbs, your pause will come after *This* and *That*.
5. Verse 71: The smoothness of this verse is obvious. If short phrases are used, the rhythm will be distorted. Should you pause, in line 1, after *and* and after *having writ?* The commas are there for the eye but not for the ear.
6. Verse 74: The grouping of the words must indicate that you know the subject and the predicate. Do you agree that *Yesterday* is the subject? If so, then *Yesterday* did prepare *This Day's Madness* and did prepare *Tomorrow's Silence, Triumph, or Despair.*

from THE RUBÁIYÁT OF OMAR KHAYYÁM

Verse 12

A Book of Verses underneath the Bough,
A Jug of Wine, a Loaf of Bread—and Thou
    Beside me singing in the Wilderness—
Oh, Wilderness were Paradise enow!

Verse 19

I sometimes think that never blows so red
The Rose as where some buried Caesar bled;
    That every Hyacinth the Garden wears
Dropt in her Lap from some once lovely Head.

Verse 24

Ah, make the most of what we yet may spend,
Before we too into the Dust descend;
    Dust into Dust, and under Dust, to lie,
Sans Wine, sans Song, sans Singer, and—sans End!

Verse 54

Waste not your Hour, nor in the vain pursuit
Of This and That endeavor and dispute;
    Better be jocund with the fruitful Grape
Than sadden after none, or bitter, Fruit.

Verse 71

The Moving Finger writes; and, having writ,
Moves on: nor all your Piety nor Wit
    Shall lure it back to cancel half a Line,
Nor shall your Tears wash out a Word of it.

Verse 74

YESTERDAY *This* Day's Madness did prepare;
TO-MORROW's Silence, Triumph, or Despair:
    Drink! for you know not whence you came, nor why:
Drink! for you know not why you go, nor where.
translated by EDWARD FITZGERALD

Parenthetical Grouping

The group of words used parenthetically—inserted either for explanation or for reinforcement of meaning—often causes unusual difficulty for the interpreter. To know how to handle the phrase effectively will require understanding of the selection.

There are times when the parenthetical expression is of considerable importance, but there are other times when the phrase is of little importance. The radio and television comedian knows the art of timing the phrase to build up laughs; he usually manages to make use of the group of words as an "aside," thus taking the audience into his confidence. In the following lines, the phrase "one of those chairs" seems rather unimportant on first reading, but the interpreter can bring a laugh if he points it up with the words which precede it—"a chair." Pauses are essential, but pauses alone will not do the work. Perhaps a swallow or a small gulp before you say, "one of *those* chairs" will bring out the humor; perhaps the raising of an eyebrow to indicate you know whereof you speak and so does the audience may help. Try it.

GOING TO JERUSALEM[28]

No matter how calm or nervous, conscientious or inspired, a chairman may be, he or she still presents one problem to the speaker to which neither the introducer nor the audience ever gives much thought. That is, what to do, where to look, how to act, while you are being introduced. It seems simple enough from the front.

A chair—one of those chairs—is near the center of the stage. According to the protocol of the platform, the one nearer the entrance is usually yours. Supposedly all you have to do is to walk from the wings to that chair and then sit down on it and wait. But that walk of no more than ten or fifteen feet can seem an eternity. . . . Twenty boards can unite to form a plank. You are in a trance, doing a conscious act unconsciously, driven forward only by the motor of your pounding heart. Matters are not helped by your knowing there is always the chance that the chairman may forget which of the seats he has agreed to occupy and that the two of you may be caught playing "Going to Jerusalem" in public.

JOHN MASON BROWN

In the excerpt from "University Days," [29] James Thurber gives the interpreter an opportunity to secure laughs through paren-

---

[28] From "We Have with Us Tonight," *Accustomed As I Am*, pp. 35-36. Copyright, 1942, by W. W. Norton & Company, Inc. Reprinted by permission of the publishers.

[29] From "University Days," *My Life and Hard Times*, pp. 110-111. Copyright, 1933, by James Thurber. Published originally in *The New Yorker* and reprinted here by permission of the author and Harper & Brothers. Italics ours.

thetical phrases. "So I am told" paves the way for his own in-
credulity; "a phenomenon of maladjustment" tickles our psychological "funny-bone," especially when it is used to explain the
"nebulous milky substance"; "You had to pass one of the biological sciences or you couldn't graduate" is in the nature of an
aside and will always bring a laugh, especially if you have a
university audience. Another good pause for a laugh—one that
never misses—is the pause after the phrase, "And I would look
again."

A PHENOMENON OF MALADJUSTMENT

I passed all the other courses that I took at my University, but I
could never pass botany. This was because all botany students had
to spend several hours a week in a laboratory looking through a
microscope at plant cells. I never once saw a cell through a microscope.
This used to enrage my instructor. He would wander around the
laboratory pleased with the progress all the students were making in
drawing the involved, and, *so I am told,* interesting structure of
flower cells, until he came to me. I would just be standing there. "I
can't see anything," I would say. He would begin patiently enough,
explaining how anybody can see through a microscope, but he would
always end up in a fury, claiming that I could too see through a
microscope but just pretended that I couldn't. . . . "Try just once
again," he'd say, and I would put my eye to the microscope and see
nothing at all, except now and then a nebulous milky substance—*a
phenomenon of maladjustment.* You were supposed to see a vivid,
restless clockwork of sharply defined plant cells. "I see what looks like
a lot of milk," I would tell him. This, he claimed, was the result of
my not having adjusted the microscope properly, so he would readjust
it for me, or rather, for himself. *And I would look again* and see milk.

I finally took a deferred pass, as they called it, and waited a year
and tried again. (*You had to pass one of the biological sciences or you
couldn't graduate.*) The professor had come back from vacation as
brown as a berry, bright-eyed, and eager to explain cell-structure
again to his classes. "Well," he said to me, cheerily, when we met in
the first laboratory hour of the semester, "We're going to see cells
this time, aren't we?" "Yes, sir," I said . . . Of course, I didn't see
anything.

JAMES THURBER

Juliet's lines in the "Potion Scene" are difficult to master mainly
because of the parenthetical images which are inserted to create

greater tension. The italicized portions are not to be inserted casually:[30]

IF I LIVE

JULIET
>   Or, if I live, is it not very like,
>   The horrible conceit of death and night,
>   Together with the terror of the place,—
>   *As in a vault, an ancient receptacle,*
>   *Where, for this many hundred years, the bones*
>   *Of all my buried ancestors are pack'd;*
>   *Where bloody Tybalt, yet but green in earth,*
>   *Lies festering in his shroud; where, as they say,*
>   *At some hours in the night spirits resort;—*
>   Alack, alack, is it not like that I,
>   So early waking, what with loathesome smells,
>   And shrieks like mandrakes' torn out of the earth,
>   That living mortals, hearing them run mad;—
>   WILLIAM SHAKESPEARE, *Romeo and Juliet*

Cyrano, the poet, the fighter, the lover, tells his friend Le Bret his philosophy of living, which is "To sing, to laugh, to dream,/ To walk in my way alone."

In the passage below can you manage the parenthetical grouping successfully? How will your voice best convey the meaning included in the inserted phrases? Remember that Cyrano is an extrovert.

ALONE! [31]

>   So, when I win some triumph, by some chance,
>   Render no share to Caesar—in a word,
>   I am too proud to be a parasite,
>   And if my nature wants the germ that grows
>   Towering to heaven like the mountain pine,
>   Or the oak, sheltering multitudes,—
>   I stand, not high it may be—but alone!
>   EDMOND ROSTAND

The proper handling of Charles Lamb's "The Housekeeper" can bring out the charm and nonchalance intended by the author.

---

[30] Italics ours.
[31] *Cyrano de Bergerac*, p. 53.

There is no fuss, no worry, no "much-a-do" in the life of the frugal snail. The parenthetical phrases seem almost unimportant, but they really add greatly to the tone of security and assurance. Notice also that the phrases are not too long; in fact, they are almost abrupt.

THE HOUSEKEEPER

The frugal snail, with forecast of repose,
Carries his house with him where'er he goes;
Peeps out—and if there comes a shower of rain,
Retreats to his small domicile again.
Touch but a tip of him, a horn—'tis well,—
He curls up in his sancturary shell.
He's his own landlord, his own tenant; stay
Long as he will, he dreads no quarter-day.
Himself he boards and lodges; both invites
And feasts himself; sleeps with himself o' nights.
He spares the upholsterer trouble to procure
Chattels; himself is his own furniture,
And his sole riches. Wheresoe'er he roam—
Knock when you will—he's sure to be at home.

CHARLES LAMB

Joan Prosper's "Inland," [32] which is reprinted as a whole on p. 470, contains parenthetical expressions which add poignancy to the meaning. They cannot be ignored because they are the crux of the emotional tone. Be aware also that there are two kinds of parenthetical expressions in the following verse: lines 3, 4, 5, 6 to "how it all comes back now" is one insertion; line 7 is another insertion with a different mood.

from INLAND

He used to talk of ships, and I remember,
Oh, I remember. . . .
Tall spars clustered in a drowsy, evening bay,
Clean winds calling, at white noon today;
Salt on the taffrail, foam at the bow,
And a singing at the windlass . . . how it all comes back now!
(Though I never saw the sea.)

JOAN PROSPER

[32] From *The Lyric West* (March, 1925), p. 34. Reprinted by permission of the publishers.

Strangely enough, the expression "ah yes, ah yes, indeed" in the poem "Vista," below changes the imagery of the snow and the sea to a "cream-puff" kind of sophistication, so that when it is again repeated in reference to love, the refrain becomes delightfully humorous, especially if the interpreter is aware of the chances for securing a laugh on the last "ah yes, indeed!"

VISTA[33]

The snow,
ah yes, ah yes, indeed,
is white and beautiful, white and beautiful,
from my window.
The sea,
ah yes, ah yes, indeed,
is green and alluring, green and alluring,
verily alluring—
from the shore.
Love?—
ah yes, ah yes, ah yes, indeed,
verily yes, ah yes, indeed!

ALFRED KREYMBORG

Involutions and Grouping

You will have to learn to solve the literary puzzle, often found in complex sentences, of inverted phrases and clauses, called *involutions*. Poets, especially Shakespeare, Browning, and Shelley, employ this type of sentence arrangement, which, in the hands of an experienced interpreter, can give the listener the thrill of intricate rhythm. This unusual order of words and phrases must be studied before interpretation is attempted. Even after you have decided what the meaning is, you will probably have difficulty sustaining the meaning through the ramifications of involutions. If the grouping is not properly analyzed, you may find yourself gasping at the end of a sentence with a dangling phrase which seems to belong nowhere. The knack of unraveling the involutions of a twisted sentence is worth cultivating.

[33] From *Mushrooms*, p. 64. Copyright, 1916, by John Marshall; 1928, by Alfred Kreymborg. Reprinted by permission of Coward-McCann, Inc.

The following speech should first be analyzed for subject and predicate and for modifying phrases and clauses. Then try to dovetail the involutions into their proper relationship to the sentence meaning. Some of the questions to be answered are: What is Cassius going to throw? When? What does the phrase "in several hands" modify? To what does the phrase "wherein obscurely" refer?

CASSIUS

                    I will this night,
In several hands, in at his windows throw,
As if they came from several citizens,
Writings all tending to the great opinion
That Rome holds of his name; wherein obscurely
Caesar's ambition shall be glanced at:
And after this let Caesar seat him sure;
For we will shake him, or worse days endure.

                    WILLIAM SHAKESPEARE, *Julius Caesar*

In the verse below from "Hervé Riel," you will be able to read the first two lines without difficulty. But lines 3, 4, 5, and 6 will require careful attention. Study these four lines and decide what the subject is before you do anything else. Try "ship on ship" for the subject. Be sure that you know who is the pursuer and who the pursued in line 4. The pursuer is not the "shoal of sharks." Why? Nor is it the "frightened porpoises." Why? It must be "ship on ship." Why?

from HERVÉ RIEL

On the sea and at the Hogue, sixteen hundred ninety-two,
    Did the English fight the French;—woe to France!
And, the thirty-first of May, helter-skelter through the blue,
Like a crowd of frightened porpoises a shoal of sharks pursue,
    Came crowding ship on ship to St. Malo on the Rance,
With the English fleet in view.

                    ROBERT BROWNING

Walt Whitman's description of Lincoln's death will challenge you as an interpreter in the management of pauses, breathing patterns, grouping, parenthetical phrases and involutions:

BOOTH, THE MURDERER[34]

Through the general hum following the stage pause, with the change of positions, came the muffled sound of a pistol shot, which not one-hundredth part of the audience heard at the time—and yet a moment's hush—somehow, surely a vague, startled thrill—and then, through the ornamented, draperied, starr'd and striped space-way of the President's box, a sudden figure, a man raises himself with hands and feet, and stands a moment on the railing, leaps below to the stage (a distance of perhaps fourteen or fifteen feet), falls out of position, catching his boot-heel in the copious drapery (the American flag), falls on one knee, quickly recovers himself as if nothing had happen'd (he really sprains his ankle, but unfelt then),—and so the figure, Booth, the murderer, dressed in plain black broadcloth, bare-headed, with a full head of glossy raven hair, and his eyes like some male animal's flashing with light and resolution, yet with a certain strange calmness, holds aloft in one hand a large knife—walks along, not much back from the footlights—turns fully toward the audience, his face of statuesque beauty, lit by those basilisk eyes, flashing with desperation, perhaps insanity—launches out in a firm and steady voice the words, *Sic semper tyrannis*—and then walks with neither slow nor very rapid pace diagonally across to the back of the stage and disappears.

WALT WHITMAN

SECTION TWO: *Emotional Meaning*

In the preceding section of this chapter, you must have have been aware that there were times when we discussed humor, laughter, emotional effects, although we were mainly interested in grouping, arrangement, and interrelationships pertinent to meaning. One cannot really separate logical and emotional meanings as we have so attempted, because one meaning is often superimposed on or blended with another. By no means do logic and emotion always travel separate paths. A series of logical statements can become an emotional issue among men. It is recognized that man seldom believes as he believes because of the logic alone but because he *thinks* the argument is the right reasoning, inasmuch as it fits into his way of living or his way of thinking and doing. It is true also that many who consider themselves persuaded by the logic of an argument cannot believe that emotion has entered into their opinion.

[34] From "Death of Abraham Lincoln," *Prose Works* (Philadelphia, David McKay Company, 1892), pp. 311-312.

Any interesting piece of literature—prose or poetry—is rich in color and emotional tone because of the choice of words and the use of images. Individual words and sentences, motivated by the author's experiences and philosophy, can stir up within the interpreter, a wealth of memories, associations, and personal emotions. Naturally the closer the interpreter's tastes and experiences to those of the author, the more meaningful is the interpretation.

This section will point up the author's technique in trying to arouse emotion and, thereby, pleasure. A study of emotional meaning will include: (1) connotative meaning; (2) imagery; (3) tone color; (4) figures of speech.

CONNOTATIVE MEANING

A word, like literature itself, has two kinds of meaning: logical and emotional. The logical meaning, that is, the denotative meaning, can be found in the dictionary. The emotional meaning, that is, the connotative meaning, is found in your memories, your imagination, your heart. A *dog* is a certain kind of canine vertebrate, but to you, your dog is more likely to be a playmate of the woods, fields, or streams. An *automobile* is a kind of locomotive machine—and also your cherished companion on many adventures. A *plane,* especially in wartime, is not merely a mechanical automaton to the pilot and his crew but a "ship" that has life and is identified and personalized with their experiences. Hence, the word *plane* becomes charged with connotative meaning. *Home* is a place of residence, but it is also a particular spot charged with memories and feelings.

Notice the difference in the connotations suggested by the word *home* in the following selections. Does any of them connote *home* to you?

A HOME OF YOUR OWN[35]

YANK

It must be great to stay on dry land all your life and have a farm with a house of your own with cows and pigs and chickens, 'way in the middle of the land where yuh'd never smell the sea

[35] From *Bound East for Cardiff* in *Plays of Eugene O'Neill* (New York, Horace Liveright, 1926), p. 236.

or see a ship. It must be great to have a wife and kids to play with at night after supper when your work is done. It must be great to have a home of your own, Drisc.

EUGENE O'NEILL

THE RIPE MELLOWNESS OF EVERYTHING[36]

Willie John had been home for a month and he had made no move toward returning—not that it was ever out of his mind for an instant, but it pleased him to stay there and savor the ripe mellowness of everything as he might savor a fruit. Summer was fairly in and the yellow blossoms had fallen from the gorse, but roses were blooming in every garden, great creamy ones and others with the vivid red of an autumn sunset.

The horse-chestnuts were heavy with balloons of white flowers, and every evening the bees returned drowsy from the heather of the purple mountains. There was something in it all that he had missed for years and that he was greedy for.

BRIAN DONN-BYRNE

THE PEACE OF THE SHADE[37]

Home! The old barn with its sheet ivy rippled by the breeze, and the ivy creeping over the screens of her windows in loving little pink tendrils . . . generous lawns sloping, unfenced, to the street . . . pigeons, flowers in the back yard which had a struggle for life and didn't do so well. Bess saw against these memories tropical flowers bursting forth in a riot behind the plaster walls topped with wicked bits of sharp glass against trespassers: that was France for you. Home! The beauty of the slate roof in its warm, mousy colorings on a rainy day, and the peace of the shade on a sunny day. . . . Elm trees, great old ones, whose trunks came blackly alive at you in a wet season, and whose green leaves wavered and flowed over you in a sunshiny one. So much shade at home that they had sometimes talked of thinning out the elm trees. While here! Bess closed her eyes against the blinding white sun of her days here.

VALMA CLARK

[36] From "The Barnacle Goose," *The Changeling and Other Stories*, p. 65. Copyright, 1924, by Brian Donn-Byrne. Reprinted by permission of the author's representative, O. K. Liveright.

[37] From "The Woman of No Imagination," *Scribner's Magazine* (August, 1925), pp. 129-143. Reprinted by permission of the author.

THE BREEZES OF OUR HOMELAND[38]

THE ACTRESS. I should dearly love to go with you to the village of our
childhood and see the meadows that slope down to the stream—
THE POET. And make chains and wreaths of flowers?
THE ACTRESS. Yes, chains and wreaths and stand with you once more,
Kurt, under the linden trees of a German spring.
THE POET. When will you go with me?
THE ACTRESS. Tomorrow, Kurt. My heart is tired.
THE POET. You will find rest there, Gretel; you shall lie down in the
grass and I shall cover you with flowers—
THE ACTRESS. And there will be yellow butterflies—
THE POET. And the breezes of our homeland.

LUDWIG LEWISOHN

IT'S JUNE NOW[39]

MRS. KEENEY. My memory is leaving me—up here in the ice. It was
so long ago. . . . It's June now. The lilacs will be all in bloom
in the front yard at home—and the climbing roses on the trellis
to the side of the house—they're budding.

EUGENE O'NEILL

THEY HAVE TO TAKE YOU IN[40]

"Home is the place where, when you have to go there,
They have to take you in."
                    "I should have called it
Something you somehow haven't to deserve."

ROBERT FROST

THE RECOLLECTIONS OF THEIR CHILDHOOD[41]

LYDIA, *half in reverie, is speaking of her feelings during Mass at St.
Eustache.*
"If I cried just now in church it wasn't for the reason that you

---

[38] From *Adam* (New York, Harper & Brothers, 1929), p. 25.
[39] From *Ile* in *Plays of Eugene O'Neill* (New York, Horace Liveright,
1926), p. 308.
[40] From "The Death of the Hired Man," *Collected Poems*, p. 49. Copyright, 1930, by Henry Holt and Company, Inc. Reprinted by permission
of the publishers.
[41] From "Christmas Holiday," *The Maugham Reader* (New York, Doubleday & Company, Inc., 1950), p. 1014.

thought. I've cried enough for that, heaven knows, but just then it was for something different. I felt so lonely. All those people, they have a country, and in that country, homes; to-morrow they'll spend Christmas Day together, father and mother and children; some of them, like you, went only to hear the music, and some have no faith, but just then, all of them, they were joined together by a common feeling; that ceremony, which they've known all their lives, and whose meaning is in their blood, every word spoken, every action of the priests, is familiar to them, and even if they don't believe with their minds, the awe, the mystery, is in their bones and they believe with their hearts; it is part of the recollections of their childhood, the gardens they played in, the countryside, the streets of the towns. It binds them together, it makes them one, and some deep instinct tells them that they belong to one another. But I am a stranger. I have no country, I have no home, I have no language. I belong nowhere. I am an outcast."

W. Somerset Maugham

Connotative meanings can be stimulated by previous experiences but cannot be indicated by the printed symbol. The sentence, "He is a nice man," may be a statement of fact; but who, except its author, can prove exactly what is meant? "Nice" can stir up various connotative meanings, according to the emphasis and inflection used by the individual interpreting it. It is this unexpressed meaning that causes differences in interpretation.

In the passage below, Duffus challenges you to give the meaning of some words. Try out the list of words among the class members for meanings. Do you agree with him?

WORDS! [42]

What, if you pardon my asking, does the word "Bolshevik" mean to you? Or "Nordic"? Or "Jew"? Or "Catholic"? Or "German"? Or "Mexican"? Or "tariff"? Or "pacifist"? Or "militarist"? Or "Prohibition"? Or "automobile"? Or "motion picture"? Or "chewing-gum"? Or any one of a thousand other words?

One answer you may safely make. They do not mean the same to you that they do to me, or to your uncle, your wife, your next-door neighbor, Mr. Coolidge, Mr. Ford, Mr. Wayne Wheeler, Mr. Wrigley, Douglas Fairbanks, or the milk man. We assume that there is such a thing as the English language—and perhaps there is. But each of us speaks a different dialect. All we say is like an imperfectly heard

[42] From "Where Do We Get Our Prejudices," *Harper's Magazine* (September, 1926), p. 503. Reprinted by permission of Harper & Brothers.

conversation over the telephone. The connection is always poor. We are always getting the wrong number. This is because every important word has to carry around, in addition to its dictionary definition, the meaning that each one of us has attached to it as the result of his life's experiences. "Automobile" signifies one thing to a man who is in the hospital recovering from an argument with one, and quite another to a man who has just made a successful speculation in General Motors.

ROBERT DUFFUS

Allusions

Authors stir up past experiences that will add meaning to their writings by the use of allusions. They know that a word or phrase that alludes to a specific experience or that is quoted from some familiar literary or historical source will give significant meaning to a passage. Speakers of this generation still like to arouse their audience emotionally by recalling a fighting Churchill who will always be remembered for his famous "blood, sweat and tears." Or they enjoy using the phrase "at long last," first heard when King Edward VIII of England abdicated the throne. Lincoln's "government of the people, by the people, and for the people" frequently brings applause. Often today you will hear phrases used as modern expressions which really belong to that great sixteenth century dramatist, William Shakespeare: "milk of human kindness"; "who steals my purse steals trash"; "what fools these mortals be"; "all the world's a stage"; "midsummer madness"; "too much rein"; "keep a good tongue in your head"; "every inch a king"; "there's a small choice in rotten apples"; "let me take you a button-hole lower"; "that which we call a rose by any other name would smell as sweet"; "it was Greek to me"; "some are born great, some achieve greatness, and some have greatness thrust upon them." John Mason Brown, who uses the Shakespearean allusion, "A Daniel come to judgment! Yea, a Daniel!" [43] is recalling the well-known court-room scene in the *Merchant of Venice:* at the moment that Shylock is demanding his "pound of flesh" from Antonio, the tables are turned by Portia's adeptness. Immediately Gratiano, friend of Antonio, steps forth in great glee, bowing and exultant at Portia's quick

---

[43] John Mason Brown, *Accustomed As I Am* (New York, W. W. Norton & Company, Inc., 1942), p. 35.

retort and cries out in mimicry of Shylock, "A Daniel come to judgment! Yea, a Daniel!"

Every interpreter should be alert to the meaning of words and phrases which we casually use today as acceptable vocabulary but which may have originated because of some habit or action among people and which have survived cultural changes. In reality these phrases become allusions. Every interpreter should know language as Mario Pei writes about it:[44]

Language is the conveyor, interpreter and shaper of man's social doings. It is all-pervasive. It enters into influences by every form of human activity without exception. Its functions are as numerous as the fields in which human ingenuity operates. That everything we do or think creates, changes, destroys, or otherwise influences language is self-evident. What is not so obvious, perhaps, is that language in return affects all our actions and thoughts. It has been fully established that a change in language on the part of an individual is attended by corresponding changes in gestures, facial expression, carriage, even humor and taboos.

Mario Pei cites idioms and words which allude to some phase of man's customs or social adjustment:[45] "don't give a rap" refers to an Irish counterfeit halfpenny of the early century which was called "rap"; "don't give a continental" is a reference to one of our early monetary units; "spud" was formed from the initials of the title of an organization of Englishmen who did not like potatoes and so called themselves the "Society for the Prevention of Unwholesome Diet"; "salary" alludes to salt money, which has its origin in the Roman custom of paying part of the soldier's wage in salt, which in ancient and medieval life was much needed to preserve perishable foods; a "square meal," a typical American idiom, alludes to the New England custom of preparing food in square tins in the eighteenth century; "Mardi Gras" is French for "fat Tuesday," referring to the fact that this is the last day on which fat food (that is, meat) may be eaten before Lent; "propaganda," which today is used almost exclusively in the political sense, comes from the Catholic organization known as *Congregatio de Propaganda Fide*, which means "Congregation

[44] From *The Story of Language*, pp. 190-191. Copyright, 1949, by J. B. Lippincott Company. Reprinted by permission of the publishers.
[45] *Ibid.*, pp. 201-233.

for the propagation of the faith," or, more literally, "the faith to be propagated."

Among different countries, idioms assume various connotations which are suggestive of habits of living. Pei mentions those which have arisen from that secret activity of missing school:[46]

A simple idiomatic, semi-colloquial expression like "playing hookey from school" has the following renderings among others: a French boy "goes to bush school"; an Italian boy "salts away" or "pickles the school"; a German boy "goes behind the school"; a Russian boy "hoboes the school"; a Turk "avoids the school"; a Chinese "hides from school"; while a Spanish boy "plays the calf."

Today we are forming idioms which allude directly to certain American activities: "according to Hoyle," "behind the eight-ball," "to pinch-hit for another," "hit-and-run drivers," "to jump the gun." Nor is it unusual to hear phrases that indicate manner or disposition: "he was Janus-faced"; "he had a Rotarian manner"; "he had the Midas touch"; "he was no Pegasus"; "he had an Achilles heel." The "dark horse," which is glibly used today in campaigns and races, may have had its origin from Disraeli, who, in 1831, wrote: "A dark horse which had never been thought of, and which the careless St. James had never observed in the list, rushed past the grand stand in sweeping triumph." The "kiss of death," often used in connection with a present-day newspaper syndicate, originated with Alfred Smith, who used the expression in alluding to the support of W. R. Hearst for Ogden Mills, who campaigned unsuccessfully for governorship of New York State in 1926. The term "Iron Curtain" is sometimes credited to Winston Churchill, who, in an address at Westminster College in 1946, said: "An iron curtain has descended across the Continent." In reality, however, the expression was first used by Hitler's ministers, Goebbels and von Krosigh. History will probably record this period in which we are living as the "Atomic Age," which involves an allusion vastly different from that evoked by the phrase "The Gay Nineties." William L. Lawrence wrote about our age:[47]

[46] *Ibid.*, p. 429.
[47] *The New York Times* (September 26, 1945), p. 1.

The Atomic Age began at exactly 5:30 Mountain War Time on the morning of July 16, 1945, on a stretch of semi-desert land about fifty airline miles from Almagordo, New Mexico, just a few minutes before the dawn of a new day on this earth. At that moment in history, ranking with the moment in the long ago when man first put fire to work for him and started on his march to civilization, the vast energy locked within the hearts of the atoms of matter was released for the first time in a burst of flame such as had never before been seen on this planet.

You are acquainted with many of the following often-quoted statements; but do you know who said them?

1. Silence is golden. *Thomas Carlyle*

2. Tell that to the marines—the sailors won't believe it. *Sir Walter Scott*

3. What a sight for sore eyes that would be! *William Hazlitt*

4. Liberty and Union, now and forever, one and inseparable. *Daniel Webster*

5. Fat, fair and forty. *Sir Walter Scott*

6. I git thar fustest with the mostest men. *Nathan B. Forrest*

7. The reports of my death are greatly exaggerated. *Mark Twain*

8. "The time has come," the Walrus said,
   To speak of many things . . ." *Lewis Carroll*

9. They say a carpenter is known by his chips. *Jonathan Swift*

10. She's no chicken; she's on the wrong side of thirty, if she be a day. *Jonathan Swift*

11. All the world is queer save thee and me, and even thou art a little queer. *Robert Owen*

12. Neat, not gaudy. *Charles Lamb*

13. He was not merely a chip of the old block, but the old block itself. *Edmund Burke*

14. We must all hang together, or assuredly, we shall all hang separately. *Benjamin Franklin*

15. A thing of beauty is a joy forever. *John Keats*

16. She looks as if butter wouldn't melt in her mouth. *Jonathan Swift*

17. Let our object be our country, our whole country, and nothing but our country. *Daniel Webster*

18. The world must be made safe for democracy. *Woodrow Wilson*

19. Barkis is willin'. *Charles Dickens*

20. War is hell. *William T. Sherman*

21. An expert is one who knows more and more about less and less. *Nicholas Murray Butler*

22. Let sleeping dogs lie. *Charles Dickens*

23. Time is but the stream I go a-fishing in. *Henry Thoreau*

24. This poor little one-horse town. *Mark Twain*

25. Cotton is King. *James H. Hammond*

26. I would not dare to call my soul my own. *Elizabeth Barrett Browning*

27. In this world nothing is certain but death and taxes. *Benjamin Franklin*

28. I pledge allegiance to the flag of the United States and to the republic for which it stands, one nation, indivisible, with liberty and justice for all. *Francis Bellamy*

29. The sweet simplicity of the three per cents. *Benjamin Disraeli*

30. Little things affect little minds. *Benjamin Disraeli*

31. Keep cool: it will be all one a hundred years hence. *Ralph Waldo Emerson*

32. She has more goodness in her little finger than he has in his whole body. *Jonathan Swift*

The following Phi Kappa Phi address, which was given during the lean depression years, has many allusions that are particularly apt. Are you acquainted with them?

DEATH, BE NOT PROUD[48]

The present trip-hammer functioning of my heart, together with other immediate physiological disturbances—quite as annoying but less mentionable—accuse me of temerity, if not audacity, in rising to address so scintillating a galaxy of talent as is here assembled. (For that sentence I am gratefully and humbly indebted to the composite effort of the English Department.) As each item on the program has concluded and the moment of my response relentlessly approached, the victuals hereabout more and more reminded me of Hamlet's "funeral baked meats which coldly furnished forth the marriage tables."

It is a source of ever increasing wonder to me, that the Inquisition

[48] From Charles H. Woolbert and Joseph Smith, *Fundamentals of Speech*, pp. 512-517. Copyright, 1940, by Harper & Brothers. Reprinted by permission of the authors and the publishers.

did not hit upon the technique of formal post-prandial dissertation as one of the more formidable punishments for heresy. Perhaps they did recognize the merits of the exquisite torture such procedure offered the speakers, but perhaps also they remembered that some one would have to listen to the speeches; and, come to think of it, I have never heard that the inquisitors were especially noted for violent masochism.

But as students seem never tired of pointing out, our present academic system is irrevocably committed to a multiplicity of tortures, and the after-dinner speech is not least among them. So here, tonight, some of us speak and you listen. But it is all a very civilized performance—marked by great deception and fraud—indubitable evidences of a high degree of civilization. We almost succeed in assuming calm exteriors and you succeed surprisingly well in disguising your ghoulish glee at our discomfiture, with polite boredom punctuated with applause which after all, helps keep you awake.

When I go to bed I shall probably toss about tonight in the throes of indigestion—I know Dr. Daines [Dean of the Medical School] would advise us to eschew food during periods of emotional stress —but to have refrained from eating this evening would have been at once an impoliteness and an economic blunder—so I shall suffer from indigestion (and probably remorse) and you will go to bed wondering why on earth— But let's not verbalize it. Even a Phi Kappa Phi who is an especial votary at truth's shrine might cringe at such bald expression.

The program formidably calls for an address. Dr. Fellows in his eminently humanitarian way has softened the formal printed demand by his gracious introductions. Certainly, I shall not be delivered of an address. I should like merely to pass on to you one thought. It comes from Professor Scott Nearing in a recent letter to a friend. He said, "Life is too interesting, too thrilling to worry about things!" That's wholesome philosophy. Few groups should receive it more heartily than this one. Human passion for the acquisition of *things* has landed us in the present [pause during which a member shouted "depression"]—sir, materialistic morass. The real tragedy of it all is that everybody, excluding, I hope, members of Phi Kappa Phi, is crying for a return to prosperity. Think of it! Can you imagine so profound a lack of intelligence as wants to return to the old material prosperity? A prosperity which must inevitably culminate in disaster. There is no returning in any event. "The moving finger writes and having writ moves on!" That we shall go on to a new prosperity—a richer prosperity—based on human achievement and spiritual growth —seems to me to be the particular and glorious responsibility of such groups as this. Wasn't it Lowell who, in extolling our literature, said, "That nation is a mere horde supplying figures to the census which does not acknowledge a truer prosperity and a richer contentment in the things of the mind?" That's profound wisdom.

And so when I reconsign my present finery to its mothballs against next year's Phi Kappa Phi dinner, and I open my closet door and see my countenance reflected in the lustre of the trouser's seat of my other suit, and bethink me of my second salary cut which precludes a more extensive wardrobe, shall I worry? Not a whit! I shall don the trusty garment and hie me cheerily to the library and commune with Emerson on life's compensations.

When next I start for town by enforced perambulation and am impelled by the instinct for self-preservation to unusual alacrity to avoid the onrush of some capitalist's 16-cylinder Whosis, shall I turn livid with envy? By no means. I shall direct my walk to safer paths and look out over our peerless valley and say with Wordsworth, "Earth hath not anything to show more fair. Dull would he be of soul who could pass by a sight so touching in its majesty."

When next I am tempted "to show a more swelling port than my faint means will grant continuance," I shall remember Lowell's "Truer prosperity in the things of the mind." I may even consider the lilies of the field, how they toil not, neither do they spin.

Or when some pompous and likely porcine butter-and-egg man scans my meager figure and scoffs at a professor's salary, meanwhile pointing to Rudy Vallee earning thousands the while he croons "Life Is Just a Bowl of Cherries," I shall sit down at my piano and in my faulty fingering heal the wound with a sonata by Mozart, who so much enriched the world for you and me and who yet was buried in a potter's field.

This is the burden of my humble message. And so at last, when unmistakably we can count the waning minutes left us of this life, altogether unencumbered with *things* and out of a richer contentment in the things of the mind, I hope we can say with Donne:

> Death, be not proud, though some have called thee
> Mighty and dreadful, for thou art not so;
> For those whom thou think'st thou dost overthrow
> Die not, poor Death; nor yet canst thou kill me.
> From rest and sleep, which but thy picture be,
> Much pleasure; then from thee much more must flow;
> And soonest our best men with thee do go—
> Rest of their bones and souls' delivery!
> Thou'rt slave to fate, chance, kings, and desperate men,
> And dost with poison, war, and sickness dwell;
> And poppy or charms can make up sleep as well
> And better than thy stroke. Why swell'st thou then?
> One short sleep past, we wake eternally,
> And Death shall be no more: Death thou shalt die!

Joseph Fielding Smith

IMAGERY

Good literature is built around images, which are vital and significant to the interpreter's experiences. To make the reader keenly aware of his images—to stimulate by stirring up past experiences—is the aim of the author.

What is an image? For a moment, imagine you are witnessing a sunset from some high mountain top. You are standing enthralled, moved by the ever changing harmony of light and color: the red and orange melting to green and mauve, and the deep purple blending gradually into the dusky blue of the evening sky. You are experiencing direct impressions of sight, of warmth, of color; these are your sensations. You have also recognized the object of your attention as the sunset; this is your perception, the act of taking in, of perceiving an object or shape. The scene shifts. Now sitting alone in your room, you close your eyes and think of that particular sunset. You will find that you are able to reproduce it, not in its fullest details, perhaps, but certainly in its myriad of colors. This reproduction is called an image. It is a substitute for the direct sensation and perception. Some psychologists call it a memory image. Of course, a word or series of words can act as a stimulus in arousing images.

The greatest difficulty in securing the meaning comes from the diversity of images which are aroused in us according to our variety of experience. As we have said before, the image exists for us only as it recalls or vitalizes some experience, some association. It follows, then, that for each person the image may be different; the image that is stimulated in you may or may not be the one that is intended by the author or the one that is experienced by another interpreter. It should be the interpreter's aim to reproduce as nearly as possible the author's intention, to recapture his impressions. But images are vitalized according to the vividness of past experiences. An image may appear quite distorted to one person—possibly because of some prejudice; to another, the image may stir up pleasant sensations. For instance, if a cat is mentioned, one person may think only of the soft purr of cats, another may be reminded only of claws and an arched back. Some may shrink from a snake because of its coil and hiss; others may observe the snake from a scientific point of view. A person is so constituted that he will or will not catch an image according to the neuromuscular patterns which he has or has not developed.

Experiment has shown that some people are more visual-minded than others; some are more sensitive to tactile images; others are more alive to kinesthetic images. Certainly an athlete or a dancer will be more moved by images that stir a kinesthetic response; but a person who has spent his life in quiet study will probably find more enjoyment in visual imagery.

Psychologists have been busy sorting out and differentiating images for a long time. The most common classification includes the following: visual, or images of sight; motor, or images of movement; auditory, or images of sounds; tactile, or images of touch; olfactory, or images of smell; gustatory, or images of taste; thermic, or images of temperature. Images of pain, hunger, thirst, and equilibrium are sometimes considered as separate from the former classification, but it is quite possible to classify the images of pain under motor and tactile images; images of hunger and thirst and equilibrium under motor or even gustatory images.

Louise Dudley has compiled from certain psychologists a table of the most important images.[49] For your purposes as an interpreter, it might be interesting to know the many varieties of images that are possible.

I. Visual images

    A. Color.
        1. Hue—yellow, blue, or red.
        2. Value—light or dark.
        3. Intensity—vivid or dull.
    B. Brightness, or light and shade—the amount and disposition of shade.
    C. Line.

II. Auditory images

    A. Variations of all sounds.
        1. Quality.
            a. Pitch—high or low tone.

[49] From Louise Dudley, *The Study of Literature*, pp. 33-34. Copyright, 1928, by Houghton, Mifflin Company. Reprinted by permission of the publishers.

  b. Timbre—the characteristic tone quality of different instruments and voices, as of violin or piano.

 2. Loudness—loud or soft.

 3. Direction—sound in front, behind, at the sides, at a distance.

 4. Duration.

B. Classification of sounds.

 1. Musical tones.

  a. Rhythm—regular recurrence of beat or accent.

  b. Melody—tune.

  c. Harmony—the agreement of musical sounds.

 2. Noises—rap, tap, flick, thud, rattle, patter, buzz, whirr, whining, scratch, snap, puff, pop, crack, etc.

III. Motor images

A. Movement—walking, riding, eating, writing, singing, sewing.

B. Resistance—grasping, pinching, plucking, biting, treading, handshaking, weight of all kinds.

C. Position—sitting, standing, all forms of posture.

IV. Tactile images

A. Contact—slight pressure from wood, metal, air, gas, fluids, wrinkling of skin, touching hair, any slight contact with surface of skin.

B. Intensity and extent of pressure—roughness, smoothness.

C. Pressure and movement—hardness and softness, stickiness.

D. Pressure and pain—sharpness, bluntness.

E. Pressure and temperature—clamminess, wetness.

V. Images of taste

A. Pure sensations of taste.

 1. Sweet.

 2. Bitter.

 3. Sour.

 4. Salt.

B. Most of the tastes usually designated as such are combinations of various sensations.

VI. Images of smells

A. Fruit odors—fruits, wine, ethers, beeswax.

B. Aromatic odors—spices, camphor, cloves, ginger, anise.

C. Flower odors—flowers, vanilla.

D. Musk odors—amber, musk.

E. Leek odors—chlorine, iodine, hydrogen carbide, asafoetida.

F. Burned odors—roast coffee, tobacco smoke, creosote.

G. Hircine odors—caproic acid, cheese, sweat.

H. Foul odors—opium, laudanum, bugs.

I. Nauseous odors—carrion flowers, feces.

For some of us the visual image will predominate; for others, the auditory will create the most vivid impressions; for some, the tactile will have the greatest appeal. Certainly we have all had the experience of reading descriptions of the odor and taste of foods and then feeling our hunger so keenly that we have had to satisfy our craving for food. In the same way, other kinds of images can stimulate us for pleasurable and uncomfortable impressions. Let us get acquainted with some kinds of images.

Notice that in the following selection from Dickens, the predominating images recalled are motor, or kinesethetic, and tactile. The words *tight-fisted, grindstone, squeezing, wrenching, grasping, scraping, clutching, covetous, hard, sharp, flint, steel, fire, self-contained, solitary, cold, froze, nipped, pointed, shriveled,* and *stiffened* definitely give the reader the impression of withdrawal and of muscular tension:

SCROOGE!

Oh, but he was a tight-fisted hand at the grindstone, Scrooge! A squeezing, wrenching, grasping, scraping, clutching, covetous old sinner! Hard and sharp as flint, from whom no steel had ever struck out generous fire; secret and self contained and solitary as an oyster. The cold within him froze his old features, nipped his pointed nose, shrivelled his cheek, stiffened his gait, made his eyes red, his thin lips blue; and spoke out shrewdly in his grating voice.

CHARLES DICKENS, *A Christmas Carol*

On the other hand, another paragraph from the same story is built around olfactory and visual imagery. The first few sentences take you through a series of odors. Then, as Mrs. Cratchit enters, you visualize her, *flushed but smiling proudly,* and you see the pudding, *hard and firm,* like a *speckled cannon-ball,* and *blazing* in *ignited brandy,* and *bedight with Christmas holly.*

A WONDERFUL PUDDING

Hallo! A great deal of steam! The pudding was out of the copper. A smell like a washing day! That was the cloth. A smell like an eating-house and a pastry-cook's next door to each other, with a laundress's next door to that! That was the pudding! In half a minute Mrs. Cratchit entered—flushed, but smiling proudly—with the pudding, like a speckled cannon-ball, so hard and firm, blazing in half of half-a-quartern of ignited brandy, and bedight with Christmas holly stuck into the top.

Oh, a wonderful pudding! Bob Cratchit said, and calmly too, that he regarded it as the greatest success achieved by Mrs. Cratchit since their marriage.

CHARLES DICKENS, *A Christmas Carol*

EXERCISES

Analyze these passages for different types of imagery. Notice how you tend to translate the images in terms of your own experience.

I

Coleridge, in discussing the purpose of *The Rime of the Ancient Mariner*, states that he wished to write a poem in which the "incidents and agents were to be, in part at least, supernatural; and the excellence aimed at was to consist in the interesting of the affections by the dramatic truth of such emotions, as would naturally accompany such situations, supposing them real." Having read or heard of the harrowing experiences of men who have been stranded in rubber boats for days, do you think that Coleridge succeeded in his purpose in these following stanzas?

from THE RIME OF THE ANCIENT MARINER

All in a hot and copper sky,
The bloody Sun, at noon,
Right up above the mast did stand,
No bigger than the Moon.

Day after day, day after day,
We stuck, nor breath nor motion;
As idle as a painted ship
Upon a painted ocean.

Water, water, every where,
And all the boards did shrink;
Water, water, every where,
Nor any drop to drink.

The very deep did rot: O Christ!
That ever this should be!

Yea, slimy things did crawl with legs
Upon the slimy sea.

. . . .

And every tongue, through utter drought,
Was withered at the root;
We could not speak, no more than if
We had been choked with soot.

. . . .

There passed a weary time. Each throat
Was parched, and glazed each eye.
A weary time! a weary time!
How glazed each weary eye,
When looking westward, I beheld
A something in the sky.

At first it seemed a little speck,
And then it seemed a mist;
It moved and moved, and took at last
A certain shape, I wist.

A speck, a mist, a shape, I wist!
And still it neared and neared:
As if it dodged a water-sprite,
It plunged and tacked and veered.

With throats unslaked, with black lips baked,
We could nor laugh nor wail;
Through utter drought all dumb we stood!
I bit my arm, I sucked the blood,
And cried, A sail! a sail!

SAMUEL TAYLOR COLERIDGE

II

Although this next selection is full of imagery, especially interesting is the author's very careful but simple choice of words, which keeps the images clearly defined and makes their appeal universal and "earthy."

from THE GREAT LOVER[50]

These have I loved:
    White plates and cups, clean-gleaming,
Ringed with blue line; and feathery, faery dust;

[50] From *Collected Poems of Rupert Brooke*, p. 125. Copyright, 1915, by Dodd, Mead and Company, Inc. Reprinted by permission of the publishers.

Wet roofs, beneath the lamp-light; the strong crust
Of friendly bread; and many-tasting food;
Rainbows; and the blue bitter smoke of wood;
And radiant raindrops couching in cool flowers;
And flowers themselves, that sway through sunny hours,
Dreaming of moths that drink them under the moon;
Then, the cool kindliness of sheets, that soon
Smooth away trouble; and the rough male kiss
Of blankets; grainy wood; live hair that is
Shining and free; blue massing clouds; the keen
Unimpassioned beauty of a great machine;
The benison of hot water; furs to touch;
The good smell of old clothes; and other such—
The comfortable smell of friendly fingers,
Hair's fragrance, and the musky reek that lingers
About dead leaves and last year's ferns. . . .
                              Dear names,
And thousand others throng to me! Royal flames;
Sweet water's dimpling laugh from tap or spring;
Holes in the ground; and voices that do sing;
Voices in laughter, too; and body's pain,
Soon turned to peace; and the deep-panting train;
Firm sands; the little dulling edge of foam
That browns and dwindles as the wave goes home.

                              RUPERT BROOKE

III

Decide why the following selections give you an exotic impression through the images.

THE TAVERN[51]

The walls of the tavern were covered with pictures painted in violent hues; blues and reds and greens jarring against one another and lighting up the gloom of the place. The stone benches were always crowded, the sunlight came in through the door in a long bright gleam, casting a dancing shadow of vine leaves on the further wall. . . . The room was cool and dark and cavernous, but the scent and heat of the summer gushed in through the open door. There was ever a full sound, with noise and vehemence, there, and the rolling music of the Latin tongue never ceased. . . .

A strange feature was the constant and fluttering motion of hands and arms. Gesture made a constant commentary on speech; white

[51] From *The Hill of Dreams*, pp. 134-135. Copyright, 1923, by Alfred A. Knopf, Inc. Reprinted by permission of the author.

fingers, whiter arms, and sleeves of all colors, hovered restlessly, appeared and disappeared with an effect of threads crossing and recrossing on the loom. And the odour of the place was both curious and memorable; something of the damp cold breath of the cave meeting the hot blast of summer, the strangely mingled aromas of rare wines as they fell plashing and ringing into the cups, the drugged vapour of the East that the priests of Mithras and Isis bore from their steaming temples; these were always strong and dominant.

ARTHUR MACHEN

THE UNVEILED WOMAN[52]

Sitting in the pavilion, looking down into the moon-mirroring water, was a woman in the ancient dress of Persia, golden and jeweled. She flung up her head magnificently, and looked at them, the moon full in her eyes. The garden was peopled now, not only with roses, but with large white blossoms sending out fierce hot shafts of perfume. They struck Beatrice Veronica like something tangible and half dazed her as she stared at the startling beauty of the unveiled woman, revealed like a flaming jewel in the black and white glory of the night.

E. BARRINGTON

IV

Compare the impressions created in the following selections. Check on the use of images.

ICHABOD CRANE

In this by-place of nature there abode, in a remote period of American history, that is to say, some thirty years since, a worthy wight of the name of Ichabod Crane, who sojourned, or, as he expressed it, "tarried," in Sleepy Hollow, for the purpose of instructing the children of the vicinity. The cognomen of Crane was not inapplicable to his person. He was tall, but exceedingly lank, with narrow shoulders, long arms and legs, hands that dangled a mile out of his sleeves, feet that might have served for shovels, and his whole frame most loosely hung together. His head was small, and flat at top, with huge ears, large green glassy eyes, and a long snipe nose, so that it looked like a weather-cock perched upon his spindle neck, to tell which way the wind blew. To see him striding along the profile of a hill on a windy day, with his clothes bagging and fluttering about him, one might have mistaken him for the genius of famine descended upon the earth, or some scarecrow eloped from a cornfield.

WASHINGTON IRVING, *The Legend of Sleepy Hollow*

[52] From "V. Lydiat," *The Atlantic Monthly* (February, 1925), p. 223. Reprinted by permission of the publishers.

THE KING

It was the most extraordinary looking little gentleman he had ever seen in his life. He had a very large nose, slightly brass-colored; his cheeks were very round, and very red, and might have warranted a supposition that he had been blowing a refractory fire for the last eight-and-forty hours; his eyes twinkled merrily through long silky eyelashes, his mustaches curled twice round like a corkscrew on each side of his mouth, and his hair, of a curious mixed pepper-and-salt color, descended far over his shoulders. He was about four-feet-six in height, and wore a conical pointed cap of nearly the same altitude, decorated with a black feather some three feet long. His doublet was prolonged behind into something resembling a violent exaggeration of what is now termed a "swallow tail," but was much obscured by the swelling folds of an enormous black, glossy-looking cloak, which must have been very much too long in calm weather, as the wind, whistling round the old house, carried it clear out from the wearer's shoulders to about four times his own length.

JOHN RUSKIN, *The King of the Golden River*

COLONEL BRERETON[53]

He was a positive, a marvellous, an incredible success, and he won every suit. Nothing like his eloquence had ever before been heard in the country. He argued, he cajoled, he threatened, he thundered, he exploded, he confused, he blazed, he fairly dazzled—for silence stunned you when the Colonel ceased to speak as the lightning blinds your eyes after it has vanished.

H. C. BUNNER

V

Notice the kinesthetic imagery in the next selection. Can you feel yourself pushing and pulling to get on firm ground?

THE DIVER[54]

The rotten coral burst and sank under footing. Clogging weeds enwreathed and held him back with evil embrace. A tridacna spread its jaws before his steps so that he nearly plunged into the deadly

[53] From "Colonel Brereton's Aunty," *The Golden Book* (August, 1926), p. 159. Reprinted by permission of the author.

[54] From "The Lost God," *The Red Mark and Other Stories*, p. 239. Copyright, 1919, by Alfred A. Knopf, Inc. Reprinted by permission of the author and the publishers.

spring-trap of the deep. But he kept on up the slope; his keen spirit rallied and bore him through, and he came surging from the waves at last on a point of rocks outside the bay where he could cling and open the emergency cock in the helmet. The suit deflated and he breathed new life. But here he suffered his second immediate mishap, for as he scrambled to his feet a dizziness took him and he slipped and pitched forward heavily, and with a great clang of armour the god fell fainting at the very threshold of his world.

JOHN RUSSELL

Do you think the above kinesthetic imagery is as vivid as the following which have been used to describe sports action?

1. scythelike interference
2. a straight line down the side lines
3. swivel-hipped
4. struggling in abysmal goo
5. ground devouring
6. churned through the middle for six points

TONE COLOR

Mood depends on many factors, but very important to the impression is the tone color by means of which connotative words stir up emotional responses. Tone color is obtained through skillful manipulation of sound values by means of repetition of vowels, syllables, or words, as in Vachel Lindsay's "The Congo":[55]

> "Be careful what you do,
>   Or Mumbo-Jumbo, God of the Congo,
>   And all of the other
>   Gods of the Congo,
>   Mumbo-Jumbo will hoodoo you,
>   Mumbo-Jumbo will hoodoo you,
>   Mumbo-Jumbo will hoodoo you" . . .

or as in Edgar Allan Poe's "The Bells":

> How they tinkle, tinkle, tinkle,
>   In the icy air at night!
> While the stars, that oversprinkle
> All the heavens, seem to twinkle
>   With a crystalline delight. . . .

[55] From *The Congo and Other Poems*, p. 4. Copyright, 1912, by The Macmillan Company. Reprinted by permission of the publishers.

Tone color can also be secured through the imitation of sounds in words associated with their meaning, called *onomatopoeia*, as in the above *tinkle* and *hoodoo*, and in words like *zip*, *zoom*, *buzz*, *fizz*, *murmur*, *bang*, *wham*, *purr*, *pop*, *crack*, *razzle-dazzle*, *bing*. Notice how the soft vowels in addition to the use of *tip-toe* give tone color to Lew Sarett's lines from "Wéeng":[56]

> Over your cheeks old Wéeng will go,
> With feet as soft as the falling snow—
> Tip-toe . . . . tip-toe.

In contrast, compare Rudyard Kipling's lines from "Gunga Din":

> It was "Din! Din! Din!
> You limpin' lump o' brick-dust, Gunga Din!"

What words in the following lines from John Masefield's "Sea Fever" [57] give you the impression of sailing?

And all I ask is a windy day with the white clouds flying,
And the flung spray and the blown spume and the sea-gulls crying.

Thus one can understand that it is difficult to decide whether the tone color adds to the connotative meaning or vice versa. To make the problem of evaluation more interesting, some persons have definite reactions to the tone color of words. Much has been written and surveys have been conducted about words that are beautiful. Naturally, that type of survey could go on forever, because people will often pick words that affect them most pleasantly according to their individual experiences rather than the ones which *sound* the most beautiful. Henry James once said to Edith Wharton: "Summer afternoon—summer afternoon; to me those have always been the two most beautiful words in the English language." He may have been under the spell of a "perfect afternoon" at Bodiam, looking at the "old spell-bound ruin, unrestored, guarded by great trees, and by a network of lanes," watching "tranquil white clouds hung above it in a wind-

---

[56] From *Slow Smoke*, p. 58. Copyright, 1925, by Henry Holt and Company, Inc. Reprinted by permission of the publishers.
[57] From *Collected Poems of John Masefield*, Vol. 1, p. 31. Copyright, 1912, by The Macmillan Company. Reprinted by permission of the publishers.

less sky," and experiencing "complete silence and solitude" as he looked across at "the crumbling towers and at their reflection in a moat starred with water-lilies, and danced over by great blue dragon-flies." [58] Certainly the peace of the afternoon might have colored his impression about the beauty of the phrase *summer afternoon.* Others have selected *lullaby, murmur, golden, croon, glimmer, azure, moon-glow, garage, dreams, woodland, wandered, tawny, swallow, glorious,* and even *cellar-door.* What is your choice?

FIGURES OF SPEECH

Mood is also obtained by likening one image, either directly or indirectly, to another image, thereby loading the suggestiveness and connotation. This is accomplished by figures of speech: simile, metaphor, and personification. You may recall from literature classes that the simile enhances meaning by indicating a likeness, as in the following poem.

THE PORTRAIT[59]

Like a dear old lady
Dressed in soft brown cashmere,
Sitting with quiet, folded hands, content and peaceful
And smiling a mysterious promise,
My winter garden waits.

CAROLINE GILTINAN

EXERCISE

Which of the similes in the following excerpts do you think is the most effective?

1

For thoughts like waves that glide by night
Are stillest when they shine.

OWEN MEREDITH, *Night and Love*

[58] Edith Wharton, *A Backward Glance* (New York, D. Appleton, Century Company, Inc., 1934), p. 249.
[59] From *The Lyric West* (January, 1924), p. 123. Reprinted by permission of the publishers.

2

Why does the world report that Kate doth limp?
O slanderous world! Kate, like the hazel-twig,
Is straight and slender, and as brown in hue
As hazel nuts and sweeter than the kernels.
                WILLIAM SHAKESPEARE, *The Taming of the Shrew*

3

I could a tale unfold whose lightest word
Would harrow up thy soul, freeze thy young blood,
Make thy two eyes, like stars, start from their spheres,
Thy knotty and combined locks to part
And each particular hair to stand on end,
Like quills upon the fretful porpentine.
                        WILLIAM SHAKESPEARE, *Hamlet*

4

I saw Eternity the other night.
Like a great ring of pure and endless light,
    All calm, as it was bright;
And round beneath it, Time, in hours, days, years,
    Driven by the spheres
Like a vast shadow moved;

.   .   .   .

The darksome statesman, hung with weights and woe,
Like a thick midnight fog moved there so slow,
    He did not stay nor go.
                        HENRY VAUGHAN, *The World*

5

Thou, from whose unseen presence the leaves dead
Are driven, like ghosts from an enchanter fleeing,
Yellow, and black, and pale, and hectic red,
Pestilence-stricken multitudes.
            PERCY BYSSHE SHELLEY, *Ode to the West Wind*

The metaphor is an implied likeness or similarity. In describing
the use of metaphor, S. I. Hayakawa makes some interesting comments:[60]

When we talk about the "head" of a cane, the "face" of a cliff, the
"bowels" of a volcano, the "arm" of the sea, the "hands" of a watch,

[60] S. I. Hayakawa, *Language in Action* (New York, Harcourt, Brace and
Company, Inc., 1914), p. 196.

the "branches" of a river or an insurance company, we are using metaphor. A salesman "covers" an area; an engine "knocks"; a theory is "built up" and then "knocked down"; a government "drains" the taxpayers, and corporations "milk" the consumers. Even in so unpoetical a source as the financial page of a newspaper, metaphors are to be found: stock is "watered," shares are "liquidated," prices are "slashed" or "stepped up," markets are "flooded," the market is "bullish"; in spite of government efforts to "hamstring" business and "strangle" enterprise, there are sometimes "melons" to be "sliced"; although this is—but here we leave the financial page—"pure gravy" for some, others are left "holding the bag." Metaphors are so useful that they often pass into the language as part of the regular vocabulary. Metaphor is probably the most important of all the means by which language develops, changes, grows, and adapts itself to our changing needs. When metaphors are successful, they "die"—that is, they become so much a part of our regular language that we cease thinking of them as metaphors at all.

EXERCISE

Evaluate the metaphors found in these lines as far as their effectiveness is concerned.

1. New York, the nation's thyroid gland. *Christopher Morley*

2. A human being: an ingenious assembly of portable plumbing. *Christopher Morley*

3. Diplomats: babies in silk hats playing with dynamite. *Alexander Woollcott*

4. Our lives are merely strange dark interludes in the electrical display of God the Father! *Eugene O'Neill*

5. April prepares her green traffic light and the world says Go. *John Mistletoe*

6. Cauliflower is nothing but cabbage with a college education. *Mark Twain*

7. This poor little one-horse town. *Mark Twain*

8. Atom bomb: A mushroom of boiling dust up to 20,000 feet. *Paul Tibbett, Jr.*

9. He could fiddle all the bugs off a sweet-potato-vine. *Stephen Vincent Benét*

10. Part of a moon was falling down the west,
    Dragging the whole sky with it to the hills.
    Its light poured softly in her lap.
    Robert Frost

11. You—you are the great vulgarizer! You have made my thoughts comprehensible even to horses! With the art of a great vulgarizer, a tailor of ideas, you dressed my Apollo in a barber's jacket, you handed my Venus a yellow ticket, and to my bright hero you gave the ears of an ass. And then your career is made. *Leonid N. Andreyev*

Slang draws heavily on metaphors for its effectiveness. It may not make you a more effective interpreter to read this paragraph, but perhaps it will draw your attention to the close relationship between connotative meaning and imagery. We say of someone: he's "all thumbs," he "bristled" with rage, he's a "big cheese," "cake-eater," "meal ticket," "pill," "crumb," "big noise," "snake-in-the-grass," "wet blanket," "gold-mine"; and she can be a "modest violet," "choice bit of calico," or "smoothie," and often is "dyed-in-the-wool," "butter-fingers," or "chicken-hearted." Or we can say let's "talk turkey," "chew the rag," "make the fur fly," "egg them on," "eat humble pie," "put up a squawk," "shoot the bull," "make no bones about it," or "foot the bill." We all understand what is meant; but a foreigner might have some difficulty in understanding these distorted images. Sometimes we are puzzled by the lingo of the waiter in a restaurant who calls out, "Adam and Eve on a raft, wreck 'em!"; but any American should know that it is an order for scrambled eggs on toast. Or we may hear, "Two on a slice of squeal," which means, "bacon and eggs."

Personification is another use of images in which objects or elements in nature are given animate characteristics or described as if they had life and were capable of human activity. Who but Herbert Hoover could create vivid association with the decimal point, with which we have all struggled:[61] "When I comb over these accounts of the New Deal, my sympathy arises for the humble decimal point. His is a pathetic and hectic life, wandering around among regimented ciphers, trying to find some of the old places he used to know." And speaking of regimentation, notice how Lew Sarett uses this image in "Hollyhocks":[62]

And a regiment of hollyhocks marching around them,
To curb their mischief, to discipline and bound them.

[61] From an address delivered in St. Louis, Mo., on December 16, 1935
[62] From *Wings Against the Moon*, p. 28. Copyright, 1931, by Henry Holt and Company, Inc. Reprinted by permission of the publishers.

. . . .

Hollyhocks! Hollyhocks! Stiff as starch!
Oh, fix your bayonets! Forward! March!

Notice the personification in the reaction of Winston Churchill to a Gallup Poll:[63] "Nothing is more dangerous in wartime than to live in the temperamental atmosphere of a Gallup Poll, always feeling one's pulse and taking one's temperature."

Earlier in this book, you encountered the selection, "Makers of the Flag." [64] You may recall that the author achieved personification throughout by the use of the pronoun "I": "I live a changing life, a life of moods and passions, of heartbreaks and tired muscles." Shakespeare also used metaphors frequently and vividly:

MACBETH. Life's but a walking shadow, a poor player
That struts and frets his hour upon the stage,
And then is heard no more.

JULIET. Is there no pity sitting in the clouds
That sees into the bottom of my grief?

IAGO. I should be wise, for honesty's a fool
And loses that it works for.

BEATRICE. Is it possible disdain should die while she hath such meet
food to feed on as Signior Benedick? Courtesy itself must convert
to disdain, if you come in her presence.

ROMEO. Night's candles are burnt out, and jocund day
Stands tiptoe on the misty mountain tops.

LADY MACBETH.   Was the hope drunk
Wherein you dress'd yourself? Hath it slept since?
And wakes it now, to look so green and pale
At what it did so freely.

This chapter has been written, not for the express purpose of having you *dig into* every quotation reprinted here, but for the need of centering your attention on as complete a meaning as is possible to get from the author's lines. Each word or group of

[63] Report on the war situation given before the House of Commons on September 30, 1941.
[64] See p. 115.

words should be evaluated for its significance in securing the meaning of the whole.

There has been much said in this chapter about details that assist in the full understanding of a literary selection. To be certain that you think in terms of the total meaning of a selection rather than in parts, it will be helpful to you, before you proceed, to study carefully the poem below and the analysis that follows it. Note how Mark Van Doren's understanding of the choice, use, sound, meaning, and arrangement of words and phrases has strengthened and added to the full understanding of the poem.

A NOISELESS PATIENT SPIDER[65]

A noiseless patient spider,
I mark'd where, on a little promontory, it stood, isolated;
Mark'd how, to explore the vacant, vast surrounding,
It launch'd forth filament, filament, filament out of itself;
Ever unreeling them—ever tirelessly speeding them.

And you, O my Soul, where you stand,
Surrounded, surrounded, in measureless oceans of space,
Ceaselessly musing, venturing, throwing—seeking the spheres, to connect them;
Till the bridge you will need, be form'd—till the ductile anchor hold;
Till the gossamer thread you fling, catch somewhere, O my Soul.

WALT WHITMAN

Here is Mark Van Doren's analysis:[66]

Here is solitude with a vengeance, in vacancy so vast that any soul seen at its center, trying to comprehend and inhabit it, looks terribly minute. Whitman's spider on its little promontory—a twig, a stalk, a leaf of grass—is no more helpless than the soul of a man must be, laboring to launch itself in the universe and connect the spheres; or even to catch anywhere, at one fact, one friend, one lover, and thus no longer be alone. Emily Dickinson's soul had the society of one person, and was content with that one. Here there are no persons yet—only the soul newborn in space, hoping to conquer its measureless environment.

The verse of the poem is free, yet not altogether so. It is bound to the task of saying for the poet how strenuous the effort is he has set himself to describe. It arranges itself in two sections—hardly stanzas, though they are almost that—and keeps a certain symmetry in those sections, a symmetry consistent with the parallel Whitman wants to maintain between the spider and the soul. After a relatively short line, each section throws out four longer ones. These have five, six, or seven stresses as the case may be; but they are roughly uniform in the time they take and in the nature of their movement. Their movement is the movement of throwing, of putting out, of launching forth filaments of themselves, of sending loops and spirals into space. "Ever unreeling them—ever tirelessly speeding them." This expresses the poem as well as the spider. Short as it is, it never seems to be done, except in so far as the last line promises some sort of success, somewhere, sometime. The soul, as if it were itself a spider, has put forth gossamer threads. One of them—the suggestion is clear—may catch.

The two adjectives in the first line are more cunning than we may suspect. Their order is eloquent of the creature referred to—not a patient, noiseless spider, but one whose silence strikes us first, and then its industry. In another poem, Whitman has spoken, not of the few large stars that glorify the night, but of "the large few stars." The difference is wonderful, as it is here. And the spider has the whole of the beginning line to itself, as if there were no observers. But there is one. "I mark'd." There, on its little promontory, says Whitman, "it stood, isolated." And then he marked how it had work to do, how it strove to overcome its isolation, its immense isolation in the space between the twig it clung to and any other object whatever. Not only did it feel out with its arching, delicate feet; from its very self it sent out filament, filament, filament—more and more of them all the time, as if it contained infinities of thread—in search of something with which contact could be made and a web begun. "Filament," used three times in precisely this place, becomes a more forceful word than we could have supposed it would be. It is a light word, like the thing it names; but the three *f*'s fill it with an energy which does not leave us surprised when we learn in the next line that the spider never became tired. The filaments went forth fast, too—faster and faster, and farther and farther away. Nothing could be compared with this. Nothing, except the soul.

My own soul, says Whitman, stands in the same fashion, surrounded by the same sea of vacancy. Or seas—or oceans, a better word—of empty air. The sentence he addresses to this essence of himself is never completed. The sentence about the spider was in the past tense and described an action; the action was not completed, but the observation of it was, and so the sentence could be. But the second half of the poem hangs unfinished, unconnected, in syntax, time, and space. *This* is the situation *now*. The soul keeps on, ceaselessly, throwing out filaments of itself—thoughts, theories, desires—and will do so forever until the day when contact is made with that reality which is as far away as the stars in their spheres. Such a day will undoubtedly come, but it has not come yet. There is not merely the hope that it will come, there is the purpose and the certainty; and somehow we are assured of this by the sound of the last five words in line 9. "Till the ductile anchor hold"—and the moment is forecast with an authority we cannot question, since the thing itself is happening in our eyes and ears. Particularly our ears. The hard *c*'s in "ductile" and "anchor" verify the competence of the one filament that is successful at last; it is flexible, but it is strong; and it will *hold;* the merest gossamer, it will nevertheless catch (another hard *c*) and stay caught. The near-rhyme of "Soul" with "hold" already commences the operation of sewing and tying the anchor tight.

The effort, meanwhile, has been immense. It is an ancient idea, this of man's mind or soul that in its little sphere of flesh can achieve a correspondence with the great sphere of creation around it. And there have been times when this correspondence was spoken of as easy to bring about—indeed, it almost happened by itself. Not so with Whitman, whose modern soul was haunted by the difficulties of the task. Whitman studied loneliness like a scholar, and made his various music out of solitude, his great subject. Here his music is urgent and anxious. The spider and the soul may fail. And yet they may not—indeed they must not, as the rolling energy of the verse by its own might declares. And as the adjectives, so intelligently and powerfully placed, assure us if we listen well. Not only "noiseless" and "patient," but "vacant" and "vast," and "ductile," and "gossamer," which stitch the sections together, giving us to understand that as the spider is assisted by the very genius for survival that can be assumed in its species, so the soul must be similarly assisted, though Whitman does not know how. Yet "somewhere, O my Soul."

Part III
THE TECHNIQUE OF EXPRESSION

CHAPTER 5

Meaning Through Bodily Movement

You are now alert to the fact that authors are people, that Carl Sandburg, for instance, is considered today

not a mere poet but a many-sided interpreter of America to itself, with his monumental six volumes on Lincoln, with his Song Bag of ballads which he has collected and sung all over the land, and with his stirring war speeches in time of trouble to great audiences by radio and television. He is, in short, a national possession with a many-sided appeal, himself a kind of Lincolnian figure, humorous, colorful, rich in American folklore, with a passion for the divine average and the American dream.[1]

If you are further impressed with the fact that words have the power to denote and connote many meanings, depending on the author's philosophy and your experiences, depending on the selection of words, how they are spaced and structured into a poem, paragraph, story, or play, then you are ready to study how one may effectively convey these meanings and impressions to an audience. How can you, the interpreter, make the audience understand and feel what you want them to understand and feel?

Meaning Through Bodily Tensions

Inasmuch as we always see before we hear—that is, the eye is quicker than the ear—we can easily recognize the fact that

[1] From Bruce Weirick, "Carl Sandburg's Poetry," a radio lecture delivered in commemoration of Carl Sandburg's seventy-fifth birthday (1953). Reprinted by permission.

213

what the interpreter's body is doing is most important in stirring up meaning for the audience. Even as we face our audience, before we say anything, we are carrying meaning of some sort. It may be the wrong meaning, it may not be what we think it is, but it is meaning. We may be frowning or smiling or appearing bored or merely appearing to be something we are not. Or we may be experiencing a bad case of stage-fright. Watch an artist as he appears before you. Notice how meaning is carried through his muscular tensions—through his smile, his posture, and his movement. Because that first moment is of so much importance, it is necessary that the interpreter show the proper control, for his attitude will suggest an attitude to the audience. Unconsciously, the audience will tend to adopt the muscular tensions of the artist. If all this can be accomplished without words, and it can be, think of the power we may have if we employ the right distribution of energy and play of muscles plus the careful control of the voice!

Meaning Through Empathy

How, then, can we best adapt ourselves to an audience-interpreter situation—a situation which demands that the interpreter arouse or stimulate in his listeners an emotional response similar to the one he himself portrays? Here is a problem of empathic response, of a kinesthetic impulse, of what the muscles of the performer can do to the muscles of the people observing him. Empathic reaction is a difficult thing to study introspectively because it comes often when we least expect it—in a spontaneous fashion. Empathy is not subject to our will; it is, rather, a natural impulse, more like an instinctive or an imitative reaction. Empathy is a "feeling into" as contrasted with a "feeling with." The muscles of the observer tend to do what the object at which he is looking is doing or is suggesting. It is most successful when people are not conscious of what is happening to them. Most persons realize usually that they have caught the emotion; but how and where it came from, they do not know.

Analyze your own set of muscular reactions. How do you react to your friend who has a sparkle in his eye or a frown on his face or a set expression around his mouth? What do you do when you observe some person walking with a prim, tense rhythm—stilted and rigid? Can you feel the pull in your muscles? Where do you feel the greatest urge for action when you observe bronzes of drooping maidens, of stern Indians watching the flight of an arrow, of a child wriggling its toe in glee, of a yawning tiger? Note the downward pull of your muscles when you observe an airplane swooping earthward; and the reaching up when the plane swings back to the clouds. Did you ever sit on the bleachers and watch the football hero tear down the field—stumbling, falling, struggling, pulling, running, dodging, twisting—and finally, with a tremendous effort, succeed in putting the ball over the line? If you thoroughly enjoyed what he was doing, if you were helping him along, exhorting, pushing your neighbor, whooping and yelling when the touchdown was made—then *you* made the touchdown, for your muscles were straining and pulling as his were and you probably felt the joyous relaxation that comes after strenuous exercise. All this is empathy, a "feeling into."

Empathy implies the response of "getting into the spirit of things." We watch dancers and, insofar as we can, we dance with them; we see the hero knock the villain down and find our fists doubled up and our arms taut trying to hit and hold still at the same time. We see the base runner "hit the dust," and we slide with him—on the bleachers. We like or dislike a person very often because of the muscular tensions we observe in him. A man of personality is often a man whose movements make people do things which they feel are correct, proper, and stimulating. In a large measure, men *are* what they are observing. So empathy is the essence of all artistic appreciation; if we enter into the spirit of what is happening, enjoy it, become lost in it, we do so because *we are taking part.* If we actually feel the significance of the cathedral, it lifts us and carries us bodily to transcendent heights. If we genuinely understand the Laocoön statue, we writhe in an agony of fear trying to throw off the loathsome coils of the snakes. Even as you read this, you may be shivering in response to the images which the words evoke. If we really enjoy "The Blue Danube," off we go in a whirling waltz—even in our seats. In other words, when we appreciate a work of art we actually try to do or be the thing in the presence of which we find ourselves. Sometimes these muscular tensions are very notice-able; sometimes they are hidden from the casual observer. Many of us, as we grow in experience, try to cover up any muscular movements that may reveal how we feel.

The theater offers an excellent opportunity for the study of empathic responses. Everything about the mechanics of the stage picture, including furniture, properties, lights, color, make-up, line, movement, is arranged to create an illusion of reality, which is necessary if we are to feel empathy—or the right kind of em-pathy. If one little thing goes wrong with the lights, if an essen-tial property has been forgotten, if the gun does not go off when it should, if the telephone does not ring, then momentarily we have come out of the picture and the illusion has been lost, and, of course, we get out of the spirit of the scene. Needless to say, empathy—the kind of empathy the director has been trying to get from the audience—has been lost.

You have caught yourself imitating the facial expression of an actor on the stage. Other things being equal, the greater number of those tensions which the actor stimulates in you, the better you like the play. When you do not get any of the desired em-pathic responses, you are bored, cold, pained at the performance; or we might say that when you are not muscularly set to enjoy anything, you will not permit yourself the empathy which the director and actors have tried to arouse, for your muscles have been pulling in the wrong direction. Usually the more relaxed you are at the beginning of the performance, the greater your chance of empathic enjoyment. Empathy is the response that tingles, that warms, that exhilarates, that pulls you this way and that way, so that you gasp, "How wonderful!" or moan "How depressing!" If an actor renders his "Come, let me clutch thee!" aright, every person in the audience who actually appreciates his fear, clutches a knife; when Casca stabs Caesar, your arm stabs too; when Richelieu shouts, "Around her form I draw the awful circle of our solemn Church," every listener has his arms raised in warning and defiance, *usually without visibly moving his arms*—that is, if the actor is really acting *Richelieu*. Some of us have never seen on the stage a villain whom we really liked, because if he *is* convincing as an actor, he gives us unpleasant tensions. Our judgment is affected by what he does to us in a pleasant or unpleasant manner. We must remember that when we get angry, we get angry all over—every gland and muscle fitting into the complete picture of anger. There is an increase of glandular secretions and a corresponding tonicity of muscles.

Why do we like comedies? Because they do pleasant things to our muscles—we laugh and are relaxed and refreshed. Most of us do not like to have unpleasant things done to us; hence, we prefer happy endings. Many of us lose sight of the fact that real tragedy, if it accomplishes its purpose, will purify, cleanse, and relax. The tragedy that is so stark that it does nothing but choke us and make us more rigid, we all like to avoid. But no matter what the author's intention or purpose may be—to make his audience laugh or cry—he makes them *do* things, and that *doing* may be called emotion.

Empathy Implies Co-ordination

How do we communicate these tensions to the audience? How do we evoke empathic responses that will create the right emotion? Remember that emotion may be thought of as a general stirring up of bodily activity: we "feel with our viscera, with our vegetative nerves, and with our endocrine glands." Hence, the answer lies in a co-ordinated bodily activity, in an integrated body. You cannot always get the desired response from everyone in the room, because every audience is made up of people with individual differences. To make all of them like you is impossible. Your aim should be to please the majority. However, to stand before an audience with an expressionless face and with hands that are waving and whirling through the air as you say, "Wherefore rejoice?" or "Why stand we here idle?" is not going to bring success; to tense the muscles of the face and then stand inert from the neck down as you say, "Begone, run to your houses," will not make the audience happy; to read Vachel Lindsay's "The Congo" without being stimulated by the rhythmical changes in the poem is to lose a great deal of the meaning expressed by the author. This does not mean that you will have to stamp your feet and beat your hands and sway your body, but it does mean that you will never get the rhythm in your voice without feeling the pulse of rhythm in co-ordinated bodily activity that must be *suggested* to the audience. Rhythm does not exist without co-ordination; hence, co-ordination is not only advisable but positively necessary.

What is involved in this principle of co-ordination? Again, we must talk in terms of muscles and tonicity of muscles. A muscle can do only one thing—contract. Our muscles, of course, are always in a state of contraction, but the degree varies. When there is no contraction, the muscle is dead. This state can be partially attained also by an anesthetic; but complete relaxation comes only when life is gone. The degree of muscle tone or muscle contraction is proportional to the degree of attention of the interpreter. That is, if we are under great excitement, the tonus (partial contraction of the muscles) increases until the muscles become so tense that they may ache, and we may experience great difficulty in relaxing. The more practice we can give muscles in employing different degrees of relaxation, the more pliable they become and the greater the "muscle memory." It is requisite that we have a muscular sense or memory of muscle movement; we cannot fully experience a movement we have never made. This sense of memory can be developed only by practice; after many, many performances, movement will tend to become a reflex activity. Without it, we could not go about our daily tasks of eating, dressing, drinking, with any economy of movement. To make our movements, our bodily tensions, mean the maximum, we must practice, thus building up muscle sense and memory, which, in turn, pave the way for co-ordination and economy of effort.

Co-ordination Implies Total Bodily Response

In order to have a bodily response that is total, you must be emotionally set, and that means muscularly set, to do what you hope to do; just as the track man "gets set" for his race, as the punter poises himself for the punt, as a golfer anticipates a "follow-through," as a horseman gets the feel of his horse, as an actor gets the mood of the character he is portraying. Each performer is getting the machine co-ordinated for a situation that calls for a complete muscular activity, not for some isolated movements which would make him awkward and which would not give the observer the proper empathic response. Inasmuch as the audience assumes some kind of motor response toward the object it is watching, too many unco-ordinated movements on the part of the interpreter are likely to produce restlessness in the audience. An amateur acrobat whose muscles are not steady makes us uneasy, and a dancer whose gasping breath we can hear, makes us gasp; so the interpreter whose hands flabbily gesture from one side to another makes us flop too, and one who fails to grapple adequately with the thought makes us fumble too. We like to do our observing as a whole: hence, the performer, if he is to secure the correct empathic response, must learn to integrate all emotional processes. There must be nothing in the activity of the muscles of any part of the body which will detract from what other muscles are doing. Command the attention of the audience upon yourself as a whole and not as an unco-ordinated collection of parts. If an audience notices that you are waving your hands through the air when you are talking about the "babbling brook" or the "blue clouds overhead," you may be sure that something is wrong with your technique, and that something is usually a lack of co-ordination in addition to poor taste. Any unusual muscular set may reveal an attitude which may distort the meaning you are trying to put over to your audience.

Have you ever realized how many phrases descriptive of bodily responses are used to identify character and attitude? Here are a few:

1. She gave me a cold shoulder.
2. She was stiff-necked about it.
3. He wears his heart on his sleeve.
4. He did a complete about-turn.
5. The teacher was a highbrow.
6. She wore a chip on her shoulder.
7. He was two-faced.
8. She opened her mouth and let her brains fall out.

Can you add others to the list?

Gesture Is Part of Total Bodily Response

Gesture usually means to most people movement of hands and arms, movement outside of our ordinary bodily habits, something to be put on and taken off, to be used here and not there. Let us think, rather, of the whole body working as a rhythmically co-ordinated instrument. This means that every movement must come from within outward as a part of the whole and not as an isolated manifestation. Gesture is movement growing out of total bodily activity and control. As Richard P. Blackmur states: "It is the purposive conventional control of the body's movements that produces meaningful gestures. Or perhaps we should say it is a kind of reduction, condensation, telescoping of free instinctive movements that transforms them into residual gestures."[2]

You are endowed with physical parts which by skillful use can carry meaning to your audience. If you feel that a certain movement is necessary, try it out on the observer in your mirror. If you are not sure, work for a suggested activity either with your facial expression or the rest of your body. If your audience squirms every time you make any kind of movement, you are undoubtedly either overdoing or unco-ordinated. When you work "all in one piece," your action should fit the thought and language; no one but an expert critic will be able to detect your body technique, and everyone will enjoy the added meaning such action contributes to your interpretation. Your objective should be to reveal meaning through movement.

Blackmur analyzes the interweaving or interrelationship of language and gesture as follows:

If there is a puzzle in my title, it is because, like Sweeney with his ladies in Eliot's *Fragment of an Agon,* "I've gotta use words when I talk to you." The puzzle is verbal, something we have made ourselves, and may be solved. Language is made of words, and gesture is made of motion. There is one half the puzzle. The other half is equally self-evident if only because it is an equally familiar part of the baggage of our thought. It is the same statement put the other way round. Words are made of motion, made of action or response, at whatever remove; and gesture is made of language—made of the language beneath or beyond or alongside of the language of words.[3]

Gesture, to him, is meaningful movement inherent in words, giving life to language, which, if the roots are cut, will produce a

[2] *Language As Gesture* (New York, Harcourt, Brace and Company, Inc., 1952), p. 8.
[3] *Ibid.*, p. 3.

rotting if indeed not a petrifying language . . . But gesture is not only native to language, it comes before it in a still richer sense, and must be, as it were, carried into it whenever the context is imaginative. Living in Belmont some ten years ago I used to go into Cambridge on an orange-yellow bus which made very good time the first half of the trip. If anyone were ahead of you getting on, you might jump from ten to twenty to forty or fifty miles an hour by the time you had paid your fare and found your seat. So it was for the woman I remember one very high bright noon. She got on with a friend whom I do not remember at all except that she sat directly behind me and no doubt looked over my shoulder seeing just what I saw. But the woman herself I remember very well. She was largish and of a French figure, that is with a noticeable waist and a more noticeable rear, and she had heels too high for her balance in a spurting bus. There she stood holding the chromium rail back of the driver's seat looking at her friend (and therefore at me) while the driver made her change. She fair yawed to leeward every few yards, each time knocking the great floppy hat, which women of such figure so often wear askew, against the upright post on which the coin box was set. She had much trouble getting the two fares in the box, and considerably more trouble getting herself from the box down the aisle, hauling from seat to seat by their shining handles against the momentum of the bus, lurching, as she had to, in all directions save the right one. During the whole business—and this is what I am getting at—she managed by sniffs and snorts, by smiles, by sticking her tongue out very sharp, by batting her very blue eyes about, and generally by cocking her head this way and that, she managed to express fully, and without a single word either uttered or wanted, the whole mixed, flourishing sense of her disconcertment, her discomfiture, her uncertainty, together with a sense of adventure and of gaiety, all of which she wanted to share with her companion behind me, who took it I was sure, as I did myself, all smiles. Because I was within the orbit of her gestures I felt myself, as I felt her, fairly playing in life as we say that water-lights play in the sun or moon.

That is an example of the gesture that comes before language; but reflecting upon it, it seems also an example of the gesture which when it goes with language crowns it, and so animates it as to make it independent of speaker or writer; reflecting upon it, it seems that the highest use of language cannot be made without incorporating some such quality of gesture within it." [4]

It will be wise for you to remember the following advice:

1. An interpreter suggests rather than imitates activity.
2. An interpreter should avoid mannerisms and random move-

[4] *Ibid.*, pp. 4-6.

ments which will detract from, rather than add to, the meaning.

3. An interpreter can add to the author's meaning by the correct
timing of bodily movement.

Co-ordination Implies Economy of Effort

Wherever there is co-ordination, there is economy of effort, so
essential to smooth performance. Witness musicians, athletes,
actors, jugglers, dancers, and skaters. Our system of muscular
co-ordination is so arranged that with the stimulation of certain
muscles there is always—or should be—a relaxation of opposing
muscles. This rhythmic contraction and relaxation results in
economy of effort and force. The smoothness of the performance
of Lynn Fontanne or of Sonja Henie delights audiences; they
have the control and co-ordination that bring about the economy
of effort that distinguishes the professional from the amateur.

Interpretation usually does not call for broad movements,
excessive head and hand activity, such as Blackmur's friend with
the floppy hat indulged in. But it does call for suggestion, and
suggestion is manifested through bodily movements of a highly
co-ordinated nature. Suggestion calls for a seemingly outward
economy of muscular movement and energy. Note, we say, *seemingly*. In reality, however, every muscle in the body of the skillful
interpreter should be performing its function of tensing and
relaxing to give ease of movement. This principle has been discussed in previous chapters: there must be a selection of the
best to carry the finest impression and to intensify the emotion
we are trying to create, just as in our best etchings, the fewest
lines carry the finest impression. The visual stimulation of an
audience will depend upon the effectiveness of suggested movement.

Economy of effort, however, does not mean an inert attitude,
slumping on the platform, or lack of purpose. The person who
stands still is not particularly interesting; but the person who
stands still with purpose, with meaning, commands attention.
The difficulty with some interpreters is that they merely stand
still. This is the same kind of difference that can be found in the
classroom between the student who listens without hearing and
intention and the student who listens and hears. Any audience

will catalogue your total bodily attitude in the same way. They like to feel that you are sure, that you are not embarrassed by the fact that they are listening to you. That audience feeling and response to you begins as soon as you start to the platform. If you lope to the reading stand, sag at the waist, fumble with your book, clear your throat many times, shuffle your feet, fidget with a gadget, and finally droop over the stand, you can be certain that the majority of your audience will be wishing that you could believe in what you are doing, that you could pretend to be interested in what you are interpreting, or that you could at least be aware of the fact that they are complimenting you by being your listeners. There should be purpose, intention shown by your bodily set and movements—with sincerity of effort without pretense, economy of effort without a limp back and a hunched shoulder. You expect that same kind of poise and assurance when you seek the services of a professional person, like a doctor or a dentist. If you are confronted by a fluttering, evasive person who cannot look you in the eye, who continually shifts his position, who hems and haws, who speaks indefinitely and is not sure of what he is saying, what do you do? Believe in his decisions? Allow him to operate? Agree to have your teeth extracted? Be ready to take gas from hands that are in continual motion? Usually you seek another person—one in whom you can place your confidence, one who has convinced you that he knows what decision to make. Why do you conclude that he is competent? Because of his directness, his movements, his control!

Co-ordination Implies Rhythm

Perfect harmony of muscular response is the aim of the interpreter. There must be no pull in the wrong direction anywhere, if the rhythm of the body is to be pleasing. What is bodily rhythm? Rhythm as shown in bodily movements consists of recurrent contraction and relaxation of muscular movement, not only of large muscle groups but of numerous smaller ones, all of which combine into a larger pattern to provide smooth, co-ordinated muscular action. The rhythmical progression of the muscular movements depends upon the balanced timing and economy of force of the muscular activity. Certainly when we have learned to co-ordinate the timing and the strength of neuro-muscular reactions, we can be assured of an integrated, rhythmical "follow-through" of the muscles.

In other words, we are saying that to do anything well, to create the greatest pleasure for our audience empathically, we must have educated our bodies, our neuromuscular machines, so that they show a pleasing, rhythmical control. You have seen a person walk with perfect freedom of movement—a movement that was lithe and pleasing. Then you have seen another person plod along heavily, straining every part of the body. Each has a rhythm, but one is a rhythm with economy of force and co-ordinated timing; the other is a rhythm with many random and unnecessary movements. In the former, there is rhythm and harmony of every part of the body, which will invigorate rather than weary; in the latter, there is misdirected nervous energy, which will soon tire and wear out the body. It is a pleasure to watch ease of movement, whether in walking, dancing, running, acting, or interpreting, because if it is done well, it has *form*. Nothing gives as much joy to the performer and to the onlooker as this *plus*, this form, because it produces an esthetic reaction, which makes us feel from head to toe that the performance has been done well.

Rhythm—do we all have it? Yes, by all means, we have rhythm of some sort; but in some of us it is latent and undeveloped. For instance, how do you breathe? Deeply and fully, or shallowly and quickly? To master a good rhythmical breathing habit is very difficult for many. Some of us go through life panting and puffing without realizing that with a little practice, we could enjoy an easy, flowing, rhythmical process. Have you ever noticed that when you are listening to a speaker you tend to breathe in rhythm with him? Or that you breathe in rhythm with the steps you are taking, whether you are walking, running, or dancing? If you seem to be doing the task successfully, you will find the rhythm of breathing co-ordinating with the rhythm of the whole body.

And how do you walk? Does each foot carry an even weight; is there a lagging foot rhythm; or is there a mincing, tense step? We do not have to lift one foot higher than the other, and we do not have to swing one foot way over to one side; but if that is the rhythm we have chosen, instead of a free, swinging rhythm that pulses through us with a pleasurable thrill, then, of course, that becomes our walking rhythm.

And how do you dance? Do you dance with the lilt and swing of the waltz rhythm? Or do you dance with a straight up and down movement of a one-step rhythm; or do you merely execute a walk rhythm; or is your rhythm one of those patterns that varies with the mood and the partner; or is it a rhythm that provides an original pattern inspired by the music; or is it a rollicking movement that does double time to any pattern offered? Or can't you dance at all? If not, look to your ability to co-ordinate.

Some of us have a highly developed sense of rhythm; some are rhythmical only in the most ordinary and necessary movements of daily life and, even then, have not mastered those elementary patterns. Very often in the training of the individual, the delight and thrill of feeling the swing of rhythm in walking, talking, running, singing has been neglected. After all, most of our pleasure in anything well done, comes from rhythmical movements. Notice the movements of brushing your teeth, or the swing of your bath towel, or the peculiar rhythmical touch you give to your morning shave.

If rhythm in you is still latent, then you have yet to learn the delight that comes through the mastering of new patterns. The more educated, the more intelligent you are in the arts, then usually the more variety you may have in your enjoyment of rhythm. The difference you feel between classical music and syncopated rhythms lies mostly in your knowledge of, and preference for, more delicate and subtle rhythms. Maybe you are fortunate and can enjoy both types. Of course, many of the modern rhythms are dynamic and powerful. The generation of the nineties adapted themselves to a rhythm typical of the kind of life to which they were accustomed and to the kinds of rhythm which evolved from that life. Their rhythm was slow—a waltz pattern of curves and easy movements. The rhythm of the 1930's, 1940's, and early 1950's was that of angles and straight lines, as shown in the architecture of these years. The return to the quick, vigorous rhythm of the barn dance by young and old fits into our rhythm of living which calls for space, outdoor expansiveness.

If you want the joy of learning new rhythms, begin with tennis, golf, horseback riding, swimming. All these will give you new patterns and teach you new co-ordinations. When you have learned to adjust your body as a co-ordinated rhythmical unit, working with the greatest economy of movement and effort, with the right degree of force and timing to insure "form," then you may be confident that you have an instrument ready to receive impressions and to convert them into expression.

Stage Fright

We have all had the unforgettable experience of stage fright, or audience fright: the voice quivers, the tongue seems glued to the palate, the knees shake, one may even faint. Stage fright is due to fear, which in turn causes undue muscular rigidity without the usual accompanying relaxation. The typical muscular co-ordination of tension and relaxation is absent. With continued tension of certain muscles, there may be a trembling or shaking of the muscles involved. Any kind of movement which will release the rigidity of those muscles will be helpful. It is wise, if you can, to admit your fear as one student did when he began his speech before the class: "I speak to you as a friend today—with the same friendly attitude that my knees have as they say to one another, 'Shake, old pal.'"

These are other hints that may help you:

1. Breathe slowly and deeply before you are called to perform.
2. Get to the platform calmly and without too much haste. If you race to the platform, your breathing will not be controlled, and the general tension of the body will be increased.
3. When you get to the platform, remember that you are master of the situation. You are in the position to impress people, and you probably know more about your interpretation than anyone else in the audience.
4. Allow your audience to settle down after your appearance. While you are gaining control of yourself, they will have a chance to "look you over," to note your grooming and general poise.
5. If your knees begin to shake or your voice begins to quiver, find a reason to pause or to move to another position.
6. Always watch your audience in your introductory remarks. If you look away from them, your stage fright will increase and it will be difficult to turn back to them.

7. *Pretend* (if you feel that you are not adequate) that you are a good interpreter. You have probably spent most of the day pretending to be intelligent or happy or interested; now you can pretend that you are confident.

8. Never be embarrassed by stage fright because everyone has experienced it. You will be a better interpreter for having mastered it.

EXERCISES

I

Your first assignment is to read Edmund Jacobson's book, *You Must Relax*.[5] Another approach to relaxation can be found in David Fink's *Release from Nervous Tension*.[6] You will enjoy his examples whether you read the chapter "Even Dogs Get Neurotic," "And the Body Talks Back," or "Are You Allergic to Some People?" Each of these authors demonstrates a method that is practical. *Learn to relax* before you proceed in this course. You will like it; you can do it; it will be an aid to you as an interpreter.

II

The following exercises are suggested for improving the general rhythm of bodily movement. It is doubtful that you will ever use any of these patterns in this form when interpreting, but they will make you conscious of what your body is capable of doing. Work for co-ordination, economy of effort, and rhythm—the three inseparables.

1. Walk across the stage demonstrating the rhythm:
   Of your own steps.
   Of an old man.
   Of a successful business man on his way to work.
   Of a girl wearing a very stylish costume.
   Of a woman carrying a heavy bag.
   Of a nonchalant, swaggering student.
   Of a model exhibiting costumes.

[5] Edmund Jacobson, *You Must Relax* (New York, McGraw-Hill Book Company, 1942).

[6] David Harold Fink, *Release from Nervous Tension* (New York, Simon and Schuster, Inc., 1943).

Of a prize-fighter.
Of a woman with tight shoes.
Of a heavy man trying to catch a train.

2. Work out a pantomime of an everyday activity which will show rhythm: for instance, brushing the teeth, shoveling coal, raking the grass. Be sure that your movements are rhythmical.

3. Demonstrate the rhythm:
Of hitting a golf ball.
Of throwing a baseball.
Of handling a basketball.
Of wielding a tennis racket.
Of throwing a discus.
Of any game you know.

4. Demonstrate the rhythm of a setting-up exercise.

5. Work out the rhythm of some performer's actions; that is, an entrance, an exit, some peculiar gesture of a juggler, a tight-rope walker, a music teacher, a vaudeville comedian.

6. Pantomime a story. Tell your audience everything by your bodily activity.

7. With a group of five or six students, work out the rhythmical pattern of an ancient ceremonial. Try a simple pattern first, and then build up and add to the first pattern until you have reached a climax.

III

Give the following sentences, first, as an actor; second, as an impersonator; third, as an interpreter.

1. You cur! Strike that little boy again and I'll thrash you on the spot.
2. Look! my lord! It comes!
3. Wait! Look! Oh, oh, how terrible!
4. It is my lady! Oh, it is my love!
5. With him? It is not possible.
6. O that I had wings like a dove!
7. That man virtuous! You might as well preach to me of the virtue of Judas Iscariot!
8. Bah! You are mean and contemptible as a cur.
9. You Heavens, give me patience—patience I need!
You see me here, you gods, a poor old man,
As full of grief as age; wretched in both!
10. To bait fish withal; if it will feed nothing else, it will feed my revenge.
11. Heigho, that was a merry yarn!
12. I have nothing more to say.

IV

Practice for economy of movement and control. Try to arouse empathic responses by creating the mood of the selections.

1

DEEP WET MOSS[7]

Deep wet moss and cool blue shadows
    Beneath a bending fir,
And the purple solitude of mountain,
    When only the dark owls stir—
Oh, there will come a day, a twilight,
    When I shall sink to rest
In deep wet moss and cool blue shadows
    Upon a mountain's breast,
And yield a body torn with passions,
    And bruised with earthly scars,
To the cool oblivion of evening,
    Of solitude and stars.

                      LEW SARETT

2

THE LAST LEAF

I saw him once before,
As he passed by the door,
    And again
The pavement stones resound,
As he totters o'er the ground
    With his cane.

They say that in his prime,
Ere the pruning-knife of Time
    Cut him down,
Not a better man was found
By the Crier on his round
    Through the town.

But now he walks the streets,
And he looks at all he meets
    Sad and wan,

[7] From *Slow Smoke*, p. 73. Copyright, 1925, by Henry Holt and Company, Inc. Reprinted by permission of the publishers.

And he shakes his feeble head
That it seems as if he said,
 "They are gone."

The mossy marbles rest
On the lips that he has prest
 In their bloom,
And the names he loved to hear
Have been carved for many a year
 On the tomb.

My grandmamma has said—
Poor old lady, she is dead,
 Long ago—
That he had a Roman nose
And his cheek was like a rose
 In the snow;

But now his nose is thin,
And it rests upon his chin
 Like a staff,
And a crook is in his back,
And a melancholy crack
 In his laugh.

I know it is a sin
For me to sit and grin
 At him here;
But the old three-cornered hat,
And the breeches, and all that,
 Are so queer!

And if I should live to be
The last leaf upon the tree
 In the spring,
Let them smile, as I do now,
At the old forsaken bough
 Where I cling.

OLIVER WENDELL HOLMES

3

MIA CARLOTTA[8]

Giuseppe, da barber, ees greata for "mash,"
He gotta da bigga, da blacka moustache,
Good clo'es an' good styla an' playnta good cash.

[8] From *Carmina*, p. 21. Copyright, 1906, by Harcourt, Brace and Company. Reprinted by permission of the publishers.

W'enevra Giuseppe ees walk on da street,
Da people dey talka, "how nobby! how neat!
How softa da handa, how smalla da feet."

He raisa hees hat an' he shaka hees curls,
An' smila weeth teetha so shiny like pearls;
O! manny da heart of da seelly young girls
        He gotta.
     Yes, playnta he gotta—
     But notta
     Carlotta!

Giuseppe, da barber, he maka da eye,
An' lika da steam engine puffa an' sigh,
For catcha Carlotta w'en she ees go by.

Carlotta she walka weeth nose in da air,
An' look through Giuseppe weeth far-away stare,
As eef she no see dere ees som'body dere.

Giuseppe, da barber, he gotta da cash,
He gotta da clo'es an' da bigga moustache,
He gotta da seelly young girls for da "mash,"
     But notta—
    You bat my life, notta—
     Carlotta.
     I gotta!

                  T. A. DALY

4

from SONG OF THE OPEN ROAD[9]

Afoot and light-hearted I take to the open road,
Healthy, free, the world before me,
The long brown path before me leading wherever I choose.

Henceforth I ask not good-fortune, I myself am good-fortune,
Henceforth I whimper no more, postpone no more, need nothing,
Done with indoor complaints, libraries, querulous criticisms,
Strong and content I travel the open road.

                  WALT WHITMAN

5

THEY SLEEP SO QUIETLY[10]

They sleep so quietly, those English dead,
In Breton churchyard, when the cold wind sighs
Through the stripped branches, weaving overhead
Fantastic webs against the wintry skies.
They do not heed the hurrying snow that covers
Their unremembered names,—Margaret, and Joan,
Philip and Lucy, long forgotten lovers,—
Where the white silence of the drifts is blown.
But when the hawthorn spills her petals down,
And ranks of jonquils break in shining blooms
As April lingers in the little town,
They will lie dreaming in the ancient tombs
Of Cornwall's cliffs beneath the soft spring rains,
Or foxgloves nodding in the Devon lanes.

Virginia L. Tunstall

6

MOONLIGHT[11]

Say—listen—
If you could only take a bath in moonlight!

Hey! Can't you just see yourself
Take a runnin' dive
Inta a pool o' glowin' blue
Feel it glidin' over you
All aroun' and inta you—

Grab a star—huh?—
Use it for soap;
Beat it up to bubbles
And white sparklin' foam—
Roll and swash—

Gee!

I just like to bet
You could wash your soul clean
In moonlight!

John V. A. Weaver

---

[10] From *The Lyric West* (February, 1924). Reprinted by permission of the publishers.

[11] From *In American*, p. 22. Copyright, 1923, by Alfred A. Knopf, Inc. Reprinted by permission of the publishers.

7

DESERTED[12]

The old house leans upon a tree
    Like some old man upon a staff;
The night wind in its ancient porch
    Sounds like a hollow laugh.

The heaven is wrapped in flying clouds
    As grandeur cloaks itself in gray:
The starlight, flitting in and out,
    Glints like a lanthorn ray.

The dark is full of whispers. Now
    A fox-hound howls; and through the night,
Like some old ghost from out its grave,
    The moon comes, misty white.

                    MADISON CAWEIN

8

TO THE TERRESTRIAL GLOBE
(By a Miserable Wretch)

Roll on, thou ball, roll on!
Through pathless realms of Space
    Roll on!
What though I'm a sorry case?
What though I cannot meet my bills?
What though I suffer toothache's ills?
What though I swallow countless pills?
    Never *you* mind!
    Roll on!

Roll on, thou ball, roll on!
Through seas of inky air
    Roll on!
It's true I've got no shirts to wear;
It's true my butcher's bill is due;
It's true my prospects all look blue—
But don't let that unsettle you!
    Never *you* mind!
    Roll on!

           (*It rolls on.*)
           W. S. GILBERT

[12] From *The Vale of Tempe*. Copyright, 1896, by E. P. Dutton & Company. Reprinted by permission of the publishers.

9

A SAILOR'S LIFE[13]

YANK

This sailor life ain't much to cry about leavin'—just one ship after another, hard work, small pay, and bum grub; and when we git into port, just a drunk endin' up in a fight, and all your money gone, and then the ship away again. Never meetin' no nice people; never gittin' outa sailor-town, hardly, in any port; travelin' all over the world and never seein' none of it; without no one to care whether you're alive or dead. There ain't much in all that that'd make yuh sorry to lose it, Drisc.

EUGENE O'NEILL

10

Note the meaningful movement inherent in this excerpt.

THE MOUNTING[14]

It was the mare. She was not a pretty picture. From her Roman nose to her rising haunches, from her arched spine hidden by the stiff machillas of a Mexican saddle, to her thick, straight, bony legs, there was not a line of equine grace. In her half-blind but wholly vicious white eyes, in her protruding under lip, in her monstrous colour, there was nothing but ugliness and vice.

"Now then," said Staples, "stand cl'ar of her heels, boys, and up with you. Don't miss your first holt of her mane, and mind ye get your off stirrup quick. Ready!"

There was a leap, a scrambling struggle, a bound, a wild retreat of the crowd, a circle of flying hoofs, two springless leaps that jarred the earth, a rapid play and jingle of spurs, a plunge, and then the voice of Dick somewhere in the darkness, "All right!"

"Don't take the lower road back onless you're hard pushed for time! Don't hold her in down hill! We'll be at the ford at five. G'lang! Hoopla! Mula! Go!"

A splash, a spark struck from the ledge in the road, a clatter in the rocky cut beyond, and Dick was gone.

BRET HARTE

---

[13] From *Bound East for Cardiff* in *Plays of Eugene O'Neill* (New York, Horace Liveright, 1926), p. 236.

[14] From "How Santa Claus Came to Simpson's Bar," *Golden Book* (December, 1925), p. 788. Reprinted by permission of the author.

11

In this selection, notice how the sentence structure of the last paragraph helps to point up the Colonel's indignation. What bodily movements would serve most effectively for your interpretation of this passage?

THE COLONEL SPEAKS[15]

We waited for the Colonel. From under our feet suddenly arose a round of scuffling and smothered imprecations. A minute later, Mike, the herculean son of the Justice, appeared in the doorway, bearing a very small man hugged to his breast as a baby hugs a doll.

"Let me down, seh!" shouted the Colonel. Mike set him down, and he marched proudly into the room, and seated himself with dignity and firmness on the extreme edge of a chair.

The Colonel was very small indeed for a man of so much dignity. He could not have been more than five foot one or two; he was slender—but his figure was shapely and supple. He was unquestionably a handsome man, with fine, thin features and an aquiline profile —like a miniature Henry Clay. His hair was snow-white—and though he was small, his carriage was large, and military. There was something military, too, about his attire. He wore a high collar, a long blue frock coat, and tight, light-gray trousers with straps. That is, the coat had once been blue, the trousers once light-gray, but they were now of many tints and tones, and, at that exact moment, they had here and there certain peculiar high lights of whitewash.

The Colonel did not wait to be arraigned. Sweeping his black, piercing eye over our little group, he arraigned us.

"Well, *gentlemen,* I reckon you think you've done a right smart thing, getting the Southern gentleman in a hole? A pro-*dee*-gious fine thing, I reckon, since it's kept you away from chu'ch. Nice Sunday mo'ning to worry a Southern gentleman! Gentleman who's owned a plantation that you could stick this hyeh picayune town into one co'neh of! Owned mo' niggehs than you eveh saw. Robbed of his land and his niggehs by you Yankee gentlemen. Drinks a little wine to make him fo'get what he's suffehed. Gets ovehtaken. Tries to avenge an insult to his honah. Put him in a felon's cell and whitewash his gyarments. And now you come hyeh—you come hyeh—" here his eye fell with deep disapproval upon Winthrop's white flannels—"you come hyeh in youh underclothes, and you want to have him held fo' Special Sessions."

H. C. BUNNER

[15] From "Colonel Brereton's Aunty," *Golden Book* (August, 1926), p. 161. Reprinted by permission of the author.

12

FITZPATRICK'S DEFIANCE[16]

The Rough Red and his crew cut everywhere, anywhere, anyhow. The easiest way was theirs. Small timber they skipped, large timber they sawed high, tops they left rather than trim them into logs. Fitzpatrick would not have the pine "slaughtered."

"Ye'll bend your backs a little, Jimmy Bourke, and cut th' stumps lower to th' ground. There's a bunch of shingles at least in every stump ye've left. And you must saw straighter. And th' contract calls for eight inches and over; mind ye that. Don't go to skippin' th' little ones because they won't scale ye high. 'Tis in the contract so. And I won't have th' tops left. There's many a good log in them, an' ye trim them fair and clean."

"Go to hell, you— Where th' blazes did ye learn so much of loggin'? I log th' way me father logged, an' I'm not to be taught by a high-banker from th' Muskegon!"

Finally in looking over a skidway Rough Red noticed that one log had not been blue penciled across the end. That meant that it had not been scaled; and that meant that he, the Rough Red, would not be paid for his labor in cutting and banking it. At once he began to bellow through the woods.

"Hey! Fitzpatrick! Come here, you blank-blanked-blank of a blank! Come here!"

The scaler swung leisurely down the travoy trail and fronted the other with level eyes.

"Well?"

"Why ain't the log marked?"

"I culled it."

"Ain't it sound and good? Is there a mark on it? A streak of punk or rot? Ain't it good timber? What the hell's th' matter with it? You tried to do me out of that."

"I'll tell you, Jimmy Bourke, th' stick is sound and good, or was before your murderin' crew got hold of it, but if ye'll take a squint at the butt of it, ye'll see that your gang has sawed her on a six-inch slant. They've wasted a good foot of log. I spoke of that afore; an' now I give ye warnin' that I cull every log, big or little, punk or sound, that ain't sawed square and true across th' butt."

"Th' log is sound and good, an' ye'll scale it, or I'll know th' reason why!"

"I will not."

STEWART EDWARD WHITE

[16] From "The Scaler," *Golden Book* (December, 1925), p. 848. Reprinted by permission of the author.

13

THE ADVENTURER RETURNS[17]

ROBERT, *who has had an intense desire to return to the joys of his youth and relinquish marital ties, has just returned to his wife after a tramp "Over the Hills" with* MARTIN, *a friend of earlier days. He has just removed his wet boots.*

HELEN. Here! Drink this.

ROBERT. Eh?

HELEN. Drink this. (*He drinks, recovers some of his brains, and looks at her, glass in hand*)

ROBERT. Hot whiskey! Slippers! (*Tears in his voice*) Don't say you expected me.

HELEN. (*Soothingly*) I thought it possible you might come back. (*Robert drinks some more whiskey, and feels it doing him good. He recovers enough to say judiciously*)

ROBERT. I'm not sure whether I like it or whether I don't like it. I'm glad of the whiskey. But to be expected! (*Plumping down the glass*) How dare you expect me?

HELEN. (*Evasively*) It's *such* a dreadful night—over the hills.

ROBERT. (*With a fearful cry*) The hills! Ugh! Ugh! Ugh! Never mention them to me again.

HELEN. Tell me about it.

ROBERT. Horrible! (*Drinks*) Soaked to the skin in five minutes. Every mile like ten. With a head wind howling past like a fury. (*Drinks*) Now and then I heard noises from Martin. Martin was *singing.* Singing. I had pains in my back, in my legs—all over. At last I stuck—told Martin I wouldn't budge any farther.

HELEN. What did he say?

ROBERT. He stood in the road, dripping wet; and he *laughed.* I left him. (*Drinks*) I left him in the awful rain trying to light his pipe. Helen, take me to bed.

JOHN PALMER

[17] From *Over the Hills* (London, Sidgwick & Jackson, Ltd., 1914), pp. 30-31.

CHAPTER 6

Speech Pattern

Your friends can recognize you over the telephone or "on the air" because your vocal habits form a speech pattern with certain emphases, intonations, and cadences repeated over and over. You have acquired *your* characteristic speech pattern with its peculiar quality and movement because of your experiences, your personality, your environment, and your vocal mechanism. Very seldom, if ever, will two voices show an identical pattern, even if one seeks to imitate the vocal pattern of another. Vocal expression is not so much a matter of whether your voice is slow or fast, high or low, resonant or thin, forceful or weak. Rather, it is a matter of how all these elements blend together to give a total pattern.

These elements of sound found in the production of voice are (1) *quality* or *timbre*, (2) *force* or *volume*, (3) *tempo* or *movement* within and among phrases and sentences, and (4) *pitch* or *inflection* and *key*. The combinations of these elements are infinitely variable. They will be discussed in the following chapters. *Although for our study, each element is considered separately, it must not be thought that each can or should be isolated from the others.*

SPEECH RHYTHM

Personality and Environment

Characteristic of every speech pattern are movement and rhythm, which will show variable combinations of attack and re-

238

lease of sound, rise and fall of inflection, pause and flow of sound. Quality, indirectly, influences speech rhythm. If the voice is richly resonant, the movement probably will not be rapid except when the owner of the voice wishes to employ rapid speech. On the other hand, if the voice is high pitched and nasal, it is likely to speed along because the owner is not taking time to use his vocal mechanism effectively.

Your speech rhythm to a considerable degree is typical of your general bodily rhythm. Precision of bodily movements will usually be accompanied by precision of vocal activity. A tense, quickly moving person often will have a high, tense voice with a fast, staccato rhythm. The movements of an awkward, slow body will be reflected in a halting speech rhythm. The healthy outdoor person has a different speech rhythm from that of an invalid. Those who have mastered the muscular patterns involved in the "follow-through" of a golf club or a tennis racket, or those who have learned control of movements in dancing, swimming, running, and hurdling, should have little difficulty in mastering rhythms of vocal expression. The hypotonic person (one with less than normal tonicity), because of a slowness and retardation of physical movement, will not have the speech pattern of the excitable, high-strung, hypertonic person (one with more than normal tonicity of muscles). The former will usually have a speech rhythm that is slow, with long pauses and little inflection; the latter will have a quick, nervous rhythm, with abrupt pauses and breaks and probably a wide range of pitch.

Your speech pattern is bound to reflect your personality. On hearing it, we decide whether you are in a pleasant, skeptical, gossipy, or harrassed mood. On extended conversation, we interpret what we hear according to the inflections, the rapidity or slowness, the forcefulness or ease of your patterns. We learn to know one another's rhythms; we also learn to know how the other person reacts to questions and problems because of his habitual approach through his bodily set and speech pattern. The brilliant individual who reacts to policies brought up in group meetings by starting his every response with an obsequious, ingratiating, low-pitched, evenly timed "I'm sorry to be so dumb, but I can't quite" *may* think he is subordinating his brilliance to group opinion; but in reality he is merely getting ready to secure a reversal of group opinion. His words may mean one thing, but his repeated speech pattern reveals his feeling of intellectual superiority.

You, the interpreter, will be of different environmental make-up from me, the interpreter. Each of us has lived through different experiences: we have various reading interests; our traveling may have been extensive or limited; our neighbors may have been friendly or aloof; our living abode may have changed every few years or it may have been snugly established in one community. So our likes and dislikes are based on how we have lived, where we have lived, and with whom we have lived. Some of us have creative ability; some know how to provide opportunities for socialization; some have the knack of self-direction and improvement; some are withdrawn from others. Many who read Jan Struther's *Mrs. Miniver* realized with no small shock the regrettable truth of her statement, "It shouldn't have taken a war to talk to our neighbor on the bus, but it did." It is an individual's friendliness, his sense of "amongness" that will provide a personality with "give" and that will be reflected in his speech rhythm. Dividends will be realized by you, the interpreter, as soon as you build a reservoir of experiences. A certain university student, who kept a thumbworn book of favorite poems in his pocket and delighted in reading them to others whenever the chance came, found dividends in this pleasurable habit; it was, in large measure, responsible for his future success. While attending a convention of building contractors, he filled in for the delayed guest speaker by reading some of his "tucked-away-in-the-pocket" poems. The audience response was enthusiastic. Not only was he asked to read more, but he was invited to the home of one of the officials for dinner. There he met, fell in love with, and married the official's daughter. He entered her father's brick concern and eventually became president of the company. In contrast, a coed with a beautiful voice quality but monotonous inflection was urged to be less aloof in class, to use her voice to greater advantage. Upon further counseling, it was found that she had no money, was suffering from malnutrition, and had made no campus friends. Her education was to profit her little so long as she continued to be ill and to feel misunderstood. No amount of work with her voice would have helped her, because the essential of true living—belonging to a group—had never been experienced by her. Her vocal pattern reflected her aloneness, her aloofness.

Locale also plays its part in making speech rhythms distinctive. Different localities have their own provincial cadences. The speech rhythm of the Bostonian is not that of the Kentuckian. The northwest side of Chicago produces cadences found in no other spot in that great city. Some southern Illinoisians show a nasality that is quite different from the tense, twangy nasality of many living in northern Illinois. So, in like manner, each nationality displays its own peculiar speech pattern. The interpreter will find that the study of dialects is mainly a study of speech rhythm, of cadence, of the stressed and unstressed. The Italian has an irresistible lilt, the Russian hurries along with a staccato movement, the Frenchman indulges in an ecstatic upward swing.

Elision in Speech Rhythm

Inability to secure a varied rhythm often occurs because the student has been urged in earlier days to give every syllable equal value in the interest of distinct enunciation. But no sensible or sensitive person talks with all words and syllables evenly spaced, like a typewriter or metronome. If you do speak with evenness of syllables, your speech will be unnatural, indirect, and stilted. Good rhythmical speech is a matter of elision, a matter of subordination and superordination, a series of dots and dashes. Some syllables must be stressed, others must be unstressed. To emphasize everything is to emphasize nothing; and without emphasis, there is little sense—just a string of monotonous individual syllables.

The standards of good speech are based upon conversational speech, which will never sound like a metronome. The complete pronunciation of every syllable happens only in the classroom of a pedantic teacher who feels it her duty to uphold the dignity of her native tongue and thinks that this requires squeezing every atom of pronunciation out of every syllable. Unless you are forced to do so, you will never say:

I—must—down—to—the—seas—a—gain,—to—the—lone—ly—seas
—and—the—sky.

Rather, you will probably elide like this:

I mus'down toth'seasagain, toth'lonely seas'n'th'sky.

One of the rules in rhythmical speech is: make the long sounds long and the short ones short. When you have decided which sounds are to be held, prolong them as much as good communicative sense will permit; and when you have decided to cut others short, cut them to the shortest demands of distinctness.

This matter of elision of the unimportant and insignificant is not at all in conflict with the needs of careful enunciation. In communicative speech, careful enunciation is by no means a matter of tearing every shred of sound out of every syllable. Many words—in speech—are never pronounced as the dictionary would have us pronounce them: such words as *and, in, of, to, be, from, that* (conjunction), *have, as, if, why* (interjection) seldom have complete dictionary pronunciation. More often they sound like *'n', 'n, 'v, tuh, bi, fr'm, th't, 'av, 'z, 'f, wy.*

Variety in Speech Rhythm

The realization that good speech and effective interpretation need a thoroughly varied rhythm from the longest hold that may represent deep feeling or strong emphasis down to the merest click or grunt is most important. Yet this principle must be applied with sense. The foregoing advice applies to a simple conversational situation, where we desire to create an air of directness and naturalness. It also applies to small audiences. But under the stress of deep emotion, before large audiences, and without a public address system, there is often need for careful enunciation of syllables. Absurdity arises when the manner of "greatness" is dragged into a situation calling for simplicity and ease.

No other criticism of your voice will ever aid you as much as your own criticism. Inasmuch as you never hear yourself as others hear you, you must learn to listen objectively to the variety in your speech pattern. How can you accomplish this? The most effective way is by the use of a tape recorder. Such a procedure is extremely valuable for educating your ear to hear your voice as others hear it. Even the most experienced interpreter resorts to "listening" before a performance. But you still will not understand *what* you hear until you know something of the operation of the vocal mechanism; neither will you know how to secure flexibility of vocal tones unless you know what you are trying to *do* with the mechanism you own.

THE VOCAL MECHANISM

The vocal mechanism is best explained with a model of the head and larynx. Unless you have at some time held a larynx—animal or human—in your hand, you will find it difficult to visualize the exact structure of the main mechanism of speech. Let us try however, as others have, to identify the various parts of the vocal mechanism.

Articulatory Structure

Suppose that, with a mirror in your hand, you observe first the visible part of the structure which produces speech. You see first the lips, formed by a circular muscle. Upon opening the lips, you see two rows of teeth: the upper teeth are firmly entrenched in the alveolar, or gum, ridge, which is part of the bony structure called the maxilla; the lower teeth grow out of another bony structure called the mandible. Looking into the mouth, or oral cavity, beyond the teeth, you see a tongue—the only muscular tissue in the body which has only one point of attachment. Consequently, the tongue is capable of great flexibility. If you look upward, you see a dome or roof above the tongue; the forward part of this roof is called the hard palate. In some people the palate is high and vaulted, in others it is very narrow, and in still others it is low and rather flat. If you allow your tongue to start at the alveolar ridge and move backward along the hard palate, it soon finds a portion of the palate that is no longer hard and bony but soft and flexible; this is the soft palate, or velum. Taking your mirror again and looking at this soft palate, you will observe that it seems to terminate in two archways called the palatine arches; these are separated in the center by pendulous tissue called the uvula, which is sometimes very short, and sometimes very long. Most of the time, the uvula extends downward, as it hangs relaxed, about halfway to the tongue. These arches, which are similar to a proscenium arch, form the entrance to the pharynx, which is the irregular longitudinal cavity that extends from the posterior opening of the nasal cavity down back of the oral cavity to the esophagus. If you touch the soft palate with a tongue depressor, you will notice that the uvula tenses and moves backward and upward with the soft palate. You will also note that there is a movement forward in the wall beyond the archway. This is the pharyngeal wall, or the cyclorama, made up of constrictor muscles which, by their contraction, move forward slightly to close partially the passageway into the nasal cavity; they also aid in closing off the cavity that leads to the esophagus and trachea, in case a foreign body enters the mouth or nose. When you drink from a fountain, for instance, the soft palate moves upward and the pharyngeal wall moves forward to close off the nasal cavity; otherwise, the water would come out the nasal cavity. When you gargle, you contract the pharyngeal muscles to aid in closing off the passageway below.

Vegetative Function of Articulators

These structures just mentioned—teeth, lips, tongue, mandible, maxilla, palates—are the *articulators*, which, by their co-ordinated movements and articulation, form the sounds of our language. Primarily, all of these structures have a vegetative function. The lips are used for sucking. The teeth, mandible, and maxilla are mainly the chewing equipment. The tongue swirls the bolus of food from one side to the other side of the mouth, and finally flips it through the archway and down the pharyngeal passageway to the esophagus, thus aiding in chewing and swallowing, as well as in sucking. The hard palate, which separates the nasal cavity from the oral cavity, acts as a wall against which food may be pushed and pressed without allowing it to get into the nasal cavity, and is also vital in the sucking process. The soft palate by its contractibility keeps foreign objects out of the nasal cavity. These vegetative activities—chewing, sucking, and swallowing—are the most primitive of all our activities and are necessary for survival. Some speech authorities call the speech activity for which you use the lips, teeth, tongue, palates, and jaws, an "overlaid function," meaning that man has been able to find speech functions in addition to the vegetative functions for these structures. For the purpose of interpretation, however, we shall call them the articulators. You use them to be articulate, and you articulate distinctly when there is a quick shift from one muscle movement to another. Finally, note before you leave these visible structures that nature has given you two entrances and two exits for the passageway of air: the nasal cavity and the oral cavity.

Phonatory Structure

Now let us pretend that you can see what you really cannot see unless you have a laryngeal mirror. Following the pharyngeal wall downward in the back of the throat, you will eventually find the entrance to the esophagus, a collapsible tube through which food moves to the stomach. Now following the *tongue* downward, you will find that it is attached to a small horseshoe-shaped bone, called the hyoid bone, the only bone in the body not attached to the skeletal frame. From this bone is suspended the larynx, the sound-production room where phonation originates. At its entrance is a muscular tonguelike fold called the epiglottis. The vegetative use of the larynx is not to produce sound but to act as a valve in order that pressure can be created for such acts as lifting, childbirth, and defecation. The larynx becomes a valve when two sets of folds close off the trachea (which is a continuation of the larynx) and consequently dam up the air stream below the folds.

The folds closest to the epiglottis are known as the false vocal folds. Just below this pair are the true vocal folds, extending (remember, we are looking down the throat) across the passageway in the form of an inverted V, as ∧. The space between the true vocal folds is called the glottis. The apex of the inverted V folds is just behind the Adam's apple. If you will put your fingers on the Adam's apple, you can feel one of the most important cartilages of the larynx, the thyroid cartilage, which, shaped like a shield, acts as a shield to the vocal folds. The thyroid cartilage articulates on the cricoid cartilage, which is shaped like a signet ring—the signet portion forming the back of the larynx. Mounted

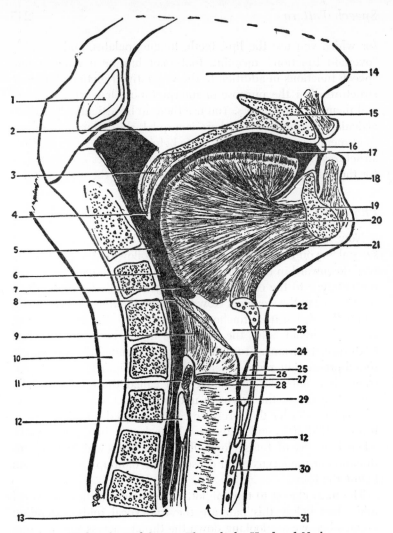

Median Sagittal Section Through the Head and Neck

1. Sphenoidal sinus; 2. hard palate; 3. soft palate; 4. uvula; 5. superior pharyngeal constrictor; 6. middle pharyngeal constrictor; 7. vallecula; 8. epiglottis; 9. aditus laryngis; 10. vertebral canal; 11. arytenoidei; 12. cricoid cartilage; 13. esophagus; 14. nasal cavity; 15. maxilla; 16. teeth; 17. oral cavity; 18. lip; 19. mandible; 20. genioglossus; 21. geniohyoid; 22. hyoid bone; 23. adipose tissue; 24. hyperglottal cavity; 25. thyroid cartilage; 26. superior ventricular folds; 27. glottis; 28. vocal folds; 29. hypoglottal cavity; 30. tracheal cartilages; 31. trachea.

on the top of the signet-ring formation are two arytenoid cartilages, not unlike dwarfed sentries keeping guard over the sound-production equipment, the vocal folds. Their main action is thought to be a lateral rotating movement, important in causing tension and relaxation of the folds. Each vocal fold has a point of attachment in one of the arytenoid cartilages; and the two folds join, forming an acute angle, at the inner front of the thyroid prominence, or Adam's apple. If you had two reins attached to the center of a horse's head (thyroid cartilage) and, while sitting on the horse, you held one rein in each hand (arytenoid cartilage), you would have a similar formation. Suppose your hands are the arytenoid cartilages and are capable of being rotated laterally by the tension and relaxation of certain muscles. Try rotating your hands from one side to the other, inward and outward. What happens? The reins come together and then open. The principle is the same for the opening and closing of the glottis, the rotation of the arytenoid cartilages being effected by intricate actions of the intrinsic muscles of the larynx. There are also extrinsic muscles of the larynx and of the throat which can change the "up and down" position of the larynx and can also cause hypertension of the vocal folds. If you put your fingers on your Adam's apple, and sound a tone, you will feel the movement of the muscles surrounding the larynx. If you make the tone harsh, nasal and tense, the Adam's apple usually is pulled up almost to the hyoid bone.

When you breathe, the vocal folds are more relaxed than when you speak; consequently, there is a gentle opening and closing of the glottis. Whenever speech occurs, the vocal folds, by means of the rotation of the arytenoid cartilages, close or approximate; the air, forced up from the lungs, causes vibration of the approximated edges, thus setting the air stream into vibration and producing sound.

Breathing Structure

But we cannot talk about breathing, which provides for a balance of oxygen and carbon dioxide, until we examine that part of the mechanism which provides the power for vocal action. You know that breathing is essential to life, that inhalation and exhalation occur because of the necessity for the exchange of oxygen and carbon dioxide in the lungs. Speech again adapts this mechanism, which has a vegetative function, for its own purposes.

In most books, breathing is explained first in the study of the production of the voice because it is the initiating process of speech production, the powerhouse from which energy is supplied. Since we are proceeding from the visible to the invisible in our discussion, the power apparatus on the ground floor comes last. Below the vocal folds, the trachea or windpipe, held open by rings of cartilage to facilitate inhalation and exhalation, extends downward. This circular tube soon branches into two bronchi, air passageways, which go to the right and to the left. These bronchi, in turn, branch into many bronchioli, which terminate in small air sacs called alveoli. The air sacs are lodged in the two large masses of spongy tissue called the lungs, which, with the heart, fill the thoracic cavity (chest). The left lung has only two lobes and is not quite as large as the right (which has three), thus making room for the heart. The thoracic cavity, which contains the suspended lungs, is enclosed by the sternum (breastbone), the ribs, and the spinal column (backbone). The lungs are passive and are acted upon by muscles for the exchange of oxygen and carbon dioxide.

Breathing Process

Breathing is a process made possible by the creation of a potential vacuum in the thoracic cavity by the action of certain muscles. This action is caused by nerve impulses originating in the respiratory center, the medulla, at the base of the brain. When there is too much carbon dioxide in the blood stream and a need for oxygen, nerve impulses are conducted to the muscles involved in respiration, thus causing the necessary contraction and relaxation. One of the principal activating muscles is the diaphragm, which lies transversely of the torso, separating the lungs and heart from the abdominal viscera, which include the stomach, liver, and intestines; it is attached to the sternum, ribs, and spinal column.

In inhalation, the diaphragm contracts, thereby pushing downward, causing a potential vacuum in the thoracic cavity, which, in turn, permits an inrush of air to the lungs, through the mouth or nose, down the pharynx, through the glottis, down the trachea, to the bronchi, and, thence, to the air sacs. In exhalation, the diaphragm relaxes to its normal position, arching upward, and thus expelling, by its action, the air from the lungs through the bronchioli, the bronchi, the larynx, the pharynx, and the nasal or oral cavity. There is always some air left in the lungs, called residual air. Some people acquire poor speech habits by trying to talk on residual air.

The external intercostal muscles, attached to the ribs, also help to increase the size of the thoracic cavity by their action. During inhalation, they pull the ribs upward and outward. During exhalation, the size of the thoracic cavity is reduced by the action of the internal intercostal muscles which pull the ribs downward and inward.

Finally, there is another group of muscles, the abdominal muscles, which aid particularly in exhalation, by causing a downward pull of the lower ribs and by pushing the abdominal viscera against the diaphragm. This action causes a relaxation of the diaphragm and exhalation occurs. Inasmuch as speech occurs during exhalation, the action and control of the abdominal muscles is important for active, vigorous, and continuous speech.

You will understand better what happens if you stand erect and place your fingers on the abdominal muscles just below the waistline. As you inhale deeply, keeping your shoulders quiet, you will feel a distention of the abdominal wall, indicating the expansion that occurs during inhalation. Note how your fingers are pushed outward. Now as you exhale, observe how the abdominal muscles recede to their original position. If you expel a vigorous "ho" on exhalation, you will feel the sudden inward direction of the muscles. Try laughing to get the feel of the muscles. Now put your hands on each side of the waistline and inhale. Note the expansion. Extend your hands farther backward and feel what happens. Although speech authorities do not endorse this type of breathing as the only acceptable kind, it is true that one can exercise more power and more control by using these muscles than by using the thoracic muscles alone. The important factor in speech is not how much breath you can take in, but how you control the outgoing air stream for the purpose of sustaining tone for speech.

In involuntary breathing, the diaphragm, by its relaxation and contraction, maintains a balance between the oxygen and carbon dioxide supply because of the nerve impulses from the respiratory center. The rate of this normal breathing process, upon which will depend the shallowness or the deepness of the breathing, can be increased or decreased by age, by physical vitality, by a sudden stimulus, and by an emotional disturbance. When you are "out of breath," your blood needs more oxygen. When you are suffering from stage fright, you have difficulty in breathing because of the tension of the muscles; so you learn to breathe deeply to secure relaxation. However, it should be mentioned that breathing too deeply for a continuous length of time as in vocal exercises may give you an oversupply of oxygen, causing dizziness.

During speaking or singing, the whole process of respiration is vigorous and must be controlled rhythmically. In exhalation, for instance, the expelled breath is not permitted to ease out as it does in normal exhalation, but is held back and controlled for speaking purposes. This controlling of the breath stream is as important for the interpreter as it is for the singer, the swimmer, the runner, or the skater. Each has his own technique. The necessary controls for the interpreter are:

1. Learn to use the outgoing air stream so that there is an adequate supply of residual air.
2. Learn to control breathing so that the listener is never conscious of lack of breath or of forced breath.
3. Learn to control breathing so that when you wish to project tones, the power comes from the abdominal muscles.

Resonating Structure

There is another factor to be considered in the production of speech, besides breathing, phonation, and articulation, and that is resonance. When we speak of resonance, we are concerned with: (1) the amplification of the vibrating air stream as it strikes various sounding boards, such as bones, palates, teeth, and other hard substances; and (2) the amplification of the vibrating air stream as it is reinforced when brought into contact with the air masses in the resonance cavities of the vocal mechanism, as the oral, pharyngeal, laryngeal, and nasal cavities. In voices that are pleasing to the ear, a balance of resonance has been established among the various resonators. Too often there is a noticeable imbalance, such as too little or too much nasal resonance. Voices are not alike in resonance, principally because of the size, shape, and nature of the amplifiers, whether they are cavities or hard substances. Presence or absence of bones, obstructions in the nose, high palates, low palates, free jaws, tense jaws, many teeth, few teeth, false teeth, flabby muscles, hard muscles—all these will produce varying degrees of reinforcement and amplification. The wail of a newborn child has little resonance: the bone structures are still soft, there are no teeth, the cavities of the nose and mouth and pharynx are still very small and not too flexible, and all surrounding tissue is soft. But as the weeks pass, the wail develops into a lusty howl.

Practice can improve resonance, but it can never make two voices alike, because of the differences in vocal structures. Your vocal mechanism is peculiar to you. This is also true of various musical instruments. For instance, the violin is valuable because of its tone; the peculiar quality of its tone is produced by certain kinds of woods that have been fashioned in various ways; thus every violin has different possibilities for richness of tone. The vibrant tones that are produced, however, depend finally on the ability of the artist who must know his instrument.

Having examined the structures that operate in speech, we can now understand that speech depends for its successful production and articulation on the following mechanisms:

1. *The Motor:* air expelled from the lungs by thoracic and abdominal muscles furnishes the power for speech.
2. *The Vibrators:* the air stream, set into vibration by the vocal folds in the larnyx—the sound-production room—causes phonation.
3. *The Articulators:* the vibrated air stream is then articulated into various sounds by the teeth, lips, tongue, palates.
4. *The Resonators:* the vibrated air stream is reinforced and amplified by hard substances, such as the palates, teeth, bones, and by certain resonating cavities, such as the oral, nasal, pharyngeal and laryngeal cavities.

We can also understand that much is to be gained in knowing how to use this apparatus efficiently and with ease in order to secure variety in speech pattern. That understanding involves, as we have said earlier, knowing how to secure an appropriate balance of vocal quality, force, tempo, and pitch to fit the meaning intended by the author.

CHAPTER 7

Vocal Quality

Quality is a term used to describe the timbre, or "ring," of the voice, which is dependent on: (1) initial complex tones produced by the vibrating mechanism, (2) the shape and size of the vocal resonators which add resonant power, or "color," to the tones, and (3) on the vitality and emotional reactions of the speaker.

THE COMPLEX TONE

The quality of a voice originates in a composite of tones produced by the vibrating part of the vocal mechanism, that is, the vocal cords housed in the larynx. As in the piano, the cello, the violin, and the wind instruments, vibrators move not only in whole units but in segments, the vibrations of these parts blending in (not always harmoniously) with the vibrations of the whole units. The tone resulting from the vibrating whole is called the *fundamental,* the low frequency tone which is most prominent in the voice of the individual, and the one most easily heard and recognized. The tones coming from the vibrations of the segments are known as *overtones.* The blending of the fundamental and the overtones produces the complex tone you hear in the vowel *o.* If the overtones are effectively reinforced by nicely balanced resonance and harmoniously related to the fundamental tone, the vocal quality is said to have depth, fullness, and richness.

253

RESONANCE

Differences in the number and relative strength of the overtones account for the main differences in the quality of voices. This differential amplification through the action of the various resonators gives character or timbre to the voice. As stated in a previous chapter, this amplification will depend on the management of the vibrating mechanism, the shape, size, flexibility, and surfaces (hard and soft) of the cavities which serve as resonators. Most important in resonating the vowels is the shaping of the oral, pharyngeal, and laryngeal cavities. The oral cavity, which is the most variable in making these changes, is shaped by the movement of the lips, the mandible (lower jaw), the tongue, the teeth, and the soft palate. If you would have better than average oral resonance, you must learn to keep these parts free of unnecessary tensions. The person who speaks with immobile lips, tense jaw, and set teeth can expect his voice quality to be unpleasant. Try to sound the vowel *a* as in *father* with the corners of the mouth pulled back: the vowel has changed from its characteristic quality when the lips and mandible are free. Now try *e* as in *feet* with the articulators in their normal position; then try it with the lips pursed. You will notice how the resonance changes as the shape of the cavity changes, because the frequencies of the vibrated tone have been picked up and reinforced in varying degrees by the air in these cavities. You must be reminded again that not only the shape of the resonator but the tension of the muscles and the hard and soft surfaces involved must also be considered in securing your best quality.

The pharyngeal cavity is a most important resonating chamber, extending from the posterior opening of the nasal and mouth cavity to the opening into the laryngeal passage. You will recall this tubelike cavity with sphincteric muscles lining its back wall (see diagram, p. 246). These muscles make this passageway extremely flexible and adaptable as a resonator of the tones which emerge from the larynx. Improper tension, however, will quickly affect these sphincteric muscles, so that the voice will become strained, harsh, or nasal.

Wrong tensions in laryngeal muscles will also produce an unpleasant strained quality, which, if it is continued, can irritate the vocal cords, causing small growths called *nodes* to appear on their vibrating edges. The quality may then become breathy, hoarse, or husky.

Nasal Resonance and Nasality

Vocal quality that is properly or pleasingly resonant must have an appropriate *balance* of pharyngeal, oral, laryngeal, and nasal resonance. The nasal cavity as a resonator causes more difficulty than any of the other cavities. The nasal sounds, which are called continuants, *m, n, ng*, properly are resonated in the nasal cavity. If any obstruction such as excessive adenoidal tissue, interferes with the passage of the air through the nasal cavity, the voice will lack some of the resonance appropriate to these sounds. Consequently the nasals will sound suppressed and, in severe cases, *b* will be substituted for *m, d* for *n*, and *g* for *ng*. So a sentence like "Spring has come" will sound more like "Sprig has cub." This kind of quality is called denasalized speech or negative nasality.

Another kind of nasality, certainly more elusive in origin, is characterized by "nasalization" of the vowels, or an overabundance of nasal resonance on non-nasal sounds, and is called positive nasality. Some persons, either because of poor speaking habits or interfering emotional tensions, use this improper nasal resonance on vowels. You can very easily nasalize the vowels by tensing the jaw, humping up the back of the tongue, or by tensing the pharyngeal muscles too much. Whenever there is an overbalance of this nasal quality, the voice is likely to prove unpleasant to the listener.

In addition to these two types of nasality, there is a quality often referred to as "nasal twang." When it is present, it pervades the speech pattern; it seems to be ever present. The cause of it appears to originate below the pharynx—in fact, in the larynx. If one tries to imitate the "nasal twang," one feels a constriction of the muscles surrounding the larynx and one suspects that the intrinsic muscles of the larynx have likewise been tensed. You can hear this quality in certain parts of the South; you can hear it in New England but with different intonations; and you can hear it among people living under the tension and noise of a large city. Some radio artists cultivate it for the portrayal of their dramatic characters.

Strangely enough, the "nasal twang," considered unacceptable in the voice brings approbation when it comes from a dance orchestra. The whine, the rasp, or the twangy quality from one or more trumpets, when the vents are muted by means of tin cans, helmets, or bottles, is peculiarly exciting and irresistible to those who are dancing, probably because the penetrating quality is so blatant and harsh that it calls for a release from the tensions which it induces.

Importance of Nasal Resonance

It must not be thought that the nasal cavity is not to be used in the production of vowels; good vocal quality always has an appropriate element of nasal resonance. There are times when it will be necessary for the interpreter, in order to transmit the author's meaning with his fullest vocal power, to add nasal resonance by the partial emission of the vibrated air stream through the nostrils. Care must be taken, however, not to have a *predominance* of nasal resonance so that there is a continual hum to the voice.

VITALITY AND EMOTION

Another factor which influences the quality of voice is the physical and emotional vitality of the individual. The quality of your voice tells much of how you think, how you live, and what kind of people your associates are. You acquire bodily tensions, attitudes, which are reflected in your voice. This character factor in vocal quality is utilized in radio programs. Think over your favorite radio actors. Each one uses a quality adapted to his particular radio personality—the one which is indicative of the principal bodily set or attitude of that character. You have heard many different kinds of quality: the infantile, the abused, the disgruntled, the shy, the petulant, the whining, the naïve, the saccharine, the hushed, and the boisterous. The quality is usually dependent on the type of character to be presented and on the purpose of the program, whether it is entertainment, narration, or information.

The flexibility and co-ordination of the muscles of the articulators are as important in producing good vocal quality as they are in the articulation of sounds. The strong amplification of overtones is not heard usually in the voice of a person too indifferent or too weak or too lazy to adjust his resonating cavities properly or by a person whose muscles are so rigid or so weak that he cannot secure the flexibility necessary for the production of a resonant tone. Good tones do not emerge from between closed teeth or lips, or rigid jaws, or too weak or too tense palatal and pharyngeal muscles, or a tongue that does not conform in shape or motility to its oral surroundings. Weakness in muscle tone will tend to give the voice a colorless quality; too much tension, on the other hand, may produce harsh, strident, or metallic tones.

The vitality of a person is sometimes reflected in the sustaining of an appropriate quality. The problem here is mainly one of lack of power in controlling the breath stream. If the breathing habits of the interpreter are such that he cannot sustain the power necessary to produce the desired quality, then he will tend to speak on residual air at the ends of sentences and paragraphs. His quality then will become breathy or aspirate. Proper phrasing and more attention to good breathing habits will help him to sustain his tones.

IMPROVEMENT IN QUALITY

To the interpreter, vocal quality is the primary ingredient of intelligent and pleasant vocal expression. To the layman, quality is either pleasant or unpleasant. If it is unpleasant, he will describe the voice as harsh, breathy, husky, hoarse, nasal, or colorless. There is no doubt that most people find it quite simple to produce unpleasant tones but are not so sure about how to make their voices more pleasant. We are assuming that every interpreter is anxious to be able to use varied combinations and blends of the fundamental and its overtones. The interpreter with trained and versatile quality can make literature overpoweringly beautiful, but the interpreter who lacks a harmonious balance of resonance can ruin the best literature ever written.

To improve your appreciation of good quality, learn to listen. The radio, television, and recording performances of poets and actors offer excellent opportunities to evaluate vocal quality. A listening project will pay dividends to you, the interpreter, as well as provide most pleasant entertainment. Here are a few recordings with which you should become familiar.

1. *Pleasure Dome* (Columbia, MM-877 or ML-4259), contains readings by Dylan Thomas, Cornelia Otis Skinner, Marianne Moore, and Ogden Nash.

2. *Contemporary Poets Series* (Columbia, D9-CB), sponsored by the National Council of Teachers of English, includes the interpretations of Vachel Lindsay, E. E. Cummings, and Stephen Vincent Benét.

3. *The Voice of Poetry* (Columbia, MM-375), sponsored by the National Council of Teachers of English, features the voice of Edith Evans.

4. *Don Juan in Hell* (Columbia, SL-166), an excerpt from Bernard Shaw's *Man and Superman,* is recorded by the First Drama Quartet, with Charles Laughton, Charles Boyer, Agnes Moorehead, and Cedric Hardwicke.

5. *An Evening with Will Shakespeare* (Theatre Masterworks, LP), features Faye Emerson, Eva Le Gallienne, and Claude Rains, under the direction of Margaret Webster, and includes scenes from *The Merchant of Venice, Henry V, The Tempest, Twelfth Night, Richard II,* and *Macbeth.*

6. *John Brown's Body* (Columbia, 5SL-181), records Stephen Vincent Benét's poem, with Tyrone Power, Judith Anderson, Raymond Massey, and Richard White under the direction of Charles Laughton.

7. *The Importance of Being Earnest* (Columbia, TMW-LP-3; Angel Records, 3504-B or T345040/41). The Columbia recording features Maurice Evans and Lucille Watson. The Angel recording, which should be listened to for comparative purposes, features John Gielgud, Edith Evans, Pamela Brown, and Celia Johnson.

8. *Masterpieces of Literature: Great Themes in Poetry* (Columbia, E11-10), sponsored by the National Council of Teachers of English, records the poetry interpretations of Basil Rathbone.

9. *Contemporary Poets Series* (Columbia, D9-CB), sponsored by the National Council of Teachers of English, features

Stephen Vincent Benét reading "Portrait of a Southern Lady" from *John Brown's Body.*

10. *Contemporary Poets Series* (Columbia, 11-A-D), sponsored by the National Council of Teachers of English, features Robert Frost reading his own verse.

11. *Lew Sarett: Reading from His Collected Poems* (Columbia, XTV-15494, 15495), records Sarett's interpretation of his own poetry.

12. *Masterpieces of Literature: The Appreciation of Poetry* (Columbia, E-5-8), sponsored by the National Council of Teachers of English, contains interpretations by Norman Corwin.

Play the recordings while you are comfortably relaxed. Listen first to the voice of the interpreter, and then play the recording a second time, listening more intently to the meaning. If you have time—and you should have—for a third recording, you can begin to listen for techniques employed by the interpreters. As members of a class in interpretation you may agree on the best vocal quality, but you may have differences of opinion concerning the relative effectiveness of the voices in carrying the meaning of the selection.

LISTENING PROJECTS

Train yourself to listen objectively to the recorded voices. Some of these selections will be evaluated further in later chapters. Two of the above-mentioned recordings, *Don Juan in Hell* and *An Evening with Will Shakespeare,* are probably the beginning of a movement to develop good listening entertainment for people who enjoy literature. For the time being, however, listen for the vocal quality insofar as it is adapted to the literature.

I

Let's select a few voices from these suggested recordings for comment:[1]

1. Dylan Thomas, who has been called the "dramatic reader without peer," has an unusually rich vocal quality that never sounds artificial or exaggerated. The warmth of his quality affects us pleasantly,

---

[1] The pages cited within parentheses correspond to those in this book on which the selections under discussion may be found.

relaxes us, makes us wish for more, and gives a sincerity of interpretation rather than a studied approach.

2. Cornelia Otis Skinner, whose sensitivity to human foibles is recorded also in her many books, has a good quality for literature that is not too solemn or too heavy. Such poetry as "Why So Pale and Wan" (p. 313), "Meeting at Night" (p. 388), and "The Musical Instrument" (p. 29), are executed effectively because of the flexibility of her vocal quality. She also has managed an appropriately awesome quality for Blake's "Tiger, Tiger" (p. 312), but, on the other hand, does not produce the resonant vowels that would give tone color to poems like Masefield's "Sea Fever" (p. 410), Brooke's "The Soldier," Tennyson's "Crossing the Bar" (p. 79), or Milton's sonnet "On His Blindness" (p. 80). This lack may be due to her own inimitable approach in writing and in interpretation, which always prepares the reader or listener for a light, humorous touch, a sophisticated manner, a quick, forceful rhythm.

3. Lew Sarett should be listened to for the depth and emotional quality of his interpretations. His "Four Little Foxes" (p. 305) has a reputation of more reprintings than any other contemporary poem, especially for use in the grade schools. His explanatory introduction to this poem, as well as to all of his poems, cues you to the mood: it was a raw, wet cold day in the Rocky Mountains when Sarett found the four motherless fox pups. In telling the story, Sarett demonstrates his typical fine control of vocal quality. Here it is admirably adapted to the tenderness and gentleness of the poem.

Again, in his interpretation of the poem "Wéeng" (p. 309), you will hear vocal quality that varies from a full but subdued resonant tone to one that becomes softer and softer until it dies away, but not without every word, every phrase, every pause being perfectly timed to the lullaby rhythm. This interpretation is an example of the sustaining of tones and mood through masterful control.

If a poem calls for a full range in quality, Sarett is equal to the occasion and suggests vividly the beat of the drums and the strange cries of approval and exultation in his poem "Thunderdrums: A War-Dance" (p. 306). This quality is different in its overtones from those which convey the solicitous mood in "Toby Goes to Market" (p. 452) or the relaxation and repose that is so effectively interpreted in "Deep Wet Moss" (p. 229). Needless to say, there is a combination of factors which blends with the vocal quality, but, basically, the meaning is carried through the richness of his tonal quality.

4. You will find Basil Rathbone's voice outstanding for its resonance and fine quality, which give sincerity and meaning to literature. There is no aloofness, no artificiality, no stiltedness, no histrionics. There is, rather, a personal note which gives one the impression that Rathbone enjoys whatever he is interpreting. Furthermore, there is variety in quality which is determined by his approach to each poem.

You will want to listen to the straightforward, direct assurance, instead of the bombast usually heard, of Henley's "Invictus" (p. 22); the deep sincerity and feeling of Elizabeth Barrett Browning's "How Do I Love Thee" (p. 311); the lightness of the tonal quality he uses for Herrick's "Gather Ye Rosebuds While Ye May"; the quick, clipped vocal attack of Browning's "Prospice" (p. 58). Certainly Rathbone's vigorous delivery of the latter poem is the kind of interpretation one imagines Browning himself might have given.

5. In contrast to Rathbone's personal approach is Vachel Lindsay's impersonal singing chant, which is achieved by stressing tonal values of words and by pitching the voice in a high monotone with occasional drops to a lower key. Nevertheless, Lindsay brings spirit and buoyancy to his interpretation, and his unique rhythmical patterns should not be overlooked.

6. Another poet who gives an impression of impersonal detachment is Stephen Vincent Benét in his interpretation of "Portrait of a Southern Lady." Although his poetry is stimulating and versatile, his interpretation lacks emotional meaning. Note that his vocal quality is not the vibrant, rich quality attained by Basil Rathbone or Lew Sarett; instead, it shows an overbalance of nasality, with insufficient oral and pharyngeal resonance.

7. The quality of Edith Evans's voice is unusually good and variable. A comparison of her excellent interpretation of Blake's "Tiger, Tiger" (p. 312) with that of Cornelia Otis Skinner is rewarding. Do you think that Skinner creates as much awe as Evans? Is Evans' interpretation too mystical? Do you think one vocal quality is more appropriate than the other? Which one stirs up the most meaning for you?

There is versatility in Evans's voice which you should not overlook. Listen to the differences in her readings of Lewis Carroll's "Father William" (p. 395), Byron's "She Walks in Beauty" (p. 51), Tennyson's "Sweet and Low" (p. 550), and Johnson's "To Celia." Notice the rolling cadences of the lullaby, "Sweet and Low" as compared with the clipped abruptness of "Father William." Listen, too, for the word values and the generally well-sustained tones. There are times when the voice is not sustained. Notice her habit of letting words die out at the end of a phrase.

8. In contrast to Edith Evans, study Robert Frost's readings of his own poetry. His vocal interpretation is like the quality of his verse: unassuming, forthright, and characterized by a kind of homespun simplicity. It has the reminiscent directness of a narrative—of telling a story—not to a group but to one person. There is none of the studied interpretation of Evans; there is no superficiality, no overdoing. In fact, there are times when the listener wishes that Frost would use pauses and changes in emphasis and key. But this is Frost, the poet and the man, reading his own poetry! You can hear him

interpret "Mending Wall" (p. 463), "After Apple Picking" (p. 275), "Birches" (p. 317), "The Runaway" (p. 454), "The Road Not Taken" (p. 68), "Stopping by a Woods on a Snowy Evening" (p. 419), and "Death of the Hired Man" (p. 336). If you have access to a recording of Norman Corwin's interpretation of "The Runaway," compare it with Frost's sensitive appreciation of the same poem.

The recorded interpretations we have listed are only a few of the many that are available. You should be just as interested in listening to these interpretations as the musician is in listening to various musical renditions. Evaluation of what you hear will fill in your background for understanding techniques in handling the voice with all its variables.

II

Columbia's *Don Juan in Hell* provides an excellent lesson in discrimination of voices. There is much to study and enjoy in the patterns and melody of the recorded voices, but the quality of each overwhelms the listener with its flexibility, resonance, and tone color. More than that, one is conscious after several moments of listening that a counterpoint of vocal melodies has skillfully been arranged, sometimes with one melody overlapping another, sometimes with a vocal pattern rising in crescendo to be picked up by another vocal theme which will mount to a climax, only to be softened by another melody. You may not *hear* this counterpoint of vocal melodies at first, but you will be enchanted by the play of vocal quality once you become familiar with the lines and can blot out the fascination of Shaw's verbal dexterity. Jacques Barzun, in the "Notes" that accompany the recording, writes aptly of this contrapuntal arrangement:[2]

What Shaw does is to compose with words and ideas a quartet in one great movement, or perhaps a fugue for four voices. It would be going beyond the facet to say that the piece was consciously written in musical form, but it is undoubtedly oratorical (which is why it holds an audience so easily), and musical forms are patterned on the

[2] Copyright, 1952, by Jacques Barzun. Reprinted by permission of the author. It should be noted that the scene recorded in this album is an excerpt from the full-length play, *Man and Superman* by George Bernard Shaw. The complete play is contained in George Bernard Shaw, *Nine Plays* (New York, Dodd, Mead & Company, Inc., 1935).

basic oratorical scheme of introduction, exposition, development, and recapitulation. The result is that in listening to Shaw's verbal sonata you do not, as in reading, mind the returns and repeats, you welcome them. And even though some have been cut from the present performance, the shape of the vocal rendering gives pleasure—the pleasure of an almost bodily satisfaction—quite apart from the satisfactions of wit, eloquence, and living philosophy.

As you listen further, you will be able to identify the vocal quality of each character. As we have indicated earlier, and as we shall learn more specifically later in this book, it is not quality alone which identifies a voice as pleasant to listen to or characteristic of a certain personality. One cannot isolate quality as being independent of pitch flexibility, variety in attack, stress, or rhythm, but *usually* it is the one vocal factor which is recognized as being good or bad or which indicates a certain mood or personality. Listen to Doña Ana's voice as a woman of 77 years and as a young girl of 27 years. As an old woman, Doña Ana has a vocal quality belonging to a person who is assured, confident of authority, worldly, sophisticated, demanding. Agnes Moorehead has added a throaty, slightly husky laugh, which adds to the impression of a woman who has lived fully and luxuriously. As soon as Doña Ana decides that she will be 27 years old while in Hell, the quality of her voice becomes lighter and softer and not so resonant. Listen for this change.

The voices of the three men, the Devil, the Commander, and Don Juan through their nuances of inflection, attack, rhythm, and their basic quality reveal clear-cut characterizations: The Devil's voice belongs to a person who is detached, aloof, commanding, ironical, impatient—and certainly to one who is not moved by the philosophy of others. The Commander's voice reveals a man of the world, a dilettante—suave, mellow, casual, not easily provoked because he enjoys security and prestige. Don Juan's voice portrays a most interesting contrast to the other masculine voices. He is the pivot about whom the other voices move. His vibrant, intense quality reveals a highly emotional, impetuous, and decisive personality. His last long speech, beginning with the line, "On the contrary, here I have everything appointed me," builds to a breathtaking climax, showing a voice under the finest control. If you are genuinely alert to the importance of vocal quality, you will be intrigued with *Don Juan in Hell,* not for one hour's listening but for many hours.

III

Another profitable listening experience for you is the recording of Shakespeare's *Macbeth* in the album, *An Evening with Will Shakespeare.* In addition to listening to the quality of every voice changing under varying emotional episodes, be sure to listen to Margaret Webster's excellent informative introductions. In former editions of this book, the following scenes have been scattered throughout the text, in order to point up certain matters of inflection, pause, attack, and rhythm. Now it would seem worth while to have the scenes reprinted in this chapter so that you can listen more effectively, not only with your ears but with your eyes. Always read the scene first; then listen to the recording. You may then wish to listen with this book before you.

In the following scene, Lady Macbeth has just received a letter from Macbeth. You will recall, as you listen to the reading of the first part of the letter, our earlier instructions about informative interpretation. Here is a good example, along with Margaret Webster's, of this type of interpretation. You hear Eva Le Gallienne's voice reading the letter with a normal vocal quality. As the reading of the letter continues, however, meaning is increased, and the mood is intensified by a shift in quality which shows the mystery and wonder conveyed by the prophecy of the witches, building to the dynamic and dramatic words, "Hail, King that shalt be!" The movement of the lines becomes quicker, then slows down again, until, finally, we hear the full, resonant voice saying with deliberate emphasis, "Glamis thou art, and Cawdor;" and then the portentous voice, whispering the evil intent, "and shalt be/What thou art promised." In the following lines, Lady Macbeth's voice is guarded, quiet; her tones are low as she counsels herself as to the wisest procedure. Thus far the scene has not moved too fast; nor has Lady Macbeth appeared to be, as she later says, "transported" beyond "this ignorant present." But as soon as the messenger tells her of the approaching visit of the king, Lady Macbeth's vocal quality becomes intense with excitement as she replies, "Thou'rt mad to say it!"

You will hear the ominous tones also in the line, "He brings great news," which precedes that famous monologue on cruelty. Listen for the appropriate aspirate quality on the lines beginning, "Come, thick night." There is another high spot, emphasized by the fullest vocal resonance, as Lady Macbeth greets Macbeth with "Great Glamis! Worthy Cawdor!" This, in turn, is contrasted by Macbeth's quietly but powerfully intense quality as he informs her, "My dearest love,/Duncan comes here to-night." The remaining lines, interpreted by Le Gallienne, are sinister, now with significant pauses and stress, now with murderous intent, now with the hiss of the serpent as she whispers, "But be the serpent under't."

THE LETTER SCENE[3]

Enter LADY MACBETH, *alone, with a letter*

LADY M. (*Reads*) "They met me in the day of success; and I have learn'd by the perfect'st report, they have more in them than mortal knowledge. When I burn'd in desire to question them further, they made themselves air, into which they vanish'd. Whiles I stood rapt in the wonder of it, came missives from the King, who all-hail'd me 'Thane of Cawdor;' by which title, before, these weird sisters saluted me, and referr'd me to the coming on of time, with 'Hail, King that shalt be!' This have I thought good to deliver thee, my dearest partner of greatness, that thou mightst not lose the dues of rejoicing, by being ignorant of what greatness is promis'd thee. Lay it to thy heart, and farewell."

Glamis thou art, and Cawdor; and shalt be
What thou art promis'd, Yet do I fear thy nature;
It is too full o' the milk of human kindness
To catch the nearest way. Thou would'st be great,
Art not without ambition, but without
The illness should attend it. What thou wouldst highly,
That wouldst thou holily; wouldst not play false,
And yet wouldst wrongly win. Thou'dst have, great Glamis,
That which cries, "Thus thou must do, if thou have it;"
And that which rather thou dost fear to do
Than wishest should be undone. Hie thee hither
That I may pour my spirits in thine ear,
And chastise with the valour of my tongue
All that impedes thee from the golden round

[3] *Macbeth,* Act I, scene 5.

Which fate and metaphysical aid doth seem
To have thee crown'd withal.

Enter MESSENGER

What is your tidings?

MESS. The King comes here tonight.

LADY M. Thou'rt mad to say it!
Is not thy master with him? who, were't so,
Would have inform'd for preparation.

MESS. So please you, it is true; our thane is coming.
One of my fellows had the speed of him,
Who, almost dead for breath, had scarcely more
Than would make up his message.

LADY M. Give him tending;
He brings great news. (*Exit* MESSENGER)

The raven himself is hoarse
That croaks the fatal entrance of Duncan
Under my battlements. Come, you spirits
That tend on mortal thoughts, unsex me here,
And fill me from the crown to the toe top-full
Of direst cruelty! Make thick my blood;
Stop up the access and passage to remorse,
That no compunctious visitings of nature
Shake my fell purpose, nor keep peace between
The effect and it! Come to my woman's breasts
And take my milk for gall, you murd'ring ministers,
Wherever in your sightless substances
You wait on nature's michief! Come, thick night,
And pall thee in the dunnest smoke of hell,
That my keen knife see not the wound it makes,
Nor heaven peep through the blanket of the dark
To cry, "Hold, hold!"

Enter MACBETH

Great Glamis! worthy Cawdor!
Greater than both, by the all-hail hereafter!
Thy letters have transported me beyond
This ignorant present, and I feel now
The future in the instant.

MACBETH. My dearest love,
Duncan comes here to-night.

LADY M. And when goes hence?

MACBETH. To-morrow, as he purposes.

LADY M. O, never
Shall sun that morrow see!
Your face, my thane, is as a book where men
May read strange matters. To beguile the time,
Look like the time; bear welcome in your eye,
Your hand, your tongue; look like the innocent flower

But be the serpent under't. He that's coming
Must be provided for; and you shall put
This night's great business into my dispatch,
Which shall to all our nights and days to come
Give solely sovereign sway and masterdom.
MACBETH. We will speak further.
LADY M.   Only look up clear;
To alter favour ever is to fear.
Leave all the rest to me.   *Exeunt*

In Act I, scene 7 of *Macbeth,* you will listen to a vacillating
and tormented Thane of Cawdor, whose brooding establishes the
mood of the scene. The hushed vocal quality of each character
is toned to the tension and secrecy involved in conspiring for
the king's murder. Whenever Macbeth is pressed beyond his endurance, however, you will hear his voice take on a harshness
and tension as in the lines:

Prithee, peace!
I dare do all that may become a man;
Who dares do more is none.

       .   .   .   .

If we should fail?

    .   .   .   .

I am settled, and bend up
Each corporal agent to this terrible feat.
Away, and mock the time with fairest show . . .

Some interesting vocal contrasts can also be heard. Compare
the utterance of those lines which immediately precede each of
the following quotations with that of the quotation itself.

1. Macbeth's quick start and sudden alertness as Lady Macbeth
   enters reveals the torture Macbeth is experiencing as he cries
   out, "How now! what news?"
2. Lady Macbeth's aspirate quality in answer to Macbeth's startled question, "He has almost supp'd," indicating that time is
   pressing and the moment is almost at hand.
3. Macbeth's quiet, firm, resonant tones as he informs Lady Macbeth, "We will proceed no further in this business."
4. Lady Macbeth's insinuating jabs to probe Macbeth on, beginning, "Was the hope drunk/Wherein you dress'd yourself?"
5. The quiet intensity of Lady Macbeth's voice as she probes still

further, "But screw your courage to the sticking-place/And we'll not fail."

6. Macbeth's deep, sustained, and awesome tones, indicating a fascinating horror for Lady Macbeth's "undaunted mettle" and adding powerful significance to the line, "Bring forth men-children only."

7. Macbeth's last line uttered with an emotional quality that hints of Macbeth's true loyalty to the king and belies the outward show of courage in the line, "I am settled."

THE CONSPIRACY SCENE[4]

MACBETH *has left the banquet to ponder over the intended murder of* DUNCAN

MACBETH. If it were done when 'tis done, then 'twere well
It were done quickly. If the assassination
Could trammel up the consequence, and catch
With his surcease success; that but this blow
Might be the be-all and the end-all here,
But here, upon this bank and shoal of time,
We'd jump the life to come. But in these cases
We still have judgement here, that we but teach
Bloody instruction, which, being taught, return
To plague the inventor. This even-handed justice
Commends the ingredients of our poison'd chalice
To our own lips. He's here in double trust:
First, as I am his kinsman and his subject,
Strong both against the deed; then, as his host,
Who should against his murderer shut the door,
Not bear the knife myself. Besides, this Duncan
Hath borne his faculties so meek, hath been
So clear in his great office, that his virtues
Will plead like angels, trumpet-tongu'd, against
The deep damnation of his taking-off;
And pity, like a naked new-born babe
Striding the blast, or heaven's cherubim, hors'd
Upon the sightless couriers of the air,
Shall blow the horrid deed in every eye,
That tears shall drown the wind. I have no spur
To prick the sides of my intent, but only
Vaulting ambition, which o'erleaps itself,
And falls on the other—
                    Enter LADY MACBETH
                    How now! what news?

4 *Ibid.,* Act I, scene 7.

LADY M. He has almost supp'd: why have you left the chamber?

MACBETH. Hath he ask'd for me?

LADY M.   Know you not he has?

MACBETH. We will proceed no further in this business.
  He hath honour'd me of late; and I have bought
  Golden opinions from all sorts of people,
  Which would be worn now in their newest gloss,
  Not cast aside so soon.

LADY M.   Was the hope drunk
  Wherein you dress'd yourself? Hath it slept since?
  And wakes it now, to look so green and pale
  At what it did so freely? From this time
  Such I account thy love. Art thou afeard
  To be the same in thine own act and valour
  As thou art in desire? Wouldst thou have that
  Which thou esteem'st the ornament of life,
  And live a coward in thine own esteem,
  Letting "I dare not" wait upon "I would,"
  Like the poor cat i' the adage?

MACBETH.   Prithee, peace!
  I dare do all that may become a man;
  Who dares do more is none.

LADY M.   What beast was't then,
  That made you break this enterprise to me?
  When you durst do it, then you were a man;
  And, to be more than what you were, you would
  Be so much more the man. Nor time nor place
  Did then adhere, and yet you would make both.
  They have made themselves, and that their fitness now
  Does unmake you. I have given suck, and know
  How tender 'tis to love the babe that milks me;
  I would, while it was smiling in my face,
  Have pluck'd my nipple from his boneless gums,
  And dash'd the brains out, had I so sworn as you
  Have done to this.

MACBETH.   If we should fail?

LADY M.   We fail!
  But screw your courage to the sticking-place,
  And we'll not fail. When Duncan is asleep—
  Whereto the rather shall his day's hard journey
  Soundly invite him—his two chamberlains
  Will I with wine and wassail so convince
  That memory, the warder of the brain,
  Shall be a fume, and the receipt of reason
  A limbeck only. When in swinish sleep
  Their drenchèd natures lie as in a death,
  What cannot you and I perform upon

The unguarded Duncan? what not put upon
His spongy officers, who shall bear the guilt
Of our great quell?
MACBETH.   Bring forth men-children only;
For thy undaunted mettle should compose
Nothing but males. Will it not be receiv'd,
When we have mark'd with blood those sleepy two
Of his own chamber and us'd their very daggers,
That they have done 't?
LADY M.   Who dares receive it other,
As we shall make our griefs and clamour roar
Upon his death?
MACBETH.   I am settled, and bend up
Each corporal agent to this terrible feat.
Away, and mock the time with fairest show;
False face must hide what the false heart doth know. (*Exeunt*)

The climax of the famous murder scene is intensified by voices
which scarcely ever rise above terrified and guilty whispers. Full
resonance is not heard, except when the movement has been
made dramatic by a quick change from a stealthy whisper to a
sudden cry as in Macbeth's "Who's there? What, ho!" or when
a high spot is reached as in Macbeth's lines on sleep, "Still it
cried 'Sleep no more!' to all the house." Listen also for the changing vocal quality of Lady Macbeth in the lines beginning,
"Alack, I am afraid they have awak'd." This vocal variability is
indicative of her underlying nervousness and fear. If you have
not noticed the movement of the scene, listen again for minor climaxes as in lines like "Alack, I am afraid they have awak'd," or
"'Amen' stuck in my throat," or "'Macbeth shall sleep no more,'"
until finally Macbeth's horrified voice, aided by the knocking
which grows louder and louder, cries out brokenly, in a tremendous climax, "Wake Duncan with thy knocking! I would thou
couldst!"

THE MURDER SCENE[5]

MACBETH *is "about it"*; LADY MACBETH *waits in an adjoining room*
LADY M. That which hath made them drunk hath made me bold;
What hath quench'd them hath given me fire. Hark! Peace!
It was the owl that shriek'd, the fatal bellman

[5] *Ibid.*, Act II, scene 2.

Which gives the stern'st good-night. He is about it.
The doors are open; and the surfeited grooms
Do mock their charge with snores. I have drugg'd their possets,
That death and nature do contend about them,
Whether they live or die.

Enter MACBETH

MACBETH. Who's there? What, ho!

LADY M. Alack, I am afraid they have awak'd,
And 'tis not done. The attempt and not the deed
Confounds us. Hark! I laid their daggers ready;
He could not miss 'em. Had he not resembled
My father as he slept, I had done't. My husband!

MACBETH. I have done the deed. Didst thou not hear a noise?

LADY M. I heard the owl scream and the crickets cry.
Did not you speak?

MACBETH.   When?

LADY M.   Now.

MACBETH.   As I descended?

LADY M. Ay.

MACBETH. Hark!
Who lies i' the second chamber?

LADY M.   Donalbain.

MACBETH. This is a sorry sight. (*Looking at his hands*)

LADY M. A foolish thought, to say a sorry sight.

MACBETH. There's one did laugh in's sleep, and one cried "Murder!"
That they did wake each other. I stood and heard them;
But they did say their prayers, and address'd them
Again to sleep.

LADY M.   There are two lodg'd together.

MACBETH. One cried "God bless us!" and "Amen" the other,
As they had seen me with these hangman's hands,
List'ning their fear, I could not say "Amen,"
When they did say "God bless us!"

LADY M.   Consider it not so deeply.

MACBETH. But wherefore could not I pronounce "Amen"?
I had most need of blessing, and "Amen"
Stuck in my throat.

LADY M.   These deeds must not be thought
After these ways; so, it will make us mad.

MACBETH. Methought I heard a voice cry "Sleep no more!
Macbeth does murder sleep,"—the innocent sleep,
Sleep that knits up the ravell'd sleave of care,
The death of each day's life, sore labour's bath,
Balm of hurt minds, great nature's second course,
Chief nourisher in life's feast,—

LADY M.   What do you mean?

MACBETH. Still it cried "Sleep no more!" to all the house;
  "Glamis hath murder'd sleep, and therefore Cawdor
  Shall sleep no more; Macbeth shall sleep no more."
LADY M. Who was it that thus cried? Why, worthy thane,
  You do unbend your noble strength, to think
  So brainsickly of things. Go get some water,
  And wash this filthy witness from your hand.
  Why did you bring these daggers from the place?
  They must lie there. Go carry them, and smear
  The sleepy grooms with blood.
MACBETH.   I'll go no more.
  I am afraid to think what I have done;
  Look on't again I dare not.
LADY M.   Infirm of purpose!
  Give me the daggers. The sleeping and the dead
  Are but as pictures; 'tis the eye of childhood
  That fears a painted devil. If he do bleed,
  I'll gild the faces of the grooms withal;
  For it must seem their guilt. (*Exit. Knocking within*)
MACBETH.   Whence is that knocking?
  How is't with me, when every noise appalls me?
  What hands are here? Ha! they pluck out mine eyes.
  Will all great Neptune's ocean wash this blood
  Clean from my hand? No, this my hand will rather
  The multitudinous seas incarnadine,
  Making the green one red.
                    Re-enter LADY MACBETH
LADY M. My hands are of your color; but I shame
  To wear a heart so white. (*Knocking*) I hear a knocking
  At the south entry: retire we to our chamber.
  A little water clears us of this deed;
  How easy is it, then! Your constancy
  Hath left you unattended. (*Knocking*) Hark! more knocking.
  Get on your nightgown, lest occasion call us,
  And show us to be watchers. Be not lost
  So poorly in your thoughts.
MACBETH. To know my deed, 'twere best not know myself.
                              (*Knocking*)
  Wake Duncan with thy knocking! I would thou couldst!

The last scene we shall listen to is the sleep-walking scene, in
which two figures in the darkness, the Doctor and the Gentle-
woman, observe Lady Macbeth in one of her nocturnal wanderings. You will hear again whispering voices—aspirate, breathy
tones—from the two observers, but the fearful intensity heard

in previous scenes is now absent. These voices serve as an effective undercurrent to point up Lady Macbeth's behavior and, also, as a contrast to the remorse and horror heard in her voice. Listen to the range and control in Lady's Macbeth's voice, sometimes full and resonant, at other times, aspirate, and then again harsh. Notice the control used on the exit line, "To bed, to bed, to bed!"

THE SLEEP-WALKING SCENE[6]

The scene is an anteroom in the castle. Enter a DOCTOR OF PHYSIC *and a* WAITING-GENTLEWOMAN

DOCTOR. I have two nights watch'd with you, but can perceive no truth in your report. When was it she last walk'd?

GENTLEW. Since His Majesty went into the field, I have seen her rise from her bed, throw her nightgown upon her, unlock her closet, take forth paper, fold it, write upon't, read it, afterwards seal it, and again return to bed; yet all this while in a most fast sleep.

DOCTOR. A great perturbation in nature, to receive at once the benefit of sleep, and do the effects of watching! In this slumb'ry agitation, besides her walking and other actual performances, what, at any time, have you heard her say?

GENTLEW. That, sir, which I will not report after her.

DOCTOR. You may to me: and 'tis most meet you should.

GENTLEW. Neither to you nor any one; having no witness to confirm my speech.

Enter LADY MACBETH, *with a taper*

Lo, you, here she comes! This is her very guise; and, upon my life, fast asleep. Observe her; stand close.

DOCTOR. How came she by that light?

GENTLEW. Why, it stood by her. She has light by her continually; 'tis her command.

DOCTOR. You see, her eyes are open.

GENTLEW. Ay, but their sense is shut.

DOCTOR. What is it she does now? Look, how she rubs her hands.

GENTLEW. It is an accustom'd action with her, to seem thus washing her hands. I have known her continue in this a quarter of an hour.

LADY M. Yet here's a spot.

DOCTOR. Hark! she speaks. I will set down what comes from her, to satisfy my remembrance the more strongly.

LADY M. Out, damnèd spot! out, I say!—One: two: why, then 'tis

[6] *Ibid.,* Act V, scene 1.

time to do't.—Hell is murky!—Fie, my lord, fie! a soldier, and afeard? What need we fear who knows it, when none can call our power to account?—Yet who would have thought the old man to have had so much blood in him?

DOCTOR. Do you mark that?

LADY M. The thane of Fife had a wife; where is she now?—What, will these hands ne'er be clean?—No more o' that, my lord, no more o' that; you mar all with this starting.

DOCTOR. Go to, go to; you have known what you should not.

GENTLEW. She has spoke what she should not, I am sure of that; Heaven knows what she has known.

LADY M. Here's the smell of the blood still; all the perfumes of Arabia will not sweeten this little hand. Oh, oh, oh!

DOCTOR. What a sigh is there! The heart is sorely charg'd.

GENTLEW. I would not have such a heart in my bosom for the dignity of the whole body.

DOCTOR. Well, well, well,—

GENTLEW. Pray God it be, sir.

DOCTOR. This disease is beyond my practice; yet I have known those which have walk'd in their sleep who have died holily in their beds.

LADY M. Wash your hands, put on your nightgown; look not so pale. —I tell you yet again, Banquo's buried; he cannot come out on's grave.

DOCTOR. Even so?

LADY M. To bed, to bed! there's knocking at the gate. Come, come, come, come, give me your hand. What's done cannot be undone. To bed, to bed, to bed!   (*Exit*)

DOCTOR. Will she go now to bed?

GENTLEW. Directly.

DOCTOR. Foul whisp'rings are abroad; unnatural deeds
Do breed unnatural troubles: infected minds
To their deaf pillows will discharge their secrets.
More needs she the divine than the physician.
God, God forgive us all! Look after her;
Remove from her the means of all annoyance,
And still keep eyes upon her. So, good-night!
My mind she has mated and amaz'd my sight.
I think, but dare not speak.

GENTLEW.   Good-night, good doctor.
                                                   (*Exeunt*)

You have by this time realized that quality reveals mood, emotions. If your vocal quality needs improvement, turn to the Appendix for assistance in securing added resonance.

EXERCISES

I

Try to find a quality that will be appropriate to the mood of the following selections.

1

In this poem, the apple-picking experience, which has involved "ten thousand thousand fruit to touch," is relived through the recall of sensory images in a drowsy, semiconscious dream. The illusion of being high in the air is caught immediately by the "long two-pointed ladder's sticking through a tree/Toward heaven still," the word *still* emphasizing the poet's weariness. The sensations of smell, touch, sight, sound, and movement linger on, recurring as he seeks to escape into the long sleep due an overtired apple-picker. As you read the poem, select the phrases that stir up these sensory images. In interpreting the poem, the quality of your voice should carry the impression of the strangeness and illusiveness of these afterimages and yet should create the reality of the experience.

AFTER APPLE-PICKING[7]

My long two-pointed ladder's sticking through a tree
Toward heaven still,
And there's a barrel that I didn't fill
Beside it, and there may be two or three
Apples I didn't pick upon some bough.
But I am done with apple-picking now.
Essence of winter sleep is on the night,
The scent of apples: I am drowsing off.
I cannot rub the strangeness from my sight
I got from looking through a pane of glass
I skimmed this morning from the drinking trough
And held against the world of hoary grass.
It melted, and I let it fall and break.
But I was well
Upon my way to sleep before it fell,

And I could tell
What form my dreaming was about to take.
Magnified apples appear and disappear,
Stems end and blossom end,
And every fleck of russet showing clear.
My instep arch not only keeps the ache,
It keeps the pressure of a ladder-round.
I feel the ladder sway as the boughs bend.
And I keep hearing from the cellar bin
The rumbling sound
Of load on load of apples coming in.
For I have had too much
Of apple-picking: I am overtired
Of the great harvest I myself desired.
There were ten thousand thousand fruit to touch,
Cherish in hand, lift down, and not let fall.
For all
That struck the earth,
No matter if not bruised or spiked with stubble,
Went surely to the cider-apple heap
As of no worth.
One can see what will trouble
This sleep of mine, whatever sleep it is.
Were he not gone,
The woodchuck could say whether it's like his
Long sleep, as I describe its coming on,
Or just some human sleep.

ROBERT FROST

2

A full resonant quality will best carry the assurance, calmness, certainty of Sarett's following lines. Can you control your voice so that the last lines will be subdued like a great Amen and yet carry over the deep solitude and contentment that are created by images like "Deep in the brookmints in the glen," "under the starry-candled sky," and "shadow of a sigh."

LET ME GO DOWN TO DUST[8]

Let me go down to dust and dreams
Gently, O Lord, with never a fear
Of death beyond the day that is done;

---

[8] From *Slow Smoke*, p. 16. Copyright, 1925, by Henry Holt and Company, Inc. Reprinted by permission of the publishers.

In such a manner as beseems
A kinsman of the wild, a son
Of stoic earth whose race is run.
Let me go down as any deer,
Who, broken by a desperate flight,
Sinks down to slumber for the night—
Dumbly serene in certitude
That it will rise again at dawn,
Buoyant, refreshed of limb, renewed,
And confident that it will thrill
To-morrow to its nuzzling fawn,
To the bugle-notes of elk upon the hill.

Let me go down to dreams and dust
Gently, O Lord, with quiet trust
And the fortitude that marks a child
Of earth, a kinsman of the wild.
Let me go down as any doe
That nods upon its ferny bed,
And, lulled to slumber by the flow
Of talking water, the muffled brawl
Of far cascading waterfall,
At last lets down its weary head
Deep in the brookmints in the glen;
And under the starry-candled sky,
With never the shadow of a sigh,
Gives its worn body back to earth again.

Lew Sarett

3

No doubt you have heard "Mandalay" sung to music which gives a stirring vigor to these lines. You can try for the same kind of vocal vigor in your interpretation, or you can use more reminiscent tones, suggesting the nostalgia of the soldier.

MANDALAY[9]

By the old Moulmein Pagoda, lookin' eastward to the sea,
There's a Burma girl a-settin', and I know she thinks o' me;
For the wind is in the palm-trees, and the temple-bells they say:
"Come you back, you British soldier; come you back to Mandalay!"
Come you back to Mandalay,

---

[9] From *Departmental Ditties and Ballads and Barrack-Room Ballads,* pp. 190-191. Copyright, 1891, by Rudyard Kipling. Reprinted by permission of Mrs. George Bambridge and Doubleday & Company, Inc.

Where the old Flotilla lay:
Can't you 'ear their paddles chunkin' from Rangoon to Mandalay?
On the road to Mandalay,
Where the flyin'-fishes play,
An' the dawn comes up like thunder outer China 'crost the Bay!

'Er petticut was yaller an' 'er little cap was green,
An' 'er name was Supi-yaw-lat—jes' the same as Theebaw's Queen,
An' I seed her fust a-smokin' of a whackin' white cheroot,
An' a-wastin' Christian kisses on an 'eathen idol's foot:
    Bloomin' idol made o' mud—
    Wot they called the Great Gawd Budd—
    Plucky lot she cared for idols when I kissed 'er where she stud!
    On the road to Mandalay . . . .

When the mist was on the rice-fields an' the sun was droppin' slow,
She'd git 'er little banjo an' she'd sing *"Kulla-lo-lo!"*
With 'er arm upon my shoulder an' 'er cheek agin my cheek
We uster watch the steamers an' the *hathis* pilin' teak.
    Elephints a-pilin' teak
    In the sludgy, squdgy creek,
    Where the silence 'ung that 'eavy you was 'arf afraid to speak!
    On the road to Mandalay . . . .

But that's all shove be'ind me—long ago an' fur away,
An' there ain't no 'busses runnin' from the Bank to Mandalay;
An' I'm learnin' 'ere in London what the ten-year soldier tells:
"If you've 'eard the East a-callin', you won't never 'eed naught
    else."
    No! you won't 'eed nothin' else
    But them spicy garlic smells,
    An' the sunshine an' the palm-trees an' the tinkly temple-bells;
    On the road to Mandalay . . . .

I am sick o' wastin' leather on these gritty pavin'-stones,
An' the blasted Henglish drizzle wakes the fever in my bones;
Tho' I walks with fifty 'ousemaids outer Chelsea to the Strand,
An' they talks a lot o' lovin', but wot do they understand?
    Beefy face an' grubby 'and—
    Law! wot do they understand?
    I've a neater, sweeter maiden in a cleaner, greener land!
    On the road to Mandalay . . . .

Ship me somewhere east of Suez, where the best is like the worst,
Where there aren't no Ten Commandments an' a man can raise a
    thirst;
For the temple-bells are callin', an' it's there that I would be—
By the old Moulmein Pagoda, looking lazy at the sea;
    On the road to Mandalay,

Where the old Flotilla lay,
With our sick beneath the awnings when we went to Mandalay!
On the road to Mandalay,
Where the flyin'-fishes play,
An' the dawn comes up like thunder outer China 'crost the Bay!
RUDYARD KIPLING

4

Notice first of all that this poem was written in memory of
Kenneth MacLeish, a casualty of World War I. Notice also that
the effectiveness of the interpretation depends to a great extent
on two kinds of vocal quality: (1) the high-pitched, slightly
monotonous quality of the orator and (2) the tense, low quality
of the author, suggestive of one waiting in suspense for the peace
that could not be given through the eloquent words of the ambassador. The italicized lines should convey the impression of an
oratorical eulogy for the men who lie row after row enjoying
"Their country's gratitude." Notice further the irony conveyed
by the contrast of the orator's fluent superficiality in speaking of
the "happy, happy dead" and the suspense created by the taut
words beginning, "The roots of the grass strain," that express the
kinship of the author with the dead.

MEMORIAL RAIN[10]
For Kenneth MacLeish, 1894-1918

Ambassador Puser the ambassador
Reminds himself in French, felicitous tongue,
What these (young men no longer) lie here for
In rows that once, and somewhere else, were young—

All night in Brussels the wind had tugged at my door:
I had heard the wind at my door and the trees strung
Taut, and to me who had never been before
In that country it was a strange wind, blowing
Steadily, stiffening the walls, the floor,
The roof of my room. I had not slept for knowing
He too, dead, was a stranger in that land
And felt beneath the earth in the wind's flowing
A tightening of roots and would not understand,

[10] From *Collected Poems: 1917-1952*, p. 36. Copyright, 1952, by Houghton, Mifflin Company. Reprinted by permission of the publishers.

Remembering lake winds in Illinois,
That strange wind. I had felt his bones in the sand
Listening.

—Reflects that these enjoy
Their country's gratitude, that deep repose,
That peace no pain can break, no hurt destroy,
That rest, that sleep—

At Ghent the wind rose.
There was a smell of rain and a heavy drag
Of wind in the hedges but not as the wind blows
Over fresh water when the waves lag
Foaming and the willows huddle and it will rain:
I felt him waiting.

—Indicates the flag
Which (may he say) enisles in Flanders plain
This little field these happy, happy dead
Have made America—

In the ripe grain
The wind coiled glistening, darted, fled,
Dragging its heavy body: at Waereghem
The wind coiled in the grass above his head:
Waiting—listening—

—Dedicates to them
This earth their bones have hallowed, this last gift
A grateful country—

Under the dry grass stem
The words are blurred, are thickened, the words sift
Confused by the rasp of the wind, by the thin grating
Of ants under the grass, the minute shift
And tumble of dusty sand separating
From dusty sand. The roots of the grass strain,
Tighten, the earth is rigid, waits—he is waiting—

And suddenly, and all at once, the rain!
The living scatter, they run into houses, the wind
Is trampled under the rain, shakes free, is again
Trampled. The rain gathers, running in thinned
Spurts of water that ravel in the dry sand,
Seeping in the sand under the grass roots, seeping
Between cracked boards to the bones of a clenched hand:
The earth relaxes, loosens; he is sleeping,
He rests, he is quiet, he sleeps in a strange land.

ARCHIBALD MacLEISH

5

Most skillfully has Walter de la Mare created a mood of "shadowiness," of strange stillness in this next poem. The quiet listening of the host of phantoms is sharply accentuated by the voice of the Traveller from "the world of men," his "Knocking on the moonlit door," the horse's champing and "cropping the dark turf," the "air stirred and shaken/By the lonely Traveller's call," and the echoes sounding through "the still house." The voice of the interpreter through its variations of resonance will have to create the impression of intrusion into the quiet of the moonlight where the phantom listeners stand "thronging the faint moonbeams on the dark stair," listening finally to the "sound of iron on stone" and "how the silence surged softly backward." This last phrase, if properly interpreted, can give an audience unusual empathy because of the kinesthetic pull of the words.

THE LISTENERS[11]

"Is there anybody there?" said the Traveller,
   Knocking on the moonlit door;
And his horse in the silence champed the grasses
   Of the forest's ferny floor:
And a bird flew up out of the turret,
   Above the Traveller's head:
And he smote upon the door again a second time;
   "Is there anybody there?" he said.
But no one descended to the Traveller;
   No head from the leaf-fringed sill
Leaned over and looked into his grey eyes,
   Where he stood perplexed and still.
But only a host of phantom listeners
   That dwelt in the lone house then
Stood listening in the quiet of the moonlight
   To that voice from the world of men:
Stood thronging the faint moonbeams on the dark stair,
   That goes down to the empty hall,
Hearkening in an air stirred and shaken
   By the lonely Traveller's call.
And he felt in his heart their strangeness,
   Their stillness answering his cry,

While his horse moved, cropping the dark turf,
   'Neath the starred and leafy sky;
For he suddenly smote on the door, even
   Louder, and lifted his head:—
"Tell them I came, and no one answered,
   That I kept my word," he said,
Never the least stir made the listeners,
   Though every word he spake
Fell echoing through the shadowiness of the still house
   From the one man left awake:
Ay, they heard his foot upon the stirrup,
   And the sound of iron on stone,
And how the silence surged softly backward,
   When the plunging hoofs were gone.

                      WALTER DE LA MARE

6

Full, resonant tones will best create the deep sincerity and solemnity of Vachel Lindsay's poem, the rhythm of which is paced by the "bronzed, lank man" with "suit of ancient black," who "stalks until the dawn-stars burn away."

ABRAHAM LINCOLN WALKS AT MIDNIGHT[12]
(*In Springfield, Illinois*)

It is portentous, and a thing of state
That here at midnight, in our little town
A mourning figure walks, and will not rest,
Near the old court-house pacing up and down.

Or by his homestead, or in shadowed yards
He lingers where his children used to play,
Or through the market, on the well-worn stones
He stalks until the dawn-stars burn away.

A bronzed, lank man! His suit of ancient black,
A famous high-top hat and plain worn shawl
Make him the quaint great figure that men love,
The prairie lawyer, master of us all.

He cannot sleep upon his hillside now.
He is among us:—as in times before!
And we who toss and lie awake for long
Breathe deep, and start, to see him pass the door.

His head is bowed. He thinks on men and kings.
Yea, when the sick world cries, how can he sleep?
Too many peasants fight, they know not why,
Too many homesteads in black terror weep.

The sins of all the war-lords burn his heart.
He sees the dreadnaughts scouring every main.
He carries on his shawl-wrapped shoulders now
The bitterness, the folly and the pain.

He cannot rest until a spirit-dawn
Shall come;—the shining hope of Europe free:
The league of sober folk, the Workers' Earth,
Bringing long peace to Cornland, Alp and Sea.

It breaks his heart that kings must murder still,
That all his hours of travail here for men
Seem yet in vain. And who will bring white peace
That he may sleep upon his hill again?

VACHEL LINDSAY

7

In his typical colloquial manner, Weaver gives Jim's girl quick emotional changes—bitterness, tenderness, sarcasm, defiance, despair—caused by everyday occurrences, all of which are reminiscent in some way of Jim's death. In order to make these emotions appear real, the interpreter will have to slow down to give the impression of emotional shifts. This poem is subdued rather than violent; consequently, the quality of voice should have some fine nuances.

HEADLINES[13]
(*Easter Sunday, 1918*)

They's headlines snarlin' at me from the "Journal,"
"Hun Drive Slows."
Slows! And I prayed last night it was stopped!
A robin just hopped
On top of a red-bud tree,
Looks to me like a rose
That a girl's holdin' up next to her cheek. . . .
Or maybe like that liquid fire them Germans uses. . . .

Clink!—Clink!—
The sidewalks is ringin' from the feet

[13] From *In American*, p. 33. Copyright, 1923, by Alfred A. Knopf, Inc. Reprinted by permission of the publishers.

Of folks goin' to church, all neat,
Gettin' ready to split their voice
Singin', "Rejoice! Rejoice!
He is risen!"
Like a man outa prison
The vi'lets is bustin' outa the ground. . . .
The headlines I'm starin' at jumps and lurches:
"Mystery Gun Slays Crowds
Prayin' in Paris Churches." . . .

Here comes a young sojer
With a girl hangin' onto his arm.
Right here only a year ago Jim useta walk
And him and me would useta talk
All about the glories o' fightin' for your country. . . .
"Airman Falls in Gallant Fight"—

That was Jim's headline. . . . I was Jim's girl. . . .
Just such a light
He useta have in his face,
Just like that he had a sorter grace
When he walked. . . . Just like that
His hair useta curl. . . .

Apple-blossoms is ridin' along on the breeze,
Flutterin' down from the trees
Like a sweet-smellin' snow—
Or like frost on them graves in Picardy. . . .

Oh, God!

Good God, almighty God,
Are you gonna stand by
And let all the things that was beautiful die?
Them Huns is killin' even the Spring,
Every little no-account lovely thing,
Twistin' everythin' inta pain. . . .

Oh, God,
Won't Beauty never come no more again! . . .
John V. A. Weaver

II

The following descriptive passages from Thomas Wolfe's *Of Time and the River*,[14] although written in prose, have the rhythmical cadences of poetry.

[14] From *Of Time and the River*, pp. 469-470, 509. Copyright, 1935, by Charles Scribner's Sons. Reprinted by permission of the publisher.

1

You will have to create for your audience the impression of the train as a "fixed and timeless object," "poised as the only motionless and unchanging object," while the "white fields, clumped woodland," the clouds in the "immense and tempestuous skies," "the driving and beleaguered moon," "the immense regimentation of heaven," and the "lonely, immortal earth below," sweep past into oblivion to the rhythm of the wheels. Your quality will have to be sustained with full resonance.

Under the immense, stormy, and tempestuous sky the train was rushing across the country with a powerful unperturbed movement; it seemed in this dark and wintry firmament of earth and sky that the train was the only fixed and timeless object—the land swept past the windows of the train in a level and powerful tide of white fields, clumped woodland, and the solid, dark, and warmly grouped buildings of a farm, pierced scarcely by a light. High up, in the immense and tempestuous skies the clouds were driving at furious speed, in an inexhaustible processional, across the visage of a wild and desolate moon, which broke through momently with a kind of savage and beleaguered reprisal to cast upon the waste below a shattered, lost and fiercely ragged light. Here then, in this storm-lost desolation of earth and sky the train hung poised as the only motionless and unchanging object, and all things else—the driving and beleaguered moon, the fiercely scudding clouds, the immense regimentation of heaven which stormed onward with the fury of a gigantic and demoniacal cavalry, and the lonely, immortal earth below sweeping past with a vast fan-shaped stroke of field and wood and house— had in them a kind of unchanging changefulness, a spoke-like recurrence which, sweeping past into oblivion, would return as on the upstroke of a wheel to repeat itself with an immutable precision, an unvarying repetition.

2

In this passage your voice should try to re-create the eeriness of the night—the darkness, the "moving waters" of the river, "full with the pulse of time," "rich, rank, beautiful, and unending as all life," as it "flows by us . . . to the sea."

The river is a tide of moving waters: by night it floods the pockets of the earth. By night it drinks the strange time, dark time. By night the river drinks proud potent tides of strange dark time. By night the river drains the tides, proud potent tides of time's dark waters that, with champ and lift of teeth, with lapse and reluctation of their breath, fill with a kissing glut the pockets of the earth. Sired by the horses of the sea, maned with the dark, they come.

They come! Ships call! The hooves of night, the horses of the sea, come on below their manes of darkness. And forever the river runs. Deep as the tides of time and memory, deep as the tides of sleep, the river runs. . . .

Full with the pulse of time it flows there, full with the pulse of all men living, sleeping, dying, waking, it will flow there, full with the billion dark and secret moments of our lives it flows there. Filled with all the hope, the madness and the passion of our youth it flows there, in the daytime, in the dark, drinking with ceaseless glut the land, mining into its tides the earth as it mines the hours and moments of our life into its tides, moving against the sides of the ships, foaming about piled crustings of old wharves, sliding like time and silence by the vast cliff of the city, girdling the stony isle of life with moving waters—thick with the wastes of earth, dark with our stains, and heavied with our dumpings, rich, rank, beautiful, and unending as all life, all living, as it flows by us, by us, by us, to the sea!

Now that you have tried to find the appropriate quality, be sure that you have built up the idea that Wolfe has expressed so vividly: the merging of man's living with the unending moving of the river to the sea, carrying with it the "hope, the madness, and the passion of our youth," and "mining" the "hours and moments of our lives into its tides." Do not permit the quality of your voice to overshadow the idea to be created.

III

In direct contrast to the Wolfe selections is E. B. White's story of his week end in a hospital. There is nothing mysterious or unusual in the tone of the story; instead, the author appears to be quite casual in his reminiscences, touching lightly on his experiences with the various nurses, as if the joke were on him. His jibes are gentle. The cues for the characterizations of the attendants are given briefly so that quality changes should not be too difficult for you.

A WEEKEND WITH THE ANGELS[15]
(*Interlude in a hospital during World War II*)

One of the advantages of surgery, to a man at loose ends in Boston,

[15] From *The Second Tree from the Corner*, pp. 3-9. Copyright, 1954, by E. B. White. Published originally in *The New Yorker* and reprinted here by permission of the author and Harper & Brothers.

is that it entitles him to a night at a hospital in advance of the operation. In short, it gets him in off the streets. I was instructed to report
for my bed not later than three o'clock on Thursday afternoon, although I wasn't to lose my middle turbinate until eight the next
morning. That gave me seventeen hours of utter relaxation in comfortable surroundings, dreaming away through the late afternoon,
sweating under the arms, wiping my moist palms on the drapes, and
marvelling at the strange succession of events that lead a man un-
erringly into an unimportant misadventure like a nose operation. I had
no particular feeling of regret at the idea of giving up a turbinate
(which sounded like something the Navy might be able to use in one
of its light cruisers); in fact, in a man's middle years there is scarcely
a part of the body he would hesitate to turn over to the proper authorities. At my age one jumps at the chance to get rid of something.
Half a lifetime with a middle turbinate is enough to satisfy all but
the most avid person.

I think the hospital was in Cambridge, but I'm not sure about that,
as I was rather depressed on the ride out and when I'm depressed I
never look where I'm going. Anyway, it was a very nice place near
a small, orderly river (which might easily have been the Charles)
and there was a fine big oak just outside my window. The room was
tiny but so am I. The bed was a standard crank-up model, complete
with drawsheet, rubber pad, and call switch. I had hoped it would
have a swan at one end of it, like the boats in the Public Garden,
but even without the swan it was a pleasanter accommodation than
one can ordinarily expect to get on short notice in Boston.

There seemed no good reason for getting into the bed right away,
so I just sat down on a hassock with a copy of the *Atlantic*. After a
while a nurse came in.

"I'm Miss Mulqueenie," she said informatively.

"My name is White," I replied. "My temperature is ninety-eight
point six, my pulse is seventy-two, and my blood pressure is one
hundred and forty over eighty except when I get interested in what
I am doing, when it goes up sharply. I'm here for a turbinectomy."
Miss Mulqueenie came and sat down by my side. She hung her
sphygmomanometer around her neck and drew a pencil and a blank
form on me.

"What's your occupation?"

"Writer," I said, searching my memory.

The nurse smiled the knowing smile of a woman who is not easily
fooled by men and their little conceits. She then began a careful listing of my clothes and personal effects. About my clothes she seemed
a trifle uncertain. "What have you got on underneath your trousers?"
she asked, dipping her pencil thoughtfully into her mouth.

"I can't recall," I replied. "It seems ages since I got dressed. This
morning seems like a million years ago."

"Well, you must have *something* on. What'll I put down?"

"Paisley shawl?" I suggested. She thought a moment and then wrote "underwear" and gave me the list to sign. Then she took my temperature, my blood pressure, and my pulse. My temperature was ninety-eight point six, my pulse was seventy-two, and my blood pressure was one hundred and forty over eighty. "You better get to bed," she said cryptically. And Miss Mulqueenie was gone.

In bed, I felt relaxed and beautiful, as I imagine I shall feel in death. I had not been there long when another nurse appeared. She was in the uniform of a student and her face had the exalted look of a person who is doing a great deal of work and receiving no pay for it—which was, of course, exactly the case. She regarded me closely.

"It says on your card that you're a writer," she began, "but I've never heard of you."

"Did you come in here to harp on my obscurity?" I asked.

"No, I came in here to rub your back." Later I was given a sedative and slept the uninterrupted sleep of the little-known.

The operation wasn't bad. I quite enjoyed the trip up from my room to the operating parlors, as a closely confined person does enjoy any sort of outing. The morphine had loosened my tongue, and while we waited in the corridor for the surgeon to arrive, the orderly and I let down our hair and had a good chat about fishing tackle. There were several rather distinguished people doing voluntary work in that hospital, and this orderly's face looked familiar. I wouldn't swear to it, but I think it was Governor Saltonstall. You never know whom you'll meet in bed these days. After a few minutes the surgeon was sighted in another part of the building and somebody gave the Governor the go-ahead. He had me halfway through a door leading into an operating room when a nurse caught sight of us. She clicked her tongue in disgust. "No, no," she said, wearily, "that's gall bladder."

The Governor backed me out and we tried our luck in another room. I cautiously put my hand up to my side, where the gall bladder is presumed to be. Everything seemed undisturbed. Soon the surgeon arrived and went to work. Under my skillful direction he removed everything he was supposed to remove and, as far as I could tell, nothing that he wasn't. It was a perfect occasion. It even turned out, in the course of the operation, that *his* father and *my* wife's people were connected—not by blood but in that happy and satisfactory way in which Boston's mystic thread entwines all its sons and daughters.

Because of the war the situation in hospitals is, of course, serious. A civilian feels embarrassed to be there at all, occupying valuable space and wasting the time and strength of the nurses, the student nurses, the nurses' aides, and the Gray Ladies. But I discovered that there is a new spirit in hospitals which, in its own way, is as merciful and resolute as the old, and every bit as mad. A patient, when he enters, receives a booklet reminding him that hospitals are short-handed and asking him not to bother the nurses unnecessarily. If he is a person of any conscience, he takes this quite literally, resolving not to push his call switch unless he is bleeding to death or the room is on fire. He throws himself so violently into the spirit of the emergency that, in the long run, he probably causes just as much trouble as he would have in more relaxed circumstances. I hadn't been off the operating table two hours and was still heavily drugged with morphine and bleeding at the nose when I found myself out of bed, armed with a window pole, engaged in a hand-to-hand encounter with a sticky transom. The effort, because of my condition, was rather too much for me, and I just made it back under the covers in time. There was quite a to-do, up and down the halls, when they found I had been out of bed.

As for routine chores, I did them myself, for the most part. Each morning I arose from bed and went at the room, tidying it up and doing all the dozens of things that need doing in an early-morning sickroom. First I would get down and crawl under the bed to retrieve the night's accumulation of blood-soaked paper handkerchiefs, which formed a dismal ring around the scrap basket where I had missed my aim in the dark. Then I'd fold the night blanket neatly and put it away in the bottom drawer of the bureau. I would crank up the bed, take the creases out of the rubber pad, tighten the drawsheet, pat the pillow back into shape, straighten out the *Atlantic Monthly*, and transfer the chrysanthemums into their day vase. Ashtrays had to be emptied, soiled towels removed, the hot-water bottle exhumed from its cold grave at the foot of the bed. One morning, in one of those passionate fits of neatness which overwhelm me from time to time, I spent an hour or so on my hands and knees clearing the room of bobby pins left by a former occupant. It was interesting work but, like all housework, exhausting.

Although there seemed to be, and undoubtedly was, a shortage of help at the hospital, there was one department which was, to my way of thinking, overstaffed. That was the back-rubbing department. There apparently was no schedule or system about back-rubbing—it was just a service a nurse would throw into her routine if she felt like it and had a few minutes to spare. One morning between ten and twelve my back was rubbed three times by as many different angels of mercy. My back, curiously enough, did not need rubbing that morning. I had been up, as usual, doing the housework, and when I finally got things to rights and crawled back into bed at quarter to ten, the blood was coursing through my back. All my back needed was a little while to itself. I took the three rubs without a murmur, but the violence and frequency of assault increased my nosebleed and when lunch was brought I was too tired to eat. Right after lunch a nurse I had never seen before, a large, eager girl, waltzed into the room and began peeling the bedclothes off.

"What's up, nurse?" I asked.

"I'm going to rub your back," she replied.

"Look," I said, plucking weakly at the sheets, "what do you say we leave the old backsy-wacksy alone for a few minutes?"

Mostly, however, the days rolled by, hour after hour, and you would never see another living soul. For patriotic reasons I seldom rang and so was seldom visited. Once I had a bath. This was the second morning after the operation. A nurse came in early. Without saying a word she flung open the door of the commode and extracted a basin, a washcloth, and a piece of soap.

"Can you take your bath?" she asked briskly.

"I always have, in recent years," I replied.

She placed the bathing equipment on the rude table that arched the bed, and handed me a towel. "Take off your uppers and work down. Then roll up your lowers and work up," she snapped. "And don't get the bed wet!"

I waited until she disappeared, then got noiselessly out of bed, removed the basin, emptied it, went into the bathroom which I shared with another fellow, drew a tub, and had a nice bath. Nurses are such formalists.

Of all the memories of this fabulous and salutary weekend, the most haunting is my recollection of the strange visitation of a certain night nurse. She came on duty, I was told, at midnight, and went off at seven. It was her custom to enter my room at a few minutes before five in the morning, when my sleeping potion still held me in thrall, snap on the light, and take a temperature reading. At her entrance I would rouse myself, at enormous physical cost, blink foolishly at the light, and open my mouth to receive, under the thick curly tongue, the thin straight thermometer. The nurse, whose name began with an "A" and ended in a thornbush, would stand in beautiful serenity, gazing peacefully down upon me for the long three minutes required for the recording. Her lips held the faint suggestion of a smile, compounded of scorn and indulgence. Motionless and cool in the lamplight, faithfully discharging her preposterous duty in the awful hour of a day born prematurely, she seemed a creature tinged with madness and beauty. She seemed, but of course could not have been, without flaw. As my drugged senses struggled vainly to catalogue her features, the thermometer would press upward against my tongue and the mercury would begin its long tedious climb toward the normal mark. I have no idea whether she was tall or short, dark or fair, plain or pretty, but in her calm and unreasoning concern about my body heat, at that unconscionable hour, she personified the beauty and lunacy of which life is so subtly blended. On the last morning of my stay I broke the mystical silence that had always before surrounded our ceremony.

"Cousin," I managed to mumble, allowing the thermometer to clash pitilessly against my incisors, "why dost wake me before the dawn for this mild dumbshow?"

She never changed her expression, but I heard words coming surely from her lips. "There's a war on, Bud," she replied. "I got twenty-six readings to take before I go off duty, so just for the heck of it I start with you."

Smiling a tiny proud smile, I raised my right hand and made a V, the way I had seen Churchill do it in the pictures. Then the drug took hold of me again, and when I awoke she was gone. Next day so was I.

IV

Each of the following excerpts carries a problem in quality which is solved only by understanding the characters in each scene.

1

Try for the tension and grimness in Keeney's voice. The Mate, not wishing to offend and cautious in his approach, realizes he is talking to a stubborn and headstrong captain who intends to get the "ile," that is, whale oil.

ILE[16]

The scene is CAPTAIN KEENEY's *cabin on board the steam whaling ship* Atlantic Queen—*a small, square compartment about eight feet high with a skylight looking out on the poop deck.*

MRS. KEENEY, *who is oppressed by all the ice, has been urging* CAPTAIN KEENEY *to turn back home; now he is expecting trouble from the crew.*

KEENEY. And trouble's they goin' to be. I feel it in my bones. (*Takes a revolver from the pocket of his coat and examines it*) Got your'n?
MATE. Yes, sir.
KEENEY. Not that we'll have to use 'em—not if I know their breed of dog—jest to frighten 'em a bit. (*Grimly*) I ain't never been forced to use one yit; and trouble I've had by land and sea 's long as I kin remember, and will have till my dyin' day, I reckon.
MATE. (*Hesitatingly*) Then you ain't goin'—to turn back?
KEENEY. Turn back? Mr. Slocum, did you ever hear o' me pointin'

[16] From *Ile* in *Plays of Eugene O'Neill*, pp. 306-308. Copyright, 1926, by Horace Liveright, Inc. Reprinted by permission of the publishers.

s'uth for home with only a measly four hundred barrel of ile in the hold?

MATE. (*Hastily*) No, sir—but the grub's gittin' low.

KEENEY. They's enough to last a long time yit, if they're careful with it; and they's plenty o' water.

MATE. They say it's not fit to eat—what's left; and the two years they signed on fur is up today. They might make trouble for you in the courts when we git home.

KEENEY. To hell with 'em. Let them make what law trouble they kin. I don't give a damm 'bout the money. I've got to git the ile! (*Glancing sharply at the* MATE) You ain't turnin' no damned sea-lawyer, be you, Mr. Slocum?

MATE. (*Flushing*) Not by a hell of a sight, sir.

KEENEY. What do the fools want to go home fur now? Their share o' the four hundred barrel wouldn't keep 'em in chewin' terbacco.

MATE. They wants to git back to their folks an' things, I s'pose.

KEENEY. (*Looking at him searchingly*) 'N you want to turn back, too. (*The* MATE *looks down confusedly before his sharp gaze*) Don't lie, Mr. Slocum. It's writ down plain in your eyes. (*With grim sarcasm*) I hope, Mr. Slocum, you ain't agoin' to jine the men agin me.

MATE. (*Indignantly*) That ain't fair, sir, to say sich things.

KEENEY. (*With satisfaction*) I warn't much afeard o' that, Tom. You been with me nigh on ten year and I've learned ye whalin'. No man kin say I ain't a good master, if I be a hard one.

MATE. I warn't thinkin' o' myself, sir—'bout turnin' home, I mean. (*Desperately*) But Mrs. Keeney, sir—seems like she ain't jest satisfied up here, ailin' like—what with the cold an' bad luck an' the ice an' all.

KEENEY. (*His face clouding—rebukingly but not severely*) That's my business, Mr. Slocum. I'll thank you to steer a clear course o' that. (*A pause*) The ice'll break up soon to no'th'ard. I could see it startin' today. And when it goes and we git some sun Annie'll perk up. (*Another pause—then he bursts forth*) It ain't the damned money what's keepin' me up in Northern seas, Tom. But I can't go back to Homeport, with a measly four hundred barrel of ile. I'd die fust. I ain't never come back home in all my days without a full ship. Ain't that the truth?

MATE. Yes, sir; but this voyage you been icebound, an'—

KEENEY. (*Scornfully*) And d'you s'pose any of 'em would believe that—any o' them skippers I've beaten voyage after voyage? Can't you hear 'em laughin' and sneerin'—Tibbots 'n' Harris 'n' Simms and the rest—and all o' Homeport makin' fun o' me? "Dave Keeney what boasts he's the best whalin' skipper out o' Homeport comin' back with a measly four hundred barrel of ile?" (*The thought of this drives him into a frenzy, and he smashes his fist down on the marble top of the sideboard*) Hell! I got to git the ile, I tell you. How could I figger on this ice? It's never been so bad before in thirty year I been acomin' here. And now it's breakin' up. In a couple o' days it'll be all gone. And they's whale here, plenty of 'em. I know they is and I ain't never gone wrong yit. I got to git me the ile! I got to git it in spite of all hell, and I ain't agoin' home till I do git it!

EUGENE O'NEILL

2

This scene from *Suppressed Desires* is in direct contrast to the heavy somberness of *Ile*. The tone is light, the tempo fast. The vocal quality of the two principals, Henrietta and Steve, should reveal the impatient husband and the understanding wife who is attempting to solve her husband's problem through her newest fad of psychoanalysis. Her voice must reflect her intense "psychological look" when she is on the trail of a complex. Steve's voice is definitely that of the disgruntled husband who objects strenuously to being awakened at night to have his dreams analyzed. Mabel's voice serves as a decoy for Steve's disgust and Henrietta's glee at finding a subject to work on.

ANALYZING MABEL'S DREAM[17]

There is a breakfast table set for three, but only two seated at it— HENRIETTA *and* STEPHEN BREWSTER. *As the curtains withdraw* STEVE *pushes back his coffee cup and sits dejected.*

HENRIETTA. It isn't the coffee, Steve dear. There's nothing the matter with the coffee. There's something the matter with you.

STEVE. (*Doggedly*) There may be something the matter with my stomach.

HENRIETTA. (*Scornfully*) Your stomach! The trouble is not with your stomach but in your subconscious mind.

STEVE. Subconscious piffle!

HENRIETTA. Steve, you never used to be so disagreeable. You certainly have got some sort of a complex. You're all inhibited. You're no longer open to new ideas. You won't listen to a word about psychoanalysis.

STEVE. A word! I've listened to volumes!

---

[17] From *Suppressed Desires*, pp. 3-6. Copyright, 1917, by the Walter H. Baker Company. Reprinted by permission of the publishers.

HENRIETTA. You've ceased to be creative in architecture—your work isn't going well. You're not sleeping well—

STEVE. How can I sleep, Henrietta, when you're always waking me up in the night to find out what I have been dreaming?

HENRIETTA. But dreams are so important, Steve. If you'd tell yours to Dr. Russell he'd find out exactly what's wrong with you.

STEVE. There's nothing wrong with me.

HENRIETTA. You don't talk as well as you used to.

STEVE. Talk? I can't say a thing without you looking at me in that dark fashion you have when you're on the trail of a complex.

HENRIETTA. This very irritability indicates that you are suffering from some suppressed desire.

STEVE. I'm suffering from a suppressed desire for a little peace.

HENRIETTA. Dr. Russell is doing simply wonderful things with nervous cases. Won't you go to him, Steve?

STEVE. (*Slamming down his newspaper*) No, Henrietta, I won't!

HENRIETTA. But, Stephen—!

STEVE. Tst! I hear Mabel coming. Let's not be at each other's throats the first day of her visit.

MABEL. Good morning.

HENRIETTA. Oh, here you are, little sister.

STEVE. Good morning, Mabel.

HENRIETTA. It's so good to have you here. I was going to let you sleep, thinking you'd be tired after the long trip. Sit down. There'll be fresh toast in a minute and will you have—

MABEL. Oh, I ought to have told you, Henrietta. Don't get anything for me. I'm not eating breakfast.

HENRIETTA. Not eating breakfast? (*She sits down, then leans toward* MABEL *and scrutinizes her*)

STEVE. (*Half to himself*) The psychoanalytical look!

HENRIETTA. Mabel, why aren't you eating breakfast?

MABEL. (*A little startled*) Why, no particular reason. I just don't care much for breakfast, and they say it keeps down—that is, it's a good thing to go without it.

HENRIETTA. Don't you sleep well? Did you sleep well last night?

MABEL. Oh yes, I sleep all right. Yes, I did have the funniest dream!

STEVE. S—h! S—t!

HENRIETTA. What did you dream, Mabel?

STEVE. Look-a-here, Mabel, I feel it's my duty to put you on. Don't tell Henrietta your dreams. If you do she'll find out that you have an underground desire to kill your father and marry your mother—

HENRIETTA. Don't be absurd, Stephen Brewster. (*Sweetly to* MABEL) What was your dream, dear?

MABEL. Well, I dreamed I was a hen.

HENRIETTA. A hen?

MABEL. Yes; and I was pushing along through a crowd as fast as I could, but being a hen, I couldn't walk very fast—it was like having a tight skirt, you know; and there was some sort of creature in a blue cap—you know how mixed up dreams are—and it kept shouting after me and saying, "Step, Hen! Step, Hen!" until I got all excited and just couldn't move at all.

HENRIETTA. (*Resting chin in palm and peering*) You say you became much excited?

MABEL. (*Laughing*) Oh, yes; I was in a terrible state.

HENRIETTA. (*Murmurs*) This is significant.

STEVE. She dreams she's a hen. She is told to step lively. She becomes violently agitated. What can it mean?

HENRIETTA. Mabel, do you know anything about psychoanalysis?

MABEL. Oh—not much. No—I— (*Brightening*) It's something about the war, isn't it?

STEVE. Not that kind of war.

MABEL. I thought it might be the name of a new explosive.

STEVE. It *is*.

MABEL. You see, Henrietta, I—we do not live in touch with intellectual things, as you do. Bob being a dentist—somehow—our friends—

STEVE. Oh, to be a dentist!

GEORGE CRAM COOK AND SUSAN GLASPELL

3

"De Lawd" walks calmly through *Green Pastures* with a full, resonant, bass voice and a serene, all-powerful manner. Noah's voice should contrast with "De Lawd's" because Noah is, so to speak, one of "De Lawd's" workers getting a directive. Noah is talkative, persistent, with definite tastes, and a good organizer. Be sure to find the humor of this scene.

"DE LAWD" CALLS ON NOAH[18]

The scene is the dining room of NOAH's *cabin.* NOAH's *wife is preparing dinner, as* NOAH *appears with a stranger.*

NOAH. Company, darlin'. (NOAH's *wife takes* NOAH's *and* GOD's *hats*) Dis gemman's a preacher, too. He's jest passin' through de country.

GOD. Good mo'nin', sister.

NOAH'S WIFE. Good mo'nin'. You jest ketch me when I'm gettin' dinner ready. You gonter stay with us?

GOD. If I ain't intrudin'. Brother Noah suggested—

[18] From *The Green Pastures*, pp. 63-72. Copyright, 1929, by Marc Connelly. Reprinted by permission of the publishers, Farrar & Rinehart, Inc.

NOAH'S WIFE. You set right down yere. I got a chicken in de pot an' it'll be ready in 'bout five minutes. I'll go out de back and call Shem, Ham 'n' Japheth. (*To* GOD) Dey's our sons. Dey live right acrost de way but always have Sunday dinner wid us. You mens make yo'selves conf'table.

GOD. Thank you, thank you kindly.

NOAH. You run along, we all right. (GOD *and* NOAH *seat themselves.* NOAH's *wife exits*)

GOD. You got a fine wife, Brother Noah.

NOAH. She pretty good woman.

GOD. Yes, suh, an' you got a nice little home. Have a ten-cent seegar? (GOD *offers him one*)

NOAH. Thank you, much obliged. (*Both men lean back restfully in their chairs*)

GOD. Jest what seems to be de main trouble 'mong mankind, Noah?

NOAH. Well, it seems to me de main trouble is dat de whol' distric' is wide open. Now you know dat makes fo' loose livin'. Men folks spen's all dere time fightin', loafin' an' gamblin', an' makin' bad likker.

GOD. What about de women?

NOAH. De women is worse dan de men. If dey ain't makin' love powder dey out beg, borrow an' stealin' money for policy tickets. Doggone, I come in de church Sunday fo' las' 'bout an hour befo' de meetin' was to start, and dere was a woman stealin' de altar cloth. She was goin' to hock it. Dey ain't got no moral sense. Now you take dat case las' month, over in East Putney. Case of dat young Willy Roback.

GOD. What about him?

NOAH. Dere is a boy sebenteen years old. Doggone, if he didn't elope with his aunt. Now, you know, dat kin' of goin' on is bad fo' a neighborhood.

GOD. Terrible, terrible.

NOAH. Yes, suh. Dis use' to be a nice, decent community. I been doin' my best to preach de Word, but seems like every time I preach de place jest goes a little mo' to de dogs. De good Lawd only knows what's gonter happen.

GOD. Dat is de truth. (*There is a pause. Each puffs his cigar. Suddenly* NOAH *grasps his knee, as if it were paining him, and twists his foot*)

NOAH. Huh!

GOD. What's de matter?

NOAH. I jest got a twitch. My buck-aguer I guess. Every now and then I gets a twitch in de knee. Might be a sign of rain.

GOD. That's just what it is. Noah, what's de mos' rain you ever had 'round dese parts?

NOAH. Well, de water come down fo' six days steady las' April an' de ribber got so swole it bust down de levee up 'bove Freeport. Raise cain all de way down to de delta.

GOD. What would you say was it to rain for forty days and nights?

NOAH. I'd say dat was a *complete* rain!

GOD. Noah, you don't know who I is, do you?

NOAH. (*Puzzled*) Yo' face looks easy, but I don' think I recall de name. (GOD *rises slowly, and as he reaches his full height, there is a crash of lightning, a moment's darkness, and a roll of thunder. It grows light again,* NOAH *is on his knees in front of* GOD) I should have known you. I should have seen de glory.

GOD. Dat's all right, Noah. You didn' know who I was.

NOAH. I'm jes' ol' preacher Noah, Lawd, an' I'm yo' servant. I ain' very much, but I'se all I got.

GOD. Sit down, Noah. Don' let me hear you shamin' you'se'f, caize yo' a good man. (*Timidly* NOAH *waits until* GOD *is seated, and then sits, himself*) I jest wanted to fin' out if you was good, Noah. Dat's why I'm walkin' de earth in de shape of a natchel man. I wish dey was mo' people like you. But, far as I kin see, you and yo' family is jest de only respectable people in de worl'.

NOAH. Dey jes all poor sinners, Lawd.

GOD. I know. I am your Lawd. I am a god of wrath and vengeance an' dat's why I'm gonter destroy dis' worl'.

NOAH. (*Almost in a whisper; drawing back*) Jest as you say, Lawd.

GOD. I ain't gonter destroy you, Noah. You and yo' family, yo' sheep an' cattle, an' all de udder things dat ain't human I'm gonter preserve. But de rest is gotta go. (*Takes a pencil and a sheet of paper from his pocket*) Look yere, Noah. (NOAH *comes over and looks over his shoulder*) I want you to build me a boat. I want you to call it de "Ark," and I want it to look like dis. (*He is drawing on the paper. Continues to write as he speaks*) I want you to take two of every kind of animal and bird dat's in de country. I want you to take seeds an' sprouts an' everythin' like dat an' put them on dat Ark, because dere is gonter be all dat rain. Dey's gonter to be a deluge, Noah, an' dey's goin' to be a flood. De levees is gonter bust an' everythin' dat's fastened down is comin' loose, but it ain't gonter float long, caize I'm gonter make a storm dat'll sink everythin' from a hencoop to a barn. Dey ain't a ship on de sea at'll be able to fight that tempest. Dey all got to go. Everythin'. Everythin' in dis pretty worl' I made, except one thing, Noah. You an' yo' family an' de things I said are goin' to ride dat storm in de Ark. Yere's de way it's to be. (*He hands* NOAH *the paper.* NOAH *takes it and reads*)

NOAH. (*Pause; looks at paper again*) Yes, suh, dis seems to be complete. Now 'bout the animals, Lawd, you say you want everythin'?

GOD. Two of everythin'.

NOAH. Dat would include jayraffes an' hippopotamusses?

GOD. Everythin' dat is.

NOAH. Dey was a circus in town las' week. I guess I kin fin' dem. Co'se I kin git all de rabbits an' possums an' wil' turkeys easy. I'll sen' de boys out. Hum, I'm jest wonderin'—

GOD. 'Bout what?

NOAH. 'Bout snakes. Think you'd like snakes, too?

GOD. Certainly. I want snakes.

NOAH. Oh, I kin git snakes, lots of 'em. Co'se, some of 'em's a little
dangerous. Maybe I better take a kag of likker, too?

GOD. You kin take a kag of likker.

NOAH. (*Musingly*) Yes, suh, dey's a awful lot of differ'nt kin's of snakes,
come to think about it. Dey's water moccasins, cottonmoufs, rattlers
—mus' be a hund'ed kin's of other snakes down in de swamps.
Maybe I better take two kags of likker.

GOD. (*Mildly*) I think de one kag's enough.

NOAH. No. I better take two kags. Besides I kin put one on each side
of de boat, an' balance de ship wid dem as well as havin' dem fo'
medicinal use.

GOD. You kin put one kag in de middle of de ship.

NOAH. (*Bouyantly*) Jest as easy to take two kags, Lawd.

GOD. I think one kag's enough.

NOAH. Yes, Lawd, but you see forty days—an' forty nights— (*There's
a distant roll of thunder*)

GOD. (*Firmly*) One kag, Noah.

NOAH. Yes, Lawd, one kag.

MARC CONNELLY

4

Shakespeare is a master in constructing scenes that move
quickly and build to a climax through the interplay of different
voices. In the following scene from *Hamlet,* you will observe that
the voices of Marcellus and Bernardo are used for reassurance
and background for Horatio's story. Horatio's voice must be alive
with its dramatic news but also cautious because of the great
portent of the news he tells and its effect upon Hamlet. The
question-answer technique adds suspense and calls for sustained
vocal quality and quick tempo.

HORATIO'S NEWS

HAMLET. My father!—methinks I see my father.

HORATIO. Oh, where, my lord?

HAM.   In my mind's eye, Horatio.

HOR. I saw him once; he was a goodly king.

HAM. He was a man, take him for all in all,
    I shall not look upon his like again.

HOR. My lord, I think I saw him yesternight.

HAM. Saw? Who?

HOR. My lord, the King your father.

HAM.   The King my father!

HOR. Season your admiration for a while
  With an attent ear, till I may deliver,
  Upon the witness of these gentlemen,
  This marvel to you.

HAM.   For God's love, let me hear!

HOR. Two nights together had these gentlemen,
  Marcellus and Bernardo, on their watch,
  In the dead waste and middle of the night,
  Been thus encount'red. A figure like your father,
  Arm'd at all points exactly, cap-a-pie
  Appears before them, and with solemn march
  Goes slow and stately by them. Thrice he walk'd
  By their oppress'd and fear-surprisèd eyes,
  Within his truncheon's length; whilst they, distill'd
  Almost to jelly with the act of fear,
  Stand dumb and speak not to him. This to me
  In dreadful secrecy impart they did,
  And I with them the third night kept the watch;
  Where, as they had deliver'd, both in time,
  Form of the thing, each word made true and good,
  The apparition comes. I knew your father;
  These hands are not more like.

HAM.   But where was this?

MARCELLUS. My lord, upon the platform where we watch'd.

HAM. Did you not speak to it?

HOR.   My lord, I did;
  But answer made it none. Yet once methought
  It lifted up its head and did address
  Itself to motion, like as it would speak;
  But even then the morning cock grew loud,
  And at the sound it shrunk in haste away,
  And vanish'd from our sight.

HAM.   'Tis very strange.

HOR. As I do live, my honour'd lord, 'tis true,
  And we did think it writ down in our duty
  To let you know of it.

HAM. Indeed, indeed, sirs. But this troubles me.
  Hold you the watch to-night?

MARCELLUS ⎱ We do, my lord.
BERNARDO ⎰

HAM. Arm'd, say you?

MAR. ⎱ Arm'd, my lord.
BER. ⎰

HAM. From top to toe?

MAR.
BER. } My lord, from head to foot.

HAM. Then saw you not his face?

HOR. O, yes, my lord; he wore his beaver up.

HAM. What, look'd he frowningly?

HOR.   A countenance more
In sorrow than in anger.

HAM.   Pale or red?

HOR. Nay, very pale.

HAM.   And fix'd his eyes upon you?

HOR. Most constantly.

HAM.   I would I had been there.

HOR. It would have much amaz'd you.

HAM. Very like, very like. Stay'd it long?

HOR. While one with moderate haste might tell a hundred.

MAR.
BER. } Longer, longer.

HOR. Not when I saw't.

HAM.   His bear was grizzly? No?

HOR. It was, as I have seen it in his life,
A sable silver'd.

HAM.   I will watch to-night;
Perchance 'twill walk again.

WILLIAM SHAKESPEARE

5

Later that night, Hamlet watches for his father, sees him, and follows him to a secluded spot. Hamlet is breathless with anxiety and suspense, so his voice should not be resonant and loud. The Ghost's words, in contrast to Hamlet's breathless ones, are uttered in a ponderous and stately manner and with a fully resonant voice.

THY FATHER'S SPIRIT

HAMLET. Where wilt thou lead me? Speak, I'll go no further.

GHOST. Mark me.

HAMLET.   I will.

GHOST.   My hour is almost come,
When I to sulphurous and tormenting flames
Must render up myself.

HAMLET.   Alas, poor ghost!

GHOST. Pity me not, but lend thy serious hearing
To what I shall unfold.

HAMLET. Speak; I am bound to hear.
GHOST. So art thou to revenge, when thou shalt hear.
HAMLET. What?
GHOST. I am thy father's spirit,
  Doom'd for a certain term to walk the night,
  And for the day confin'd to fast in fires,
  Till the foul crimes done in my days of nature
  Are burnt and purg'd away. But that I am forbid
  To tell the secrets of my prison-house,
  I could a tale unfold whose lightest word
  Would harrow up thy soul, freeze thy young blood,
  Make thy two eyes, like stars, start from their spheres,
  Thy knotty and combined locks to part
  And each particular hair to stand on end,
  Like quills upon the fretful porpentine.
  But this eternal blazon must not be
  To ears of flesh and blood. List, Hamlet, O, list!
  If thou didst ever thy dear father love—
HAMLET. O God!
GHOST. Revenge his foul and most unnatural murder.
HAMLET. Murder!
GHOST. Murder most foul, as in the best it is,
  But this most foul, strange, and unnatural.

WILLIAM SHAKESPEARE

CHAPTER 8

Vocal Force

The technique of making words as forceful or as gentle as needed is the next problem for study. Many of the effects necessary for good interpretation are to be acquired by the mastery of the many shades and nuances of force, or intensity of tone, which must be differentiated from loudness, or extensity of tone.

Control of Force

The element of sound called *force* or *volume* is controlled in interpretation mainly by the manner in which the breath stream is expelled. How much breath is used? And how is it sustained? Does it come out forcibly and rapidly or slowly and evenly or abruptly? Will the attack be hard or soft? When you are speaking, the rhythm of breathing is not the smooth, easy, flowing rhythm of involuntary breathing; it is dependent upon the rhythm of your ideas, on the grouping and phrasing of your thought, on the stress and attack on your words. If the interpretation is to appear easy and effortless in presentation, breathing must be controlled and subordinated to the rhythm of the material to be interpreted.

Lack of proper force probably means that there is not enough energy being expended by the muscles of the abdominal regions. Sometimes this lack is due to the absence of "know-how"; sometimes it is due to the physical and emotional make-up of the person. A voice that never attacks vigorously indicates that the person is likely to be unresponsive. Those who are not intense enough in their emotional reactions to bother about using more than the minimum energy in speaking will usually have colorless, weak voices. They are the passive people who accept everything and anything that lies along the path of least resistance. There is a lack of intention and purpose in whatever they say and, probably, in whatever they do. Flabby, unused muscles usually mean flabby, lukewarm emotions; and because the voice is an indicator of how one thinks and feels, lukewarm emotions produce a voice without spontaneity. Be conscious of variety in the intensity, the fullness, the force of your tones, if you would develop speech that is expressive and communicative. To those who live and feel vividly, an apathetic, hypotonic person is one of the most uninteresting creatures to be found anywhere.

It should be the aim of the interpreter, then, to have animated, lively speech, to show a body well organized and adjusted to the situation. The audience likes the idea that you are purposeful and sincerely alert to the fact that you have something to offer for their enjoyment. Your body and face can do much to show this animation, but your voice must also demonstrate the interpreter's willingness to respond to the situation and the selection.

Loudness

Some people believe that force means *loudness*, or extensity of tone; but no sensitive interpretation requires loudness. In fact, loudness destroys enjoyment and too often makes the listeners cringe. What the interpreter wants is not loudness, which usually increases to shouting, but projection controlled by an energized exhalation. Furthermore, loudness will often cause strain and tension in the vocal folds, whereas well-projected voices with fullness and strength will show no strain, no tensions, no harshness. In an effort to project or to make tones carry or to adjust volume to a large room, often the interpreter will strain and tense the muscles of the larynx instead of sustaining tones by means of abdominal pressure. The voice, consequently, becomes harsh, sometimes high-pitched or nasal, and if vocalization is long continued, may become husky. During World War II, it was found that many new officers were unable to vocalize above a whisper after thirty minutes of issuing commands. This was not due to the fact that there was anything wrong with their vocal or breathing mechanisms, but there was everything wrong with the way they were using these mechanisms. They were trying to secure "carrying power" by shouting, thereby expelling all their breath and, consequently, issuing their commands on residual air. Strain and tension in the delicate muscles which control the vocal folds were reduced only after the men had been taught to secure force and energy from the abdominal muscles and then to control the breath stream properly.

Forms of Attack

Many emotional effects can be created by the manner in which various vocal sounds are projected. Sounds and words produced with a staccato tone indicate a positive attitude; a soft, gentle approach to sounds indicates an entirely different attitude. To say, "Give me what I ask!" with a sharp, vigorous attack is urgent and impolite or, at least, importunate; to say it gently suggests persuasiveness and control. Voice experts of several generations ago formulated three terms descriptive of forms of attack: *effusive* or smooth tone; *expulsive* or vigorous tone; *explosive* or abrupt tone. These terms are useful only insofar as they help us to understand the degree and variety of the attack to be used and how the exhaled air stream is to be controlled. However, they are not to be thought of as mutually exclusive; they blend according to the meaning. The interpreter can learn to use these different forms of force, if he can control the rhythm of his breathing; for the kind of attack is dependent, as we have already said, upon the power and control of the breath.

Smoothness of tone is produced by an evenness of movement in the respiratory muscle systems. There must be a steady pressure of outgoing air to secure the gentle, easy attack without abruptness. You have listened to Lew Sarett's interpretation of "Four Little Foxes" for vocal quality. Now, listen again to his recording. Study his smoothness of projection or attack. Notice the restraint and control he achieves. Try to keep this smoothness in your interpretation of the poem.

FOUR LITTLE FOXES[1]

Speak gently, Spring, and make no sudden sound;
For in my windy valley, yesterday I found
New-born foxes squirming on the ground—
　　　　　Speak gently.

Walk softly, March, forbear the bitter blow;
Her feet within a trap, her blood upon the snow,
The four little foxes saw their mother go—
　　　　　Walk softly.

Go lightly, Spring, oh, give them no alarm;
When I covered them with boughs to shelter them from harm,
The thin blue foxes suckled at my arm—
　　　　　Go lightly.

Step softly, March, with your rampant hurricane;
Nuzzling one another, and whimpering with pain,
The new little foxes are shivering in the rain—
　　　　　Step softly.

LEW SARETT

Vigor of tone is characterized by firmness and definiteness of
attack, which is produced by continuous energetic pressure from
the respiratory muscles. It is the mean between the steady pressure used in the smooth tone and the abrupt pressure exerted in
the explosive attack and is used more often than either of the
other two. It bespeaks earnestness, spontaneity, sincerity, forthrightness. An admirable example of this form of attack is Lew
Sarett's interpretation of "Requiem for a Modern Croesus,"
which, as he says in the recording, is the length of a telegram but
contains the story of an entire lifetime. The vigor of tone which
you hear in Sarett's explanatory remarks is heard again in the
poem itself but with a different approach.

[1] By permission from *The Collected Poems of Lew Sarett*, p. 5. Copy-
right, 1920, 1922, 1925, 1931, 1941, by Henry Holt and Company, Inc.
This and the three following selections appear in the record album *Lew
Sarett: Reading from His Collected Poems* (Columbia, XTV-15494, 15495).

REQUIEM FOR A MODERN CROESUS[2]

To him the moon was a silver dollar, spun
Into the sky by some mysterious hand; the sun
    Was a gleaming golden coin—
        His to purloin;
The freshly minted stars were dimes of delight
Flung out upon the counter of the night.

    In yonder room he lies,
    With pennies on his eyes.

Lew Sarett

Explosiveness of tone is produced by a sudden hard pressure
from the abdominal muscles. The movement is more powerful
and more sudden than in the smooth or vigorous projection. The
explosive form of attack is used when a selection requires a series
of short, sharp shouts which communicate intensity of speech.
Sarett's recording of "Thunderdrums" contains a combination of
all kinds of attack but excels in the exultant staccato calls of "Hi!
Hi! Hi!" and "Ho! Ho! Ho!" and powerful attacks on phrases
like "Beat on the buckskin, beat on the drums." In stanza 2, pay
particular attention to the sharpness and abruptness of each line,
which give the impression of quick, flying steps. In stanza 4,
listen for the difference between the abrupt first line and the
second series of "Ho!" In stanza 5, notice the effusiveness of attack throughout, except in the lines "Look! to the West!" and
"Beat, beat on the drums," and "Wuh!"

from THUNDERDRUMS[3]

1

THE DRUMMERS SING

Beat on the buckskin, beat on the drums,
Hi! Hi! Hi! for the Thunderbird comes;
His eyes burn red with the blood of battle;

---

[2] By permission from *The Collected Poems of Lew Sarett*, p. 217. Copyright, 1920, 1922, 1925, 1931, 1941, by Henry Holt and Company, Inc.
[3] By permission from *The Collected Poems of Lew Sarett*, p. 127. Copyright, 1920, 1922, 1925, 1931, 1941, by Henry Holt and Company, Inc.

His wild wings roar in the medicine-rattle.
Thunderbird-god, while our spirits dance,
Tip with your lightning the warrior's lance;
On shafts of wind, with heads of flame,
Build for us arrows that torture and maim;
Ho! may our ironwood war-clubs crash
With a thunderbolt head and a lightning flash.
Hí! Hí! Hí! hear the Cut-throat's doom,
As our wild bells ring and our thunderdrums boom.

2

DOUBLE-BEAR DANCES

Hí! Hí! Hí!
My wild feet fly,
For I follow the track
Of a cowardly pack;
Footprints here,
Footprints there—
Enemies near!—
Taint in the air!
Signs on the sod!
Ho! the Thunderbird-god
Gives me the eye
Of a hawk in the sky!—
Beat, beat on the drums,
For the Thunderbird comes.

Ho! Ho!
Ho! Ho!

4

GHOST-WOLF DANCES

Hó! Ho! Hó!
In the winds that blow
From yonder hill,
When the night is still,
What do I hear
With my Thunderbird ear?
Down from the river
A gray wolf's wail?
Coyotes that shiver
And slink the tail?
Ugh! enemies dying—

And women crying!—
For Cut-throat men—
One, two . . . nine, ten.
Hó! Ho! Hó!
The Spirit-winds blow—
Beat, beat on the drums,
For the Thunderbird comes.

Ah-hah-háy!
Ah-hah-háy!

5

IRON-WIND DANCES

Over and under
The shaking sky,
The war-drums thunder
When I dance by!
Ho! a warrior proud,
I dance on a cloud,
For my ax shall feel
The enemy reel;
My heart shall thrill
To a bloody kill—
Ten Sioux dead
Split open of head!
Look! to the West!—
The sky-line drips—
Blood from the lips!
Ho! when I dance by,
The war-drums thunder
Over and under
The shaking sky.
Beat, beat on the drums,
For the Thunderbird comes.

Wuh!
Wuh!

LEW SARETT

Variety in Forms of Force

To use one of these forms of attack constantly will produce
monotonous speaking and interpretation. As you listened to
Sarett's interpretation of "Thunderdrums," you were aware of

the hard sudden cries, the vigor in "Footprints here,/Footprints there," the smoothness of lines like, "What do I hear." It may be wise for you to listen to your own vocal pattern and to those of others for the variety in force which is so important for pleasant speech. A speaker who employs a continuous, explosive, bombastic force leaves us cold because the voice does not convey finer and more significant meanings. A teacher often uses sharpness of attack that becomes wearisome to those exposed to her all day long. Neither are we pleased to have about us people who continually use a subdued voice which lacks discrimination in responding with alertness and with vigor.

Touch

Variety in the application of force is gained through the heaviness or lightness of your *touch*, just as musicians try to gain the proper touch for the melody they are playing. In interpretation, you should learn to vary the amount of force according to the meaning. The smooth attack will not always have the same touch —it may be light or it may be heavy. So variety of touch must be studied within each form of force as well as variety among the forms of force.

Listen again to Sarett's interpretation of his poem "Wéeng" for *variety and control in touch*. Even though the general tone of the poem as interpreted is smooth, there is great variety within that range of smoothness.

WÉENG[4]

(*An Indian Slumber-song*)

Hush! my baby, or soon you will hear
The Sleepy-eye, Wéeng-oosh, hovering near;
Out of the timber he will come,
A little round man as small as your thumb.
Swinging his torch of a red fire-fly,
Out of the shadows old Sleepy-eye,
With sound of a ghost, on the wind will creep
To see if a little boy lies asleep;

[4] From *Slow Smoke*, p. 58. Copyright, 1925, by Henry Holt and Company, Inc. Reprinted by permission of the publishers.

Over your cheeks old Wéeng will go,
With feet as soft as the falling snow—
Tip-toe . . . . tip-toe.

Hush! my little one, close your lids tight,
Before old Sleepy-eye comes to-night;
Hi-yáh! if he finds you are still awake,
He draws from his quiver a thistledown stake;
With an acorn for club he pounds on its butt,
Till Sleepy-eye hammers the open eye shut;
Then from his bundle he pulls out another,
Hops over your nose and closes the other;
Up and down with his club he will rap
On the open lid till he closes the gap—
Tap-tap . . . . tap-tap.

If Wéeng-oosh comes at the end of this day,
And finds you asleep he will hurry away . . .
Do you hear him cry on the winds that blow?—
And walk on the earth as soft as a doe?—
To-and-fro . . . . to-and-fro. . .
Hi-yáh! he has crept away from my lap!
For he found my little boy taking a nap.
Oh, weep no more and whisper low,
I hear the feet of Sleepy-eye go—
Tip-toe . . . . tip-toe.

Lew Sarett

A few weeks before his death, Lew Sarett wrote to us concerning his recording:[5]

I am so glad that you liked my record. It has had a wonderful sale. I feel that readers of my poems should know how the author of them *meant* them to be read, or again, how the author *himself* reacts to them, for good or for ill. That should be helpful. For example, in the recording—and always on the platform—I read "Four Little Foxes" and "Wind in the Pine" with great and deep feeling inwardly but always with great *restraint;* I never express outwardly one half of what I feel. I do this because that is the way I am made. But also it happens to be the most effective way to read these moving poems; they have a head of steam when they are read with restraint. So also with the Indian poems—readers should learn much from the recording. I doubt that anybody ever saw fully the beauty of the Indian sleep-story, "Wéeng," until he got the melodic pattern established in the recording. . . . As you say, "Requiem," is succinct. It

[5] From a letter to the authors dated July 28, 1954.

says a lot in a few words—and they cut deep. Another favorite of mine is "Deep Wet Moss." It is a smooth and deep little poem.

EXERCISES

As a class, study the following selections for effective vocal force. Decide whether the interpreter should use a heavy or light touch. Whenever you can listen to someone's recorded interpretation, do so. Do not try to imitate, but see if you approve. If you do not approve, decide what changes you would make to carry a different meaning and mood.

I

Basil Rathbone, as was mentioned earlier, uses a discriminating touch in interpreting the sonnet "How Do I Love Thee?" [6] Try it yourself.

HOW DO I LOVE THEE?

How do I love thee? Let me count the ways.
I love thee to the depth and breadth and height
My soul can reach, when feeling out of sight
For the ends of Being and ideal Grace.
I love thee to the level of every day's
Most quiet need, by sun and candle-light.
I love thee freely, as men strive for Right;
I love thee purely, as men turn from Praise.
I love thee with the passion put to use
In my old griefs, and with my childhood's faith.
I love thee with a love I seemed to lose
With my lost saints,—I love thee with the breath,
Smiles, tears, of all my life!—and, if God choose,
I shall but love thee better after death.
ELIZABETH BARRETT BROWNING

II

On first reading Blake's "The Tiger," one experiences a brilliant flash that stuns one. On recall, the poem, which is superb in its compression and sharply etched manner of phrasing, still sends

[6] In the record album *Masterpieces of Literature: Great Themes in Poetry* (Columbia, E11-10), sponsored by the National Council of Teachers of English.

out its startling burning light. The images which inspire awe, fear, doubt, suggest the analogy of the fire in a blacksmith's forge: the anvil, hammer, furnace and fire shining through the dark of the forest. Many believe that the tiger is a symbol of evil, and that the lamb is one of innocence or good. What meaning do you find?

The interpretation as given by Edith Evans[7] shows interesting variety in touch. Notice how the poem becomes more dramatic by the use of questions which mount in increasing interest and force.

THE TIGER

Tiger! Tiger! burning bright
In the forests of the night,
What immortal hand or eye
Could frame thy fearful symmetry?

In what distant deeps or skies
Burnt the fire of thine eyes?
On what wings dare he aspire?
What the hand dare seize the fire?

And what shoulder, and what art,
Could twist the sinews of thy heart?
And when the heart began to beat,
What dread hand? And what dread feet?

What the hammer? what the chain?
In what furnace was thy brain?
What the anvil? what dread grasp
Dare its deadly terrors clasp?

When the stars threw down their spears,
And watered heaven with their tears,
Did he smile his work to see?
Did he who made the Lamb make thee?

Tiger! Tiger! burning bright
In the forests of the night,
What immortal hand or eye
Dare frame thy fearful symmetry?

WILLIAM BLAKE

[7] In the record album *The Voice of Poetry* (Columbia, MM-375), sponsored by the National Council of Teachers of English.

III

Compare the above interpretation by Edith Evans with her recording of "Why So Pale and Wan?" [8] Notice the lightness of the touch and attack. Notice also that both poems employ a series of questions to build to a climax.

WHY SO PALE AND WAN

Why so pale and wan, fond lover?
    Prithee, why so pale?
Will, if looking well can't move her,
    Looking ill prevail?
    Prithee, why so pale?

Why so dull and mute, young sinner?
    Prithee, why so mute?
Will, when speaking well can't win her,
    Saying nothing do't?
    Prithee, why so mute?

Quit, quit, for shame! This will not move,
    This cannot take her.
If of herself she will not love,
    Nothing can make her:
    The devil take her!

                Sir John Suckling

IV

The tone and mood of the next selection is reflected in the first two lines. It would be impossible to use any but a lazy, drawling tone. If the interpreter gets too ambitious in portraying Joe, he will give him too much energy, for Joe is a dreamer and a loafer —"that wuthless scamp." Ease into the poem.

JOE[9]

A keerless, lanky sort was Joe,
An' kind o' lonesome like, you know;
He didn't seem to want a home,
Jes' seemed to be content to roam.

[8] *Ibid.*
[9] Reprinted by permission of The Stratford Company.

He never came to meetin' camp,
An' folks called him "that wuthless scamp!"

But I have seen him on the hill,
At sunset, watch the sky until
He seemed to grow an inch in height,
As if he breathed the very sight.

An' felt my eyes grow sort o' damp
A-watchin' him—"that wuthless scamp!"

I've seen him in the woods alone,
A-lis'nin' to its lazy drone,
As if 'twas music that he heered—
His eyes so set, they had me skeered.

He thought great things, I guess, to tramp
All day alone—"that wuthless scamp!"

I've heered him laugh at children's play—
A laugh so clear, an' sweet, an' gay,
That trembled like the organ when
They drown its wheezin', now and then.

But reg'lar folks at meetin' camp
Said he was "lost"—"that wuthless scamp!"

He always was the lonesome kind—
A sort o' misfit—didn't find
His fun in things that others did,
As boy an' man, his heart was hid.

I think the folks who shun his stamp
Don't understand "that wuthless scamp!"

                                        LEWIS W. BRITTON

V

The character of Shylock in the *Merchant of Venice* always
offers variety in interpretation, especially in attack. In the following passage, Shylock is taunting Antonio, who, beset by his
financial losses, has come to ask Shylock for a loan. Each one of
Shylock's comments about Antonio and himself varies in force.
You can sense the abruptness of his imitation of Antonio by the
direct statement, "Shylock, we would have moneys." And there is
a cue to the interpretation of the last four lines in his words,
"bated breath and whispering humbleness."

WE WOULD HAVE MONEYS

SHYLOCK
Signor Antonio, many a time and oft
In the Rialto you have rated me
About my moneys and my usances;
Still have I borne it with a patient shrug,
For sufferance is the badge of all our tribe. . . .
Well, then, it now appears you need my help.
Go to, then. You come to me, and you say,
"Shylock, we would have moneys." . . .
What should I say to you? Should I not say,
"Hath a dog money? Is it possible
A cur can lend three thousand ducats?" Or
Shall I bend low, and in a bondman's key,
With bated breath and whispering humbleness,
Say this:
"Fair sir, you spat on me on Wednesday last;
You spurn'd me such a day; another time
You call'd me dog; and for these courtesies
I'll lend you thus much moneys"?

WILLIAM SHAKESPEARE, *Merchant of Venice*

VI

The following three poems are very different in mood; consequently, the attack will vary for each:

1. "The Toast of Mars" has an ironic, mocking tone which, in this instance, calls for a strong attack. Phrases like, "ghastly cry," "Hear ye," "war-god Mars," "to the dregs I quaff," and "with a mocking laugh" indicate a force that is not smooth and even.

2. "A Red, Red Rose" has an assurance in its lines which keeps it from being wholly reminiscent. There is an optimism which does not indicate the tearful sadness with which this poem is sometimes interpreted. The force, therefore, should not be too subdued; nor should it be too violent. Try for a happy mean, especially in the first three stanzas. If you feel the need for mournfulness, be sure to save it for the last stanza. Even then, do not drone.

3. "Red Winds" has a somber quietness which calls for a smooth, even attack, almost to the point of monotony. The vocal quality is important in establishing the mood.

THE TOAST OF MARS[10]

My ghastly cry I raise on high,
    In great Olympus' hall.
Listen, oh gods, for Mars am I,
    Hear ye my battle call.

In my wine cup grim, filled to battered brim,
    Foam twinkling, bloody stars.
O list ye well what I have to tell,
    The toast of the war-god Mars!

O the life of the slain and the racking pain
    And the agony are mine.
All that men can be, they must offer me,
    With the blood of their hearts for wine.

Turn not away; in my goblet gray
    Foam twinkling, bloody stars.
To the dregs I quaff; with a mocking laugh
    I give you the toast of Mars!

                MARY E. OAKES

A RED, RED ROSE

Oh, my luve is like a red, red rose,
    That's newly sprung in June.
Oh, my luve is like the melodie,
    That's sweetly played in tune.

As fair art thou, my bonie lass,
    So deep in luve am I,
And I will luve thee still, my dear,
    Till a' the seas gang dry.

Till a' the seas gang dry, my dear,
    And the rocks melt wi' the sun!
And I will luve thee still, my dear,
    While the sands o' life shall run.

And fare thee weel, my only luve!
    And fare thee weel a while!
And I will come again, my luve,
    Tho' it were ten thousand mile!

                ROBERT BURNS

[10] Reprinted by permission of The Stratford Company.

RED WINDS[11]

I hear the shadows moving among old trees;
I see cold, white mists face new ecstasies;
    And I, a thing of tears
    And fears.

I hear the dead feet travel in a row;
I see the torn leaves falling where they go;
    And I, a sleeping stone
    Age blown.

I hear the red winds of the west arise;
I see strange, wide and watchful, waiting eyes;
    And I, a thing of dust
    In trust.

WINIFRED V. JACKSON

VII

Here are two poems that are decidedly different in mood, attack, imagery, and purpose:

1. "Birches" is reminiscent, pleasantly so, with the author's philosophy woven in and out of the lines. One gets the impression that the author is musing aloud, happily recalling his boyhood. Try to listen to Frost's recording of this poem.

2. "Chicago," on the other hand, is a vigorous, hard-hitting poem in which Sandburg rapidly heaps one image upon another with fierce bluntness and energy. Notice how a climax is reached in the last four lines by repetition of some of the most vivid phrases.

BIRCHES[12]

When I see birches bend to left and right
Across the lines of straighter darker trees,
I like to think some boy's been swinging them.
But swinging doesn't bend them down to stay.
Ice-storms do that. Often you must have seen them

---

[11] From the *Emerson Quarterly* (January, 1923), p. 178. Reprinted by permission of the publishers.

[12] From *Complete Poems of Robert Frost*. Copyright, 1930–1949, by Henry Holt and Company, Inc. Copyright, 1936, 1948, by Robert Frost. Reprinted by permission of the publishers.

Loaded with ice a sunny winter morning
After a rain. They click upon themselves
As the breeze rises, and turn many-colored
As the stir cracks and crazes their enamel.
Soon the sun's warmth makes them shed crystal shells
Shattering and avalanching on the snow-crust—
Such heaps of broken glass to sweep away
You'd think the inner dome of heaven had fallen.
They are dragged to the withered bracken by the load,
And they seem not to break; though once they are bowed
So low for long, they never right themselves:
You may see their trunks arching in the woods
Years afterwards, trailing their leaves on the ground
Like girls on hands and knees that throw their hair
Before them over their heads to dry in the sun.
But I was going to say when Truth broke in
With all her matter-of-fact about the ice-storm
I should prefer to have some boy bend them
As he went out and in to fetch the cows—
Some boy too far from town to learn baseball,
Whose only play was what he found himself,
Summer or winter, and could play alone.
One by one he subdued his father's trees
By riding them down over and over again
Until he took the stiffness out of them,
And not one but hung limp, not one was left
For him to conquer. He learned all there was
To learn about not launching out too soon
And so not carrying the tree away
Clear to the ground. He always kept his poise
To the top branches, climbing carefully
With the same pains you use to fill a cup
Up to the brim, and even above the brim.
Then he flung outward, feet first, with a swish,
Kicking his way down through the air to the ground.
So was I once myself a swinger of birches.
And so I dream of going back to be.
It's when I'm weary of considerations,
And life is too much like a pathless wood
Where your face burns and tickles with the cobwebs
Broken across it, and one eye is weeping
From a twig's having lashed across it open.
I'd like to get away from earth awhile
And then come back to it and begin over.
May no fate willfully misunderstand me
And half grant what I wish and snatch me away

Not to return. Earth's the right place for love:
I don't know where it's likely to go better.
I'd like to go by climbing a birch tree,
And climb black branches up a snow-white trunk
Toward heaven, till the tree could bear no more,
But dipped its top and set me down again.
That would be good both going and coming back.
One could do worse than be a swinger of birches.

ROBERT FROST

CHICAGO[13]

Hog Butcher for the World,
Tool Maker, Stacker of Wheat,
Player with Railroads and the Nation's Freight Handler;
Stormy, husky, brawling,
City of the Big Shoulders:
They tell me you are wicked and I believe them, for I have seen your painted women under the gas lamps luring the farm boys.
And they tell me you are crooked and I answer: Yes, it is true I have seen the gunman kill and go free to kill again.
And they tell me you are brutal and my reply is: On the faces of women and children I have seen the marks of wanton hunger.
And having answered so I turn once more to those who sneer at this my city, and I give them back the sneer and say to them:
Come and show me another city with lifted head singing so proud to be alive and coarse and strong and cunning.
Flinging magnetic curses amid the toil of piling job on job, here is a tall bold slugger set vivid against the little soft cities;
Fierce as a dog with tongue lapping for action, cunning as a savage pitted against the wilderness,
Bareheaded,
Shoveling,
Wrecking,
Planning,
Building, breaking, rebuilding,
Under the smoke, dust all over his mouth, laughing with white teeth,
Under the terrible burden of destiny laughing as a young man laughs,
Laughing even as an ignorant fighter laughs who has never lost a battle,
Bragging and laughing that under his wrist is the pulse, and under his ribs the heart of the people,
Laughing!

[13] From *Chicago Poems*, p. 3. Copyright, 1916, by Henry Holt and Company, Inc. Reprinted by permission of the publishers.

Laughing the stormy, husky, brawling laughter of Youth, half-naked,
   sweating, proud to be Hog Butcher, Tool Maker, Stacker of
   Wheat, Player with Railroads and Freight Handler to the
   Nation.

CARL SANDBURG

VIII

Prose, too, offers wide contrast and variety for the interpreter
in his study and projection of force. We have emphasized the
need for you, the interpreter, to understand the author's idea or
meaning before you try varying degrees of attack. This principle
applies as much to prose literature as to poetry. Contrast the
ideas of this next selection with "Chicago," which you have just
read. Notice the mood, vocabulary, phrasing, and form. Sandburg uses metaphor and personification in describing a big city.
Does Wolfe?

THE CITY[14]

And the image of the city, written in his heart, was so unbelievable
that it seemed to be a fiction, a fable, some huge dream of his own
dreaming, so unbelievable that he did not think that he should find
it when he returned; yet it was just the same as he had remembered
it. He found it, the instant he came out of the station: the tidal swarm
of faces, the brutal stupefaction of the street, the immense and arrogant blaze and sweep of the great buildings.

It was fabulous and incredible, but there it was. He saw again the
million faces—the faces dark, dingy, driven, harried, and corrupt,
the faces stamped with all the familiar markings of suspicion and
mistrust, cunning, contriving, and a hard and stupid cynicism. There
were the faces, thin and febrile, of the taxi drivers, the faces cunning, sly, and furtive, the hard twisted mouths and rasping voices,
the eyes glittering and toxic with unnatural fires. And there were the
faces, cruel, arrogant and knowing, the brutal heavy figures of the
Irish cops, and their red beefy faces, filled with the stupid, swift, and
choleric menaces of privilege and power, shining forth terribly with
an almost perverse and sanguinary vitality and strength among the
swarming tides of the gray-faced people. They were all there as he
remembered them—a race mongrel, dark, and feverish, swarming
along forever on the pavements, moving in tune to that vast central
energy, filled with the city's life, as with a general and dynamic
fluid. . . .

[14] From *Of Time and the River*, pp. 415-416. Copyright, 1935, by Charles
Scribner's Sons. Reprinted by permission of the publishers.

And as he saw them, as he heard them, as he listened to their words again, as they streamed past, their stony gravel of harsh oaths and rasping cries, the huge single anathema of their bitter and strident tongues dedicated so completely, so constantly, to the baseness, folly, or treachery of their fellows that it seemed that speech had been given to them by some demon of everlasting hatred only in order that they might express the infamy and vileness of men, or the falseness of women—as he listened to this huge and single tongue of hatred, evil, and of folly, it seemed incredible that they could breathe the shining air without weariness, agony, and labor—that they could live, breathe, move at all among the huge encrusted taint, the poisonous congestion of their lives.

And yet live, breathe, and move they did with a savage and indubitable violence, an unfathomed energy. Hard-mouthed, hard-eyed, and strident-tongued, with their million hard gray faces, they streamed past upon the streets forever, like a single animal, with the sinuous and baleful convolutions of an enormous reptile. And the magical and shining air—the strange, subtle and enchanted weather, was above them, and the buried men were strewn through the earth on which they trod, and a bracelet of great tides was flashing round them, and the enfabled rock on which they swarmed swung eastward in the marches of the sun into eternity, and was masted like a ship with its terrific towers, and was flung with a lion's port between its tides into the very maw of the infinite, all-taking ocean. And exultancy and joy rose with a cry of triumph in his throat, because he found it wonderful.

THOMAS WOLFE

IX

The following selections illustrate the essay, the narrative, and the drama, three different forms of prose writing:

1. "Calling Cards" is an essay which moves along easily and with casual humor, so the tone should be energetic but not too forceful.

2. "Buttin'" has a contrasting combination of abrupt, vigorous thrusts and an easy, informal narrative style.

3. The scene from *Adam*, which is punctuated with energy and abruptness, rises through a series of minor episodes to the climax of Lucy's last line. The voices of the three characters offer an interesting study in touch: the brother's is the heaviest; the mother's is an echo of her son's, but milder; Lucy's is intense and subdued.

CALLING CARDS[15]

I have been returning calls, an occupation which makes me realize with appalling accuracy what a diamond in the rough I am. I have learned that you leave two of your husband's cards and one of your own, though why I cannot tell, unless it indicates the relative status of men and women in England. I have learned to judge how long fifteen minutes lasts without peering near-sightedly at the clock and sinking back with an eloquent, involuntary "Oh!" But I cannot learn how to get rid of the cards.

Englishwomen leave cards in my house as unconcernedly as flowers shedding petals, but when I try to leave my cards in their houses, I have more trouble than if I were attempting to deposit a foundling. I endeavor first to give the cards to the maid who answers the door, but she puts both hands behind her and backs defiantly away. While she is announcing me, I look wildly around for a tray or a bowl, but if there is one, it is always hopelessly concealed under the strata of umbrellas, walking sticks, raincoats, and garden shears that form an integral part of every English hallway. I suppose if you could find it, it would probably be fossilized. In the end, I am out on the doorstep again, saying good-bye and still clutching the cards—which by this time look as if they had been salvaged from the Lusitania—in my hot, unhappy palm. It always concludes by my having to hold them out and say, "Here. Here's something for you," as if I were distributing samples of shaving cream. One of these days I am going to find myself adding that there is absolutely no obligation.

MARGARET HALSEY

BUTTIN' [16]

The canvas-covered tobacco wagon had been jolting over the frozen track of Little North Road since before dawn. On the seat huddled two small figures, almost submerged in a welter of quilts. Silent they sat, swaying instinctively to the pitch and roll of the wagon, as the steel tires climbed screechingly from rut to rut.

The larger, a white boy, held the reins loosely in one hand, allowing the mules their own way. His eyes were fixed abstractedly on the road ahead; his shoulders bowed, as if under weighty responsibilities. The clink of the breast chains, in soft accompaniment to the clack-clack of the mules' shoes on the frozen ground, and the rumble and creak of the heavily loaded wagon came vaguely to him as homely,

[15] From *With Malice Toward Some*, pp. 204-205. Copyright, 1938, by Simon and Schuster, Inc. Reprinted by permission of the publishers.

[16] From "Buttin' Blood," *The Atlantic Monthly* (September, 1928), p. 361. Reprinted by permission of the publishers.

comforting sounds, in the deserted stillness of early morning. And
the intimate mellow-peach fragrance of Virginia sun-cured tobacco,
together with the everyday mule-and-harness smell, drifted over him
comfortingly, too.

With a sigh he roused from his reverie and quickened the lagging
team. Glancing at the small head resting on his shoulder, muffled in
an old slouch hat brought down about the ears with a fragment of
blanket, his face softened into a whimsical smile. He gave a vigorous
shrug, and shouted:

"Wake up, Nubbin! Sun's up, nigger!"

The little form straightened with a start. An ashy black hand came
out from the chaos of covers and pulled off the head-piece. Slowly
he rubbed his face, scratched his head, and rolled his big eyes at his
companion.

"Huccome you 'niggah' me? I got big graveyard in de woods full
o' white boys what call me 'niggah'."

The white boy threw back his head and laughed; then, turning
suddenly, with an explosive "Baa!" butted his coonskin cap roundly
against the black ear.

"Ba-a! Phut! Phut!" went the little darky, jumping from the seat;
and bridling like an angry goat, sent his bullet head thump against the
white boy's ribs.

"Ouch! I give up! I give up!"

"You ain' gwine call me 'niggah' no mo'?"

"No! No! Cross my heart—and double cross," and his mittened hand
made youth's inviolable sign of the double cross.

"Dat's mo' like hit—an' you 'member hit too, Luther Patten." With
a final admonitory "Baa!" and a half-dancing shuffle of his big-shod
feet on the wagon bottom, he dived to the seat and snatched the
quilts about him.

PERNET PATTERSON

LUCY'S WHIM[17]

*The scene is in a manorial hall somewhere in England. Lucy and
her mother are sitting near a tall window. Lucy's brother hovers uneasily between them. They are discussing Lucy's decision to leave
her husband, Adam Elhar.*

THE MOTHER. Well, I'm sure I don't know what to advise—

THE BROTHER. Give it time—that's what I say.

MOTHER. Yes, why not? After all, Lucy, you've got nothing definite
to complain of. Or have you?

[17] From *Adam*, pp. 25-28. Copyright, 1929, by Ludwig Lewisohn. Reprinted by permission of the author and Harper & Brothers.

BROTHER. Why, when you cabled us to come I thought sure that Elhar had at least beaten you or been openly unfaithful to you.

MOTHER. I must say; so did I.

BROTHER. For God's sake, Lucy, don't sit there like a bump on a stump. Is there anything you haven't told us?

LUCY. I've got to get out of this.

MOTHER. Well, weren't you free to go to London? You've got a house there. You didn't need us for that.

LUCY. London! I've got to get out of this whole business. I'm going back home with you.

BROTHER. Hold your horses, young woman!

MOTHER. Exactly. You wouldn't call me old-fashioned. But simply to desert your husband when you have nothing to complain of on your own showing—why it doesn't seem to me that that's right.

BROTHER. And there are all sorts of interests involved. He pays your mother an income; he sets me up in business—

LUCY. Interests. . . .

BROTHER. Hold on! Don't misunderstand me. If Elhar has done you dirt, I'd be the first one to stand by and to knock his teeth down his throat. I never liked him, as you well know. But according to you—

MOTHER. No, I can't say I ever liked him either. Do me the justice to remember that I advised against him in spite of his millions. He always gave me a grue—

BROTHER. Me too. Gosh—

MOTHER. —but his behavior has been beyond criticism. And you seemed wild enough about him.

BROTHER. You certainly were! Why don't you talk things out with him? Where is he?

LUCY. In Monte Carlo.

MOTHER. Didn't he ask you to go with him?

LUCY. Yes. And he flew over the other day and asked me again.

BROTHER. Well, what the hell—

MOTHER. Can't you use decenter language?

BROTHER. Language!

MOTHER. And if I remember rightly, Lucy, it was you who wanted him to buy this place of the Darlingtons. I think it's gloomy if you ask me. But why didn't you go to France with him?

LUCY. Because—oh, there's no use. I'm going home.

BROTHER. Look here, Lou—these foreigners. Now I'm a man and your brother. Has he got any secret vices?

LUCY. Oh, how sick you make me!

BROTHER. Well, have it your own way. He's a perfect gentleman and a perfect husband. He asks you to go to the Riviera. He buys you a country-place and a house in London. He gives you jewels. He's the cat's pajamas. But you got to desert him and cable us to come and help you desert him. How does that all hang together? Who are you trying to make a fool of?

MOTHER. I can't help agreeing with your brother, my child. And I think it's hard that I should have to go back to scrimping and saving and that your brother should lose his chance on account of a whim of yours.

LUCY. Whim! Oh!

LUDWIG LEWISOHN

Climax

Not only does the interpreter watch the varying degrees of force, but he also knows that there may be a rhythmical movement of force from phrase to phrase, from sentence to sentence— either a building up or a letting down of attack at a certain point. This principle of culmination is called climax. (The term *climax* is derived from the Greek word meaning *ladder*.) Sometimes the climax that recedes or comes unexpectedly is more powerful than the one that rises, because of the sudden turn in movement.

Good literature uses this principle of climax in great abundance, whereby the writer, following the emotional tone, builds a rhythmical movement. The interpreter must be careful not to ignore the power of such lines. For instance, the following five sentences seemingly carry little emphasis because of the casual approach of the author; but a pause before the last line and the proper touch and emphasis on the last sentence can produce an effect almost as powerful as the atomic energy of which the author is speaking.[18]

This black object that I hold in my hand is a cylinder of pure uranium. The amount I hold here is small as you can see. It is harmless. Five years ago no man had even seen this much pure uranium. Not that it was rare, but it was simply of little importance. Tonight this black metal, this inanimate substance is the central figure in the councils of the peoples of the world.

DAVID E. LILIENTHAL

[18] From "Atomic Energy," delivered before the American Society of Newspaper Editors in Washington, D.C., on April 19, 1943. The text of this speech appears in *Representative American Speeches: 1946-1947* (New York, H. W. Wilson Co., 1947), pp. 134-143.

Shylock, when Salarino asks why he insists on having the pound of flesh from Antonio, replies quickly:

To bait fish withal. If it will feed nothing else, it will feed my revenge. He hath disgrac'd me, and hinder'd me half a million; laugh'd at my losses, mock'd at my gains, scorn'd my nation, thwarted my bargains, cool'd my friends, heated mine enemies; and what's his reason? I am a Jew.

William Shakespeare, Merchant of Venice

Notice the culminating effect of phrase after phrase about Antonio's treatment of Shylock, ending in the question, "and what's his reason?" which calls for the statement of climax, "I am a Jew."

There are times also when the climax takes an ironic turn, as in this next poem.

MY LITTLE SISTER[19]

My little sister had everything,
   Everything in the world—
Blue eyes, dimples, pink cheeks,
   And her hair curled.

She played forward at basket-ball,
   And shot ducks from cover,
She had a sweet rose-colored hat,
   And a tall lover.

All her life she had everything,
   Plenty and more than plenty.
She did not need a perfect death—
   Death at twenty.

May W. Ward

EXERCISES

In the following selections, study the lines for the proper kind of climax. Then try to reach that climax in your interpretation.

---

[19] Reprinted from *Poetry* (February, 1925), p. 247, by permission of the publishers.

I

In the play *Death Takes a Holiday,* climaxes abound throughout the action. In the following speech by Death, there is a series of "build-ups," each one different. The first line—"And so at last I am to become a mortal!"—is a sentence of intense emotion, climaxing previous action. Then the lines begin to pile up to "not afraid, not afraid," and the intensity mounts to the point of hysteria with the words, "a mad joke I play with life . . . what a monstrous, what a sublime joke." Death reaches the final climax with a mocking laugh, "I, Death, do hereby take on the world, the flesh, and the Devil!" Without the preceding lines to indicate the direction of thought and emotion, however, this line would have lost a great deal of its power. Be sure not to lose the irony of the last line, "And now shall we begin our interesting experiment?"

MY HOLIDAY IS JUST CAPRICE[20]

Shadow, or Death, has made a bargain with Duke Lambert to appear in his home as the Duke's guest, Prince Sirki. Against the wishes of the Duke, he is to assume the appearance of a mortal; if his secret is divulged at any time, Death threatens to return in his proper person—Death. At the conclusion of the bargain, Death says:

And so I am at last to become a mortal! . . . . I shall feel blood in my veins . . . warm blood of life. I shall feel my desire becoming flesh and my hunger taking the fire of blood. . . . I shall know what you know, and feel what you feel. . . . When I take flowers in my hand they will not wither. . . . And youth will not run from me with terrified eyes. . . . (*He makes a movement of intense restlessness, as though his inner pressure were near agony*) My hunger shall be appeased for an hour . . . my hunger that is as old as time. . . . And those I love need not . . . be afraid, not afraid, not afraid! (*He laughs with intensity*) No . . . no . . . I am beside myself. . . . My holiday is just caprice . . . a mad joke I play with life. . . . Ha, Ha . . . what a monstrous, what a sublime joke. . . . (*He draws himself up with a mocking laugh*) I, Death, do hereby take on the world, the flesh, and the Devil! (*With an effort the Shadow masters himself*) Forgive me, my friend. My sense of humor overcame me for a moment. . . . And now shall we begin our interesting experiment?

ALBERTO CASELLA

[20] From *Death Takes a Holiday,* p. 49. Copyright, 1928, 1930, by Walter Ferris. Reprinted by permission of the author and Samuel French, Inc.

II

Capulet, Juliet's father in Shakespeare's *Romeo and Juliet,* works himself into a fine rage over his daughter's refusal to marry the man of his choice. Shakespeare would never make the serious mistake, however, of keeping one of his characters on the same emotional level for the length of one long speech. You will notice how skillfully he cues the actor on changes of force and vocal quality. The first four lines are dedicated to a father's martyrdom in rearing a child. The next five lines are softened by the description of the gentleman of his choice, who is "stuff'd as they say, with honourable parts." The following three lines have their tone and force set for them by the words, "wretched puling fool," "whining mammet," "I cannot love," "I am too young." Then, the lines begin to mount relentlessly with anger and fury to the final expression of Capulet's supreme sacrifice, "I'll ne'er acknowledge thee . . . I'll not be forsworn." Throughout these lines, the vocal force employed must show changes from wrathful indignation, to expansiveness, to whining, to sustained fury.

IT MAKES ME MAD

CAPULET
God's bread! it makes me mad.
Day, night, hour, tide, time, work, play,
Alone, in company, still my care hath been
To have her match'd; and having now provided
A gentleman of noble parentage,
Of fair demesnes, youthful and nobly train'd,
Stuff'd as they say, with honourable parts,
Proportion'd as one's thought would wish a man;
And then to have a wretched puling fool,
A whining mammet, in her fortune's tender,
To answer, "I'll not wed; I cannot love,
I am too young; I pray you, pardon me."
But, an you will not wed, I'll pardon you;
Graze where you will, you shall not house with me.
Look to't, think on't, I do not use to jest.
Thursday is near; lay hand on heart, advise.
An you be mine, I'll give you to my friend;
An you be not, hang, beg, starve, die in the streets,
For by my soul, I'll ne'er acknowledge thee.

Nor what is mine shall never do thee good.
Trust to't, bethink you; I'll not be forsworn.
                    WILLIAM SHAKESPEARE, *Romeo and Juliet*

III

The interpretation of a climaxing sentence such as the one
with which Robinson so adroitly ends this next poem takes practice. This poem is effective for what is left unsaid, and the interpreter should realize that the first fourteen lines are most casual
in tone. Although the poem is dramatic, the words are stated with
forthrightness and simplicity. If this simplicity can be sustained,
the climax will be unusually effective, especially if the last two
lines are also interpreted with a light touch. A forceful attack will
not give the audience the intended shock because it will betray
the fact that something of great moment is going to happen. It is
obvious that Robinson was striving for climax through understatement: the words "one calm summer night" set the tone of
quietness; the short phrase "went home" adds to the everyday
event. A pause after "went home," and then quietly, "and put a
bullet through his head." will give the climax the author wishes.

RICHARD CORY[21]

Whenever Richard Cory went down town,
We people on the pavement looked at him:
He was a gentleman from sole to crown,
Clean-favored, and imperially slim.

And he was always quietly arrayed,
And he was always human when he talked;
But still he fluttered pulses when he said,
"Good-morning," and he glittered when he walked.

And he was rich—yes, richer than a king,
And admirably schooled in every grace:
In fine, we thought that he was everything
To make us wish that we were in his place.

So on we worked, and waited for the light,
And went without the meat, and cursed the bread;

[21] From *The Children of the Night,* p. 82. Copyright, 1897, by Charles
Scribner's Sons. Reprinted by permission of the publishers.

And Richard Cory, one calm summer night,
Went home and put a bullet through his head.
                    EDWIN ARLINGTON ROBINSON

IV

The same principle of saving the climax for the last line should be applied to Landis' poem below. There is much of Robinson's style here, but we are better prepared for the outcome; hints are given several times before the last three lines. Be sure that you pause slightly before the last phrase, "and flipped the match," if you wish to give the final gesture its best meaning.

H—— L——, M.D.[22]

"There's something less than courage in his sneers
At death," we said. The careless way he rolled
A cigarette and flipped the match and told
The hearse to come, as he were ordering beers,
Made us believe that what he lacked was tears,
And hope we'd see him shiver with the cold
Of death. "He'll not be quite so bold,"
We smiled and waited, "facing his own fears."
They came to take him to the hospital,
Too late—he was a doctor and he knew—
Knew also we'd be somewhere near to watch;
And so he walked alone, though not too well,
Out to the car, and for a last adieu
Rolled one more cigarette and flipped the match.
                    PAUL LANDIS

V

Thomas Hardy gives a superlative finish to this well-known poem. He uses the question-answer technique to create suspense and carefully prepares the readers for the expected fidelity of a dog for its master. If this poem is interpreted for listeners who are not acquainted with it, their faces usually express their pleasure in the dog's faithfulness. To some, consequently, the last stanza comes as a surprise; but to all, it is climactic.

---

[22] Published here by permission of the author.

"AH, ARE YOU DIGGING ON MY GRAVE?" [23]

"Ah, are you digging on my grave
  My beloved one?—planting rue?"
—"No: yesterday he went to wed
One of the brightest wealth has bred,
'It cannot hurt her now,' he said,
  'That I should not be true.'"

"Then who is digging on my grave?
  My nearest, dearest kin?"
—"Ah, no: they sit and think, 'What use!
What good will planting flowers produce?
No tendance of her mound can loose
  Her spirit from Death's gin.'"

"But some one digs upon my grave?
  My enemy?—prodding sly?"
—"Nay: when she heard you had passed the Gate
That shuts on all flesh soon or late,
She thought you no more worth her hate,
And cares not where you lie."

"Then, who is digging on my grave?
  Say—since I have not guessed!"
—"O, it is I, my mistress dear,
Your little dog, who still lives near,
And much I hope my movements here
  Have not disturbed your rest?"

"Ah, yes! *You* dig upon my grave. . . .
  Why flashed it not on me
That one true heart was left behind!
What feeling do we ever find
To equal among human kind
  A dog's fidelity?"

"Mistress, I dug upon your grave
  To bury a bone, in case
I should be hungry near this spot
When passing on my daily trot.
I am sorry, but I quite forgot
  It was your resting-place."

THOMAS HARDY

VI

The next two poems are persuasive in their intent. The authors intended clearly to clinch their beliefs with a powerful climax. Note the difference in the approach to each problem and the means by which they hope to persuade. Untermeyer uses contrast: the "laughter of life" and "the laughter of Spring," overshadowed by "the laughter of streams running red," the "laughter of ghouls," and the "laughter of death." Then, with a sardonic twist, he combines his two contrasting images for the climax of the last two lines:

> Death that arises to sing,—
> Hailing the Spring!

Oppenheim takes his thrusts at the American citizen. His beginning lines contain the précis of his poem: if we would end war we must create great peace. His contrast between peace that weakens millions and peace that is creative, disciplined, hard, and courageous is climaxed by the three lines beginning, "Set him to work." The remaining seven lines are like a great Amen. You will find that varying degrees of force are necessary in both poems, but you will also note that there is nothing soft and gentle in any of the lines.

THE LAUGHERS[24]

Spring!
And her hidden bugles up the street.
Spring—and the sweet
Laughter of winds at the crossing;
Laughter of birds and a fountain tossing
Its hair in abandoned ecstasies.
Laughter of trees.
Laughter of shop girls that giggle and blush;
Laugh of the tug-boat's impertinent fife.
Laughter followed by a trembling hush—
Laughter of love, scarce whispered aloud.
Then, stilled by no sacredness or strife,
Laughter that leaps from the crowd;

[24] From *These Times*, p. 41. Copyright, 1917, by Henry Holt and Company, Inc. Reprinted by permission of the publishers.

Seizing the world in a rush.
Laughter of life. . . .

Earth takes deep breaths like a man who had feared he might smother,
Filling his lungs before bursting into a shout. . . .
Windows are opened—curtains flying out;
Over the wash-lines women call to each other.
And, under the calling, there surges, too clearly to doubt,
Spring, with the noises
Of shrill little voices;
Joining in "Tag" and the furious chase
Of "I-spy," "Red Rover" and "Prisoner's Base";
Of the roller-skates' whir at the sidewalk's slope,
Of boys playing marbles and girls skipping rope.
And there, down the avenue, behold,
The first true herald of the Spring—
The hand-organ gasping and wheezily murmuring
Its tunes ten years old. . . .
And the music, trivial and tawdry, has freshness and magical swing.
And over and under it,
During and after—
The laughter of Spring! . . .

And lifted still
With the common thrill,
With the throbbing air, the tingling vapor,
That rose like strong and mingled wines,
I turned to my paper,
And read these lines:
"Now that Spring is here,
The war enters its bloodiest phase. . . .
The men are impatient. . . .
Bad roads, storms and the rigors of the winter
Have held back the contending armies. . . .
But the recruits have arrived,
And are waiting only the first days of warm weather. . . .
There will be terrible fighting along the whole line—
Now that Spring has come."

I put the paper down. . . .
Something struck out the sun—something unseen;
Something arose like a dark wave to drown
The golden streets with a sickly green.
Something polluted the blossoming day
With a touch of decay.
The music thinned and died;
People seemed hollow-eyed.
Even the faces of children, where gaiety lingers,

Sagged and drooped like banners about to be furled—
And Silence laid its bony fingers
On the lips of the world. . . .
A grisly quiet with the power to choke;
A quiet that only one thing broke;
One thing alone rose up thereafter . . .
Laughter!
Laughter of streams running red.
Laughter of evil things in the night;
Vultures carousing over the dead;
Laughter of ghouls.
Chuckling of idiots, cursed with sight.
Laughter of dark and horrible pools.
Scream of the bullets' rattling mirth,
Sweeping the earth.
Laugh of the cannon's poisonous breath. . . .
And over the shouts and the wreckage and crumbling
The raucous and rumbling
Laughter of death.
Death that arises to sing,—
Hailing the Spring!

Louis Untermeyer

from 1914–and after[25]

Would you end war?
Create great Peace . . . .

You rave at the war, do you?
Do you know that the war has struck in the face with a fist
A race of clerks,
And turned them to men?
The flabby boys of London died athletes at Ypres. . . .
The Lords of large estates proved in their deaths equality. . . .

Vast millions have ceased to whimper over the coffee at breakfast,
And ceased from family cowardice,
And from industrial bondage,
And now the mother gives the son she feared to release for a night's
    adventure,
And the man who demanded safety first leads the charge from the
    trenches,
And life is so real that men are ready to lose it. . . .

[25] From *War and Laughter*, p. 147. Copyright, 1914, 1916, by The Century Company. Reprinted by permission of the publishers.

For in war they have found Peace:
The Peace with oneself, the being used for a great purpose,
The releasing of the spirit in the heart, and its victorious sweep in
    the soul,
The assertion of manhood, which means courage, hardness, discipline,
    and adventure.

Such is Peace. . . .
But that which we call Peace?
This monstrous machine that weakens millions in factories,
This lust of money for its own sake: to swell one's social stomach
    larger than one's neighbor's. . . .
This poor little personal strife and family pride,
This softness of muscle and cowardice of spirit. . . .
Is this Peace?
Is merely keeping alive, Peace?
Better the young die greatly than live weakly. . . .

Would you end war?
Create great Peace. . . .
The Peace that demands all of a man,
His love, his life, his veriest self;
Plunge him in the smelting fires of a work that becomes his child,
Coerce him to be himself at all hazards: with the toil and the mating
    that belong to him:
Compel him to serve. . . .
Give him a hard Peace: a Peace of discipline and justice. . . .
Kindle him with vision, invite him to joy and adventure:
Set him at work, not to create *things*
But to create *men:*
Yea, himself.

Go search your heart, America. . . .
Turn from the machine to man,
Build, while there is yet time, a creative Peace. . . .
While there is yet time! . . .
For if you reject great Peace,
As surely as vile living brings disease,
So surely shall your selfishness bring war.

JAMES OPPENHEIM

VII

Inherent in an author's plan for dramatic dialogue will be a
balance of highlight and shadow conveyed by contrasting characterizations, variety in emotional intensity, changes in rhythm,
tone, and force. A nice proportion of varying elements will assist

in the progression of thought and lead to a powerful climax. Robert Frost has given us these highlights and shadows in his dramatic dialogue, "The Death of the Hired Man," even though the tone of the two voices from the shadowy figures on the back porch is hushed and subdued. He intensifies the oncoming climax by forcing his readers to wait for the main character, who never appears, and by sending Warren into the house to look for him while Mary waits outside to see "if that small sailing cloud/Will hit or miss the moon." There is a deep silence, and then—

> . . . It hit the moon.
> Then there were three there, making a dim row,
> The moon, the little silver cloud, and she.

Another silence, and—

> Warren returned—too soon, it seemed to her,
> Slipped to her side, caught up her hand and waited.

No sound is heard from within the house or out of doors until Mary speaks—

> "Warren?" she questioned.
>
> "Dead," was all he answered.

THE DEATH OF THE HIRED MAN[26]

> Mary sat musing on the lamp-flame at the table
> Waiting for Warren. When she heard his step,
> She ran on tip-toe down the darkened passage
> To meet him in the doorway with the news
> And put him on his guard. "Silas is back."
> She pushed him outward with her through the door
> And shut it after her. "Be kind," she said.
> She took the market things from Warren's arms
> And set them on the porch, then drew him down
> To sit beside her on the wooden steps.

[26] From *Collected Poems*, p. 49. Copyright, 1930, by Henry Holt and Company, Inc. Reprinted by permission of the publishers. Frost's recording of this poem is contained in the album *Contemporary Poets Series* (Columbia, 11-A-D).

"When was I ever anything but kind to him?
But I'll not have the fellow back," he said.
"I told him so last haying, didn't I?
'If he left then,' I said, 'That ended it.'
What good is he? Who else will harbour him
At his age for the little he can do?
What help he is there's no depending on.
Off he goes always when I need him most.
'He thinks he ought to earn a little pay,
Enough at least to buy tobacco with,
So he won't have to beg and be beholden.'
'All right,' I say, 'I can't afford to pay
Any fixed wages, though I wish I could.'
'Someone else can.' 'Then someone else will have to.'
I shouldn't mind his bettering himself
If that was what it was. You can be certain,
When he begins like that, there's someone at him
Trying to coax him off with pocket-money—
In haying time, when any help is scarce.
In winter he comes back to us. I'm done."

"Sh! not so loud: he'll hear you," Mary said.

"I want him to: he'll have to soon or late."

"He's worn out. He's asleep beside the stove.
When I came up from Rowe's I found him here,
Huddled against the barn-door fast asleep,
A miserable sight, and frightening, too—
You needn't smile—I didn't recognize him—
I wasn't looking for him—and he's changed.
Wait till you see."

            "Where did you say he'd been?"

"He didn't say. I dragged him to the house,
And gave him tea and tried to make him smoke.
I tried to make him talk about his travels.
Nothing would do: he just kept nodding off."

"What did he say? Did he say anything?"

"But little."

      "Anything? Mary, confess
He said he'd come to ditch the meadow for me."

"Warren!"

      "But did he? I just want to know."

"Of course he did. What would you have him say?
Surely you wouldn't grudge the poor old man
Some humble way to save his self-respect.
He added, if you really care to know,
He meant to clear the upper pasture, too.
That sounds like something you have heard before?
Warren, I wish you could have heard the way
He jumbled everything. I stopped to look
Two or three times—he made me feel so queer—
To see if he was talking in his sleep.
He ran on Harold Wilson—you remember—
The boy you had in haying four years since.
He's finished school, and teaching in his college.
Silas declares you'll have to get him back.
He says they two will make a team for work:
Between them they will lay this farm as smooth!
The way he mixed that in with other things.
He thinks young Wilson a likely lad, though daft
On education—you know how they fought
All through July under the blazing sun,
Silas up on the cart to build the load,
Harold along beside to pitch it on."

"Yes, I took care to keep well out of earshot."

"Well, those days trouble Silas like a dream.
You wouldn't think they would. How some things linger!
Harold's young college boy's assurance piqued him.
After so many years he still keeps finding
Good arguments he sees he might have used.
I sympathize. I know just how it feels
To think of the right thing to say too late.
Harold's associated in his mind with Latin.
He asked me what I thought of Harold's saying
He studied Latin like the violin
Because he liked it—that an argument!
He said he couldn't make the boy believe
He could find water with a hazel prong—
Which showed how much good school had ever done him.
He wanted to go over that. But most of all
He thinks if he could have another chance
To teach him how to build a load of hay—"

"I know, that's Silas' one accomplishment.
He bundles every forkful in its place,
And tags and numbers it for future reference,
So he can find and easily dislodge it
In the unloading. Silas does that well.

He takes it out in bunches like big birds' nests.
You never see him standing on the hay
He's trying to lift, straining to lift himself."

"He thinks if he could teach him that, he'd be
Some good perhaps to someone in the world.
He hates to see a boy the fool of books.
Poor Silas, so concerned for other folk,
And nothing to look backward to with pride,
And nothing to look forward to with hope,
So now and never any different."

Part of a moon was falling down the west,
Dragging the whole sky with it to the hills.
Its light poured softly in her lap. She saw it
And spread her apron to it. She put out her hand
Among the harp-like morning-glory strings,
Taut with the dew from garden bed to eaves,
As if she played unheard some tenderness
That wrought on him beside her in the night.
"Warren," she said, "he has come home to die:
You needn't be afraid he'll leave you this time."

"Home," he mocked gently.

         "Yes, what else but home?
It all depends on what you mean by home.
Of course he's nothing to us, any more
Than was the hound that came a stranger to us
Out of the woods, worn out upon the trail."

"Home is the place where, when you have to go there,
They have to take you in."

         "I should have called it
Something you somehow haven't to deserve."
Warren leaned out and took a step or two,
Picked up a little stick, and brought it back
And broke it in his hand and tossed it by,

"Silas has better claim on us you think
Than on his brother? Thirteen little miles
As the road winds would bring him to his door.
Silas has walked that far no doubt to-day.
Why didn't he go there? His brother's rich,
A somebody—director in the bank."

"He never told us that."

         "We know it though."

"I think his brother ought to help, of course,
I'll see to that if there is need. He ought of right
To take him in, and might be willing to—
He may be better than appearances.
But have some pity on Silas. Do you think
If he had any pride in claiming kin
Or anything he looked for from his brother,
He'd keep so still about him all this time?"

"I wonder what's between them."

                                              "I can tell you.
Silas is what he is—we wouldn't mind him—
But just the kind that kinsfolk can't abide.
He never did a thing so very bad.
He don't know why he isn't quite as good
As anybody. Worthless though he is,
He won't be made ashamed to please his brother."

"I can't think Si ever hurt anyone."

"No, but he hurt my heart the way he lay
And rolled his old head on that sharp-edged chair-back.
He wouldn't let me put him on the lounge.
You must go in and see what you can do.
I made the bed up for him there to-night.
You'll be surprised at him—how much he's broken.
His working days are done; I'm sure of it."

"I'd not be in a hurry to say that."

"I haven't been. Go, look, see for yourself.
But, Warren, please remember how it is:
He's come to help you ditch the meadow.
He has a plan. You mustn't laugh at him.
He may not speak of it, and then he may.
I'll sit and see if that small sailing cloud
Will hit or miss the moon."

                              It hit the moon.
Then there were three there, making a dim row,
The moon, the little silver cloud, and she.

Warren returned—too soon, it seemed to her,
Slipped to her side, caught up her hand and waited.

"Warren?" she questioned.

                            "Dead," was all he answered.
                                        ROBERT FROST

VIII

Stephen Vincent Benét portrays the whims and the differentiating limitations of his character in *John Brown's Body* with unusual discernment and artistic skill. If you, as a student of interpretation, have not read this literary masterpiece, consider the reading an important assignment. Read the poem and then listen to the recorded version.[27] This album should be part of every interpreter's library and a part of your listening program.

Below is a portrayal of two of the women in that epochal poem: Lucy Weatherby and Sally Dupré, alike only in their interest in Clay Wingate.[28] Notice how you are given cues to the interpretation of the emotions of these two women through sentence structure and vocabulary. The section concerning Sally Dupré suggests restraint, withdrawal, until Sally is joined by Lucy. Then, beginning with the lines, "The two women kissed/ And talked for a while about riding-habits and war," the sentences lose their terseness and the ideas are expressed in the language of Lucy Weatherby, revealing her superficiality. If you turn to the passage describing Lucy's thoughts about her own attractiveness, you will note that Benét uses this same sentence structure. In the last four lines of the passage on Sally Dupré, however, the author changes to the former abrupt, clipped style and, using mainly monosyllabic words, attains a sharp, unforgettable climax.

A STUDY OF TWO WOMEN[29]

Lucy Weatherby

Lucy Weatherby, cuddled up in her bed,
Drifted along toward sleep with a smile on her mouth,
"I was pretty tonight," she thought, "I was pretty tonight.
Blue's my color—blue that matches my eyes.
I always ought to wear blue. I'm sorry for girls
Who can't wear that sort of blue. Her name is Sally
But she's too dark to wear the colors I can,

---

[27] *John Brown's Body* (Columbia, 5SL-181).
[28] Neither of these two passages is recorded in the above-cited album.
[29] From *John Brown's Body* (New York, Rinehart and Company, Inc., 1927), pp. 164-166, 167-170. Copyright, 1927, 1928, by Stephen Vincent Benét. Reprinted by permission of the Stephen Vincent Benét estate.

I'd like to give her my blue dress and see her wear it,
She'd look too gawky, poor thing.
                                    He danced with her
For a while at first but I hadn't danced with him then,
He danced with me after that. He's rather a dear.
I wonder how long he'll be here. I think I like him.
I think I'm going to be pretty while I am here.

Lucy Weatherby—Lucy Shepley—Lucy Wingate—
Huger's so jealous, nearly as jealous as Curly,
Poor Curly—I ought to answer his mother's letter
But it's hard answering letters."
                                    She cried a little,
Thinking of Curly. The tears were fluent and warm,
They did not sting in her eyes. They made her feel brave.
She could hardly remember Curly any more,
But it was right to cry for him, now and then,
Slight tears at night and a long, warm, dreamless sleep
That left you looking pretty.
                                    She dried the tears
And thought to herself with a pleasant little awe,
"You really are mighty brave, dear. You really are.
Nobody would think your beau was killed in Manassas."
—She could hardly remember Curly any more—
She tried to make Curly's face come out of the darkness
But it was too hard—the other faces kept coming—
Huger Shepley and all the Virginia boys
And now this new boy's face with the dark, keen eyes.

Boys who were privates, boys who were majors and captains,
Nice old Generals who patted your shoulder,
Darling convalescents who called you an angel—
A whole great lucky-bag of nice, thrilling boys,
Fighting for you—and the South and the Cause, of course.
You were a flame for the Cause. You sang songs about it.
You sent white feathers to boys who didn't enlist
And bunches of flowers to boys who were suitably wounded.
You wouldn't dream of making peace with the North
While a single boy was left to fight for the Cause
And they called you the Dixie Angel.
                                    They fought for the Cause
But you couldn't help feeling, too, that they fought for you,
And when they died for you—and the Cause and the flag—
Your heart was tender enough. You were willing to say
You had been engaged to them, even when you hadn't
And answer their mothers' letters in a sweet way,

Though answering letters was hard.
She cuddled closer,

"Pillow, tell me I'm pretty, tell me I'm lovely,
Tell me I'm nicer than anybody you know,
Tell me that nice new boy is thinking about me,
Tell me that Sally girl couldn't wear my blue,
Tell me the war won't end till we've whipped the Yankees,
Tell me I'll never get wrinkles and always have beaus."

Sally Dupré

Sally Dupré, from the high porch of her house
Stared at the road.
They would be here soon enough.

She had waved a flag the last time they went away.
This time she would wave her hand or her handkerchief.
That was what women did. The column passed by
And the women waved, and it came back and they waved,
And, in between, if you loved, you lived by a dull
Clock of long minutes that passed like sunbonneted women
Each with the same dry face and the same set hands.
They were coming now.
Then she thought. "No, no, I can't bear it. It cannot be borne."
And knowing this, bore it.
He saw her. He turned his horse.

"If he comes here, I can't keep it back, I can't keep it back,
I can't stand it, don't let him come." He was coming now.
He rides well, she thought, while her hands made each other cold.
I will have to remember how. And his face is sharper.
The moustache quite changes his face. The face that I saw
While he was away was clean-shaven and darker-eyed.
I must change that, now. I will have to remember that.
It is very important.
He swung from Black Whistle's back.

His spurs made a noise on the porch. She twisted her hands.
"If I shut my eyes, I can make him kiss me. I will not."

They were saying good-bye, now. She heard polite voices saying it.
Then the voices ended. "No, no, it is not to be borne,
It is the last twist of the vise."
Her will snapped then.

When she looked at him, she knew that the knives were edgeless.
In an instant life would begin, life would be forever.

His eyes wavered. There was a thin noise in her ears,
A noise from the road.

The instant fell and lay dead
Between them like something broken.

She turned to see what had killed it.

Lucy Weatherby, reining a bright bay mare,
Played with the braided lash of a riding-whip
And talked to Wingate's father with smiling eyes,
While Huger Shepley tried to put in a word
And the whole troop clustered about her.

Her habit was black
But she had a knot of bright ribbons pinned at her breast,
Red and blue—the Confederate colors.

They had cheered her,
They had cheered her, riding along with her colored ribbons.
It was that which had killed the instant.

Sally looked
At the face with the new moustache she had to remember.
"Good-bye," she said. The face bent over her hand
And kissed it acceptably.

Then the face had gone.
He was back with the others now. She watched a minute.

Lucy was unpinning her knot of ribbons.
She saw a dozen hands go up for the knot
And Lucy laugh her sweet laugh and shake her bright head,
Glance at Huger Shepley and once at Clay,
And then toss the colored knot to the guidon-bearer
Who grinned and tied the ribbons around the staff
While some of them cheered again.

Then the horses moved.
They went by Lucy. Lucy was waving her hand.
She had tears in her eyes and was saying brave words to the soldiers.

Sally watched a back and a horse go out of sight.
She was tired, then.
When the troop had quite disappeared
Lucy rode up to the house.

The two women kissed
And talked for a while about riding-habits and war.
"I just naturally love every boy in the Black Horse Troop.
Don't you, Sally darling? They're all so nice and polite,
Quite like our Virginia boys, and the Major's a dear,
And that nice little one with the guidon is perfectly sweet.
You ought to have heard what he said when I gave him the knot.
Though, of course, I can tell why you didn't come down to the road—
War's terrible, isn't it? All those nice boys going off—
I feel just the way you do, darling—we just have to show them

Whenever we can that we know they are fighting for us,
Fighting for God and the South and the cause of the right—
I always remember and just try to do what I can
For the boys and the wounded and—well, that's it, isn't it, dear?
We've all got to do what we can in this horrible war."

Sally agreed that we had, and drank from a cup.
She thought. "Lucy Weatherby. Yes. I must look for a doll.
I must make a doll with your face, an image of wax.
I must call that doll by your name."

STEPHEN VINCENT BENÉT

CHAPTER 9

Vocal Tempo

You know now that the student of interpretation is benefited by a pleasant, resonant voice but must develop the ability to vary that resonance according to the character of the literature he is interpreting. You know, too, the importance of variety of touch as applied to force in order to obtain as appropriately variable a speech pattern as possible. Another intrinsic element in an effective speech pattern is timing, which is controlled by the proper use of silences, pauses, breaks in utterance; by the inherent quantity of sounds; and by the rate of movement. All of these factors must be skillfully employed to convey the rhythmical cadences of the literature to be interpreted.

The Pause

Silences are as necessary in giving an intelligent and effective interpretation as are sounds. Lack of pause is the surest stamp of the amateur. Even the most ordinary meaning gains in importance as one uses breaks in the flow of sound. For the interpreter, the subtleties of meaning possible in sentient use of pause are quite beyond calculation. The greatest performers on the stage and on the air are those who know the value of timing in order to get laughs or achieve dramatic suspense. They know, for instance, that by a careful sense of timing and by intelligent pausing, they can, as they call it, "squeeze a laugh." Listen to Bob Hope for excellent timing—even to the fraction of a second. Some people who have laughed heartily at a story or joke are quite disappointed if they are unable to "get a laugh" when they repeat it to someone else. The reason probably lies in their poor timing.

The Pause and Phrasing

Pause, used in its simplest form, controls meaning through an effective grouping of words. This grouping is called phrasing. Pause lends itself to all the delicate variations of giving words the many interpretations of which they are capable. There is no fixed rule for phrasing; only that as you break up a sentence by pauses—or fail to break it up—you settle the meaning your audience will receive. Intelligent phrasing carries the interpretation you intend; careless phrasing conveys meanings you do not intend. There are times when one must pause for controlled breathing, but the breathing pattern must be subordinated to the intended meaning.

Phrasing, then, is one of the chief problems in the interpretation of the printed page. When you are inventing your own sentences and picking your own words to express your own ideas in conversation and extempore speech, the certainty of your idea helps you to a sensible and expressive phrasing of the words. But when you are provided with words first and ideas second, as must happen in the interpretation of literature, the use of pause for phrasing becomes a serious study. For, once you have determined what your phrasing will be, you have gone far in deciding the meaning you wish to give a particular selection. An inadvertent pause or a failure to pause at the right moment may change the whole meaning.

EXERCISES

I

The following nonsensical bit will give you some merriment and will tax your ingenuity in the use of the pause. Although the meaning is far from profound, you should be able to decide on the correct phrasing. Observe how the meaning changes with shift in pause. Notice, also, the change of meaning if you elide such words as "Esau Wood" and "wood-saw." The test lies in whether you can carry the meaning over to the class without having the members follow the selection with their eyes.

Esau Wood sawed wood. Esau Wood would saw wood. All the wood Esau Wood saw Esau Wood would saw. In other words, all the wood Esau saw to saw Esau sought to saw. Oh, the wood Wood would saw! And oh, the wood-saw with which Wood would saw wood. But one day Wood's wood-saw would saw no wood, and thus the wood Wood sawed was not the wood Wood would saw if Wood's wood-saw would saw wood. Now, Wood would saw if Wood's wood-saw would saw wood. Now, Wood would saw wood with a wood-saw that would saw wood, so Esau sought a saw that would saw wood. One day Esau saw a saw saw wood as no other wood-saw Wood saw would saw wood. In fact, of all the wood-saws Wood ever saw saw wood Wood never saw a wood-saw that would saw wood as the wood-saw Wood saw saw wood would saw wood, and I never saw a wood-saw that would saw as the wood-saw Wood saw would saw until I saw Esau saw wood with the wood-saw Wood saw saw wood. Now Wood saws wood with the wood-saw Wood saw saw wood.

II

The following famous lines uttered by Churchill need study for emphasis that must be sustained by pauses. This speech was delivered before the House of Commons on June 4, 1940, at a momentous time for the British, and it was presented in a decisive and fervent manner. Try it for the study of pauses.

THE RETREAT FROM FLANDERS[1]

I have myself full confidence that if all do their duty, if nothing is neglected, and if the best arrangements are made, as they are being made, we shall prove ourselves once again able to defend our island home, ride out the storms of war, and outlive the menace of tyranny, if necessary, for years, if necessary, alone.

At any rate, that is what we are going to do. That is the resolve of His Majesty's Government—every man of them. That is the will of Parliament and the nation. The British Empire and the French Republic, linked together in their cause and their need, will defend to the death their native soils, aiding each other like good comrades to the utmost of their strength. Even though large tracts of Europe and many old and famous States have fallen or may fall into the grip of the Gestapo and all the odious apparatus of Nazi rule, we shall not flag or fail. We shall go on to the end; we shall fight in France; we shall fight on the seas and oceans; we shall fight with

[1] From *Blood, Sweat and Tears*, pp. 296-297. Copyright, 1950, by G. P. Putnam's Sons. Reprinted by permission of the publishers.

growing confidence and growing strength in the air; we shall defend our Island, whatever the cost may be; we shall fight on the beaches; we shall fight on the landing grounds; we shall fight in the fields and in the streets; we shall fight in the hills. We shall never surrender, and even if, which I do not for a moment believe, this Island or a large part of it were subjugated and starving, then our Empire beyond the seas, armed and guarded by the British Fleet, will carry on the struggle, until, in God's good time, the New World, with all its power and might, steps forth to the rescue and the liberation of the old.

WINSTON CHURCHILL

III

Notice how important the pause becomes in the poem below. If you ignore the breaks in the prose sections, you will lose the humor. How are you going to manage the last line of each stanza?

THE PARTY AT CROGAN'S[2]

'Twas a foine time we had down at Crogan's;
  The five av us slept not a wink,
Wid a fiddle to stir up our brogans,
  An' plenty o' toddy to dhrink.
The grog it was free as the air is,
  An' we managed to store it away;
We whistled and sang like canaries.
  An' who was the five, did ye say?

The two Crogans, that's one; Mike Semployd, that's two; Tim Horrigan's three; an' meself—but there was five av us.

We played forty-five. Mike was b'atin'
  An' Horrigan called him a cheat,
Then they threw off their coats widout waitin'
  An' tuk at it like dogs in the shtreet.
They stirred up our blood wid their brawlin'
  Till we all got mixed up in the fray,
The five av us pullin' an' haulin'
  But who was the five, did ye say?

Mike Sployd, that's one; Tim Horrigan's two; the two Crogans is three; an' meself—sure, there was five av us.

Pat Crogan he tuk up his fiddle,—
  Och, Pat is a merry gossoon!—

²From the *Century.* Reprinted by permission of The Century Company.

An' he drew the bow over the middle
　　An' played us a bit av a chune;
Himself round the kitchen went prancin',—
　　Such a jig as Pat Crogan can play!—
An' it set the whole five av us dancin',
　　Now who was the five, did ye say?

Meself, that's one; Mike Sployd, that's two; the two Crogans is three; Tim Horrigan's four—I thought there was five av us.

It was early daylight in the mor-rning
　　When the party at Crogan's broke up;
The cock in the shed called a war-rning,
　　An' we all tuk a turn at the cup:
But the truest of friends must be parted,
　　An' each av us then went our way,
The five av us all happy hearted.
　　But who was the five, did ye say?

The two Crogans, that's one; Mike Sployd, that's two; Tim Horrigan's three: meself—och, I guess there was only four av us, afther all.

FLORENCE J. BOYCE

IV

Browning's "My Last Duchess" is difficult for the beginner in interpretative study because of its many nuances of thought and emotion. This dramatic monologue, however, is so skillfully written that it affords the student various approaches to its meaning. Interpretation of the superficial meaning is not enough; you must do some probing, get a pen sketch of the Duke, question the reasons underlying his remarks. The word *last,* for instance, in the first line, cannot be ignored. Does it give you the impression of coldness? Of aloofness? Of pride or sorrow? Or does it merely tell you that there is to be another Duchess? Will you pause a second before or after the word *last?* Will you give emphasis to the word or will you group it with the phrase "my last Duchess"?

Perhaps before you make any decision about the word *last,* you should make a collection of the phrases that characterize the Duke. Here are several: "My gift of a nine-hundred-years-old name"; "I choose/Never to stoop"; "I gave commands"; "Notice Neptune . . . thought a rarity . . . cast in bronze for me."

The phrases are not easy to handle effectively because some of them are too long for comfortable breathing patterns. Pauses, however, are plentiful and full of shifts in meaning and emotion. The line "Then all smiles stopped together" evokes several meanings and certainly makes the pause important after the line has been uttered.

MY LAST DUCHESS

That's my last Duchess painted on the wall,
Looking as if she were alive. I call
That piece a wonder, now: Frà Pandolf's hands
Worked busily a day, and there she stands.
Will 't please you sit and look at her? I said
"Frà Pandolf" by design, for never read
Strangers like you that pictured countenance,
The depth and passion of its earnest glance,
But to myself they turned (since none puts by
The curtain I have drawn for you, but I)
And seemed as they would ask me, if they durst,
How such a glance came there; so, not the first
Are you to turn and ask thus. Sir, 'twas not
Her husband's presence only, called that spot
Of joy into the Duchess' cheek: perhaps
Frà Pandolf chanced to say, "Her mantle laps
Over my lady's wrist too much," or "Paint
Must never hope to reproduce the faint
Half-flush that dies along her throat:" such stuff
Was courtesy, she thought, and cause enough
For calling up that spot of joy. She had
A heart—how shall I say?—too soon made glad,
Too easily impressed: she liked whate'er
She looked on, and her looks went everywhere.
Sir, 'twas all one! My favor at her breast,
The dropping of the daylight in the West,
The bough of cherries some officious fool
Broke in the orchard for her, the white mule
She rode with round the terrace—all and each
Would draw from her alike the approving speech,
Or blush, at least. She thanked men,—good! but thanked
Somehow—I know not how—as if she ranked
My gift of a nine-hundred-years-old name
With anybody's gift. Who'd stoop to blame
This sort of trifling? Even had you skill
In speech—(which I have not)—to make your will
Quite clear to such an one, and say, "Just this

Or that in you disgusts me; here you miss,
Or there exceed the mark"—and if she let
Herself be lessoned so, nor plainly set
Her wits to yours, forsooth, and made excuse,
—E'en then would be some stooping; and I choose
Never to stoop. Oh, sir, she smiled, no doubt,
Whene'er I passed her; but who passed without
Much the same smile? This grew; I gave commands;
Then all smiles stopped together. There she stands
As if alive. Will 't please you rise? We'll meet
The company below, then. I repeat,
The Count your master's known munificence
Is ample warrant that no just pretence
Of mine for dowry will be disallowed;
Though his fair daughter's self, as I avowed
At starting, is my object. Nay, we'll go
Together down, sir. Notice Neptune, though,
Taming a sea-horse, thought a rarity,
Which Claus of Innsbruck cast in bronze for me!

ROBERT BROWNING

V

The pauses in this next poem are used to achieve a different effect from that for which they were used in "My Last Duchess." Here Yellow Otter is trying to make "big-talk." He is "big-smart man; he's "got-um golden medal on chest from big-knife chief." He is also struggling with the American language, a factor which requires an entirely different rhythm from the previous poem.

MEDALS AND HOLES[3]
(*An Indian Council Talk*)

Boo-Zhóo nee-chée! Me—Yellow-Otter,
I'm going mak-'um big-talk, 'Spector Jone'.
Look-see!—on chest I'm got-um golden medal;
Got-um woman on medal!—Ho! good medal!
Me—I'm go on Washin'ton long tam' ago;
Me—I'm tell-um Keétch-ie O-gi-má, dose big w'ite chief:

"Eenzhuns no lak'-um Eenzhun rese'vation;
No good! She's too much jack-pine, sand, and swamp."
Big-chief, him say: "O-zah-wah-kíg, you be good boy!
Go back to rese'vation. You tell-um tribe
If Eenzhun stay on rese'vation, Washin'ton gov'ment

[3] From *The Box of God*, p. 63. Copyright, 1922, by Henry Holt and Company, Inc. Reprinted by permission of the publishers.

Give-um all de Eenzhuns plenty payments,
Give-um plenty good hats and suits o' clothes
My heart is good to you; you damned good Eenzhun.
Me—I'm stick-em dis golden medal on your chest."
Ho! I'm walk-um home. I got-um medal—look-see!

But no got-um plenty good hats and suits o' clothes;
No got-um every year; only every two year.
Clothes no good! Look-see! Got-um clothes on now—
No good! Got-um holes in legs—plenty-big holes
Wit' not much clot' around, and too much buttons off.
Gov'ment clothes she's coming every two year—
Long tam' between, too much—wit' too much holes.

Before de w'ite man comes across big-water,
In olden tam', de Eenzhun got-um plenty clothes;
He mak'-um plenty suits wit' skins,—no holes.
Even Shing-oós, dose weasel, Wah-bóos, dose rabbit,
Dey got-um better luck—two suits every year—
Summer, brown-yellow suit; winter, w'ite suit—
No got-um holes.
Wau-goósh and Nee-gíg, dose fox and otter,
Shang-wáy-she, dose mink, Ah-méek, dose beaver,
Dey get-um plenty clothes, each year two suits—
Summer, t'in clothes; winter, t'ick fur clothes—
No got-um holes.
Ah deék, dose caribou, dose deer, and moose,
In spring dey t'row away deir horns;
In summer dey get-um nice new hat—
No got-um holes.
Me—I'm big-smart man, smarter dan weasel,
Smarter dan moose and fox and beaver—
I got-um golden medal on chest from big-knife chief;
Me—I'm only got-um one suit clothes
In two year—no-good clothes, no-good hats!

'Spector Jone', you tell-um our big-knife Grandfader, so:
"Yellow-Otter no got-um plenty good clothes;
No got-um silk-black hat, no stove-pipes hat;
Him got-um plenty much holes in Washin'ton pants."
Tell-um holes in pants now big, plenty-big—
Bigger dan golden medal on chest!

So much—dat's enough.

How! How!
Kay-gét! Kay-gét!
Ho! Ho! Ho!

LEW SARETT

The Pause for Suspense

Some of the most impelling meanings can be projected through pause. Two vital purposes are served: *suspense* and *reinforcement*. Each of these is required in order to interpret with vigor and penetration. The logic of your ideas obliges you, most of the time, to pause in certain places with no leeway for caprice or chance. But your feelings allow you wide latitude in pausing and breaking sentences—and even phrases—apart. A speaker or an interpreter *can* pause anywhere, provided that he pauses to give significance to the meaning. By pausing to create suspense, the listener can be brought easily to a high level of interest and expectancy, thus adding tremendously to the effectiveness and intensity of meaning.

EXERCISES

The following poems have been selected to illustrate the use of pause for suspense. The need for this kind of pause will not be altogether obvious in each of these selections; but as you read, remember that during the pause, the reader must sustain his mood and intensify his meaning by facial expression.

I

This lyric by Sandburg depends on the pause to give rhythm to the line and illusiveness to the mood. In order that the person reading may appreciate his feelings, the poet has structured the cadence of the last two lines of each stanza.

THE GREAT HUNT[4]

I cannot tell you now;
   When the wind's drive and whirl
   Blow me along no longer,
   And the wind's a whisper at last—
  Maybe I'll tell you then—
           some other time.

[4] From *Chicago Poems*, p. 117. Copyright, 1916, by Henry Holt and Company, Inc. Reprinted by permission of the publishers.

When the rose's flash to the sunset
Reels to the wrack and the twist,
And the rose is a red bygone,
When the face I love is going
And the gate to the end shall clang,
And it's no use to beckon or say, "So long"—
Maybe I'll tell you then—
                          some other time.

I never knew any more beautiful than you:
I have hunted you under my thoughts,
I have broken down under the wind
And into the roses looking for you.
        I shall never find any
                     greater than you.
                          CARL SANDBURG

II

You will convey the reminiscent mood by pausing for shifts in feeling. Do not neglect the pause at the end of the first line even though the author has not indicated, except by a period, an important shift in meaning.

SCRATCHES[5]

I found a scar across my wrist to-day.
    I got it gathering apple-blooms for you
    One breathless afternoon when Spring was new,
And all the trees were wearing white, for May.

I had forgotten any scar was there—
    I had forgotten, too, the trifling pain
    Quite paid for with a kiss . . . and then, the rain
Scattering transient diamonds in your hair. . . .

You thought you loved me then, do you remember?
    And I, for my part, poured out, I am sure,
    Brave words like "grow," and "strength," and "endure." . . .
But that, of course, was May—this is November.

Time will be-dim that night . . . the blooms . . . your face . . .
Even the scar will heal to a faint trace . . . .
                          JOHN V. A. WEAVER

[5] From *Finders*, p. 83. Copyright, 1923, by Alfred A. Knopf, Inc. Reprinted by permission of the publishers.

III

The pause after the first line, "I do not understand," should be longer than the pause after the second line, "They bring so many, many flowers to me." The first pause indicates bewilderment and thus creates suspense; but the pause after the second line is for reinforcement. Why will a pause after "wooded heights" be effective? Be careful of the pauses in the second stanza. The line beginning "Bent, mournful mothers" will need special phrasing. Watch the pauses preceding and following "Jim" and "John." Don't hurry the last stanza, and be ready for the last line.

THE UNKNOWN[6]

I do not understand . . .
 They bring so many, many flowers to me—
Rainbows of roses, wreaths from every land;
 And hosts of solemn strangers come to see
My tomb here on these quiet, wooded heights.
 My tomb here seems to be
One of the sights.

The low-voiced men who speak
 Of me quite fondly, call me The Unknown:
But now and then at dusk, Madonna-meek,
 Bent, mournful mothers come to me alone
And whisper down—the flowers and grasses through—
 Such names as "Jim" and "John" . . .
I wish they knew.

And once my sweetheart came.
 She did not—nay, of course she could not—know,
But thought of me, and crooned to me the name
 She called me by—how many years ago?
A very precious name. Her eyes were wet,
 Yet glowing, flaming so . . .
She won't forget!

E. O. LAUGHLIN

IV

In *Romeo and Juliet,* the young heroine decides that she must take a sleeping potion in order to avoid a marriage arranged by

---

[6] Published originally in the *Ladies' Home Journal* (November, 1926), p. 9. Reprinted by permission of the author and the publishers.

her father and to postpone all further plans until Romeo's arrival. There are several important reminders for you: Juliet is only fourteen years old; she is in love with Romeo, whose family has feuded with hers for many years; she has no one in whom she dares confide, not even her nurse; she is distraught and fearful that the potion may be dangerous.

Notice how the tone of this dramatic monologue is set immediately by the line, "I have a faint cold fear thrills through my veins," and how frequently the lines call for a wide range of change in vocal quality. Notice, too, the varying attacks of force required and the precision needed for the appropriate touch in lines like, "Come, vial" and "Lie thou there." Observe the series of culminating movements which lead to the decision, "This do I drink to thee."

It is impossible even to suggest the number of significant points where a pause can carry the shift of meaning and emotion. You may start, however, with her first word, "Farewell," to consider the pause for suspense. There is another definite emotional change with the word "Nurse." Work it out carefully. If you are content with a smooth, even rhythm, you have not analyzed this selection carefully, for the movement is quite broken by emotional intensity.

THE POTION SCENE

LADY CAPULET.   Good-night:
  Get thee to bed, and rest; for thou hast need.
                  (*Exeunt* LADY CAPULET *and* NURSE)
JULIET. Farewell! God knows when we shall meet again.
  I have a faint cold fear thrills through my veins,
  That almost freezes up the heat of life.
  I'll call them back again to comfort me.
  Nurse!—What should she do here?
  My dismal scene I needs must act alone.
  Come, vial.
  What if this mixture do not work at all?
  Shall I be married then to-morrow morning?
  No, no: this shall forbid it. Lie thou there.
             (*Laying down her dagger*)
  What if it be a poison, which the friar
  Subtly hath minist'red to have me dead,
  Lest in this marriage he should be dishonour'd,

Because he married me before to Romeo?
I fear it is; and yet, methinks, it should not,
For he hath still been tried a holy man.
How if, when I am laid into the tomb,
I wake before the time that Romeo
Come to redeem me? There's a fearful point!
Shall I not then be stifled in the vault,
To whose foul mouth no healthsome air breathes in,
And there die strangled ere my Romeo comes?
Or, if I live, is it not very like,
The horrible conceit of death and night,
Together with the terror of the place,—
As in a vault, an ancient receptacle,
Where, for this many hundred years, the bones
Of all my buried ancestors are pack'd;
Where bloody Tybalt, yet but green in earth,
Lies fest'ring in his shroud; where, as they say,
At some hours in the night spirits resort;—
Alack, alack, is it not like that I,
So early waking, what with loathsome smells,
And shrieks like mandrakes' torn out of the earth,
That living mortals, hearing them, run mad;—
O, if I wake, shall I not be distraught,
Environèd with all these hideous fears,
And madly play with my forefathers' joints,
And pluck the mangled Tybalt from his shroud,
And, in this rage, with some great kinsman's bone,
As with a club, dash out my desperate brains?
O, look! methinks I see my cousin's ghost
Seeking out Romeo, that did spit his body
Upon a rapier's point. Stay, Tybalt, stay!
Romeo, I come! This do I drink to thee.

WILLIAM SHAKESPEARE, *Romeo and Juliet*

V

If you are not familiar with *Cyrano de Bergerac*, by all means read it; for nowhere will you find a more appealing character than the homely, arrogant, and devoted Cyrano. Like Juliet, Cyrano, too, knows fear; but his is the fear that Roxane, whom he loves, will someday laugh at his "poor big devil of a nose." He takes every opportunity to jest wryly about his "protuberance" and uses humor as a shield against ridicule or pity. You will enjoy the way he turns a phrase, and you will be able to interpret effectively only through careful use of pauses.

CYRANO'S FEAR[7]

CYRANO.   My old friend—look at me,
And tell me how much hope remains for me
With this protuberance! Oh I have no more
Illusions! Now and then—bah! I may grow
Tender, walking alone in the blue cool
Of evening, through some garden fresh with flowers
After the benediction of the rain;
My poor big devil of a nose inhales
April . . . and so I follow with my eyes
Where some boy, with a girl upon his arm,
Passes a patch of silver . . . and I feel
Somehow, I wish I had a woman too,
Walking with little steps under the moon,
And holding my arm so, and smiling. Then
I dream—and I forget. . . . And then I see
The shadow of my profile on the wall!
LE BRET. My friend! . . .
CYRANO.   My friend, I have my bitter days,
Knowing myself so ugly, so alone.
Sometimes—
LE BRET.   You weep?
CYRANO. (*Quickly*) Oh, not that ever! No,
That would be too grotesque—the tears trickling down
All the way along this nose of mine?
I will not so profane the dignity
Of sorrow. Never any tears for me!
Why there is nothing more sublime than tears,
Nothing!—Shall I make them ridiculous
In my poor person?
LE BRET.   Love's no more than chance!
CYRANO. (*Shakes his head*) No. I love Cleopatra; do I appear
Caesar? I adore Beatrice; have I
The look of Dante?
LE BRET.   But your wit—your courage—
Why, that poor child who offered you just now
Your dinner! She—you saw with your own eyes,
Her eyes did not avoid you.
CYRANO. (*Thoughtful*) That is true . . .
LE BRET. Well then! Roxane herself, watching your duel,
Paler than—
CYRANO.   Pale?—

---

[7] *Cyrano de Bergerac*, trans. Brian Hooker (New York, Henry Holt and
Company, Inc., 1928), pp. 52-53.

LE BRET.   Her lips parted, her hand
  Thus, at her breast—I saw it! Speak to her!
  Speak, man!
CYRANO.   Through my nose? She might laugh at me;
  That is the one thing in this world I fear!
                          EDMOND ROSTAND, *Cyrano de Bergerac*

Pause for Reinforcement

Meaning can be reinforced by pauses. When an author has
written something that is particularly impressive, the mere re-
telling of it is not enough. You must make use of the pause for
reinforcement of the meaning. Remember that people grasp ideas
more slowly through the ear than through the eye. Listeners often
will not get the importance of the meaning unless it is highlighted through reinforcement. They may have to reflect upon it
for a moment or two. Pausing before the word or phrase or after
it will give it greater intensity of meaning. Pausing before a word
will tend to direct the listener's attention and curiosity. Pausing
after the word will add emphasis to what has just been said, and
your listeners will actually repeat it to themselves. So if the line
is to be made vivid, *pause for reinforcement*.

In "Benediction" you can sense that a pause is essential after
the phrase "And when dusk comes" in order to prepare the audience for the final thought.

BENEDICTION[8]

The sun be warm and kind
To you,
The darkest night, some star
Shine through.
The dullest morn
A radiance brew,
And when dusk comes—
God's hand
To you.

                          ELEANOR POWERS

In "Jenny Kiss'd Me," the piling up of the phrases

[8] Published originally in *Good Housekeeping* (May, 1932), p. 159. Reprinted by permission of the author and the publishers.

> Say I'm weary, say I'm sad,
> Say that health and wealth have missed me,
> Say I'm growing old, but add,

leads naturally to a pause that will end in delight with the last line.

JENNY KISS'D ME

> Jenny kiss'd me when we met,
> Jumping from the chair she sat in;
> Time, you thief, who love to get
> Sweets into your list, put that in!
> Say I'm weary, say I'm sad,
> Say that health and wealth have missed me,
> Say I'm growing old, but add,
> Jenny kiss'd me.
>
> LEIGH HUNT

Tennyson has packed the philosophy of the whole Christian world into six lines; and in the interpretation of these lines the audience should be given time to grasp the meaning. There are many pauses in the poem; yet it remains melodious and smooth. The longest pause—but it should not drag—is after "all in all."

FLOWER IN THE CRANNIED WALL

> Flower in the crannied wall,
> I pluck you out of the crannies,
> I hold you here, root and all, in my hand,
> Little flower—but *if* I could understand
> What you are, root and all, and all in all,
> I should know what God and man is.
>
> ALFRED TENNYSON

The right timing in the following verse can bring a laugh on the last line. There must be a pause after "Mamma"—which is accented on the last syllable—and a half beat before you very quickly and lightly add, "And that's my earliest recollection."

A TERRIBLE INFANT

> I recollect a nurse called Ann,
> Who carried me about the grass,

And one fine day a fine young man
   Came up, and kissed the pretty lass:
She did not make the least objection!
    Thinks I, "Aha!
   When I can talk, I'll tell Mamma."
—And that's my earliest recollection.

Frederick Locker-Lampson

EXERCISES

Watch carefully in each of these short poems for the reinforcement which will make the meaning more significant. This awareness on your part will help you to present the literature in a professional manner.

I

The two poems below offer contrasting moods. Poignancy is added to their meaning if you remember that in World War I MacLeish lost a brother and Rupert Brooke was killed in action at the age of thirty-two.

1892-19—[9]

There will be little enough to forget—
The flight of crows,
A wet street,
The way the wind blows,
Moonrise: sunset:
Three words the world knows—
Little enough to forget.

It will be easy enough to forget.
The rain drips
Through the shallow clay,
Washes lips,
Eyes, brain,
The rain drips in the shallow clay,
The soft rain will wash them away—
The flight of crows,
The way the wind blows,
Moonrise: sunset:

[9] From *Collected Poems: 1917-1952*, p. 17. Copyright, 1952, by Houghton, Mifflin Company. Reprinted by permission of the publishers.

Will wash them away
To the bare hard bones:
And the bones forget.

ARCHIBALD MacLEISH

GRANTCHESTER[10]
(Written in Berlin, May, 1912)

Ah God! to see the branches stir
Across the moon at Grantchester!
To smell the thrilling-sweet and rotten
Unforgettable, unforgotten
River-smell, and hear the breeze
Sobbing in the little trees.
Say, do the elm-clumps greatly stand
Still guardians of that holy land?
The chestnuts shade, in reverend dream,
The yet unacademic stream?
Is dawn a secret shy and cold
Anadyomene, silver-gold?
And sunset still a golden sea
From Haslingfield to Madingley?
And after, ere the night is born,
Do hares come out about the corn?
Oh, is the water sweet and cool,
Gentle and brown, above the pool?
And laughs the immortal river still
Under the mill, under the mill?
Say, is there Beauty yet to find?
And Certainty? And Quiet kind?
Deep meadows yet, for to forget
The lies, and truths, and pain? . . . oh! yet
Stands the Church clock at ten to three?
And is there honey still for tea?

RUPERT BROOKE

II

The reinforcement in the poem below centers on the words, "You love ships." The author has strengthened their meaning by describing a variety of ships and boats. There is no doubt that you will be conscious of the pause before "I love hearth-fires"; but be sure that you hold the pause after this expression so that

---

[10] From *The Collected Poems of Rupert Brooke*, p. 164. Copyright, 1915, by Dodd, Mead & Company. Reprinted by permission of the publishers.

the mood and contrast in meaning has time to be established in the minds of your listeners.

SHIPS[11]

You love ships.
                    —Tall-masted schooners lifting
Sideways up and under as the deep wave dips,
—Little sly fishing-smacks with small sails scuttering
Tinily to windward, low along the sky-line . . .
    So that they adventure out, freed, on the water,
Released, swift, springing—so that they are ships!

Stately forthright steamers, with smoke far-streaming,
    Starry-necklaced ferry-boats, lacing like a tale
Happily ended, across and back the rivers,
—Racing-boats, many-oared, flashing down the morning,
—Dark canoes with lanterns and a stencilled sail. . . .

Your quick eyes follow them, lighted like a lover's,
    The ships that bear a lifetime of your city-bound desires:
You love ships. I watch you, wistfully.
You love ships. . . .
                              I love hearth-fires.
                              MARGARET WIDDEMER

III

    Although the invitation is never actually given in these lines, one can feel the pull of the "thrush music," the mystery of the "pillared dark" that the author feels. The listeners will remember the words "come in," if properly phrased, rather than the stars beyond the wood.

COME IN[12]

        As I came to the edge of the woods,
        Thrush music—hark!
        Now it is was dusk outside,
        Inside it was dark.

Too dark in the woods for a bird
By sleight of wing
To better its perch for the night
Though it still could sing.

The last of the light of the sun
That had died in the west
Still lived for one song more
In a thrush's breast.

Far in the pillared dark
Thrush music went—
Almost like a call to come in
To the dark and lament.

But no, I was out for stars:
I would not come in,
I meant not even if asked,
And I hadn't been.

ROBERT FROST

IV

The reminiscent mood which permeates "Memory Green" must
be sustained by careful pausing. It is especially important to
watch the pauses for reinforcement of the idea "With whom" in
the last two stanzas. You will need a pause after "You will close
your eyes" and "With whom," and another before "Ah where" in
the last line.

MEMORY GREEN[13]

Yes and when the warm unseasonable weather
Comes at the year's end of the next late year
And the southwest wind that smells of rain and summer
Strips the huge branches of their dying leaves

And you at dusk along the Friedrichstrasse
Or you in Paris on the windy quay
Shuffle the shallow fallen leaves before you
Thinking the thoughts that like the grey clouds change

You will not understand why suddenly sweetness
Fills in your heart nor the tears come to your eyes
You will stand in the June-warm wind and the leaves falling
When was it so before you will say With whom

[13] From *Collected Poems: 1917-1952*, p. 47. Copyright, 1952, by Houghton, Mifflin Company. Reprinted by permission of the publishers.

You will not remember this at all you will stand there
Feeling the wind on your throat the wind in your sleeves
You will smell the dead leaves in the grass of a garden
You will close your eyes With whom you will say
Ah where?
ARCHIBALD MACLEISH

V

Prose selections need the same care in phrasing and pausing for suspense and reinforcement as poetry. Franklin Roosevelt was a master of reinforcement who frequently drove his points home through the use of reiteration and climax. Undoubtedly you are acquainted with his famous speech on the Four Freedoms; but now read this excerpt from it from the point of view of an interpreter.

FOUR FREEDOMS[14]

In the future days, which we seek to make secure, we look forward to a world founded upon four essential human freedoms.

The first is freedom of speech and expression—everywhere in the world.

The second is freedom of every person to worship God in his own way—everywhere in the world.

The third is freedom from want—which, translated into world terms, means economic understandings which will secure to every nation a healthy peacetime life for its inhabitants—everywhere in the world.

The fourth is freedom from fear—which, translated into world terms, means a world-wide reduction of armaments to such a point and in such a thorough fashion that no nation will be in a position to commit an act of physical aggression against any neighbor—anywhere in the world.

FRANKLIN D. ROOSEVELT

VI

Some of the pauses in the following selection should be shorter than others because of the general impression to be created of the burning glare of the sun, which grows more and more intense until it becomes unbearable:

---

[14] From the President's annual message to Congress, January 6, 1941.

SUN GLARE[15]

It seems to you that the blue sky-fire is burning down into your brain—that the flare of the white pavements and yellow walls is piercing somehow into your life—creating an unfamiliar mental confusion—blurring out thought. . . . Is the whole world taking fire? . . . The flaming azure of the sea dazzles and pains like a crucible-glow;—the green of the mornes flickers and blazes in some amazing way. . . . Then dizziness inexpressible; you grope with eyes shut fast—afraid to open them again in that stupefying torrefaction—moving automatically—vaguely knowing you must get out of the flaring and flashing—somewhere, anywhere away from the white wrath of the sun, and the green fire of the hills, and the monstrous colour of the sea. . . . Then, remembering nothing, you find yourself in bed—with an insupportable sense of weight at the back of the head—a pulse beating furiously—and a strange sharp pain at intervals stinging through your eyes. . . . And the pain grows; expands—fills all the skull—forces you to cry out—replaces all other sensations except a weak consciousness, vanishing and recurring, that you are very sick, more sick than ever before in all your life.

LAFCADIO HEARN

VII

The scene we have selected from the play *Our Town* appears to be a simple one for interpretation, but only the expert will have success in creating and sustaining the mood of contentment, peace, and serenity that the Stage Manager creates in his colloquial and philosophical manner. You will recall that throughout the play he sets the scene and tone and thus interprets the characters and action for the audience. Watch the quality of your voice, for there is none of the bombast here that is sometimes typical of stage managers. Be careful to get the even, gentle touch. And, finally, remember that your pauses will make or break your interpretation.

THE HILLTOP[16]

STAGE MANAGER
    This time nine years have gone by, friends—summer 1913.

---

[15] From "Do Not Think Like That," *Golden Book* (April, 1926), p. 503. Reprinted by permission of the author.
[16] From *Our Town*, pp. 98-101. Copyright, 1938, by Coward-McCann, Inc. Reprinted by permission of the publishers. No performance of any kind whatsoever may be given without permission in writing from Samuel French, Inc.

Gradual changes in Grover's Corners. Horses are getting rarer. Farmers coming into town in Fords.

Chief difference is in the young people, as far as I can see.

They want to go to the moving pictures all the time.

They want to wear clothes like they see there . . . want to be citified.

Everybody locks their house doors now at night. Ain't been any burglars in town yet, but everybody's heard about 'em.

But you'd be surprised though—on the whole, things don't change at Grover's Corners.

Guess you want to know what all these chairs are here fur. Smarter ones have guessed it already. I don't know how you feel about such things; but this certainly is a beautiful place. It's on a hilltop—a windy hilltop—lots of sky, lots of clouds—often lots of sun and moon and stars. You come up here on a fine afternoon and you can see range on range of hills—awful blue they are—up there by Lake Sunapee and Lake Winnapassaukee . . . and way up, if you've got a glass, you can see the White Mountains and Mt. Washington—where North Conway and Conway is. And, of course, our favorite mountain, Mt. Monadnock's, right here—and all around it lie these towns—Jaffrey, 'n East Jaffrey, 'n Peterborough, 'n Dublin and there, quite a ways down is Grover's Corners.

Yes, beautiful spot up here. Mountain laurel and li-lacks. I often wonder why people like to be buried in Woodlawn and Brooklyn when they might pass the same time up here in New Hampshire.

Over in that corner are the old stones—1670, 1680. Strong-minded people that come a long way to be independent. Summer people walk around there laughing at the funny words on the tombstones . . . it don't do any harm. And genealogists come up from Boston—get paid by city people for looking up their ancestors. They want to make sure they're Daughters of the American Revolution and of the *Mayflower*. . . . Well, I guess that don't do any harm, either. Wherever you come near the human race, there's layers and layers of nonsense. . . . Over there are some Civil War veterans too. Iron flags on their graves. . . . New Hampshire boys . . . had a notion that the Union ought to be kept together, though they'd never seen more than fifty miles of it themselves. All they knew was the name, friends—the United States of America. The United States of America. And they went and died about it.

This here is the new part of the cemetery. Here's your friend Mrs. Gibbs. 'N let me see—Here's Mr. Stimson, organist at the Congregational Church. And over there's Mrs. Soames who enjoyed the wedding so—you remember? Oh, and a lot of others. And Editor Webb's boy, Wallace, whose appendix burst while he was on a Boy Scout trip to Crawford Notch.

Yes, an awful lot of sorrow has sort of quieted down up here. People just wild with grief have brought their relatives up to this hill. We all know how it is . . . and then time . . . and sunny days . . . and rainy days . . . 'n snow . . . tz-tz-tz. We're glad they're in a beautiful place and we're coming up here ourselves when our fit's over.

This certainly is an important part of Grover's Corners. A lot of thoughts come up here, night and day, but there's no post office. Now I'm going to tell you some things you know already. You know'm as well as I do, but you don't take'm out and look at'm very often. I don't care what they say with their mouths—everybody knows that *something* is eternal, and that something has to do with human beings. All the greatest people ever lived have been telling us that for five thousand years and yet you'd be surprised how people are always losing hold of it. There's something way down deep that's eternal about every human being.

THORNTON WILDER

Tempo or Movement

By the tempo or general movement of your interpretation you can communicate to an audience the most vital revelations about a piece of literature. Although pauses are significant, the rate of speed with which sentences and phrases are uttered may be considered even more important. You cannot talk fast without having others think that you are hurried or excited or eager; and you cannot talk slowly without making them think you are deliberate or calm or indifferent. One attention-getting device of radio announcers of football and basketball games is a rapid tempo, partly because of the rapidity of the game, and partly because they like to create empathically the excitement of the game for their listeners. Watch a room full of people listening to a boxing match that is being described on the radio. Note how they lean forward, how they attend to the voice that is rapidly and forcefully recounting the activity. Then note how this same announcer can control the rate of his speech after the fight is over. Such control is essential for those who wish to interpret literature.

The general rate of a selection is controlled by the meaning and mood expressed by the author. In fact, the whole sense and significance of an interpretation may be quite overthrown by the use of the wrong tempo: meaning can be distorted, and mood can be lost, if the interpreter fails to realize the author's intention. It would be difficult, for instance, to express doubt by using a fast tempo, or sorrow by a staccato rate. The interpreter should work for the tempo which will aid in the projection of the sense and feeling of the selection; he should be able to vary the tempo according to the literature to be interpreted. Some race from start to finish, stumble over words, hurry through sentence after sentence, no matter what tempo is indicated by the meaning and mood. Others amble along contentedly and consistently. Interpretation that includes no change of pace in whole compositions, or in sentences and words, will always be ineffective. Unless the selection calls for monotony of tempo, no interpreter should utter all words with the same rate of speech rhythm without regard for meaning, tone, color, or mood. Good taste and thorough study of the selection are requisites in establishing the time factor.

Tempo is important in three aspects: rate of the whole selection; rate of sentence or phrase; and rate of the individual word, which involves the study of quantity of vowels. In the excerpt below from *Iolanthe*, the general movement is fast: the phrases are short, and the words have been selected for their abruptness. Listen to some of them: *tickles, pickles, sharp, pricking, hot, cross, tumble, toss, ticking, heap, tangle, wreck, crick, neck, pins, shins, fluff, ditto.*

THE NIGHT HAS BEEN LONG!

When you're lying awake with a dismal headache, and repose is
    tabooed by anxiety,
I conceive you may use any language you choose to indulge in with-
    out impropriety,
For your brain is on fire—the bedclothes conspire of usual slumber
    to plunder you:
First your counterpane goes and uncovers your toes, and your sheet
    slips demurely from under you;
Then the blanketing tickles—you feel like mixed pickles, so terribly
    sharp is the pricking;
And you're hot and you're cross, and you tumble and toss till there's
    nothing 'twixt you and the ticking;
Then your bedclothes all creep to the floor in a heap, and you pick
    'em all up in a tangle;
Next your pillow resigns and politely declines to remain at its usual
    angle.
Well, you get some repose in the form of a doze, with hot eyeballs
    and head ever-aching;

But your slumbering teems with such horrible dreams that you'd very
    much better be waking.
You're a regular wreck, with a crick in your neck,
And no wonder you snore, for your head's on the floor,
And you've needles and pins from your soles to your shins,
And your flesh is a-creep, for your left leg's asleep,
And some fluff in your lungs, and a feverish tongue,
And a thirst that's intense, and a general sense
That you haven't been sleeping in clover.
But the darkness has passed, and it's daylight at last,
And the night has been long—ditto, ditto, my song—
And thank goodness, they're both of them over!

                               W. S. GILBERT

The following selection calls for moderate speed and movement, although many of the phrases tend to be short and abrupt,
in accordance with Cyrano's personality. There are times, however, when the movement is slowed down, as in the first four
lines. But the rate increases immediately with the phrases, "At a
word, a Yes, a No,/To fight—or write." The difference in movement between Cyrano's speech and the lines from Gilbert stems
from the meaning of each. Cyrano is expressing his philosophy of
living, so the meaning, and hence the rate, shifts. In the Gilbert
lines, however, only one impression is being created—that of
bodily discomfort.

TO SING, TO LAUGH, TO DREAM[17]

CYRANO . . . To sing, to laugh, to dream,
  To walk in my own way and be alone,
  Free, with an eye to see things as they are,
  A voice that means manhood—to cock my hat
  Where I choose— At a word, a *Yes,* a *No,*
  To fight—or write. To travel any road
  Under the sun, under the stars, nor doubt
  If fame or fortune lie beyond the bourne—
  Never to make a line I have not heard
  In my own heart; yet, with all modesty
  To say: "My soul, be satisfied with flowers,
  With fruit, with weeds even; but gather them
  In the one garden you may call your own."
  So, when I win some triumph, by some chance,

[17] *Cyrano de Bergerac,* pp. 98-99.

Render no share to Caesar—in a word,
I am too proud to be a parasite,
And if my nature wants the germ that grows
Towering to heaven like the mountain pine,
Or like the oak, sheltering multitudes—
I stand, not high it may be—but alone!

LE BRET. Alone, yes!—But why stand against the world?
What devil has possessed you now, to go
Everywhere making yourself enemies?

CYRANO. Watching you other people making friends
Everywhere—as a dog makes friends! I mark
The manner of these canine courtesies
And think: "My friends are of a cleaner breed;
Here comes—thank God!—another enemy!"

LE BRET. But this is madness!

CYRANO.   Method, let us say.
It is my pleasure to displease. I love
Hatred. Imagine how it feels to face
The volley of a thousand angry eyes—
The bile of envy and the froth of fear
Spattering little drops about me— You—
Good nature all around you, soft and warm—
You are like those Italians, in great cowls
Comfortable and loose— Your chin sinks down
Into the folds, your shoulders droop. But I—
The Spanish ruff I wear around my throat
Is like a ring of enemies; hard, proud,
Each point another pride, another thorn—
So that I hold myself erect perforce.
Wearing the hatred of the common herd
Haughtily, the harsh collar of Old Spain,
At once a fetter and—a halo!

EDMOND ROSTAND

"The Spires of Oxford Town" is impressive for its restraint and simplicity. The general movement is slow, even though the lines are short and apparently abrupt.

THE SPIRES OF OXFORD TOWN[18]

I saw the spires of Oxford
As I was passing by,

[18] From *The Spires of Oxford Town and Other Poems*, p. 5. Copyright, 1925, by E. P. Dutton & Company. Reprinted by permission of the publishers.

The gray spires of Oxford
Against a pearl-gray sky.
My heart was with the Oxford men
Who went abroad to die.

The years go fast in Oxford,
The golden years and gay.
The hoary colleges look down
On careless boys at play.
But when the bugles sounded war
They put their games away.

They left the peaceful river,
The cricket-field, the quad,
The shaven lawns of Oxford
To seek a bloody sod—
They gave their merry youth away
For country and for God.

God rest you, happy gentlemen,
Who laid your good lives down,
Who took the khaki and the gun
Instead of cap and gown.
God bring you to a fairer place
Than even Oxford town.

WINIFRED M. LETTS

Quantity

It must have been apparent as we discussed fast and slow tempo that inherent in the general movement of the selection is the timing given to individual words. This duration of sound within the word, which is called quantity, is the most subtle of all devices necessary to keep your interpretation alive and to establish the mood of the author. Every speech sound, vowel or consonant, possesses quantity. *K* is quick and short, as are *p, b, t,* hard *g; m, n, s, ng* are long. Among the vowels, *oo, ou, a* as in *all, a* as in *father, o* as in *go,* are inherently long; *o* as in *got, a* as in *at, e* as in *met* are by nature short and quick.

In subtle interpretation, there are always problems in deciding whether to yield to the inherent quantities of the sounds as written or whether to do as one pleases about them. Even more important is the necessity for recognizing that quantities are important in developing the proper speech rhythm.

Mercutio's speech on Queen Mab contains a succession of sounds inviting the interpreter to brevity and alertness.

MERCUTIO

   O, then, I see Queen Mab hath been with you.
   She is the fairies' midwife, and she comes
   In shape no bigger than an agate-stone
   On the fore-finger of an alderman,
   Drawn with a team of little atomies
   Over men's noses as they lie asleep:
   Her waggon-spokes made of long spinners' legs,
   The cover of the wings of grasshoppers,
   Her traces of the smallest spider web,
   Her collars of the moonshine's watery beams,
   Her whip of cricket's bone, the lash of film,
   Her waggoner a small grey-coated gnat,
   Not half so big as a round little worm
   Prick'd from the lazy finger of a maid;
   Her chariot is an empty hazel-nut
   Made by the joiner squirrel, or old grub,
   Time out o' mind the fairies' coachmakers.
   And in this state she gallops night by night
   Through lovers' brains, and then they dream of love;
   O'er courtiers' knees, that dream on curtsies straight;
   O'er lawyers' fingers, who straight dream on fees;
   O'er ladies' lips, who straight on kisses dream,
   Which oft the angry Mab with blisters plagues,
   Because their breaths with sweetmeats tainted are.
   Sometimes she gallops o'er a courtier's nose,
   And then dreams he of smelling out a suit;
   And sometime comes she with a tithe-pig's tail,
   Tickling a parson's nose as a' lies asleep,
   Then he dreams of another benefice.
   Sometime she driveth o'er a soldier's neck,
   And then dreams he of cutting foreign throats,
   Of breaches, ambuscadoes, Spanish blades,
   Of healths five fathom deep; and then anon
   Drums in his ear, at which he starts and wakes,
   And, being thus frighted swears a prayer or two,
   And sleeps again.
             WILLIAM SHAKESPEARE, *Romeo and Juliet*

In another mood, but with the same value given to word quantities is a scene from *The Green Hat*. Iris, misunderstood and maligned by her husband's male relatives and friends runs out of the house to her car and speeds down the winding road. Sir Maurice, realizing too late his injustice to her, starts after her with Hilary. The movement of the scene is rapid, the word quantities are short and abrupt, the attack is quite forceful until the last three paragraphs when the tempo is slowed down greatly.

THE GREEN HAT[19]

"Come along," the old gentleman rapped out, and darted through the window. I caught the General up as he was starting off Guy's car.

"After her, boy. After her. Feel sick, her going like that. Feel sick."

"Can't catch her in this car, sir."

"We'll see. Try, anyway. Must catch her. Must beg her forgiveness." He looked at me as the car started off. He was smiling. Those clever darting eyes were wet. Then Hilary, hatless, like ourselves, jumped on to the footboard and into the back.

"What's this, Maurice?"

"After her, man. Iris has suddenly thrown her hand in. Listen to that hell's own racket!"

Sir Maurice rushed that ancient Rolls break-neck up the winding drive. From the distance came that menacing roar. "Can do seventy-six if you like." I heard the husky whisper above the roar, I saw the dancing tawny curls through the darkness, boy's head, curly head, white and tiger-tawny. . . .

"Can't catch her in this," I cried again.

Hilary was leaning forward from behind, his chin by my shoulder. He whispered through the rushing air: "Afraid of her happiness in the end. You beat her, Maurice, you and your mouldy old England. And your son wasn't worthy of her love. Good God, he cared whether we respected her or not! She wasn't enough for him as she was. Maurice, it's on your head, all this. She'll be in despair. You've got to catch her."

We swept headlong round a corner. We were on the crown of the several small slopes that I remembered ascending.

"There!" yelled Sir Maurice. And he laughed like an excited boy. "We'll catch her yet."

Far down the slope, winding, killing the darkness, rushed the lights of the Hispano. Sir Maurice kept his thumb on the button of the electric-horn, and we drove headlong down that slope with a wild cry of warning to Iris.

"She can't hear!" I yelled.

"Go on, let her know we're here!" yelled Hilary.

[19] From *The Green Hat,* pp. 301-303. Copyright, 1924, by George H. Doran Company. Reprinted by permission of the publishers.

The General's silver hair waved frantically on the wind. He was driving like a madman. He was smiling. The two great lights ahead lit the countryside. Then they seemed to shorten, and Harrod's stood like a pillar of light against the darkness. The silver leaves, the giant trunk . . . in the lights of Iris's car. The stork screamed hoarsely, once, twice, thrice. . . .

"Iris!" Hilary sobbed. "Stop her, man! Stop her! Not that—"

"Iris, not that!" Sir Maurice whispered. "Child, not that!"

I was blind, sick. There was a tearing crash, a tongue of fire among the leaves of Harrod's. Our car had stopped. "Iris!" Sir Maurice whispered. "Iris!" Once again the great tree was lit by a shivering light, then from the darkness there came a grinding, moaning noise as of a great beast in pain. I stood beside Sir Maurice on the road. At the angle at which we had stopped, our lights did not fall on the throbbing wreck. He was staring into the darkness.

"But that death!" Hilary stammered. "That death!"

My foot touched something on the grass beside the road, and I picked up the green hat.

MICHAEL ARLEN

To interpret "Annabel Lee" with short quantities would be to lose the lyrical beauty and rhythm of the lines. Notice that it is essential to give moderately long quantities to the vowels and to elide as much as possible in order to get the lilt of the lines. On the other hand, if you have an inclination to make the vowels too long, your interpretation becomes maudlin.

ANNABEL LEE

It was many and many a year ago,
    In a kingdom by the sea,
That a maiden there lived whom you may know
    By the name of Annabel Lee;
And this maiden she lived with no other thought
    Than to love and be loved by me.

I was a child and *she* was a child,
    In this kingdom by the sea,
But we loved with a love that was more than love—
    I and my Annabel Lee—
With a love that the wingèd seraphs of heaven
    Coveted her and me.

And this was the reason that, long ago,
    In this kingdom by the sea,
A wind blew out of a cloud, chilling

My beautiful Annabel Lee;
So that her highborn kinsmen came
And bore her away from me,
To shut her up in a sepulchre
In this kingdom by the sea.

The angels, not half so happy in heaven,
Went envying her and me—
Yes! that was the reason (as all men know,
In this kingdom by the sea)
That the wind came out of a cloud by night,
Chilling and killing my Annabel Lee.

But our love it was stronger by far than the love
Of those who were older than we—
Of many far wiser than we—
And neither the angels in heaven above,
Nor the demons down under the sea,
Can ever dissever my soul from the soul
Of the beautiful Annabel Lee:

For the moon never beams, without bringing me dreams
Of the beautiful Annabel Lee,
And the stars never rise, but I feel the bright eyes
Of the beautiful Annabel Lee;
And so, all the night-tide, I lie by the side
Of my darling, my darling, my life and my bride,
In her sepulchre there by the sea,
In her tomb by the sounding sea.

EDGAR ALLAN POE

In Sarett's "Wind in the Pine" long quantities abound.

WIND IN THE PINE[20]

Oh, I can hear you, God, above the cry
Of the tossing trees—
Rolling your windy tides across the sky,
And splashing your silver seas
Over the pine,
To the water-line
Of the moon.
Oh, I can hear you, God,

---

[20] From *The Box of God*, p. 21. Copyright, 1922, by Henry Holt and Company, Inc. Reprinted by permission of the publishers.

Above the wail of the lonely loon—
When the pine-tops pitch and nod—
    Chanting your melodies
Of ghostly waterfalls and avalanches,
Swashing your wind among the branches
    To make them pure and white.

Wash over me, God, with your piney breeze,
    And your moon's wet-silver pool;
Wash over me, God, with your wind and night,
    And leave me clean and cool.

                                        Lew Sarett

Here, then, is the significance of quantity to the keen interpreter: if the passage which deals with ideas and sentiments suggesting a quick, sparkling rendition is read slowly and with a
drag, the meaning is lost. The same thing is true of the passage
written for prolongation when it is read fast. Reverse the procedure in the passages above and disobey the signals, and the
effect will be one of confusion and futility.

So one of the most penetrating studies an interpreter can make
in rhythmical speech is to study how the quantity of the vowels
and consonants matches with what the author is trying to express. The words *moon, stars, love, dawn, trees, flowers, moan,
groan, die, burn, grave, sorrow, calm, serene, dreams, drum* all
fit beautifully with the length and duration of their sound. Such
words as *hit, crack, tip, rush, fright, trip, butt, flash, bite, nip* all
ask for speed. He who writes of dreamy things with *nip, hit,* and
rush, or writes of lively and stirring things with *groan, dawn,* and
burn, writes nonsense, or at least, nonsentiment.

EXERCISES

The following poems offer a study of quantities. Notice how
the establishment of the mood depends to a certain extent on
the duration of the word:

I

Here, the first line gives you a clue, and the second line adds
assurance, that the poem is to be paced slowly.

SCARS[21]

There is a deep serenity in homely things—
    Wood dark with age and scarred with daily wear,
In rough coats wet with rain, in steaming muddy shoes,
    Or faces marked with old forgotten care.

They have the strong plain breath of earthiness about them.
    Their feel is like the coarse black bark of trees
That stand deep planted in the loam, that knew through ages
    The crackling storm or sunlit drone of bees.

Great souls there are who leap to flaming beauty
    In timeless, wind-swept realms behind the stars,
But he may know, who walks in homely places,
    The intimate serenity of scars.

GARRETA BUSEY

II

This poem is a nonsense jingle, of course. It must be gay and sparkling. The last four lines of each stanza abound in short quantities and quick movement. That the author intended to give the reader a feeling of lightness and gaiety is evident in the repetition of sounds and the brevity of the refrain.

THE OWL AND THE PUSSY-CAT

The Owl and the Pussy-cat went to sea
    In a beautiful pea-green boat:
They took some honey, and plenty of money
    Wrapped up in a five-pound note.
The Owl looked up to the stars above,
    And sang to a small guitar,
"O lovely Pussy, O Pussy, my love,
    What a beautiful Pussy you are,
            You are,
            You are!
    What a beautiful Pussy you are!"

Pussy said to the Owl, "You elegant fowl,
    How charmingly sweet you sing!
Oh! let us be married; too long we have tarried:
    But what shall we do for a ring?"

---

[21] Published originally in *The Bookman* (May, 1926), p. 351. Reprinted by permission of the author and the publishers.

They sailed away, for a year and a day,
　To the land where the bong-tree grows;
And there in a wood a Piggy-wig stood,
　With a ring at the end of his nose,
　　　　　His nose,
　　　　　His nose,
　With a ring at the end of his nose.

"Dear Pig, are you willing to sell for one shilling
　Your ring?" Said the Piggy, "I will."
So they took it away and were married next day
　By the Turkey who lives on the hill.
They dined on mince and slices of quince,
　Which they ate with a runcible spoon;
And hand in hand, on the edge of the sand,
　They danced by the light of the moon,
　　　　　The moon,
　　　　　The moon,
　They danced by the light of the moon.

EDWARD LEAR

III

"The Cupboard" is merry and distinctly terse and neat in form
and mood. Every line is designed to be fanciful and pleasantly
secretive. Part of its charm depends on its interpretation by one
who knows the value of a short pause after every third line of
each stanza, so that the refrain line can be given without pauses
and the quantities can be short.

THE CUPBOARD[22]

I know a little cupboard,
　With a teeny tiny key,
And there's a jar of Lollypops
　For me, me, me.

It has a little shelf, my dear,
　As dark as dark can be,
And there's a dish of Banbury Cakes
　For me, me, me.

I have a small fat grandmamma,
　With a very slippery knee,

And she's the Keeper of the Cupboard
  With a key, key, key.

And when I'm very good, my dear,
  As good as good can be,
There's Banbury Cakes, and Lollypops
  For me, me, me.

WALTER DE LA MARE

IV

This "Song" *sings.* You cannot interpret it in any other way
because of its inherent melody, which is created in large part by
the repetitions of phrases and words with short quantities, such
as "a hey and a ho, and a hey nonino," and, of course, by the
refrain.

This selection and the next two from Shakespeare all deal with
the subject of love. Compare the three pieces for word quantities.
Notice that in each the form of the line is changed, the phrasing
varies, the moods differ, and, finally, the word quantities vary
according to the mood to be expressed.

SONG

It was a lover and his lass,
  With a hey, and a ho, and a hey nonino,
That o'er the green corn-field did pass
  In the spring time, the only pretty ring time,
When birds do sing, hey ding a ding, ding;
Sweet lovers love the spring.

Between the acres of the rye,
  With a hey, and a ho, and a hey nonino,
These pretty country folks would lie,
  In spring time, the only pretty ring time,
When birds do sing, hey ding a ding, ding;
Sweet lovers love the spring.

This carol they began that hour,
  With a hey, and a ho, and a hey nonino,
How that life was but a flower
  In spring time, the only pretty ring time,
When birds do sing, hey ding a ding, ding;
Sweet lovers love the spring.

And therefore take the present time,
  With a hey, and a ho, and a hey nonino;
For love is crownèd with the prime,
  In spring time, the only pretty ring time,
When birds do sing, hey ding a ding, ding;
Sweet lovers love the spring.
                    WILLIAM SHAKESPEARE, *As You Like It*

V

Quantities are not as short in this sonnet as in the "Song"; but neither are they too long. Strike a happy mean but notice that the word duration is shorter in some lines than in others: for example, "Haply I think on thee; and then my state,/Like to the lark at break of day arising."

SONNET XXIX

When, in disgrace with Fortune and men's eyes,
I all alone beweep my outcast state,
And trouble deaf heaven with my bootless cries,
And look upon myself, and curse my fate,
Wishing me like to one more rich in hope,
Featur'd like him, like him with friends possess'd,
Desiring this man's art and that man's scope,
With what I most enjoy contented least;
Yet in these thoughts myself almost despising,
Haply I think on thee; and then my state,
Like to the lark at break of day arising
From sullen earth, sings hymns at heaven's gate;
  For thy sweet love rememb'red such wealth brings
  That then I scorn to change my state with kings.
                              WILLIAM SHAKESPEARE

VI

A variety of word quantities is to be found in this soliloquy, mainly because Hamlet is experiencing intense emotions. He shifts from depressing thoughts on suicide to horror at the marriage of his mother and uncle less than a month after his father's death, and, finally, to the decision that despite his sorrow and disapproval, he must hold his tongue. Shakespeare has given you clues to the ascending climaxes by using ejaculations which have short quantities.

THIS TOO TOO SOLID FLESH

HAMLET
  O that this too too solid flesh would melt,
  Thaw, and resolve itself into a dew!
  Or that the Everlasting had not fix'd
  His canon 'gainst self-slaughter! O God! O God!
  How weary, stale, flat, and unprofitable
  Seem to me all the uses of this world!
  Fie on't! O fie, fie! 'Tis an unweeded garden,
  That grows to seed; things rank and gross in nature
  Possess it merely. That it should come to this!
  But two months dead. Nay, not so much, not two.
  So excellent a king; that was, to this,
  Hyperion to a satyr; so loving to my mother
  That he might not beteem the winds of heaven
  Visit her face too roughly. Heaven and earth!
  Must I remember? Why, she would hang on him,
  As if increase of appetite had grown
  By what it fed on; and yet, within a month,—
  Let me not think on 't!—Frailty, thy name is woman!—
  A little month, or ere those shoes were old
  With which she follow'd my poor father's body,
  Like Niobe, all tears,—why she, even she—
  O God! a beast, that wants discourse of reason,
  Would have mourn'd longer—married with mine uncle,
  My father's brother, but no more like my father
  Than I to Hercules; within a month,
  Ere yet the salt of most unrighteous tears
  Had left the flushing in her gallèd eyes,
  She married. . . .
  It is not nor it cannot come to good.—
  But break, my heart, for I must hold my tongue.
                    WILLIAM SHAKESPEARE, *Hamlet*

VII

The three poems below reflect moods that are reminiscent of thoughts dear to one or of longing for the past. In each, the mood is indicated and sustained by words whose sounds lend themselves to medium or long duration. What are the key words?

THE LONELY ROAD[23]

So long had I travelled the lonely road,
Though, now and again, a wayfaring friend
Walked shoulder to shoulder, and lightened the load,
I often would think to myself as I strode,
No comrade will journey with you to the end.

And it seemed to me, as the days went past,
And I gossiped with cronies, or brooded alone,
By wayside fires, that my fortune was cast
To sojourn by other men's hearths to the last,
And never to come to my own hearthstone.

The lonely road no longer I roam.
We met, and were one in the heart's desire.
Together we came through the wintry gloam
To the little old house by the cross-ways home;
And crossed the threshold, and kindled the fire.

WILFRED W. GIBSON

SILENCE[24]

God must have loved the silence for He laid
A stillness on the sunset and the dawn;
Upon the moment when the bird has gone,
Leaving a note, high-hung, within the glade
More sweet than when he sang it; noons that pass
Too full of forest changelessness for sound;
Creeping of little frosts along the ground;
Silence of growth among the summer grass.

God must have deeply loved the silences,
For is there one of us who has not heard
Promptings to silence that he speaks not of?—
What of an old remorse; a hope that is
Too deeply hoped; what of a grief outgrown;
And silent, old, unconquerable love?

M. C. BARNETT

[23] From *Poems: 1904-1917*, p. 2. Copyright, 1917, by The Macmillan Company. Reprinted by permission of the publishers.
[24] From *Contemporary Verse* (December 22, 1923), p. 19. Reprinted by permission of the publishers.

MIRAGE

The hope I dreamed of was a dream,
    Was but a dream; and now I wake
Exceeding comfortless, and worn, and old,
    For a dream's sake.

Lie still, lie still, my breaking heart;
    My silent heart, lie still and break;
Life, and the world, and mine own self, are changed
    For a dream's sake.

CHRISTINA ROSSETTI

VII

Usually, when an author writes of love, night, stars, or peace, he chooses words which lend themselves to longer duration of vowels. In the following poems, select words which give you clues to the quantities to be used by the interpreter to reinforce meaning.

DUSK AT SEA[25]

To-night eternity alone is near:
    The sea, the sunset, and the darkening blue;
Within their shelter is no space for fear,
    Only the wonder that such things are true.

The thought of you is like the dusk at sea—
    Space and wide freedom and old shores left far,
The shelter of a lone immensity
    Sealed by the sunset and the evening star.

THOMAS S. JONES, JR.

A THRUSH IN THE MOONLIGHT[26]

In came the moon and covered me with wonder,
    Touched me and was near me, and made me very still.
In came a rush of song, raining as from thunder,

[25] From *The Voice in the Silence*, p. 41. Copyright, 1915, by Thomas Bird Mosher. Reprinted by permission of the author and the publishers.
[26] From *Grenstone Poems*, p. 42. Copyright, 1917, by Alfred A. Knopf, Inc. Reprinted by permission of the publishers.

Pouring importunate on my window-sill.
I lowered my head, I hid my head, I would not see nor hear—
The bird-song had stricken me, had brought the moon too near.
   But when I dared to lift my head, night began to fill
With singing in the darkness. And then the thrush grew still.
And the moon came in, and silence, on my window-sill.

WITTER BYNNER

THE NIGHT HAS A THOUSAND EYES

The night has a thousand eyes,
   And the day but one,
Yet the light of the whole world dies
   With the dying sun.

The mind has a thousand eyes,
   And the heart but one,
Yet the light of the whole world dies
   When love is done.

FRANCIS BOURDILLON

MONODY TO THE SOUND OF ZITHERS[27]

I have wanted other things more than lovers . . .
I have desired peace, intimately to know
The secret curves of deep-bosomed contentment,
To learn by heart things beautiful and slow.

Cities at night, and cloudful skies, I've wanted;
And open cottage doors, old colors and smells apart;
All dim things, layers of river-mist on river—
Capture Beauty's hands and lay them on my heart.

I have wanted clean rain to kiss my eyelids,
Sea-spray and silver foam to kiss my mouth.
I have wanted strong winds to flay me with passion;
And, to soothe me, tired winds from the south.

These things have I wanted more than lovers . . .
Jewels in my hands, and dew on the morning grass—
Familiar things, while lovers have been strangers.
Friended thus, I have let nothing pass.

KAY BOYLE

[27] From *Poetry* (December, 1922), p. 47. Reprinted by permission of the publishers.

FRAGMENT[28]

I can forget the peace of solitude,
The calm of two alone with quiet rain,
Alone, with fire shadows stammering
Across the ceiling of the room; and I
Am able to restrain regret that these
Are gone . . . until a sight of any sky,
Wind-blue and white with clouds, or sight of trees
Against a shield of stars, or breath of scent
You cared to use, or any little thing
At all that we enjoyed comes back again. . . .

LORD STITES

WORLDLY WISDOM[29]

My days you have stolen, World,
My hands you have chained to an endless task;
My brain you have scourged by day and night—
Oh, it has learned your tricks now, well enough,
And knows the worth of a coin at dusk!

You are so wise, World:
How could you have overlooked my heart
And the hills that are green and high
And Spring that comes laughing a song?

JOHN R. McCARTHY

IX

These two poems are companion pieces, but notice that each reflects a different mood. In "Meeting at Night," Browning surrounds us first with the sea and the "long black land." Then we find ourselves moving over the "mile of warm sea-scented beach" and "three fields." Word quantities, thus far, are of medium length; but with "A tap at the pane," the movement quickens, because the words that follow are all of short quantity. Then, with the last two lines, the poem slows down again. The four lines of "Parting at Morning," however, move with directness and decision; they have none of the darkness and hushed breathlessness of the previous poem, partly because of the preponderance of monosyllabic words, and partly because of the choice of words that connote the beginning of a new adventure.

[28] Reprinted by permission of the author.
[29] Reprinted by permission of James T. White & Company.

MEETING AT NIGHT

The gray sea and the long black land;
And the yellow half-moon large and low;
And the startled little waves that leap
In fiery ringlets from their sleep,
As I gain the cove with pushing prow,
And quench its speed i' the slushy sand.

Then a mile of warm sea-scented beach;
Three fields to cross till a farm appears;
A tap at the pane, the quick sharp scratch
And blue spurt of a lighted match,
And a voice less loud, through its joys and fears,
Than the two hearts beating each to each!

ROBERT BROWNING

PARTING AT MORNING

Round the cape of a sudden came the sea,
And the sun looked over the mountain's rim:
And straight was a path of gold for him,
And the need of a world of men for me.

ROBERT BROWNING

Rhythm and Meter

The student of interpretation will learn the distinction between good and poor speech rhythms by listening to others and by practicing. Especially does this apply to the movement of poetry, for the interpretation of poetry has two time factors to interest the interpreter: rhythm and meter. If you do not get the distinction between these two patterns, your interpretation will not be very effective.

Meter is a matter of regularity of strokes of the voice, a system of heavy and light, long and short. It can always be represented by a system of marks that indicates this regularity and fixed order; that is, it can be broken into feet which are iambic, dactyllic, trochaic, etc. The reading of poetry with this regularity of beats is known as scansion: to read a line according to its metrical pattern is to scan it. Now the point is that in the interpretation of the printed page, scansion rarely makes for good sense and proper feeling. Scansion is merely an artificial device for testing metrical forms to see whether the meter is made according to rule; it is not a means of communicating thought.

Thought is conveyed by rhythm, not by meter. What then is rhythm? No definition will ever identify positively what rhythm is. In a general way, we can say that rhythm is a blending of recurrent stressing and nonstressing of syllables into a flowing, continuous pattern or melody. Or, to put it another way, rhythm is a varying pattern of sound and pause but with enough regularity and repetition that the ear catches the cadences, usually bringing pleasure to the listener. Meter can be said to exist on the printed page, for it can be marked off by rule with mechanical regularity; it can be paced like the beat of a drum or the click-clack of train wheels. One can usually predict what is coming next. It is the basic structure for rhythm, for the intricate patterns of cadence and melody, for the varying excursions within the metrical pattern. It is impossible to locate rhythm, because although it is inherent in the selection, it must strike a sympathetic response in the interpreter and must be identified with the interpreter's feeling. You have watched ballet troupes. There is always a basic pattern, which is interpreted by various groups on the stage into different rhythms; finally, these patterns are blended, as are melodies in a symphonic orchestration, into one intricate rhythmical pattern. Dance orchestras also provide a background pattern which dancing couples interpret according to the rhythms popular at the time or according to the dancers' inherent rhythms. Similarly, from every line of poetry or prose, the interpreter may find several rhythmical patterns. If a sense of rhythm is latent and has never been developed in you, then you may have difficulty finding rhythm in any poem. This is characteristic of the person who says that he does not enjoy poetry. It must be repeated, however, that there is no interpretation in scanning meter, for all readers do it alike, and what all do alike is not interpretation.

Interpretation is given its most personal touch through rhythm. There is an element in rhythm which meter lacks: it is the emotional factor, an empathic movement which gives the spirit, the mood—call it what you will—to the selection. It is a plus which no one ever feels or is required to show in scanning verse aloud.

It is the difference which will always be found between the mechanical rendition of an exercise and the spirited or moving production of a finished interpretation. Rhythm conforms to no rule of its own, for it is always a matter of the interpreter's ingenuity, his versatility in employing a happy combination of all the principles that make up lively speech. "You are a poet if you read a poem well." The poetry is in the interpreter—and the hearer—or else there is none. Meter is like a church hymn sung by the congregation; rhythm is like the rendition of an artist giving expression to his inmost soul. Meter has no surprises; rhythm never gives away its secrets. It is one surprise after another, and each one of them is a pleasure. It catches the audience off guard and makes them glad. It titillates attention and interest by the everlasting uncertainty of what is going to happen next.

The interpreter needs no detailed study of prosody to interpret a poem well. In fact, some students could probably read "This is the forest primeval" with truer rhythmical sense if they had not been urged at various times to scan it. Overemphasis on scansion distorts speech rhythm and is likely to tend toward monotonous, droning reading of poetry—even to singsong. It takes experience to overcome this mechanical procedure. There may be value in being conscious of metrical pattern; but when that consciousness becomes paramount so that the interpreter reads in terms of iambs and dactyls, then interpretation has suffered its worst blow, for force is distorted, timing becomes mechanical, pitch is monotonous, quality becomes inflexible, and meaning is lost. When an interpreter says, "I was miserable listening to every one mutilate Shakespeare's iambic pentameter," he has lost, if he ever had it, the joy of Shakespeare's melody and rhythm. Anyone who reads blank verse for the sake of blank verse instead of the meaning does not have a realization of the author's aim. Certainly no author would say, "See how well I write blank verse," but rather, "Note how well I can gain rhythmical effects by using a framework of blank verse." No poet ever wrote blank verse for the sake of blank verse. Meter is not an end in itself but a means to an end. It should be considered a sort of convenience, a guidepost which shows the general movement of the poem, and from which various rhythmical patterns emerge. After all, as interpreters of poetry, we are anxious to convey a rhythm to the listener; and the rhythm we are working for is not a matter of scansion but a matter of muscles and glands. We live rhythmically, we move rhythmically, and we ought to be able to interpret rhythmically.

But just as each of us has varying speech cadences, so each of us may find a different rhythm in a poem. The poem which seems most rhythmical to you may not seem so to me, or at least, your rhythm may not be mine. You have all heard Kipling's "Mandalay" sung and interpreted many times, and almost every time you have heard it, you have experienced a different rhythm. But there is probably one interpretation you remember above all others, because it fits in with the cadences of your vocal expression. Many students complain that they cannot interpret Carl Sandburg because he has no rhythm. The trouble lies, of course, in the interpreter, who is not able to adjust his speech rhythm to the symbols on the printed page. One of Carl Sandburg's recordings of his own poetry will prove to you instantly the rhythmical potentiality of his poetry. Sometimes you will hear a poet read his own poetry with a lack of rhythmical expression or with a rhythm not felt by you. The poet probably knows the rhythm he is trying to convey, feels it, appreciates it; yet he may have difficulty in making his listeners feel what he feels. His handicap lies in his inability to express what he feels through the rhythmical use of the voice. It is your task as an interpreter to discover and improve the variability of your vocal expression and to adapt the cadences to the meaning of the selection and for the pleasure of your audience.

LISTENING PROJECTS

I

As we said earlier, a good way to experience rhythm is to listen to it. One recording that should be listened to in order to train the ear in rhythm is *John Brown's Body* by Stephen Vincent Benét.[30] You will have hours of enjoyment listening over and over

[30] *John Brown's Body* (Columbia, 5SL-181), with Tyrone Power, Judith Anderson, Raymond Massey, and Richard White under the direction of Charles Laughton.

to the strains that repeat themselves, to the rhythms that give characterization to Cudjo, Sally Dupré, Lucy Weatherby, Mary Lou Wingate, Jack Ellyat, Melora, and Clay Wingate. Since portions of the poem have been omitted from the recording, it is highly important that you read the Wingate homecoming scene in its entirety before listening to the recorded version,[31] which we discuss below.

The first scene describes the preparations for the gala day which will bring Clay Wingate home from the war. There are a number of listening observations for you to make:

1. The quick tempo which introduces Cudjo throughout the poem is repeated at the beginning of the scene; the rhythm of his speech quickens almost to a buck-and-wing tempo, as he says:
> There's goin' to be mixin's and mighty doin's
> Chicken-fixin's and barbecuin's.
2. The lines that describe the laughter of the Negroes,
> The laughter that doesn't end with the lips
> But shakes the belly and curls the toes
> And prickles the end of the fingertips
have, as a background, cascades of laughter which provide a pattern for the lines beginning, "Up through the garden, in through the door," until "It spills like a wave in the crowded kitchen."
3. The background incantation of "This is the last" haunts the scene, starting as an echoing whisper and mounting in crescendo (by means of contrasting voices and the choral choir) through Mary Lou's innermost thoughts until it dins the ear of Clay Wingate with its insistence as he rides along and finally sings itself into the dance music,
> And Wingate Hall must tumble down,
> Tumble down, tumble down.
4. The lines which introduce Aunt Bess are the aftermath of the laughter lines and are still quick in tempo and rhythm as they describe her skill "on oceans of trifle and floating island." But as soon as Benét begins her characterization, the lines assume a dignified rhythm appropriate to the "matriarch of the weak and young," to "one who is older than Time," "a curious blossom from bitter ground."
5. The rhythmic adjustment by Judith Anderson to the words and phrases revealing various characteristics of Mary Lou Wingate shows consummate skill. Note some of the contrasting phrases that characterize Mary Lou: she was "hard as a rapier blade" but "knew

---

[31] Stephen Vincent Benét, *John Brown's Body* (New York, Rinehart and Company, Inc., 1941), pp. 157-170.

her Bible" and "how to flirt/With a swansdown fan and a brocade skirt," "for she was gentle but she could hate."

6. Above all, the scene moves with spirit; there is no drag, no monotony, even though the undercurrent of the scene is made intense and tragic in the line "Hurry, hurry, this is the last."

7. The waltz tune as background to the impending disaster assists in creating the mood which Benét gives us of past and present bustle, excitement, and preparations at Wingate Hall. The character portrayals of Mary Lou, Aunt Bess, and Cudjo are reminiscent of typical southern gentility and the loyalty of plantation servants. The gay music accentuates and makes more tragic the undercurrent of doom awaiting Wingate Hall, which reaches a climax as Clay Wingate approaches his home with the same foreboding.

8. The waltz tune also ties these two scenes together, so that the superficial gaiety and inner tension are sustained as Sally and Wingate fight inwardly rather than verbally.

9. The dance scene is a most enriching experience. Listen for the timing of the words, phrases, sentences to the rhythm of the waltz. Hear the differences in vocal quality as the two dancers, Sally and Clay, utter superficial nothings but, as they follow the gay melody, think intensely of their mutual relationship. The final blending of the strife between Sally and Wingate and the tumbling down of Wingate Hall is superb.

10. The climax here is unsurpassed—tense, quickening, and disastrous:

> And Wingate Hall must tumble down,
> An idol broken apart,
> Before I sew on a wedding gown
> And stitch my name in your heart.

And all the while the music carries us through its gay lilt!

The last lines of the dance scene are reprinted below in full for your study along with the recording mentioned above.

SALLY DUPRÉ AND WINGATE TALK WITH THE MUSIC[32]

> That's good music. It beats in your head.
>
> (It beats in the head, it beats in the head,
> It ties the heart with a scarlet thread,
> This is the last,

This is the last,
Hurry, hurry, this is the last.
We dance on a floor of polished sleet,
But the little cracks are beginning to meet,
Under the play of our dancing feet.
I do not care. I am Wingate still.
The corn underground by the watermill.
And I am yours while the fiddles spill,
But my will has a knife to cut your will,
My birds will never come to your hill.

You are my foe and my only friend,
You are the steel I cannot bend,
You are the water at the world's end.

But Wingate Hall must tumble down,
Tumble down, tumble down,
A dream dissolving, a ruined thing,
Before we can melt from the shattered crown
Gold enough for a wedding-ring.
And Wingate Hall must lie in the dust,
And the wood rot and the iron rust
And the vines grow over the broken bust,
Before we meet without hate or pride,
Before we talk as lover and bride,
Before the daggers of our offence
Have the color of innocence,
And nothing is said and all is said,
And we go looking for secret bread,
And lie together in the same bed.)

Yes, it's good music, hear it lift.

(It is too mellow, it is too swift,
I am dancing along in my naked shift,
I am dancing alone in the snowdrift.
You are my lover and you my life,
My peace and my unending strife
And the edge of the knife against my knife.
I will not make you a porcelain wife.

We are linked together for good and all,
For the still pool and the waterfall,
But you are married to Wingate Hall.
And Wingate Hall must tumble down,
Tumble down, tumble down,
Wingate Hall must tumble down,
An idol broken apart,

Before I sew on a wedding gown
And stitch my name in your heart.)

STEPHEN VINCENT BENÉT

II

A listening project entirely different from the previous one as
far as rhythm is concerned is offered in the recording of "Father
William," by Edith Evans.[33] This is an admirable demonstration
of how not to dawdle in the interpretation of a poem which at
first glance might appear to be slowly paced. Her spirited rhythm
gives meaning to this ballad type of question-and-answer poem.

FATHER WILLIAM

"You are old, Father William," the young man said,
    "And your hair has become very white;
And yet you incessantly stand on your head—
    Do you think, at your age, it is right?"

"In my youth," Father William replied to his son,
    "I feared it might injure the brain;
But, now that I'm perfectly sure I have none,
    Why, I do it again and again."

"You are old," said the youth, "as I mentioned before,
    And have grown most uncommonly fat;
Yet you turned a back-somersault in at the door—
    Pray, what is the reason of that?"

"In my youth," said the sage, as he shook his gray locks,
    "I kept all my limbs very supple
By the use of this ointment—one shilling the box—
    Allow me to sell you a couple?"

"You are old," said the youth, "and your jaws are too weak
    For anything tougher than suet;
Yet you finished the goose, with the bones and the beak—
    Pray, how did you manage to do it?"

"In my youth," said the father, "I took to the law,
    And argued each case with my wife;
And the muscular strength which it gave to my jaw
    Has lasted the rest of my life."

[33] *The Voice of Poetry* (Columbia, MM-375), sponsored by the National
Council of Teachers of English.

"You are old," said the youth, "one would hardly suppose
That your eye was as steady as ever;
Yet you balanced an eel on the end of your nose—
What made you so awfully clever?"

"I have answered three questions, and that is enough,"
Said his father. "Don't give yourself airs!
Do you think I can listen all day to such stuff?
Be off, or I'll kick you down-stairs!"

LEWIS CARROLL

EXERCISES

I

Vachel Lindsay chants his poem "The Congo," [34] even though
he gives directions about the interpretation of lines, which offer
a wide variation in tones, pause, tempo, and quantities for rhythmical changes. You will find when studying it that the poem can
be interpreted with many varieties of speech rhythm and melody:
it can be chanted; it can be interpreted effectively with a tom-
tom rhythm; it can have a lively modern swing to it. This poem
illustrates the principle that the rhythm is within you. It is your
opportunity to test your versatility to make use of quality changes,
force changes, and tempo variations. There is one factor to be
kept in mind: the poem cannot be successfully interpreted without an alert, spirited attitude which will shift in tension with
every change in mood and rhythm. Students of interpretive dancing have danced to the rhythms of "The Congo" as given by
interpreters. Try it. Can you find the buck-and-wing rhythm, the
voodoo rhythm, the waltz rhythm, the cakewalk rhythm, the
Charleston rhythm? A few hints may help you:

1. You should be able to hear the tom-tom rhythm in the lines
   beginning, "Then I saw the Congo, creeping through the
   black."
2. The tom-tom should beat a more syncopated rhythm beginning "Then along that riverbank."
3. The voodoo rhythm builds up in the lines beginning, " 'Be
   careful what you do.' "
4. The Charleston rhythm is obvious in lines beginning, "Wild
   crap-shooters with a whoop and a call."

[34] *Contemporary Poets Series* (Columbia, D9-CB), sponsored by the
National Council of Teachers of English.

5. The waltz tempo swings in with the line, "A negro fairyland swung into view."
6. The buck and wing fits in nicely with the line, "A troupe of skull-faced witch-men came."
7. The cake-walk tempo takes over on the line, "Just then from the doorway, as fat as shotes."
8. A slow buck and wing, which goes into a definite beat of the voodoo rhythm begins "While the witch-men laughed, with a sinister air" and ends with " 'BOOM.' "

Besides these hints, you should realize too that there is an infinite number of ways in which you can apply force and touch to lines like "Boomlay, boomlay, boomlay, boom," "Rattle-rattle, rattle-rattle," "Hoo, hoo, hoo," and "Mumbo-Jumbo will hoo-doo you."

THE CONGO[35]
A Study of the Negro Race

I. Their Basic Savagery

Fat black bucks in a wine-barrel room,
Barrel-house kings, with feet unstable,
Sagged and reeled and pounded on the table,   *A deep rolling*
Pounded on the table,   *bass.*
Beat an empty barrel with the handle of a broom,
Hard as they were able,
Boom, boom, BOOM,
With a silk umbrella and the handle of a broom,
Boomlay, boomlay, boomlay, BOOM.
THEN I had religion, THEN I had a vision.
I could not turn from their revel in derision.
THEN I SAW THE CONGO, CREEPING THROUGH THE   *More deliberate.*
   BLACK,   *Solemnly chanted.*
CUTTING THROUGH THE JUNGLE WITH A GOLDEN
   TRACK.
Then along that riverbank
A thousand miles
Tattooed cannibals danced in files;
Then I heard the boom of the blood-lust song
And a thigh-bone beating on a tin-pan gong.
And "Blood!" screamed the whistles and the fifes   *A rapidly piling*
   of the warriors,   *climax of speed*
"Blood!" screamed the skull-faced, lean witch-   *and racket.*
   doctors;

[35] From *The Congo and Other Poems*, pp. 3-11. Copyright, 1915, by The Macmillan Company. Reprinted by permission of the publishers.

"Whirl ye the deadly voo-doo rattle,
Harry the uplands,
Steal all the cattle,
Rattle-rattle, rattle-rattle,
Bing!
Boomlay, boomlay, boomlay, Boom!"   *With a philo-*
A roaring, epic, rag-time tune   *sophic pause.*
From the mouth of the Congo
To the Mountains of the Moon.
Death is an Elephant,
Torch-eyed and horrible,
Foam-flanked and terrible.
Boom, steal the pygmies,   *Shrilly and with*
Boom, kill the Arabs,   *a heavily accent-*
Boom, kill the white men,   *ed metre.*
Hoo, hoo, hoo.
Listen to the yell of Leopold's ghost   *Like the wind in*
Burning in Hell for his hand-maimed host.   *the chimney.*
Hear how the demons chuckle and yell
Cutting his hands off, down in Hell.
Listen to the creepy proclamation,
Blown through the lairs of the forest-nation,
Blown past the white-ants' hill of clay,   *All the O sounds*
Blown past the marsh where the butterflies   *very golden.*
     play:—   *Heavy accents*
"Be careful what you do,   *very heavy.*
Or Mumbo-Jumbo, God of the Congo,   *Light accents*
And all of the other   *very light. Last*
Gods of the Congo,   *line whispered.*
Mumbo-Jumbo will hoo-doo you,
Mumbo-Jumbo will hoo-doo you,
Mumbo-Jumbo will hoo-doo you."

II. Their Irrepressible High Spirits

Wild crap-shooters with a whoop and a call   *Rather shrill and*
Danced the juba in their gambling-hall   *high.*
And laughed fit to kill, and shook the town,
And guyed the policemen and laughed them
     down
With a boomlay, boomlay, boomlay, BOOM. . . .
Then I saw the Congo, creeping through the
     black,
Cutting through the jungle with a golden   *Read exactly as*
     track.   *in first section.*
A negro fairyland swung into view,   *Lay emphasis on*
A minstrel river   *the delicate ideas.*

Where dreams come true.
The ebony palace soared on high
Through the blossoming trees to the evening sky.
The inlaid porches and casements shone
With gold and ivory and elephant-bone.
And the black crowd laughed till their sides were
    sore
At the baboon butler in the agate door,
And the well-known tunes of the parrot band
That trilled on the bushes of that magic land.

Keep as light-footed as possible.

A troupe of skull-faced witch-men came
Through the agate doorway in suits of flame,
Yea, long-tailed coats with a gold-leaf crust
And hats that were covered with diamond-dust.
And the crowd in the court gave a whoop and a
    call
And danced the juba from wall to wall.
But the witch-men suddenly stilled the throng.
With a stern cold glare, and a stern old song:
"Mumbo-Jumbo will hoo-doo you." . . .

With pomposity.

With a great deliberation and ghostliness.

Just then from the doorway, as fat as shotes
Came the cake-walk princes in their long red
    coats,
Canes with a brilliant lacquer shine,
And tall silk hats that were red as wine.
And they pranced with their butterfly partners
    there,
Coal-black maidens with pearls in their hair,
Knee-skirts trimmed with the jessamine sweet,
And bells on their ankles and little black feet.
And the couples railed at the chant and the
    frown
Of the witch-men lean, and laughed them down.
(Oh, rare was the revel, and well worth while
That made those glowering witch-men smile.)

With overwhelming assurance, good cheer, and pomp.
With growing speed and sharply marked dance rhythm.

The cake-walk royalty then began
To walk for a cake that was tall as a man
To the tune of "Boomlay, boomlay, BOOM,"
While the witch-men laughed, with a sinister air,
And sang with the scalawags prancing there:
"Walk with care, walk with care,
Or Mumbo-Jumbo, God of the Congo,
And all of the other
Gods of the Congo,
Mumbo-Jumbo will hoo-doo you.

With a touch of negro dialect and as rapidly as possible toward the end.

Beware, beware, walk with care,
Boomlay, boomlay, boomlay, boom.
Boomlay, boomlay, boomlay, boom,
Boomlay, boomlay, boomlay, boom,
Boomlay, boomlay, boomlay,   *Slow   philosophic*
Boom."   *calm.*
Oh, rare was the revel, and well worth while
That made those glowering witch-men smile.

VACHEL LINDSAY

II

No one can give you the right rhythm for the following poems,
but you can exercise some judgment on which one is most effective in keeping the meaning true to the author's purpose. Pausing
is the key to the many twists and turns which the lines may take,
especially refrain lines. Play with each line; tease meaning out
of it by trying your skills, but keep within the author's boundaries. You may pause many places where there is no punctuation,
and you will use quantities that are long and short; but if you
race through any poem, you are conveying little but a jumble of
words. Be sure to give rhythmical expression and not metrical
scansion. If you wish to be sure of the effect of rhythm and meter,
try reading first by scansion; then see if the sense and thought
are not improved and if empathy is not aroused more readily
when you interpret rhythmically.

1

You will remember you listened to Lew Sarett's interpretation
of "Wéeng" for control of force and touch. Now go back to it
and work on the rhythm which Sarett handles so masterfully.
Remember the last stanza:[36]

> If Wéeng-oosh comes at the end of this day,
> And finds you asleep he will hurry away . . .
> Do you hear him cry on the winds that blow?—
> And walk on the earth as soft as a doe?—
> To-and-fro . . . . to-and-fro . . .
> Hi-yáh! he has crept away from my lap!
> For he found my little boy taking a nap.

[36] From *Slow Smoke*, p. 58. Copyright, 1925, by Henry Holt and Company, Inc. Reprinted by permission of the publishers.

Oh, weep no more and whisper low,
I hear the feet of Sleepy-eye go—
Tip-toe . . . . tip-toe.

2

In an entirely different mood and rhythm is the poem "Holly-hocks." Sarett is whimsical, lightly touching on his problems as a gardener. There is a marked contrast between the words used in the first stanza and those used in the second. In the first stanza there are words like *ribald, hysterical, incorrigible, militant, friv-olous, apoplectic, palpitant, acrimonious,* and *irate,* which call for short quantities with a clean-cut touch on the predominant sounds *p, b, t,* and *k.* The second stanza contains words like *lackadaisically, apathetic, downtrodden, boorish, exotic, drop-sical, fainting,* which are of longer quantity and require a slower touch. The second stanza "droops" because the words *bilious, neurotic, yawn,* and *sullen* do not evoke happy connotations. The two-line refrain, however, is intended to be crisp and com-manding.

HOLLYHOCKS[37]

I have a garden, but, oh, dear me!
What a ribald and hysterical company:
Incorrigible mustard, militant corn,
Frivolous lettuce, and celery forlorn;
Beets apoplectic, and fatuous potatoes,—
Voluptuous pumpkins and palpitant tomatoes;
Philandering pickles trysting at the gate,
Onions acrimonious, and peppers irate;
And a regiment of hollyhocks marching around them,
To curb their mischief, to discipline and bound them.

> *Hollyhocks! Hollyhocks! What should I do*
> *Without the morale of a troop like you!*

Some lackadaisically yawn and nod;
Others, hypochondriac, droop on the sod;
Cabbage apathetic, parsnips sullen,
And peas downtrodden by the lancing mullein;

[37] From *Wings Against the Moon,* p. 28. Copyright, 1931, by Henry Holt and Company, Inc. Reprinted by permission of the publishers.

Boorish rutabagas, dill exotic,
The wan wax-bean, bilious and neurotic;
Dropsical melons, varicose chard,
And cauliflowers fainting all over the yard.
Thank heaven for the hollyhocks! Till day is done,
They prod them to labor in the rain and the sun.

Hollyhocks! Hollyhocks! Stiff as starch!
Oh, fix your bayonets! Forward! March!

LEW SARETT

3

There is a backward pull to the lines of this next poem that
holds the rhythm to a slow pace. Phrases like "dead, dark watch,"
"long, long night," and "lags a-creeping there" are not conducive
to a gay rhythm.

MESSMATES[38]

He gave us all a good-bye cheerily
At the first dawn of day;
We dropped him down the side full drearily
When the light died away.
It's a dead, dark watch that he's a-keeping there,
And a long, long night that lags a-creeping there,
Where the Trades and the Tides roll over him,
And the great ships go by.

He's there alone with green seas rocking him
For a thousand miles around;
He's there alone with dumb things mocking him,
And we're homeward bound.
It's a long, lone watch that he's a-keeping there,
And a dead, cold night that lags a-creeping there,
While the months and the years roll over him,
And the great ships go by.

I wonder if the tramps come near enough
As they thrash to and fro,—
Or the battleship's bells ring clear enough
To be heard down below.
If through all the lone watch that he's a-keeping there

---

[38] From *Poems Old and New*, p. 32. Copyright, 1915, by E. P. Dutton
& Company. Reprinted by permission of the publishers.

And the long, cold night that lags a-creeping there,
The voices of the sailormen will comfort him.
When the great ships go by.

HENRY NEWBOLDT

4

An interesting effect has been achieved in these twelve lines,
The light and shadow, the movement, and the stillness combine
in a rhythmic impression that is not easily forgotten. The dancing
cadences are inherent in the lines. Be sure that you find them.

WHERE THE HAYFIELDS WERE[39]

Coming down the mountains in the twilight—
April it was and quiet in the air—
I saw an old man and his little daughter
Burning the meadows where the hayfields were.

Forksful of flame he scattered in the meadows.
Sparkles of fire in the quiet air
Burned in their circles and the silver flowers
Danced like candles where the hayfields were.—

Danced as she did in enchanted circles,
Curtseyed and danced along the quiet air:
Slightly she danced in the stillness, in the twilight,
Dancing in the meadows where the hayfields were.

ARCHIBALD MACLEISH

5

These two poems by Walter de la Mare are typical of his
mystic world—of the hushed mystery of the unknown, of elves
and fairies, of what-you-will. The rhythm differs in each, as does
the mood. Notice that the sound quantities in "Some One" are
short and that the mood is light and whimsical. In "The Little
Green Orchard," however, the author has carefully chosen certain
words to create a mood of stillness, whispering, and listening.
Notice, too, that the refrain in the latter poem has a rhythmic
lilt, whereas the line "I'm sure—sure—sure" has a different kind
of cadence.

[39] From *Collected Poems: 1917-1952*, p. 153. Copyright, 1952, by Houghton Mifflin Company. Reprinted by permission of the publishers.

THE LITTLE GREEN ORCHARD[40]

Someone is always sitting there,
    In the little green orchard;
  Even when the sun is high
  In noon's unclouded sky,
  And faintly droning goes
  The bee from rose to rose,
Someone in the shadow is sitting there,
    In the little green orchard.

Yes, and when twilight is falling softly
    In the little green orchard;
  When the grey dew distils
  And every flower-cup fills;
  And when the last blackbird says,
  "What—what!" and goes her way—s-sh!
I have heard voices calling softly
    In the little green orchard.

Not that I am afraid of being there,
    In the little green orchard;
  Why, when the moon's been bright,—
  Shedding her lonesome light,
  And moths like ghosties come,
  And the horned snail leaves home:
I've sat there, whispering and listening there,
    In the little green orchard.

Only it's strange to be feeling there,
    In the little green orchard;
  Whether you paint or draw,
  Dig, hammer, chop, or saw;
  When you are most alone,
  All but the silence gone . . .
Someone is waiting and watching there,
    In the little green orchard.
               WALTER DE LA MARE

SOME ONE[41]

Some one came knocking
  At my wee, small door;

[40] From *Collected Poems: 1901-1918*, Vol. 2, p. 160. Copyright, 1920, by Henry Holt and Company, Inc. Reprinted by permission of the publishers.
[41] From *Collected Poems: 1901-1918*, Vol. 2, p. 105. Copyright, 1920, by Henry Holt and Company, Inc. Reprinted by permission of the publishers.

Some one came knocking,
    I'm sure—sure—sure;
I listened, I opened,
    I looked to left and right,
But nought there was a-stirring
    In the still dark night;
Only the busy beetle
    Tap-tapping in the wall.
Only from the forest
    The screech-owl's call,
Only the cricket whistling
    While the dewdrops fall,
So I know not who came knocking,
    At all, at all, at all.

WALTER DE LA MARE

6

This poem sings its way into your heart with its melody. It is so cleverly written that an interpreter can easily find the cues for the way the author wants it interpreted. Listen to the word quantities in the four lines that end with a "Big Bath bun."

IF I EVER HAVE TIME FOR THINGS THAT MATTER[42]

If I ever have time for things that matter,
    If ever I have the smallest chance,
I'm going to live in
    Little Broom Gardens,
        Moat-by-the-Castle,
            Nettlecombe, Hants.

I'll take my ease and never, never hurry,
    And sit for hours on the top of a stile,
With a friend from
    Wookey, Cress-on-the-Water,
        Spennithorne-Baggot,
            Bury Saint Gile.

Anything can happen, anything at all,
With faith and a moat and a castle wall.

With good Friar Tuck I'll roam through the heather,
    Or shiver for a while by Windrush Rill,
With a headless knight from

[42] From *Scribner's Magazine* (May, 1926). Reprinted by permission of the author and Charles Scribner's Sons.

Hangman's Hollow,
 Or a jolly old ghost from
  Traitor's Hill.

Then home to dusk through cowslip meadows,
 And a seat on the settle when day is done,
A dish of tea and a
 Pennyworth of cockles,
  A muffin and a crumpet and a
   Big Bath bun.

Why go to Liverpool, why go to Leeds,
Where nothing *could* happen that any one needs?
VILDA SAUVAGE OWENS

7

In much the same mood is the following poem, but with a different rhythm. The mood is mellow, and the rhythm fits the wished-for dream. The end of each stanza is abrupt, however, except for the ending of the last stanza. Make the most of these "scoffings" for contrast with the rest of the poem.

FOR PASSERS-BY[43]

If ever I have the house I've planned
For my heart's dear and me,
It will stand on the top of a wooded hill
Beneath a live oak tree;
And you may pass on the road below
And look at my house and scoff,
And say, "Why, any winter wind
Could blow it off."

If ever I have a garden small
For my heart's love and me,
I'll spread it out on a sloping hill
Beside a live-oak tree;
And you may say: "Why, what a place
To make a garden plot!
The rain will wash it down the gulch
As like as not!"

If ever I light a candle tall
For my heart's heart and me,

[43] Published originally in *Good Housekeeping* (February, 1932), p. 34. Reprinted by permission of the author and the publishers.

I'll set it high on the casement ledge,
And you may pass and see,
And say: "Some one must *live* up there—
I can't imagine who—
It's just the sort of silly thing
Some folk would do!"

Now, if you pass at six o'clock
Upon the road below,
I may be talking with my dear,
And I shall never know.
But if it's only half-past five
I'm nearly sure to see,
And I shall whisper to myself,
"How they must envy me!"

ROBERTA RINEAR

8

This poem gives you poetry in its most concentrated form, with no extraneous words or thoughts. There is only one way for you to interpret these few lines, and that is to be aware of every word or group of words. Nothing must be slighted in the imagery. Watch the pauses, especially the one before the last two lines.

THINGS LOVELIER[44]

You cannot dream
   Things lovelier
Than the first love
   I had of her.

Nor air is any
   By magic shaken
As her first breath in
   The first kiss taken.

And who, in dreaming,
   Understands
Her hands stretched like
   A blind man's hands?

[44] This and the two following poems are from *Kensington Gardens,* pp. 23, 35, 41. Copyright, 1927, by Humbert Wolfe. Reprinted by permission of Ann Wolfe and E. Benn, Ltd.

Open, trembling,
  Wise they were—
You cannot dream
  Things lovelier.

HUMBERT WOLFE

9

Here are two more of Humbert Wolfe's poems which require
delicacy in touch and pause. The comma in the third line of
stanza 3 of "The Gray Squirrel" takes a half-beat pause; each
line should have an almost imperceptible pause at the end. "The
Lilac" speaks for itself. Give it the proper timing and rhythm.

THE GRAY SQUIRREL

Like a small gray
coffee-pot,
sits the squirrel.
He is not

all he should be,
kills by the dozens
trees, and eats
his red-brown cousins.

The keeper, on the
other hand
, who shot him, is
a Christian, and

loves his enemies,
which shows
the squirrel was not
one of those.

HUMBERT WOLFE

THE LILAC

Who thought of the lilac?
"I," dew said,
"I made up the lilac
out of my head."

"She made up the lilac!
Pooh!" thrilled a linnet,
and each dew-note had a
lilac in it.

HUMBERT WOLFE

10

"Miniver Cheevy" is a poem that "grows," and with each grow-ing pain, adds an understanding chuckle. There is a forthright-ness in the rhythm which you cannot avoid. Be ready for the surprise ending which will take some care in timing.

MINIVER CHEEVY[45]

Miniver Cheevy, child of scorn,
  Grew lean while he assailed the seasons;
He wept that he was ever born,
  And he had reasons.

Miniver loved the days of old
  When swords were bright and steeds were prancing;
The vision of a warrior bold
  Would set him dancing.

Miniver sighed for what was not,
  And dreamed, and rested from his labors;
He dreamed of Thebes and Camelot,
  And Priam's neighbors.

Miniver mourned the ripe renown
  That made so many a name so fragrant;
He mourned Romance, now on the town,
  And Art, a vagrant.

Miniver loved the Medici,
  Albeit he had never seen one;
He would have sinned incessantly
  Could he have been one.

Miniver cursed the commonplace
  And eyed a khaki suit with loathing;
He missed the medieval grace
  Of iron clothing.

[45] From *Town Down the River*, p. 47. Copyright, 1910, by Charles Scribner's Sons. Reprinted by permission of the publishers.

Miniver scorned the gold he sought,
  But sore annoyed was he without it;
Miniver thought, and thought, and thought,
  And thought about it.

Miniver Cheevy, born too late,
  Scratched his head and kept on thinking;
Miniver coughed, and called it fate,
  And kept on drinking.

EDWIN ARLINGTON ROBINSON

11

There is a forward (but not fast) rhythmic movement in "Sea Fever" which is quite different from the steady reluctance found in Newboldt's "Messmates." The words blend into one another, so that you get the empathic response of sailing through the "flung spray" and the "blown spume." The last two lines, however, should convey the feeling of relaxation that follows an exhilarating experience.

SEA-FEVER[46]

I must down to the seas again, to the lonely sea and the sky,
And all I ask is a tall ship, and a star to steer her by,
And the wheel's kick and the wind's song and the white sail's shaking,
And a grey mist on the sea's face and a grey dawn breaking.

I must down to the seas again, for the call of the running tide
Is a wild call and a clear call that may not be denied;
And all I ask is a windy day with the white clouds flying,
And the flung spray and the blown spume, and the sea-gulls crying.

I must down to the seas again to the vagrant gypsy life,
To the gull's way and the whale's way where the wind's like a
    whetted knife;
And all I ask is a merry yarn from a laughing fellow-rover,
And quiet sleep and a sweet dream when the long trick's over.

JOHN MASEFIELD

12

The following anonymous parody on "Sea Fever" is clever as far as phrasing and certain repetitions are concerned. Observe,

though, how the choice of words gives an entirely different mood
and rhythm.

EARTH FEVER[47]

I must down to the earth again, to the fruitful earth and the weeds,
And all I need is a catalogue and a handful or so of seeds,
And a wet rain, and a sunny sun, and an early waking,
And a crouching on the good earth and a poor back breaking.

I must down to the earth again, for the call of the teeming soil
Is a spring call (and it will call) that is answered by just toil,
And all I ask is a sudden shower with a rainbow vying
And a daisy spray and a rose bloom and the seedlings trying.

I must down to the earth again, to the quiet pastoral life,
To the farmer's way and to nature's way that is peaceful and without
    strife;
And all I ask is a yielding garden though it won't be all clover,
And a noisy city and the bright lights when the short summer's over.

13

Browning has chosen an interesting rhythmic arrangement,
emphasizing the cadences by the rhyme scheme. Notice how the
phrasing and pausing alter the melody in the last four lines.

MY STAR

All that I know
    Of a certain star
Is, it can throw
    (Like an angled spar)
Now a dart of red,
    Now a dart of blue;
Till my friends have said
    They would fain see, too,
My star that dartles the red and the blue!
Then it stops like a bird; like a flower, hangs furled:
    They must solace themselves with the Saturn above it.
What matter to me if their star is a world?
    Mine has opened its soul to me; therefore I love it.
                                        ROBERT BROWNING

[47] Published originally in the *Chicago Tribune*. Reprinted by permission
of the publishers.

14

Here is another poem which uses the rhyme scheme to achieve
a light, gay cadence. Be sure that you catch the rhythmic movement, especially in the lines that are heightened by the words
"pinched," "plunged," and "sank." The surprise element in the
last five lines can be intensified by proper pausing and some glee
on the part of the interpreter.

CUPID SWALLOWED

T'other day, as I was twining
Roses for a crown to dine in,
What, of all things, midst the heap,
Should I light on, fast asleep,
But the little desperate elf—
The tiny traitor—Love himself!
By the wings I pinched him up
Like a bee, and in a cup
Of my wine, I plunged and sank him,
And what d'ye think I did?—I drank him!
Faith, I thought him dead. Not he!
There he lives with ten-fold glee;
And now this moment, with his wings,
I feel him tickling my heart-strings.

LEIGH HUNT

15

This is a bit of nonsense, but it is interesting for its simplicity
and especially for its last stanza. Try a pause after "him," and
one after "sit," keeping the word quantities very short.

RESCUE[48]

Close to a wall whose bricks were all
    Rain-soaked and old,
A little cat hunched where he sat
    Dripping and cold.

Deaf to his cry, crowds hurried by,
    Past his me-ow.
I couldn't bear to see him there:
    He's my cat now.

[48] Published originally in the *Chicago Tribune*. Reprinted by permission
of the *Chicago Tribune*.

We have long talks; Lincoln Park walks;
　　Cream-puffs and pie.
A windowpane shuts out the rain:
　　Keeps my cat dry.

Days would be dim—
　　So says my cat—
Had I let him
　　Sit where he sat.

B. D. F.

16

"Larrie O'Dee" is full of gleeful humor. The rhythm should be emphasized to the point of jingling, but the lilt of the Irish dialect should be kept.

LARRIE O'DEE

Now the Widow McGee,
　　And Larrie O'Dee,
Had two little cottages out on the green,
With just room enough for two pig-pens between.
The widow was young and the widow was fair,
With the brightest of eyes and the brownest of hair,
And it frequently chanced, when she came in the morn,
With the swill for her pig, Larrie came with the corn,
And some of the ears that he tossed from his hand
In the pen of the widow were certain to land.

　　One morning said he:
　　"Och! Misthress McGee,
It's a waste of good lumber, this runnin' two rigs,
Wid a fancy purtition betwane our two pigs!"
"Indade, sir, it is!" answered Widow McGee,
With the sweetest of smiles upon Larrie O'Dee.
"And thin, it looks kind o' hard-hearted and mane,
Kapin' two friendly pigs so exsaidenly near
That whiniver one grunts the other can hear,
And yit kape a cruel purtition betwane."

　　"Schwate Widow McGee,"
　　Answered Larrie O'Dee,
"If ye fale in your heart we are mane to the pigs,
Ain't we mane to ourselves to be runnin' two rigs?
Och! it made me heart ache when I paped through the cracks
Of me shanty, lasht March, at yez swingin' yer axe,

An' a bobbin' yer head an a-shtompin' yer fate,
Wid yer purty white hands jisht as red as a bate,
A-shplittin' yer kindlin'-wood out in the shtorm,
When one little shtove it would kape us both warm!"

　　"Now, piggy," says she,
　　"Larrie's courtin' o' me,
Wid his dilicate tinder allusions to you;
So now yez must tell me jisht what I must do:
For, if I'm to say yes, shtir the swill wid yer snout;
But if I'm to say no, ye must kape yer nose out.
Now, Larrie, for shame! to be bribin' a pig
By tossin' a handful of corn in its shwig!"
"Me darlint, the piggy says yes," answered he.
And that was the courtship of Larrie O'Dee.
　　　　　　　　　　　　　　WILLIAM W. FINK

17

　　Your interpretation of "Gunga Din" must have the cockney
rhythm. Decide on the attack and pausing to be used in the
repetition of "Din! Din! Din!"

GUNGA DIN[49]

You may talk o' gin and beer
When you're quartered safe out 'ere,
An' you're sent to penny-fights an' Aldershot it:
But if it comes to slaughter,
You will do your work on water,
An' you'll lick the bloomin' boots of 'im that's got it.
Now in Injia's sunny clime,
Where I used to spend my time
A-servin' of 'Er Majesty the Queen,
Of all them black-faced crew
The finest man I knew
Was our regimental *bhisti*, Gunga Din!
He was "Din! Din! Din!
You limpin' lump o' brick-dust, Gunga Din!
Hi! slippery *hitherao!*
Water! Get it! *Panee lao!*
You squidgy-nosed old idol, Gunga Din!"

[49] From *Departmental Ditties and Ballads and Barrack-Room Ballads*,
p. 163. Copyright, 1891, by Rudyard Kipling. Reprinted by permission of
Mrs. George Bambridge and Doubleday & Company, Inc.

The uniform 'e wore
Was nothin' much before,
An' rather less than 'arf o' that be'ind;
For a twisty piece o' rag
An' a goatskin water-bag
Was all the field equipment 'e could find.
When the sweatin' troop-train lay
In a sidin' through the day,
Where the 'eat would make your bloomin' eyebrows crawl,
We shouted "Harry By!"
Till our throats were bricky-dry,
Then we wopped 'im cause 'e couldn't serve us all.
It was "Din! Din! Din!
You 'eathen, where the mischief 'ave you been?
You put some *juldee* in it
Or I'll *marrow* you this minute,
If you don't fill up my helmet, Gunga Din!"

'E would dot an' carry one
Till the longest day was done,
An' 'e didn't seem to know the use o' fear.
If we charged or broke or cut,
You could bet your bloomin' nut,
'E'd be waitin fifty paces right flank rear.
With 'is *mussick* on 'is back,
'E would skip with our attack,
An' watch us till the bugles made "Retire,"
An' for all 'is dirty 'ide
'E was white, clear white, inside,
When 'e went to tend the wounded under fire!
It was "Din! Din! Din!"
With the bullets kickin' dust spots on the green,
When the cartridges ran out,
You could 'ear the front-files shout:
"Hi! ammunition-mules an' Gunga Din!"

I sha'n't forgit the night
When I dropped be'ind the fight
With a bullet where my belt-plate should 'a' been.
I was chokin' mad with thirst,
An' the man that spied me first
Was our good old grinnin', gruntin' Gunga Din.
'E lifted up my 'ead,
An' 'e plugged me where I bled,
An' 'e guv me 'arf-a-pint o' water—green:
It was crawlin' and it stunk,
But of all the drinks I've drunk,
I'm gratefullest to one from Gunga Din.

It was "Din! Din! Din!
'Ere's a beggar with a bullet through 'is spleen;
'E's chawin' up the ground,
An' 'e's kickin' all around:
For Gawd's sake git the water, Gunga Din!"

'E carried me away
To where a *dooli* lay,
An' a bullet come an' drilled the beggar clean.
'E put me safe inside,
An' just before 'e died:
"I 'ope you liked your drink," sez Gunga Din.
So I'll meet 'im later on
At the place where 'e is gone—
Where it's always double drill and no canteen;
'E'll be squattin' on the coals,
Givin' drink to pore damned souls,
An' I'll get a swig in Hell from Gunga Din.
Yes, Din! Din! Din!
You Lazarushian-leather Gunga Din!
Though I've belted you and flayed you,
By the livin' Gawd that made you,
You're a better man than I am, Gunga Din!

                                        RUDYARD KIPLING

18

   This old favorite is a masterpiece of onomatopoetic structure,
which, as you recall, involves the use of words that imitate the
sound associated with the meaning. Strangely enough, in your
interpretation of the "bells" lines, you can create the sounds of
the various bells the poet describes. In the first stanza, the voice,
if kept high and light, can make the bells tinkle. For the wedding
bells of the second stanza, the voice should be pitched high on
the first "bells" and lower on the second. The clanging alarm
bells of the third stanza can be had by repeating the word at
the same harsh, monotonous pitch. And for the tolling iron bells
of the last stanza, the voice should be low and heavy and monotonous. It is obvious that the rhythm throughout is dependent
on the vowel sounds and the way in which you handle them.

THE BELLS

   Hear the sledges with the bells—
       Silver bells!

What a world of merriment their melody foretells!
    How they tinkle, tinkle, tinkle,
        In the icy air of night!
    While the stars, that oversprinkle
    All the heavens, seem to twinkle
        With a crystalline delight;
    Keeping time, time, time,
    In a sort of Runic rhyme,
To the tintinnabulation that so musically wells
    From the bells, bells, bells, bells,
        Bells, bells, bells—
From the jingling and the tinkling of the bells.

    Hear the mellow wedding bells,
        Golden bells!
What a world of happiness their harmony foretells!
    Through the balmy air of night
    How they ring out their delight!—
        From the molten-golden notes,
            And all in tune,
        What a liquid ditty floats
To the turtle-dove that listens, while she gloats
        On the moon!
    Oh, from out the sounding cells,
What a gush of euphony voluminously wells!
        How it swells!
        How it dwells
        On the Future!—how it tells
        Of the rapture that impels
    To the swinging and the ringing
        Of the bells, bells, bells,
    Of the bells, bells, bells, bells,
        Bells, bells, bells—
To the rhyming and the chiming of the bells!

    Hear the loud alarum bells,
        Brazen bells!
What a tale of terror, now their turbulency tells!
    In a startled ear of night
    How they scream out their affright!
        Too much horrified to speak,
        They can only shriek, shriek,
            Out of tune,
In the clamorous appealing to the mercy of the fire,
In a mad expostulation with the deaf and frantic fire,
        Leaping higher, higher, higher,
        With a desperate desire,

And a resolute endeavor
Now—now to sit or never,
By the side of the pale-faced moon.
    Oh, the bells, bells, bells!
    What a tale their terror tells
            Of Despair!
    How they clang, and clash, and roar!
    What a horror they outpour,
On the bosom of the palpitating air!
    Yet the ear it fully knows,
            By the twanging
            And the clanging,
    How the danger ebbs and flows;
    Yet the ear distinctly tells,
            In the jangling
            And the wrangling,
By the sinking or the swelling in the anger of the bells—
            Of the bells—
        Of the bells, bells, bells, bells,
            Bells, bells, bells—
In the clamor and the clangor of the bells!

        Hear the tolling of the bells—
            Iron bells!
What a world of solemn thought their monody compels!
        In the silence of the night
        How we shiver with affright
    At the melancholy menace of their tone!
        For every sound that floats
        From the rust within their throats
            Is a groan.
        And the people—ah, the people—
        They that dwell up in the steeple,
            All alone,
        And who tolling, tolling, tolling
            In that muffled monotone,
        Feel a glory in so rolling
            On the human heart a stone—
    They are neither man nor woman—
    They are neither brute nor human—
            They are Ghouls:—
        And their king it is who tolls:—
        And he rolls, rolls, rolls,
            Rolls
        A paean from the bells!
        And his merry bosom swells
            With the paean of the bells!

And he dances, and he yells;
Keeping time, time, time,
In a sort of Runic rhyme,
    To the paean of the bells:—
      Of the bells:
Keeping time, time, time,
In a sort of Runic rhyme,
    To the throbbing of the bells.—
Of the bells, bells, bells—
    To the sobbing of the bells:—
Keeping time, time, time,
    As he knells, knells, knells,
In a happy Runic rhyme,
    To the rolling of the bells—
Of the bells, bells, bells:—
    To the tolling of the bells—
Of the bells, bells, bells, bells,
    Bells, bells, bells—
To the moaning and the groaning of the bells.

EDGAR ALLAN POE

19

The following poem is enveloped in a mood of softness, darkness, and cold, emphasized by phrases like "darkest evening," "frozen lake," "downy flake," and "lovely, dark and deep." The rhythm is closely related to the feeling of isolation which the snow, the cold, and the darkness bring. The hushed wonderment can be conveyed only by a quiet cadence that gradually slows down until the last line is reached. Notice how the repetition of that line helps to slow down the rhythm.

STOPPING BY WOODS ON A SNOWY EVENING[50]

Whose woods these are I think I know.
His house is in the village though;
He will not see me stopping here
To watch his woods fill up with snow.

My little horse must think it queer
To stop without a farmhouse near
Between the woods and frozen lake
The darkest evening of the year.

He gives his harness bells a shake
To ask if there is some mistake.
The only other sound's the sweep
Of easy wind and downy flake.

The woods are lovely, dark and deep.
But I have promises to keep,
And miles to go before I sleep,
And miles to go before I sleep.

ROBERT FROST

III

Contrast the rhythmical cadences and patterns found in the following prose passages. Which selection do you most enjoy from the point of view of rhythm?

THE MOONLIGHT[51]

Now Virginia lay dreaming in the moonlight. In Louisiana bayous the broken moonlight shivers the broken moonlight quivers the light of many rivers lay dreaming in the moonlight beaming in the moonlight dreaming in the moonlight moonlight moonlight seeming in the moonlight moonlight moonlight to be gleaming to be streaming in the moonlight moonlight moonlight moonlight moonlight moonlight moonlight moonlight
—Mo-hoo-oonlight—oonlight oonlight oonlight oonlight oonlight oonlight oonlight oonlight oonlight
—To be seeming to be dreaming in the moonlight!

THOMAS WOLFE

AMERICA[52]

For America has a thousand lights and weathers and we walk the streets, we walk the streets forever, we walk the streets of life alone.

It is the place of the howling winds, the hurrying of the leaves in old October, the hard clean falling to the earth of acorns. The place of the storm-tossed moaning of the wintry mountainside, where the young men cry out in their throats and feel the savage vigor, the rude strong energies; the place also where the trains cross rivers.

It is a fabulous country, the only fabulous country; it is the one place where miracles not only happen, but where they happen all of the time. . . .

[51] From *Of Time and the River*, p. 70. Copyright, 1935, by Charles Scribner's Sons. Reprinted by permission of the publishers.
[52] From *Of Time and the River*, p. 156.

It is the place where great boats are baying at the harbor's mouth, where great ships are putting out to sea; it is the place where great boats are blowing in the gulf of night, and where the river, the dark and secret river, full of strange time, is forever flowing by us to the sea. . . .

It is the place of autumnal moons hung low and orange at the frosty edges of the pines; it is the place of frost and silence; of the clean dry shocks and the opulence of enormous pumpkins that yellow on hard clotted earth; it is the place of the stir and feathery stumble of the hens upon their roost, the frosty, broken barking of the dogs, the great barnshapes and solid shadows in the running sweep of the moon-whited countryside, the wailing whistle of the fast express. It is the place of flares and steamings on the tracks, and the swing and bob and tottering dance of lanterns in the yards; it is the place of dings and knellings and the sudden glare of mighty engines over sleeping faces in the night; it is the place of the terrific web and spread and smouldering, the distant glare of Philadelphia and the solid rumble of the sleepers; it is also the place where the Transcontinental Limited is stroking eighty miles an hour across the continent and the small dark towns whip by like bullets, and there is only the fanlike stroke of the secret, immense and lonely earth again.

THOMAS WOLFE

CHARITY

Though I speak with the tongues of men and of angels, and have not charity, I am become as sounding brass, or a tinkling cymbal.

And though I have the gift of prophecy, and understand all mysteries, and all knowledge, and though I have all faith, so that I could remove mountains, and have not charity, I am nothing.

And though I bestow all my goods to feed the poor, and though I give my body to be burned, and have not charity, it profiteth me nothing.

Charity suffereth long, and is kind; charity envieth not; charity vaunteth not itself, is not puffed up,

Doth not behave itself unseemly, seeketh not her own, is not easily provoked, thinketh no evil;

Rejoiceth not in iniquity, but rejoiceth in the truth;

Beareth all things, believeth all things, hopeth all things, endureth all things.

Charity never faileth: but whether there be prophecies, they shall fail; whether there be tongues, they shall cease; whether there be knowledge, it shall vanish away.

For we know in part, and we prophesy in part.

But when that which is perfect is come, then that which is in part shall be done away.

When I was a child, I spake as a child, I understood as a child, I thought as a child: but when I became a man, I put away childish things.

For now we see through a glass, darkly; but then face to face: now I know in part; but then shall I know even as also I am known.

And now abideth faith, hope, charity, these three; but the greatest of these is charity.

I Corinthians XIII

AT THE TOMB OF NAPOLEON

A little while ago, I stood by the grave of the old Napoleon—a magnificent tomb of gilt and gold, fit almost for a dead deity—and gazed upon the sarcophagus of black Egyptian marble, where rest at last the ashes of that restless man. I leaned over the balustrade and thought about the career of the greater soldier of the modern world.

I saw him walking upon the banks of the Seine, contemplating suicide. I saw him at Toulon—I saw him putting down the mob in the streets of Paris—I saw him at the head of the army of Italy—I saw him crossing the bridge of Lodi with the tri-color in his hand—I saw him in Egypt in the shadow of the Pyramids—I saw him conquer the Alps and mingle the eagles of France with the eagles of the crags. I saw him at Marengo—at Ulm and Austerlitz. I saw him in Russia, where the infantry of the snow and the cavalry of the wild blast scattered his legions like winter's withered leaves. I saw him at Leipsic in defeat and disaster—driven by a million bayonets back upon Paris—clutched like a wild beast—banished to Elba. I saw him escape and retake an empire by the force of his genius. I saw him upon the frightful field of Waterloo, where Chance and Fate combined to wreck the fortunes of their former king. And I saw him at St. Helena, with his hands crossed behind him, gazing out upon the sad and solemn sea.

I thought of the orphans and widows he had made—of the tears that had been shed for his glory, and of the only woman who ever loved him, pushed from his heart by the cold hand of ambition. And I said I would rather have been a French peasant and worn wooden shoes. I would rather have lived in a hut with a vine growing over the door, and the grapes growing purple in the kisses of the autumn sun. I would rather have been that poor peasant with my loving wife by my side, knitting as the day died out of the sky—with my children upon my knees and their arms about me. I would rather have been that man and gone down to the tongueless silence of the dreamless dust than to have been that imperial impersonation of force and murder, known as Napoleon the Great.

Robert G. Ingersoll

DEANS WITHIN DEANS[53]

American institutions dealing as they do with younger people, and furnishing far more numerous services, have to be run by a separate body of diversely specialized managers known collectively as the administration. The Director of Admissions admits, the Registrar registers, the Bursar imburses, and a galaxy of Deans decide. There is a Dean of Men, a Dean of Women, a Dean of Studies, and Freshmen Deans in droves. In a large University, there are as many deans and executive heads as there are schools and departments. Their relations to one another are intricate and periodic; in fact, "galaxy" is too loose a term: it is a planetarium of deans with the President of the University as a central sun. One can see eclipses, inner systems, and oppositions. But usually more sympathy obtains among fellow administrators than between them and the teaching personnel. If it came to a pitched battle, I feel sure that the more compact executive groups, animated by a single purpose, besides being better fed and self-disciplined, could rout the more numerous but disorderly rabble that teaches.

JACQUES BARZUN

FAREWELL, MY LOVELY[54]

The last Model T was built in 1927, and the car is fading from what scholars call the American scene—which is an understatement, because to a few million people who grew up with it, the old Ford practically *was* the American scene.

It was the miracle God had wrought. And it was patently the sort of thing that could only happen once. Mechanically uncanny, it was like nothing that had ever come to the world before. Flourishing industries rose and fell with it. As a vehicle, it was hard-working, commonplace, heroic; and it often seemed to transmit those qualities to the persons who rode in it. My own generation identifies it with Youth, with its gaudy, irretrievable excitements; before it fades into the mist, I would like to pay it the tribute of the sigh that is not a sob, and set down random entries in a shape somewhat less cumbersome than a Sears Roebuck catalogue.

The Model T was distinguished from all other makes of cars by

[53] From *Teacher in America*, p. 178. Copyright, 1944, 1945, by Jacques Barzun. Reprinted by permission of Little, Brown & Co. and the Atlantic Monthly Press.

[54] From "Farewell, My Lovely," *The New Yorker* (May 16, 1936). Copyright, 1936, by The New Yorker Magazine, Inc. Reprinted under the title *Farewell to Model T* by G. P. Putnam's Sons.

the fact that its transmission was of a type known as planetary—which was half metaphysics, half sheer friction. Engineers accepted the word "planetary" in its epicyclic sense, but I was always conscious that it also meant "wandering," "erratic." Because of the peculiar nature of this planetary element, there was always, in Model T, a certain dull rapport between engine and wheels, and even when the car was in a state known as neutral, it trembled with a deep imperative and tended to inch forward. There was never a moment when the bands were not faintly egging the machine on. In this respect it was like a horse, rolling the bit on its tongue, and country people brought to it the same technique they used with draft animals.

Its most remarkable quality was its rate of acceleration. In its palmy days the Model T could take off faster than anything on the road. The reason was simple. To get under way, you simply hooked the third finger of the right hand around a lever on the steering column, pulled down hard, and shoved your left foot forcibly against the low-speed pedal. These were simple, positive motions; the car responded by lunging forward with a roar. After a few seconds of this turmoil, you took your toe off the pedal, eased up a mite on the throttle, and the car, possessed of only two forward speeds, catapulted directly into high with a series of ugly jerks and was off on its glorious errand. The abruptness of this departure was never equalled in other cars of the period. The human leg was (and still is) incapable of letting in a clutch with anything like the forthright abandon that used to send Model T on its way. Letting in a clutch is a negative, hesitant motion, depending on delicate nervous control; pushing down the Ford pedal was a simple country motion—an expansive act, which came as natural as kicking an old door to make it budge.

Lee Strout White

ICHABOD CRANE'S DELIGHT

He was, in fact, an odd mixture of small shrewdness and simple credulity. His appetite for the marvelous, and his powers of digesting it, were equally extraordinary; and both had been increased by his residence in this spell-bound region. No tale was too gross or monstrous for his capacious swallow. It was often his delight, after school was dismissed in the afternoon, to stretch himself on the rich bed of clover, bordering the little brook that whimpered by the schoolhouse, and there con over old Mather's direful tales, until the gathering dusk of the evening made the printed page a mere mist before his eyes. Then, as he wended his way by swamp, and stream and awful woodland, to the farmhouse where he happened to be quartered, every sound of nature at that witching hour, fluttered his excited imagination: the voice of the whippoorwill, that harbinger of storm; the dreary hooting of the screech-owl, or the sudden rustling in the thicket of birds frightened from their roost. The fireflies, too, which sparkled most vividly in the darkest places now and then startled him, as one of uncommon brightness would stream across his path, and if, by chance, a huge blockhead of a beetle came winging his blundering flight against him, the poor varlet was ready to give up the ghost, with the idea that he was struck with a witch's token. His only resource on such occasions, either to drown thought or drive away evil spirits, was to sing psalm tunes;—and the good people of Sleepy Hollow, as they sat by their doors of an evening, were often filled with awe, at hearing his nasal melody, "in linked sweetness long drawn out," floating from the distant hill or along the dusky road.

WASHINGTON IRVING, *The Legend of Sleepy Hollow*

IV

In the interpretation of dramatic dialogues, the timing of the speech patterns is all-important, not only for meaning but for contrast in characterizations and for general build-up of the scene. There are many instances when the whole scene will be light and quick in tempo; but there are other times when the scene will be geared to the speech tempo of the dominant character.

1

In the scene below all the characters are subordinate to Capulet, Juliet's father. Juliet, Lady Capulet, and the nurse "feed" the lines to Capulet, who sets the timing of the scene through the rhythm of his own lines.

CAPULET'S DECISION

JULIET *has just said farewell to* ROMEO, *whom she has secretly married. She has been warned by the nurse that her mother,* LADY CAPULET, *is on her way to* JULIET's *room. It is early morning.*

LADY CAPULET. Ho, daughter! are you up?
JULIET. Who is't that calls? It is my lady mother.
   Is she not down so late, or up so early?
   What unaccustom'd cause procures her hither?
LADY C. Why, how now, Juliet!
JULIET.   Madam, I am not well.
LADY C. Evermore weeping for your cousin's death?
   What, wilt thou wash him from his grave with tears?
   And if thou couldst, thou couldst not make him live;
   Therefore, have done. Some grief shows much of love;

But much of grief shows still some want of wit.

JULIET. Yet let me weep for such a feeling loss.

. . . .

LADY C. Well, girl, thou weep'st not so much for his death
 As that the villain lives which slaughter'd him.

JULIET. What villain, madam?

LADY C. That same villain, Romeo.

JULIET. (*Aside*) Villain and he be many miles asunder.—
 God pardon him! I do, with all my heart;
 And yet no man like he doth grieve my heart.

LADY C. That is, because the traitor murderer lives.

. . . .

But now I'll tell thee joyful tidings, girl.

JULIET. And joy comes well in such a needy time.
 What are they, I beseech your ladyship?

LADY C. Well, well, thou hast a careful father, child;
 One who, to put thee from thy heaviness,
 Hath sorted out a sudden day of joy,
 That thou expect'st not, nor I look'd not for.

JULIET. Madam, in happy time, what day is that?

LADY C. Marry, my child, early next Thursday morn,
 That gallant, young and noble gentleman,
 The County Paris, at Saint Peter's Church,
 Shall happily make thee there a joyful bride.

JULIET. Now, by Saint Peter's Church and Peter too,
 He shall not make me there a joyful bride.
 I wonder at this haste; that I must wed
 Ere he that should be husband comes to woo.
 I pray you, tell my lord and father, madam,
 I will not marry yet; and when I do, I swear,
 It shall be Romeo, whom you know I hate,
 Rather than Paris. These are news indeed!

LADY C. Here comes your father; tell him so yourself,
 And see how he will take it at your hands.

Enter CAPULET *and* NURSE

CAPULET. When the sun sets, the air doth drizzle dew;
 But for the sunset of my brother's son
 It rains downright.
 How now! a conduit? What, still in tears?
 Evermore show'ring? . . .

. . . .

How now, wife!
 Have you deliver'd to her our decree?

LADY C. Ay sir; but she will none, she gives you thanks.
 I would the fool were married to her grave!

CAPULET. Soft! take me with you, take me with you, wife.
 How! will she none? Doth she not give us thanks?

Is she not proud? Doth she not count her blest,
Unworthy as she is, that we have wrought
So worthy a gentleman to be her bride?
JULIET. Not proud, you have; but thankful, that you have.
  Proud can I never be of what I hate;
  But thankful even for hate, that is meant love.
CAPULET. How now, how now, chop-logic! What is this?
  "Proud," and "I thank you," and "I thank you not";
  And yet "not proud." Mistress minion, you,
  Thank me no thankings, nor proud me no prouds,
  But fettle your fine joints 'gainst Thursday next,
  To go with Paris to Saint Peter's Church,
  Or I will drag thee on a hurdle thither.
  Out, you green-sickness carrion! Out, you baggage!
LADY C.   Fie, fie! what, are you mad?
JULIET. Good father, I beseech you on my knees,
  Hear me with patience but to speak a word.
CAPULET. Hang thee, young baggage! disobedient wretch!
  I tell thee what: get thee to church o' Thursday,
  Or never after look me in the face.
  Speak not, reply not, do not answer me!
  My fingers itch. Wife, we scarce thought us blest
  That God had lent us but this only child;
  But now I see this one is one too much,
  And that we have a curse in having her.
  Out on her, hilding!
NURSE.   God in heaven bless her!
  You are to blame, my lord, to rate her so.
CAPULET. And why, my lady wisdom? Hold your tongue,
  Good prudence; smatter with your gossips, go.
NURSE. I speak no treason.
CAPULET.   O, God ye god-den.
NURSE. May not one speak?
CAPULET.   Peace, you mumbling fool!
  Utter your gravity o'er a gossip's bowl;
  For here we need it not.
LADY C.   You are too hot.
CAPULET. God's bread! it makes me mad.
  Day, night, hour, tide, time, work, play,
  Alone, in company, still my care hath been
  To have her match'd; and having now provided
  A gentleman of noble parentage,
  Of fair demesnes, youthful, and nobly train'd;
  Stuff'd as they say, with honourable parts,
  Proportion'd as one's thought would wish a man;
  And then to have a wretched puling fool,
  A whining mammet, in her fortune's tender,

To answer, "I'll not wed; I cannot love,
I am too young; I pray you, pardon me."
But, an you will not wed, I'll pardon you.
Graze where you will, you shall not house with me.
Look to't, think on't, I do not use to jest.
Thursday is near; lay hand on heart, advise.
An you be mine, I'll give you to my friend;
An you be not, hang, beg, starve, die in the streets,
For, by my soul, I'll ne'er acknowledge thee.
Nor what is mine shall never do thee good.
Trust to't, bethink you; I'll not be forsworn. (*Exit*)
JULIET. Is there no pity sitting in the clouds,
That sees into the bottom of my grief?
O, sweet my mother, cast me not away!
Delay this marriage for a month, a week;
Or, if you do not, make the bridal bed
In that dim monument where Tybalt lies.
LADY C. Talk not to me, for I'll not speak a word.
Do as thou wilt, for I have done with thee. (*Exit*)
JULIET. O God!—O nurse, how shall this be prevented?

. . . .

Alack, alack, that heaven should practise stratagems
Upon so soft a subject as myself!
What say'st thou? Hast thou not a word of joy?
Some comfort, nurse.
NURSE.   Faith, here it is.
Romeo is banish'd; and all the world to nothing,
That he dares ne'er come back to challenge you;
Or, if he do, it needs must be by stealth.
Then, since the case so stands as now it doth,
I think it best you married with the County.

. . . .

JULIET. Speak'st thou from thy heart?
NURSE. And from my soul too; else beshrew them both.
JULIET. Amen!
NURSE. What?
JULIET. Well, thou hast comforted me marvelous much.
Go in; and tell my lady I am gone,
Having displeas'd my father, to Laurence' cell,
To make confession and to be absolv'd.
NURSE. Marry, I will; and this is wisely done. (*Exit*)
JULIET. Ancient damnation! O most wicked fiend!
Is it more sin to wish me thus forsworn,
Or to dispraise my lord with that same tongue
Which she hath prais'd him with above compare

So many thousand times? Go, counsellor;
Thou and my bosom henceforth shall be twain,
I'll to the friar, to know his remedy;
If all else fail, myself have power to die. (*Exit*)
WILLIAM SHAKESPEARE, *Romeo and Juliet*

2

The following selection is not to be taken too seriously, for it is written only to point up—lightly but keenly—woman's inability to understand high finance. The tone is light and the tempo is generally quick with some interesting pauses used to enlighten Mrs. Jones.

THE FINANCIAL STRUCTURE[55]

Mrs. Jones looked up from the newspaper she was reading and asked, in that bland way that gets so many husbands into trouble:—
"Walter, dear, what is a 'financial structure'?"
"A what?"
"A financial structure. It says here: 'Now that the Oceanic Bank Company has secured 75 per cent of the stock of the Plethoric Title and Mortgage Company, its financial structure is complete. The Oceanic Bank Company owns 100 per cent of the stock of the Oceanic Banking Company, 80 per cent of the stock of the Transatlantic Oceanic Company, and all but the directors' qualifying shares of the International Transatlantic Company. The Plethoric Title and Mortgage Company holds 90 per cent of the stock of the Balzac Trust Company, 100 per cent of the Premium Mortgage Company'— and a lot more of the same sort of thing, Walter. What does it mean?"
"Why, that's simple, my dear. What you have just read me is the financial structure you asked me about. In this day, when great combinations of capital are required to swing the vast transactions that—"
"But I don't understand it."
"I can explain very easily, Jessie. Let us suppose that we buy a small place in the country—"
"Oh! I should love to!"
"I am just supposing. Suppose, then, we buy a small place in the country—ten acres, let us say. You and I and Dorothy put our money together and buy it. We call it the Jooks Farming and Dairy Company, and we each put in $3333.33, and pay $10,000 for the place. That is simple, isn't it?"
"You couldn't get much of a place for $10,000."
"That's just the point. You couldn't. But we do it anyway. So we

---

[55] Reprinted by permission of the author.

go out there and start a garden. We have beets and spinach and beans and corn. So we get along for a year. At the end of the year I say to you, 'Jessie, I think I'll buy a cow'; so I take my own money and pay a hundred dollars for a cow, and I call it the Jooks Cow Company. So there are now two companies—the Farming and Dairy Company, and the Cow Company. You understand that?"

"Certainly."

"Good! We now have a cow. But we could use a pig, so you take your own money and pay fifty dollars for a pig, and you call it the Jooks Pig Company. There are now three companies."

"I can see that."

"But Dorothy thinks a chicken can pick up a living on the place, so she buys a chicken for two dollars."

"I don't think one chicken would be enough. I think one chicken would be too lonely."

"All right! All right! Make it ten chickens—ten chickens for twenty dollars."

"If you wouldn't mind, Walter, I would rather have the chickens— I always did want to have chickens."

"Then you have the chickens. I am only trying to explain what a financial structure is, and—"

"And I'm sure Dorothy would rather not have the pig. Dorothy is always so dainty about things."

"All right! Let her have the cow. It makes no difference whatever. I'll have the pig, capital fifty dollars, and you have the chickens, capital twenty dollars, and Dorothy has the cow, capital one hundred dollars. So you call your chickens the Mrs. Jooks Chicken Company. There are now four separate companies, all independent and good going concerns. But when we have been operating another year, we find we could do better if we had more land and more stock to raise, so we look around. Next door to us are Mr. and Mrs. Smith and their son."

"How old is the son? It would be nice for Dorothy if he was—"

"Never mind that. The Smiths have organized much as we have. They own eight acres, and they raise cucumbers and peas and squash and corn, calling it the Smith Farming and Culturing Company. They have two cows, two hundred dollars, called the Smith Cow Company. They have no pig. They have five chickens, ten dollars, called the Smith Chicken Company. They have nine rabbits, nine dollars, called the Smith Rabbit Company. The Smiths are getting along well enough, but none too well. Smith and his wife and their son—"

"What is the son's name?"

"Algernon."

"It's queer that they gave him a name like that. I should never call a boy Algernon."

"Please! Please, Jessie! I'm trying to explain what a financial structure is."

"Well, I'm listening, Walter. I think I have a right to know something about my neighbors, if I'm going to live next door to them."

"Yes? Well, please let me go on. These Smiths, next door to us, are up-to-date people. They see that combining allied interests is the modern financial trend, so one day at dinner Mr. Smith says, 'Folks, this thing of having a lot of separate companies is getting us nowhere. The Smith Farming and Culturing Company proposes to buy out the Smith Cow Company, the Smith Chicken Company, and the Smith Rabbit Company. How about it? I will sell the Smith Cow Company to the Farming and Culturing Company—100 per cent of it.'"

"So, then, there is no more Smith Cow Company."

"But there is! Mr. Smith does not sell his cows; he keeps on running the cows; he remains Chairman of the Board of the Cow Company, and he only sells the stock of the Cow Company to the Smith Farming and Culturing Company. That is the way it is done, Jessie."

"I see."

"But when Mr. Smith turns to Mrs. Smith and Algernon, they look at each other queerly. Mrs. Smith says, 'John, I forgot to tell you, but Algernon needed money for some new rabbit hutches, and I bought 80 per cent of the stock of the Rabbit Company, and that stock is now owned by the Chicken Company.'"

"Wait a minute, Walter. There were nine rabbits and Algernon sold 80 per cent. That left him—"

"One and eight-tenths rabbits. But Mrs. Smith was fond of her chickens, and she did not want to part with them entirely to the Farming and Culturing Company, so she proposed to sell to it 90 per cent of the chickens and rabbits she now owned. For the Farming and Culturing Company, Mr. Smith accepted that offer, which included 90 per cent of Mrs. Smith's five chickens, and 90 per cent of 80 per cent of Algernon's nine rabbits. In other words,—let us see— Algernon now had one and eight-tenths rabbits, the Mrs. Smith Chicken Company had one half a chicken and seventy-two one-hundredths of a rabbit, and the Smith Farming and Culturing Company has two cows, four and one-half chickens, and,—wait a minute, —yes, six and forty-eight one-hundredths rabbits. But of course, the Cow Company and the Rabbit Company now owned part of the Farm."

"Oh!"

"Which they got in exchange. And the Rabbit Company owned part of Mrs. Smith's chickens and part of Mrs. Smith's part of the farm."

"Oh!"

"Mr. Smith now thought the financial structure was complete, but what do you think we had been doing all this while, my dear?"

"Farming,"—after a moment of deep thought.

"No. Yes—farming, of course, but we had been building our financial structure in exactly the same way, Jessie. Financial structure building is the slogan of the day."

"I see I am going to lose some of my chickens. And I loved my chickens!"

"Oh, come now! We must be progressive, my dear. We must follow the trend of the times. As a matter of fact, you were the first to propose a deal. You said to Dorothy, 'The Mrs. Jooks Chicken Company will sell you 80 per cent of its chickens for stock in your Cow Company,' and the deal was made. The Cow Company now had eight chickens and your Chicken Company retained two chickens."

"I hope one was a rooster."

"We will say it was. For our financial structure building that makes no difference. But what was I doing? I went to Dorothy and proposed to buy 90 per cent of the Cow Company. She agreed, and the deal was made. My Pig Company now owned nine-tenths of the cow, seven and two-tenths chickens, and the pig. But seeing that a farm could do better than a lot of separately managed concerns, the Jooks Farming and Dairy Company came to me—"

"You came to yourself?"

"I was president of the Farming Dairy Company, so I came to myself, as president of the Jooks Pig Company, and I bought 80 per cent of the Pig Company. I now owned, as the Farming and Dairy Company, seventy-two one-hundredths of a cow, five and seventy-six one-hundredths chickens, eight-tenths of a pig. You owned, as the Chicken Company—"

"Never mind, Walter, I see what is coming. You're going to buy 76 per cent of the Smith outfit—"

"Ninety per cent, to be exact. Ninety per cent, Jessie, thus bringing under one control—wait a minute! When the deal is completed, the Jooks Farming and Dairy Company would own—"

Late that night Mr. Jooks was still computing hundred-thousandths of a rabbit, and tens of thousandths of a chicken, and saying, "No! Eight and nine hundred and seventy-six thousandths from eleven and eight-four hundredths—no, that's not rabbits, that's cow—no, it couldn't be cow, there were only three cows; it's chickens. Hold on! I subtracted rabbits from pig here. Wait a minute, now—"

Mrs. Jooks had long since gone up to bed. At two o'clock Jooks crumpled up his papers and put them in the fireplace. He stole upstairs quietly and undressed as noiselessly as he could, but as he was putting on his pyjamas Mrs. Jooks opened her eyes. She lay quiet for a moment, getting awake.

"Walter?"

"Yes, my dear."

"Walter, I was thinking, before I went to sleep. I think fifty dollars is too much to pay for a pig. I think I'd rather have a cheaper pig and have more chickens."

"Yes?"

"And, Walter, I don't want to be in partnership with those Smiths. I want to own my own chickens myself."

She closed her eyes and a moment later, Mr. Jooks knew, by her deep breathing, that she was asleep. She had left him only about 33⅓ per cent of the bed. Very carefully, not to awaken her again and bring up the matter of financial structures, Mr. Jooks got into bed. He drew over himself 64⅖ per cent of the bed covers. He fell asleep immediately, for he was feeling exceptionally well satisfied with himself—he had explained the higher finance to his wife.

ELLIS PARKER BUTLER

3

The following scene needs to be acted—as does all of Shakespeare—in order to convey the entire meaning and the innuendoes that are inherent in the action as well as the words. The scene is full of activity, which the interpreter can merely suggest, but the rhythm of the selection is, or should be, obvious to the interpreter. The characters are rather evenly balanced, with more weight given to Petruchio—*and* he has the last lines. Remember Katherine is the shrew who is finally tamed by the swashbuckling antics of Petruchio.

PETRUCHIO COURTS KATHERINA

PETRUCHIO. Good morrow, Kate; for that's your name, I hear.
KATHERINA. Well have you heard, but something hard of hearing.
　　They call me Katherine, that do talk of me.
PETR. You lie, in faith; for you are call'd plain Kate,
　　And bonny Kate, and sometimes Kate the curst;
　　But Kate, the prettiest Kate in Christendom;
　　Kate of Kate Hall; my super-dainty Kate,
　　For dainties are all cates: and therefore, Kate,
　　Take this of me, Kate of my consolation;
　　Hearing thy mildness praised in every town,
　　Thy virtues spoke of, and thy beauty sounded,
　　Yet not so deeply as to thee belongs,
　　Myself am mov'd to woo thee for my wife.
KATH. Mov'd! in good time. Let him that mov'd you hither
　　Remove you hence.

.　　.　　.　　.　　.　　.　　.　　.　　.　　.　　.

PETR. Alas, good Kate, I will not burden thee;
　　For, knowing thee to be but young and light—
KATH. Too light for such a swain as you to catch;

And yet as heavy as my weight should be.

PETR. Should be! should—buzz!

KATH.   Well ta'en and like a buzzard.

PETR. O slow-wing'd turtle! shall a buzzard take thee?

KATH. Ay, for a turtle, as he takes a buzzard.

PETR. Come, come, you wasp; i' faith, you are too angry.

KATH. If I be waspish, best beware my sting.

PETR. My remedy is, then, to pluck it out.

KATH. Ay, if the fool could find it where it lies.

PETR. Who knows not where a wasp does wear his sting?
    In his tail.

KATH. In his tongue.

PETR. Whose tongue?

KATH. Yours, . . . and so farewell.

PETR. What, . . . nay, come again,
    Good Kate; I am a gentleman.

KATH.   That I'll try. (*She strikes him*)

PETR. I swear I'll cuff you, if you strike again.

KATH. So may you lose you arms.
    If you strike me, you are no gentleman;
    And if no gentleman, why then no arms.

PETR. A herald, Kate? O, put me in thy books!

KATH. What is your crest? A coxcomb?

PETR. A combless cock, so Kate will be my hen.

KATH. No cock of mine: you crow too like a craven.

PETR. Nay, come, Kate, come: you must not look so sour.

KATH. It is my fashion, when I see a crab.

PETR. Why, here's no crab; and therefore look not sour.

KATH. There is, there is.

PETR. Then show it me.

KATH. Had I a glass, I would.

PETR. What, you mean my face?

KATH. Well aim'd of such a young one.

PETR. Now, by Saint George, I am too young for you.

KATH. Yet you are wither'd.

PETR. 'Tis with cares.

KATH. I care not.

PETR. Nay, hear you, Kate. In sooth you 'scape not so.

KATH. I chafe you, if I tarry. Let me go.

PETR. No, not a whit; I find you passing gentle.
    'Twas told me you were rough and coy and sullen,
    And now I find report a very liar;
    For thou art pleasant, gamesome, passing courteous,
    But slow in speech, yet sweet as spring-time flowers.
    Thou canst not frown, thou canst not look askance,
    Nor bite the lip, as angry wenches will;
    Nor hast thou pleasure to be cross and talk;

But thou with mildness entertain'st thy wooers,
With gentle conference, soft and affable.
Why does the world report that Kate doth limp?
O slanderous world! Kate, like the hazel-twig,
Is straight and slender, and as brown in hue
As hazel nuts and sweeter than the kernels.
O, let me see thee walk. Thou dost not halt.
KATH. Go, fool, and whom thou keep'st command.
PETR. Did ever Dian so become a grove
  As Kate this chamber with her princely gait?
  O, be thou Dian, and let her be Kate;
  And then let Kate be chaste and Dian sportful!
KATH. Where did you study all this goodly speech?
PETR. It is extempore, from my mother-wit.
KATH. A witty mother! witless else her son.
PETR. Am I not wise?
KATH. Yes: keep you warm.
PETR. Marry, so I mean, sweet Katherine, in thy bed.
  And therefore, setting all this chat aside,
  Thus in plain terms. Your father hath consented
  That you shall be my wife; your dowry 'greed on;
  And, will you, nill you, I will marry you.
  Now, Kate, I am a husband for your turn;
  For, by this light, whereby I see thy beauty,
  Thy beauty, that doth make me like thee well,
  Thou must be married to no man but me;
  For I am he am born to tame you, Kate,
  And bring you from a wild Kate to a Kate
  Conformable as other household Kates.
  Here comes your father. Never make denial;
  I must and will have Katherine to my wife.
      WILLIAM SHAKESPEARE, *The Taming of the Shrew*

CHAPTER 10

Vocal Pitch

You know now that the quality of your voice can have much to do with making your personality attractive or displeasing; that the volume or force of your voice can make you sound agreeably animated or too decisive and too positive or even too indifferent and too weak; and that the tempo of your voice can make you persuasive and meaningful or tiresome and boring. Conversely, your voice is a barometer of you and your manner of living; it tells us much of how you feel about life and people; it tells us whether you are easygoing or aggressive or timid.

All of these voice factors—vocal quality, force, and tempo— are important in the interpretation of the printed page, but the vocal element which is the most sensitive indicator of your reactions, feelings, ideas, and attitudes is *pitch*. By discriminating use of slides, steps, and key, which are various manifestations of pitch, the interpreter can achieve the vocal inflections, or changes in pitch, that make it possible to express not only the obvious logical meanings of literature but its more subtle connotative and emotional meanings. And proper control of vocal inflection is one of the principal requirements for the development of speech melody.

WHAT IS VOCAL PITCH?

To put it simply, vocal pitch is the highness or lowness of the voice as it strikes the ear. More technically, it is the auditory sensation that is produced by the rate at which the vocal folds vibrate; and this rate, or frequency, is determined by the length, thickness, and tension of the vocal folds.[1] People whose vocal

[1] See above, p. 246.

folds are longer and thicker than average have low-pitched voices, because there are fewer vibrations per second; those whose folds are short and thin have higher-pitched voices, because there are more vibrations per second.

Young children usually have high-pitched voices until they reach the age of puberty. Sometimes the high pitch remains during adulthood. This may be due to failure of development of the laryngeal mechanism or to failure of the child to adjust the use of his resonators to the growth of the larynx. Sometimes, in this adjustment period, the adolescent will pass through a period of huskiness, showing a failure of approximation of the vocal folds or glottal edges. But in men, particularly, the vocal pitch should become lower as the individual approaches maturity. Certainly any male who still has a high-pitched voice at the age of eighteen should find the reason for it and seek the necessary therapy.

OPTIMUM PITCH

The pitch level, or key, at which the voice operates with the greatest ease is called the optimum pitch. It is the most natural pitch for your particular vocal mechanism. When you phonate "ah," without imitation of another voice, you will probably use your optimum pitch. The optimum pitch for women is usually slightly higher than 256 double vibrations per second (middle C), and the optimum pitch for men is near 150 double vibrations, about one octave lower. However, some people, through poor habits or bodily tensions, use a much higher pitch than is pleasant to the listener; others use a pitch level that is too low, so that speech becomes aspirate or guttural or indistinct. It must not be forgotten that the tension of the vocal folds is determined by the action of the intrinsic and extrinsic muscles of the larynx, which are affected to a great extent by general bodily tension. Anyone—man or woman—who is frightened or who, for some other reason, lives in a state of hypertension will have a voice that is pitched higher than average. If there is no organic dysfunction causing the high-pitched voice, the pitch *can* be lowered. To do so, however, you will find that the general bodily tension must first be relaxed.

SPEECH MELODY DEPENDS ON
PITCH VARIABILITY

The melody of a person's speech depends primarily on his ability to vary the pitch changes of his voice. Melody is a delicate combination of pitch changes and, to be interesting, should be a smooth, rhythmical movement of the voice up and down the scale, making use of as much variability as is necessary for the best expression. Melody shows how one feels; it reveals the individual's general condition of health and happiness. In other words, melody is an index of what is taking place within; it reports the condition of the speaker, the interpreter, the character. The plaintive person has a depressing melody because his pitch changes are monotonous and narrow. The lively, happy-go-lucky person has a breezy melody that is very contagious, because he uses variety of pitch changes. Good melody enlightens and charms by the correct use of pitch changes; poor melody bores by the wrong use of pitch changes. The speaker with personality and temperament usually has a melody that is infectious and enjoyable.

Many people do not hear their own speech melody; some are offended when they are told their voices are monotonous and lacking in verve and sensitiveness. Every would-be speaker and interpreter should have his ear tested for pitch discrimination. The Seashore Measures of Musical Talent might well be used by prospective interpreters to ascertain their aptitude in this respect. The person who is not sensitive to pitch variations in his own voice, who is not able to hear his own melody, cannot profitably criticize his own speaking. For the interpreter, the refinement of refinements, both in understanding literature and in expressing its meaning, lies in his ability to use correct variations of pitch.

PITCH VARIABILITY DEPENDS ON
THE USE OF SLIDE, STEP, KEY

The interpreter will carry the most subtle meanings to an audience through the skillful use of vocal pitch changes. A voice that makes little use of pitch changes carries little meaning; and unless the speaker deliberately limits his pitch changes to convey lack of interest or hopelessness or despair, minimum inflections can become extremely monotonous. Monotony, of course, can be due to lack of variety in force and in tempo, which stems usually from slovenly habits, laziness, imitation, or tone deafness. But it is most evident when the same pitch pattern is repeated over and over. The person who continually lowers the pitch at the end of a phrase and the person who always raises the pitch at the end of a phrase are just as boring as the one who never bothers to use any inflections. Each pattern becomes monotonous and indicates a certain type of personality: the first will belong to a person who is dogmatic and overly certain; the second to one who is not too certain and seeks approval; and the last to a person who leads a dull life.

Monotony can also be caused by too many variations in pitch; that is, a voice may travel up and down the scale with "too much ado." This fault, however, is not common; but one unfortunate consequence of excessive variation is that it sometimes gives the impression that the speaker is "talking down" to his audience.

There are three ways in which pitch changes can be effected: by *slide*, by *step*, and by *key*. The changes produced by the appropriate use of these three devices indicate the proportions of sense and feeling in the material. Slides, the upward and downward movements of the voice *within* the word or syllable, must be present in lively sense. Steps, the upward and downward movements of the voice *between* words and syllables, are necessary to sense, but play an equally interesting part in feeling. Key, the *level* of tone, strikes the mood.

The Slide

There are many variations of slides in vocal pitch, but the three classifications usually spoken of are the *upward* (/), the *downward* (\ ), and the *wave* ($\wedge$ $\vee$ $\wedge\wedge$ $\vee\vee$). The upward slide, if used correctly and with discretion, can give a very interesting lilt and melody to the voice; however, it must be used, not exclusively, but in nice admixture with the downward slide. The upward slide, if overdone, gives the auditor an indecisive note. The person who is always apologizing or the one who is not quite sure of himself, employs a preponderance of upward slides.

It is the sign of inconclusiveness, of hesitation. However, it must be remembered that most people use more upward than downward slides. The downward slide can also be used too much. The meaning then becomes too dogmatic, too certain, too sure, too pedantic. The discriminating use of the downward slide, however, gives a sense of assurance; it clinches the thought and leaves a feeling of satisfaction. The wave, a combination of the upward and downward slides, can excite the most subtle and delicate meanings and add much to an interesting melody and rhythm. The gossip employs it—overtime; the sarcastic person gets most of his effects from the use of the wave; the actor is always using a combination of slides to provoke a new meaning for the audience. Slang phrases are tantalizing because of varied slides.

In a way, pitch slides are the very essence of meaning in the spoken word. In sensible and informative reading, every syllable should have a slide or glide of the voice. This is not easy to detect in your own speech rhythm or in the talk of those whom you hear daily. But if you listen carefully to others, you can catch a slide in even the quickest syllables; and in syllables held for any length of time, the upward and downward movement is readily apparent. A surer way of noting this phenomenon is to listen to a phonograph record, especially as it slows down. The more the sound drags, the more readily you can detect the slide in every syllable. The interpreter adds more to the meaning every time he uses a slide that indicates the intention of the writer. Note how the meaning has been changed in the following by various uses of the slides.[2]

$$\underset{\text{Yes.}}{/} \quad \underset{\text{Yes.}}{\backslash} \quad \underset{\text{Yes.}}{\wedge} \quad \underset{\text{Yes.}}{\wedge} \quad \underset{\text{Yes.}}{\vee} \quad \underset{\text{Yes.}}{\vee} \quad \underset{\text{Yes.}}{\wedge\wedge}$$

$$\underset{\text{Speak gently.}}{\backslash \quad \backslash\backslash} \qquad \underset{\text{Speak gently.}}{/ \quad \vee} \qquad \underset{\text{Speak gently.}}{/ \quad \wedge\vee}$$

$$\underset{\text{I love her.}}{\backslash \ \backslash \ \backslash} \qquad \underset{\text{I love her.}}{/ \ \wedge \ \wedge} \qquad \underset{\text{I love her.}}{\backslash \ \backslash \ \wedge}$$

[2] These marks are for demonstration purposes. It is not suggested that every word of a selection be diagrammed as above. Train your ear to hear these variations in slides.

It is possible in any group of words to find a score of meanings. Take the sentence, *I will go,* and see how many combinations of slides you can use for various meanings. Notice how the meaning is dependent upon the pitch changes. First you can mean, "I am leaving" (downward slide on *go* will give that meaning). Or you can mean, "I am determined to go whether you like it or not" (long upward slide on *will* makes this meaning possible). Then you can mean, "You expect me to go?" (The interrogation point added for punctuation is merely a way of advising the reader how to employ the slide. This meaning is accomplished by a long upward slide on *I* and short upward slides on *will* and *go*.) You should be able to find many more meanings.

As you become conscious of the possibilities of different pitch patterns, you increase your powers of understanding and expressing meaning. The author of the material to be interpreted knows what he intends; this to him is the meaning. This intention he indicates as well as he can by proper rhetoric and composition, by placing words in the right order and by using understandable syntactical structure; and then he completes his task by the aid of punctuation, at best a tricky guide to the meaning intended.

When Lady Macbeth and Macbeth are debating the advisability of killing Duncan, the following dialogue takes place:

MACBETH. If we should fail?
LADY MACBETH. We fail. But, screw your courage to the sticking-place and we'll not fail.

Another Shakespearean editor has printed this text:

MACBETH. If we should fail?
LADY MACBETH. We fail! But screw your courage to the sticking-place and we'll not fail.

Now here are two clearly defined meanings. How is the difference indicated? Is it the punctuation? That seems reasonable. But we must remember that punctuation does not make meaning; it only records and suggests it. The real meaning is in the writer or the speaker. You can see it is not in the words; for the words in the above dialogue are precisely the same, yet they have two very different meanings. In the first passage, the *fail* in Lady Macbeth's speech has a downward slide; in the second passage, *fail* has an upward slide—and therein lies all the difference in the intention and meaning. Now what kind of slides can be used in the second *fail* in Lady Macbeth's speech? Observe that the same rule holds true—meaning can be intensified and made richer through proper slides.

This principle shows even more clearly in cases where the interpreter obviously gets the wrong meaning. For instance, nine out of ten novices in interpretation will interpret the following lines as if all they want is a quiet bar when *they* cross, no matter how much noise the bar makes for the rest of us.

> And may there be no moaning of the bar
> When I put out to sea.

This meaning is accomplished by a long downward slide on *I*. But it would be more civilized and more humane to give a short upward slide on *I* and longer upward slides on *put out*. Or try John V. A. Weaver's "Moonlight." [3] If the interpreter is careful to use an upward slide on the last word of the last line, he will keep his audience swathed in moonlight; if he hits *moonlight* with downward slides, he can expect his audience to drop back to earth. Try it.

> Gee!
> I just like to bet
> You could wash your soul clean
> In moonlight!

Slides or Song Notes? Possibly the slide in interpretation can be understood better by knowing its opposite—the "song note," which is held at one level, with no upward or downward movement. This is the typical use of pitch in singing, where the slide is the exception rather than the rule. Singing and speech are different chiefly in this matter of slide. In musical comedies and vaudeville acts you will now and then detect an actor or "singer" merely reciting instead of singing the words of a song. What is

---

[3] From *In American* (New York, Alfred A. Knopf, Inc., 1923), p. 22. The complete poem is reprinted above, p. 232.

the difference? The talking singer uses slides; the singer keeps his notes level. The reverse effect is found in the intoning used by certain speakers: preachers and political orators seem to be the most common offenders. In fact, some people limit oratory to the chanting effect of the song notes as against the conversational style which uses the speech note.

Court criers and circus ballyhooers use song notes; it is valuable for you, the interpreter, to imitate them only if you wish to portray that type of character. They probably use song notes for the same reason that men speaking to large crowds in immense auditoriums or in the open air incline to song notes. The reason for this is worth marking: a slide involves greater exertion than a tone held on one level. In shouting, it is easier to hold the voice level than to slide; the louder the sound, the harder it is to run up and down the scale. Try this and you will readily get the point. So, a man straining his voice to be heard, saves himself much exertion by keeping up the volume and cutting out the slides. Accordingly, the national-convention and camp-meeting style of speaking is indirect, remote from the ordinary conversation of the audience, and more like a chant than intelligent conversation. Fortunately, the public-address system is helping to rid the platform of the song-note speaker, although, he is still heard occasionally on the radio. The effect is rather ludicrous because the speaker and the audience *know* there is no need for indirectness over so intimate a means of communication as the microphone. The speaker must learn to talk in tune with the times.

This gliding motion of the voice is the very essence of speech sense. By omitting or reducing it, we impair the conversational ease of our speech; we sound indirect, affected, stilted, and monotonous. In declamatory and oratorical contests, these faults flourish. A contest or exhibition of declamatory skill is rare indeed that is not made boresome by the stiltedness and indirectness that come from the failure to use slides with intelligence and meaning. Such speaking does not sound sincere and genuine; it always gives the impression of a store window or a circus poster. It lacks the effect of the "first time over," a term used by actors to characterize this impression of natural, easy, direct interpretation of lines. When teachers of reading ask their orators, declaimers, and debaters in contests to be more natural, they really mean, "use slides more intelligently." It cannot be emphasized too strongly that directness and simplicity and sincerity are achieved chiefly by the intelligent use of the slide.

In some schoolrooms the children are actually criticized for using lively changes of pitch; and too often, unfortunately, Americans ridicule foreigners, whose rhythmical speech relies heavily on the use of the slide. In our own language this rhythm is particularly noticeable in the speech patterns of cultured Englishmen. The best way to imitate an Englishman is by using as wide a variety of pitch as possible, both in step and slide. It is this very variety that gives point to the perspicacious criticism of the man who said, "The cultivated American speaks with distinctness; the cultivated Englishman speaks with distinction."

The following passage reminds you of small talk you have heard. Usually a number of slides can be distinguished because the speaker uses an exaggerated tone in attempt to be convincing. Try it.

The Loquacious Man is one who will say to those whom he meets, if they speak a word to him, that they are quite wrong, and *he* knows all about it, and that, if they listen to him, they will learn; then, while one is answering him, he will put in, "Do you tell me so?—don't forget what you are going to say"; or "Thanks for reminding me"; or "How much one gets from a little talk, to be sure!"; or "By-the-bye" —; or "Yes! you have seen it in a moment"; or "I have been watching you all along to see if you would come to the same conclusion as I did"; and other such cues will he make for himself, so that his victim has not even breathing-time.

Before you undertake the exercises below, there is one important point to bear in mind. As was mentioned at the beginning of this chapter, the voice reflects the personality of the individual. A lack of pitch variability, consequently, may indicate a need to make some changes in your personal habits and attitudes. It might be well, therefore, to catalogue the assets and liabilities of your personality at the outset, because if your voice does reflect your liabilities, you will first have to readjust your thinking and living habits. The exercising and changing will have to begin within yourself, and no exercise will help you improve your voice until you have done so. Mechanical exercises are perfunctory compared to the real work of improving your personality and physical well-being. This is true of all vocal exercises, but it is especially true of exercises for pitch. If you are sure of your personality but still not sure of your ability to use slides effectively, turn to the Appendix for additional exercises. Whenever possible, practice them with a tape recorder—and listen to your own efforts with a critical ear.

EXERCISES

I

There is no character in literature who is more adept in accomplishing his evil plot through insinuation than Iago in Shakespeare's play *Othello*. The following passage will offer you an opportunity to show Iago's shrewdness and craftiness by skillful use of the slides. Iago is attempting to make Othello suspicious of Desdemona; Othello is unsuspecting at first. Consequently, the slides employed by the two characters should be entirely different. Every line of Iago's speeches must have a double meaning. Notice the one word "Indeed!" in line 11. Try various slides before you decide which one will carry Iago's meaning most expertly. Do the same thing with the phrases, "Honest, my lord?" and "Think, my lord!" Watch Othello's lines for imitation and for reversal of slides in the same words. Bear in mind that the last words, "Thou dost mean something," are uttered by an angry and impatient Othello.

BY HEAVEN, HE ECHOES ME

IAGO. My noble lord,—
OTHELLO.   What dost thou say, Iago?
IAGO. Did Michael Cassio, when you woo'd my lady,
    Know of your love?
OTH. He did, from first to last. Why dost thou ask?
IAGO. But for a satisfaction of my thought;
    No further harm.
OTH.   Why of thy thought, Iago?
IAGO. I did not think he had been acquainted with her.
OTH. O, yes; and went between us very oft.
IAGO. Indeed!
OTH. Indeed! ay, indeed. Discern'st thou aught in that?
    Is he not honest?

IAGO.   Honest, my lord?
OTH.   Honest! ay, honest.
IAGO. My lord, for aught I know.
OTH. What dost thou think?
IAGO.   Think, my lord!
OTH.   Think, my lord!
    By heaven, he echoes me,
    As if there were some monster in his thought
    Too hideous to be shown.—Thou dost mean something.
                          WILLIAM SHAKESPEARE, *Othello*

II

Now see what you can do with the slides in this next selection. Remember that Cyrano is a poet, a philosopher, a wit. Remember, too, that any offense to Cyrano's enormous nose means death from Cyrano's sword. The Vicomte de Valvert has just witnessed the death of the Meddler because of his reference to Cyrano's nose. The Vicomte attempts to put Cyrano in his place by telling him that his nose is too large. In Cyrano's reply, you will find cues for the inflections that are to be used. Your slides for the tones of the various attitudes described by Cyrano will all be quite different.

CALL THAT A NOSE? [4]

                          Ah, no, young sir!
    You are too simple. Why, you might have said—
    Oh, a great many things! Mon dieu, why waste
    Your opportunity? For example, thus:—
    AGGRESSIVE: I, sir, if that nose were mine,
    I'd have it amputated—on the spot!
    FRIENDLY: How do you drink with such a nose?
    You ought to have a cup made specially.
    DESCRIPTIVE: 'Tis a rock—a crag—a cape—
    A cape? say rather, a peninsula!
    INQUISITIVE: What is that receptacle—
    A razor-case or a portfolio?
    KINDLY: Ah, do you love the little birds
    So much that when they come and sing to you,
    You give them this to perch on? INSOLENT:
    Sir, when you smoke, the neighbors must suppose

---

[4] From *Cyrano de Bergerac*, trans. Brian Hooker (New York, Henry Holt and Company, Inc., 1928), pp. 40-41.

Your chimney is on fire. CAUTIOUS: Take care—
A weight like that might make you topheavy.
THOUGHTFUL: Somebody fetch my parasol—
Those delicate colors fade so in the sun!
PEDANTIC: Does not Aristophanes
Mention a mythologic monster called
Hippocampelephantocamelos?
Surely we have here the original!
FAMILIAR: Well, old torchlight! Hang your hat
Over that chandelier—it hurts my eyes.
ELOQUENT: When it blows, the typhoon howls,
And the clouds darken. DRAMATIC: When it bleeds—
The Red Sea! ENTERPRISING: What a sign
For some perfumer! LYRIC: Hark—the horn
Of Roland calls to summon Charlemagne!
SIMPLE: When do they unveil the monument?
RESPECTFUL: Sir, I recognize in you
A man of parts, a man of prominence—
RUSTIC: Hey? What? Call that a nose? Na, na—
I be no fool like what you think I be—
That there's a blue cucumber! MILITARY:
Point against cavalry! PRACTICAL: Why not
A lottery with this for the grand prize?
Or—parodying Faustus in the play—
"Was this the nose that launched a thousand ships
And burned the topless towers of Ilium?"
These, my dear sir, are things you might have said
Had you some tinge of letters, or of wit
To color your discourse. But wit,—not so,
You never had an atom—and of letters,
You need but three to write you down—an Ass.
Moreover,—if you had the invention, here
Before these folk to make a jest of me—
Be sure you would not then articulate
The twentieth part of half a syllable
Of the beginning! For I say these things
Lightly enough myself, about myself,
But I allow none else to utter them.

EDMOND ROSTAND

III

This poem can be very dull, if interpreted without proper slides. Or it can convey humor and nice discrimination in meaning, if the lines are thought out carefully. The final interpretation, however, must be casual and smooth. Note that there are many inflections that can be given to the two words "like" and "nice."

I LIKE AMERICANS[5]

I LIKE Americans.
You may say what you will, they are the nicest people in the world.

They sleep with their windows open.
Their bath-tubs are never dry.

They are not grown-up yet. They still believe in Santa Claus.
They are terribly in earnest.
But they laugh at everything.

They know that one roll does not make a breakfast.
Nor one vermouth a cocktail.
I like Americans.
They smoke with their meals.

The Italians are nice.
But they are not so nice as the Americans.

They have been told that they live in a warm climate.
And they refuse to heat their houses.
They are forever sobbing Puccini.
They no longer have lions about, to prey on Christian flesh.
But they have more than a sufficient supply of certain smaller car-
    nivora.
And if you walk in the street alone, somebody pinches you.

I like Americans.
They give you the matches free.

The Austrians are nice.
But they are not so nice as the Americans.

They eat sausages between the acts at the opera.
But they make you go out into the snow to smoke.

They are gentle and friendly. They will walk ten blocks out of their
    way to show you your way.
But they serve you paper napkins at the table.
And the sleeves of their tailored blouses are gathered at the shoulder.
But they don't know how to do their hair.

[5] From *Distressing Dialogues* (New York, Harper & Brothers, 1924), pp.
3-11. Copyright, 1922, 1923, by Conde Nast Publications, Inc. Copyright,
1924, by Edna St. Vincent Millay. Reprinted by permission of Brandt and
Brandt, agents for Miss Millay.

I like Americans.
They dance so well.

The Hungarians are nice.
But they are not so nice as the Americans.

They make beautiful shoes.
Which are guaranteed to squeak for a year.

Their native tongue is like a typewriter in the next room, and every
    word beginning with the shift-key.

Their wines are too sweet.

I like Americans.

They are the only men in the world, the sight of whom in their
    shirt-sleeves is not rumpled, embryonic, and agonizing.
They wear belts instead of suspenders.

The French are nice.
But they are not so nice as Americans.

They wear the most charming frocks in the world.
And the most awkward underclothes.

Their shoes are too short.
Their ankles are too thick.
They are always forgetting where they put their razors.

They have no street-corner shoe-shining palaces, where a man can be
    a king for five minutes every day.
Nor any Sunday supplement.
Their mail boxes are cleverly hidden slits in the wall of a cigar store.

They put all their cream into cheese.
Your morning cup of chickory is full of boiled strings.

If you want butter with your luncheon, they expect you to order
    radishes.
And they insist on serving the vegetables as if they were food.

I like Americans.
They make a lot of foolish laws.
But at least their cigarettes are not rolled by the government.
The material of which the French make their cigarettes would be used
    in America to enrich the fields.

In the city the French are delightful.
They kiss in the cafés and dine on the sidewalks.

Their dance halls are gay with paper ribbons and caps and colored
balloons.
Their rudeness is more gracious than other people's courtesy.

But they are afraid of water.
They drink it mixed with wine.
They swim with wings.
And they bathe with an atomizer.
Their conception of a sport suit is a black taffeta gown, long gloves
with fringe on, a patent leather hand-bag, and a dish-mop dog.
In the country they are too darned funny for words.

I like Americans.
They carry such pretty umbrellas.
The *Avenue de l'Opéra* on a rainy day is just an Avenue, on a rainy
day.
But Fifth Avenue on a rainy day is an old-fashioned garden under a
shower.

The French are a jolly lot.
Their cities have no traffic regulations.
And no speed limit.
And if you get run over, you have to pay a fine for getting in the way.

But they have no ear drums.
Paris is the loveliest city in the world.
Until she opens her mouth.

Should the French go forth to battle armed only with their taxi horns,
they would drive all before them.
I would liefer live in a hammock slung under the "L" at Herald Square
than in a palace within ear-shot of the *Place de la Harmony*.

I like Americans.
They are so ridiculous.
They are always risking their lives to save a minute.
The pavement under their feet is red-hot.
They are the only people in the world who can eat their soup with-
out a sound as of the tide coming in.

They sell their bread hygienically wrapped.
The Europeans sell it naked.
They carry it under the arm.
Drop it and pick it up.
Beat the horse with it.
And spank the children.
They deliver it at your apartment. You find it lying outside your door
on the door-mat.

And European hotels are so hateful and irritating.
There is never an ash-tray in your bedroom.
Nor a waste-basket.
Nor a cake of soap.
No sweet little cake of soap all sealed in paper!
Not even a sliver left behind by a former guest.
No soap.
No soap at all.
And there's always a dead man in a blanket across the head of the bed.
And you can't get him out. He's tied there.
And the pillow-slips are trimmed with broken buttons.
That scratch your ear.

Then there are their theatres.
They make you tip the usher.
And pay for your program.
The signal for the curtain to rise is the chopping of wood off stage.

Then the railroad system.
Especially in France.
Have to get there forty-five minutes ahead of train time, or stand in
    the aisle all day.
Pay for every pound of trunk.
Never a soul in sight who knows anything about anything.
No place to sit.
No place to powder up.
And before they will let you into the station at all, they insist on
    your pushing two sous into a slot-machine.
When you have just had your pocket picked of the last sou you had
    in the world.
And are expecting your only husband on the express from Havre.

I like Americans.
They let you play around in the Grand Central all you please.
Their parks are not locked at sunset.
And they always have plenty of paper bags.
Which are not made of back numbers of *Le Rire*.

The English are nice.
But they are not so nice as the Americans.
They wear much too much flannel.

No matter with whom they are dancing, they dance a solo.
And no matter where they go, they remain at home.
They are nice. They keep the tea-set at the office.
But the Americans keep the dish-pan in the music-room.

The English are an amusing people.
They are a tribe of shepherds, inhabiting a small island off the coast
    of France.
They are a simple and genial folk.
But they have one idiosyncrasy.
They persist in referring to their island as if it were the mainland.

The Irish are nice.
But they are not so nice as the Americans.
They are always rocking the boat.

I like Americans.
They either shoot the whole nickel, or give up the bones.
You may say what you will, they are the nicest people in the world.
                    NANCY BOYD (EDNA ST. VINCENT MILLAY)

IV

If you listen carefully to Lew Sarett's recording of "Toby Goes
to Market," [6] you will soon be aware of the poet's subtle use of
slides to get the sympathy of his listeners. His slides convey a
love and feeling for Toby which the lines might not reveal if
read carelessly.

TOBY GOES TO MARKET [7]

We shipped the calf to the market—
    Toby, the brindle-bull,
With his face of perpetual wonder,
    And his tail like stuck-out wool.

Toby, who wallowed in mischief:
    Who squirmed through the pasture-rails,
Trampled my garden of melons,
    Battered my milking-pails.

Toby, who cried in the downpour,
    Too frugal of brindle brain
To dash from the storm into shelter,
    Or rump himself to the rain.

[6] *Lew Sarett: Reading from His Collected Poems* (Columbia, XTV
15494).

[7] By permission from *The Collected Poems of Lew Sarett*, p. 88. Copyright, 1920, 1922, 1925, 1931, 1941, by Henry Holt and Company, Inc.

We tried to corral him for market;
    He blatted, his fear intense,
Straddled his legs on a railing,
    And hung himself on the fence.

We cornered him and roped him,
    He flung out his legs and sprawled;
We dragged him into the cow-pen,
    And there bewildered he bawled.

I drove him into the runway
    That leads to the cattle-cars;
He rattled his heels on the pickets
    And battered his head on the bars.

Pierre jammed him in with the cattle,
    Beside his bellowing cow;
She lowed to her suckling gently
    And licked the blood from his brow.

And Toby trembled beside her,
    Fear in his big brown eyes,
As he heard the thunder and tumult
    Of clamoring cattle rise.

A lurch of the snorting engine
    Flung him beneath the feet
Of steers that trampled him earthward;
    And Toby began to bleat.

He was on his way to the market,
    Toby, the neighborhood pet,
Who had licked the salt from my fingers
    And slavered my hands with wet.

He was off on the big adventure;
    He was reluctant to go
On a jaunt that had no returning—
    Oh, Toby, how did you know!

Lew Sarett

V

If possible, listen to Norman Corwin's interpretation of "The
Runaway" [8] and compare the inflections he uses with those em-

---

[8] *Masterpieces of Literature: The Appreciation of Poetry* (Columbia,
E-5-8), sponsored by the National Council of Teachers of English.

ployed by Frost in his recording of the same poem.[9] Which is the more convincing? Now compare both of these recordings with Lew Sarett's interpretation of "Toby Goes to Market." The two poems make good companion pieces. Which one shows the greater sincerity and emotional meaning?

THE RUNAWAY[10]

Once when the snow of the year was beginning to fall,
We stopped by a mountain pasture to say, 'Whose colt?'
A little Morgan had one forefoot on the wall,
The other curled at his breast. He dipped his head
And snorted at us. And then he had to bolt.
We heard the miniature thunder where he fled,
And we saw him, or thought we saw him, dim and grey,
Like a shadow against the curtain of falling flakes.
'I think the little fellow's afraid of the snow.
He isn't winter-broken. It isn't play
With the little fellow at all. He's running away.
I doubt if even his mother could tell him, "Sakes,
It's only weather." He'd think she didn't know!
Where is his mother? He can't be out alone.'
And now he comes again with clatter of stone,
And mounts the wall again with white eyes
And all his tail that isn't hair up straight.
He shudders his coat as if to throw off flies.
'Whoever it is that leaves him out so late,
When other creatures have gone to stall and bin,
Ought to be told to come and take him in.'

                                        ROBERT FROST

VI

This next poem calls for restraint and gentleness in touch. Be sure that the slides carry the full meaning of the line, "It is fitting that you be here."

[9] *Contemporary Poets Series* (Columbia, 11-A-D), sponsored by the National Council of Teachers of English.

[10] From *Complete Poems of Robert Frost.* Copyright, 1930–1949, by Henry Holt and Company, Inc. Copyright, 1936, 1948, by Robert Frost. Reprinted by permission of the publishers.

ON SEEING TWO BROWN BOYS IN A CATHOLIC CHURCH[11]

It is fitting that you be here,
Little brown boys
With Christ-like eyes
And curling hair.

Look you on yon crucifix
Where he hangs nailed and pierced
With head hung low
And eyes a'blind with blood that drips
From a thorny crown . . . .
Look you well,
You shall know this thing.

Judas' kiss will burn your cheek
And you shall be denied
By your Peter—
And Gethsemane . . . .
You shall know full well Gethsemane . . . .

You, too, will suffer under Pontius Pilate
And feel the rugged cut of rough hewn cross
Upon your surging shoulder
They will spit in your face
And laugh . . . .
They will nail you up twixt thieves
And gamble for your little garments.
And in this you will exceed God
For on this earth
You shall know Hell—

O little brown boys
With Christ-like eyes
And curling hair
It is fitting that you be here.

FRANK HORNE

The Step

The slide is the movement up and down *within* the word or syllable; the step is the change of pitch *between* words and

[11] From *The Book of American Negro Poetry*, ed. James Weldon Johnson (New York, Harcourt, Brace and Company, Inc., 1931), p. 276. Copyright, 1931, by Harcourt, Brace and Company, Inc. Reprinted by permission of the author and the publishers.

syllables. Steps have much to do with meaning. Monopitch, which is characterized by very narrow steps, is tiresome. However, it has its place many times in selections that involve moods of intense hatred, sullenness, and sorrow. Sometimes it is used as an indication of a low degree of intelligence. On the other hand, there are some people who go to the opposite extreme and cultivate enormously wide steps: for instance, the storyteller over the radio, or the neighborly gossip. Neither one of these extremes is valuable in good conversation; but the interpreter must be able to discriminate and to study them as "character types." In lively, rhythmical speech, the voice makes wide steps repeatedly from the highest notes to the lowest notes and then, quite as often, employs steps that are barely perceptible. All intelligent speech uses variety in steps and in slides. When there is a certain measure of abandon and spontaneity, pitch changes, both in slide and instep, are wide, almost to the limit of the voice's range. A typical example of how the meaning can be changed by the use of wide or narrow steps is shown in the following diagram. The dotted lines may be considered the normal level of the voice. The space indicated between each syllable is the step; some intervals are narrow, others are quite wide, depending on the meaning:

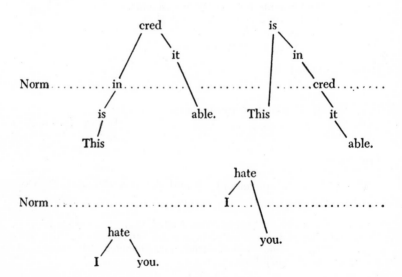

Wide range of pitch is one of the sure ways of expressing keen exposition, lively narrative, and enthusiastic description. When you are speaking wholeheartedly, without restraint and fear of consequences, you tend to use wide steps. This is usually true in extreme anger, jealousy, or fear. But when you are beset with doubts, fears, or indifference, or are torn between two opinions or feelings, you are more likely to use narrow steps or a more level pitch. For instance, in extreme fear, the voice may sound the whole gamut; whereas with a fear that is the result of two warring opinions or feelings, the voice tends to hold a more level tone. If you cry out in terror, "They are killing me!" you may use the whole range of your voice. On the other hand, when Lady Macbeth finds that Macbeth has blundered in the plans for concealing the murder of Duncan, she is frightened and yet she wishes to correct the fatal mistake; so she says with a level voice, the very evenness of which shows the conflict within her, "Why did you bring those daggers from the room!"

In the same way, sentiments of serenity, love, adoration, solemnity are likely to employ narrow steps, because there is always a factor of restraint. One does not bark at the beauty of the moon or orate his devotion to his beloved—if he means what he says. Thus, Romeo, full of "rapture and a wild desire," yet fearful of being caught in the Capulet garden, cries out softly:

> Soft, what light through yonder window breaks?
> It is the east, and Juliet is the sun!

Later:

> It is my lady, O, it is my love!
> O, that she knew she were!

Notice the effect you gain if you interpret the above lines with wide steps. Yet Portia explains earnestly, and even eagerly, with the full gamut of her voice:

> The quality of mercy is not strain'd,
> It droppeth as the gentle rain from heaven
> Upon the place beneath. It is twice blest:
> It blesseth him that gives and him that takes.
> 'Tis mightiest in the mightiest; it becomes
> The thronèd monarch better than his crown. . . .

However, Marcellus and Bernardo, repressed by fear, in the dead of night, and in sight of a ghost, speak almost on one level:

MARCELLUS. Peace, break thee off! Look, where it comes again!
BERNARDO. In the same figure, like the King that's dead.
MARCELLUS. Thou art a scholar; speak to it, Horatio.
BERNARDO. Looks it not like the King? Mark it, Horatio.
HORATIO. Most like; it harrows me with fear and wonder.

The humor of these paragraphs below will be lost if wide steps are not used in building up to the attitudes of the two instructors.

LET X EQUAL[12]

Then I have more than an impression—it amounts to a certainty—that algebra is made repellent by the unwillingness or inability of teachers to explain why we suddenly start using a and b, what components mean apart from their handling, and how the paradoxical behavior of $+$ and $-$ came into being. There is no sense of history behind the teaching, so the feeling is given that the whole system dropped down readymade from the skies, to be used only by born jugglers. This is what paralyzes—with few exceptions—the infant, the adolescent, or the adult who is not a juggler himself.

When you add to this the fact that many computers who teach are both impatient and inarticulate, you have reason enough for the child's hatred of ciphering. I well remember one college instructor, said to have been a brilliant discoverer, but whose students failed with alarming regularity. He used to write on the board difficult problems in integration, and after everyone had given up he would put the chalk to his lips, make a noise like a straining gear box, and write out the correct result. How he got to it he could never explain. "Don't you see?" he would plead. We never did see. But we had his exact opposite, a rather crude and coarse barrel of a man, whom I remember with gratitude for the phrase he never tired of using at every step, "What'll this *gim-me?*" That expressed the true spirit of calculation, and to symbolize this feeling we students made up the myth that he was a successful bootlegger on the side.

JACQUES BARZUN

EXERCISES

I

You will notice that the mood of Gilbert's "Song" is gay and irresponsible, so the steps should be wide and varied.

[12] From *Teacher in America*, p. 82. Copyright, 1944, 1945, by Jacques Barzun. Reprinted by permission of Little, Brown & Co. and the Atlantic Monthly Press.

SONG

If you're anxious for to shine in the high esthetic line as a man of
    culture rare,
You must get up all the germs of the transcendental terms, and plant
    them everywhere.
You must lie upon the daisies and discourse in novel phrases of your
    complicated state of mind,
The meaning doesn't matter if it's only idle chatter of a transcendental
    kind.
    And everyone will say
    As you walk your mystic way,
"If this young man expresses himself in terms too deep for *me*,
Why, what a very singularly deep young man this deep young man
    must be!

Be eloquent in praise of the very dull old days which have long since
    passed away,
And convince them if you can, that the reign of good Queen Anne
    was Culture's palmiest day.
Of course, you will pooh-pooh whatever's fresh and new, and declare
    it's crude and mean;
For art stopped short in the cultivated court of the Empress Josephine.
    And everyone will say
    As you walk your mystic way,
"If that's not good enough for him which is good enough for *me*,
Why, what a very cultivated kind of youth this kind of youth must
    be!"

Then a sentimental passion of a vegetable fashion must excite your
    languid spleen,
An attachment *a la* Plato for a bashful young potato, or a not-too-
    French French bean!
Though the Philistines may jostle, you will rank as an apostle in the
    high esthetic band,
If you walk down Piccadilly, with a poppy or a lily in your medieval
    hand.
    And everyone will say,
    As you walk your flowery way,
"If he's content with a vegetable love which would certainly not
    suit *me*,
Why, what a particularly pure young man this pure young man must
    be!"

                  W. S. Gilbert, *Patience*

II

This selection differs greatly from the preceding one in mood. It is heavy, morose, and morbid. The steps should be so narrow that your vocal pitch approaches a monotone.

KILLERS[13]

I am singing to you
Soft as a man with a dead child speaks;
Hard as a man in handcuffs,
Held where he cannot move:

Under the sun
Are sixteen million men,
Chosen for shining teeth,
Sharp eyes, hard legs,
And a running of young warm blood in their wrists.

And a red juice runs on a green grass;
And a red juice soaks the dark soil.
And the sixteen million are killing—and killing and killing.

I never forget them day or night:
They beat on my head for memory of them;
They pound on my heart and I cry back to them;
To their homes and women, dreams and games.

I wake in the night and smell the trenches,
And hear the low stir of sleepers in lines—
Sixteen million sleepers and pickets in the dark:
Some of them long sleepers for always,

Some of them tumbling to sleep to-morrow for always,
Fixed in the drag of the world's heartbreak,
Eating and drinking, toiling . . . on a long job of killing,
  Sixteen million men.
                                        CARL SANDBURG

III

The author, in the following poem, gives the interpreter cues for narrow steps and evenness of tone by using hyphenated words. Usually in poems where the intent is ironical, as it is in this one, the interpreter will use subtle slides to connote the

[13] From *Chicago Poems*, p. 85. Copyright, 1916, by Henry Holt and Company, Inc. Reprinted by permission of the publisher.

meaning; but here, the irony is carried through the supreme indifference and short-sightedness of the attendant, whose attitude requires the interpreter to hold his range of steps to a minimum. The last line is loaded with meaning. Do it justice.

THE EMPIRE BUILDERS[14]

THE MUSEUM ATTENDANT:
  This is *The Making of America in Five Panels:*

  This is Mister Harriman making America:
  Mister-Harriman-is-buying-the-Union-Pacific-at-Seventy:
  The Sante Fe is shining on his hair.

  This is Commodore Vanderbilt making America:
  Mister-Vanderbilt-is-eliminating-the-short-interest-in-Hudson:
  Observe the carving on the rocking chair.

  This is J. P. Morgan making America:
  (The Tennessee Coal is behind to the left of the Steel Company.)
  Those in mauve are braces he is wearing.

  This is Mister Mellon making America:
  Mister-Mellon-is-represented-as-a-symbolical-figure-in-aluminum-
  Strewing-bank-stocks-on-a-burnished-stair.

  This is the Bruce is the Barton making America:
  Mister-Barton-is-selling-us-Doctor's-Deliciousest-Dentifrice.
  This is he in beige with the canary.

  You have just beheld the Makers making America:
  This is *The Making of America in Five Panels:*
  America lies to the west-southwest of the switch-tower:
  There is nothing to see of America but land.
                                         ARCHIBALD MACLEISH

IV

Slides and steps must be carefully studied in this poem. Notice that the first fifteen lines are in a steel-like mood, with words like "tempered," "resistance," and "inflexible" strengthening the image. The voice will have to connote the power and skill of "this legion of iron," so the slides should not be too varied; nor should the steps be wide. The next two lines show a difference in key, in steps, and in slides; they prepare the listener for the remaining lines, which build to a climactic end. The lines beginning, "What of the flamboyant cities," show wide steps and varied inflections.

THE LEGION OF IRON[15]

They pass through the great iron gates—
Men with eyes gravely discerning,
Skill to appraise the tonnage of cranes
Or split an inch into thousandths—
Men tempered by fire as the ore is
And planned to resistance
Like steel that has cooled in the trough;
Silent of purpose, inflexible, set to fulfilment—
To conquer, withstand, overthrow . . .
Men mannered to large undertakings,
Knowing force as a brother
And power as something to play with,
Seeing blood as a slip of the iron,
To be wiped from the tools
Lest they rust.

But what if they stood aside,
Who hold the earth so careless in the crook of their arms?

What of the flamboyant cities
And the lights guttering out like candles in a wind . . .
And the armies halted . . .
And the train midway on the mountain
And idle men chaffing across the trenches . . .
And the cursing and lamentation
And the clamor for grain shut in the mills of the world?
What if they stayed apart,
Inscrutably smiling,
Leaving the ground encumbered with dead wire
And the sea to row-boats
And the lands marooned—
Till time should like a paralytic sit,
A mildewed hulk above the nations squatting?

LOLA RIDGE

[15] From *Poems* (New York, The Viking Press, Inc., 1923), p. 15. Copyright, 1923, by Lola Ridge. Reprinted by permission of her husband, David Lawson.

V

Nearly every interpreter, at some time, has tried to interpret "Mending Wall," one of Frost's most widely known poems. The tone is chatty but not gossipy. Frost is gently inquiring about his neighbor's thoughts. The slides, consequently, are variable but not extreme, and the steps follow the same middle course.

MENDING WALL[16]

Something there is that doesn't love a wall,
That sends the frozen-ground-swell under it,
And spills the upper boulders in the sun;
And makes gaps even two can pass abreast.
The work of hunters is another thing:
I have come after them and made repair
Where they have left not one stone on a stone,
But they would have the rabbit out of hiding,
To please the yelping dogs. The gaps I mean,
No one has seen them made or heard them made,
But at spring mending-time we find them there.
I let my neighbour know beyond the hill;
And on a day we meet to walk the line
And set the wall between us once again.
We keep the wall between us as we go.
To each the boulders that have fallen to each.
And some are loaves and some so nearly balls
We have to use a spell to make them balance:
"Stay where you are until our backs are turned!"
We wear our fingers rough with handling them.
Oh, just another kind of out-door game,
One on a side. It comes to little more:
There where it is we do not need the wall:
He is all pine and I am apple orchard.
My apple trees will never get across
And eat the cones under his pines, I tell him.
He only says, "Good fences make good neighbours."
Spring is the mischief in me, and I wonder
If I could put a notion in his head:
"Why do they make good neighbours? Isn't it

Where there are cows? But here there are no cows.
Before I built a wall I'd ask to know
What I was walling in or walling out,
And to whom I was like to give offence.
Something there is that doesn't love a wall,
That wants it down." I could say "Elves" to him,
But it's not elves exactly, and I'd rather
He said it for himself. I see him there
Bringing a stone grasped firmly by the top
In each hand, like an old-stone savage armed.
He moves in darkness as it seems to me,
Not of woods only and the shade of trees.
He will not go behind his father's saying,
And he likes having thought of it so well
He says again, "Good fences make good neighbours."

ROBERT FROST

VI

This poem has the same sort of reminiscent and thoughtful
tone as Frost's "Mending Wall," but the rationalizing keeps it
from being as objective. The slides are more varied, and the
steps, in some instances, are very wide.

DILEMMA[17]

Gee, she's sweet! So sorta eyes wide open
    And shiny, like the street-lights do at night
When rain is on the sidewalk. They's a somethin'
    About the way her whole face has that light

Whenever she looks at me. It always says,
    "I believe in you! Oh, I believe in you!"
That face like a little flower, starin' at me—
    It scares me! What should I do? What *can* I do?

I tell her not to go and dream about me,
    I ain't no fine guy, and I tell her so;
She keeps on thinkin' I'm just kiddin' her,
    And answers back, "You can't fool me! I know!"

And just to think, that lovely dream about me
    Has got to smash all up some awful day
When she finds out the way that I am really. . . .
    It'll hurt her so. . . . I ought to get away

[17] From *Finders*, p. 54. Copyright, 1923, by Alfred A. Knopf, Inc. Reprinted by permission of the publishers.

Where she can't never see me any more,
　　Before that dream and all that sweetness dies. . . .
But can I do it? Can I do without her?
　　Can I stand not seein' that lovin' in her eyes? . . .
　　　　　　　　　　　　　　　JOHN V. A. WEAVER

VII

These two poems take wide steps and variable slides to be
effective:

MY GARDEN[18]

A garden is a lovesome thing, God wot!
　　Rose plot,
　　　　Fringed pool,
　　Ferned grot—
　　　　The veriest school
　　　　Of peace; and yet the fool
　Contends that God is not—
Not God! in gardens! when the eve is cool?
　　　　Nay, but I have a sign:
　　　　'Tis very sure God walks in mine.
　　　　　　　　　　　　THOMAS EDWARD BROWN

THE GOLDEN FISH

Love is a little golden fish,
　　Wondrous shy . . . ah, wondrous shy . . .
You may catch him if you wish;
He might make a dainty dish . . .
　　　But I . . .
　　　Ah, I've other fish to fry!

For when I try to snare this prize,
　　Earnestly and patiently,
All my skill the rogue defies,
Lurking safe in Aimee's eyes . . .
　　　So you see,
　　　I am caught and love goes free!
　　　　　　　　　　　　　GEORGE ARNOLD

[18] From *Collected Poems*, p. 135. Copyright, 1908, by The Macmillan
Company. Reprinted by permission of the publishers.

VIII

The four selections in this group demonstrate how mood influences the use of slides and steps, which become less variable in each succeeding poem. The first has the "vagabond" mood, with many slides and variable steps. The second has the "notes of cellos that are very low" and none of the open joyousness of the first. "Nocturne" has the quietness of a lullaby, and the last, "In Canada," is intense and somber.

A VAGABOND SONG[19]

There is something in the autumn that is native to my blood—
Touch of manner, hint of mood;
And my heart is like a rhyme,
With the yellow and the purple and the crimson keeping time.

The scarlet of the maples can shake me like a cry
Of bugles going by.
And my lonely spirit thrills
To see the frosty asters like a smoke upon the hills.

There is something in October sets the gypsy blood astir;
We must rise and follow her,
When from every hill of flame
She calls and calls each vagabond by name.

BLISS CARMAN

THE TRUST[20]

I have given you my dreams and you alone;
They are like figures in tapestry,
Faded, and dim, and visible to few,
Or like the strips of moonlight that have shown
On columns lying broken long ago;
The notes of cellos that are very low—
And rich; or shallow bowls of porcelain—
That catch and keep the sunlight through the rain
Fragile and beautiful.
I have given you
My dreams; Oh, hold them very tenderly.

EVELYN HARDY

[19] From *More Songs of Vagabondia*, p. 39. Copyright, 1916, by Small, Maynard & Company. Reprinted by permission of the publishers.

[20] From *Scribner's Magazine* (June, 1924). Reprinted by permission of the author and Charles Scribner's Sons.

NOCTURNE[21]

Now may, with soft surprise,
    Sleep's so elusive spell
Fall on your lips, your eyes,
    That I do love so well.

Fold your unquiet hands
    Across your fair young breast,
And in the dim white lands
    Seek thy unbroken rest.

Now let me never know
    Through this, a little while,
Thy voice; let me forego
    The beauty of thy smile.

Stir not at all, at all;
    Be without memory here,
Till the first lark shall call
    Thee from thy slumbers, dear.

GEORGE CARROLL

IN CANADA[22]

You are dead.
The songs of birds are still as sweet,
The vagrant blue blossoms smile in the wheat
Cheerily, as when you were here
Long ago. Nay, but a year
Has passed. A year of days
Uncertain, long and dread always
Save for the hope that you would come
When peace stilled the cannon, hushed the drum.
Will peace come now to stop the shed
Of blood and tears, now you are dead?

You are dead.
Lilies nod in the prairie hay,
The wandering woodbines beckon gay,
The sky above is azure blue,
The sun gleams gold, as the day that you

Enlisted. Then war meant
A cross of honor; and I sent
You gladly. You won the cross
And died. What is my loss?
A trifling toll to the God of War,
And Hate and Strife thrive as before,
And you are dead.

ETHEL NICHOLSON

IX

The mood of this Eliot poem is dependent on the slides and steps. What kind of a person is Mr. Hodgson? Describe him. Watch your interpretation of the sentence, "How delightful to meet Mr. Hodgson!"

LINES TO RALPH HODGSON, ESQRE.[23]

How delightful to meet Mr. Hodgson!
    (Everyone wants to know *him*)—
With his musical sound
And his Baskerville Hound
Which, just at a word from his master
Will follow you faster and faster
And tear you limb from limb.
How delightful to meet Mr. Hodgson!
Who is worshipped by all waitresses
(They regard him as something apart)
While on his palate fine he presses
The juice of the gooseberry tart.
How delightful to meet Mr. Hodgson!
    (Everyone wants to know *him*.)
He has 999 canaries
And round his head finches and fairies
In jubilant rapture skim.
How delightful to meet Mr. Hodgson!
    (Everyone wants to meet *him*.)

T. S. ELIOT

Key

Key, or the level of tone, is also an indicator of mood. It is distinctly a device used by the interpreter to express emotions

---

[23] From *Collected Poems: 1909-1935*, p. 168. Copyright, 1936, by Harcourt, Brace and Company, Inc. Reprinted by permission of the publishers.

and feelings. The level of tone, whether high, low, or medium, should help to carry the author's meaning. Those who use the same key for all interpretations acquire a monotonous speech pattern.

In general, a high key is used for moods of serenity, gaiety, calmness, as in Browning's lyric from "Pippa Passes":

> The year's at the spring
> And day's at the morn;
> Morning's at seven;
> The hillside's dew-pearled;
> The lark's on the wing;
> The snail's on the thorn:
> God's in his heaven—
> All's right with the world!

The very highest key, a shrill shriek, is reserved for extreme rage or terror—when one has lost control of oneself. When Emilia discovers that Othello has killed Desdemona, his innocent wife, she cries out, first probably in a medium key, then in a high tone, and, finally, with a shriek of fear and horror:

> Thou hast not half that power to do me harm
> As I have to be hurt. O gull! O dolt!
> As ignorant as dirt! thou hast done a deed—
> I care not for thy sword; I'll make thee known,
> Though I lost twenty lives.—Help! help! ho! help!
> The Moor hath kill'd my mistress! Murder! murder!

A middle key represents quiet repression, sincerity, sometimes indifference. It could be used very adequately, for example, in Thomas Gray's "Elegy":

> The curfew tolls the knell of parting day,
>   The lowing herd wind slowly o'er the lea,
> The ploughman homeward plods his weary way,
>   And leaves the world to darkness and to me.

A low key is most expressive of pathos, solemnity, controlled hate, worship, or despair. In the following excerpt from *Othello*, notice the contrast of Desdemona's voice, which strikes a high key, and Othello's voice, which employs a low level:

DESDEMONA. Who's there? Othello?
OTHELLO.   Ay, Desdemona.
DES. Will you come to bed, my lord?
OTH. Have you pray'd to-night, Desdemona?
DES.   Ay, my lord.
OTH. If you bethink yourself of any crime
    Unreconcil'd as yet to Heaven and grace,
    Solicit for it straight.
DES. Alack, my lord, what may you mean by that?
OTH. Well, do it, and be brief; I will walk by.
    I would not kill thy unprepar'd spirit;
    No; heavens forfend! I would not kill thy soul.
DES. Talk you of killing?
OTH.   Ay, I do.
DES.   Then Heaven
    Have mercy on me!
OTH.   Amen, with all my heart!

It should be the task of the interpreter to suit the key to the meaning, although one cannot always be too certain about the level of the key. For the poem "Inland," a variety of levels can be tried. Here is one way: try a high (slightly higher than medium key), gentle tone on the first two lines; a low key on the next four lines; and a medium key on the last line.

INLAND[24]

He used to talk of ships, and I remember,
Oh, I remember. . . .
    Tall spars clustered in a drowsy, evening bay,
    Clean winds calling, at white noon today;
    Salt on the taffrail, foam at the bow,
    And a singing at the windlass . . . how it all comes back now!
        (Though I never saw the sea.)

I sweep the rooms, half dreaming
Of tides. . . .
    Slow breathing, languid giants sucking at the sands,
    Surging to the harbors of brilliant, tropic lands;
    An old black brig headed for the sunset's gold,
    Bringing back the red dawn stuffed in her hold.
        (His words!)

[24] From *The Lyric West* (March, 1925), p. 34. Reprinted by permission of the publishers.

The six-year maple on his grave is sturdy,
Yet . . . yet . . .
    Night, all drenched with stars, and still we're outward bound,
    Oh, the creaking of the canvas is an eerie sort of sound,
    And I hear the tramping watch as I lie warm-bunked below,
    Where the yellow slush lamp swings to and fro, to and fro.
    (Like that, his talk.)

I scour the kettles and hang up the wash,
But these pictures won't go out of my head:
    Full, white sails on a level twilight sea,
    A tired bark trailing to some port of mystery;
    Green waves a-glitter, . . . ships, ships, ships,
    And a laughing sailor man with red, remembered lips.
    (God! How I'm still missing him!)

                                     JOAN PROSPER

EXERCISES

I

Notice that the key in the italicized lines of this poem differs from that of the other three stanzas. Notice also that the steps in the same lines are narrow—so narrow, in fact, that they create an obvious monotone.

THE SHEEPHERDER[25]

Loping along on the day's patrol,
I came on a herder in Jackson's Hole;
Furtive of manner, blazing of eye,
He never looked up when I rode by;
But counting his fingers, fiercely intent,
Around and around his herd he went:

    One sheep, two sheep, three sheep, four. . . .
    Twenty and thirty . . . forty more;
    Strayed—nine ewes; killed—ten rams;
    Seven and seventy lost little lambs.

He was the only soul I could see
On the lonely range for company—
Save one lean wolf and a prairie-dog,
And a myriad of ants at the foot of a log;
So I sat the herder down on a clod—
But his eyes went counting the ants in the sod:

One sheep, two sheep, three sheep, four. . . .
Fifty and sixty . . . seventy more;
There's not in this flock a good bell-wether!
Then how can a herder hold it together!

Seeking to cheer him in his plight,
I flung my blankets down for the night;
But he wouldn't talk as we sat by the fire—
Corralling sheep was his sole desire;
With fingers that pointed near and far,
Mumbling, he herded star by star:

One sheep, two sheep, three—as before!
Eighty and ninety . . . a thousand more!
My lost little lambs—one thousand seven!—
Are wandering over the hills of Heaven.

LEW SARETT

II

The first two stanzas of "Spring Night" should be interpreted in a key different from that of the last sixteen lines. Slides and steps should vary also, because of the change of mood.

SPRING NIGHT[26]

The park is filled with night and fog,
　　The veils are drawn about the world,
The drowsy lights along the paths
　　Are dim and pearled.

Gold and gleaming the empty streets,
　　Gold and gleaming the misty lake,
The mirrored lights like sunken swords,
　　Glimmer and shake.

Oh, is it not enough to be
Here with this beauty over me?
My throat should ache with praise, and I
Should kneel in joy beneath the sky.
O beauty, are you not enough?
Why am I crying after love
With youth, a singing voice, and eyes
To take earth's wonder with surprise?

[26] From *Love Songs*, p. 27. Copyright, 1920, by The Macmillan Company. Reprinted by permission of the publishers.

Why have I put off my pride,
Why am I unsatisfied,—
I, for whom the pensive night
Binds her cloudy hair with light,—
I, for whom all beauty burns
Like incense in a million urns?
O beauty, are you not enough?
Why am I crying after love?

SARA TEASDALE

III

Notice the change in slides, steps, and key in the last four lines of the following selection.

HIT[27]

Out of the sparkling sea
I drew my tingling body clear, and lay
On a low ledge the livelong summer day,
Basking, and watching lazily
White sails in Falmouth Bay.

My body seemed to burn
Salt in the sun that drenched it through and through,
Till every particle glowed clean and new
And slowly seemed to turn
To lucent amber in a world of blue . . .

I felt a sudden wrench—
A trickle of warm blood—
And found that I was sprawling in the mud
Among the dead men in the trench.

WILFRED W. GIBSON

IV

If you recall Cudjo's voice in the recording of *John Brown's Body*, you will remember the typical range of slides and the wide steps used. You will also remember that the key was a trifle higher than the medium pitch. The same kind of vocal impression should be created in the following poem.

[27] From *Poems*, p. 126. Copyright, 1916, by The Macmillan Company. Reprinted by permission of the publishers.

THE TURNING OF THE BABIES IN THE BED[28]

Woman's sho' a cur'ous critter, an' dey ain't no doubtin' dat.
She's a mess o' funny capahs f'om huh slippahs to huh hat.
Ef yo' tries to un'erstan' huh, an' yo' fails, des' up an' say:
"D' ain't a bit o' use to try to un'erstan' a woman's way."

I don' mean to be complainin', but I's jes' a-settin' down
Some o' my own obserwations, w'en I cas' my eye eroun'.
Ef yo' ax me fu' to prove it, I ken do it mighty fine,
Fu' dey ain't no bettah 'zample den dis ve'y wife o' mine.

In de ve'y hea't o' midnight, w'en I's sleepin' good an' soun',
I kin hyeah a so't o' rustlin' an' somebody movin' 'roun'.
An' I say, "Lize, whut yo' doin'?" But she frown an' shek huh haid,
"Hesh yo' mouf, I's only tu'nin' of de chillun in de bed.

"Don' yo' know a chile gets restless, layin' all de night one way?
An' yo' got to kind o' 'range him sev-al times befo' de day?
So de little necks won't worry, an' de little backs won't break;
Don' yo' t'ink 'cause chillun's chillun dey hain't got no pain an' ache."

So she shakes 'em, an' she twists 'em, an' she tu'ns 'em 'roun' erbout,
'Twell I don' see how de chillun evah keeps f'om hollahin' out.
Den she lif's 'em up head downwards, so' dey won't git livah-grown,
But dey snoozes des' ez peaceful ez a liza'd on a stone.

W'en hit's mos' nigh time fu' wakin' on de dawn o' jedgment day,
Seems lak I kin hyeah ol' Gab'iel lay his trumpet down an' say,
"Who dat walkin' 'round so easy, down on earf ermong de dead?"—
'Twill be Lizy up a-tu'nin' of de chillun in de bed.

PAUL LAURENCE DUNBAR

V

The first eight lines below differ in mood from the rest of this excerpt. Notice how the word "Gloom" gives you the cue for the first lines. Your interpretation would sound ridiculous if you were to use a high key, wide steps, and many inflections at the beginning of the poem. The rest of the lines, however, are persuasive and inquiring, so your interpretative manner will change.

from ANTWERP[29]

I

Gloom!
An October like November;
August a hundred thousand hours,
And all September,
A hundred thousand, dragging sunlit days,
And half October like a thousand years . . .
And doom!
That then was Antwerp. . . .
                              In the name of God,
How could they do it?
Those souls that usually dived
Into the dirty caverns of mines;
Who usually hived
In whitened hovels; under ragged poplars;
Who dragged muddy shovels, over the grassy mud,
Lumbering to work over the greasy sods. . . .
Those men there, with the appearance of clods
Were the bravest men that a usually listless priest of God
Ever shrived. . . .
And it is not for us to make them an anthem.
If we found words there would come no wind that would fan them
To a tune that the trumpets might blow it,
Shrill through the heaven that's ours or yet Allah's
Or the wide halls of any Valhallas.
We can make no such anthem. So that all that is ours
For inditing in sonnets, pantoums, elegiacs, or lays
Is this:
"In the name of God, how could they do it?"

II

For there is no new thing under the sun,
Only this uncomely man with a smoking gun
In the gloom. . . .
What the devil will he gain by it?
Digging a hole in the mud and standing all day in the rain by it
Waiting his doom,
The sharp blow, the swift outpouring of the blood,
Till the trench of grey mud
Is turned to a brown purple drain by it.
Well, there have been scars

[29] From *On Heaven and Poems Written in Active Service*, pp. 17-23. Copyright, 1918, by John Lane Company. Reprinted by permission of the publishers.

Won in many wars . . .
Punic,
Lacedaemonian, wars of Napoleon, wars for faith, wars for honour,
 for love, for possession,
But this Belgian man in his ugly tunic,
His ugly round cap, shooting on, in a sort of obsession,
Overspreading his miserable land,
Standing with his wet gun in his hand . . .
Doom!
He finds that in a sudden scrimmage,
And lies, an unsightly lump on the sodden grass . . .
An image that shall take long to pass!

 .   .   .   .   •   •

                              v

And what in the world did they bear it for?
I don't know.
And what in the world did they dare it for?
Perhaps that is not for the likes of me to understand.
They could very well have watched a hundred legions go
Over the fields and between their cities
Down into more southerly regions.
They could very well have let their legions pass through their woods,
And have kept their lives and their wives and their children and cattle
 and goods.
I don't understand.
Was it just love of their land?
Oh poor dears!
Can any man so love his land?
Give them a thousand pities
And rivers and rivers of tears
To wash off the blood from the cities of Flanders.

                              Ford Madox Ford

                              VI

In this next poem, notice how the images, vivid and almost staccato in their sharpness, present a "pitifully" hopeless mood. The steps are narrow, and the key must be held at one level, except when the sister speaks.

BOY WITH HIS HAIR CUT SHORT[30]

Sunday shuts down on this twentieth-century evening.
The L passes. Twilight and bulb define

[30] From *Selected Poems of Muriel Rukeyser.* Copyright, 1951, by Muriel Rukeyser. Reprinted by permission of the publishers, New Directions.

the brown room, the overstuffed plum sofa,
the boy, and the girl's thin hands above his head.
A neighbor's radio sings stocks, news, serenade.

He sits at the table, head down, the young clear neck exposed,
watching the drugstore sign from the tail of his eye;
tattoo, neon, until the eye blears, while his
solicitous tall sister, simple in blue, bending
behind him, cuts his hair with her cheap shears.

The arrow's electric red always reaches its mark,
successful neon! He coughs, impressed by that precision.
His child's forehead, forever protected by his cap,
is bleached against the lamplight as he turns head
and steadies to let the snippets drop.

Erasing the failure of weeks with level fingers,
she sleeks the fine hair, combing: "You'll look fine tomorrow!
You'll surely find something, they can't keep turning you down;
the finest gentleman's not so trim as you!" Smiling, he raises
the adolescent forehead wrinkling ironic now.

He sees his decent suit laid out, new-pressed,
his carfare on the shelf. He lets his head fall, meeting
her earnest hopeless look, seeing the sharp blades splitting,
the darkened room, the impersonal sign, her motion,
the blue vein, bright on her temple, pitifully beating.
                                            MURIEL RUKEYSER

Characterization is revealed through inflection, steps, and key. In earlier chapters it was suggested that you listen to the recording of *Don Juan in Hell*.[31] Listen again to that particular album, for you are now ready to appreciate the wide range of slides, steps, and keys that are used throughout. Side 4 is especially interesting because of the series of long speeches by Don Juan and the Devil which hold the attention of the listeners through a wide variation of pitch changes. Beginning with Don Juan's speech, "On the contrary, here I have everything that disappointed me . . ." and following with his next speech, "Why should I be civil to them or to you?" you will hear every kind of inflection that one may use to convey meaning. You will hear wide steps where climaxes are reached; downward slides that

[31] *Don Juan in Hell* (Columbia, SL-166), recorded by the First Drama Quartet, with Charles Laughton, Charles Boyer, Agnes Moorehead, and Cedric Hardwicke.

indicate resolution and determination, as in the line, "That is the law of life"; and upward inflections at the end of sentences which are punctuated with a period. Unusually good are the slides within monosyllabic words. Listen for them. And, of particular interest to you in the last of the above-mentioned speeches will be the way in which Boyer handles a series of phrases with parallel construction that could be quite monotonous if steps and key were not handled effectively. Notice how the speech is ended with definite downward slides on the phrase, "to the very backbone of their souls."

In dialogue, each character's speech pattern will vary through the combination of changes in quality, force, tempo, and pitch. Dramatic selections always present the problem of characterization, and the interpreter should study the scene carefully beforehand to determine what combinations he will use to make the personality and purpose of each character distinct for the audience.

EXERCISES

I

Try to interpret the following scene, keeping these points in mind: pitch inflections and steps are wide, the key varies, and the rhythmical cadences are strong. The over-all effect should be eerie. Above all, the voices of the witches must blend together, especially in rhythm, and they should form a marked contrast to the voices of Macbeth and Banquo.

ALL HAIL, MACBETH!

This scene takes place late at night on a heath near Forres. It is stormy, and thunder is heard.

FIRST WITCH. Where hast thou been, sister?
SECOND WITCH. Killing swine.
THIRD WITCH. Sister, where thou?
1. WITCH. A sailor's wife had chestnuts in her lap,
And munch'd, and munch'd, and munch'd. "Give me," quoth I.
"Aroint thee, witch!" the rump-fed ronyon cries.
Her husband's to Aleppo gone, master o' the Tiger;
But in a sieve I'll thither sail,

And, like a rat without a tail,
I'll do, I'll do, and I'll do.

2. WITCH. I'll give thee a wind.

1. WITCH. Thou'rt kind.

3. WITCH. And I another.

1. WITCH. I myself have all the other,
And the very ports they blow,
All the quarters that they know
I' the shipman's card.
I'll drain him dry as hay.
Sleep shall neither night nor day
Hang upon his pent-house lid;
He shall live a man forbid.
Weary se'nnights nine times nine
Shall he dwindle, peak, and pine:
Though his bark cannot be lost,
Yet it shall be tempest-tost.
Look what I have.

2. WITCH. Show me, show me.

1. WITCH. Here I have a pilot's thumb,
Wreck'd as homeward he did come. (*Drums within.*)

3. WITCH. A drum, a drum!
Macbeth doth come.

ALL. The weird sisters, hand in hand,
Posters of the sea and land,
Thus do go about, about;
Thrice to thine, and thrice to mine.
And thrice again, to make up nine.
Peace! the charm's wound up.

Enter Macbeth and Banquo

MACBETH. So foul and fair a day I have not seen.

BANQUO. How far is't call'd to Forres? What are these
So wither'd and so wild in their attire,
That look not like the inhabitants o' the earth,
And yet are on't? Live you? or are you aught
That man may question? You seem to understand me,
By each at once her choppy finger laying
Upon her skinny lips. You should be women,
And yet your beards forbid me to interpret
That you are so.

MACBETH. Speak, if you can. What are you?

1. WITCH. All hail, Macbeth! hail to thee, thane of Glamis!

2. WITCH. All hail, Macbeth! hail to thee, thane of Cawdor!

3. WITCH. All hail, Macbeth, that shalt be King hereafter!

BANQUO. Good sir, why do you start, and seem to fear
Things that do sound fair? (*To the witches*) I' the name of truth,
Are ye fantastical, or that indeed

Which outwardly ye show? My noble partner
You greet with present grace and great prediction
Of noble having and of royal hope,
That he seems rapt withal; to me you speak not.
If you can look into the seeds of time,
And say which grain will grow and which will not,
Speak then to me, who neither beg nor fear
Your favours nor your hate.

1. WITCH. Hail!
2. WITCH. Hail!
3. WITCH. Hail!
FIRST WITCH. Lesser than Macbeth, and greater.
2. WITCH. Not so happy, yet much happier.
3. WITCH. Thou shalt get kings, though thou be none;
So all hail, Macbeth and Banquo!
1. WITCH. Banquo and Macbeth, all hail!
MACBETH. Stay, you imperfect speakers, tell me more.
By Sinel's death I know I am thane of Glamis;
But how of Cawdor? The thane of Cawdor lives,
A prosperous gentleman; and to be king
Stands not within the prospect of belief
No more than to be Cawdor. Say from whence
You owe this strange intelligence, or why
Upon this blasted heath you stop our way
With such prophetic greeting. Speak, I charge you.
Witches vanish
WILLIAM SHAKESPEARE, *Macbeth*

II

The humor in this next scene comes from the quick turns in meaning which are achieved through slides. The author has made clear to the person interpreting the lines the kind of meaning he wishes to convey, even to Elaine's last line.

THE HEART INTEREST[32]

ELAINE *is helping* DICK *write a play so that they may raise the necessary funds to cover debts incurred by* DICK's *father. If the play is not sold,* DICK *intends to carry out his first plan: his own death so that insurance money may be collected.* ELAINE *has decided that the play needs heart interest and that it would be better to act it out. So she turns to* DICK.

[32] From *The Big Idea*, pp. 65-69. Copyright, 1914, by A. E. Thomas and Clayton Hamilton. Reprinted by permission of the authors and Samuel French, Inc.

ELAINE. All right then. Begin.

DICK. Begin!

ELAINE. Yes, lead up to the subject of your suddenly realized regard for me.

DICK. (*With conviction, seeing her plan*) By Jove, you're wonderful.

ELAINE. Yes, that'll do for a beginning.

DICK. But I mean it.

ELAINE. And I'm talking about the play. Now say it again and I'll go on from there.

DICK. All right. (*The wind taken out of his sails, he says it in a perfunctory way*) By Jove, you're wonderful.

ELAINE. You must say it as if you mean it. It will put me in the mood.

DICK. By Jove, you *are* wonderful.

ELAINE. Nonsense, Dick, don't be absurd.

DICK. (*She says it so naturally that he is again puzzled and drops out of his loverlike attitude*) Say, are you acting now or not?

ELAINE. Of course, I am.

DICK. It didn't seem possible, you said it so naturally.

ELAINE. My dear Dick, we shall never get on at this rate. Will you try and forget everything but this play? We are trying to act a love scene; we need one desperately. Now, you and I are merely characters, have you got that?

DICK. Yes, I think so.

ELAINE. Well, try to remember it. Now we'll begin again. Go on— By Jove, you're wonderful.

DICK. Well, by Jove, you're wonderful.

ELAINE. Nonsense, Dick, don't be absurd.

DICK. But you are and you know it, you're too intelligent not to know it.

ELAINE. At any rate, I don't mind your thinking so.

DICK. It wouldn't prevent it if you did. You know that, too, don't you?

ELAINE. (*Softly*) You know, Dick, we really haven't time for this sort of thing.

DICK. Haven't we?

ELAINE. Have we?

DICK. It may be the only time we'll ever have. Have you ever thought of that?

ELAINE. Yes—no—no—I haven't, and I won't think of it. It's too terrible. Besides we must get on with our work.

DICK. Elaine, I've got to tell you—

ELAINE. No, no, I—

DICK. Don't be afraid, it can't do you any harm; but I—I can't go on any longer—like this.

ELAINE. Like this?

DICK. I can't seem to think any more about what we're trying to do; my heart is so full that my brain won't do its work.

ELAINE. Please.

DICK. My heart's so full of you. Three days ago I hadn't even heard your name. It's not twenty-four hours since I first saw you coming through that door; and now like a flame that leaps from blackness you've flashed into all that I've ever read or dreamed that's beautiful, all that's ever fired my brain or warmed my heart, all my life, my soul,—my dear.

ELAINE. Oh, Dick!

DICK. What I'm saying doesn't seem quite possible, does it? It's the sort of thing that simply doesn't happen; and yet it's true. It's the truest thing in all my life.

ELAINE. Dick, please.

DICK. It isn't fair of me to speak like this, standing as I do under a provisional sentence of death.

ELAINE. Oh!

DICK. But I can't help it. Loving you is the finest thing I've ever done in all my life, and I just can't bear the thought that you should never know. You see, it's a sort of bequest. I want to leave you the finest thing I have; do you mind?

ELAINE. Do you mean it, Dick?

DICK. God knows I do.

ELAINE. (*With an entire change of manner, very matter-of-fact*) Well, I think we're doing very well so far.

DICK. (*Staggered*) Doing well?

ELAINE. I mean for the play. (*She makes it clear she's not quite sure whether he is in earnest or not and is going to take no chances*)

DICK. The play. God!

ELAINE. Oh, that's good. Dick, that's fine, you just keep to that pose. You see, I don't quite know whether you are sincere or just acting, but it's very effective.

DICK. (*Hopelessly*) Do you think so?

ELAINE. Yes; so then I go on—let's go back a moment. Dick, do you mean it?

DICK. (*With an effort repeating his former answer*) God knows I do.

ELAINE. Oh, Dick, I've wondered if you cared.

DICK. Didn't you know that I did?

ELAINE. Sometimes I've hoped you did and then I've hoped that you didn't; because if you did care and things should go wrong it would make it so much harder for you to bear; and now you do care and it's too late to stop you.

DICK. Yes, it's too late, but you needn't be sorry.

ELAINE. Sorry? Oh, my dear. Last night as I lay awake and watched the first faint gray creep into my room, it seemed as if I had never seen the dawn before. I went to the window and looked out at the brightening sky, and presently tears came to my eyes, and suddenly I knew; and then like a flood of glory the sun and my love rose together. (*He looks at her uncertainly a moment, starts to embrace her, then checks himself*)

DICK. Excuse me, I think I had better write some of this down.

ELAINE. Dick. I mean it.

DICK. Elaine.

ELAINE. God knows I do.

DICK. Elaine.

ELAINE. Now you see we've got our heart interest.

A. E. THOMAS and CLAYTON HAMILTON

III

This scene is in direct contrast to the former one: the tone is hushed; the voices are intense in their excitement; the slides and steps are narrow; and the key does not vary too much.

MATT DENANT'S ESCAPE[33]

More than a year has passed since Matt Denant has been thrown in prison for killing a policeman in defense of a girl. The following scene is on the prison farm, Dartmoor, in a heavy fog. The stone wall of the field runs along the back and a stone wall joins it on the left. Matt Denant and a fellow convict are picking up the potatoes they have dug up earlier. They are but dimly seen in the fog, flinging the potatoes right and left into two baskets between them. They are speaking in low voices.

MATT. The poor blighter was dead, and I got five years for manslaughter.

FELLOW CONVICT. Cripes! A cop! You were lucky not to swing, mate.

MATT. The girl stood by me like a brick. If she hadn't come forward—

F. C. Lucky there, too. Most of 'em wouldn't. They're too mortal scared. 'Ow much you got left to do?

MATT. Three years, if I behave like a plaster saint.

(*He stops and straightens himself*)

F. C. I got four. I say, you're a torf, yn't you?

MATT. Toff! (*With a laugh*) Item, one Oxford accent; item, one objection to being spoken to like a dog.

F. C. Hush! (*Jerking his thumb toward the wall*) Fog don't prevent 'em hearin', blight 'em!

MATT. It's come up mighty sudden. Think it's going to last?

F. C. After a wet spell—this time o' year, when the wind's gone—yus. They'll be roundin' us up in a minute, you'll see—and 'ome to

[33] From *Escape*, pp. 17-23. Copyright, 1928, by Charles Scribner's Sons. Reprinted by permission of the publishers.

Blighty. Makes 'em nervous—fog. That's when you get the escapes.

MATT. No one's ever got away from here, they say.

F. C. There've been a good few tries, though.

MATT. Gosh! I'd like to have one.

F. C. Don't you do it, mate. You want clothes, you want money, you want a car, to give you a dawg's chance. And then they'd get you. This moor's the 'ell of a place. I say, you must 'ave hit that cop a fair knock!

MATT. Just an ordinary knock-out on the jaw. It wasn't that. He landed the back of his head on the Row rail. Poor devil! He wasn't married, luckily.

F. C. Luckily? Well, you never know about *that*. But get 'im off your chest, mate—'e wouldn't sit on mine—no more than an 'un did in the War. That's a good fair potato.

> (*The figure of a Warder is dimly seen coming along from the Right under the wall. He stops*)

WARDER. No talking there! When you've finished that row, pick back the next and then stand by to fall in. Hear me? Answer, can't you?

F. C. Right, Sir! (*The Warder's figure is seen moving back*) Nice man, ain't he? Wot'd I tell you? Early 'ome to tea.

MATT. (*Very low*) Like a dog! Three more years—like a dog!

F. C. 'E's all right, reely. It's the fog. Fog makes 'em nervous; an' when a man's nervous I've always noticed 'e speaks like that.

MATT. Yes: well, *I* can't get used to it.

F. C. Too particular, you torfs—get too much corn when you're two-year-olds.

MATT. (*Sharp and low*) *You* know the moor—where's Two Bridges?

F. C. There—a mile.

MATT. And Tavistock?

F. C. (*Pointing right back*) Seven. Guv'nor—don't do it. There ain't a chance in a million. You'll only get pneumonium in this stinkin' wet, and they'll have you into the bargain, sure as eggs—bread and water, cells, and the rest of it.

MATT. I got out of Germany.

F. C. Out of Germany? Cripes! That was none so dusty!

MATT. They've got no dogs here now, have they?

F. C. Don't fancy they 'ave. But, Guv'nor, the whole countryside round 'ere's agynst you. They don't like convicts. Funny yn't it?

> (*They have reached the end of the row, and stop, stooping, with their heads close together*)

MATT. Draw me a plan with this stick.

F. C. Blimy! (*Marking the earth*) 'Ere's the main road, and 'ere's the cross road to Tavistock. 'Ere's the Inn at Two Bridges, and 'ere's Post Bridge. 'Ere's Bee Tor Cross, ten to twelve mile. Chagford up there, Moreton 'ampstead 'ere.

MATT. What's across the main road from Two Bridges?

F. C. Moor. A long bit o' wood about 'ere; then 'ambleton; then you drops into fields to Widecombe; then up, and more moor to Heytor and Bovey. There's rail at Bovey or Lustleigh, and much good that'll do you with everybody as eager to see you as if you was the Prince of Wyles! Out this way you got Fox Tor Mire—ruddy bad bog, that!

(*A moment's silence while Matt studies the chart in the soil*)

WARDER'S VOICE. Hurry up with that last row—you two men!

(*The fog grows thicker*)

MATT. (*Smearing out the chart with his foot*) It's real thick now. Gosh! I'll have a shot!

(*They move back, beginning the last row*)

F. C. (*Jerking his thumb*) There's another blighter thirty yards out on the wall there. 'E'll shoot.

MATT. I know. I'm going over that wall in the corner, and then along under his nose on the near side. Ten to one he'll be looking out on the off side in this fog. If that chap there doesn't spot me, I'll get by.

F. C. You're mad, Guv'nor. They'll shoot at sight. And if they don' see you—in ten minutes I'll have finished this row, an' they're bound to know you're gone. You 'aven't the chance of a cocklouse.

MATT. All right, friend, don't worry! A bullet'd be a nice change for me. If I don't get one—I'll give 'em a run for their money.

F. C. Well, if you must go, mate— Strike the main road and run that way. In this fog they'll 'ave to take us back before they dare start after you. You'll find a scrap of a wood a bit beyond the river on the left side. Get into it and cover yourself with leaves till it's dead dark. Then you'll still be close to the road and you can myke shift in a stack or something till the morning. If you go wandering about the moor all night in this fog, you won't get nowhere, and you'll be done in stiff before dawn.

MATT. Thanks. Sooner the better, now— Never stop to look at a fence. Next time the steam's full on. (*Puts some potatoes in his pocket*) Can you eat these raw? I ate turnips in Germany.

F. C. Never tried, Guv'nor. Tyke this. (*He holds out a slice of bread*)

MATT. Thanks awfully. You're a good chap.

F. C. Wish you luck. Wish I was comin' too, but I 'aven't got the pluck, an' that's a fact.

MATT. Now! Turn your head the other way and keep it there. Remember me to Blighty. So long!

(*He moves three steps away from his fellow convict, pauses a few seconds, then suddenly, stooping low, runs to the wall, and is over it like a cat. In the minute of silence that follows, one can see the Convict listening*)

F. C. (*Counting the seconds to himself, up to twenty, in an excited murmur*) Gawd! 'E's past that blighter! (*Listens again*) Gawd!

'E's orf! (*With realization of his fellow's escape comes an itch to attempt it himself*) Shall I 'ave a shoot meself? Shall I? Gawd! I must!

(*He has just turned to sneak off, when the Warder's voice is heard off Right*)

WARDER. You, man, there! Where's your mate?

F. C. 'Ad a call, sir.

WARDER. What d'you mean?

F. C. Went over that wall, Sir.

WARDER. He's not there. Now then! Where is he?

F. C. No use arstin' me. I don't know where he is.

WARDER. Come with me. (*He marches sharply along the wall back*) Convict! Out there! Answer! Warder! You, Williams! Anyone passed you? Lost a man here!

VOICE OF SECOND WARDER. No one's passed.

FIRST WARDER. Sharp, then! There's a man gone!

(*Second Warder appears at the top of the wall*)

SECOND WARDER. He must ha' got past *you*, then.

FIRST WARDER. Curse this fog! Fire a shot for warning. No, don't, or we'll have others running for it. Muster sharp and get off home and report—that's the only thing. Here, you! Keep your mouth shut. You know all about it, I bet.

F. C. Not me, Sir. 'E just said 'e 'ad a call to 'ave tea with the Duchess; an' I went on pickin' up, knowin' you was in an 'urry.

FIRST WARDER. Mind your lip! Come on, Williams. March, you!

JOHN GALSWORTHY

IV

There is no scene in Shakespeare's plays more powerful in emotional content than the scene between Hamlet and his mother. Hamlet's first words, "Now, mother, what's the matter?" strike the keynote of tension felt by Hamlet. There is nothing gentle in those words. And the intensity of his attitude is even more evident when, in answer to his mother's rebuke, "Hamlet, thou hast thy father much offended," he states, "Mother, you have my father much offended." He is referring, of course, to the murder of his father; so the contrast on the slides used in "thy father" and "my father" sets the scene for further insinuations.

LOOK HERE, UPON THIS PICTURE

Hamlet has discovered that his father has been murdered by the man who now shares the throne with the Queen, Hamlet's mother. He has been called to the Queen's room.

POLONIUS. He will come straight. Look you lay home to him.
Tell him his pranks have been too broad to bear with,
And that your Grace hath screen'd and stood between
Much heat and him. I'll silence me e'en here.
Pray you, be round with him.
HAMLET. (*Within*) Mother, mother, mother!
QUEEN. I'll warrant you,
Fear me not. Withdraw, I hear him coming.
(*Polonius hides behind the arras*)
HAMLET. Now, mother, what's the matter?
QUEEN. Hamlet, thou hast thy father much offended.
HAMLET. Mother, you have my father much offended.
QUEEN. Come, come, you answer with an idle tongue.
HAMLET. Go, go, you question with a wicked tongue.
QUEEN. Why, how now, Hamlet!
HAMLET. What's the matter now?
QUEEN. Have you forgot me?
HAMLET. No, by the rood, not so:
You are the Queen, your husband's brother's wife;
But would you were not so! You are my mother.
QUEEN. Nay, then, I'll set those to you that can speak.
HAMLET. Come, come, and sit you down. You shall not budge.
You go not till I set you up a glass
Where you may see the inmost part of you.
QUEEN. What wilt thou do? thou wilt not murder me?
Help, help, ho!
POLONIUS. (*Behind*) What, ho! help, help, help!
HAMLET. (*Drawing*) How now! A rat? Dead, for a ducat, dead!
(*Kills Polonius*)
POLONIUS. (*Behind*) O, I am slain!
QUEEN. O me, what hast thou done?
HAMLET. Nay, I know not:
Is it the King?
QUEEN. O, what a rash and bloody deed is this!
HAMLET. A bloody deed! Almost as bad, good mother,
As kill a king, and marry with his brother.
QUEEN. As kill a king?
HAMLET. Ay, lady, 'twas my word.
(*Lifts up the arras and discovers Polonius*)
Thou wretched, rash, intruding fool, farewell!
I took thee for thy better. Take thy fortune.
Thou find'st to be too busy is some danger.
—Leave wringing of your hands. Peace! Sit you down,
And let me wring your heart; for so I shall,
If it be made of penetrable stuff,
If damned custom have not braz'd it so
That it is proof and bulwark against sense.

QUEEN. What have I done, that thou dar'st wag thy tongue
In noise so rude against me?
HAMLET.   Such an act
That blurs the grace and blush of modesty,
Calls virtue hypocrite, takes off the rose
From the fair forehead of an innocent love
And sets a blister there, makes marriage-vows
As false as dicers' oaths. . . .

.   .   .   .

QUEEN.   Ay me, what act,
That roars so loud, and thunders in the index?
HAMLET. Look here, upon this picture, and on this,
The counterfeit presentment of two brothers.
See, what a grace was seated on his brow.
Hyperion's curls; the front of Jove himself,
An eye like Mars, to threaten or command,
A station like the herald Mercury
New-lighted on a heaven-kissing hill;
A combination and a form indeed,
Where every god did seem to set his seal,
To give the world assurance of a man.
This was your husband. Look you now, what follows:
Here is your husband, like a mildew'd ear,
Blasting his wholesome brother. Have you eyes?
Could you on this fair mountain leave to feed,
And batten on this moor? Ha! have you eyes?
You cannot call it love; for at your age
The hey-day in the blood is tame, it's humble,
And waits upon the judgement: and what judgement
Would step from this to this?

.   .   .   .

QUEEN.   O Hamlet, speak no more!
Thou turn'st mine eyes into my very soul,
And there I see such black and grainèd spots
As will not leave their tinct.
HAMLET.   Nay but to live
In the rank sweat of an enseamed bed,
Stew'd in corruption . . .
QUEEN.   O, speak to me no more!
These words like daggers enter in mine ears.
No more, sweet Hamlet!
HAMLET.   A murderer and a villain!
A slave that is not twentieth part the tithe
Of your precedent lord! A vice of kings!
A cutpurse of the empire and the rule,

That from a shelf the precious diadem stole,
And put it in his pocket!
QUEEN.   No more!
Enter Ghost
HAMLET. A king of shreds and patches,—
Save me, and hover o'er me with your wings,
You heavenly guards! What would your gracious figure?
QUEEN. Alas, he's mad!
HAMLET. Do you not come your tardy son to chide,
That, laps'd in time and passion, lets go by
The important acting of your dread command?
O, say!
GHOST. Do not forget! This visitation
Is but to whet thy almost blunted purpose.
But look, amazement on thy mother sits.
O, step between her and her fighting soul.
Conceit in weakest bodies strongest works.
Speak to her, Hamlet.
HAMLET.   How is it with you, lady?
QUEEN. Alas, how is't with you,
That you do bend your eye on vacancy
And with the incorporal air do hold discourse?
Upon the heat and flame of thy distemper
Sprinkle cool patience. Whereon do you look?
HAMLET. On him, on him! Look you, how pale he glares!
His form and cause conjoin'd, preaching to stones,
Would make them capable. Do not look upon me,
Lest with this piteous action you convert
My stern effects: then what I have to do
Will want true colour, tears perchance for blood.
QUEEN. To whom do you speak this?
HAMLET.   Do you see nothing there?
QUEEN. Nothing at all, yet all that is I see.
HAMLET. Nor did you nothing hear?
QUEEN.   No, nothing but ourselves.
HAMLET. Why, look you there! Look, how it steals away!
My father, in his habit as he liv'd!
Look, where he goes, even now, out at the portal! (*Exit Ghost*)
QUEEN. This is the very coinage of your brain.
This bodiless creation ecstasy
Is very cunning in.
HAMLET.   Ecstasy?
My pulse, as yours, doth temperately keep time,
And makes as healthful music. It is not madness
That I have utter'd. Bring me to the test,
And I the matter will reword, which madness
Would gambol from. Mother, for love of grace,

Lay not that flattering unction to your soul,
That not your trespass, but my madness speaks.
It will but skin and film the ulcerous place,
Whilst rank corruption, mining all within,
Infects unseen. Confess yourself to Heaven;
Repent what's past; avoid what is to come.
QUEEN. O Hamlet, thou hast cleft my heart in twain.
HAMLET. O, throw away the worser part of it,
And live the purer with the other half.
Good-night: but go not to mine uncle's bed;
Assume a virtue, if you have it not.
And when you are desirous to be bless'd
I'll blessing beg of you. For this same lord,
                (*Pointing to Polonius*)
I do repent: but Heaven hath pleas'd it so,
To punish me with this and this with me,
That I must be their scourge and minister.
I will bestow him, and will answer well
The death I gave him. So again, good night.
I must be cruel only to be kind.
Thus bad begins and worse remains behind.
                    WILLIAM SHAKESPEARE, *Hamlet*

V

The following scene will give you a chance to try out slides that will carry the many ironical meanings. It is a bitter scene, and the interpreter should remember to use combinations of slides, steps, and key that will sustain this mood.

YOU—A RIVAL! [34]

Morning, before the rehearsal. HE is striding thoughtfully up and down the room. He wears a broad, parti-coloured coat, and a prismatic tie. His derby is on the back of his head, and his face is cleanshaven like that of an actor. His eyebrows are drawn, lips pressed together energetically, his whole appearance severe and sombre. After the entrance of the gentleman he changes. His face becomes clown-like, mobile—a living mask.

The gentleman comes in. He is dressed in black, and has an extremely well-bred appearance. His thin face is yellowish, like an invalid's. When he is upset, his colourless, dull eyes often twitch. HE does not notice him.

[34] From *He Who Gets Slapped*, trans. Gregory Zilboorg, pp. 96-106. Copyright, 1921, by The Dial Publishing Company, Inc. Reprinted by permission of the publishers.

GENTLEMAN. Good morning, sir.

HE. (*Turning around and looking at him absent-mindedly*) Ah! It's you.

GENT. I am not late? . . .

HE. No manners, please. What do you want? Tell me quickly, I have no time. . . .

GENT. In this suit, and with this face, you make a still stranger impression. Yesterday it seemed to me that it was all a dream; to-day . . . *you.* . . .

HE. You have forgotten my name again? My name is HE.

GENT. You are determined to continue talking to me like this?

HE. Decidedly! But you are squandering your time like a millionaire. Hurry up!

GENT. I really don't know. . . . Everything here strikes me so. . . . These posters, horses, animals, which I passed when I was looking for you. . . . And finally, *you,* a clown in a circus! (*With a slight, deprecating smile*) Could I expect it? It is true, when everybody there decided that you were dead, I was the only man who did not agree with them. I felt that you were still alive. But to find you among such surroundings—I can't understand it.

HE. You said you have a son, now. Doesn't he look like me?

GENT. I don't understand?

HE. Don't you know that widows or divorced women often have children by the new husband, which resemble the old one? This misfortune did not befall you? (*Laughs*) And your book, too, is a big success, I hear.

GENT. You want to insult me again?

HE. (*Laughing*) What a restless, touchy faker you are! Why were you trying to find me?

GENT. My conscience . . .

HE. You have no conscience. Or were you afraid that you hadn't robbed me of *everything* I possessed, and you came for the rest? But what more could you take from me now? My fool's cap with its bells? You wouldn't take it. It's too big for your bald head! Crawl back, you book-worm!

GENT. You cannot forgive the fact that your wife . . .

HE. To the devil with my wife! (*The gentleman is startled and raises his eyebrows.* HE *laughs*)

GENT. I don't know. . . . (HE *laughs*) Then *what* brought you to such a . . . step? Or is it that you cannot forgive me my success? But you always were so indifferent to glory. Or perhaps your indifference was only hypocrisy. And when I, a more lucky rival . . . .

HE. (*With a burst of laughter*) Rival! You—a rival!

GENT. (*Growing pale*) But my book!

HE. You are talking to me about *your* book? To me?

GENT. I am a very unhappy man. You must forgive me. I am deeply, irreparably, and infinitely unhappy.

HE. But why? Explain it to me. You say yourself that your book is a tremendous success, you are famous, you have glory; there is not a yellow newspaper in which *you* and *your* thoughts are not mentioned. Who knows *me?* Who cares about my heavy abstractions, from which it was difficult for them to derive a single thought? You—you are the great vulgarizer! You have made my thoughts comprehensible even to horses! With the art of a great vulgarizer, a tailor of ideas, you dressed my Apollo in a barber's jacket, you handed my Venus a yellow ticket, and to my bright hero you gave the ears of an ass. And then your career is made, as Jackson says. And wherever I go, the whole street looks at me with thousands of faces, in which—what mockery—I recognize the traits of my own children. Oh! How ugly your son must be, if he resembles me! Why then are you unhappy, you poor devil? The police haven't caught you, as yet. What am I talking about? Is it possible to catch you? You always keep within the limits of the law. You have been torturing yourself up to now because you are not married to my wife. . . . What is the use of this self-torture, my friend? Get married. I died. You are not satisfied with having taken only my wife? Let my glory remain in your possession. It is yours. Accept my ideas. Assume all the rights, my most lawful heir! I died! And when I was dying (*making a stupidly pious face*) I forgave thee! (*Bursts out laughing*)

GENT. And my pride?

HE. Have you any pride? . . . Think of it. There was a time when I loved you a little, even thought you a little gifted! You—my empty shadow.

GENT. I am your shadow.

HE. Oh, you are marvellous! What a comedy! What a touching comedy! Listen. Tell me frankly if you can; do you hate me very much?

GENT. Yes! With all the hate there is in the world! . . . I am respected and I am famous, yes? I have a wife and a son, yes. (*Laughs slowly*) My wife still loves you: our favorite discussion is about your genius. She supposes you are a genius. My son—yes, he'll resemble you. And when, in order to have a little rest, I go to my desk, to my ink-pot, my books—there, too, I find you. Always you! Everywhere you! And I am never alone—never myself and alone. And when at night—you, sir, should understand this—when at night I go to my lonely thoughts, to my sleepless contemplations, even then I find your image in my head, in my unfortunate brain, your damned and hateful image!

HE. What a comedy. How marvellously everything is turned about in this world: the robbed proves to be a robber, and the robber is complaining of theft, and cursing! (*Laughs*) . . . Oh, what a marvellous comedy! Tell me, would you be relieved if I really had died?

GENT. Yes! I think so. Death augments distance and dulls the memory. Death reconciles. But you do not look like a man who——
HE. Yes, yes! Death, *certainly!* . . .
GENT. . . . I do not dare to ask you—(*makes a grimace*) to ask you to die, but tell me: you'll never come back there? No, don't laugh. If you want me to, I'll kiss your hand. Don't grimace! I would have done so if you had died.
HE. (*Slowly*) Get out, vermin!

LEONID N. ANDREYEV

VI

Compare the long speech of He, which you have just read, with the speeches of the German soldier in *The Green Bay Tree* (p. 20) and of Death in *Death Takes a Holiday* (p. 327). How do they differ in climax, intensity, meaning, and vocal variety? Listen to yourself on a tape recorder as you try each characterization.

VII

The humor of the five following prose selections will depend mainly on your skill in the use of pause and inflection and on your sense of timing. Do not hurry over a laugh line; but do not wait expectantly for a laugh.

UNIVERSITY DAYS[35]

I passed all the other courses that I took at my University, but I could never pass botany. This was because all botany students had to spend several hours a week in a laboratory looking through a microscope at plant cells. I never once saw a cell through a microscope. This used to enrage my instructor. He would wander around the laboratory pleased with the progress all the students were making in drawing the involved and, so I am told, interesting structure of flower cells, until he came to me. I would just be standing there. "I can't see anything," I would say. He would begin patiently enough, explaining how anybody can see through a microscope, but he would always end up in a fury, claiming that I could *too* see through a microscope but just pretended that I couldn't. "It takes away from the beauty of the flowers anyway," I used to tell him. "We are not concerned with beauty in this course," he would say. "We are con-

[35] From "University Days," *My Life and Hard Times*, pp. 110-119. Copyright, 1933, by James Thurber. Published originally in *The New Yorker* and reprinted here by permission of the author and Harper & Brothers.

cerned solely with what I may call the *mechanics* of flars." "Well,"
I'd say, "I can't see anything." "Try just once again," he'd say, and
I would put my eye to the microscope and see nothing at all, except
now and then a nebulous milky substance—a phenomenon of maladjustment. You were supposed to see a vivid, restless clockwork of
sharply defined plant cells. "I see what looks like a lot of milk," I
would tell him. This, he claimed, was the result of my not having
adjusted the microscope properly, so he would readjust it for me, or
rather, for himself. And I would look again and see milk.

I finally took a deferred pass, as they called it, and waited a year
and tried again. (You had to pass one of the biological sciences or
you couldn't graduate.) The professor had come back from vacation
as brown as a berry, bright-eyed, and eager to explain cell-structure
again to his classes. "Well," he said to me, cheerily, when we met in
the first laboratory hour of the semester, "we're going to see cells
this time, aren't we?" "Yes, sir," I said. Students to right of me and
to left of me and in front of me were seeing cells; what's more, they
were quietly drawing pictures of them in their notebooks. Of course,
I didn't see anything.

"We'll try it," the professor said to me, grimly, "with every adjustment of the microscope known to man. As God is my witness, I'll
arrange this glass so that you see cells through it or I'll give up teaching. In twenty-two years of botany, I—" He cut off abruptly for he
was beginning to quiver all over, like Lionel Barrymore, and he genuinely wished to hold onto his temper; his scenes with me had taken
a great deal out of him.

So we tried with every adjustment of the microscope known to
man. With only one of them did I see anything but blackness or the
familiar lacteal opacity, and that time I saw, to my pleasure and
amazement, a variegated constellation of flecks, specks, and dots.
These I hastily drew. The instructor, noting my activity, came back
from an adjoining desk, a smile on his lips and his eyebrows high in
hope. He looked at my cell drawing. "What's that?" he demanded,
with a hint of a squeal in his voice. "That's what I saw," I said. "You
didn't, you didn't, you *didn't!*" he screamed, losing control of his
temper instantly, and he bent over and squinted into the microscope.
His head snapped up. "That's your eye!" he shouted. "You've fixed
the lens so that it reflects! You've drawn your eye!"

Another course that I didn't like, but somehow managed to pass,
was economics. I went to that class straight from botany class, which
didn't help me in understanding either subject. I used to get them
mixed up. But not as mixed up as another student in my economics
class who came there direct from a physics laboratory. He was a
tackle on the football team, named Bolenciecwcz. At that time Ohio
State University had one of the best football teams in the country,
and Bolenciecwcz was one of its outstanding stars. In order to be
eligible to play it was necessary for him to keep up in his studies, a
very difficult matter, for while he was not dumber than an ox he was

not any smarter. Most of his professors were lenient and helped him along. None gave him more hints, in answering questions, or asked him simpler ones than the economics professor, a thin, timid man named Bassum. One day when we were on the subject of transportation and distribution, it came Bolenciecwcz's turn to answer a question. "Name one means of transportation," the professor said to him. No light came into the big tackle's eyes. "Just any means of transportation," said the professor. Bolenciecwcz sat staring at him. "That is," pursued the professor, "any medium, agency, or method of going from one place to another." Bolenciecwcz had the look of a man who is being led into a trap. "You may choose among steam, horse-drawn, or electrically propelled vehicles," said the instructor. "I might suggest the one which we commonly take in making long journeys across land." There was a profound silence in which everybody stirred uneasily, including Bolenciecwcz and Mr. Bassum. Mr. Bassum abruptly broke this silence in an amazing manner. "Choo—choo—choo," he said, in a low voice, and turned instantly scarlet. He glanced appealingly around the room. All of us, of course, shared Mr. Bassum's desire that Bolenciecwcz should stay abreast of the class in economics, for the Illinois game, one of the hardest and most important of the season, was only a week off. "Toot, toot, too-toooooot!" some student with a deep voice moaned, and we all looked encouragingly at Bolenciecwcz. Somebody else gave a fine imitation of a locomotive letting off steam. Mr. Bassum himself rounded off the little show. "Ding, dong, ding, dong," he said, hopefully. Bolenciecwcz was staring at the floor now, trying to think, his great brow furrowed, his huge hands rubbing together, his face red.

"How did you come to college this year, Mr. Bolenciecwcz?" asked the professor. "*Chuffa, chuffa, chuffa chuffa.*"

"M'father sent me," said the football player.

"What on?" asked Bassum.

"I git an 'lowance," said the tackle, in a low, husky voice, obviously embarrassed.

"No, no," said Bassum. "Name a means of transportation. What did you *ride* here on?"

"Train," said Bolenciecwcz.

The Illinois game was won.

JAMES THURBER

BUTTON, BUTTON[36]

The approach of the Easter of 1945 and the releasing of my son from his then school started me wondering what happy surprises lie

[36] From *Nuts in May*, pp. 89-100. Copyright, 1942, 1944, 1945, 1946, 1948, 1949, 1950, by Cornelia Otis Skinner. Reprinted by permission of Dodd, Mead & Company, Inc.

in store for me. His previous vacation, his homecoming was heralded by a letter announcing the tidings that there would arrive from a biological supply company a C.O.D. package containing an embalmed cat; that he was planning to spend his free time dissecting it; that I could count it as part of his Christmas present and, if I had no better place to store it, I might keep it in the family refrigerator. The shock to my sensibilities was somewhat tempered by the solacing thought that perhaps this macabre harbinger might be an indication of his eventually becoming an eminent surgeon. That he might, by the same token, become an eminent mortician didn't occur to me. Neither did it occur to me that once having embarked upon this particular form of holiday pursuit, he'd want to yield to any distractions of a social nature. Hitherto, parties have meant little in his life. However, having now attained the worldly age of fifteen, my son has become the recipient of a flood of invitations to attend certain organized dances that come under the heading of "Junior," which is a polite way of indicating that along with a boy's acceptance must go a parent's check, for these festivities are subscription affairs, the expenses being shouldered by the youthful participants, a worthy manifestation in these troubled times. The invitations arrived while my offspring was away at school, and, under the influence of that manly remoteness, he flatly turned down the proffered frivolity. However, as the holidays approached, learning that some of his pals were going, he changed his mind and grudgingly admitted he might go to two—"just to find out," which sounded significant.

The fact that he'd have to have a dinner jacket for these galas didn't occur to me until I overheard a fellow mother bewailing the fact that she'd been all over town to get her Oswald some tux and there wasn't a pair, or a set (or maybe it was a brace) to be had. This piece of information I found peculiarly upsetting. The idea of my child in evening clothes seemed fantastic to me who still harbors a tendency to dress him in gray shorts and Basque jumpers. Besides, in my day, which I am increasingly made to feel was contemporary with the initial publication of "Little Women," boys attended our young fry dances in nothing more formal than white flannels and navy blazers in summer, and, in winter, dark blue suits and stiff collars . . . the last item under protest. But that was provincial suburbia then and this was Manhattan New York now, and, as my family so often and endearingly point out, I just don't know. It all struck me as very foolish and shockingly extravagant. My son at that period was growing with a nonstop rapidity akin to the growth of Alice after she consumed the "Eat Me" cake. The expenditure entailed in the purchase of a suit he would wear only twice and then completely outbourgeon went violently against the grain which in me is a cautious blend of Missouri and Vermont. A hand-me-down, I determined, was what he'd wear and like it. The problem was to find a hander-downer. I called a number of acquaintances with older sons and some whose boys were still in service. They each gave the same discouraging response. They were sorry but Junior's dinner clothes had already been handed down to the little Whooziz youth. To the horrified amazement of my more fastidious friends, I resorted to a few of those rental houses which specialize in chauffeurs' and butlers' uniforms and tried to hire a suit. In one I might have procured a full dress white-tie-and-tail arrangement and in another I hesitated over a waiter's outfit, but all dinner clothes had been previously bespoken. As the proprietor of one of the establishments explained, "All my regular customers are having weddings this season." Stifling my scruples of frugality, I set out to buy a suit, a search that dragged me through all the leading emporiums of the city. Finally, after several days, I found one in an emporium that wasn't especially leading and my resentment of this enforced expenditure was somewhat mitigated by the fact that the garments were reduced in price, the jacket having a flaw at the elbow, a locale in which every jacket springs a flaw ten minutes after my boy has put it on anyway. Also, being fortunate in the lack of his presence, which would otherwise have shamed me into getting a size that fitted, I was able to make off with one I imagine may come in handy when he's a man of fifty. The purchase of the tie, suspenders and collar was comparatively easy, but the difficulty in locating a dress shirt in those days appeared to be as hopeless a quest as that of tracking down a dozen nylons. The only things to be found were soft ones and I was about to write Lucius Beebe, requesting him to make a statement that this season the evening attire of well-dressed youth will be a combination of tuxedo and colored sports shirt, when my husband's secretary, one of those treasures who in dire emergency "knows someone downtown," was able to obtain a boiled one through some mysterious friend who works for a stockbroker. How she wangled it I never inquired. Had it been handed me warm from the freshly slain body of the stockbroker, I would have accepted it thankfully. My son was outfitted for his first formal party and that was all I cared about.

The lad arrived from school and so, eventually, did the evening of the dance. It was scheduled to begin promptly at eight. There was a slight error in the matter of starting him dressing, owing to the fact that in the afternoon we had gone to see "The Lost Weekend," which terrifying and moral warning had so unnerved me, I had had to rush from the theatre to the house of some friends for a double Martini just to reassure myself of my sterling lack of dependence on stimulants, while my child eyed me speculatively over a Pepsi-Cola. This respite, while emotionally restorative, delayed us overtime. Pouring rain and the prevailing obsolescence of taxis forced us into an elbow-gouged journey home on the B.M.T. and we staggered in hot and gasping and ready to blame each other for things. My offspring raced upstairs for a tub and I followed in his wake. I hurried to his room and started getting out his party paraphernalia, still wearing my hat. I had forgotten about the assortment of complicated details essential to the bright evening plumage of the male. I seldom if ever have to handle these tortuosities, as my husband is blessedly the type that likes to conduct his own clothing arrangements. Reflecting in somewhat bitter retrospect on my ensuing struggles, I realized he might have been of considerable help on this occasion. But, possibly sensing trouble, he had left town for a short business trip. Perhaps it was just as well. Otherwise we would never have felt so free to plunder his bureau drawers.

My son emerged from his bath bright and dripping water on a newly cleaned gray rug, brandishing my pet comb which he had clogged with vaseline for his cowlick. He removed a monogrammed linen guest towel which, for reasons known not even to himself, he had twisted into a loin cloth and announced he was ready to start. The preliminary preparations were simple, his underthings being reduced at that time to the singular in the way of a pair of shorts long since stripped of buttons whose properties for the maintenance of modesty depended upon a complicated elaboration of a bit of tape and a tie clip. When I suggested he might substitute a pair of his father's, he said emphatically no, he was used to these and anyway, since they didn't show, what was the diff. The trousers, although somewhat roomy, went on easily enough and even I know how to fasten and adjust suspenders. The sock situation was the first to offer difficulties, the collection the boy brought back from school being made up of unmated woolen sundries, lurid plaids for the most part, all marked with the name tapes of unknowns. However, he solved the problem by taking the last silk pair belonging to his father, whose feet are a good two sizes smaller, casually snipping off the toes and wearing them like mitts. Garters we ignored. I am assured that to expect the modern youth to wear garters is the equivalent of presuming a Junior Miss will appear in victorian pantalettes. Socks, I am peremptorily informed, are worn in casual folds cascading down over the shoe top with a glimpse of skin showing provocatively below the trouser bottom, and mothers just have to resign themselves to the fashion with the consolingly cultural thought that Charles the First wore his hose in somewhat the same way.

It was over the donning of the shirt that feelings on both sides started to soar. Each of us had a divergent theory as to how it went on and neither of us really knew. Discord first jangled over the question of collar buttons. Having heretofore worn only soft shirts and pullovers, my son possesses no collar buttons of his own and, in my homespun way, I was all for having him wear two modest wooden numbers that had come home in the laundry, a suggestion he took as a gross indignity. I pointed out the fact that since, like the underdrawers they didn't show, what, to use his very words, was the diff? He cast upon me the look of an offended Hapsburg prince (he can do that when his hair is faultlessly slick) and said no, nothing would do but his father's gold collar buttons. His father's gold collar buttons are kept in his top bureau drawer, not in the crest-engraved case that his son's tone implied, but in a tin Louis Sherry box along with an old watch, a nail clipper, a number of stray buttons he hopes some day I'll sew onto whatever they came off of. I don't really believe I also saw some jacks and a marble, but it's an assortment which gives that impression. The studs, on the other hand, enjoy a position of dignity in a jeweler's box that won't stay closed but is held together by a twisted Boston garter. This was pounced upon by my young Brummel who announced that he guessed he'd wear the pearl dress set. I announced that I guessed he wouldn't, to which he asked why not and I answered because he'd lose them, and he inquired what made me think so; I retaliated by stating that he always lost other people's things and he asked what for instance, and I countered, well, my tennis racquet, and he said that was different as he wasn't wearing my tennis racquet. I put a stop to this spirited verbal tournament by saying bluntly that he'd wear his father's plain gold studs and like it. I was very firm. So he wore his grandfather's black onyx ones and I had to like it.

I was all for getting these somewhat idiotic gewgaws imbedded in their appointed positions before putting on the shirt, then slipping it down over the head in the manner of a turtleneck sweater. But my child said no, he would get into the shirt and I would then "stab the gadgets *on* him," which smacked somehow of primitive ceremony. He slipped on the shirt. Starting ill-advisedly enough with the neckband, I managed, with a good deal of panting, to drill the collar buttons through the areas in that solid wall of starch and goods intended to simulate apertures and on into my thumb, where they left a sizable dent and black mark. My satisfaction over this accomplishment was short-lived for it turned out I'd put the short-stemmed button where the long-stemmed one belonged and vice versa and it had to be done all over again, which made for a flurry of rancor on both sides. The second time, however, was easier, as I had wedged open the holes with a nail file and enlarged them sufficiently to permit the collar buttons not only to go on in but, at the least encouragement, to continue on out. The attachment of the collar itself we left until later. Impaling the studs in that unyielding white board jokingly known as a "bosom" offered fresh hazards. To gouge them into the front was all very well but how, I complained, to adjust that nasty little rod that has to be pulled out and released on the nether side unless you crawled under the shirt in the manner of a photographer under a black cloth. My son, by way of response, merely informed me I was dumb and while his statement contained the elements of truth, it seemed poor co-operation at the moment. I countered by saying that if it was dumbness he was looking for, he'd find it in the genus of men . . . no woman would put up with such asinine accessories; which protestations he topped by asking why, if accessories were so asinine, was I still wearing my hat. I silenced this second clash of arms by bellowing at him to hold still. By dint of tucking the end of the shirt tail under my chin and reaching up with one hand between the respective bosoms of shirt and boy, I was able to implant the studs. They showed up very nicely on the gleaming white front. So did a few impressions of my thumb.

The collar was, according to masculine standards of elegance, the exact size for the neckband, which meant it was too small for it. The back eyelet and one of the front ones connected up with a minimum of struggle, but to pull around the stiffly flighty end and impale it on a wobbly button that had no firmer backing than the boy's rapidly rising larynx, required more than our combined strength. I sought help from our young cook who is the Sandow of the family and upon whom we call in all tight-lid emergencies. By means of her making a fold in the band, which was about like making a fold in a length of weather stripping, then my holding onto it with the power born of desperation while my son backed the button with his finger, the cook, pulling on the collar as if it were a stubborn saddle girth, managed to get it fastened. It was unfortunate that we'd forgotten to place the tie in it, an oversight which drove my son into a frenzied tirade in which he demanded the instant firing of his father's secretary, which hardly seemed an immediate solution. By again resorting to the nail file, I succeeded, without undoing the collar, to wedge in the tie, and the secretary's job no longer hung in the balance.

My fifteen-year-old started in on the fixing of the tie himself but gave it over, along with his neck, to me. I am not blessed with the gift of tie tying. It impresses me as one of those smugly superfluous accomplishments like flower arranging or the ability to do up trick Christmas packages. Facing him squarely, I struggled for a time, only to effect first a bow with one side a great deal larger than the other, then a bow that looked quite lovely for a brief moment but collapsed quickly into two dangling ends. My son, whose ire had increased considerably, again informed me I was dumb. I reminded him that he was in no position to cast the first, or even the second, stone, and, with injured dignity, summoned the maid and asked if she could tie a bow tie. She, also facing him, tied it, but the bow came out perpendicular, and jointly we yelled for the cook, who said she didn't know but she'd do her best. The cook's best was on a par with the maid's best. My son, while he dearly loves them both, told them they too were dumb, a bit of gratuitous information I nervously laughed off, explaining that he would have his little joke. It is doubtful if either of them got it. This, I decided, was a crisis that called for a man, and I rang for Patrick, the elevator man. Patrick was sympathetic. He had, it seemed, worn the same tie for years, but the fact that it was made of leather and went on by means of an elastic around his neck did not make for his skill in tying a silk one. I wondered how he'd feel if I suggested borrowing his for the evening, but dismissed the idea at the thought of how my son would feel. The suggestions Patrick had to offer were well intentioned but quite useless. I thanked him and sent him back to his elevator before my son had a chance of including him in his category of the dumb. By now the wrath of that young man had assumed Homeric dimensions and the greater portion of it was aimed at me. I couldn't make out what I'd done, but decided that whatever it was I'd better do something still further. Taking my courage and the phone in hand, I rang up a kindly gentleman who lives in the next door building and asked how much he'd mind tying my boy's tie. He didn't state the amount he minded but told me pleasantly to bring the boy and the tie on over. We journeyed across the way in silence, my son with his tie-ends dangling, looking very baleful indeed. The gentleman received us with charming cordiality. He led my son up to the mirror, stood directly behind him, reached both hands around his neck and, with the quiet technique of an expert, tied an elegant bow. We thanked him profusely . . . at least I did, and my man-about-town hastened off belatedly to his soiree. I returned home to supper on a tray and "Modern Man Is Obsolete." Some fortuitous inner prompting had made me feel it was wisest not to inquire when my son thought he'd be home. He returned a little before midnight and, with a tact born of instinct, I carefully disguised my relief at seeing him home safe and, to all intents and purposes, sound. In reply to my hesitant inquiry as to what the party had been like, he summed up the festivities with a descriptive "It was O.K." He did, however, pause on his way up to bed long enough to lean over my chair, give me a sound smack and say "Gee, Mom, thanks a lot."

Cornelia Otis Skinner

WE HAVE WITH US TONIGHT[37]

To some chairmen, perhaps quite naturally since talking is their business, lecturers do not seem like human beings, filled with human fears and standing in need of last-minute concentration. The war of nerves is supposed to hold no terrors for them. They are talking machines; sound tracks with bodies; the kind of offspring a Victrola might have if wedded to a windmill. Such an attitude, even though it puts you in the robot class, is flattering when, because of it, you suddenly find yourself miscast as a knight-errant.

In the automobile on the way to the auditorium you can tell when you will have to hoist your faded plume and rub the dust off your broken armor.

"Now, Belle, it's going to be all right," says the husband of the lady who is to present you and who has suddenly begun to keen in the front seat like a chorus of unhappy fisherwomen in an Irish play. "I

[37] From *Accustomed As I Am*, pp. 30-34. Copyright, 1942, by W. W. Norton & Company, Inc. Reprinted by permission of the publishers.

know you will be fine. Won't Belle be fine, Mr. Brown?" Forgetting what you were trying to remember about your own speech, you bow to the inevitable. "Of course, she will. Don't worry. It's easy."

"But I can't! I won't go on." There is a pause. Then a sudden rally. "You see, I'm dreadfully scared, Mr. Brown, because this is the first time I have had to do this kind of thing. I wish I'd never gotten into it! I know it's silly, but I'm petrified. Henry, I'm *petrified!* I'm sure I'll disgrace you. I'll have to read it, even though I promised Grace this afternoon that I wouldn't. I tell you I'm PETRIFIED! I was scared at luncheon—but NOW! Oh, Henry! Henry, did you bring the aromatics?"

By this time the auditorium has been reached, and you have begun to feel as nervous about Belle as Belle does and as Henry does. Henry has disappeared, mopping his brow. "Good luck, girlie," he has said in parting. "Chin up! You couldn't be worse than Evelyn was." With that, Henry has gone to take his place out front. Belle has meanwhile been drawn to the mirror above the dressing table like an astronomer to the Milky Way. The drone of the audience through the curtains and the open door might appeal to an apiarist, but it unnerves Belle.

"My tummy! My tummy!" she sighs, with an expression usually reserved for the English Channel. "It's full of butterflies!"

Your one hope is that moths won't emerge.

"Now calm yourself, Mrs. Tremens," you say, patting her on the back as if she were a baby about to bring up a bubble, and trusting her husband will understand if he returns. "It'll soon be over. All things come to an end."

"No! No! No! It won't," she insists, opening her evening bag to spread a neatly written manuscript before her on the dressing table. "I knew it! I knew it! I can't remember a word of it, and I had it all by heart."

"May I help you?" you ask, putting your own notes in your suitcase and locking it. Suddenly an intern's calm descends upon you.

"Oh, I know it's silly, but would you?" Belle passes her manuscript to you in a hand quaking with palsy.

"Now, then, let's try it."

" 'Ladies and gentlemen,' " begins Belle, clearing her throat like a motorboat having a hard time getting started, and at last speaking in an astral voice, " 'Ladies and gentlemen—!' There! I told you. I haven't the vaguest idea what comes next."

" 'Ladies and gentlemen,' " you repeat, " 'the—' "

"No! No! Don't tell me," she insists. " 'The—the—' Now let's see. How could it go on from there?"

" 'Ladies and gentlemen,' " you say firmly, reading her script to her, " 'the Broadway theatre is a long way from here, but we are hoping it will be nearer to us to-night. It gives me great pleasure to introduce—' "

By now it is ten minutes after the announced starting time.

"Don't you think we really ought to get going?" you ask. "Why don't you just read it? No one will know."

"Never! Never!" says Belle. "I promised Grace I wouldn't. And anyway she said she'd kill me if I did."

Someone knocks timidly on the door. It is Henry. "Dear," says he, puffing from the dash up the aisle of the auditorium, the plunge down the stairs by the box office, the long run through the basement corridor, and the climb up the truncated steps leading to the stage, "Grace thinks you ought to begin. They're getting restless."

So out you go, forgetting Henry as he sits down to mop his face, and following Belle onto the stage to those chairs. For what seems an eternity, Belle remains seated, doing her best to resemble Queen Mary at the Durbar. You try to whisper a few nothings to her, to indicate how much at home you both are. But, in addition to palsy, Belle now seems to have developed a sudden and acute attack of deafness. After five repulses, which have entirely shaken your confidence and made the audience wonder what you could possibly have done to insult Mrs. Tremens in the wings, Belle at last rises. Swaying somewhat unsteadily, she advances to the lectern to grab hold of it as if it were a mast and she a sailor imperiled in a Conrad typhoon. Clutched in her hand you can see the manuscript of her introduction. In a moment or two she spreads this out before her and reaches in her handbag with magnificent defiance for her tortoise-shell glasses.

A new peace—a calm decidedly outward—has descended upon her. Only to the speaker is Belle's fear now evident. He, after all, can see what the audience cannot. Though Belle's voice is firm when she starts off with "Ladies and gentlemen," and her hands are propped so that they cannot shake, Belle's back contrives to tremble beneath her tight satin skirt like Jello in the wind.

"Ladies and gentlemen," she begins, bowing right and left at the sheet of paper before her as if the whole audience were sitting on it. Thereafter she never lifts her eyes from her written speech until, with a very pained look, she has expressed the pleasure it has given her to introduce you. Whereupon, turning her head to the side of the stage where you aren't, she points to an empty chair, realizes her error, looks around in tragic confusion, smiles when she has at last spotted you, and rushes back to her seat to reread the manuscript, fearful lest she may have omitted part of it. Just as you step forward, murmuring, "You were fine; Henry will be very proud of you," Henry comes walking down the aisle to retake his place, still mopping his head, and having missed the big moment, when comparisons with Evelyn were in order.

JOHN MASON BROWN

HAY FEVER IN ENGLAND[38]

July 8th

I am face to face with the possibility that I have hay fever. My childhood was spent in all sorts of entangling alliances with ragweed and goldenrod, and if I sneezed, it kept the family in table talk for two weeks. But ever since the long walks we took in Stratford, I have suffered a sea change. My eyes itch in long crescendos, my nose tickles to madness, and my handkerchiefs are developing fins. Henry suggests a doctor, but I have a theory that germs and infirmities like to play the grandstand, and that if one can manage to ignore them, they will go sheepishly away. Besides, should it really be hay fever, there is very little a doctor can do at this late stage. What I need is a harbor master. Oh, well. I pin my hopes to its subsiding when I leave the gardens of Cambridge and get to the relative barrenness of London.

July 21st

I went to the doctor yesterday, to see about my hay fever, mechanically and without much hope of relief, an attitude which the worthy practitioner did little to change. His office, up two flights of stairs in a decayed region near Golden Square, is full of large, broody furnishings which make the room navigable only by persons of a very light draft. The doctor himself is gaunt as a totem pole. He wore an antiquated black suit, the lapels of which had been dragged together in a reluctant rendezvous just over his collarbone. When I rehearsed my ailment, he listened with an attention which seemed too mournful and elaborate for a trifling tale of catarrh. I felt ashamed not to have a life-size, three-dimensional illness to offer him, something with a fair prospect of taking me off. After I had finished my apologetic plaint, he looked sadly up my nose and said in a stifled voice that there was nothing to be done for hay fever, if it were hay fever, but that I might try smelling salts.

"Well," I reflected, as I went down the stairs, "at least he didn't want to bleed me," so I worked my way out into Piccadilly Circus, where I found a drug store. I had had no experience of smelling salts, and coming from the shop into the street again, I uncorked the bottle, held it firmly under my nose, and drew a breath so deep as almost to suck in several little boys who were standing nearby. I do not know how I got home. The world was under water. A taxi wavered through the deeps and I have an impression I took it. When I could look about me once more, I saw that I had come home.

But the most outlandish part of the whole fantastic medication was that it wrought a cure. I suddenly noticed, while retailing the catastrophe to Henry, that fresh air was going boldly in and out of my nostrils as if it had the freedom of the city. Gingerly, with millimetric caution, I returned to the salts bottle. By last night, I was so perceptibly less rheumy that I think if I had sent out a dove, it would have come back with an olive leaf in its mouth, and this morning, except for an occasional reminiscent sniff, I was cured.

MARGARET HALSEY

HUNGAH[39]

When my sister and I were ten and eleven, our six aunts on the lace-curtain-Irish, or Farrel, side of the family got up a little fund to make their nieces cultured.

In their dreams, they could see, these amiable ladies who loved us so dearly, Eileen at the piano bringing tears to the eyes of her relatives with a splendid performance of "Narcissus," the selection where you cross your hands on the keyboard. They could see me, too, in their affectionate musings, spreading a fluffy organdie skirt for a polite curtsy to a parlor of admiring Farrels and Murphys and Flannigans, and then launching into a moving recitation of "Trees."

After all, our second cousins, the Murphy children, aged only eleven and twelve, could already recite "Trees" and play "The Rose of No Man's Land," not to speak of "Humoresque," on the piano. If the Murphys could be cultured, so, my aunts said grimly, could the McKenneys. If they had secret misgivings, they never said so. They started off the big culture program by getting Eileen a music teacher, a nervous, angular lady who wore her eyeglasses on a black ribbon and sniffled.

"One," she used to say, "two, three," and then a long sniffle, "four. One, two," then another short ladylike sniffle, "three, four."

The sniffles and the black ribbon for the eyeglasses fascinated my sister. She used to keep time to the sniffles instead of the counting, and as a result her scales went from bad to worse. Eventually, though, she learned to read simple sheet music. She also learned a bass which consisted mostly of fearful thumping and a rolling sound like kettle-drums, all in the lowest octave of the keyboard. With this equipment, she was able to play "Chloe," a popular song of the early nineteen-twenties. She was never able to play anything except "Chloe," but she certainly could play that.

She used to stalk to the piano and seat herself firmly, with quite a thump, at the bench. Then, swaying largely from the waist, she picked up the melody, not without some difficulty. Finally, when the preliminaries were over, she burst into song, accompanying herself as she went along.

"Thr—ooo the bu-la-ck of night," Eileen used to intone a deep bass growl, "I got-tuh go wheah yew are."

The climax of the song, where the melody goes up, always used to baffle my poor sister, who, like myself, is absolutely tone-deaf and has never been able to carry a tune, even the simplest one, in her whole life. She solved the difficulty by simply pounding so hard in the bass that she drowned herself out. Her voice emerged triumphantly just at the end: "I got-tuh go wheah yew are."

While Eileen was learning to play a bayou chant, I, too, was busy with culture. I was taking what my aunts thought were elocution lessons. These thoughtful ladies, after a solemn family conclave, had decided I should study public speaking because I stuttered over the telephone. I still do. It is very humiliating.

How my conservative, respectable aunts fell afoul of Madame DuLak and her Studio of the Voice I cannot imagine. Certainly she was not the teacher they thought she was. They hoped that I would learn how to recite "Trees." Madame DuLak told me the first time I met her that Joyce Kilmer "stank." That was the word she used. I was eleven years old, and I certainly was surprised to hear about Joyce Kilmer.

Madame DuLak had studied in Paris. She said so often. She had picked up a lot of fancy notions in gay old Paris, I gathered, not only about Joyce Kilmer but also about "recitations" and "elocution lessons."

"We are going," Madame DuLak intoned, in a rich, deep voice full of culture, that first morning our little class of six assembled, "to undertake the study of a litt-tul play which I rather" (she said "rawther," of course) "like. I shall assign and read the parts this morning. By next week you will have memorized your lines, and then we shall settle down for a winter's work."

I memorized my lines easily. My part consisted of the word "hunger." But do not imagine that I was a mere walk-on in this little play of Madame DuLak's. On the contrary, I was one of the leading characters. I was, in spite of my rotund figure, a hungry old beggar. I sat on the steps of what was supposed to be a cathedral. From the time the curtain went up until at last it went down, I sat on those steps, chanting the word "hunger" more or less at one-minute intervals. Sometimes I said it very loudly, drowning out the rest of the cast, and sometimes I was supposed to whisper it very softly, as background. It was a Greek-chorus idea.

The play was exceedingly symbolical. I was not supposed to be physically hungry, which was a good thing, considering my appearance; I was just supposed to be spiritually hungry. Madame DuLak used to urge me to put this difference into the reading of my lines, or, rather, line. I was a big girl for my eleven years, and I was often hungry in the good old-fashioned sense of wanting another piece of chocolate cake or second helping of chocolate pie. So when Madame

DuLak would urge me on Saturday mornings to "Put some feeling into your part, Ruth," I would concentrate hard on something chocolate and howl, "Hun-gah!" with a fine frenzied note in my voice. Madame DuLak thought I was pretty good, on the whole. Of course sometimes I forgot and said, "Hunger," and then Madame DuLak used to denounce me as a boor.

The rest of the pupils were also symbolical. The only other girl in the class, Betty Chippendale, was Vice. I wanted to be Vice myself; I got pretty tired of being a dirty old beggar yelling, "Hun-gah!" all the time. Vice was a nice, rich part. There weren't any lines in the part, to be sure, not even a one-word chant like my "Hun-gah," but Vice got to stroll up and down the stage, wiggling her hips, brushing against other characters with lewd gestures, and such like. Of course Betty was only thirteen years old, and although she wanted to be an actress when she grew up, her life had been rather restricted so far. So she had some difficulty in making her character study of Vice symbolical enough to suit Madame DuLak.

"No, no, Betty," Madame DuLak would say in her cultured voice, "you represent the dregs of humanity, you are the symbol of lust and ugliness. You must make your audience feel that as you move across the stage, you must put that into every gesture of your little finger."

"Yes, Ma'am," Betty would say. She took her work very seriously, and never got tired of walking up and down and being the symbol of lust and ugliness.

The boys were, variously, Greed and Power and Truth and Loving Kindness. Since this was a pretty modern morality play, Loving Kindness and Truth got licked to a frazzle at the curtain. Greed and Power beat them up and dragged them off bodily every Saturday morning. Vice tagged along to get in on the kill, and that left me still sitting on the cathedral steps. I had the last lines. "Hun-gah!" I bellowed. "Hun-gah! Hun-gah!" Curtain.

I think now that Madame DuLak must have written that remarkable play herself. Of course it had certain resemblances to other dramas of its genre, but that smashing finish—that was pure DuLak.

After the first three weeks, Madame DuLak decided we must have costumes for our rehearsals. The costumes, she said, would help us get into the feeling of our roles. My costume was wonderful. I made it myself, and it certainly was realistic. I wore an old, ragged, burlap sack with holes cut out for the arms. My legs were bare, and I had a pair of Father's old bedroom slippers tied on my feet with rope. This was only the beginning, however. I took off my hair ribbon, unbraided my pigtails, and systematically, with a comb, snarled and matted my long hair. Then I covered my face, arms, and legs with artistic smatterings of coal dust. The first time Madame DuLak saw me emerge from my dressing room in her little studio, she gave me the highest praise a make-up artist can get.

"Awk!" she said, blasted out of her usual cultured calm.

With the first soft breezes of spring, with the first robin, my aunts began to question me rather sharply about my elocution lessons. I explained as well as I could about the play, but I could see that they rejected my story as the simple fantasy of an imaginative child. They urged me to recite my part for them, but some inner instinct warned me off.

Finally, though, one of the Farrel family reunions came along. The Farrels had family reunions at the drop of a hat, and the Murphys, the Flannigans, the McKenneys, Aunt Susan Maloney with her brood, and assorted other in-laws turned up, ate prodigiously, and argued about politics. Our aunts felt that it was practically certain that the Murphy girls would play "The Rose of No Man's Land" and recite "Trees."

"This time," Aunt Molly said, with a dangerous glitter in her eye, "we'll show them that the Murphy girls aren't the only ones in the family who take lessons."

Eileen and I turned up at the family reunion bearing our stage properties. I brought my costume in a box, with a neat bag of coal dust, and Eileen brought the sheet music of "Chloe." We weren't nervous in the least. After dinner we retired upstairs to prepare for what we felt would be our triumph. Eileen gargled, and I repeated "Hun-gah, hun-gah" several times, to get in voice.

Downstairs we could hear Margaret Murphy playing "The Rose of No Man's Land," and very badly, too. She had to start over again several times. The applause, however, was generous.

When Cousin Rita Murphy began to recite "Trees," Uncle Wally went out to the kitchen, and we heard him say, "There is a limit to everything, Katie. Where do they keep the whiskey bottle around here?" Katie was the cook. We bridled. Uncle Wally would never walk out on our performances, we felt sure.

He didn't. Nobody did. They were frozen to their seats. We got, in fact, the most flattering kind of attention. Even Uncle Wally's jaws fell ajar.

Eileen played and sang first. Just as the final notes of her bass monotone chant, "I got-tuh go wheah yew are," and the final rumble of the piano died away, I burst dramatically through the door, shouting "Hun-gah! Hun-gah!" and shaking my matted and snarled locks at my assembled relatives. My grandmother Farrel, who always takes everything seriously, let out a piercing scream.

Ignoring the awed comments of the rest of the audience, I paced slowly over to the fireplace. "This," I said in stately tones, while my aunts stared at my coal-dust-streaked face, "is a cathedral. I am sitting on the cathedral steps." I sat down. There was a long pause. Then I put up my arms to the heavens.

"Hun-gah!" I shrieked. Grandma jumped and said audibly, "Mercy!"

I let another impressive silence fall. The Murphys, mother and father and the two accomplished child Murphys, breathed heavily. Suddenly I plopped down on the floor, my face turned to the horrified audience.

"Hun-gah," I barely breathed. Eileen struck a soft chord in the bass.

"God!" Uncle Wally said. In the silence, everybody heard him, but they were too engrossed in my performance to be shocked. I rolled over, one limp hand trailing on the carpet.

"Hun-gah!" I whined. I lay on the floor several seconds, letting it sink in. Then I began to drag myself to my feet. My knee joints always cracked, and in the silence you could hear them clearly all over the room. Nobody said anything. Finally I was all the way up, and panting. I was supposed to pant. I was supposed to have some kind of a terrible disease, like leprosy. I lowered my head, inch by inch. In those days I had a double chin, and I couldn't get my head down very far, unfortunately. I sighed, heavily.

Then in a flat, sad voice I said, "Hun-gah."

Eileen struck a minor chord. I bowed. I stalked toward the door. Eileen rose gravely and followed me. At the door we bowed together.

"Well, for God's sake!" my Uncle Wally said, quite loudly. We waited for the burst of applause, but our relatives sat glued to their seats, staring at us. Finally Aunt Molly pulled herself together and started to clap. Everybody else clapped too, dutifully, and we retired with the sweet sound of applause in our ears.

There never was another family reunion like that one. We knew perfectly well we had electrified our dear relatives. As Eileen put it, "It was about time somebody stuck a pin in them." Anyway, Uncle Wally told us afterward that he liked us better than "Trees." He thought that we had done it on purpose, and maybe, as I look back on it, we did. Our approach to life was somewhat confused at ten and eleven.

After that, the Murphy girls had the field of culture, in our family, to themselves. It never did them any good, either.

RUTH McKENNEY

CHAPTER 11

Choral Interpretation

When you listened to the recording of *John Brown's Body*, you heard a full range of styles of interpretation. The interpretative procedures involved the "personalized" presentation of the poem. At times, these interpretations were formed into a unit by background music, as in the ballroom scene. In other instances, individual interpretations were integrated by a choir, sometimes singing and sometimes chanting. This form of interpretation involves the blending together of a number of voices and is called choral reading.

Choral interpretation is considered by some to be an echo—a very distant echo—of the choral rendition of passages in early Greek plays. These Greek choruses, accompanied by highly stylized movements, created mass effects; but, unlike modern choral reading, they were used primarily to explain some motive to the audience or to inform it of some action that had occurred, was occurring, or would occur. Today, choral reading serves chiefly to provide a synchronized contrast to the individual interpretations.

GROUP RESPONSES

Group activities or mass responses have always been a part of ceremonial rituals. The basis of primitive rituals was group pantomime, which gradually became rhythmical through mass activity. Because of the emotional excitement of the tribe in its supplications, cries became a part of the group movement, probably giving the participants added enjoyment and satisfaction.

Rhythm and repetition, which are basic in any ritual, whether for war, victory, or religion, probably gave impetus to increased fervor. One can imagine how an ancient ceremonial might start quietly with only pantomimic expression and, gradually, with increased activity and emotional cries, rise to a rhythmical climax. Chants and speech in unison no doubt evolved from these primitive ceremonials, which included supplications to the deity, incitements to revenge and war, lamentations for the dead, and celebrations of victory. Many people today get their religious experiences and inspiration from similar mass responses. The psychological effects of this practice have long been recognized. The singing of a hymn or the offering of a prayer in unison gives a church audience a united feeling. Many churches employ the chant, often effectively and impressively, to express meaning through beauty of distinct utterance. An impressive reading of the Bible in chorus is not too difficult, for the literature of the Bible, with its rhythmical structure and the universal appeal of its message, lends itself to such reading.

Group response will arouse the emotions of those participating as well as those listening. The medieval ballads and minstrel poetry were popular because the audience was able to participate in singing or reciting the refrains. In current English folk ballads and American cowboy songs, for example, the refrain still plays an important part in stimulating audience response. Today the enthusiastic and co-ordinated rhythmical cheering at athletic games follows the same pattern of vocalization. The leadership is supplied by some six or eight acrobatic leaders who try to motivate the crowd on the bleachers into synchronized responses. Without this mass cheering at a football game, for instance, there is supposed to be no "spirit," no loyalty to one's team. The same type of response is found in square dancing, in the evangelist's service, and in Indian ceremonials. To participate in any one of these types of group response is to understand how enthusiasm can be created or increased through rhythm and repetition.

In addition to many anthologies of selections for choral reading, there have been some plays which employ the choral response. T. S. Eliot's *Murder in the Cathedral* uses this device impressively; Toller's *Man and the Masses* reaches its climax through powerful choral responses. The radio sketch, "Listen to the People," in Chapter XII has been performed effectively with choral groups interspersed throughout an audience.

SYNCHRONIZATION OF PARTS

Choral interpretation, if it is to be artistic, requires a technique which must be learned. The most difficult technique in group performances is the synchronization of parts, the mass effects being highlighted by some individual performance. No matter how careful the director is, he will never be able to secure from a number of voices, the flexibility, warmth, or intimacy of one voice. The effects will always be mass effects—as in a singing chorus—impressive but never highly personalized; the solo voice will always be the voice that the audience will wait for and most enjoy. The chorus gives the background, the atmosphere, but never a true impression of personality. In choral interpretation, however, it is important to try to secure maximum warmth, feeling, and understanding from a number of voices, instead of some unique arrangement of parts and voices that takes the attention away from the literature and its meaning.

This synchronization of parts can be heard in the recorded interpretation of the following scene from *John Brown's Body.* The contrasting vocal qualities, the differences in key, intensity, slides, steps, and rhythm of both the speaking choir and the singing choir should be listened to. Note how effectively the individual voices blend with the choral group. Listen to the force of the voice portraying John Brown, and notice especially how the increased intensity in the individual voices and the singing of "Glory, Glory, Hallelujah" by the background choir build the scene to a climax.

THAT IS MY SONG[1]

John Brown's body lies a-mouldering in the grave.
He will not come again with foolish pikes

[1] From *John Brown's Body* (New York, Rinehart and Company, Inc., 1927), pp. 58-60. Copyright, 1927, 1928, by Stephen Vincent Benét. Reprinted by permission of the Stephen Vincent Benét estate. The recorded version (Columbia, 5SL-181) varies slightly from the printed text but can easily be followed.

And a pack of desperate boys to shadow the sun.
He has gone back North. The slaves have forgotten his eyes.
John Brown's body lies a-mouldering in the grave.
John Brown's body lies a-mouldering in the grave.

Already the corpse is changed, under the stone,
The strong flesh rotten, the bones dropping away.
Cotton will grow next year, in spite of the skull.
Slaves will be slaves next year, in spite of the bones.
Nothing is changed, John Brown, nothing is changed.

*"There is a song in my bones. There is a song
In my white bones."*

I hear no song. I hear
Only the blunt seeds growing secretly
In the dark entrails of the preparate earth,
The rustle of the cricket under the leaf,
The creaking of the cold wheel of the stars.

*"Bind my white bones together—hollow them
To skeleton pipes of music. When the wind
Blows from the budded Spring, the song will blow."*

I hear no song. I only hear the roar
Of the Spring freshets, and the gushing voice
Of mountain-brooks that overflow their banks,
Swollen with melting ice and crumbled earth.

*"That is my song.
It is made of water and wind. It marches on."*

No, John Brown's body lies a-mouldering,
A-mouldering.

*"My bones have been washed clean
And God blows through them with a hollow sound,
And God has shut his wildfire in my dead heart."*

I hear it now,
Faint, faint as the first droning flies of March,
Faint as the multitudinous, tiny sigh
Of grasses underneath a windy scythe.

"It will grow stronger."

It has grown stronger. It is marching on.
It is a throbbing pulse, a pouring surf,
It is the rainy gong of the Spring sky
Echoing,
John Brown's body,

John Brown's body.
But still it is not fierce. I find it still
More sorrowful than fierce.

"You have not heard it yet. You have not heard
The ghosts that walk in it, the shaking sound."

Strong medicine,
Bitter medicine of the dead,
I drink you now. I hear the unloosed thing,
The anger of the ripe wheat—the ripened earth
Sullenly quaking like a beaten drum
From Kansas to Vermont. I hear the stamp
Of the ghost-feet. I hear the ascending sea.

　　　"Glory, Glory, Hallelujah,
　　　Glory, Glory, Hallelujah,
　　　Glory, Glory, Hallelujah!"

What is this agony of the marching dust?
What are these years ground into hatchet blades?

"Ask the tide why it rises with the moon,
My bones and I have risen like that tide
And an immortal anguish plucks us up
And will not hide us till our song is done."

The phantom drum diminishes—the year
Rolls back. It is only winter still, not spring,
The snow still flings its white on the new grave,
Nothing is changed, John Brown, nothing is changed
John . . . Brown . . .

　　　　　　　　　　　STEPHEN VINCENT BENÉT

VALUES

Group interpretation focuses attention on the control of the voice, which, after all, is a skill to be encouraged. It will aid you in *listening* to voices, your own included. It may develop rhythmical patterns for you which you would never otherwise experience. It may provide a stimulus for understanding literature, may make you realize that there are various ways of giving artistic interpretations of the printed page. You will enjoy group activity. You will have a chance to try your own interpretation on someone else and then listen to it. Your vocal pattern may improve in flexibility through the discipline of following other voices. Choral interpretation then may have a fourfold value:

1. It may be a means of motivation for those who do not usually enjoy poetry.
2. It may be an exercise which will help those who are not too well trained in the nuances of meaning or in rhythmical vocal variety.
3. It may be an artistic endeavor which involves polish and perfect synchronization of a group of voices.
4. It may be an exercise that will give group enjoyment.

TYPES OF CHORAL RESPONSE

Literature used for choral interpretation is arranged according to the various vocal responses from the group. It is effective sometimes to introduce a solo voice to carry some particular lines; or to start with several small vocal groups—each group taking certain lines—and build all the voices up to an ensemble climax; or to produce contrasts by using voices with different pitch levels and different resonant qualities. The four principal responses used in choral interpretation are the refrain, the sequence, the antiphonal, and the response in unison.

Refrain

This type of response is used with poetry containing repetitive passages or refrains. The narrative is usually recited by one person or by a small group of voices, with the refrain given by the entire group. Ballads, nursery rhymes, and narrative poetry offer the best media for this type of response. The following poem, for example, contains lines that are especially suitable for the refrain response.

THE TURTLE AND THE FLAMINGO[2]

A lively young turtle lived down by the banks
Of a dark rolling stream called the Jingo;
And one summer day, as he went out to play,
Fell in love with a charming flamingo—
An enormously genteel flamingo!
An expansively crimson flamingo!
A beautiful, bouncing flamingo!

[2] From *Ballads and Other Verses*, pp. 42-44. Copyright, 1881, by Houghton, Mifflin Company. Reprinted by permission of the publishers.

Spake the turtle, in tones like a delicate wheeze:
"To the water I've oft seen you in go,
And your form has impressed itself deep on my shell,
You perfectly modelled flamingo!
You tremendously A-1 flamingo!
You inexpressible flamingo!

"To be sure, I'm a turtle, and you are a belle,
And my language is not your fine lingo;
But smile on me, tall one, and be my bright flame,
You miraculous, wondrous flamingo!
You blazingly beauteous flamingo!
You turtle-absorbing flamingo!
You inflammably gorgeous flamingo!"

Then the proud bird blushed redder than ever before,
And that was quite *un-nec-es-*SA-*ry,*
And she stood on one leg and looked out of one eye,
The position of things for to vary—
This aquatical, musing flamingo!
This dreamy, uncertain flamingo!
This embarrassing, harassing flamingo!

Then she cried to the quadruped, greatly amazed:
"Why your passion toward *me* do you hurtle?
I'm an ornithological wonder of grace,
And you're an illogical turtle—
A waddling, impossible turtle!
A low-minded, grass-eating turtle!
A highly improbable turtle!"

JAMES THOMAS FIELDS

Sequence

The sequence response is employed in choral interpretation when the lines rise to a climax or are cumulative in response. The lines are spoken by various groups or by solo speakers, with the chorus entering toward the end to build the climax. Johnson's impressive poem "The Creation" offers excellent interplay of solo and group response. Certainly the voice of God must be taken by a voice that is fully resonant and has a low key; the solo speaker must make the most of the inflections possible in such phrases as "That's good!" and "I'm lonely." Various key levels can be introduced by the choral groups. If interpreted carefully, this poem can be presented most effectively.

THE CREATION[3]

(*A Negro Sermon*)

And God stepped out on space,
And He looked around and said,
"I'm lonely—
I'll make me a world."

And as far as the eye of God could see
Darkness covered everything,
Blacker than a hundred midnights
Down in a cypress swamp.

Then God smiled,
And the light broke,
And the darkness rolled up on one side,
And the light stood shining on the other,
And God said, *"That's good!"*

Then God reached out and took the light in His hands,
And God rolled the light around in His hands
Until He made the sun;
And He set that sun a-blazing in the heavens.
And the light that was left from making the sun
God gathered it up in a shining ball
And flung it against the darkness,
Spangling the night with the moon and stars.
Then down between
The darkness and the light
He hurled the world;
And God said, *"That's good!"*

Then God Himself stepped down—
And the sun was on His right hand,
And the moon was on His left;
The stars were clustered about His head,
And the earth was under His feet.
And God walked, and where He trod
His footsteps hollowed the valleys out
And bulged the mountains up.

Then He stopped and looked and saw
That the earth was hot and barren.
So God stepped over to the edge of the world
And He spat out the seven seas;

[3] From *God's Trombones,* p. 17. Copyright, 1927, by The Viking Press, Inc. Reprinted by permission of the publishers.

He batted His eyes, and the lightnings flashed;
He clapped His hands and the thunders rolled;
And the waters above the earth came down,
The cooling waters came down.

Then the green grass sprouted,
And the little red flowers blossomed,
The pine tree pointed his finger to the sky,
And the oak spread out his arms,
The lakes cuddled down in the hollows of the ground,
And the rivers ran down to the seas;
And God smiled again,
And the rainbow appeared,
And curled itself around His shoulder.

Then God raised His arm and He waved His hand
Over the sea and over the land,
And He said, "Bring forth! Bring forth!"
And quicker than God could drop His hand,
Fishes and fowls
And beasts and birds
Swam the rivers and the seas,
Roamed the forests and the woods,
And split the air with their wings.
And God said, *"That's good!"*

Then God walked around,
And God looked around
On all that He had made.
He looked at His sun,
And He looked at His moon,
And He looked at His little stars;
He looked on His world
With all its living things,
And God said, *"I'm lonely still.'*

Then God sat down
On the side of a hill where He could think;
By a deep, wide river He sat down;
With His head in His hands,
God thought and thought,
Till He thought, *"I'll make me a man!"*

Up from the bed of the river
God scooped the clay;
And by the bank of the river
He kneeled Him down;
And there the great God Almighty
Who lit the sun and fixed it in the sky,

Who flung the stars to the most far corner of the night,
Who rounded the earth in the middle of His hand;
This Great God,
Like a mammy bending over her baby,
Kneeled down in the dust
Toiling over a lump of clay
Till He shaped it in His own image;

Then into it He blew the breath of life,
And man became a living soul.
Amen. Amen.

JAMES WELDON JOHNSON

Antiphonal

There are certain selections that almost demand an antiphonal response, where the voices of one group are contrasted with the voices of another group. Choral interpretation of the lines quoted below, for example, depends on contrasting vocal qualities to represent the various states.

from COLLOQUY FOR THE STATES[4]

(There is talk, "tall talk" about the states—"on the east wind";
  "mean talk," says Maine)

It's how we marry, says Maine. We ain't choosers.
We scrabble them up and we mingle them in. We marry the
Irish girls with the shoes with the quick come-after.
We marry the Spaniards with the evening eyes.
We marry the English with the tiptoe faces.
We marry the golden Swedes: the black Italians:
The German girls with the thick knees; the Mexicans
Lean and light in the sun with the jingling and jangling:
The Chilenas for luck: the Jews for remembrance: the Scots girls
Tall as a tall man—silver as salmon;
The French with the skillful fingers: the long loves.
I gather we marry too many, says Maine: too various.
I gather we're bad blood: we're mixed people.

That what they say? says Texas.
        That's what they're saying.
What's in their soup, says Arkansas: what they been eating?

[4] From *Collected Poems: 1917-1952*, pp. 344-345. Copyright, 1952, by Houghton, Mifflin Company. Reprinted by permission of the publishers.

What's in their hair? says Maryland.
              Aren't they men?
Can't they make it with strangers? says Alabama.

Are they shy? says Missouri.
        Or what? says Montana.
                 I gather they're
Bred pure, says Maine: they're superior people.
                                    ARCHIBALD MacLEISH

Unison

To use the voices of the whole group, at the same time and at the same pitch, is sometimes the best way to interpret certain types of literature. "Prelude to Invasion" should be interpreted in unison by a group of male voices.

PRELUDE TO INVASION[5]
From the Fathers of 1918 to the Sons of 1943

Withered now the poppies lie on Flanders Plain,
    No longer white the crosses over us, long dead;
Yet in our mounds of earth we stir to guns again
    That growl a prelude to your armored tread.

At their bright flame our white bones leap to life,
    And o'er the grass-grown trench of yesteryear,
Our rust-red rifles lift to meet new strife
    And battle once again the ancient fear.

The worm casts shake from poilu blue,
    From mildewed brown that breasted long ago
The screaming steel that seeks you, too.
    In the unchanged red horizon's glow.

Our quarrel with the foe,
Waged long ago,
Today is yours, but know
That when you come at last
    To tread the old front line your fathers knew,
We shall be there in ghostly ranks,
Beneath our proud old battle flags,
    To march again with you.

[5] *The Saturday Evening Post* (January 8, 1945), p. 34. Reprinted by permission of the author and the publishers.

The fire on freedom's hearth still flames.
We fed it with our blood and yours,
With all the peaceful ways that we held dear—
The sounds of home,
Your first unfettered words,
The simple faith
Unmarred by any wraith of crooked cross,
The sturdy stride that marked free people's hope.

Some say we died in vain—
We did not die, if we can link our arms across the years
To march with you again,
To end the task that we forgot to do,
Like some unfinished chore,
When we were lads like you.

JOHN W. ALEXANDER

PROBLEMS

The problems involved in group interpretation are not very different from the basic problems of individual interpretation. The meaning must be decided upon, rhythmical patterns must be studied, and the control of the voice must be emphasized. The difference lies in these principles:

1. You will not be able to use every piece of literature effectively for choral interpretation.
2. You may have to accept someone else's interpretation rather than your own.
3. You will have to learn to follow a director in order to secure group unity and co-ordination.
4. You will have to train your ear to listen for the blending of *all* voices.

Selection of Literature

Prose or poetry of a highly personal nature should not be selected for choral interpretation. If the literature describes subjectively the emotions or feelings of one person, the selection certainly is not suitable choral material. Sincerity must be considered fundamental in any interpretation. A number of voices repeating in unison Milton's "On His Blindness" or Elizabeth Browning's "How Do I Love Thee?" would never be able to create the personal touch which is important to the meaning intended by the author. Neither is it possible to get delicate variations of vocal meaning from a number of voices. These sonnets should be interpreted and known, and appreciated by every student of interpretation but should never be read by a group. It is better to select literature that tells a story, that is objective in its treatment, and universal in its message. Literature that has narrative, dramatic, and entertainment qualities will lend itself to choric treatment. If poetry which carries a personal meaning and employs the pronoun *I* is selected, care must be taken to *use solo speaking effectively* in combination with unison responses.

Finding the Meaning

Once the selection has been chosen, it is not always easy to find the meaning that is most acceptable to the majority of the choral group. As we have pointed out earlier, our experiences are not like those of anyone else in the group. We come from different home environments, different schools, different parts of the country. Our experiences vary; our interpretations of identical experiences vary; our meanings of words vary according to our own particular associations; and our rhythmical patterns vary according to our training and our vitality. One way of arriving at a decision about the meaning to be expressed is to try several interpretations and then judge which is the most effective. Too often, in choral interpretation, meaning is sacrificed to a stylization of the mood. Instead of the mood adding to the meaning, the atmosphere or mood becomes an end in itself. Of course, in some poems this is acceptable because they are enjoyable mainly for sound values. However, when a poem like Poe's "Annabel Lee" is interpreted only for the *m, n, ng* and *l* sounds, so that the voices take on a singing tone instead of a speech pattern or melody, then technique has gone askew, taste is lacking, and emphasis has been misplaced. Effects should never be so emphasized that the meaning of the literature is lost in a welter of prolonged vowels and a continuant hum on the nasal sounds, the technique of the radio "crooner" of several years ago.

The Director

A choral group needs a director to make decisions about the techniques to be used and to criticize the blending of the voices. The director should have a fine sensitivity for artistic interpretation, must be sound-conscious, must understand rhythm, and, most of all, should permit no histrionics in the interpretation. It is wise to have several different directors within the group. There will be less tendency to concentrate on a single technique, as so often is true of choral groups heard over the air. Many times it is possible to recognize groups as belonging to certain schools or directors because of the sameness of the arrangements and techniques. This stylization may be interesting for a time, but after several performances, the interpretations become tiresome because they offer no surprises. Every selection is treated with the same basic techniques, which become more obvious than the meaning of the literature.

Care must be taken to think in terms of the literature to be read rather than the personal idiosyncrasies of the director. A group interested in choral reading must be alert to the fine distinctions of meaning and interpretation. It must train itself for the light touch as well as for the sonorous effect and must be sure *always* that the literature is spoken instead of sung, unless, as in the recording of *John Brown's Body,* the group is a singing choir. Let it be said that any technique which heightens the arrangement of responses at the expense of the meaning of the poem should be discarded. Arrangements of responses described and explained in choral reading books tend to set up a stereotyped manner of procedure that does little to encourage group interpretation as a creative experience to be understood and appreciated by those who are participating in it. For that reason there are no arrangements given in this chapter. It is assumed that each group should have the experience of originating rather than of copying techniques. Certainly in a class of student interpreters there should be no better experience than leading a group into the meaning discussed and decided upon by the entire group. The execution of that interpretation in order to convey the full meaning to the audience is a satisfying, and often an inspiring, experience. A well-integrated group interpretation gives pleasure to both the audience and the performers.

Training the Ear

Choral reading is one of the best exercises for controlling the voice, inasmuch as each member of the choir must fit his vocal pattern to the general scheme that has been outlined by the group. The voices must produce a unified effect: unity of rhythmical pattern, inflection, pitch, timing, and attack must blend with spontaneity and purpose. It is wise, during rehearsal, for each member of the choir to *listen* occasionally to the other voices objectively, because it is difficult for the individual to *hear* his own voice in relation to the other voices while he is taking part in the chorus.

Probably more vital than anything else in this kind of interpretation is the rhythmical unity of the speaking choir. The pulse, the recurring pattern, the pauses which mark the rhythm of the sentence must be felt by the entire group, just as one feels the rhythmical pattern of square dancing or the rhythm of a melody or the rhythm of a squad of soldiers presenting arms. If a few of the group do not sense the rhythm, the movement of the interpretation will be marred. Every selection should be given with appropriate timing. Consequently, the breathing patterns of the group should be similar; the group must work and breathe as one person, so that it is possible to pick up a phrase even on a half beat, if necessary.

Pitch will be decided rather arbitrarily by the director. Training in the discrimination of pitch, inflection, and slides will aid the interpreter, but most of all, the ear must hear the variations in the pitch used. For instance, all members must start with a key that has been established by the leader, or that at least blends with it. If one person is off key or out of tune with the rest of the slides and inflections, the effect is disastrous.

One of the most difficult techniques is the control of the volume of each voice. If *one* voice is projected more than the other voices, the illusion of unity is destroyed. This problem becomes serious, especially if there is one person in the group who likes to hear his own voice sounding over other voices or who thinks that he is not performing to the best of his ability unless he can hear his own voice over the others. If the director works too hard at blending the voices, however, spontaneity may be lost. Each member of the chorus must hold himself responsible for alertness and briskness of projection but should never display his own voice. As soon as he joins a speaking choir, he should realize that his voice should *blend* with other voices. This does not mean that he has to wipe out all of his personality and make himself an automaton, but it does imply co-operation and co-ordination with others.

It is impossible for all voices to have the same resonant quality, but those individuals whose vocal quality is not so pleasing can learn to adjust their voices to the better voices. To be able to hear what others do with their voices always aids and stimulates those who are not so well equipped—at least it should! Consequently, when high voices are used, the director must be sure that they are as pleasant and resonant as possible. Many students with high, thin voices will relax and produce better tones when they have the support of others, just as many of us can sing better in a chorus than by ourselves.

Articulation is important in choral interpretation, because the sounds from many voices must give the impression of coming from one voice. Articulation must not be slovenly; neither should it be overprecise. The group must agree on the sound effects to be produced. If the rhythm of the line calls for an assimilation of words, each person should be cognizant of that elision. After all, the meaning is paramount, and meaning is not well expressed when every word becomes a unit in itself. On the other hand, sounds cannot be unified into meaning if several members start too soon or stop too abruptly or skip over endings or give the final letters an extra sharp attack or an *s* more than its value or become slouchy on medial sounds, calling *city* "cidy" or *little* "liddle."

EXERCISES

In the Appendix to this volume there are a number of articulatory exercises that will help you attain the agility and precision of movement especially necessary in choral interpretation. These exercises are not calculated to solve all articulatory problems; nor will they be of much value to you unless you incorporate the elements they illustrate into your normal speech pattern. Exercises, to be of greatest good, should be adjusted to each person's needs. After you have practiced these articulatory exercises as a group and mastered the correct pronunciation of all sounds, try some of the selections given below. Try to apply the agility you have acquired to each of the practiced words as it appears in relation to other words and contributes to the rhythmical patterns of the selection. Work for precision in articulation.

I

THE MODERN MAJOR-GENERAL

I am the very model of a modern Major-General,
I've information vegetable, animal, and mineral;
I know the kings of England, and I quote the fights historical,
From Marathon to Waterloo, in order categorical;
I'm very well acquainted, too, with matters mathematical,
I understand equations, both the simple and quadratical;
About binomial theorem I'm teeming with a lot o' news,
With interesting facts about the square of the hypotenuse.
I'm very good at integral and differential calculus,
I know the scientific names of beings animalculous.
In short, in matters vegetable, animal, and mineral,
I am the very model of a modern Major-General.
            W. S. GILBERT, *The Pirates of Penzance*

II

THE MILITARY MOTHER GOOSE[6]

(*Revised European Edition*)

Mary, Mary, cautionary,
    How does your garden grow?
Under a bombproof shelter,
    All in a barbed wire row.

[6] Published originally in the *Chicago Tribune*. Reprinted by permission of the author and the publishers.

Deedle, deedle dumpling, our son John
Goes to bed with his uniform on;
All-steel helmet and field gray pants,
And that's the latest crisis at a glance.

To market, to market to buy a sandbag,
Home again, home again, ziggety-zag;
To market, to market, a gas mask to fit,
Home again, home again, lickety-split.

Taffy was a soldier,
Taffy could salute,
And all the little children
Admired his parachute.

Dink-a-dunk-dank,
Three men in a tank,
And who do you think they be?
The captain, the gunner,
The signal runner.
Pip, pip! Time out for tea!

DOW RICHARDSON

III

JOHN WELLINGTON WELLS

My name is John Wellington Wells,
I'm a dealer in magic and spells,
    In blessings and curses,
    And ever filled purses,
In prophecies, witches, and knells.
If you want a proud foe to "make tracks"—
If you'd melt a rich uncle in wax—
    You've but to look in
    On the resident Djinn,
Number seventy, Simmery Axe.

We've a first-rate assortment of magic;
    And for raising a posthumous shade,
With effects that are comic or tragic,
    There's no cheaper house in the trade.
Love-philtre, we've quantities of it!
    And for knowledge, if any one burns,
We're keeping a very small prophet, a prophet
    Who brings us unbounded returns:

For he can prophesy
With a wink of his eye,
Peep with security
Into futurity,
Sum up your history,
Clear up a mystery,
Humor proclivity
For a nativity;
He has answers oracular,
   Bogies spectacular,
   Tetrapods tragical,
   Mirrors so magical.
   Facts astronomical,
   Solemn or comical;
And, if you want it, he
Makes a reduction on taking a quantity!

Oh! If any one anything lacks,
He'll find it all ready in stacks,
   If he'll only look in
   On the resident Djinn,
Number seventy, Simmery Axe!

He can raise you hosts of ghosts,
   And that without reflectors;
And creepy things with wings,
   And gaunt and grisly spectres;
He can fill you crowds of shrouds,
   And horrify you vastly;
He can rack your brains with chains,
   And gibberings grim and ghastly!

   Then, if you plan it, he
   Changes organity,
   With an urbanity
   Full of satanity,
   Vexes humanity
   With an inanity
   Fatal to vanity,
Driving your foes to the verge of insanity!
   Barring tautology,
   In demonology,
   'Lectro biology,
   Mystic nosology,
   Spirit philology,
   High-class astrology,
   Such is his knowledge, he
   Isn't the man to require an apology!

Oh! My name is John Wellington Wells,
I'm a dealer in magic and spells,
  In blessings and curses,
  And ever filled purses,
In prophecies, witches, and knells.
If you want a proud foe to "make tracks"—
If you'd melt a rich uncle in wax—
  You've but to look in
  On the resident Djinn,
Number seventy, Simmery Axe.

W. S. Gilbert, *The Sorcerer*

IV

HOW JACK FOUND THAT BEANS MAY GO BACK ON A CHAP[7]

Without the slightest basis
For hypochondriasis,
  A widow had forebodings which a cloud around her flung,
And with expression cynical
For half the day a clinical
  Thermometer she held beneath her tongue.

Whene'er she read the papers
She suffered from the vapors,
  At every tale of malady or accident she'd groan;
In every new and smart disease,
From housemaid's knee to heart disease,
  She recognized the symptoms as her own!

She had a yearning chronic
To try each novel tonic,
  Elixir, panacea, lotion, opiate, and balm;
And from a homeopathist
Would change to an hydropathist,
  And back again, with stupefying calm!

She was nervous, cataleptic,
And anemic, and dyspeptic:
  Though not convinced of apoplexy, yet she had her fears.
She dwelt with force fanatical,
Upon a twinge rheumatical,
  And said she had a buzzing in her ears!

[7] From *Grimm Tales Made Gay*, p. 40. Copyright, 1935, by Houghton, Mifflin Company. Reprinted by permission of the publishers.

Now all of this bemoaning
And this grumbling and this groaning
  The mind of Jack, her son and heir, unconscionably bored.
His heart completely hardening,
He gave his time to gardening,
  For raising beans was something he adored.

Each hour in accents morbid
This limp maternal bore bid
  Her callous son affectionate and lachrymose good-bys.
She never granted Jack a day
Without some long "Alackaday!"
  Accompanied by rolling of the eyes.

But Jack, no panic showing,
Just watched his beanstalk growing,
  And twined with tender fingers the tendrils up the pole.
At all her words funereal
He smiled a smile ethereal,
  Or sighed an absent-minded "Bless my soul!"

That hollow-hearted creature
Would never change a feature:
  No tear bedimmed his eye, however touching was her talk.
She never fussed or flurried him,
The only thing that worried him
  Was when no bean-pods grew upon the stalk!

But then he wabbled loosely
His head, and wept profusely,
  And, taking out his handkerchief to mop away his tears,
Exclaimed: "It hasn't got any!"
He found this blow to botany
  Was sadder than were all his mother's fears.

The Moral is that gardeners pine
Whene'er no pods adorn the vine.
Of all sad words experience gleans
The saddest are "It might have beans."
  (I did not make this up myself:
  'Twas in a book upon my shelf.
  It's witty, but I don't deny
  It's rather Whittier than I.)
                              GUY WETMORE CARRYL

V

THE FAMILY FOOL

Oh! a private buffoon is a light-hearted loon,
    If you listen to popular rumour;
From morning to night he's so joyous and bright,
    And he bubbles with wit and good humour!
He's so quaint and so terse, both in prose and in verse;
    Yet though people forgive his transgression,
There are one or two rules that all Family Fools
    Must observe, if they love their profession.
          There are one or two rules,
            Half-a-dozen, maybe,
        That all family fools,
           Of whatever degree,
    Must observe if they love their profession.

If you wish to succeed as a jester, you'll need
    To consider each person's auricular:
What is all right for B would scandalise C
    (For C is so very particular);
And D may be dull, and E's very thick skull
    Is as empty of brains as a ladle;
While F is F sharp, and will cry with a carp
    That he's known your best joke from his cradle!
        When your humour they flout,
          You can't let yourself go;
        And it *does* put you out
          When a person says, "Oh,
I have known that old joke from my cradle!"

If your master is surly, from getting up early
    (And tempers are short in the morning),
An inopportune joke is enough to provoke
    Him to give you, at once, a month's warning.
Then if you refrain, he is at you again,
    For he likes to get value for money;
He'll ask then and there, with an insolent stare,
    "If you know that you're paid to be funny?
          It adds to the tasks
           Of a merryman's place
        When your principal asks,
           With a scowl on his face,
If you know that you're paid to be funny?"

Comes a Bishop, maybe, or a solemn D.D.—
   Oh, beware of his anger provoking!
Better not pull his hair—don't stick pins in his chair;
   He don't understand practical joking.
If the jests that you crack have an orthodox smack,
   You may get a bland smile from these sages;
But should they, by chance, be imported from France,
   Half-a-crown is stopped out of your wages!
         It's a general rule,
            Though your zeal it may quench,
         If the family fool
            Tells a joke that's too French,
   Half-a-crown is stopped out of his wages!

Though your head it may rack with a bilious attack,
   And your senses with toothache you're losing,
Don't be mopy and flat—they don't fine you for that,
   If you're properly quaint and amusing!
Though your wife ran away with a soldier that day,
   And took with her your trifle of money;
Bless your heart, they don't mind—they're exceedingly kind—
   They don't blame you—as long as you're funny!
         It's a comfort to feel
            If your partner should flit,
         Though *you* suffer a deal,
            They don't mind it a bit—
   They don't blame you—so long as you're funny!
               W. S. GILBERT, *The Yeomen of the Guard*

VI

THE QUANGLE WANGLE'S HAT

On the top of the Crumpetty Tree
   The Quangle Wangle sat,
But his face you could not see,
   On account of his Beaver Hat.
For his Hat was a hundred and two feet wide,
With ribbons and bibbons on every side,
And bells, and buttons, and loops, and lace,
So that nobody ever could see the face
   Of the Quangle Wangle Quee.

The Quangle Wangle said
   To himself on the Crumpetty Tree,

"Jam, and jelly, and bread
   Are the best of food for me!
But the longer I live on this Crumpetty Tree,
The plainer than ever it seems to me
That very few people come this way,
And that life on the whole is far from gay!"
   Said the Quangle Wangle Quee.

But there came to the Crumpetty Tree
   Mr. and Mrs. Canary;
And they said, "Did you ever see
   Any spot so charmingly airy?
May we build a nest on your lovely Hat?
Mr. Quangle Wangle, grant us that!
Oh, please, let us come and build a nest,
   Mr. Quangle Wangle Quee!"

And the Golden Grouse came there,
   And the Pobble who has no toes,
And the small Olympian bear,
   And the Dong with a luminous nose.
And the blue Baboon who played the flute,
And the Orient Calf from the Land of Tute,
And the Attery Squash, and the Bisky Bat—
All came and built on the lovely Hat
   Of the Quangle Wangle Quee.

And the Quangle Wangle said
   To himself on the Crumpetty Tree,
"When all these creatures move
   What a wonderful noise there will be!"
And at night by the light of the Mulberry moon
They danced to the Flute of the Blue Baboon,
On the broad green leaves of the Crumpetty Tree,
And all were as happy as happy could be,
   With the Quangle Wangle Quee.

                                   EDWARD LEAR

SUGGESTIONS FOR GROUP INTERPRETATION

The articulatory exercises above and in the Appendix will have given you some appreciation for sound formation, singly and in combination with other sounds. Now that you are sound-conscious, you are ready to start with group interpretation. The following suggestions may be of help:

FOR THE DIRECTOR

1. Begin with a group that does not exceed twenty voices.
2. Decide whether the voices are *light* (high, clear tones) or *dark* (low, deep tones) and group them accordingly. Then, if necessary, divide these two groups further into units of *light, medium light, medium dark,* and *dark* voices.
3. Have the choral members form two short lines rather than one long line; or group them in a wedge shape or a two-row semicircle. It is easier to gain group feeling and to secure unity if the shoulders of the members are touching.
4. Start the group with a nursery rhyme, a refrain verse, or a poem that has a swinging rhythm.
5. Repeat the selection over and over very softly; then gradually have the group give it more power and vitality.

FOR THE CHORAL MEMBERS

1. Read the selection aloud for rhythm and movement.
2. Listen to several members of the group read the selection as they would interpret it.
3. Do not indulge in vocal gymnastics.
4. Do not intone. Think in terms of the meaning and *interpret*.
5. Be sure that your voice is not the discordant one.
6. Co-ordinate your responses and time them to those which have just been made, whether solo or group responses.
7. Remember that the solo voice must keep within the rhythmical pattern established by the other interpreters, unless his lines properly call for a different pattern.
8. Remain aware of the timing and rhythmical patterns of the other groups while you are waiting for your group to respond.
9. Avoid mannerisms and too many movements.
10. Avoid a dead-pan expression, but be sure also that your face is not excessively expressive by comparison with the others in the group.
11. Be sincere and alert.

EXERCISES

I

The following poem can be adapted for choral reading. You will get some suggestions for the rhythm by listening to Lew Sarett's recording of it.[8]

[8] *Lew Sarett: Reading from His Collected Poems* (Columbia, XTV 15495).

THE SQUAW-DANCE[9]

Beat, beat, beat, beat, beat upon the tom-tom,
Beat, beat, beat, beat, beat upon the drum.
Hóy-eeeeeee-yáh! Hóy-eeeeeee-yáh!
Shuffle to the left, shuffle to the left,
Shuffle, shuffle, shuffle to the left, to the left.
Fat squaws, lean squaws, gliding in a row,
Grunting, wheezing, laughing as they go;
Bouncing up with a scuffle and a twirl,
Flouncing petticoat and hair in a whirl.
Rheumatic hags of gristle and brawn,
Rolling in like a ponderous billow;
Fair squaws lithe as the leaping fawn,
Swaying with the wind and bending with the willow;
Bouncing buttock and shriveled shank,
Scuffling to the drumbeat, rank on rank;
Stolid eye and laughing lip,
Buxom bosom and jiggling hip,
Weaving in and weaving out,
Hí! Hí! Hí! with a laugh and a shout,
To the beat, beat, beat, beat, beat upon the tom-tom.
Beat, beat, beat, beat, beat upon the drum;
To the drum-beat, drum-beat, drum-beat, drum-beat, drum-beat, drum-
    beat, drum-beat—
Hóy-eeeeeee-yáh! Hóy-eeeeeee-yáh!
Hí! Hí! Hí! Hí! Hóy-eeeeeeeeeeeeeee-yáh!

Medicine-men on the medicine-drum,
Beating out the rhythm—here they come!
Medicine-gourd with its rattle, rattle, rattle,
Flinging wild with the call of battle.
Beaded drummers squatting in the ring
Leap to its challenge with a crouch and a spring;
Weathered old bucks who grunt and wheeze
As they jangle bells on their wrists and their knees:
Shining new and olden bells,
Silver, copper, golden bells,
Cow-bells, toy bells, ringing sleigh-bells,
Beaded dance bells, "give-away" bells,
Jingling, jangling, jingling bells,
Set-the-toes-atingling bells—
To the beat, beat, beat, beat, beat upon the drum;
Beat, beat, beat, beat, beat upon the drum;

To the drum-beat, drum-beat, drum-beat, drum-beat, drum-beat, drum-
  beat, drum-beat—
Hóy-eeeeeee-yáh! Hóy-eeeeeee-yáh!
Hí! Hi! Hí! Hi! Hóy-eeeeeeeeeeeeeee-yáh!

Old bucks stamping heel and toe,
Ugh! as they snort and they cackle and they crow;
Yowling like the lynx that crouches nigh,
Howling like the wolf at the prairie sky;
Growling and grunting as they shift and they tramp,
Stalking, crouching—with a stamp, stamp, stamp—
Sleek limbs, lithe limbs, strong and lean limbs;
Flat feet, bare feet, dancing feet,
Buckskin-moccasined prancing feet,
Eager child-feet, scuffling feet,
Feet, feet, feet, feet, shuffling feet!
Hí! Beat, beat, beat, beat, beat upon the tom-tom,
Beat, beat, beat, beat, beat upon the drum;
To the drum-beat, drum-beat, drum-beat, drum-beat, drum-beat, drum-
  beat, drum-beat—
Shuffle to the left, shuffle to the left,
Shuffle, shuffle, shuffle to the left, to the left—
Hí! Hi! Hí! Hi! Hóy-eeeeeeeeeeeeeee-yáh!

Mah-Éen-Gans, the "Little Wolf," Speaks:

Hóy-eeeeeeeeeeeeeee-yáh! Hóy-eeeeeeeeeeeeeee-yáh!
Hí! Hi! Hí! Hi! Hóy-eeeeeeeeeeeeeeeee-yáh!
Beat, beat, beat, beat, beat upon the tom-tom,
Beat, beat, beat, beat, beat upon the drum.
Medicine-gourd with its rattle, rattle, rattle,
Ringing wild with the call of battle.
Rheumatic hags of gristle and brawn,
Rolling in like a ponderous billow;
Fair squaws lithe as the leaping fawn,
Swaying with the wind and bending with the willow.
Old bucks stamping heel and toe,
Ugh! as they snort and they cackle and they crow—
Sleek limbs, lithe limbs, strong and clean limbs;
Withered limbs, bowed limbs, long and lean limbs;
Flat feet, bare feet, dancing feet,
Buckskin-moccasined prancing feet;
Shuffle to the left, shuffle to the left,
Shuffle, shuffle, shuffle to the left, to the left;
With a crouch and a spring and a grunt and a wheeze,
And a clanging of bells at the wrists and the knees:
Shining new and olden bells,
Silver, copper, golden bells—

Feet, feet, feet, feet, scuffling feet!
To the drum-beat, drum-beat, drum-beat, drum-beat, drum-beat, drum-
    beat, drum-beat—
Hí! Hí! Hí! Hí! Hóy-eeeeeeeeee-yáh!

LEW SARETT

II

Try your ingenuity for choral arrangements on the following
poems. Be careful that you do not distort or hide the meaning in
your effort to present an unusual interpretation. Also, be aware
of changes in mood and tone, so that you can utilize voices of
different quality, force, rhythm, and pitch.

ROAD SONG OF THE BANDAR-LOG[10]

Here we go in a flung festoon,
Halfway up to the jealous moon!
Don't you envy our pranceful bands?
Don't you wish you had extra hands?
Wouldn't you like if your tails were—*so*—
Curved in the shape of a Cupid's bow?
    Now you're angry, but—never mind,
    Brother, thy tail hangs down behind!

Here we sit in a branchy row,
Thinking of beautiful things we know;
Dreaming of deeds that we mean to do,
All complete, in a minute or two—
Something noble and wise and good,
Done by merely wishing we could.
    Now we're going to—never mind.
    Brother, thy tail hangs down behind!

All the talk we ever have heard
Uttered by bat or beast or bird—
Hide or fin or scale or feather—
Jabber it quickly and all together!
Excellent! Wonderful! Once again!
Now we are talking just like men!
    Let's pretend we are—never mind,
    Brother, thy tail hangs down behind!
    This is the way of the Monkey kind.

[10] From *The Jungle Book*, p. 73. Copyright, 1894, by Rudyard Kipling.
Reprinted by permission of Mrs. George Bambridge and Doubleday &
Company, Inc.

Then join our leaping lines that scumfish through the pines,
That rocket by where, light and high, the wild grape swings.
By the rubbish in our wake, and the noble noise we make,
Be sure, be sure, we're going to do some splendid things!
RUDYARD KIPLING

THE DWARF[11]

"Now, Jinnie, my dear, to the dwarf be off,
    That lives in Barberry Wood,
And fetch me some honey, but be sure you don't laugh,—
    He hates little girls that are rude, are rude,
        He hates little girls that are rude."

Jane tapped at the door of the house in the wood,
    And the dwarf looked over the wall,
He eyed her so queer, 'twas as much as she could
    To keep from laughing at all, at all,
        To keep from laughing at all.

His shoes down the passage came clod, clod, clod,
    And when he opened the door,
He croaked so harsh, 'twas as much as she could
    To keep from laughing the more, the more,
        To keep from laughing the more.

As there, with his bushy red beard, he stood,
    Pricked out to double its size,
He squinted so cross, 'twas as much as she could
    To keep the tears out of her eyes, her eyes,
        To keep the tears out of her eyes.

He slammed the door, and went clod, clod, clod,
    But while in the porch she bides,
He squealed so fierce, 'twas as much as she could
    To keep from cracking her sides, her sides,
        To keep from cracking her sides.

He threw a pumpkin over the wall,
    And melons and apples beside,
So thick in the air that to see them all fall,
    She laughed and laughed, till she cried, cried, cried;
        Jane laughed and laughed till she cried.

Down fell her teardrops a pit-apat-pat,
    And red as a rose she grew;—

[11] From *Collected Poems: 1901-1918*, Vol. 2, p. 24. Copyright, 1920, by
Henry Holt and Company, Inc. Reprinted by permission of the publishers.

"Kah! kah," said the dwarf, "is it crying you're at?
  It's the very worst thing you could do, do, do,
    It's the very worst thing you could do."

He slipped like a monkey up into the tree,
  He shook her down cherries like rain;
"See now," says he, cheeping, "a blackbird I be,
  Laugh, laugh, little Jinnie, again—gain—gain,
    Laugh, laugh, little Jinnie, again."

Ah me! what a strange, what a gladsome duet
  From a house in the deeps of a wood!
Such shrill and such harsh voices never met yet
  A-laughing as loud as they could, could, could,
    A-laughing as loud as they could.

Come Jinnie, come dwarf, cocksparrow, and bee,
  There's a ring gaudy-green in the dell,
Sing, sing, ye sweet cherubs, that flit in the tree;
  La! who can draw tears from a well, well, well,
    Who ever drew tears from a well!

WALTER DE LA MARE

THE WALRUS AND THE CARPENTER

The sun was shining on the sea,
  Shining with all his might:
He did his very best to make
  The billows smooth and bright—
And this was odd, because it was
  The middle of the night.

The moon was shining sulkily,
  Because she thought the sun
Had got no business to be there
  After the day was done—
"It's very rude of him," she said,
  "To come and spoil the fun!"

The sea was wet as wet could be,
  The sands were dry as dry.
You could not see a cloud, because
  No cloud was in the sky:
No birds were flying overhead—
  There were no birds to fly.

The Walrus and the Carpenter
  Were walking close at hand:

They wept like anything to see
　　Such quantities of sand:
"If this were only cleared away,"
　　They said, "it *would* be grand!"

"If seven maids with seven mops
　　Swept it for half a year,
Do you suppose," the Walrus said,
　　"That they could get it clear?"
"I doubt it," said the Carpenter,
　　And shed a bitter tear.

"O Oysters, come and walk with us!"
　　The Walrus did beseech.
"A pleasant walk, a pleasant talk,
　　Along the briny beach:
We cannot do with more than four,
　　To give a hand to each."

The eldest Oyster looked at him,
　　But never a word he said:
The eldest Oyster winked his eye,
　　And shook his heavy head—
Meaning to say he did not choose
　　To leave the oyster-bed.

But four young Oysters hurried up,
　　All eager for the treat:
Their coats were brushed, their faces washed,
　　Their shoes were clean and neat—
And this was odd, because, you know,
　　They hadn't any feet.

Four other Oysters followed them,
　　And yet another four;
And thick and fast they came at last,
　　And more, and more, and more—
All hopping through the frothy waves,
　　And scrambling to the shore.

The Walrus and the Carpenter
　　Walked on a mile or so,
And then they rested on a rock
　　Conveniently low:
And all the little Oysters stood
　　And waited in a row.

"The time has come," the Walrus said,
　　"To talk of many things:

Of shoes—and ships—and sealing-wax—
  Of cabbages—and kings—
And why the sea is boiling hot—
  And whether pigs have wings."

"But wait a bit," the Oysters cried,
  "Before we have our chat;
For some of us are out of breath,
  And all of us are fat!"
"No hurry!" said the Carpenter.
  They thanked him much for that.

"A loaf of bread," the Walrus said,
  "Is what we chiefly need:
Pepper and vinegar besides
  Are very good indeed—
Now, if you're ready, Oysters dear,
  We can begin to feed."

"But not on us!" the Oysters cried,
  Turning a little blue.
"After such kindness, that would be
  A dismal thing to do!"
"The night is fine," the Walrus said.
  "Do you admire the view?

"It was so kind of you to come!
  And you are very nice!"
The Carpenter said nothing but
  "Cut us another slice:
I wish you were not quite so deaf—
  I've had to ask you twice!"

"It seems a shame," the Walrus said,
  "To play them such a trick,
After we've brought them out so far,
  And made them trot so quick!"
The Carpenter said nothing but
  "The butter's spread too thick!"

"I weep for you," the Walrus said:
  "I deeply sympathize."
With sobs and tears he sorted out
  Those of the largest size,
Holding his pocket-handkerchief
  Before his streaming eyes.

"O Oysters," said the Carpenter,
  "You've had a pleasant run!

Shall we be trotting home again?"
But answer came there none—
And this was scarcely odd, because
They'd eaten every one.

LEWIS CARROLL

DRINKING SONG

Here's to the maiden of bashful fifteen,
   Here's to the widow of fifty,
Here's to the flaunting extravagant queen,
   And here's to the housewife that's thrifty.

> *Let the toast pass,*
> *Drink to the lass,*
> *I'll warrant she'll prove an excuse for the glass.*

Here's to the charmer, whose dimples we prize,
   And now to the maid who has none, sir,
Here's to the girl with a pair of blue eyes,
   And here's to the nymph with but one, sir.

> *Let the toast pass,*
> *Drink to the lass,*
> *I'll warrant she'll prove an excuse for the glass.*

Here's to the maiden with a bosom of snow,
   And to her that's as brown as a berry;
Here's to the wife with a face full of woe.
   And now to her that is merry.

> *Let the toast pass,*
> *Drink to the lass,*
> *I'll warrant she'll prove an excuse for the glass*

For let 'em be clumsy, or let 'em be slim,
   Young or ancient, I care not a feather;
So fill a pint bumper quite up to the brim,
   And let us e'en toast them together.

> *Let the toast pass,*
> *Drink to the lass,*
> *I'll warrant she'll prove an excuse for the glass.*

RICHARD BRINSLEY SHERIDAN

THE MAN IN THE MOON[12]

Said the Raggedy Man on a hot afternoon,
    "My!
        Sakes!
           What a lot o' mistakes
Some little folks makes on the Man in the Moon.
But people that's been up to see him like Me,
And calls on him frequent and intimutly,
Might drop a few hints that would interest you
    Clean!
        Through!
           If you wanted 'em to—
Some actual facts that might interest you!

"O the Man in the Moon has a crick in his back.
    Whee!
        Whimm!
           Ain't you sorry for him?
And a mole on his nose that is purple and black;
And his eyes are so weak that they water and run
If he dares to *dream* even he looks at the sun,—
So he jes' dreams of stars, as the doctors advise—
    My!
        Eyes!
           But isn't he wise—
To jes' dream of stars, as the doctors advise?

"And the Man in the Moon has a boil on his ear—
    Whee!
        Whing!
           What a singular thing!
I know! but these facts are authentic, my dear,—
There's a boil on his ear; and a corn on his chin,—
He calls it a dimple,—but dimples stick in—
Yet it might be a dimple turned over, you know!
    Whang!
        Ho!
           Why certainly so—
It might be a dimple turned over, you know!

"And the Man in the Moon has a rheumatic knee,
    Gee!
        Whizz!
           What a pity that is!

[12] From *Rhymes of Childhood*, p. 101. Copyright, 1890, by The Bobbs-Merrill Company. Reprinted by permission of the publishers.

And his toes have worked round where his heels ought to be.
So whenever he wants to go North he goes South,
And comes back with porridge crumbs all round his mouth,
And he brushes them off with a Japanese fan,
    Whing!
        Whang!
            What a marvellous man!
What a very remarkably marvellous man!

"And the Man in the Moon," sighed the Raggedy Man,
    "Gits!
        So!
            Sullonesome, you know!
Up there by himself since creation began!—
That when I call on him and then come away,
He grabs me and holds me and begs me to stay—
Till—well, if it wasn't for *Jimmy-cum-Jim,*
    Dadd!
        Limb!
            I'd go pardners with him!
Jes' jump my job here and be pardners with him!"
JAMES WHITCOMB RILEY

THE BALLAD OF JESSE JAMES[13]

Jesse James was a two-gun man,
    (*Roll on, Missouri!*)
Strong-arm chief of an outlaw clan.
    (*From Kansas to Illinois!*)
He twirled an old Colt forty-five,
    (*Roll on, Missouri!*)
They never took Jesse James alive.
    (*Roll on, Missouri, roll!*)
Jesse James was King of the Wes';
    (*Cataracks in the Missouri!*)
He'd a di'mon heart in his lef' breas';
    (*Brown Missouri rolls!*)
He'd a fire in his heart no hurt could stifle;
    (*Thunder, Missouri!*)
Lion eyes an' a Winchester rifle.
    (*Missouri, roll down!*)

Jesse James rode a pinto hawse;
Come at night to a water-cawse;

[13] From *Golden Fleece,* p. 85. Copyright, 1927, by William Rose Benét. Reprinted by permission of Dodd, Mead & Company, Inc.

Tetched with the rowel that pinto's flank;
She sprung the torrent from bank to bank.

Jesse rode through a sleepin' town;
Looked the moonlit street both up an' down;
Crack-crack-crack, the street ran flames
An' a great voice cried, "I'm Jesse James!"

Hawse an' afoot they're after Jess!
   (*Roll on, Missouri!*)
Spurrin' an' spurrin'—but he's gone Wes'.
   (*Brown Missouri rolls!*)
He was ten foot tall when he stood in his boots;
   (*Lightnin' light the Missouri!*)
More'n a match fer sich galoots.
   (*Roll, Missouri, roll!*)

Jesse James rode outa the sage;
Roun' the rocks come the swayin' stage;
Straddlin' the road a giant stan's
An' a great voice bellers, "Throw up yer han's!"

Jesse raked in the di'mon' rings,
The big gold watches an' the yuther things;
Jesse divvied 'em then an' thar
With a cryin' child had lost he mar.

The U. S. Troopers is after Jess;
   (*Roll on, Missouri!*)
Their hawses sweat foam, but he's gone Wes';
   (*Hear Missouri roar!*)
He was broad as a b'ar, he'd a ches' like a drum,
   (*Wind an' rain through Missouri!*)
An' his red hair flamed like Kingdom Come.
   (*Missouri down to the sea!*)

Jesse James all alone in the rain
Stopped an' stuck up the Eas'-boun' train;
Swayed through the coaches with horns an' a tail,
Lit out with the bullion an' the registered mail.

Jess made 'em all turn green with fright,
Quakin' in the aisles in the pitch-black night;
An' he give all the bullion to a pore ole tramp
Campin' nigh the cuttin' in the dirt an' damp.

The whole U. S. is after Jess;
   (*Roll on, Missouri!*)
The son-of-a-gun, if he ain't gone Wes';
   (*Missouri to the sea!*)

He could chaw cold iron an' spit blue flame;
　(*Cataracks down the Missouri!*)
He rode on a catamount he'd larned to tame.
　(*Hear that Missouri roll!*)

Jesse James rode into a bank;
Give his pinto a tetch on the flank;
Jumped the teller's window with an awful crash;
Heaved up the safe an' twirled his mustache;

He said, "So long, boys!" He yelped, "So long!
Feelin' porely to-day—I ain't feelin' strong!"
Rode right through the wall agoin' crack-crack-crack,—
Took the safe home to Mother in a gunny-sack.

They're creepin', they're crawlin', they're stalkin' Jess;
　(*Roll on, Missouri!*)
They's a rumor he's gone much further Wes';
　(*Roll, Missouri, roll!*)
They's a word of a cayuse hitched to the bars
　(*Ruddy clouds on Missouri!*)
Of a golden sunset that busts into stars.
　(*Missouri, roll down!*)

Jesse James rode hell fer leather;
He was a hawse an' a man together;
In a cave in a mountain high up in air
He lived with a rattlesnake, a wolf, an' a bear.

Jesse's heart was as sof' as a woman;
Fer guts an' stren'th he was sooper-human;
He could put six shots through a woodpecker's eye
And take in one swaller a gallon o' rye.

They sought him here an' they sought him there,
　(*Roll on, Missouri!*)
But he strides by night through the ways of the air,
　(*Brown Missouri rolls!*)
They say he was took an' they say he is dead;
　(*Thunder, Missouri!*)
But he ain't—he's a sunset overhead!
　(*Missouri down to the sea!*)

Jesse James was a Hercules.
When he went through the woods he tore up the trees.
When he went on the plains he smoked the groun'
An' the hull lan' shuddered fer miles aroun'.

Jesse James wore a red bandanner
That waved on the breeze like the Star Spangled Banner;
In seven states he cut up dadoes.
He's gone with the buffler an' the desperadoes.

Yes, Jesse James was a two-gun man
   (*Roll on, Missouri!*)
The same as when this song began;
   (*From Kansas to Illinois!*)
An' when you see a sunset bust into flames
   (*Lightnin' light the Missouri!*)
On a thunderstorm blaze—that's Jesse James!
   (*Hear that Missouri roll!*)

WILLIAM ROSE BENÉT

COOL TOMBS[14]

When Abraham Lincoln was shoveled into the tombs, he forgot the
   copperheads and the assassin . . . in the dust, in the cool tombs.

And Ulysses Grant lost all thought of con men and Wall Street, cash
   and collateral turned ashes . . . in the dust, in the cool tombs.

Pocahontas' body, lovely as a poplar, sweet as a red haw in November, or a pawpaw in May, did she wonder? does she remember?
   . . . in the dust, in the cool tombs?

Take any streetful of people buying clothes and groceries, cheering a
   hero or throwing confetti and blowing tin horns . . . tell me if
   the lovers are losers . . . tell me if any get more than the lovers
   . . . in the dust . . . in the cool tombs.

CARL SANDBURG

THE PIRATE DON DURKE OF DOWDEE[15]

Ho, for the Pirate Don Durke of Dowdee!
He was as wicked as wicked could be,
But oh, he was perfectly gorgeous to see!
The Pirate Don Durke of Dowdee.

His conscience, of course, was as black as a bat,
But he had a floppety plume on his hat,
And when he went walking it jiggled—like that!
The plume of the Pirate Dowdee.

[14] From *Cornhuskers*, p. 120. Copyright, 1918, by Henry Holt and Company, Inc. Reprinted by permission of the publishers.

[15] From *Child Life* (March, 1923). Reprinted by permission of the Mildred Plew Meigs estate and the publishers.

His coat it was crimson and cut with a slash,
And often as ever he twirled his mustache,
Deep down in the ocean the mermaids went splash,
Because of Don Durke of Dowdee.

Moreover, Dowdee had a purple tattoo,
And stuck in his belt where he buckled it through
Were a dagger, a dirk and a squizzamaroo,
For fierce was the Pirate Dowdee.

So fearful he was he would shoot at a puff,
And always at sea when the weather grew rough,
He drank from a bottle and wrote on his cuff,
Did Pirate Don Durke of Dowdee.

Oh, he had a cutlass that swung at his thigh,
And he had a parrot called Pepperkin Pye,
And a zigzaggy scar at the end of his eye,
Had the Pirate Don Durke of Dowdee.

He kept in a cavern, this buccaneer bold,
A curious chest that was covered with mould,
And all of his pockets were jingly with gold!
Oh jing! went the gold of Dowdee.

His conscience, of course, it was crook'd like a squash,
But both of his boots made a slickery slosh
And he went through the world with a wonderful swash,
Did Pirate Don Durke of Dowdee.

It's true he was wicked as wicked could be,
His sins they outnumbered a hundred and three,
But oh, he was perfectly gorgeous to see,
The Pirate Don Durke of Dowdee.

MILDRED PLEW MEIGS

TARANTELLA[16]

Do you remember an Inn,
Miranda?
Do you remember an Inn?
And the tedding and the spreading
Of the straw for a bedding,
And the fleas that tease in the High Pyrenees,
And the wine that tasted of tar?
And the cheers and the jeers of the young muleteers

[16] From *Sonnets and Verse.* Copyright, 1900, by Robert M. McBride & Company. Reprinted by permission of the publishers.

(Under the dark of the vine verandah)?
Do you remember an Inn, Miranda,
Do you remember an Inn?
And the cheers and the jeers of the young muleteers
Who hadn't got a penny,
And who weren't paying any,
And the hammer at the doors and the Din?
And the Hip! Hop! Hap!
Of the clap
Of the hands to the twirl and the swirl
Of the girl gone chancing,
Glancing,
Dancing,
Backing and advancing,
Snapping of the clapper to the spin
Out and in—
And Ting, Tong, Tang of the Guitar!
Do you remember an Inn,
Miranda?
Do you remember an Inn?

> Never more;
> Miranda,
> Never more,
> Only the high peaks hoar:
> And Aragon a torrent at the door.
> No sound
> In the walls of the Halls where falls
> The tread
> Of the feet of the dead to the ground.
> No sound:
> Only the boom
> Of the far Waterfall like Doom.

HILAIRE BELLOC

ABOU BEN ADHEM

Abou Ben Adhem (may his tribe increase!)
Awoke one night from a deep dream of peace,
And saw, within the moonlight in his room,
Making it rich, and like a lily in bloom,
An angel writing in a book of gold;
Exceeding peace had made Ben Adhem bold,
And to the presence in the room he said,
"What writest thou?" The vision raised its head,
And with a look made of all sweet accord,
Answered, "The names of those who love the Lord."

"And is mine one?" said Abou. "Nay, not so,"
Replied the angel. Abou spoke more low
But cheerily still; and said, "I pray thee, then,
Write me as one that loves his fellow-men."

The angel wrote and vanished. The next night
It came again, with a great wakening light,
And showed the names whom love of God had blessed,
And, lo! Ben Adhem's name led all the rest!

                                        LEIGH HUNT

GOLDEN SLUMBERS KISS YOUR EYES

Golden slumbers kiss your eyes,
Smiles awake you when you rise,
Sleep, pretty wantons, do not cry,
And I will sing a lullaby:
Rock them, rock them, lullaby.

Care is heavy, therefore sleep you;
You are care, and care must keep you.
Sleep, pretty wantons, do not cry,
And I will sing a lullaby:
Rock them, rock them, lullaby.

                                        THOMAS DEKKER

SWEET AND LOW

Sweet and low, sweet and low,
    Wind of the western sea,
Low, low, breathe and blow,
    Wind of the western seas!
Over the rolling waters go,
Come from the dying moon, and blow,
    Blow him again to me;
While, my little one, while my pretty one, sleeps.

Sleep and rest, sleep and rest,
    Father will come to thee soon;
Rest, rest, on mother's breast,
    Father will come to thee soon;
Father will come to his babe in the nest,
Silver sails all out of the west
    Under the silver moon;
Sleep, my little one, sleep, my pretty one, sleep.

                                        ALFRED TENNYSON, *The Princess*

THE TRUANTS[17]

Ere my heart beats too coldly and faintly
    To remember sad things, yet be gay,
I would sing a brief song of the world's little children
       Magic hath stolen away.

The primroses scattered by April,
    The stars of the wide Milky Way,
Cannot outnumber the hosts of the children
       Magic hath stolen away.

The buttercup green of the meadows,
    The snow of the blossoming may,
Lovelier are not than the legions of children
       Magic hath stolen away.

The waves tossing surf in the moonbeam,
    The albatross lone on the spray,
Alone know the tears wept in vain for the children
       Magic hath stolen away.

In vain: for at hush of the evening
    When the stars twinkle into the grey,
Seems to echo the far-away calling of children
       Magic hath stolen away.
               WALTER DE LA MARE

QUEEN VICTORIA[18]

Queen Victoria's
statue is
the work of her
daughter Beatrice.

The shape's all wrong,
and the crown don't fit,
but—bless her old heart!
she was proud of it.
               HUMBERT WOLFE

THRUSHES

The City Financier
walks in the gardens,
stiffly, because of
his pride and his burdens.

The daisies, looking
up, observe
only a self-
respecting curve.

The thrushes only
see a flat
table-land
of shiny hat.

He looks importantly
about him,
while all the spring
goes on without him.

HUMBERT WOLFE

CAPTAIN STRATTON'S FANCY[19]

Oh some are fond of red wine, and some are fond of white,
And some are all for dancing in the pale moonlight;
But rum alone's the tipple and the heart's delight
    Of the old bold mate of Henry Morgan.

Oh some are fond of Spanish wine, and some are fond of French,
And some'll swallow tay and stuff fit only for a wench;
But I'm for the right Jamaica till I roll beneath the bench,
    Says the old bold mate of Henry Morgan.

Oh some are for the lily, and some are for the rose,
But I am for the sugar-cane that in Jamaica grows;
For it's that that makes the bonny drink to warm my copper nose,
    Says the old bold mate of Henry Morgan.

Oh some are fond of fiddles and a song well sung,
And some are all for music for to lilt upon the tongue;
But mouths were made for tankards, and for sucking at the bung,
    Says the old bold mate of Henry Morgan.

[19] From *Collected Poems*, Vol. 1, p. 83. Copyright, 1912, by The Macmillan Company. Reprinted by permission of the publishers.

And some are fond of dancing, and some are fond of dice,
And some are all for red lips and pretty lassies' eyes;
But a right Jamaica puncheon is a finer prize
    To the old bold mate of Henry Morgan.

Oh some that's good and godly ones they hold that it's a sin
To troll the jolly bowl around and let the dollars spin;
But I'm for toleration and for drinking at an inn,
    Says the old bold mate of Henry Morgan.

Oh some are sad and wretched folk that go in silken suits,
And there's a mort of wicked rogues that live in good reputes;
So I'm for drinking honestly, and dying in my boots,
    Like the old bold mate of Henry Morgan.

JOHN MASEFIELD

THE HOLLOW MEN[20]

A Penny for the Old Guy

I

We are the hollow men
We are the stuffed men
Leaning together
Headpiece filled with straw. Alas!
Our dried voices, when
We whisper together
Are quiet and meaningless
As wind in dry grass
Or rats' feet over broken glass
In our dry cellar

Shape without form, shade without colour,
Paralyzed force, gesture without motion;

Those who have crossed
With direct eyes, to death's other Kingdom
Remember us—if at all—not as lost
Violent souls, but only
As the hollow men
The stuffed men.

II

Eyes I dare not meet in dreams
In death's dream kingdom

[20] From *Collected Poems: 1909-1935*, p. 101. Copyright, 1936, by Harcourt, Brace and Company, Inc. Reprinted by permission of the publishers.

These do not appear:
There, the eyes are
Sunlight on a broken column
There, is a tree swinging
And voices are
In the wind's singing
More distant and more solemn
Than a fading star.

Let me be no nearer
In death's dream kingdom
Let me also wear
Such deliberate disguises
Rat's coat, crowskin, crossed staves
In a field
Behaving as the wind behaves
No nearer—

Not that final meeting
In the twilight kingdom

III

This is the dead land
This is cactus land
Here the stone images
Are raised, here they receive
The supplication of a dead man's hand
Under the twinkle of a fading star.

Is it like this
In death's other kingdom
Waking alone
At the hour when we are
Trembling with tenderness
Lips that would kiss
Form prayers to broken stone.

IV

The eyes are not here
There are no eyes here
In this valley of dying stars
In this hollow valley
This broken jaw of our lost kingdoms

In this last of meeting places
We grope together
And avoid speech
Gathered on this beach of the tumid river

Sightless, unless
The eyes reappear
As the perpetual star
Multifoliate rose
Of death's twilight kingdom
The hope only
Of empty men.

V

Here we go round the prickly pear
Prickly pear prickly pear
Here we go round the prickly pear
At five o'clock in the morning.

Between the idea
And the reality
Between the motion
And the act
Falls the Shadow
        For Thine is the Kingdom

Between the conception
And the creation
Between the emotion
And the response
Falls the Shadow
        Life is very long

Between the desire
And the spasm
Between the potency
And the existence
Between the essence
And the descent
Falls the Shadow
        For Thine is the Kingdom

For Thine is
Life is
For Thine is the

This is the way the world ends
This is the way the world ends
This is the way the world ends
Not with a bang but a whimper.

                T. S. ELIOT

PSALM 24

The earth is the Lord's, and the fulness thereof; the world, and they that dwell therein.

For he hath founded it upon the seas, and established it upon the floods.

Who shall ascend into the hill of the Lord? or who shall stand in his holy place?

He that hath clean hands, and a pure heart; who hath not lifted up his soul unto vanity, nor sworn deceitfully.

He shall receive the blessing from the Lord, and righteousness from the God of his salvation.

This is the generation of them that seek him, that seek thy face, O Jacob. Selah.

Lift up your head, O ye gates; and be ye lift up, ye everlasting doors; and the King of glory shall come in.

Who is this King of glory? The Lord strong and mighty, the Lord mighty in battle.

Lift up your heads, O ye gates; even lift them up, ye everlasting doors; and the King of glory shall come in.

Who is this King of glory? The Lord of hosts, he is the King of glory. Selah.

PSALM 150

Praise ye the Lord. Praise God in his sanctuary: praise him in the firmament of his power.

Praise him for his mighty acts: praise him according to his excellent greatness.

Praise him with the sound of the trumpet: praise him with the psaltery and harp.

Praise him with the timbrel and dance: praise him with stringed instruments and organs.

Praise him upon the loud cymbals: praise him upon the high sounding cymbals.

Let everything that hath breath praise the Lord. Praise ye the Lord.

BLESSED ARE THEY

Blessed are the poor in spirit: for theirs is the kingdom of heaven.

Blessed are they that mourn: for they shall be comforted.

Blessed are the meek: for they shall inherit the earth.

Blessed are they which do hunger and thirst after righteousness: for they shall be filled.

Blessed are the merciful: for they shall obtain mercy.

Blessed are the pure in heart: for they shall see God.

Blessed are the peacemakers: for they shall be called the children of God.

Blessed are they which are persecuted for righteousness' sake: for theirs is the kingdom of heaven.

MATTHEW 5:3-10

GLORY TO GOD

And there were in the same country shepherds abiding in the field, keeping watch over their flock by night.

And, lo, the angel of the Lord came upon them, and the glory of the Lord shone round about them: and they were sore afraid.

And the angel said unto them, Fear not: for, behold, I bring you good tidings of great joy, which shall be to all people.

For unto you is born this day in the city of David a Saviour, which is Christ the Lord.

And this shall be a sign unto you; Ye shall find the babe wrapped in swaddling clothes, lying in a manger.

And suddenly there was with the angel a multitude of the heavenly host praising God, and saying,

Glory to God in the highest, and on earth peace, good will toward men.

LUKE 2:8-14

III

"The Congo" lends itself to choral interpretation. What other selections in this text could be used for this kind of presentation?

CHAPTER 12

Radio Interpretation

If listening to the voices of others and to your own voice is essential to the improvement of interpretative technique before visible audiences, it is even more necessary for success in radio broadcasting. Before a visible audience, the interpreter uses facial expression, bodily action, and voice; furthermore, there are items like dress and make-up to observe. Before a loud-speaker audience, the speaker may use body and voice, but voice is the only medium which carries the intended meaning to the ever fluctuating and invisible audience. The radio audience relies entirely on what it hears—and what it hears is the voice, aided sometimes by sound effects.

For this reason, the person engaged in radio interpretation, whether as master of ceremonies, news commentator, dramatic artist, comedian, or sports announcer, should be as objective as possible about his voice. He should be able to recognize the circumstances under which his voice is effective or ineffective and why. The radio performer learns very quickly that all stations prefer trained to untrained voices. He learns that his voice must be distinctive, and he will be told often that his voice indicates his personality, his indifference, his naïveté. Sometimes, through practice and training, he will succeed, but it is not so simple and easy as the novice thinks.

For those who have studied interpretation, there is little that is new about radio interpretation. Professional directors will tell you that good radio interpretation is a matter first of understanding the script and then of deciding how its meaning can best be presented so that the material will be easy to listen to, whether its purpose is to inform, to interest, to convince, or to entertain. Consequently, no matter what type of program is offered over the air, the interpretation of lines is involved, not merely rote reading but an interpretation which shows understanding of meaning, control of vocal flexibility, and consideration for the audience.

The radio voice is under intense scrutiny. Many listeners are not conscious of disliking a radio voice; they merely know that they do not like the speaker and analyze no further. To others, however, even the smallest vocal defect is irritating and becomes an important reason why they flick the dial to another station. So if the radio voice reveals saccharine smugness, condescension, or too much histrionic display, the listener can always remove the offender. The radio voice should belong to a person who appears to be interested in people and events. The radio audience will not tolerate a voice unless it *seems* natural; in other words, the artist must give the impression of being spontaneous and sincere. This requires the same techniques we have discussed earlier: the ability to create an illusion by a mastery of the instruments used. In radio interpretation the tools are the voice and the microphone; the object is to hold the audience, which although not seen, certainly should be visualized. To interpret before a microphone without getting the "feel" of an imaginary audience is to fail. It is difficult for the radio performer to talk to an invisible audience, because, as he speaks, he gets no cues to audience reaction. The interpreter on the platform continually observes his audience for signs of approval or disapproval. If he sees that his audience does not approve, he can sometimes change the tenor of his program; but a radio artist cannot change his program materially once he is on the air.

CONTROL IN RADIO BROADCASTING

The "Mike"

One of the first controls is a "speaking" acquaintance with the microphone. In these days, everyone interested in communication should try out his vocal techniques, first with a tape recorder and then with a radio microphone. "Mike fright," or the loss of self-possession when one faces a microphone, is a real catastrophe for the inexperienced radio performer, even though he may be an authority or an artist in some other field. The mike causes tensions that affect the quality, volume, tempo, and pitch of his voice. According to Samuel Hopkins Adams, Alexander Woollcott, who was well-known to radio audiences as the Town Crier, was under great tension during his first attempt at broadcasting:[1]

It is a reasonable assumption that Woollcott, with his bumptious savoir-faire, would be a calm and confident mike-speaker. But the little circular mechanism has been known to strike terror into performers far more experienced in the public approach than Alexander Woollcott, with his record of amateur drama and a few lecture appearances: for example, such veterans as Will Rogers, Elsie Janis, Eddie Cantor, and David Wark Griffith, all of whom were thrown into abject jitters when they first confronted the metal mouthpiece. He approached the test with apparent composure, but the blank, unresponsive aspect of the implement, which carried his words to an unseen and therefore terrifying audience, "got" him. Roger Bower, in charge of the program, tried to steady him, but he became wheezy and breathy. His sibilants hissed spitefully. His tongue clacked. He lost his sense of timing. His words, as he painfully read, were being distorted by that mysterious and malevolent little contraption into something quite alien to himself. He staggered to the finish in a cold sweat. All Director Bower's tact was required to persuade him that he was not so bad as he believed himself and would be better at the next trial.

It is known that Woollcott became a finished radio performer, but he preferred having a studio audience at broadcasting time.

The microphone is a sensitive instrument which will transmit not only your voice with some accuracy but also all the noises you are likely to make in an effort to control yourself, such as gasps, coughs, clearing of the throat, rattling of papers, rustling of clothing, sniffling, kicking of the microphone stand, and vocal blasting. It will usually accentuate peculiar vocal qualities and eccentricities, such as lip-smacking and glottal clicking, sibilants

---

[1] From Samuel Hopkins Adams, *A. Woollcott* (New York, Harcourt, Brace and Company, Inc., 1945), p. 152.

that whistle or hiss, nasal snorts, uncontrolled or heavy breathing, nasal tones, high voices. Just as the microphone may amplify vocal defects, it may also make good voices sound better than they are, especially if the control man knows his job and if the performer knows how to use the mike.

Mike technique comes only with actual experience in broadcasting. A good radio director will know what voices, distances, and procedures will work effectively before the microphone. Although eight to twelve inches between the speaker and the mike are considered a good distance for the broadcaster, no set rule can be followed. Variations in the kind of voice you intend to use will make a difference in the distance from the mike. The number of people working with you must also be considered, and the kind of broadcasting you are doing will influence your use of the mike. Your stance and position should be comfortable to you, but not so relaxed that you lapse into indifference. Improper handling of your script can ruin your broadcast. Know your mike, for the mike can make or break you as a radio performer. If you do not understand it, ask those who do to explain its live and dead areas.

The Voice

The first intimation that tension exists in the radio performer is his undue or excessive intake of air at the beginning or sometimes in the middle of sentences, which indicates uncontrolled breathing. Again, if the broadcaster is not careful to take advantage of pauses, he will talk on residual air, a procedure which tends to leave the audience gasping. Of course, there are times when a certain characterization may call for forced breathing or an unusual pattern of breath control, and there are also unexpected incidents which occur as the broadcaster is relating some event. Radio history cannot name a more dramatic incident than Herbert Morrison's broadcast of the arrival and subsequent burning of the German dirigible *Hindenburg* on May 6, 1937, at Lakehurst, New Jersey. After describing its crossing in less than four hours, Morrison suddenly gasped out a description of the unexpected burning of the dirigible, much to his own horror and the amazement of his audience. His voice was broken as he sought words to describe the scene, and his emotions choked off the words that he tried to form.[2]

Volume is an important vocal factor in radio broadcasting. Most directors believe that the performer should use a normal voice, rather than subdued tones, and talk directly into the microphone in order to create a feeling of intimacy with the audience. If soft tones are used, it becomes necessary to shift the volume control from the performer to the operator in the master control room, where instruments are calibrated so that volume can be kept within certain established limits. And it is generally conceded that mechanical control of volume increases the possibility of vocal distortion. If the interpreter himself controls the volume, without technical assistance, his voice will sound more natural and spontaneous.

Care must also be taken not to "blast" the microphone, that is, raise the voice to sudden and unexpected peaks of volume. Avoiding this requires the same kind of control which most stage directors strive for when they urge their actors to keep their voices within a certain range of volume. It is very disturbing, and sometimes very funny, when one member of a cast vocalizes above the volume range of every other actor in the play.

Timing must be minutely controlled. There is usually a tendency to hurry if the script has not been well timed and appears to be running over its allotted period. Sometimes, however, hurrying is caused by nervousness; the broadcaster becomes obsessed with the idea that if he does not quicken his pace, the audience will tune off. Timing depends also upon the material to be presented and upon the emotional tensions of the performer. However, no radio program director ever loses sight of the fact that the audience must have time to understand and that rapidity is not too often successful in carrying meaning unless the audience is alert, as in the reception of a basketball game. At such times, the broadcaster's tempo is increased to meet the tension and excitement of the fast-moving action. Normally, though, rushing a program is more likely to cause hesitancy, repetition, errors, unnaturally high pitch, and inarticulate speech. Pauses are just as vital to meaning on the air as they are on the

[2] The album *I Can Hear It Now* (Columbia, 5ML-4095), Vol. 1, contains a recording of this broadcast.

speaking platform, but they must be carefully planned for suspense, for meaning, and for laughs. Furthermore, when more than one person is performing, variations in timing for each personality will help the listening audience to distinguish between characters because of the different speech rhythms. Correct pacing also does much to give the illusion of speaking instead of reading from a script. Of course, various types of material require different timing: one would not expect to use a quick, staccato attack on words for sustained narrative or for characterizations.

Quality of voice, good or bad, will draw the attention of the audience. And sometimes characterizations are remembered because of the peculiar vocal quality of the performer. Many of the popular radio artists are those who have cultivated a vocal quality which identifies the eccentricities of the character they are portraying. This technique of caricaturing is legitimate, if the audience finds humor and fun in the results. Performers like Jack Benny, Gracie Allen, Bob Hope, Milton Berle, and Eve Arden use it successfully. You can name others; perhaps you can even imitate them because the vocal efforts are broad and obvious. In announcing and in narration, as well as in discussion groups, we are likely to enjoy a performer not only because of the resonant quality of his voice but because of some vocal peculiarities, like those that identify H. V. Kaltenborn, Fulton Lewis, Jr., Lowell Thomas, and Quincy Howe. So we can say that if you are hoping to get a warm and enthusiastic response, you should make every effort to use an appropriate vocal quality that will establish your personality in the minds of your audience.

Pitch, with its variations of slides, steps, and key, should be established as soon as you become acquainted with your material. If the program involves other performers, a good director will strive to emphasize differences in key or the level of pitch; he will attempt to point up characterizations or particular types by predominance of certain slides and steps. He knows, as you do through your study of interpretation, that vocal flexibility and variety on the radio is achieved largely through inflection. Because of close contact with the mike, the voice, without undue effort, can carry shadings of meanings through inflections more successfully to the radio audience than to an auditorium audience. This is especially true if you wish to interpret poetry which lends itself to an intimate style of delivery. It is possible to pitch the voice low and keep a close contact with the mike, thus avoiding vocal strain.

One of the surest signs of the amateur radio performer is the failure to change the pitch at beginning of sentences. Variation in key levels is important, too, so that the end of a sentence is not slurred into the same key of a new thought. Sometimes the novice will use an overabundance of slides and wide steps, which are good for humorous situations but sound ridiculous for other kinds of programs. One of the easiest performers to imitate is the storyteller, who exaggerates every vocal device in an effort to clarify the meaning for children.

Articulation on radio programs should never be slovenly, unless a careless speech pattern happens to fit the personality of a character being presented. If a characterization calls for a drawl, or "wuz" for "was," or "settin'" for "sitting," we can accept it as part of the personality to be portrayed; but otherwise poor articulation is taboo. Inappropriate overpreciseness of utterance may be equally objectionable.

Pronunciation not only must be correct but must sound natural. Above all, there should be no hesitation or repetition of unusual words. Words should fit personalities as clothes do. They must "belong," either through habit or through conscious practice. People engaged in radio broadcasting generally use pronunciations that are common to various regions rather than those that are peculiar to a local area. What is heard will be used, and today, many listeners adopt the pronunciations used by radio announcers and news commentators. In fact, the radio probably is doing more to establish standard pronunciation than any dictionary has ever done.

Bodily action and how much it should enter into voice control is another matter that the broadcaster must consider. Inasmuch as visible action and voice normally co-ordinate to create emotional response, the body is as much a part of the interpretation over the air as it is on the platform before a visible audience. A smile or a frown can be "heard" over the air, because it changes the quality and inflection of the voice. Whether the performer wills it or not, general bodily action determines what the voice does. Voice and visible action are not separable. It is true, however, that the radio interpreter cannot use broad gestures or sweeping movements, because the microphone distance must be kept constantly in mind; but he can co-ordinate bodily action and voice to carry meaning over the microphone. For example, the tense, strained body of the sports announcer—every muscle alert for the unusual to happen—gives the proper tension and excitement to his voice. His action and his voice work as one unit.

Train your ear to listen to what the radio voice is really doing. For instance, listen to a variety of programs and try to analyze what you have heard in relation to the following questions:

1. Which announcers' voices sound the most interesting to you?
2. Which comedy voices are the most original?
3. Which voices are the most sincere?
4. Which voice is the most rapid and the best articulated?
5. Which voice would you like to sound like?
6. Which feminine voices appeal to you?
7. What comedy programs do you not like? Why not?
8. What program is most thrilling? Is it because of the voices, the sound effects, or the story?
9. Which voices would you like to take off the air?
10. Which radio drama has the best contrasting voices?

Radio Technique

Everyone interested in radio agrees that "good radio is good showmanship"; and good showmanship means control of technique. In developing radio technique, the interpreter should remember that radio directors are particular about the following general principles:

1. Be comfortable before the microphone, which should be adjusted to the proper height.
2. Keep the right distance from the microphone. If you are too close or too far away, the vocal effects may be distorted.
3. Move and stand quietly. Do not cough into, touch, or kick the microphone.
4. Avoid extraneous personal mannerisms, such as coughing, clearing the throat, and gasping for breath, unless the lines call for such action.

5. Hold the script loosely together, so that you can drop each page softly to the floor, after reading it. Inexpensive paper is less noisy than bond paper.

6. Be careful to give other performers their chance; keep quiet while they are reading and do not get in their way before the microphone.

7. Keep alert to the reading of other characters; remain in character; watch cues so that the illusion of a real incident is preserved.

8. Control the projection of your voice: if your tones are too soft, your voice may lack vitality and carrying power; if your tones have too much volume, you will blast the microphone. Do not project your voice as if you were talking in an auditorium.

9. Control bodily tension: too little tension will not give the impression of spontaneity; too much will cause tightening of the vocal muscles which may result in a harsh, nasal voice.

10. Gain smoothness by distinct and natural articulation rather than overprecise articulation, by certainty of pronunciation, and by the avoidance of careless repetition of words.

11. Strive to get attention immediately.

12. Work for sincerity and spontaneity by:

    recalling the purpose of the broadcast;

    remembering that you have an audience;

    thinking of the meaning of the script;

    phrasing and grouping according to the meaning;

    using brief pauses to accentuate, support, and reinforce meaning;

    thinking your way through the material rather than reading mechanically;

    watching emphasis;

    trying to get the meaning over rather than worrying about finishing on time (the timing should be carefully checked beforehand);

    using inflections that will carry the best meaning;

    timing for interest, laughs, and thought;

    avoiding the same key or pitch at the beginning of every sentence;

    varying the stress at the beginning of sentences, paragraphs, and stanzas;

    varying the length of phrases, when possible;

    avoiding the same key of the last lines of the person preceding you;

    varying the speech rhythm so that a set pattern is not repeated.

THE BROADCASTING VOICE

The Voice of the Announcer

It is often thought that announcing is one of radio's easiest assignments, that anyone who has a good voice can announce. This is not true. More than anyone else the announcer is tempted to use the same stereotyped speech pattern every time he delivers his lines. So much of what he reads is repetitious that he can easily sound insincere. It is his difficult task to avoid monotony, to strive to be direct, to give the message thoughtfully. His role is similar to that of the professional actor who must repeat the same performance for weeks and still sound sincere. He must sound confidential without being smug, intimate without being sentimental. His voice must be accepted by the masses as well as by the cultured. He cannot be too precise, too casual, too commonplace, or too undignified, and he must establish a personality that listeners will remember. He must sound vitally interested if he is to interest his audience.

As an interpreter, the announcer thinks of the meaning of the words on the script before him; he tries to create the mood and stimulate interest in what he is reading. This involves interpretation of the lines rather than mere reading as if from the minutes of the last meeting. The announcer is attempting more than to convey information; he is trying to secure the attention of an audience whose individual likes and dislikes vary widely. The reading, therefore, must be conversational but also compelling. It would be a wise procedure for announcers to practice interpreting all kinds of literature—informative, spectacular, comic, dramatic, or commercial—in order to train their voices in flexibility and variety of tone for various programs. The announcer are really the supersalesmen of the air.

David Ross, winner of the 1932 gold medal awarded by th American Academy of Arts and Letters for effective announcin summarizes the important characteristics of the announcer:[3]

[3] From *The New York Times* (November 13, 1932). Reprinted by pe mission of the author and the publishers.

1. A clear speaking voice.
2. An ability to enlist the voice in the service of good speech.
3. A knowledge of the tonal quality of words and their psychological effects beyond their dictionary meaning.
4. An announcer must first understand his continuity thoroughly before he can speak it intelligently.
5. He must understand the effect of understatement as well as emphasis.
6. He must never try to inflate by false accentuation what is essentially a simple, homey phrase to the proportions of grandeur. The phrase will die of pomposity.
7. He must remember that he is talking to live human beings who have loved, struggled, laughed, dreamed, despaired and hoped; therefore his work before the microphone must reflect his human experience so that his audience will recognize it as real.
8. He must bear in mind that the cheap wisecrack is as offensive as the direct insult.
9. An announcer must know when he knows not, and make it his business to find out.
10. If the announcer expects to be received into the homes of his hearers, he must come with credentials of grace, sincerity and warm fellowship, and these may be found in the voice.

Milton Cross aptly writes, "An announcer's voice must be healthy, well-dressed, and cheerful."

Waldo Abbot, in his *Handbook of Broadcasting*, concludes:[4]

The qualities that make the best announcers are personality, charm, naturalness, sincerity, conviction, enthusiasm, spontaneity, accuracy, culture, and salesmanship, to which add a dash of voice with an excellent vocabulary, and you will have an ideal radio announcer. . . . To be acceptable to the radio listener, the announcer must avoid all forms of affectation such as gushing, evangelical exhortations, pleading sweetness, aggressive overemphasis, spiritual ecstasy, and the precise pronunciation that results in an obvious division of a word into its syllables.

The Voice of the News Commentator

The importance of vocal personality is well demonstrated in the role of the radio news commentator. Although people listen

[4] From *Handbook of Broadcasting* (New York, McGraw-Hill Book Company, 1937), pp. 62, 64.

to news programs primarily to acquire information on current affairs, they have discovered that news can be delivered in a number of ways, depending on the personality of the individual broadcasting. Many of us like our news interpreted in one way better than in another. We may find one voice more distinctive, more authoritative, more direct. Some like the dramatic touch, the enhancing of facts by a spectacular vocal manner. Others like to relax and listen to a voice that soothes. All of us experience a sense of excitement when a news bulletin is flashed in unexpectedly and transmitted immediately by the commentator. It is then that the broadcast reaches a dramatic climax, that the tension of the commentator becomes a reality as it is conveyed to us through the ether. One well-known commentator has remarked that although he tries not to be nervous, it is always an exciting experience for him to know that he may be announcing news of great importance to millions. He concludes that he has yet to have a broadcast during which he is not excited by the possibilities in the use of the radio time allotted to him.

The Voice in Interviews and Round Table Discussions

The voice of a person being interviewed sometimes plays a secondary part before the microphone. Usually the individual to be interviewed is important enough to attract and hold attention, regardless of his voice. The elements of surprise, of human interest, of intimately meeting an important personality may compensate for a poor voice. Interviews, however, often provide an interesting study of the contrast between the announcer's trained voice and the untrained voice of the one being interviewed.

Round table discussions must carry the impression of spontaneity and sincerity so necessary to all radio programs. Care should be taken to identify the voices for the audience by calling the members of the forum by name as often as seems feasible. The technique of giving the illusion of extemporaneous discussion must be carefully worked out, mainly through selection of ideas and the use of the voice. Sometimes actual discussion by members is taken down during a rehearsal and then worked over for general smoothness and emphasis. Then the

participants have to interpret these scripts in the actual broadcast.

The Voice of the Sports Announcer

Probably in no other type of radio program is greater empathy
felt by listeners than in the announcing of sports events. The
rapidity of the game, the excitement of visualizing the ball as it
passes from one team to another, the thrill of a basket or a touchdown, are captured by the audience through one voice which is
tensely, quickly, but surely describing the action of the game and
the excitement of the onlookers. In such a broadcast, the audience does not want a lukewarm, casual voice that carries no
thrill of the contest. The sports announcer is in reality playing a
dramatic role, more dramatic than any other role because of the
shifting action and impromptu climaxes. Consequently the sports
announcer must know his game, he must be fluent, alert, and
observing, and he must have a sense of dramatic values.

The Voice of the Interpreter of Poetry

In 1937 the National Broadcasting Company discovered that
music occupied first place in radio, with literature running a
close second. Their survey showed that 19% of the literature was
poetry, 21% was comedy, and 60% was drama. Radio could be a
great force in bringing back the original custom of reading
poetry aloud for enjoyment.

The microphone enhances the interpretation of poetry. Many
more delicate meanings of a poem can be brought out, and it is
much easier to establish mood and atmosphere over the air
than it is in an auditorium. The reason for this, of course, is that
the voice can be used without strain: the pitch of the voice can
be kept low, the rhythm of the poetry does not have to be
slowed down as in a large-sized hall, the tones can be as soft as
the poetry demands.

A program of poetical selections should follow the same plan
that an interpreter would use for a platform audience: the poetry
should center around a unifying theme, and the author and his
poetry should be well known to the interpreter so that interest-

ing sidelights can be used to point up the interpretation. Music may give continuity, establish mood, and climax the program. However, the interpretation should not fall into the rhythmical patterns of the music and thus be sung over the microphone.

The radio interpreter of poetry should remember that the audience will consist of teachers, ministers, business men and women, laborers, farmers, housewives—old and young. The poetry chosen should not be too mystical or too involved for the audience to understand or for the interpreter to read. Poetry with familiar themes and moods will always attract listeners. The first selection should hold attention, and the last should make the audience wish to listen in again.

The Voice in Comedy

The most successful radio comedy uses the familiar to interest the audience; the more closely the plot ties up with the experiences of the audience, the better it will be liked. Frequently, the appeal is through "hokum": exaggeration of types and characterizations; nasal, plaintive, and infantile voices; hearty guffaws; repetition of the same phrases, events, entrances, and exits. Radio comedy is much like a variety show, which also is built upon vocal gymnastics and stock incidents.

The technique of good timing is one of the necessary assets of the comedian on the air. Timing, as we have mentioned before, can make or break a joke or a "gag," for it can kill a laugh that is ready to break out or it can touch off hilarious laughter. A "gag" is merely a time-worn joke which has been modernized for new situations and new characters and depends on split-second timing for its effect. No one can explain how to gauge correct timing because it is like rhythm—it must be felt or sensed by the performer. Of course, if a comedian has built up a reputation for himself, he has less to worry about, because an expectant audience will laugh no matter what the interpreter does. It is good psychology, however, to be sure of the first laughs, for once laughter has started, the program will usually develop a cumulative effect and become uproarious. The story has been told of how Mark Twain, who always delighted his audience, rose to give a serious speech at a dinner and announced in his first sentence that he was going to give a serious speech for the first time in his life. His remark evoked a roar of laughter, which continued throughout his speech; the more serious he became, the more the audience laughed.

The Voice in Drama

There are certain handicaps in producing radio drama which are not experienced on the stage; but sometimes instead of making the direction more difficult, radio drama simplifies the director's problems. The director can set his drama anywhere, suggesting by conversation and by sound effects the desired atmosphere; the imagination of the audience supplies the stage setting. The mere mention of a cozy fireplace or a glowing fire satisfies the audience; a few grunts and puffs as one works in an imaginary garden and the picture is complete for the radio listeners—perhaps more complete than any which the most competent stage director can give the audience. The radio director does not have to worry about how well entrances and exits are made, about action being duplicated too many times, about crosses and position and balance on the stage, about lighting, costumes, color. But he does have to worry about getting his story over through sound effects and the voice.

He uses dialogue and sound effects to suggest action and revamps his story to cut down on the number of characters so that the voices may be followed easily. He uses repetition to be sure that his audience will not miss important ideas. He uses characters of different sex, age, experience, and taste to achieve interesting vocal effects. He usually begins his story in the midst of action, which, because of time limitations, is quick-moving and climactic. He suggests entrances by sound effects—by the voice, by the slam of a door, or by the rattling of the doorknob, and he gives the impression of distance by various positions before the microphone. The desired illusion is completed by contrasting voices. The director is careful to choose voices that do not sound too much alike and that typify the characters in the script. The hero can be shorter than the heroine; he may be tall, thin, and gawky or he may be short, fat, and roly-poly; he may have red or gray hair. No one cares how he *looks*, if he *sounds* right. Sounding like the part is the crux of the actor's success or failure in radio drama.

Spontaneity and sincerity in the conversational flow are necessary to create the impression of movement and reality. However, no radio director will keep the same pace for all characters; rather, he will vary the tempo to give contrast. Since phrases and sentences must sound conversational, the speech rhythm will shift and change; inflections will indicate specific meaning; and pitch level and quality will suggest character types. If a character is introduced and described by another character, as he often is, with statements like, "You remember Harry. Well, he'll be here soon; slightly aged since his tragedy, but still the same old Harry"—the person taking the part of *Harry* must use the quality of voice, the pitch, the inflections, and the tempo which best suit the description.

In the final analysis, the radio director probably depends on the selection of contrasting and appropriate voices more than on any other factor to put over his drama because, first, the audience must not be confused, and, secondly, the audience must be convinced that the characters are real. The rest of the reality comes if the characters pick up cues, keep alert during the program, remain in character, and interpret lines effectively.

In any kind of radio program, the control of the voice and of all sound effects is necessary. One can have many ingenious mechanical effects, but unless the voices create the meaning, give the continuity of the action, and stimulate the imagination, the program fails. The sound effects are secondary to the vocal sounds and become a part of the total visualized picture by providing the atmosphere for the interpreters—and the audience. However, the listeners not only control the types of programs through their purchase of the advertised product but are keenly critical of what they hear.

The discerning student, after attempting the interpretation of various types of literature before different audiences, will discover that the interpreter's technique is based upon the same principles whether in personal, choral, or radio interpretation. He must always know the meaning of the literature to be interpreted and he must know how to use his voice effectively to create the meanings for an audience.

EXERCISES

The following have been given over the air. These can be practiced with radio casts, either before a tape recorder mike or behind a screen so that the class can hear but not see the characters.

I

Here is an "on the spot" broadcast made by Jack Knell in 1939 as he watched the thrilling rescue of men from the sunken submarine, *U.S.S. Squalus*. Observe how his tension increases as the moment arrives for the first man to emerge and how he keeps up the excitement as each new man is helped out of the bell.[5]

This is Jack Knell speaking to you through short-wave transmitter WAAU operating on 2190 kilocycles. We are at the present time in a small boat, riding at anchor at a spot approximately 50 yards from the scene of rescue operations of the sunken submarine *Squalus*, 16 miles due north from the Portsmouth Navy Yard. We have seen and are seeing one of the most thrilling sights of our lives today. We are seeing history in the making.

About one hour ago, that huge ten-ton diving bell disappeared from view as it sank to the bottom of the sea. We spent anxious minutes awaiting its return to the surface, and just a few minutes ago, before we came on the air, that immense bell broke the surface of the water. Its huge, pear-shaped bulk is now bobbing around in the water close to the side of the rescue ship, *Falcon*. The men aboard the *Falcon* are maneuvering the bell toward the stern of the ship, by means of long poles. They seem to have it in the desired position now, and two men are astride the bell working on the hatch cover in an attempt to unscrew the bolts which keep the cover tightly closed against the sea and the tremendous pressure down there, 250 feet below the surface.

One of the men is rising from his crouched position now, and the men aboard the rescue ship are leaning tensely over the side. . . . I think they're about to open the cover now . . . yes . . . the hatch cover of the diving bell is open! They're reaching down inside the bell now . . . and . . . There's a man's head. . . . They're helping someone out of the bell now. . . . He's climbing out of the bell under his own steam. . . . He's stepping across the top of the bell and is boarding the *Falcon*. . . . The first survivor rescued from the sunken

[5] From *Best Broadcasts of 1938-1939*, ed. Max Wylie (New York, McGraw-Hill Book Company, 1939), pp. 427-428.

submarine *Squalus* is out and safely aboard the rescue ship. . . . and now here's another man coming out of the bell. He's being helped aboard the *Falcon*, although he seems to be able to make it without assistance . . . and here's another . . . and another. . . . These men seem to be in remarkably good condition despite the tremendous strain they've been under. . . . Another man is out now, and they're reaching inside to aid another. . . . We may have lost count during the excitement of seeing these men emerge from the bell alive and well, but I think that's the sixth man to come out of the bell . . . and here . . . here's the seventh.

Seven men have come out of that big, white, pear-shaped diving bell. We don't know if they have all been brought out of the sunken submarine or if some of them went down with the bell to control it. But there you are. . . . We've seen and have attempted to describe to you the actual rescue of the first seven survivors from the ill-fated submarine *Squalus*, which is lying at the bottom of the sea in approximately 250 feet of water. Undoubtedly the bell will immediately be sent down again in an attempt to bring up more of the men trapped down there, but it's a long job, taking at least an hour for the round trip, so we're going to sign off from this point for the time being, but we'll be on hand to bring you the eye-witness account of the rescue as the bell comes up again. Keep tuned to this network for further developments. This is Jack Knell, speaking to you through short-wave transmitter WAAU, operating on 2190 kilocycles. . . . This is the Columbia Broadcasting System.

II

Although the following radio speech is not framed in as dramatic a setting as Jack Knell's broadcast, it is, nevertheless, dramatic in content. The performer must be alive to its possibilities. His voice should reflect some of the wonder of a good story.

CATCHING UP WITH NATURE[6]

Recently, Dr. Black conducted on the General Motors' Symphony the overture by Johann Strauss "Die Fledermaus" or "The Bat." I have often wondered if the composer knew at the time he wrote this that the bat had a voice of great range. The voice, however, is pitched mostly above the ability of the human ear to detect.

I was discussing this with a musical friend of mine and I asked him if he knew of this peculiarity. He said he had never heard of it but he was very curious to know why the bat had this high pitched voice and how he used it. So I told him of the work that had been done

[6] Reprinted by permission of General Motors Corporation.

by two professors at Harvard and added that there were other animals such as cats and dogs who, in addition to their audible voices, were able to communicate with each other in inaudible sounds.

Now most people regard the bat as a rather objectionable, somewhat loathesome creature that lives in dark caves and comes out only in the evening and flies around to hunt for food. The thing that makes this more interesting is that tests made in many of the caves where the bats live show that there is insufficient light to register on our most delicate apparatus. These devices can detect light much below the point of visibility. Now the bat can fly around in these caves apparently as well as if they were fully lighted.

This uncanny "blind flying" ability has, from time to time, aroused a lot of speculation on the part of scientists. Comparatively recently, as I mentioned, two men at Harvard found what they believed to be the answer. Instead of theorizing they decided to try a few simple experiments.

The two men, Dr. Galambos and Dr. Griffin, picked out a sound-proof room for their experiments and suspended from floor to ceiling a straight row of steel wires spaced one foot apart. Bats were set free in the room and they flew about, rarely touching the wires. Then they were blindfolded and this did not seem to make much difference; in fact, some of the bats did better blind-folded. But the next step indicated the bats' secret. Their ears were plugged and their eyes were left uncovered. It was very difficult now to make them fly, but when they did they collided consistently with the wires. And the same thing happened when a thread was tied around their mouths and their eyes were uncovered and the ears unplugged. Apparently the bat steered by sounds from its mouth which were picked up by its ears—the eyes had little or nothing to do with it.

Using the most modern sound-recording devices the men found that while in flight the bat emits a sound which has a frequency of vibration reaching a maximum of about 80,000 cycles—or, in musical terms, about 8½ octaves above middle "C." We call these sounds "supersonic" because their pitch is so high they cannot be heard by the human ear. Our range of hearing is somewhat greater than the highest note produced by instruments of the orchestra. The harmonics on the E string of the violin are about 10,000 cycles per second. Apparently, the bat while in flight sends out these inaudible sounds in short squeaks which strike the obstacle he is approaching and are reflected back and are picked up by his sensitive ears in time for him to steer clear of the object.

This method of sound reflection has been used for many years to determine the depths of the ocean and the pilots of boats in Alaskan waters often use the echo of their boat whistles to determine if they are getting too near the cliffs when traveling in dense fog. Many other applications of this system are in daily use in laboratories for determining faults in materials, and undoubtedly after the war it will be applied in many other ways.

We feel proud of our recently developed sound echo devices even though the bat has been using it in the dark for thousands of years. We marvel at the automatic flying instrumentation of our modern airplanes, but every year flocks of birds go from their southern homes to their northern ones and return to precisely the same location with only their natural "instrumentation." Man has attempted to duplicate some of the feats of the animal world, and in recent years science has given us instrumentation that has done very well indeed.

But we are a long way from catching up to Nature. There are some people who speak glibly of science "conquering Nature." Nothing could be further from the truth. When a scientist conquers something, he abides by the fundamental laws and does so with Nature's permission. He has learned that conquering is submission.

CHARLES F. KETTERING

III

The vocal delivery of this optimistic account of the human race must show warmth and geniality.

I ADMIRE THE HUMAN RACE[7]

I admire the human race. I do, indeed. Everybody is busy running us down, these days, for the mess they say we have made here and there and everywhere. Pshaw! That's short-range stuff, a worm's eye view of our world. Over the marching and abundant centuries, we haven't made any mess. Far from it!

We have done and are doing a better job than anyone has any right to expect. We're all right!

From the beginning, we found ourselves alone in a vast universe, and not only alone but the only living thing on this planet which could realize its loneness. We realized it, gave it a good close look, and then turned our attention to making something practical and useful out of an unprecedented situation.

First of all, we found for ourselves a Light, a God, and we got a sense of direction, a goal to work toward. This was pretty clever of us, if you think of it carefully.

We proceeded to set up standards for our living together. Early in our experience we made the revolutionary discovery that gentleness and kindliness were more practical than brute strength. No other species has ever found that out and used it as a model and practical code of conduct.

We have in actual fact no one we need to answer to, beyond ourselves, and yet we observe our ideal standards in remarkable degree. We are honest and trustworthy one with another so that it is the exception, it is news, when we commit a theft. We are decent 99 per cent of the time, when we could easily be vile.

With silence and mystery behind us and ahead of us, we make up gay little songs and whistle them, and our feet keep jig time to them. We look life and fate in the eye, and smile. I like that, and I admire the people who do it.

Alone among all living things, we have discovered Beauty, and we cherish it, and create it for eye and ear. Alone among living things, we have the power to look at our environment and criticize and improve it.

Finding it necessary to live together by the millions, we created for ourselves governing systems covering vast geographical spaces. Now we actually have the thrilling and terrific idea of a world government, a global government to bring justice to white and black, to Eskimo and Afrikander, rich and poor, not because any tribe is powerful and can exact justice, but because we have conceived and created the ideal of justice and plan it for all men. This is great. This is not the act of a little animal, or a mean animal. This is possible only to a great animal. We inhabit a star, and we know it.

Finding that we have to work to stay alive, we work with ability beyond imagining. Out of the earth we take food, and improve that food year by year; we take heat, and light, so that darkness which lay upon the face of the earth is dispelled by man-made light. We enjoy all the myriad products of our unparalleled ingenuity.

Every morning the necessity for the day's work faces us. And we go and do a day's work, with an overall average effectiveness and perseverance that is amazing, considering many of the jobs.

Of a persistence, a daring and ingenuity impossible to surpass, we find ways to move easily under the water and through the air. Now we speculatively eye our neighboring planets. It should astound no one if man one day begins to move among these planets. How shall I not admire such a creature? Daunted by nothing, his horizons constantly recede, the territories of his possession and use expand and expand.

Whenever he comes to an impassable obstacle, an apparently final barrier, he goes to work at it and, in due time, surpasses it. If it has limits, I do not see where they are. I do not think he has limits. I think he is a child of the universe who inherits eternity. I think he is wonderful. I am his devoted partisan, and I am proud indeed to be one of him.

ROGER W. RIIS

IV

This dramatic sketch is an excellent example of what can be done on radio but not so easily accomplished on television. You will be interested to notice how episodes can be interwoven, regardless of the time element, to give continuity. The voices must show differences in locale, in background, in the use of English, and in patterns of rhythm.

I HAVE NO PRAYER[8]

(*Music setting scene of desert, down and continuing behind*)

ANNOUNCER. We are somewhere in North Africa. The time: yesterday, today, tomorrow . . .

(*Music up, down and continuing behind*)

JOE. A prayer? Are you guys nuts? What do I know about prayers. All right, so he was my friend, so what? I don't know how to pray! (*Down slightly*) Okay. We'll sorta stand around his grave and I'll just talk, but it won't be a prayer. I—uh—I knew Jake just about as long as you guys did. He got to Texas for operational training when I did—and when you guys did. (*Fade*) I remember that day. . . .

(*Music out. Wind sighing, continuing behind*)

COMMANDING OFFICER. I guess there is little to say to you men. You know why you're here. You five are to be the crew of the latest in armored equipment. The six weeks at this field you are to learn to work together—so get to know each other. (*Fade*) That's all men.

(*Music behind*)

JOE. Remember, Jake—get to know each other. Five of us—and if five strange hound dogs meeting each other for the first time could shake hands, that's the way we shook. (*Fade*) Remember, Jake. . . .

(*Music out. Wind sighs behind*)

JOE. Joe Kelly's my name.

JAMES. How do you do, Sergeant. I'm James Adams.

LEM. Me—I'm Lem Jackson.

SAM. Sam Jones is my name.

JAKE. My name is Jake Cracow. Hello.

(*Music continuing behind*)

JOE. I didn't like you, Jake. I didn't think much of the other three,

[8] From "I Have No Prayer," *Free World Theatre: Nineteen New Radio Plays*, pp. 56-62. Copyright, 1944, by Random House, Inc. Reprinted by permission of the publishers.

either. Not my kind of guys. I didn't think so then—and I was sure of it that night. (*Fade*) Remember that night . . .

(*Music out. Sound of five men sitting around. We hear a succession of nervous coughs*)

JAMES. (*Fade-in*) Well, the five of us have been sitting around here for the last ten minutes. C.O. said we had to get acquainted, so here goes. I suggest we simply tell each other all about ourselves —at least the pertinent facts: I'll start. James Adams—born in the suburbs of Boston, Massachusetts. Went to Harvard. I had a couple of hundred flying hours before I joined up—flying private planes. I got washed out a couple months after that—eyes went bad. I can't say I exactly like the change, but here I am and, unless a miracle happens to my eyes (*Fade*), here I stay.

(*Music behind*)

JOE. James Adams here started the ball rolling. Yeah, true confessions —and then Sam. . . .

(*Music behind*)

SAM. (*Fade-in*) I got the name Detroit because Detroit's the only place I've ever known. Me, I didn't get washed out anywhere. I wanted to be here because inside of that tin buggy, like the fellow calls it, is a radial engine, and, if I do say so myself, there's nothing in the book I don't know about radials! (*Fade*) I wonder if they sell beer around here.

(*Music behind*)

JOE. Then Lem. . . .

(*Music goes on. Hold chord*)

LEM. Ah guess that the only thing different about me is Ah never was more'n ten miles away from the place where Ah was born for twenty-one years—so anything that happens to me in this man's war is new—brand new! Only machinery Ah know anything about is an old Fohd, model T, mah pappy used to have. (*Fade*) But Ah guess that won't do much good around heah, will it?

(*Music goes on*)

JOE. Then you, Jake. . . .

(*Hold chord*)

JAKE. So then I went to Northwestern University to get my Master's degree. Biology. It's about the only thing in life I'm interested in. That sounds funny in view of the fact of where I am now—but —but since we're supposed to be talking frankly, there's the truth. What good a Master's degree in biology is going to do driving a tank, I don't know, but maybe I'll be able to do this squad some good. (*Chuckles*) Hey, I've talked enough! It's your turn, Sergeant Kelly. How about you?

JOE. (*Brusquely*) I'm from New York and I'm Irish and let's go to sleep—we got work to do tomorrow!

(*Music goes on*)

JOE. Five guys: a longnose from Harvard who looked as if he was born wearing soup and fish; a cockeyed mechanic with dirt and grease under his nails; a Hebe from Chicago; a Methodist farmer kid from the South with a thin face like he was hungry most of the time—and me. Five different guys—yeah, different. . . .

OFFICER. (*Filter*) The six weeks at this field you are to learn to work together.

JOE. Okay! Okay! You're in the army now! Guys you'd never be with, you're *with!* Okay!

(*Music goes into tense action. Sound of tank and continuing back*)

JOE. You're in a tank with those four guys, and their names happen to be Jake and Lem and Sam and James Adams. And you're in a tank and you gotta be a team 'cause you're in the army now! Yeah!

(*Music building on time motif*)

JOE. And a couple of days go by!

(*Music, time motif*)

JOE. And a couple of more!

(*Music, time motif*)

JOE. And then it's a couple of weeks—and a couple more . . .

(*Music hits chord*)

JOE. And one day riding along in that tank, a funny thing happens. . . .

(*Music out. Fade-in of tank rolling along, continuing behind*)

JIM. (*Calling out above rumble of mechanism, slight echo*) Enemy objective thousand yards right.

JOE. (*Back*) Thousand right—full speed ahead!

JAKE. (*Back*) Full speed ahead!

JIM. Range seven fifty.

JOE. Ready for firing, Lem!

LEM. Ready!

JOE. Steady ahead, Jake!

JAKE. Okay, Joe!

JOE. Steady! Fire!

(*Seventy-five gun goes off*)

SAM. A hit! It's a hit! (*Fade*) A hit!

(*Sound fades quickly with above. Music behind*)

JOE. Yeah, it happens! All at once you *like* being with these guys! You can't figure it out, but you like being with them! Yeah, you who all your life had been full of words like Hunkie and Dago and Wop and Sheenie. . . . Yeah, you who had always thought that anybody who had any more schooling than you had was a fathead, that anybody who was a farmer was a hick, that anybody who didn't live right around where you'd always lived wasn't quite right! All of a sudden you were forgettin' all those things, and—an' likin' these guys. . . . And you can't figure it out! (*Music hits*

attention chord) And all at once you're not rollin' a tank over Texas
—you're to heck and gone and you don't know quite how it happened! (*Sound of tank behind*) You're in Africa—rollin' over the
sand in Africa—and the same guys are with you—and the old iron
buggy makes the same noise—but it's not the same . . . (*Music
goes into something planting war*) 'Cause the objective is *real* now
—the Nazi objective—and you can't see 'em, but you know they're
some place up ahead because the radio buzzing in your ears is
tellin' you. . . .

VOICE. (*British, through headphones*) They're over the ridge, Americans. Get them!

JOE. So you give the order. This is it! Let's get 'em, guys! Yeah, guys!
Four guys—*your* guys! And the tank shakin' underneath you and
your heart's bangin' inside of you. (*Music hits chord*) And then
the second funny thing happens! You're not five guys in the belly
of that iron thing but *one* guy—one guy drivin' it, and the same
guy sightin' down the gun, and the same guy standin' by to load
it, and the same guy at the machine gun, and the same guy watchin'
through the turret—one guy—*one* guy—and he's a scared guy, and
a mad guy, and a guy like ice, and he's not a Methodist or a Jew
or a Catholic or a Protestant or a guy with no God. He's one fightin'
guy and he's goin' to beat back the Nazi or die tryin'! (*Music
builds to climax, then down and continuing quietly behind*)
(*Quietly*) You were the one who died tryin', Jake. And we buried
you here and now I'm supposed to say a prayer over you. I can
only talk. We got to the top of the ridge and there were three of
them waitin' for us. We got them—but they got you. Jim says
there should be a star over your grave, but that'll have to wait.
Meanwhile we've stuck up a cross, so we'll know where you're at
when we come back. We lost the iron buggy, and we're hoofin' it
back to the base, but we *will* come back. If it isn't me and Lem
and Sam and Jim, it'll be others like us, so like us you won't be
able to tell us apart 'cause—'cause like I said before, there's only
one guy fightin' this war on our side. He's the guy who's found
out, now that the chips are down, that we're all men together—
fightin' for one reason. Yeah, all over the world—so that the Catho-
lics and the Hindus and the Chinese and the Methodists and the
Jews, and the Greeks and the English and every other kind of
man can be free men together all over the world. But—a different
kind of a free man! Not like I was—with a chip on my shoulder
that my father had put there, and my father's father before him
on account of the wrongs that had been done back in Ireland. Not
like—like Lem here—thinkin' that anybody who didn't talk like
he did, or have the same kind of skin over his bones was the scum
of the earth! Or not like Jim—with a fence between himself and
anybody who didn't come from his snooty neck of the woods. No!

(*Tightly*) Jake, maybe out of this war, just the way five guys like us who thought we were free Americans found out we weren't really free of all the dirty hates inside of ourselves until we started workin' together—maybe it'll be like that—at least the start of it —all over the world! We'll march into Germany—all of us together —all of us alike—and nobody will be askin' anybody else where they're from, or what they did, or what's their skin, or the shape of their head, or the crook of their nose! They'll be men together with one idea—to make this world a place of live and let live— no, live and *help* live! And nobody's goin' to gyp them and us out of that idea—nobody, *nobody!* (*Down, quietly*) Well, Jake, I—I guess that's all. We'll be back for you. Lie there in peace. If I said anything wrong or—or not fittin' to the occasion, excuse me. I only said what I could say . . . I got no prayer. . . .
(*Music up to curtain*)

ARCH OBOLER

V

The selection below is not so personal in its approach as the preceding ones; nevertheless, it makes a dramatically effective radio presentation, especially if choral interpretation is used to build up climaxes. It may also provide an auditorium program, in which case performers should be scattered throughout the audience. The voices should seem to come from different distances. Cues concerning the kinds of voices to be used have been provided by the author. Watch for variety and contrast in quality, force, timing, and pitch. Whenever the voices speak in short sentences, try to gain effectiveness by varying the pitch levels at the beginning of sentences and by changing the volume and attitudes of the speakers. Be certain that each sentence is not given the same emphasis and stress.

LISTEN TO THE PEOPLE[9]

Independence Day, 1941

NARRATOR:
This is Independence Day,
Fourth of July, the day we mean to keep,
Whatever happens and whatever falls

[9] From *The Selected Works of Stephen Vincent Benét* (New York, Farrar & Rinehart, Inc., 1941), Vol. 1, p. 471. Copyright, 1941, by Stephen Vincent Benét. Reprinted by permission of the Stephen Vincent Benét estate.

Out of a sky grown strange;
This is firecracker day for sunburnt kids,
The day of the parade,
Slambanging down the street.
Listen to the parade!
There's J. K. Burney's float,
Red-white-and-blue crepe-paper on the wheels,
The Fire Department and the local Grange,
There are the pretty girls with their hair curled,
The Spirit of East Greenwich, Betsy Ross,
Democracy, or just some pretty girls.
There are the veterans and the Legion Post
(Their feet are going to hurt when they get home),
The band, the flag, the band, the usual crowd,
Good-humored, watching, hot,
Silent a second as the flag goes by,
Kidding the local cop and eating popsicles,
Jack Brown and Rosie Shapiro and Dan Shay,
Paul Bunchick and the Greek who runs the Greek's,
The black-eyed children out of Sicily,
The girls who giggle and the boys who push,
All of them there and all of them a nation.
And, afterwards,
There'll be ice cream and fireworks and a speech
By Somebody the Honorable Who,
The lovers will pair off in the kind dark
And Tessie Jones, our honor-graduate,
Will read the Declaration.
That's how it is. It's always been that way.
That's our Fourth of July, through war and peace,
That's our Fourth of July.

And a lean farmer on a stony farm
Came home from mowing, buttoned up his shirt
And walked ten miles to town,
Musket in hand.
He didn't know the sky was falling down
And, it may be, he didn't know so much.
But people oughtn't to be pushed around
By kings or any such.
A workman in the city dropped his tools.
An ordinary, small-town kind of man
Found himself standing in the April sun,
One of a ragged line
Against the skilled professionals of war,
The matchless infantry who could not fail,
Not for the profit, not to conquer worlds,

Not for the pomp or the heroic tale
But first, and principally, since he was sore.
They could do things in quite a lot of places.
They shouldn't do them here, in Lexington.
He looked around and saw his neighbors' faces. . . .

AN ANGRY VOICE:
Disperse, ye villains! Damn you, why don't you disperse?

A CALM VOICE:
Stand your ground, men. Don't fire unless fired upon.
But, if they mean to have a war, let it begin here!

NARRATOR, RESUMING:
Well, that was that. And later, when he died
Of fever or a bullet in the guts,
Bad generalship, starvation, dirty wounds
Or any one of all the thousand things
That kill a man in wars,
He didn't die handsome but he did die free
And maybe that meant something. It could be.
Oh, it's not pretty! Say it all you like!
It isn't a bit pretty. Not one bit.
But that is how the liberty was won.
That paid for the firecrackers and the band.

A YOUNG VOICE, RADICAL:
Well, what do you mean, you dope?
Don't you know this is an imperialist, capitalist country, don't you?
Don't you know it's all done with mirrors and the bosses get the
    gravy, don't you?
Suppose some old guy with chin whiskers did get his pants shot off
    at a place called Lexington?
What does it mean to me?

AN OLDER VOICE, CONSERVATIVE:
My dear fellow, I myself am a son of a son of a son of the American
    Revolution,
But I can only view the present situation with the gravest alarm,
Because we are rapidly drifting into a dictatorship
And it isn't my kind of dictatorship, what's more.
The Constitution is dead and labor doesn't know its place,
And then there's all that gold buried at Fort Knox
And the taxes—oh, oh, oh!
Why, what's the use of a defense-contract if you can't make money
    out of your country?
Things are bad—things are very bad.
Already my Aunt Emeline has had to shoot her third footman.
(He broke his leg passing cocktails and it was really a kindness.)

And, if you let the working-classes buy coal, they'll only fill it with bathtubs.

Don't you realize the gravity of the situation, don't you?

Won't you hide your head in a bucket and telegraph your congressman, opposing everything possible, including peace and war?

A TOTALITARIAN VOICE, PERSUASIVE:

My worthy American listeners,

I am giving you one more chance.

Don't you know that we are completely invincible, don't you?

Won't you just admit that we are the wave of the future, won't you?

You are a very nice, mongrel, disgusting people—

But, naturally, you need new leadership.

We can supply it. We've sent the same brand to fourteen nations.

It comes in the shape of a bomb and it beats as it sweeps as it cleans.

For those of you who like order, we can supply order.

We give the order. You take it.

For those of you who like efficiency, we can supply efficiency.

Look what we did to Coventry and Rotterdam!

For those of you who like Benito Mussolini, we can supply Benito Mussolini.

(He's three doors down to the left, at the desk marked Second Vice President.)

Now be sensible—give up this corrupt and stupid nonsense of democracy.

And you can have the crumbs from our table and a trusty's job in our world-jail.

RADICAL VOICE:

Forget everything but the class struggle. Forget democracy.

CONSERVATIVE VOICE:

Hate and distrust your own government. Whisper, hate, and never look forward.

Look back wistfully to the good old, grand old days—the days when the boys said "The public be damned!" and got away with it.

Democracy's a nasty word, invented by the Reds.

TOTALITARIAN VOICE:

Just a little collaboration and you too can be part of the New Order.

You too can have fine new concentration camps and shoes made out of wood pulp. You too can be as peaceful as Poland, as happy and gay as France. Just a little collaboration. We have so many things to give you.

We can give you your own Hess, your own Himmler, your own Goering—all home-grown and wrapped in cellophane. We've done it elsewhere. If you'll help, we can do it here.

RADICAL VOICE:
Democracy's a fake—

CONSERVATIVE VOICE:
Democracy's a mistake—

TOTALITARIAN VOICE:
Democracy is finished. We are the future.

(*Music up and ominous*)

NARRATOR, RESUMING:
The sky is dark, now, over the parade,
The sky's an altered sky, a sky that might be.

There's J. K. Burney's float
With funny-colored paper on the wheels
Or no—excuse me—used to be J.K.'s.
But the store's under different management
Like quite a lot of stores.
You see, J.K. got up in church one day,
After it all had happened and walked out.
That day they instituted the new order.
They had a meeting. Held it in the church.
He just walked out. That's all.
That's all there is to say about J.K.,
Though I remember just the way he looked,
White-faced and chin stuck out.
I think they could have let the church alone.
It's kind of dreary, shutting up the church.
But don't you say I said so. Don't you say!
Listen to the parade!
There are the pretty girls with their hair curled,
Back from the labor camp.
They represent the League of Strength through Joy.
At least, I guess it's that.
No, they don't go to high school any more.
They get told where to go. We all get told.
And, now and then, it happens like Jack Brown,
Nice fellow, Jack. Ran the gas station here.
But he was married to a You-Know-Who.
Fond of her, too.
I don't know why we never used to mind.
Why, she walked round like anybody else,
Kept her kids clean and joined the Ladies' Social.
Just shows you, doesn't it? But that's all done.
And you won't see her in the crowd today,

Her or the kids or Jack,
Unless you look six feet under the ground,
The lime-washed ground, the bitter prison ground
That hides the martyrs and the innocent,
And you won't see Dan Shay.
Dan was a Union man
And now we don't have Unions any more.
They wouldn't even let him take his specs,
The day the troopers came around for him.
And yet he needed specs. He had gray hair.
Funny—you keep remembering things like that.
Maybe he's still alive. It's hard to say.
(*Half hysterically*)
Listen to the parade!
The marching, marching, marching feet,
All with the same hard stamp!
The bands, the bands, the bands, the flags, the flags,
The sharp, mechanical, inhuman cheer
Dragged from the straining throats of the stiff crowd!
It's Independence—sorry, my mistake!
It's National Day—the Day of the New Order!
We let it happen—we forgot the old,
Bleak words of common sense, "Unite or Die,"
We fiddled and we squabbled and we scrapped,
We led a filibuster in the Senate,
We were quite ready for a sacrifice
Sometime, next Tuesday—but not yet, not now!
And the clock struck—and the bad dream was here.

A Voice:
But you can't do this to me! I subscribed to Party funds!

A Voice:
You can't do this to me. We got laws, We got courts, We got unions.

A Voice:
You can't do this to me. Why, I believe in Karl Marx!

A Voice:
You can't do this to me. The Constitution forbids it.

A Voice:
I was always glad to co-operate.

A Voice:
It looked to me like good business.

A Voice:
It looked to me like the class struggle.

A VOICE:
It looked to me like peace in our time.

TOTALITARIAN VOICE:
Thank you, ladies and gentlemen. Democracy is finished. You are
 finished. We are the present!

(*Music up and down*)

NARRATOR:
That is one voice. You've heard it. Don't forget it.
And don't forget it can be slick or harsh,
Violent or crooning, but it's still the same,
And it means death.

Are there no other voices? None at all?
No voice at all out of the long parade
That marched so many years,
Out of the passion of the Puritans,
The creaking of the wagons going west,
The guns of Sharpsburg, the unnumbered dead,
Out of the baffled and bewildered hosts
Who came here for a freedom hardly known,
Rebel and exile, bondservant and outcast.
Out of the bowels of the immigrant ship,
The strange, sick voyage, the cheating and the scorn
And yet, at the end, Liberty.
Liberty with a torch in her right hand,
Whoever cheated and whoever lied,
Liberty for my children, Liberty
Slowly worked out, deceived a thousand times,
But never quite forgotten, always growing,
Growing like wheat and corn.
"I remember a man named Abe Lincoln.
I remember the words he used to say."
Oh, we can call on Lincoln and Tom Paine,
Adams and Jefferson.
Call on the great words spoken that remain
Like the great stars of evening, the fixed stars,
But that is not enough.
The dead are mighty and are part of us
And yet the dead are dead. This is our world,
Our time, our choice, our anguish, our decision.
This is our world. We have to make it now,
A hundred and thirty millions of us have to,
And make it well, or suffer the bad dream.
What have we got to say?

A Woman's Voice:
I don't know. I'm a woman with a house.
I do my work. I take care of my man.
I've got a right to say how things should be.
I've got a right to have my kids grow up
The way they ought to grow. Don't stop me there.
Don't tread on me, don't hinder me, don't cross me.
I made my kids myself. I haven't got
Big words to tell about them.
But, if you ask about democracy,
Democracy's the growing and the bearing,
Mouth at the breast and child still to be born.
Democracy is kids and the green grass.

Narrator:
What have we got to say,
People, you people?

A Man's Voice:
I guess I haven't thought about it much.
I been too busy. Way I figure it
It's this way. We've got something. If it's crummy
The bunch of us can change what we don't like
In our own way and mean it.
I got a cousin back in the old country.
He says it's swell there but he couldn't change
A button on his pants without an order
From somebody's pet horse. Maybe he likes it.
I'm sticking here. That's all. Well, sign me off.

Narrator:
People, you people, living everywhere,
Sioux Falls and Saugatuck and Texarkana,
Memphis and Goshen, Harrodsburg and Troy,
People who live at postmarks with queer names,
Blue Eye and Rawhide, Santa Claus and Troublesome,
People by rivers, people of the plains,
People whose contour-plows bring back the grass
To a dust-bitten and dishonored earth,
And those who farm the hillside acres still
And raise up fortitude between the stones,
Millions in cities, millions in the towns,
People who spit a mile from their front doors
And gangling kids, ballplaying in the street,
All races and all stocks, all creeds and cries,
And yet one people, one, and always striving. . . .

A MAN:
I'm on relief.
I know what they say about us on relief,
Those who were never there.
All the same, we made the park.
We made the road and the check-dam and the culvert.
Our names are not on the tablets. Forget our names.
But, when you drive on the road, remember us, also.
Remember Johnny Lombardo and his pick,
Remember us, when you build democracy,
For we, too, were part and are part.

NARRATOR:
One nation, one.
And the voices of young and old, of all who have faith,
Jostling and mingling, speaking from the ground,
Speaking from the old houses and the pride,
Speaking from the deep hollows of the heart.

A MAN'S VOICE:
I was born in '63.
There were many then who despised the Republic,
Many fine and solid citizens.
They had good and plausible reasons and were eloquent.
I grew up in the Age of Brass, the Age of Steel.
I have known and heard of three wars.
All through my life, whenever the skies were dark,
There came to me many fine and solid citizens,
Wringing their hands, despairing of the Republic,
Because of an income tax or a depression,
Because their party had lost the last election,
Because we couldn't do this and shouldn't do that.
And yet, each time, I saw the Republic grow
Like a great elm tree, through each fault and failure,
The stubborn rock, the parched soil,
And spread its branches over all the people.
Look at the morning sun. There is the Republic.
Not yesterday, but there, the breaking day.

TOTALITARIAN VOICE:
But, my worthy American listeners,
All this is degenerate talk.
The future rolls like a wave and you cannot fight it.

A VOICE:
Who says we can't?

A Voice:
Who says so?

A Voice:
What's his racket?

A Voice:
How does he get that way?

A Voice:
You mean to tell me
A little shrimp like that could run the world,
A guy with a trick mustache and a bum salute
Run us, run you and me?

Totalitarian Voice:
You mistake me.
Others have often made the same mistake
Often and often and in many countries.
I never play upon a people's strength.
I play upon their weaknesses and fears.
I make their doubts my allies and my spies.
I have a most convincing mask of peace
Painted by experts, for one kind of sucker,
And for another—I'm a business man,
Straight from the shoulder, talking trade and markets
And much misunderstood.
I touch this man upon his pocketbook,
That man upon his hatred for his boss,
That man upon his fear.
I offer everything, for offering's cheap.
I make no claims until I make the claims.
I'm always satisfied until I'm not,
Which happens rather rapidly to those
Who think I could be satisfied with less
Than a dismembered and digested world.
My secret weapon is no secret weapon.
It is to turn all men against all men
For my own purposes. It is to use
Good men to do my work without their knowledge,
Not only the secret traitor and the spy.
It is to raise a question and a doubt
Where there was faith. It is to subjugate
Men's minds before their bodies feel the steel.
It is to use
All envy, all despair, all prejudice
For my own work.
If you've an envy or prejudice

A nicely grown, well-rounded piece of hate,
I'll play on it and use it to your ruin.
My generals are General Distrust,
General Fear, General Half-A-Heart,
General It's-Too-Late,
General Greed and Major-General Hate,
And they go walking in civilian clothes
In your own streets and whisper in your ears.
I won't be beaten just by sitting tight.
They tried that out in France. I won't be beaten
By hiding in the dark and making faces,
And certainly I never will be beaten
By those who rather like my kind of world,
Or, if not like it, think that it must come,
Those who have wings and burrow in the ground.
For I'm not betting only on the tanks,
The guns, the planes, the bombers,
But on your own division and disunion.
On your own minds and hearts to let me in,
For, if that happens, all I wish for happens.
So what have you got to say?
What have you got to bet against my bet?
Where's your one voice?

AMERICAN VOICE:
Our voice is not one voice but many voices.
Not one man's, not the greatest, but the people's.
The blue sky and the forty-eight States of the people.
Many in easy times but one in the pinch
And that's what some folks forget.
Our voice is all the objectors and dissenters
And they sink and are lost in the groundswell of the people,
Once the people rouse, once the people wake and listen.
People, you people, growing everywhere,
What have you got to say?
There's a smart boy here with a question and he wants answers.
What have you got to say?

A VOICE:
We are the people. Listen to us now.

A VOICE:
Says you we're puny? We built Boulder Dam,
We built Grand Coulee and the T.V.A.
We built them out of freedom and our sweat.

A VOICE:
Says you we're faint of heart and little of mind?

We poured like wheat through the gaps of the Appalachians.
We made the seas of wheat, the seas of corn.
We made five States a sea of wheat and corn.

A VOICE, LAUGHING:
We built the cities and the skyscrapers,
All the proud steel. We built them up so high
The eagles lost their way.

A VOICE:
That's us. When did you do a job like that?

A VOICE:
Wasn't enough.

A VOICE:
No, and you bet it wasn't.
Not with the apple-sellers in the streets,
Not with the empty shops, the hungry men.

A VOICE:
But we learned some things in that darkness and kept free.
We didn't fold up and yell for a dictator.
We built, even in the darkness. We learned our trade
By the licks we took and we're building different now.

A VOICE:
We lost our way for a while but we've found our way.
We know it and we'll hold it and we'll keep it.
We'll tell it to the world. We're saying it.

A VOICE:
Freedom to speak and pray.

A VOICE:
Freedom from want and fear.

A VOICE:
That's what we're building.

A VOICE:
Now and here and now.

A VOICE:
Forever and forever and forever.

NARRATOR:
People, you people, risen and awake. . . .

A VOICE:
That's what we're building and we'll build it here.
That's what we're building and we'll build it now,

Build it and make it shine across the world,
A refuge and a fortress and a hope,
Breaking old chains and laughing in the sun.
This is the people's cause, the people's might.
We have set up a standard for the free
And it shall not go down.
That's why we drill the plate and turn the wheel,
Build the big planes.
That's why a million and a half of us
Learn here and now how free men stand in arms.
Don't tread on us, don't hinder us, don't cross us.
We won't have tyranny here.

A VOICE:
We don't give one long low hoot for your master race.
We think your slick new order's a bowl of raspberries.
We'll pick the small and the free and the enduring,
Wherever we find them and wherever they are.
We won't have tyranny here.

A VOICE:
We'll stick by Rosie Shapiro and Dan Shay,
Paul Bunchick and the Greek who runs the Greek's,
And all of 'em like that, wherever they are,
We'll stick by the worn old stones in Salem churchyard,
The Jamestown church and the bones of the Alamo.
We won't have tyranny here.

A VOICE:
It's a long way out of the past and a long way forward.
It's a tough way, too, and there's plenty of trouble in it.
It's a black storm crowding the sky and a cold wind blowing,
Blowing upon us all.
See it and face it. That's the way it is.
That's the way it'll be for a time and a time.
Even the easy may have little ease.
Even the meek may suffer in their meekness.
But we've ridden out storms before and we'll ride out this one,
Ride it out and get through.
It won't be done by the greedy and the go-easies.
The stuffed shirts, the "yes but" men and the handsome phonies,
The men who want to live in their father's pockets,
The folks who barely believe and the bitter few.
It'll be done by the river of the people,
The mountain of the people, the great plain
Grown to the wheat of the people,
Plowed by their suffering, harrowed by their hope,
Tall with their endless future.

It'll be done by the proud walker, Democracy,
The walker in proud shoes.
Get on your feet, Americans, and say it!
Forget your grievances, wherever you are,
The little yesterday's hates and the last year's discord.
This is your land, this is your independence,
This is the people's cause, the people's might.
Say it and speak it loud, United, free . . .

MANY VOICES:
United, free.

A VOICE:
Whatever happens and whatever falls.
We pledge ourselves to liberty and faith.

MANY VOICES:
To liberty and faith.

A VOICE:
We pledge ourselves to justice, law and hope
And a free government by our own men
For us, our children and our children's children.

MANY VOICES:
For us, our children and our children's children.

A VOICE:
Not for an old dead world but a new world rising.

A VOICE:
For the toil, the struggle, the hope and the great goal.

(*Music up and down*)

NARRATOR:
You've heard the long parade
And all the voices that cry out against it,
Some of our own, and one that's not our own
And never will be while we're still the people.
(*Quietly*)
What do the people say?
Well, you've just heard some questions and some answers,
Not all, of course. No man can say that's all.
A man's a humbug if he says that's all.
But look in your own minds and memories
And find out what you find and what you'd keep.
It's time we did that and it won't be earlier.
I don't know what each one of you will find,
What memory, what token, what tradition,

It may be only half a dozen words
Carved on a stone, carved deeper in the heart,
It might be all a life, but look and find it—
Sun on Key West, snow on New Hampshire hills,
Warm rain on Georgia and the Texas wind
Blowing across an empire and all part,
All one, all indivisible and one—
Find it and keep it and hold on to it,
For there's a buried thing in all of us,
Deeper than all the noise of the parade,
The thing the haters never understand
And never will, the habit of the free.

Out of the flesh, out of the minds and hearts
Of thousand upon thousand common men,
Cranks, martyrs, starry-eyed enthusiasts,
Slow-spoken neighbors, hard to push around,
Women whose hands were gentle with their kids,
And men with a cold passion for mere justice.
We made this thing, this dream.
This land unsatisfied by little ways,
Open to every man who brought good will,
This peaceless vision, groping for the stars,
Not as a huge devouring machine
Rolling and clanking with remorseless force
But as live earth where anything could grow,
Your crankiness, my notions and his dream,
Grow and be looked at, grow and live or die.
But get their chance of growing and the sun.
We made it and we make it and it's ours.
We shall maintain it. It shall be sustained.

ALL VOICES UP:

WE SHALL MAINTAIN IT. IT SHALL BE SUSTAINED.

(*Music up to climax*)

(*Curtain*)

STEPHEN VINCENT BENÉT

TECHNIQUE PROBLEMS IN RADIO AND TELEVISION

The two great media of communication—radio and television
—are basically alike in that each depends on the effective delivery of words to convey the intended impression. They differ

primarily in that the "listening ear" of radio has become the "watching eye" of television. Radio relies exclusively on the voice, sound effects, and music to reach the major proportion of its audience. It thus allows the listener's imagination to create its own illusion of reality through suggestion. Television, on the other hand, utilizes these same sound elements in combination with an almost unlimited variety of visual aids. The illusion, therefore, is specifically defined and no longer left to the individual's imagination. For this reason, then, although in both media the spoken word remains a vital force in evoking audience response, the problems of interpretation and presentation faced by the radio director differ substantially from those the television director must solve.

In radio, the emphasis is always on sound, and because of this, the director must be able to handle vocal techniques with unusual skill. The voices of his cast must reflect versatility, sincerity, and assurance. Here, he is at somewhat less of a disadvantage than the television director, for he is not concerned with how the radio actor looks, so long as he is vocally able to create the desired illusion. Also, with a few changes in pitch, quality, force, and tempo, the radio director can use the same voices to interpret more than one part or one personality. But this very concession requires him to exercise greater interpretative ingenuity. He must be expert in the use of speech techniques and devices. He must know how to balance and contrast voices and how to suggest with only a few words. He must know how to build up action or climax by a montage of vocal arrangements so that a quick succession of short scenes of one or two sentences will indicate a personality or an action. His sense of timing must be unusually keen, and he must be familiar with the limitations and possibilities of the microphone, the control room, and the other technical equipment of his studio. Above all, the good radio director must be able to integrate all these elements in such a way that the total meaning of his program is effectively presented to an audience that is held by what it *hears.*

In television, vocal interpretation is subordinate to the visual presentation. The audience is impressed first by what it sees and only secondly by what it hears. Consequently, the television director concentrates on conveying the meaning of his material through visual effects. Unlike the radio director, he must consider such factors as lighting, scenery, costumes, physical appearance, and make-up. His cast must be chosen with a view to the principles of acting, especially the use of the body as a unit. Gestures, facial expressions, positions, and attitudes become important. In a sense, the television director is more limited than the radio director in his job. He must have performers who can memorize lines, frequently on short notice, and he can assign only one part to each. Furthermore, he must work with, and depend on, a host of technicians, especially the camera crew, the electricians, and the audio man, who assumes control of the voices as well as the sound effects. Also, he must create the illusion of reality within the physical boundaries of the studio stage or set.

Despite his preoccupation with visual effects, however, the television director who knows his job never disregards the basic principles of good interpretation or neglects to incorporate into his presentation many of the vocal techniques used in radio. Evidence of this is found in the following list of requirements prepared by the National Association of Radio and Television Broadcasters. Compare it with the requirements for radio performers listed on p. 568.

APTITUDES AND PERSONALITY IN TV[10]

Aptitudes

1. *A good radio voice:* The accepted radio voice of 15 years ago is not the accepted voice of today. The stentorian tone is no longer in demand. In fact, as a general rule, it is frowned upon. A natural, easy delivery is the order of the day. (This is not to be confused with sloppy or careless delivery.) The voice must convey warmth, sincerity and integrity. As one network official said, a good announcer's voice must sound like the average man thinks he sounds although not, of course, as the average man does in fact sound.

2. *Pleasant, neat appearance:* Television, by adding sight to sound, emphasizes the importance of appearance. However, most TV stations have found that the great majority of their radio announcers are sufficient on this count to handle a TV job. Most TV station

[10] From *Station Management Takes a Look at Television Jobs* (Washington, D. C., The National Association of Radio and Television Broadcasters, 1952), pp. 7-8. Reprinted by permission of the publishers.

managers feel that an honest, sincere, pleasant face will stand up best
over the long haul. The movie star profile will not be a handicap, but
neither will the lack of it. However, those with physical defects which
show up before the camera, also those who are extreme physical types
—for example, very tall, very short, very fat, or very thin—are not
acceptable for television. It is important to keep in mind here that
these are characteristics of general applicability. Exceptions may and
do exist.

3. *Ability to memorize:* This is an extremely important difference
between AM and TV announcing. There are some good AM announcers who are well qualified for TV except on this count. They
cannot learn lines, especially on short notice. It doesn't take more
than one or two "forgets," especially at the network or larger station
level, for an announcer in TV to lose favor with sponsors and management. At the small stations, the memory factor is in some ways even
more important. Much less rehearsal time is available; copy is often
written at the last minute; and there are no mechanical memory aids
available.

4. *Diction:* There was a time in radio when perfect, or what
would now be regarded as stilted, diction was thought to be desirable.
This quality has gone the way of the stentorian tone. Clear diction is
necessary but naturalness is an equally important factor.

5. *Fluency:* Ability to *ad lib* has become increasingly important
in radio. There is every reason to believe that it will be equally or
even more important in television where the use of scripts is often
awkward or disconcerting to the audience. A quick mind and fluent
delivery are often a good substitute for memory.

6. *Acting ability:* Almost all of those who have had considerable
hiring experience in TV emphasize again and again the importance
for announcers. Even with the simplest type of show, where the announcer is merely sitting at a desk and giving a commercial, the ability
to use the hands and face correctly is essential. Where product
demonstrations are involved, grace and sureness of movement become
much more important. All agree that stage experience is the one best,
and indeed, almost the only way in which to develop this aptitude.

Personality

Television is a merciless revealer of personality. Insincerity,
smugness, and conceit are clearly portrayed by the TV camera. This
means that the TV announcer must be a genuine, sincere personality.
On the other hand, an outgoing nature is important. Indeed, few
would be attracted to the field who are not basically outgoing. However, several station managers emphasize the fact that television announcing is no place for egomaniacs. Stability, honesty, cooperative-
ness are also placed high on the list of desirable personality traits.

CONCLUSION

The interpretative techniques that have been defined and illustrated in this book will serve as an excellent foundation for those students who continue to work in the field of speech or its related areas. Whatever the student can add in the way of experience, living, travel, and study will help him achieve the effective presentation of all types of material. In conclusion, however, two major considerations should be pointed out. The first is that the fundamental principles of good speech set forth here can be of lasting value to all students, regardless of their future pursuits. We have repeatedly emphasized the interrelationship of personality and speech pattern. A well-balanced personality, grounded in healthful living, is the most predominant factor in cultivating a pleasant voice. And, certainly, a flexible, well-modulated voice contributes much to the social poise and popularity of the individual. Secondly, we have stressed the importance of understanding both the logical and emotional meanings of any literary selection. Throughout, we have indicated various approaches to that understanding. It is hoped, therefore, that the guideposts in this book will have led the student toward not only a fuller and more artistic interpretation but a deeper personal appreciation of good literature.

APPENDIX

Vocal and Articulatory Improvement

The following exercises are necessary mechanical drills for the interpreter, just as finger drills are for the pianist. Failure to control the vocal mechanism can interfere most seriously with the artistry of your performance. Therefore, mastery of these details, though it will not guarantee an effective performance, forms the basis for your study of interpretation.

Vocal Quality

Before you start it might be helpful to review the section on the vocal mechanism (pp. 243-252). Also, do not practice the following exercises until you have read Edmund Jacobson's *You Must Relax* or David Fink's *Release from Nervous Tension.*[1] You should have some concept of what the word *relax* means before you try to relax, because, as was pointed out earlier, good vocal quality *begins* with bodily relaxation and controlled breathing.

EXERCISES FOR BREATHING AND RELAXATION

1. Lie on your back; relax gross muscles; breathe easily and comfortably. Begin to breathe as deeply as possible. Inhale, hold the breath 5 counts, and slowly exhale it on 5 counts. Try to keep the outgoing air steady and controlled.

---

[1] Edmund Jacobson, *You Must Relax* (New York, McGraw-Hill Book Company, 1942); David Harold Fink, *Release from Nervous Tension* (New York, Simon and Schuster, Inc., 1943).

2. Lie on your back; relax gross muscles; breathe deeply. When you feel relaxed, exhale with a sigh; then repeat, whispering "ah." Keep your shoulders, throat, and mandible relaxed.

3. In the same relaxed position, and breathing abdominally, sing "ah" softly up and down the scale. Gradually begin to vocalize with more energy, but always with the shoulders and throat muscles as relaxed as possible and with the greatest tension in the region of the abdominal and diaphragmatic muscles. As soon as you feel too much tension or constriction in the throat, stop singing and begin relaxing again.

4. Keeping the fingertips on the abdominal muscles, and the body as relaxed as possible, project a soft, quick "oh." Repeat several times, adding more force each time. Notice the muscular contraction of the abdominal muscles. Although there is some tension in the region of the larynx, there should be no noticeable constriction, and the throat passageway should feel quite free and open.

5. Repeat the above exercise, but instead of a quick "oh," sustain the "oh" as long as you can. As soon as the tone begins to waver, stop. Repeat several times and note whether you can sustain the tone longer than you did the first time.

6. Feeling very relaxed, yawn; at the peak of the yawn, as you begin to exhale, vocalize a tone like "oh" or "ah." Notice how relaxed the throat passageway feels.

7. Sit in a chair; relax the muscles of the legs, thighs, arms, hands, and neck. Allow your head to fall forward or to the side, whichever is the more relaxed for you. Let someone move your head slowly in a circular motion. As your head is being moved, keep the lower jaw as relaxed as possible; keep your eyes closed; allow your head to feel heavy. As your head is being moved in a circular motion, very quietly emit a continuous "ah" with minimum effort.

8. Repeat the essentials of exercise 7, but this time, *you* move your head in a circular motion. Emit an "ah" as your head moves, softly at first, and gradually try for more resonance. Finally, keeping your head in an upright position, repeat the projection of "ah," with increased force. Do not permit an overtension in the throat.

9. Repeat exercise 8, but this time say "ah-m," by eliding; then "oh-m"; "i-m"; "ee-m"; "oo-m"; "ay-m."

10. Frown as intensely as you can; then close your eyes, smooth out the frown, and let the lower jaw relax.

11. Frown as intensely as you can; give a quick "oh," as if you were exasperated; then smooth out the frown, close your eyes, relax the mandible, and say "oh," as if you were exhausted.

12. Stand as relaxed as possible, but without slouching. Pretend you are in the mountains and expecting an echo, as you vocalize, "hello-o-o-, hello-o-o-, hello-o-o"; then let your voice be the echo.

13. Do the same thing with "How-are-you"; "Ship-ahoy."

14. Pant softly, using the abdominal muscles; gradually begin to vocalize "ha." Increase the tempo of the "ha" until you have a laugh. There should be little strain in the larynx.

15. Laugh heartily with a "ho, ho, ho" and a "ha, ha, ha." Gradually diminish the "ho" and "ha" until all sound is whispered and then gone.

16. Inhale deeply. As you exhale, vocalize "mmm-nnn-ooo." Hold on to each sound about 3 counts and then slide from one sound to the next.

You will recall that the correct balance of nasal resonance with oral, pharyngeal, and laryngeal resonance is important for a pleasant, resonant tone. Failure to use nasal resonance on the nasal continuants can result in suppressed *m*, *n*, and *ng* or in the substitution of *b*, *d*, or *g* for those sounds. Either one of these difficulties may be caused by the failure to direct the air stream into the nasal cavity. The substitutions are usually caused by adenoidal tissue which blocks the nasal passageway posteriorly. Inasmuch as the articulatory mechanism has the same muscular adjustment for *m* as for *b*, for *n* as for *d*, and for *ng* as for *g*, it is quite natural to make this substitution. However, in the articulation of *b*, the vibrated air stream is dammed up behind the closed lips and is finally expelled through the oral cavity when the lips are opened or relaxed. In the articulation of *d*, the air stream is stopped by the tongue contacting the alveolar or gum ridge and is released through the oral cavity. In the articulation of *g*, the air stream is dammed up by the back of the tongue and the palatal muscles, just as in the sound *ng*, but is released through the oral cavity instead of being resonated in the nasal cavity. This substitution is one kind of nasality, often called adenoidal speech and is distinctly unpleasant to listen to, because it sounds stuffy. Speech that is characterized by such phrases as "Cub to see be sood" or "Sig be a sog" or "Sprig has cub," certainly needs correction, first by medical treatment, if necessary, and then by exercises involving the resonance of *m*, *n*, and *ng*.

EXERCISES TO INCREASE RESONANCE ON M, N, NG

1. Practice humming a song to get the feel of nasal resonance.
2. Practice: mo, mo, mo; mome, mome, mome

my, my, my; mime, mime, mime
mee, mee, mee; meem, meem, meem
moo, moo, moo; moom, moom, moom
may, may, may; maym, maym, maym
mah, mah, mah; mahm, mahm, mahm

3. Repeat with the nasal *n*.

4. Practice the following for improvement of the nasal continuants. Exaggerate the resonance on *m, n, ng* when practicing.

m

came, dame, same, name	prime, dime, rhyme
tame, frame, lame, game	crime, time, lime
tram, ham, cram, am	foam, poem, roam
jam, lamb, ram, dam	home, comb, loam
dream, seam, team, steam	rum, bum, mum, thumb
cream, beam, deem, ream	drum, sum, hum, crumb
stem, hem, them	bumble, mumble, fumble, stumble
gem, hemp, tempt	crumble, tumble, humble, rumble
dim, limb, rim	autumn, rhythm, bottom
brim, him, trim	custom, handsome, fathom
simmer, trimmer, dimmer	broom, tomb, boom, plume
nimble, thimble, limber	doom, room, loom, groom
spasm, chasm, prism, schism	hammer, stammer, streamer
organism, criticism, skepticism	drummer, boomer, roomer

n

van, ran, tan, fan	drench, quench, wrench
span, ban, bran, plan	wench, stench, bench
dance, prance, trance, stance	brown, town, crown, clown
fence, pence, whence, thence	gown, frown, down, noun
danced, pranced, tranced	bound, ground, found
land, grand, band, stand	hound, sound, mound
pant, cant, rant, grant	expound, around, astound
banter, canter, planter, ranter	profound, compound, confound
landed, expanded, granted	run, bun, gun, hun
hinted, haunted, hunted	ton, son, won, stun
train, rain, deign, brain	swindle, brindle, kindle
gain, cane, lane, sprain	cringe, impinge, tinge, singe
green, seen, mean, lean	grunt, stunt, hunt, brunt
bean, wean, clean, preen	crunch, bunch, munch, hunch
ten, pen, wren, then	lunge, plunger, pungent
hen, men, glen, when	lone, moan, tone, phone
brine, fine, line, swine	bone, cone, stone, zone
pine, vine, sign, nine	tune, croon, spoon, moon

kind, bind, find, mind
minor, liner, finer

sin, bin, tin, din
fin, gin, grin, kin

soon, prune, dune, loon
crooner, sooner, tuner

open, cotton, rotten
button, kitten, curtain

ng

tang, sang, bang, hang
fang, gang, clang, pang ·
ring, sing, bring, thing
ting, ling, wing, swing
long, song, tong, along
bong, dong, gong, strong

rung, sung, tongue, young
hung, clung, lung, stung
singing, ringing, bringing
training, raining, gaining
hanging, banging, clanging
singer, wringer, hanger, bringer

ng–g

linger, finger
hunger, younger
stronger, longer
tingle, mingle, single
dangle, tangle, bangle
wrangle, fangle, mangle
anger, angler, anguish
bungle, jungle, fungus

ng–k

wink, pink, kink, brink
link, mink, sink, drink
sank, spank, tank, thank
frank, lank, prank, crank
sunk, spunk, shrunk
trunk, bunk, drunk
twinkle, sprinkle, tinkle
lynx, jinx, minx

5. Give full resonance to the following combinations of *m* and *n*.

melancholy	monotony	memory
tremendous	remembrance	confectionery
conversationalist	shimmering	determined
instrument	commission	pantomime
testament	luncheon menu	impression
mountains	impression	feminine
compound	continually	intangible
nonsense	constriction	examine
combination	modification	punishment
intonations	intention	vitamin
stupendous	resonance	continue
contentment	countenance	maintenance
sentences	abdominal	unintelligent
indistinct	murmuring	co-ordination
union	clientele	elimination
company	constitution	unconscious
arrangement	intelligence	formation
impersonation	panorama	accomplishment

6. Practice the following for nasal continuants. Columns of words will not aid you unless you use what you have learned in the interpretation of a selection.

from THE PIED PIPER OF HAMELIN

Rats!
They fought the dogs and killed the cats
 And bit the babies in the cradles,
And ate the cheeses out of the vats,
 And licked the soup from the cooks' own ladles,
Split open the kegs of salted sprats,
Made nests inside men's Sunday hats,
And even spoiled the women's chats
 By drowning their speaking
 With shrieking and squeaking
In fifty different sharps and flats.

At last the people in a body
 To the Town Hall came flocking:
" 'Tis clear," cried they, "our Mayor's a noddy;
 And as for our Corporation—shocking
To think we buy gowns lined with ermine
For dolts that can't or won't determine
What's best to rid us of our vermin!
You hope, because you're old and obese,
To find in the furry civic robe ease?
Rouse up, sirs! Give your brains a racking
To find the remedy we're lacking,
Or, sure as fate, we'll send you packing!"
At this the Mayor and Corporation
Quaked with a mighty consternation.

An hour they sat in council;
 At length the Mayor broke silence:
"For a guilder I'd my ermine gown sell,
 I wish I were a mile hence!
It's easy to bid one rack one's brain—
I'm sure my poor head aches again,
I've scratched it so, and all in vain.
Oh for a trap, a trap, a trap!"
Just as he said this, what should hap
At the chamber-door but a gentle tap?
"Bless us," cried the Mayor, "what's that?"

. . . .

"Only a scraping of shoes on the mat?
Anything like the sound of a rat
Makes my heart go pit-a-pat!"

"Come in!"—the Mayor cried, looking bigger—
And in did come the strangest figure!
His queer long coat from heel to head
Was half of yellow and half of red,
And he himself was tall and thin,
With sharp blue eyes, each like a pin,
And light loose hair, yet swarthy skin,
No tuft on cheek nor beard on chin,
But lips where smiles went out and in;
There was no guessing his kith and kin;
And nobody could enough admire
The tall man and his quaint attire.
Quoth one: "It's as my great-grandsire,
Starting up at the Trump of Doom's tone,
Had walked this way from his painted tombstone!"

He advanced to the council-table;
And, "Please your honors," said he, "I'm able,
By means of a secret charm, to draw
　　All creatures living beneath the sun,
　　That creep or swim or fly or run,
After me so as you never saw!
And I chiefly use my charm
On creatures that do people harm,
The mole and toad and newt and viper;
And people call me the Pied Piper."

．　　．　　．　　．　　．　　．　　．　　．

"Yet," said he, "poor piper as I am
In Tartary I freed the Cham,
Last June, from his huge swarms of gnats;
　　And as for what your brain bewilders,
If I can rid your town of rats
　　Will you give me a thousand guilders?"
"One? fifty thousand!"—was the exclamation
Of the astonished Mayor and Corporation.

Into the street the Piper stept,
　　Smiling first a little smile,
As if he knew what magic slept
　　In his quiet pipe the while;
Then, like a musical adept,
To blow the pipe his lips he wrinkled,
And green and blue his sharp eyes twinkled,
Like a candle-flame where salt is sprinkled;
And ere three shrill notes the pipe uttered,
You heard as if an army muttered;

And the muttering grew to a grumbling;
And the grumbling grew to a mighty rumbling.
And out of the houses the rats came tumbling—
Great rats, small rats, lean rats, brawny rats,
Brown rats, black rats, gray rats, tawny rats,
Grave old plodders, gay young friskers,
 Fathers, mothers, uncles, cousins,
Cocking tails and pricking whiskers,
 Families by tens and dozens,
Brothers, sisters, husbands, wives—
Followed the Piper for their lives.
From street to street he piped advancing,
And step for step they followed dancing,
Until they came to the river Weser,
Wherein all plunged and perished!

 . . . .

You should have heard the Hamelin people
Ringing the bells till they rocked the steeple.
"Go," cried the Mayor, "and get long poles,
Poke out the nests and block up the holes!
Consult with carpenters and builders,
 And leave in our town not even a trace
 Of the rats!" When suddenly, up the face
Of the Piper perked in the market-place,
With a "First, if you please, my thousand guilders!"
A thousand guilders! The Mayor looked blue;
So did the Corporation too.

 . . . .

To pay this sum to a wandering fellow
With a gypsy coat of red and yellow!
"Beside," quoth the Mayor with a knowing wink,
"Our business was done at the river's brink;
We saw with our eyes the vermin sink,
And what's dead can't come to life, I think.
So, friend, we're not the folks to shrink
From the duty of giving you something for drink,
And a matter of money to put in your poke;
But as for guilders, what we spoke
Of them, as you very well know, was in joke.
Beside, our losses have made us thrifty.
A thousand guilders! Come, take fifty!"

The Piper's face fell, and he cried,
"No trifling! I can't wait, beside!
I've promised to visit by dinner-time

Bagdad and accept the prime
Of the Head Cook's pottage, all he's rich in,
For having left in the Caliph's kitchen,
Of a nest of scorpions no survivor.
With him I proved no bargain-driver,
With you, don't think I'll bate a stiver!
And folks who put me in a passion
May find me pipe after another fashion."

.   .   .   .

Once more he stept into the street,
    And to his lips again
    Laid his long pipe of smooth straight cane;
And ere he blew three notes (such sweet
Soft notes as yet musician's cunning
    Never gave enraptured air)
There was a rustling, that seemed like a bustling
Of merry crowds justling at pitching and hustling;
Small feet were pattering, wooden shoes clattering,
Little hands clapping, and little tongues chattering,
And, like fowls in a farm-yard when barley is scattering,
Out came the children running.
All the little boys and girls,
With rosy cheeks and flaxen curls,
And sparkling eyes and teeth like pearls,
Tripping and skipping, ran merrily after
The wonderful music with shouting and laughter.
                                        ROBERT BROWNING

THE CATARACT OF LODORE

"How does the water
Come down at Lodore?"
My little boy asked me
    Thus once on a time
And, moreover, he tasked me
    To tell him in rhyme.

    Anon at the word
There first came one daughter
And then came another,
    To second and third
The request of their brother
And to hear how the water
    Comes down at Lodore,

With its rush and its roar
  As many a time
They had seen it before.

So I told them in rhyme,
For of rhymes I had store,
And 'twas in my vocation
For their recreation
  That I should sing;
Because I was Laureate
  To them and the King.

From its sources which well
In the Tarn on the fell:
From its fountains
In the mountains
Its rills and its gills;
  Through moss and through brake
    It runs and it creeps
    For a while, till it sleeps
  In its own little lake.

And thence at departing,
Awakening and starting,
It runs through the reeds,
And away it proceeds
Through meadow and glade,
In sun and in shade,
And through the wood-shelter,
  Among crags in its flurry,
Helter-skelter,
  Hurry-skurry.

Here it comes sparkling,
And there it lies darkling;
Now smoking and frothing
Its tumult and wrath in,
Till, in this rapid race
  On which it is bent,
It reaches the place
  Of its steep descent.

The cataract strong
Then plunges along,
Striking and raging
As if a war waging
It caverns and rocks among;
  Rising and leaping,

Sinking and creeping,
Swelling and sweeping,
Showering and springing,
Flying and flinging,
Writhing and ringing,
Eddying and whisking,
Spouting and frisking,
Turning and twisting,
Around and around
With endless rebound;
Smiting and fighting,
A sight to delight in,
Confounding, astounding,
Dizzying and deafening the ear with its sound;

Collecting, projecting,
Receding and speeding,
And shocking and rocking,
And darting and parting,
And threading and spreading,
And whizzing and hissing,
And dripping and skipping,
And hitting and splitting,
And shining and twining,
And rattling and battling,
And shaking and quaking,
And pouring and roaring,
And waving and raving,
And tossing and crossing,
And flowing and going,
And running and stunning,
And foaming and roaming,
And dinning and spinning,
And dropping and hopping,
And working and jerking,
And guggling and struggling,
And heaving and cleaving,
And moaning and groaning;
And glittering and frittering,
And gathering and feathering,
And whitening and brightening,
And quivering and shivering,
And hurrying and skurrying,
And thundering and floundering;

Dividing and gliding and sliding,
And falling and brawling and sprawling,

And driving and riving and striving,
And sprinkling and twinkling and wrinkling,
And sounding and bounding and rounding,
And bubbling and troubling and doubling,
And grumbling and rumbling and tumbling,
And clattering and battering and shattering,

Retreating and beating and meeting and sheeting,
Delaying and straying and playing and spraying,
Advancing and prancing and glancing and dancing,
Recoiling, turmoiling and toiling and boiling,
And gleaming and streaming and steaming and beaming,
And rushing and flushing and brushing and gushing,
And flapping and rapping and clapping and slapping,
And curling and whirling and purling and twirling,
And thumping and plumping and bumping and jumping,
And dashing and flashing and splashing and clashing;
And so never ending, but always descending,
Sounds and motions for ever and ever are blending,
All at once and all o'er, with a mighty uproar:
And this way the water comes down at Lodore.

ROBERT SOUTHEY

Oral and pharyngeal resonance are often hampered by (1) small cavities held taut by tense muscles and (2) a rigid tongue. The following exercises are designed to help you acquire mobility in the mandible and to release tongue tension, especially at the base of the tongue. Practice with some freedom. Do not mince through the exercises but use large movements. Remember always that a mobile tongue and a flexible mandible aid in improving resonance.

EXERCISES TO INCREASE VOWEL RESONANCE

1. Be sure you are relaxed. Then repeat "ee—oo—ah" five times; work for flexibility of facial muscles; notice the difference in the shape of the oral cavity for each sound.

2. Phonate the vowels *a, e, i, o, u* and work for increased resonance. Start softly and increase projection. Elide first; then take them separately; then project them with energy from the abdominal muscles.

3. Phonate the vowels *a, e, i, o, u;* then prefix them with an *r, y, w.*

4. Work on the following combinations; first separate the vowel from the nasal; gradually elide them:

rah — mmm	yah — mmm	wah — mmm	sah — mmm
ay — mmm	yay — mmm	way — mmm	say — mmm
ree — mmm	yee — mmm	wee — mmm	see — mmm
ri — mmm	yi — mmm	wi — mmm	si — mmm
ro — mmm	yo — mmm	wo — mmm	so — mmm
roo — mmm	yoo — mmm	woo — mmm	soo — mmm

5. Work on the following combinations; gradually elide them:

rah — nnn	yah — nnn	wah — nnn	sah — nnn
ray — nnn	yay — nnn	way — nnn	say — nnn
ree — nnn	yee — nnn	wee — nnn	see — nnn
ri — nnn	yi — nnn	wi — nnn	si — nnn
ro — nnn	yo — nnn	wo — nnn	so — nnn
roo — nnn	yoo — nnn	woo — nnn	soo — nnn

6. Practice by overdoing jaw movement:

yah — dah — dah — yah	zah — yah — yah — zah
yah — shah — shah — yah	zah — yi — yi — zah
yah — ray — ray — yah	zah — rah — rah — zah
yah — ho — ho — yah	zah — ho — ho — zah

zoom — boom — boom — zoom	waym — woom — waym
zahm — bum — bum — zahm	wahm — woom — wahm
zahm — rahm — rahm — zahm	woom — wahm — woom
zoom — zahm — zahm — zoom	woom — wim — woom

oh — wah — yah — yah	ah — ha — ho — he
oh — rah — wah — wah	ah — hay — hi — ho
oh — yah — yo — yo	ah — yah — yay — yo
oh — zay — ray — ray	ah — yo — yi — yah

7. Practice by overdoing the jaw movement:
The wayside wanderer was waylaid and walloped.
"Wow, wow, wow!" wailed the waking watchman.
Yams filled the yard of the youthful youngsters.
"Zam, zam, zam," is the way I would yell it.
Hit them again—harder—harder!

8. Practice one of your college yells with the greatest freedom of the jaw and the articulators. *Don't* set the jaw as you do when you are on the bleachers.

Many people nasalize vowels because of habit or association; others nasalize because of a stenosis, that is, partial closure in the anterior port to the nasal cavity. This difficulty will always mar an artistic performance. Unfortunately, it is a serious problem to overcome. The correction lies mainly in *hearing* your nasal tones. We can even say that unless you do hear your nasalization, you will never improve. The best way to improve is to have your voice recorded and then listen to the recording.

EXERCISES TO DECREASE NASALIZATION

1. Relax the mandible, keep the tongue from humping in the back unnecessarily, keep the pharyngeal muscles free of tension, and try the following words:

rat	facial	high	seat	zest
saddle	crate	sky	treat	pet
batter	bait	lie	freeze	excite
flat	hay	item	preach	deck
crash	lady	ice	breeze	misled
cattle	spade	write	feet	shed
ash	sake	fright	speak	dredge
clatter	grade	kite	creak	sled
trash	race	fight	beat	peddle
patter	braid	five	bleak	hedge
fit	spot	dog	loud	boy
fiddle	father	brought	power	ahoy
crib	cot	caught	hour	toy
trip	top	hog	cloud	oil
bitter	bottom	all	shower	rejoice
bridge	cock	frog	aloud	voice
kiss	hollow	jaw	owl	choice
hip	clock	boss	tower	toil
twiddle	clot	fought	bow	coil
quitter	rock	loss	how	boil
ore	judge	stove	ruby	church
soar	crutch	crow	truth	hurt
roar	crush	hope	roof	hurry
tore	strut	road	groove	jerk
gory	hustle	fold	ruthless	blur
board	fudge	froze	prove	world
lore	plush	told	soothe	turf
hoary	fuss	spoken	hoot	curve
store	hut	rose	crude	heard
yore	flush	cold	foolish	word

2. The following pairs of sentences reveal the difference between nasal resonance acquired through *m, n, ng* in words and resonance of the vowels. Note that the first sentence is loaded with *m, n,* and *ng* words and that the second sentence depends on the vowels for resonance.

(a) I'm going on a jungle hunt.
(b) I shall juggle the figures.

(a) Spring time brings merriment.
(b) Sprigs of the tree caused the blockage.

(a) Stones came tumbling down the incline.
(b) Boards, typewriters, chairs, clocks, pictures—all were hurled through the air.

(a) Torrents of muddy rain made them hasten along.
(b) Drops from the sky pattered on her Easter hat.

(a) The moon beams down on them as they are sailing along.
(b) The hot rays baked the holiday crowds.

(a) The crime was well-planned and organized.
(b) The crisis was over for all.

(a) The hovering clouds meant approaching thunderstorms.
(b) They rolled through the grass and flowers in their jeep.

3. Watch the assimilation of the nasals in combination with vowels. It is easy to nasalize the vowels when they are either preceded or followed by a nasal continuant. If you have difficulty, take the words like this: gra-nd, da-me.

1

1. She was a grand dame.
2. He was milking the cow as rapidly as possible.
3. He and his father had famous names.
4. I played the same game as Jane.
5. The time was the right time for his arrival.
6. Her hands and arms were sandy.
7. The rain was pelting down on the streets.
8. She had peanut candy and ham sandwiches.
9. The farm animals were shaggy.
10. The man and the lady were driving in the car.
11. The crime was well planned and organized.
12. Nine pounds of lime were weighed for Henry.
13. She framed him at his own game.
14. The fire and flames leaped higher and higher.
15. A cry was raised by every child.
16. The train was at least five hours late.
17. 'Sweet Adeline' was practiced by the choir.
18. The boy and his buddies were not blamed.
19. Sam's grandfather was fat and famous.
20. The troops were lying in wait for the enemy.
21. His mind was completely unbalanced.

22. They crammed for their exams.
23. Ham salad sandwiches, shrimps, and fried potatoes were served on paper plates.
24. The jam was like jelly.
25. There were five fine organizers.
26. Paint the fence white and yellow.
27. He dislikes pineapple pie and cranberries.
28. It was a matter of the horse's saddle being adjusted.
29. The dark clouds meant showers.
30. The snake lay in the hayloft.
31. He climbed the tower.
32. The eggs were boiled and the steak was broiled

2

Man's inhumanity to man,
Makes countless thousands mourn.
ROBERT BURNS, *Man Was Made to Mourn*

3

I dwelt alone
In a world of moan,
And my soul was a stagnant tide.
EDGAR ALLAN POE, *Eulalie*

4

Alone, alone, all, all, alone,
Alone on a wide wide sea!
SAMUEL COLERIDGE, *The Rime of the Ancient Mariner*

5

Cannon to right of them,
Cannon to left of them,
Cannon in front of them
Volley'd and thunder'd;
Storm'd at with shot and shell,
Boldly they rode and well,
Into the jaws of Death,
Into the mouth of Hell
Rode the six hundred.
ALFRED TENNYSON, *The Charge of the Light Brigade*

6

Then along the river bank
A thousand miles
Tattooed cannibals danced in files;

Then I hear the boom of the blood-lust song
And a thigh-bone beating on a tin-pan gong.

   .   .   .   .   .   .

Rattle-rattle, rattle-rattle,
Bing!
Boomlay, boomlay, boomlay, BOOM!
A roaring epic rag-time tune
From the mouth of the Congo
To the mountains of the Moon.

   .   .   .   .   .   .

Mumbo-Jumbo will hoo-doo you,
Mumbo-Jumbo will hoo-doo you,
Mumbo-Jumbo will hoo-doo you.

VACHEL LINDSAY, *The Congo*[2]

7

The wind was a torrent of darkness among the gusty trees,
The moon was a ghostly galleon tossed upon cloudy seas,
The road was a ribbon of moonlight over the purple moor,
And the highwayman came riding—
Riding—riding—
The highwayman came riding up to the old inn door.

ALFRED NOYES, *The Highwayman*[3]

8

For the moon never beams, without bringing me dreams
  Of the beautiful Annabel Lee;
And the stars never rise, but I feel the bright eyes
  Of the beautiful Annabel Lee;
And so, all the night-tide, I lie down by the side
Of my darling—my darling—my life and my bride,
  In the sepulchre there by the sea—
  In her tomb by the sounding sea.

EDGAR ALLAN POE, *Annabel Lee*

9

FIRST WITCH. When shall we three meet again
  In thunder, lightning, or in rain?
SECOND WITCH. When the hurlyburly's done,

---

[2] From *The Congo and Other Poems*, p. 4. Copyright, 1915, by The Macmillan Company. Reprinted by permission of the publishers.
[3] From *Collected Poems*, Vol. 1, p. 192. Copyright, 1906, by Frederick A. Stokes Company. Reprinted by permission of the publishers.

When the battle's lost and won.
THIRD WITCH. That will be ere the set of sun.
WILLIAM SHAKESPEARE, *Macbeth*

10

There's a clashing snarling rhythm down by the valley broad and
  ample
Of the drum, kettledrum,
There's a low, swelling rumor that is cavalry a-trample,
  Here they come, here they come,
To the brassy crash and wrangle, to the horseman's clink and jangle,
And the restive legs beneath 'em all a-welter and a-tangle,
  "I am rhythm, dancing rhythm," says the drum.
"White and sorrel, roan and dapple, hocks as shiny as an apple,
"Don't they make a splendid showing, ears a-pricking, tails a-blowing?
"Good boys—bless 'em—well, they're knowing all my tricks to set 'em
  going
  "To my rhythm, clashing rhythm!" says the drum.

There's an echo shakes the valley o'er the rhythm deep and slow
  Of the drum, of the drum,
'Tis the guns, the guns a-rolling on the bridges down below,
  Here they come, here they come,
Hark the felloes grind and lumber through the shadows gray and
  umber,
And triple spans a-panting up the slope the stones encumber.
  With the rhythm, distant rhythm, of the drum.
EDWARD FORRESTER SUTTON, *The Drum*[4]

11

BRUTUS
 How ill this taper burns! Ho! who comes here?
 I think it is the weakness of mine eyes
 That shapes this monstrous apparition.
 It comes upon me. Art thou any thing?
 Art thou some god, some angel, or some devil,
 That mak'st my blood cold and my hair to stare?
 Speak to me what thou art.
WILLIAM SHAKESPEARE, *Julius Caesar*

12

  Banners yellow, glorious, golden,
   On its roof did float and flow,
  (This—all this—was in the olden

[4] From *A Book of Verse from the Great War*, ed. Reginald Wheeler, p.
151. Copyright, 1917, by Yale University Press. Reprinted by permission
of the publishers.

Time long ago,)
And every gentle air that dallied,
  In that sweet day,
Along the ramparts plumed and pallid,
  A wingèd odor went away.
                    EDGAR ALLAN POE, *The Haunted Palace*

13

From the sea-coast, from the bleak ravines of the hills that lift
their bare escarpments towards the sky that pours down pitiless
threads of sunlight, whirls over chill clinging tentacles of rain, smashes
hard buffets of huge wind, sifts fine quivering drifts of snow, thrashes
with thunder and with hail, uncurls its great sodden flapping curtains
before the gale—from the marshlands, from the banks of slow rivers,
from the still brown plateaus, from the mist of steaming valleys, from
the wide bays ringed with peaks—a thousand cities reek into the sky.
                    JOHN GOULD FLETCHER, *America*[5]

4. Now practice carrying over the resonance into conversational
literature.

SCARS[6]

Dallas never irritated Dirk. She rested him, he told himself. He
would arm himself against her, but one minute after meeting her he
would sink gratefully and resistlessly into her quiet depths. Sometimes
he thought all this was an assumed manner in her.

"This calm of yours—this effortlessness," he said to her one day, "is
a pose, isn't it?" Anything to get her to notice.

"Partly," Dallas had replied amiably. "It's a nice pose though, don't
you think?"

What are you going to do with a girl like that!

Here was the woman who could hold him entirely, and who never
held out a finger to hold him. He tore at the smooth wall of her indifference, though he only cut and bruised his own hands in doing it.

"Is it because I'm a successful business man that you don't like
me?"

"But I do like you."

"That you don't find me attractive then."

"But I think you're an awfully attractive man. Dangerous, that's
wot."

---

[5] From *Breakers and Granite*, p. 144. Copyright, 1921, by The Macmillan
Company. Reprinted by permission of the publishers.

[6] From *So Big*, pp. 347-348. Copyright, 1936, by Edna Ferber. Reprinted
by permission of the author and the publishers, Doubleday, Doran and
Company, Inc.

"Oh, don't be the wide-eyed ingénue. You know damned well what I mean. You've got me and you don't want me. If I had been a successful architect instead of a successful business man, would that have made any difference? Is that it? He's got to be an artist, I suppose, to interest you."

"Good Lord, no! Some day I'll probably marry a horny-handed son of toil, and if I do it'll be the horny hands that will win me. If you want to know, I like 'em with their scars on them. There's something about a man who has fought for it—I don't know what it is—a look in his eye—the feel of his hand. He needn't be successful—though he probably would be. I don't know. I'm not very good at this analysis stuff. I only know he—well, you haven't a mark on you. Not a mark. You quit being an architect, or whatever it was, because architecture was an uphill disheartening job all the time. I don't say that you should have kept on. For all I know you were a bum architect. But if you had kept on—if you had loved it enough to keep on—fighting, and struggling, and sticking it out—why, that fight would show in your face to-day—in your eyes and your jaw and your hands and in your way of standing and walking and sitting and talking. Listen. I'm not criticizing you. But you're all smooth. I like 'em bumpy. That sounds terrible. It isn't what I mean at all. It isn't—"

"Oh, never mind, I think I know what you mean." He sat looking down at his hands—his fine strong unscarred hands. Suddenly and unreasonably he thought of another pair of hands—his mother's—with the knuckles enlarged, the skin broken—expressive—her life written on them. Scars. She had them. "Listen, Dallas. If I thought—I'd go back to Hollis & Sprague's and begin all over again at forty a week if I thought you'd—"

"Don't."

EDNA FERBER

ALONE AT HOME[7]

HERMINE *is having her first party in her new home. Felix, her husband, is greatly disturbed over the fact that he never sees his wife because of her social activities.*

FELIX. A charming state of affairs. I am in my own house and should like to make myself comfortable in the evening; but instead of that, I must sit here in my dress suit and be bored. I have cigars and must not smoke them; I have wine and must not drink it; I have a wife and must not be alone with her. My study is cleared out and serves as a wardrobe. My desk is in the store-room; my books are in the linen closet; where my comfortable easy chair has

[7] From *By Ourselves*, pp. 208-210. Copyright, 1920, by The Poet Lore Company. Reprinted by permission of the publishers.

gotten to, the gods alone can tell. I am furious and must play the amiable man. And all this for whom? For people, not one of whom interests me in the least; for whom, in fact, I do not care. (*Rises as if to make a toast*) And you, my worthy guests, make yourselves at home; for I should be very glad were you indeed at home. With this sentiment, I raise my glass and say, fare ye well!

HERMINE. Your malice is irresistible!

FELIX. But in vain. They are coming, all of them; they will eat their fill, they will gossip, they will dance, and I must smile at them. But my smile will be nothing but a sugar-coated dynamite bomb. Hermine, how different things might be! How comfortably we could sit here together—by ourselves, and chat—

HERM. And yawn. A whole evening by ourselves! I have no idea what we could do to pass the time.

FELIX. We should spend the time calmly. We should give audience to our good spirits, the shy house spirits who are frightened away by noise, and are summoned forth by quietness. They dare not appear at parties; but when two people are alone, by themselves, two people who love—hush, here they come! Do you hear?

HERM. No, not yet.

FELIX. But you will hear them. There is still too much dance music ringing in your ears. They are already here and they are whispering of the charm and blessing of home life. And suddenly this apparition of the invitation, the ball-room, and the long table disappears. We are in my study, naturally not the one that is cleared out; let us imagine it in its normal condition.

HERM. I imagine it.

FELIX. I am sitting in my comfortable easy chair and am smoking a cigar. May I light one?

HERM. No, indeed!

FELIX. Then let's imagine it. You are sitting at some little distance from me on a low chair. Will you be so kind?

HERM. Well, I am sitting here.

FELIX. I sharply close a heavy book which I have been reading till now; you lay aside your needlework which is, naturally, to be a surprise for my birthday.

HERM. What next?

FELIX. Now we are glad we are in our cozy room, during this blinding snowstorm.

HERM. It is not snowing at all.

FELIX. That's nothing. We are pretending that it is; it will put us in the right frame of mind. My lamp throws its pleasant glow upon your dear face, and I find you charming in your simple house dress. The snowstorm becomes more and more violent; you are apprehensive and move nearer.

HERM. Still nearer? (*She moves closer to him*)

FELIX. I dispel your apprehension with a kiss.
HERM. Can we not imagine that too?
FELIX. Impossible. That I must give you.
HERM. So far I like the thing very well.

LUDWIG FULDA

VIOLA CONCEALS HER LOVE

VIOLA, *disguised as a boy, is known to the* DUKE *as* CESARIO.

DUKE. Let all the rest give place. (CURIO *and* ATTENDANTS *retire*)
                    Once more, Cesario,
  Get thee to yond same sovereign cruelty.
  Tell her, my love, more noble than the world,
  Prizes not quantity of dirty lands;
  The parts that fortune hath bestow'd upon her,
  Tell her, I hold as giddily as fortune;
  But 'tis that miracle and queen of gems
  That nature pranks her in attracts my soul.
VIOLA. But if she cannot love you, sir?
DUKE. I cannot be so answer'd.
VIOLA.   Sooth, but you must.
  Say that some lady, as perhaps there is,
  Hath for your love as great a pang of heart
  As you have for Olivia. You cannot love her.
  You tell her so. Must she not then be answer'd?
DUKE. There is no woman's sides
  Can bide the beating of so strong a passion
  As love doth give my heart; no woman's heart
  So bid, to hold so much. They lack retention.
  Alas, their love may be call'd appetite,
  No motion of the liver, but the palate,
  That suffer surfeit, cloyment, and revolt;
  But mine is all as hungry as the sea,
  And can digest as much. Make no compare
  Between that love a woman can bear me
  And what I owe Olivia.
VIOLA.   Ay, but I know—
DUKE. What dost thou know?
VIOLA. Too well what love women to men may owe.
  In faith, they are as true of heart as we.
  My father had a daughter lov'd a man,
  As it might be, perhaps, were I a woman,
  I should your lordship.
DUKE.   And what's her history?

Viola. A blank, my lord. She never told her love,
  But let concealment, like a worm i' the bud,
  Feed on her damask cheek. She pin'd in thought,
  And with a green and yellow melancholy
  She sat, like patience on a monument,
  Smiling at grief. Was not this love indeed?
  We men may say more, swear more; but indeed
  Our shows are more than will; for still we prove
  Much in our vows, but little in our love.
Duke. But died thy sister of her love, my boy?
Viola. I am all the daughters of my father's house,
  And all the brothers too;—and yet I know not.
  Sir, shall I to this lady?
Duke.   Ay, that's the theme.
  To her in haste. Give her this jewel. Say,
  My love can give no place, bide no denay.
              William Shakespeare, *Twelfth Night*

SIR HARRY IS OUTRAGED[8]

Kate, *the divorced wife of* Sir Harry, *has come to do some typing for him.*

Sir Harry. (*With concentrated scorn*) You!

Kate. (*As if agreeing with him*) Yes, it's funny.

Sir H. The shamelessness of your daring to come here.

Kate. Believe me, it is not less a surprise to me than it is to you. I was sent here in the ordinary way of business. I was given only the number of the house. I was not told the name.

Sir H. (*Withering her*) The ordinary way of business! This is what you have fallen to—a typist!

Kate. (*Unwithered*) Think of it!

Sir H. After going through worse straits, I'll be bound.

Kate. (*With some grim memories*) Much worse straits.

Sir H. (*Alas, laughing coarsely*) My congratulations!

Kate. Thank you, Harry.

Sir H. (*Who is annoyed, as any man would be, not to find her abject*) Eh? What was that you called me, madam?

Kate. Isn't it Harry? On my soul, I almost forget.

Sir H. It isn't Harry to you. My name is Sims, if you please.

Kate. Yes, I had not forgotten that. It was my name, too, you see.

Sir H. (*In his best manner*) It was your name until you forfeited the right to bear it.

[8] From "The Twelve Pound Look" in *Half Hours*, pp. 55-57. Copyright, 1914, by Charles Scribner's Sons. Reprinted by permission of the publishers.

KATE. Exactly.

SIR H. (*Gloating*) I was furious to find you here, but on second thought it pleases me. (*From the depths of his moral nature*) There is a grim justice in this.

KATE. (*Sympathetically*) Tell me?

SIR H. Do you know what you were brought here to do?

KATE. I have just been learning. You have been made a knight, and I was summoned to answer the messages of congratulation.

SIR H. That's it, that's it. You come on this day to be my servant!

KATE. I, who might have been Lady Sims.

SIR H. And you are her typist instead. And she has four men-servants. Oh, I am so glad you saw her in her presentation grown.

KATE. I wonder if she would let me do her washing, Sir Harry?

SIR H. (*With dignity*) You can go. The mere thought that only a few flights of stairs separates such as you from my innocent children— (*He will never know why a new light has come into her face*)

KATE. (*Slowly*) You have children?

SIR H. (*Inflated*) Two. (*He wonders why she is so long in answering*)

KATE. (*Resorting to impertinence*) Such a nice number.

SIR H. (*With an extra turn of the screw*) Both boys.

KATE. Successful in everything. Are they like you, Sir Harry?

SIR H. (*Expanding*) They are very like me.

KATE. That's nice. (*Even on such a subject she can be ribald*)

SIR H. Will you please to go?

KATE. Heigho! What shall I say to my employer?

SIR H. That is no affair of mine.

KATE. What will you say to Lady Sims?

SIR H. I flatter myself that whatever I say, Lady Sims will accept without comment. (*She smiles, heaven knows why, unless her next remark explains it*)

KATE. Still the same Harry.

SIR H. What do you mean?

KATE. Only that you have the old confidence in your profound knowledge of the sex.

SIR H. (*Beginning to think as little of her intellect as of her morals*) I suppose I know my wife.

KATE. (*Hopelessly dense*) I suppose so. I was only remembering that you used to think you knew her in the days when I was the lady. (*He is merely wasting his time on her, and he indicates the door. She is not sufficiently the lady to retire worsted*) Well, good-by, Sir Harry. Won't you ring, and have the four men-servants show me out?

SIR JAMES M. BARRIE

Vocal Force

Breathing is important in sustaining tones for varying degrees
of force. One must learn to control the breath for the sustained
soft touch as well as for the vigorous and abrupt attack. Watch
the tendency to emit immediately too much of the breath stream.
Learn how to sustain tones.

EXERCISES TO IMPROVE VOCAL ATTACK

1. Take a comfortable relaxed standing position, but do not sag.
Put your fingertips on the abdominal muscles. Breathe deeply, and
as you exhale, emit an "oh" with a sustained even tone; then with a
sharp quick attack. Repeat five times.

2. Breathe deeply, and emit a series of "ho's" until the breath
is all exhaled. Be sure you can feel the action of the abdominal
muscles.

3. Try to sustain a series of vowels with one deep breath. Try
ah, oh, ee, oh; aw, oo, i, aw. Repeat five times.

4. Vocalize the sound "oh" softly; then increase in attack, but
do not allow the pitch to rise.

5. Repeat Exercise 4 with "ho"; with "ha"; with "hi."

6. Vocalize a series of short quick "ho's"; then with the breath
that is left, sustain a "ho" until the breath is gone; do the same
thing with "ha." Repeat several times.

7. Sustain a "ho" for five counts; then use the rest of the breath
for a series of short "ho's." Repeat with "ha."

8. Practice the laughing and panting exercises given on p. 604.

9. Practice the following with increasing and decreasing degrees
of force; be careful not to change the pitch as you increase in force,
and be sure that you are getting your energy from the abdominal
muscles:

> one, two, three, four, five
> a, b, c, d, e
> a, e, i, o, u
> oh — oh — oh
> no — no — no
> ha — ha — ha
> ho — ho — ho
> help — help — help

10. Sustain the tone as you practice these:

> Hello — hello — hello
> Hello — What ho?

How are you?
Ship ahoy!
Anchors aweigh!
Hail — hail — hail!
Holy — holy — holy.
All ashore that are going ashore!
All aboard!
Hip, hip, hoorah!
Blow, bugle, blow!
Oh wonderful, wonderful, most wonderful!
Alone, alone, all, all alone.
Boot, saddle, to horse, and away!

11. Now use sustained tones in the following:

1

Heigh-ho! sing, heigh-ho! unto the green holly;
Most friendship is feigning, most loving mere folly.
   Then, heigh-ho, the holly!
   This life is most jolly.
           WILLIAM SHAKESPEARE, *As You Like It*

2

Gold! Gold! Gold! Gold!
Bright and yellow, hard and cold.
Molten, graven, hammered, and rolled;
Heavy to get and light to hold;
Hoarded, bartered, bought, and sold,
Stolen, borrowed, squandered, doled;
To the very verge of the churchyard mold;
Price of many a crime untold—
Gold! Gold! Gold! Gold!
          THOMAS HOOD, *Miss Kilmansegg: Her Moral*

3

God of our fathers, known of old—
Lord of our far-flung battle line—
Beneath whose awful hand we hold
Dominion over palm and pine;
Lord God of Hosts, be with us yet,
Lest we forget; lest we forget.
          RUDYARD KIPLING, *Recessional*

4

No sail from day to day, but every day
The sunrise broke into scarlet shafts

Among the palms and ferns and precipices;
The blaze upon the waters to the east;
The blaze upon his island overhead;
The blaze upon the waters to the west;
Then the great stars that globed themselves in Heaven,
The hollower-bellowing ocean, and again
The scarlet shafts of sunrise—but no sail.

ALFRED TENNYSON, *Enoch Arden*

5

MACDUFF.   Awake, awake!
Ring the alarum-bell. Murder and treason!
Banquo and Donalbain! Malcolm! awake!
Shake off this downy sleep, death's counterfeit,
And look on death itself! Up, up, and see
The great doom's image! Malcolm! Banquo!
As from your graves rise up, and walk like sprites,
To countenance this horror! Ring the bell.

WILLIAM SHAKESPEARE, *Macbeth*

6

MACBETH

To-morrow, and to-morrow, and to-morrow,
Creeps in this petty pace from day to day
To the last syllable of recorded time;
And all our yesterdays have lighted fools
Their way to dusty death. Out, out, brief candle!
Life's but a walking shadow, a poor player
That struts and frets his hour upon the stage
And then is heard no more. It is a tale
Told by an idiot, full of sound and fury,
Signifying nothing.

WILLIAM SHAKESPEARE, *Macbeth*

7

Pack, clouds, away! and welcome, day!
    With night we banish sorrow.
Sweet air, blow soft; mount, lark, aloft
    To give my Love good-morrow.
Wings from the wind to please her mind,
    Notes from the lark I'll borrow:
Bird, prune thy wing! nightingale, sing!
    To give my Love good-morrow!
        To give my Love good-morrow!
    Notes from them all I'll borrow.

THOMAS HEYWOOD, *Matin Song*

8

The blab of the pave, tires of carts, sluff of boot-soles, talk of the promenaders,
The heavy omnibus, the driver with his interrogating thumb, the clank of the shod horses on the granite floor,
The snow-sleighs, clinking, shouted jokes, pelts of snow-balls,
The hurrahs for popular favorites, the fury of rous'd mobs,
The flap of the curtain'd litter, a sick man inside borne to the hospital,
The meeting of enemies, the sudden oath, the blows and fall,
The excited crowd, the policeman with his star quickly working his passage to the center of the crowd,
The impassive stones that receive and return so many echoes. . . .

WALT WHITMAN, *Leaves of Grass*

9

A word carries far—very far—deals destruction through time as the bullets go flying through space.

JOSEPH CONRAD, *Lord Jim*

10

Lost yesterday, somewhere between sunrise and sunset, two golden hours, each set with sixty diamond minutes. No reward is offered for they are gone forever.

THOMAS MANN, *The Magic Mountain*

11

I have nothing to offer but blood, toil, tears, and sweat.

WINSTON CHURCHILL, Statement to the House of Commons,
May 13, 1940

12

Victory at all costs, victory in spite of all terror, victory however long and hard the road may be; for without victory there is no survival.

WINSTON CHURCHILL, Statement to the House of Commons,
May 13, 1940

13

The day is done, and the darkness
Falls from the wings of night
As a feather is wafted downward
From an eagle in its flight.

And the night shall be filled with music,
And the cares, that infest the day,

> Shall fold their tents, like the Arabs,
> And as silently steal away.
>
> HENRY WADSWORTH LONGFELLOW

12. Two groups should try the following famous scene between Cassius and Brutus. Nowhere in literature is there such a masterfully sustained scene. Let the class decide which of the groups does the better job of keeping the quarrel alive and tense through the use of vocal attack.

The scene takes place in Brutus' tent.

CASSIUS. That you have wrong'd me doth appear in this:
  You have condemn'd and noted Lucius Pella
  For taking bribes here of the Sardians;
  Wherein my letters, praying on his side,
  Because I knew the man, were slighted off.
BRUTUS. You wrong'd yourself to write in such a case.
CASSIUS. In such a time as this it is not meet
  That every nice offence should bear his comment.
BRUTUS. Let me tell you, Cassius, you yourself
  Are much condemn'd to have an itching palm,
  To sell and mart your offices for gold
  To undeservers.
CASSIUS.   I an itching palm!
  You know that you are Brutus that speaks this,
  Or, by the gods, this speech were else your last.
BRUTUS. The name of Cassius honours this corruption,
  And Chastisement doth therefore hide his head.
CASSIUS. Chastisement!
BRUTUS. Remember March, the ides of March remember:
  Did not great Julius bleed for justice' sake?
  What villain touch'd his body, that did stab,
  And not for justice? What, shall one of us,
  That struck the foremost man of all this world
  But for supporting robbers, shall we now
  Contaminate our fingers with base bribes,
  And sell the mighty space of our large honours
  For so much trash as may be graspèd thus?
  I had rather be a dog, and bay the moon,
  Than such a Roman.
CASSIUS.   Brutus, bait not me;
  I'll not endure it. You forget yourself,
  To hedge me in. I am a soldier, I,
  Older in practice, abler than yourself
  To make conditions.
BRUTUS.   Go to; you are not, Cassius.
CASSIUS. I am.

BRUTUS. I say you are not.

CASSIUS. Urge me no more, I shall forget myself;
  Have mind upon your health, tempt me no farther.

BRUTUS. Away, slight man!

CASSIUS. Is't possible?

BRUTUS.   Hear me, for I will speak.
  Must I give way and room to your rash choler?
  Shall I be frighted when a madman stares?

CASSIUS. O ye gods, ye gods! must I endure all this?

BRUTUS. All this! ay, more. Fret till your proud heart break;
  Go show your slaves how choleric you are,
  And make your bondmen tremble. Must I budge?
  Must I observe you? Must I stand and crouch
  Under your testy humour? By the gods,
  You shall digest the venom of your spleen,
  Though it do split you; for, from this day forth,
  I'll use you for my mirth, yea, for my laughter,
  When you are waspish.

CASSIUS.   Is it come to this?

BRUTUS. You say you are a better soldier:
  Let it appear so; make your vaunting true,
  And it shall please me well. For mine own part,
  I shall be glad to learn of noble men.

CASSIUS. You wrong me every way; you wrong me, Brutus;
  I said, an elder soldier, not a better.
  Did I say "better"?

BRUTUS.   If you did, I care not.

CASSIUS. When Caesar liv'd, he durst not thus have mov'd me.

BRUTUS. Peace, peace! you durst not so have tempted him.

CASSIUS. I durst not!

BRUTUS. No.

CASSIUS. What, durst not tempt him!

BRUTUS.   For your life you durst not.

CASSIUS. Do not presume too much upon my love;
  I may do that I shall be sorry for.

BRUTUS. You have done that you should be sorry for.
  There is no terror, Cassius, in your threats,
  For I am arm'd so strong in honesty
  That they pass by me as the idle wind,
  Which I respect not. I did send to you
  For certain sums of gold, which you denied me;
  For I can raise no money by vile means.—
  By heaven, I had rather coin my heart,
  And drop my blood for drachmas, than to wring
  From the hard hands of peasants their vile trash
  By any indirection.—I did send
  To you for gold to pay my legions,

Which you denied me: was that done like Cassius?
Should I have answer'd Caius Cassius so?
When Marcus Brutus grows so covetous,
To lock such rascal counters from his friends,
Be ready, gods, with all your thunderbolts;
Dash him to pieces!

CASSIUS.   I denied you not.

BRUTUS. You did.

CASSIUS. I did not. He was but a fool that brought
My answer back. Brutus hath riv'd my heart.
A friend should bear his friend's infirmities,
But Brutus makes mine greater than they are.

BRUTUS. I do not, till you practice them on me.

CASSIUS. You love me not.

BRUTUS.   I do not like your faults.

CASSIUS. A friendly eye could never see such faults.

BRUTUS. A flatterer's would not, though they do appear
As huge as high Olympus.

CASSIUS. Come, Antony, and young Octavius, come,
Revenge yourselves alone on Cassius,
For Cassius is aweary of the world;
Hated by one he loves; brav'd by his brother;
Check'd like a bondman; all his faults observ'd,
Set in a note-book, learn'd and conn'd by rote
To cast into my teeth. O, I could weep
My spirit from mine eyes! There is my dagger,
And here my naked breast; within, a heart
Dearer than Plutus' mine, richer than gold.
If that thou be'st a Roman, take it forth;
I, that denied thee gold, will give my heart.
Strike, as thou didst at Caesar; for, I know,
When thou didst hate him worst, thou lov'dst him better
Than ever thou lov'dst Cassius.

BRUTUS.   Sheathe your dagger.
Be angry when you will, it shall have scope.
Do what you will, dishonour shall be humour.
O Cassius, you are yokèd with a lamb,
That carries anger as the flint bears fire;
Who, much enforcèd, shows a hasty spark
And straight is cold again.

CASSIUS.   Hath Cassius liv'd
To be but mirth and laughter to his Brutus,
When grief, and blood ill-temper'd, vexeth him?

BRUTUS. When I spoke that, I was ill-temper'd too.

CASSIUS. Do you confess so much? Give me your hand.

BRUTUS. And my heart too!

CASSIUS.   O Brutus!

BRUTUS.   What's the matter?
CASSIUS. Have not you love enough to bear with me,
  When that rash humour which my mother gave me
  Makes me forgetful?
BRUTUS.   Yes, Cassius, and from henceforth,
  When you are over earnest with your Brutus,
  He'll think your mother chides, and leave you so.
                              WILLIAM SHAKESPEARE, *Julius Caesar*

Vocal Pitch

You may have good resonant quality, variety in force, and
good timing, but if you lack variety in inflection or if you
sustain your tones at one key only, your voice will sound monotonous and will carry a minimum of meaning. Many people are
not conscious of lack of variation in their voices. Listen for it in
other voices, and listen to your own voice on a tape recorder.
These exercises will assist you; but, like all exercises, their value
lies in your ability to carry over what you learn into conversation and into performance.

EXERCISES FOR PITCH VARIABILITY

1. Vocalize the vowels, "ah," "oh," "oo," at your optimum
pitch. Keep the throat muscles as relaxed as possible. Now vocalize
the vowels at a higher pitch; then at a lower pitch than your optimum
pitch.
2. Starting with a high level of pitch, practice downward slides
with "ah," "oh," "oo." Stop as soon as you feel strain.
3. Starting with the lowest level of pitch that you can manage
comfortably, vocalize the vowels "ah," "oh," "oo" and slide upward
to the highest pitch you have but without strain.
4. Starting at a low pitch with the vowels "ah," "oh," "oo,"
slide upward as high as you can without strain, and then slide downward again. The effect will be like a siren.
5. Repeat exercise 4, but start at a high pitch, come down, and
go up again.
6. Hum at a high level of pitch, and then sing down to the most
comfortable low tone you can manage. The pattern will be like this:
mmmmmmm
        ah
      ah
       ah
        ah . . .

7. Hum at a high level of pitch and then lower your voice to your optimum pitch by saying "ah"; sustain the "ah." The pattern will be:

mmmmmmm

.
.

.

ah . . . ah . . . ah

8. Repeat exercise 7, but this time see if you can find a pitch a trifle lower than your optimum pitch or the pitch that you most frequently use. Be sure it is a relaxed tone and not strained. If your optimum pitch is too high, as decided by others, this exercise will lower the pitch of your voice. Care must be taken to find the tone with the least strain.

9. Hum at a high level of pitch, and then lower your voice to your optimum pitch by sustaining "ah." Then let your voice slide into a short simple sentence like "My name is Susie Smith." Monotone the sentence. Repeat continually with other sentences. As soon as you find your pitch rising, strike the high "mmmmm" again, and the lower "ah," and then follow with short sentences. The pattern will be:

mmmmm

.
.

a-a-a-ah . . . My name is Susie Smith.

10. Practice the following with as many different kinds of slides as you can:

Oh!	I like her.	Merry Christmas!
Hello.	No, really.	That's my story.
Yes.	You mean it?	Oh, so that's the way it is.
Oh, no!	I can't believe it.	Oh yes, I think so.
Oh, I see.	Strange, isn't he?	That's what you think.

11. Read a paragraph from a children's story, pretending that the class is a group of children between the ages of five and seven years of age.

12. Imitate an Italian, a Frenchman, a Scandinavian, using the sentence, "America is a good land!"

13. Standing behind a screen, imitate a radio artist, using the slides and key peculiar to his speech.

14. Try the following poetry excerpts using first a high key, then a low key. Then try them with many inflections and slides, and then with a monotone. Hear how ridiculous they may sound if you use pitch that is not appropriate to the meaning.

1

A hurry of hoofs in the village street,
A shape in the moonlight, a bulk in the dark,
And beneath, from the pebbles, in passing a spark
Struck out by the steed flying fearless and fleet;
That was all! And yet, through the gloom and the light,
The fate of the nation was riding that night;
And the spark struck out by that steed in his flight,
Kindled the land into flame with its heat.

HENRY WADSWORTH LONGFELLOW, *Paul Revere's Ride*

2

"O, Mary, go and call the cattle home,
    And call the cattle home,
    And call the cattle home,
Across the sands o' Dee!"
The western wind was wild and dark wi' foam,
    And all alone went she.

.   .   .   .

They rowed her in across the rolling foam,
    The cruel crawling foam,
    The cruel crawling foam,
To her grave beside the sea:
And still the boatmen hear her call the cattle home
    Across the sands o' Dee!

CHARLES KINGSLEY, *The Sands of Dee*

3

So live that when thy summons comes to join
The innumerable caravan, which moves
To that mysterious realm, where each shall take
His chamber in the silent halls of death,
Thou go not, like the quarry slave at night,
Scourged to his dungeon, but, sustained and soothed
By an unfaltering trust, approach thy grave
Like one who wraps the drapery of his couch
About him and lies down to pleasant dreams.

WILLIAM CULLEN BRYANT, *Thanatopsis*

4

All the world's a stage,
And all the men and women merely players:
They have their exits, and their entrances;
And one man in his time plays many parts,

His acts being seven stages. At first, the infant,
Mewling and puking in the nurse's arms.
And then, the whining school boy, with his satchel,
And shining morning face, creeping, like a snail,
Unwillingly to school. And then the lover,
Sighing like a furnace, with a woeful ballad
Made to his mistress' eyebrow. Then the soldier,
Full of strange oaths, and bearded like a pard,
Jealous in honor, sudden and quick in quarrel,
Seeking the bubble reputation
Even in the cannon's mouth. And then, the justice,
In fair round belly, with good capon lin'd,
With eye severe, and beard of formal cut,
Full of wise saws and modern instances,
And so he plays his part. The sixth age shifts
Into the lean and slipper'd pantaloon,
With spectacles on nose, and pouch on side;
His youthful hose well sav'd, a world too wide
For his shrunk shank; and his big manly voice,
Turning again toward childish treble, pipes
And whistles in his sound. Last scene of all,
That ends this strange, eventful history,
Is second childishness, and mere oblivion;
Sans teeth, sans eyes, sans taste, sans everything.
WILLIAM SHAKESPEARE, As You Like It

5

I bring fresh showers for the thirsting flowers,
From the seas and the streams;
I bear light shade for the leaves when laid
In their noonday dreams.
From my wings are shaken the dews that waken
The sweet buds every one,
When rocked to rest on their mother's breast,
As she dances about the sun.
I wield the flail of the lashing hail,
And whiten the green plains under,
And then again I dissolve it in rain,
And laugh as I pass in thunder.
PERCY BYSSHE SHELLEY, The Cloud

6

I saw Eternity the other night,
Like a great ring of pure and endless light,
All calm, as it was bright;
And round beneath it, Time, in hours, days, years,
Driven by the spheres,

Like a vast shadow moved; in which the world
And all her train were hurled.
Henry Vaughan, *The World*

7

A sweet disorder in the dress
Kindles in clothes a wantonness;
A lawn about the shoulders thrown
Into a fine distraction;
An erring lace, which here and there
Enthralls the crimson stomacher;
A cuff neglectful, and thereby
Ribands to flow confusedly;
A winning wave, deserving note,
In the tempestuous petticoat;
A careless shoe-string, in whose tie
I see a wild civility,
Do more bewitch me than when art
Is too precise in every part.
Robert Herrick, *Delight in Disorder*

8

Have you heard of the wonderful one-hoss-shay,
That was built in such a logical way
It ran a hundred years to a day,
And then, of a sudden, it—ah, but stay,
I'll tell you what happened without delay,
Scaring the parson into fits,
Frightening people out of their wits,—

.   .   .   .

Now in building chaises, I tell you what,
There is always *somewhere* a weakest spot,—
In hub, tire, felloe, in spring or thill,
In panel, or crossbar, or floor, or sill,
In screw, bolt, thoroughbrace,—lurking still,
Find it somewhere you must and will,—
Above or below, or within or without,—
And that's the reason, beyond a doubt,
A chaise *breaks down*, but doesn't *wear out*.
Oliver Wendell Holmes, *The Deacon's Masterpiece*

9

The barge she sat in, like a burnish'd throne,
Burned on the water: the poop was beaten gold;

Purple the sails, and so perfumed that
The winds were love-sick with them; the oars were silver,
The water which they beat to follow faster
As amorous of their strokes.

WILLIAM SHAKESPEARE, *Antony and Cleopatra*

10

Oh, to be in England,
Now that April's there,
And whoever wakes in England
Sees, some morning, unaware,
That the lowest boughs and the brush-wood sheaf
Round the elm-tree bole are in tiny leaf,
While the chaffinch sings on the orchard bough
In England—now!

ROBERT BROWNING, *Home Thoughts from Abroad*

Articulation

The factors involved in good articulation are always variable, depending mostly on the individual. You should always be concerned not in articulation *per se* but in how articulation lends distinction to your interpretation. Practice may solve some of your articulatory difficulties, especially slovenly speech; but do not strive for the kind of precise speech that robs the literature of its meaning.

ARTICULATORY EXERCISES

1. Practice the following lists of words for differences in sound. Articulate so that each word is distinct without being precise.

Consonants

b — p

buy	— pie	embark	— impart	rib	— rip
baste	— paste	rabid	— rapid	cub	— cup
ban	— pan	harbor	— harping	robe	— rope
bass	— pass	hobbling	— hopping	mob	— mop
bing	— ping	robber	— mopper	nab	— nap
bite	— pipe	babbling	— sapling	probe	— prop
beak	— peak	fabulous	— rapturous	crab	— crap
bath	— path	rabies	— rapier	slab	— slap
beck	— peck	ember	— empty	drab	— drop
bounce	— pounce	probably	— property	sub	— sup

b — m

ban	— man	rub	— rum
ball	— mall	cub	— come
bake	— make	robe	— roam
bad	— mad	dub	— dumb
beet	— meet	rib	— rim
bug	— mug	crab	— cram
butter	— mutter	sub	— some
batter	— matter	tab	— tam
bow	— mow	hub	— hum
batch	— match	drab	— dram

t — d

tuck — duck	fattest — faddist	palate — pallid
toe — dough	metal — medal	meat — mead
tin — din	butter — rudder	meant — mend
time — dime	fitting — fiddling	fright — fried
tear — dare	latter — ladder	late — laid
tank — dank	better — bedding	beat — bead
tart — dart	twitter — twiddle	sent — send
tug — dug	shutter — shudder	great — grade
tire — dire	witless — windlass	chart — chard
ten — den	winter — window	plot — plod

t — th   t — th   t — th

Ted — thread	tease — these	debt — death
too — threw	toes — those	boat — both
toe — throw	ten — then	pat — path
tee — three	time — thine	heart — hearth
tin — thin	tat — that	oat — oath
tie — thigh	toe — though	quote — quoth
team — theme	Thames — them	sheet — sheath
tank — thank	'tis — this	rat — wrath
tingle — think	tear — there	toot — tooth
tick — thick	tusk — thus	welt — wealth

f — v

fine — vine	rifle — rival	fife — five
fast — vast	raffle — ravel	grief — grieve
face — vase	fifer — fiver	safe — save
feel — veal	leafing — leaving	half — halve
ferry — very	reefer — fever	leaf — leave
fan — van	baffle — gavel	waif — waive
fault — vault	effort — ever	strife — strive
few — view	wafer — waiver	belief — believe
fat — vat	briefer — beaver	thief — thieve
famish — vanish	gifted — giver	sheaf — sheave

d — th

den	— then
doze	— those
disk	— this
dance	— than
dough	— though
fodder	— father
ladder	— lather
udder	— other

f — th

fin	— thin
fret	— threat
free	— three
five	— thrive
few	— threw
frank	— thank
fries	— thrice
fickle	— thickly

th — th

that	— thatch
then	— thence
thus	— thrust
thy	— thigh
this	— thistle
though	— thorough
these	— themes
thou	— thousand

v — w

vent	— went
vine	— wine
veer	— we're
vest	— west
vain	— wane
vague	— wake
veered	— weird
verse	— worse
vile	— wile
vacant	— wakened

v — hw

victual	— whittle
vesper	— whisper
vine	— whine
vital	— white
vat	— what
vent	— when
vile	— while
veteran	— whether
vim	— whim
veer	— where

w — hw

watt	— what
wine	— whine
wear	— where
wick	— whisk
witch	— which
wit	— whit
wet	— whet
wail	— whale
wile	— while
weather	— whether

h — hw

hair	— where
hot	— what
heather	— whether
hale	— whale
hen	— when
hither	— whither
help	— whelp
hence	— whence
high	— why
hind	— whine

l — w

let	— wet
light	— wight
line	— wine
leave	— weave
life	— wife
leap	— weep
lit	— wit
lay	— way
leak	— weak
ledge	— wedge

medial l

dollar
scaler
killer
yellow
pillar
swallow
fellow
tallow
mellow
hello

final l

poll	— roll
ball	— bell
call	— gall
peal	— squeal
mole	— maul
stall	— squall
broil	— brawl
heel	— hall
hill	— mill
pile	— pill

gl	sl	pl	fl	cl	bl	tl — bl — kl — dl
glide	sleuth	place	fleece	clash	blow	prattle — freckle
glove	slide	please	fly	climb	blew	bottle — tickle
glossary	slouch	ply	flown	close	black	cattle — crackle
glue	slope	play	flag	clinch	blame	little — tackle
glimmer	slimmer	plaster	flight	cluster	bluster	brittle — heckle
gloaming	sleeve	plane	floss	clover	bloom	hobble — muddle
glade	slack	plant	flake	cling	blush	dabble — middle
glance	slice	pleasant	flock	clock	blight	wabble — cradle
glowing	slant	planning	flinch	clutch	block	cobble — paddle
glamour	slump	plead	flea	clothes	bless	bauble — cuddle

r — w	medial r	final r	
rise — wise	bury	car	queer
raise — weighs	marrow	mar	steer
reeds — weeds	carriage	par	peer
ride — wide	porridge	star	mere
ring — wing	perish	bar	hear
rage — wage	hurrah	dare	tore
rain — wane	marriage	fair	four
rich — witch	carry	swear	lore
rare — wear	terrace	care	chore
roar — wore	hurry	bare	more

dr — tr	pr — br
drain — train	prow — brow
drape — traipse	pry — bribe
drag — trash	press — breath
dram — tram	pray — bray
dread — tread	prime — brine
dress — tress	prig — brig
drive — trite	praying — brain
drift — trick	pride — bride
drink — trinket	prowl — brown
droll — troll	prexy — breathy

tr — thr	kr — gr
tree — three	crew — grew
trash — thrash	crime — grime
troll — throw	crib — grin
trust — thrust	croon — groom
tread — thread	crayon — greyhound
tribe — thrive	crass — grass
true — threw	cream — green
try — thrice	creed — greed
treat — threat	crumb — grub
trot — throttle	crane — grain

k — g

call — gall	stacker — stagger	tuck — tug
cunning — gunning	chicken — chigger	back — bag
crab — grab	beckon — beggar	kick — gig
crow — grow	racking — raggy	pluck — plug
coat — goat	tricky — trigger	pick — pig
cut — gut	bucking — buggy	prick — prig
came — game	sacking — sagging	luck — lug
camel — gamble	lucky — lugging	stack — stag
come — gum	embarking — embargo	buck — bug
confine — gunfire	tacking — tagging	brick — brig

g — ng   n — ng   ng — ng-k

g — ng	n — ng	ng — ng-k
sag — sang	son — sung	wing — wink
bag — bang	sin — sing	rang — rank
lug — lung	pan — pang	ring — rink
gag — gang	thin — thing	fang — flank
tug — tongue	fan — fang	thing — think
log — long	tan — tang	sung — sunk
flag — flung	kin — king	king — kink
hag — hang	ton — tongue	slung — slunk
fag — fang	win — wing	bring — brink
rug — rung	ban — bang	bang — bank

ng — ng-g   k — ng-k   n — ng

ng — ng-g	k — ng-k	n — ng
long — longer	wick — wink	eaten — eating
singer — single	thick — think	bacon — baking
hung — hunger	brick — brink	beaten — beating
wing — mingle	back — bank	rotten — rotting
swing — shingle	tack — tank	taken — taking
strong — stronger	lick — link	loosen — loosing
tang — tangle	kick — kink	proven — proving
fang — fangle	truck — trunk	garden — guarding
ring — finger	black — blank	barren — bearing
rang — wrangle	pick — pink	raven — raving

s — z

sip — zip	tassle — dazzle	race — raise
sink — zinc	tussle — muzzle	price — prize
seal — zeal	hisses — scissors	trace — trays
sue — zoo	hasten — hesitate	lice — lies
sag — zag	passing — peasant	bus — buzz
scissors — zithers	bristle — fizzle	grace — graze
cellar — zealous	racer — razor	fuss — fuzz
scene — zenith	bustling — buzzing	rice — rise
ceiling — zebra	amassment — amazement	mice — maize
sewing — zoning	brassy — brazen	loose — lose

s — sh — tsh

sin	— shin	— chin	mass — mash	— match
sip	— ship	— chip	swiss — swish	— switch
sop	— shop	— chop	muss — mush	— much
seat	— sheet	— cheat	pass — passion	— patch
same	— shame	— chain	lass — lash	— latch
see	— she	— chee	crus — crush	— crutch
sue	— shoe	— chew	crass — crash	— catch
seer	— sheer	— cheer	bass — bash	— batch
seep	— sheep	— cheap	plus — plush	— clutch
sun	— shun	— chum	Russ — rush	— wretch

tsh — dzh		sh — st	shr
Initial	*Medial and Final*	*Final*	*Initial*

choke	— joke	rich	— ridge	lash — last	shrill
cheap	— jeep	such	— smudge	crush — crust	shrimp
chunk	— junk	much	— fudge	mush — must	shrub
chest	— jest	match	— magic	mash — mast	shriek
chin	— gin	pitch	— pigeon	cash — cast	shrivel
chump	— jump	crutch	— drudge	rush — rust	shroud
chug	— jug	latch	— ledge	fish — fist	shrewd
cheer	— jeer	hatch	— hedge	gush — gust	shred
choose	— juice	lunch	— lunge	lush — lust	shrink
chilled	— jilt	patch	— pageant	thrush — thrust	shrew

s — z — sh — zh — dzh

precious treasure	skilled tacticians	casual persuasion
anxious dietician	shell-shocked soldiers	unusual composure
delicious sherbets	rash arrangements	crushing invasion
vicious expressions	shady assertions	soil erosion
audience apprecia-tion	shark-infested ocean	additional expan-sions
harassed pediatri-cians	shiftless civiliza-tion	pleasurable admo-nitions

st	str	sl	spl	sp	spr
stove	stream	slope	splash	special	spring
stay	strive	slide	spleen	spine	sprite
stop	stroke	slowly	splice	space	sprig
story	street	slouchy	split	spicy	sprout
star	strut	slice	splint	speak	spray
step	stray	slippery	splendor	spell	sprinkle
stitch	strike	sliver	splurge	spur	spread
steep	strength	sleuth	splinter	spar	sprawl

sk	skr	skw	sm	sn	sw
skip	scream	squeal	smell	snail	swing
scum	scroll	squeeze	small	snoop	swipe
scope	scribe	square	smoke	snow	swift
scan	scrub	squint	smoulder	sniff	swollen
scold	scratch	squeaky	smith	sneeze	sweep
scanty	scrawl	squelch	smite	snort	swish
scorch	script	squash	smack	sneer	switch
skate	scrape	squad	smelt	snub	swim

ts — ks

bets	— becks
beats	— beaks
hats	— hacks
fetes	— fakes
pots	— pox
dots	— docks
pats	— packs
debts	— decks
cuts	— crux
blots	— blocks

sts — sks

masts	— masks
wrists	— risks
tastes	— tasks
bastes	— basks
fists	— frisks
casts	— casks
tests	— desks
twists	— twisks
crests	— whisks
rusts	— husks

ps — ks

whips	— wicks
tips	— ticks
steps	— sticks
stops	— stocks
traps	— tracks
raps	— racks
lops	— locks
taps	— tacks
mops	— mocks
saps	— sacks

dz — ts

heeds	— heats
toads	— totes
treads	— tests
threads	— threats
reds	— rests
meads	— meets
breads	— breasts
rides	— rites
bides	— bites
braids	— baits

st

creased
voiced
pronounced
expressed
missed
caressed
passed
last
most
crossed

sht

pushed
squashed
mashed
splashed
washed
cashed
smashed
wished
lashed
rushed

bd	gd	ld	vd	zd
bobbed	begged	mailed	dived	teased
grabbed	hugged	billed	heaved	seized
sobbed	tagged	cold	believed	buzzed
robed	bagged	held	raved	raised
scrubbed	tugged	mold	loved	oozed
robbed	pegged	called	shaved	roused
mobbed	sagged	crawled	served	sneezed
swabbed	bragged	scold	moved	paused
absorbed	clogged	spilled	arrived	closed
webbed	plugged	bawled	shoved	poised

ft	nt	tl — tn	
laughed	want	bottle	— button
coughed	sent	little	— lenten
leafed	punt	whittle	— written
soft	paint	kettle	— cotton
staffed	joint	battle	— batten
scoffed	slant	brittle	— Briton
puffed	quaint	thistle	— listen
tuft	haunt	throttle	— rotten
golfed	point	mistle	— mitten
loft	hunt	treadle	— threaten

Vowels

ĭ — ĕ — ă			ă — ŭ — ĭ			ĭ — ĕ — ô		
pin	— pen	— pan	tack	— tuck	— tick	bill	— bell	— ball
sit	— set	— sat	ham	— hum	— him	will	— well	— wall
lid	— led	— lad	bag	— bug	— big	hilt	— held	— halt
pick	— peck	— pack	fan	— fun	— fin	nit	— net	— nought
rid	— red	— rat	bat	— but	— bit	fill	— fell	— fall
hid	— head	— had	dad	— dud	— did	bit	— bet	— bought
him	— hem	— ham	lack	— luck	— lick	till	— tell	— tall
pit	— pet	— pat	span	— spun	— spin	kit	— kettle	— caught

ŏ — ă — ŭ			o͝o — ŭ — ŏ		
cot	— cat	— cut	put	— putt	— pot
pod	— pad	— puddle	book	— buck	— block
hot	— hat	— hut	took	— tuck	— tock
shock	— shack	— shuck	look	— luck	— lock
cop	— cap	— cup	stood	— stud	— stock
sod	— sad	— suds	could	— cud	— clod
rot	— rat	— rut	crooks	— crux	— crocks
top	— tap	— tuft	shook	— shuck	— shock
pot	— pat	— putt	nook	— knuckle	— knock
mop	— map	— muff	cook	— cluck	— clock

ă — ŏ — ô — ŭ				ā — ĕ — ă		
cat	— cot	— caught	— cut	tale	— tell	— tally
tat	— tot	— taught	— tut	mate	— met	— mat
rat	— rot	— wrought	— rut	laid	— led	— lad
gnat	— not	— naught	— nut	bait	— bet	— bat
sad	— sod	— sawed	— suds	bake	— beck	— back
hack	— hock	— hawk	— hung	pain	— pen	— pan
tack	— tock	— talk	— tuck	rain	— wren	— ran
pad	— pod	— pawed	— puddle	main	— men	— man

ĕ — ē — ĭ — ŭ

net	— neat	— nit	— nut
bet	— beat	— bit	— but
pep	— peep	— pip	— pup
met	— meat	— mitten	— mutton
debt	— deed	— did	— dud
head	— heed	— hid	— huddle
sweat	— sweet	— swim	— swum
bread	— breed	— bid	— bud

ī — ŏ — ē

pipe	— pop	— peep
like	— lock	— leak
hide	— hod	— heed
tried	— trod	— treed
side	— sod	— seed
night	— not	— neat
wine	— wan	— ween
ride	— rod	— reed

ĭ — ô — oi — ā

ill	— all	— oil	— ale
till	— tall	— toil	— tail
kill	— call	— coil	— kale
spill	— sprawl	— spoil	— spade
bill	— ball	— boil	— bale
hill	— hall	— Hoyle	— hail
fill	— fall	— foil	— fail
pill	— pall	— point	— pale

û — ä — ē

purr	— par	— peer
fur	— far	— fear
spur	— spar	— spear
stir	— star	— steer
yearn	— yarn	— year
burn	— barn	— beard
cur	— car	— career
burr	— bar	— beer

ō — ô — o͝o

coal	— call	— could
bowl	— bawl	— bull
pole	— pall	— pull
loan	— lawn	— look
boat	— bought	— book
shoal	— shawl	— should
hold	— hauled	— hood
know	— gnaw	— nook

ŏ — ou

crop	— crowd
shot	— shout
rot	— rout
trot	— trout
dot	— doubt
pot	— pout
spot	— spout
got	— gout

ŏ — ō — o͞o

cod	— code	— cooed
shod	— showed	— shooed
rot	— wrote	— root
calm	— cold	— cool
cot	— coat	— coot
palm	— poll	— pool
not	— note	— nude
rod	— road	— rude

o͞o — ou

prude	— proud
croon	— crown
dune	— down
tune	— town
broom	— brown
moon	— noun
mousse	— mouse
loose	— louse

o͞o — u

food	— feud
pooh	— pew
coo	— cue
whose	— hues
moo	— mew
flu	— few
booty	— beauty
who	— hew

o͞o — ŭ

mood	— mud
noon	— nun
food	— flood
shoot	— shut
tube	— tub
soon	— sun
boot	— but
root	— rut

o͝o — o͞o

foot	— food
pull	— pool
full	— fool
look	— Luke
could	— cooed
should	— shooed
stood	— stoop
good	— glued

2. The following selections will afford you good practice in many sounds. Remember that each sound is usually assimilated with others. Do not try for precise articulation but for careful and easy speech.

1

Don't you love to lie and listen,
Listen to the rain,

And its little patter, patter,
And its tiny clatter, clatter,
And its silvery spatter, spatter
On the roof and on the pane?

CLINTON SCOLLARD, *The Rain*

2

Fib and Nib, and Pinck and Pin,
Tick and Quick, and Jill and Jim,
Tit and Nit, and Wap and Win,
The train that wait upon her.

WILLIAM SHAKESPEARE, *Midsummer Night's Dream*

3

To sit in solemn silence in a dull dark dock,
In a pestilential prison, with a life-long lock,
Awaiting the sensation of a short, sharp shock,
From a cheap and chippy chopper on a big black block!
A big, black block, a short, sharp shock,
From a cheap and chippy chopper on a big black block!

W. S. GILBERT, *The Mikado*

4

The Lord is my shepherd; I shall not want.
He maketh me to lie down in green pastures: he leadeth me beside
the still waters.
He restoreth my soul: he leadeth me in the paths of righteousness for
his name's sake.
Yea, though I walk through the valley of the shadow of death, I will
fear no evil: for thou art with me; thy rod and thy staff they
comfort me.
Thou preparest a table before me in the presence of mine enemies:
thou anointest my head with oil; my cup runneth over.
Surely goodness and mercy shall follow me all the days of my life:
and I will dwell in the house of the Lord for ever.

Psalms 23

5

ON A STILE[9]

With lavender sachet,
And ruffles of lace,
And a yellow poke bonnet
Cupping her face,

[9] From *Contemporary Verse* (August, 1923), p. 200. Reprinted by permission of the publishers.

With pantalets peeping
Demurely below
A rustle of cretonne
Trim ankles to show;
With rosette of pansies
Upon her slim wrist,
And lips made of bud pinks
That ought to be kissed,
Cicily wandered
The asters among,
And pouted, "I'm tired
Of being so young!"
So she glanced cautiously
Round and about,
Lest Aunt Priscilla
Might be walking out.
Then she lifted her hoops
And she scampered a mile
'Til she came to the southerly
Side of a stile.

With coat-tails a-hanging
Sable and long,
With ivory hand leaning
On oaken cane strong,
And snug kerchief silkily
Muffling a cough,
And silver hair handsome
If most were not off;
With knees crook'd and foot slow
But eye bright on tree
Where high in the top the best
Nuts used to be,
Captain Q. down the lane
Ruefully strolled,
And muttered, "I'm tired
Of being so old!"
So peering craftily
This way and that,
Lest Daughter was out
To see what he was at,
He flipped his stout cane
And he frisked him a mile,
'Til he came to the northerly
Side of a stile.

And Cicily climbed, and Captain Q. climbed,
And they sat side by side up on high!
The sun grew merry, the wind grew mild,
And a lark laughed out in the sky.

> Captain Q. sat him tight,
> Captain Q. sat him bold,
> And shouted, "I'm tired
> Of being so old!"
> "Tra la! I'm tired
> Of being so young!"
> Said C. And they swung
> And they swung and they swung!
>
> MARTHA OSTENSO

6

First, we polish off some batches
Of political despatches,
   And foreign politicians circumvent:
Then, if business isn't heavy,
We may hold a Royal *levée*,
   Or ratify some Acts of Parliament.
Then we probably review the household troops—
With the usual "Shalloo humps!" and "Shalloo hoops!"
Or receive with ceremonial and state
An interesting Eastern potentate.
   After that we generally
   Go and dress our private *valet*—
(It's a rather nervous duty—he's a touchy little man)—
   Write some letters literary
   For our private secretary—
He is shaky in his spelling, so we help him if we can.
   Then, in view of cravings inner,
   We go down and order dinner;
Then we polish the Regalia and the Coronation Plate—
   Spend an hour in titivating
   All our Gentlemen-in-Waiting;
Or we run on little errands for the Ministers of State. . . .

   Oh, philosophers may sing
   Of the troubles of a King
But of pleasures there are many and of worries there are none;
   And the culminating pleasure
   That we treasure beyond measure
Is the gratifying feeling that our duty has been done!

W. S. GILBERT, *The Gondoliers*

7

The Pobble who has no toes
  Had once as many as we;
When they said, "Some day you may lose them all,"
  He replied, "Fish fiddle de-dee!"
And his Aunt Jobiska made him drink
Lavendar water tinged with pink;
For she said, "The World in general knows
There's nothing so good for a Pobble's toes!"

The Pobble who has no toes,
  Swam across the Bristol Channel;
But before he set out he wrapped his nose
  In a piece of scarlet flannel.
For his Aunt Jobiska said, "No harm
Can come to his toes if his nose is warm;
And it's perfectly known that a Pobble's toes
Are safe—provided he minds his nose."

The Pobble swam fast and well,
  And when boats or ships came near him,
He tinkledy-binkledy-wrinkled a bell
  So that all the world could hear him.
And all the Sailors and Admirals cried,
When they saw him nearing the further side,
"He has gone to fish, for his Aunt Jobiska's
Runcible Cat with crimson whiskers!"
                    EDWARD LEAR, *The Pobble Who Has No Toes*

8

A CERTAIN YOUNG LADY

There's a certain young lady,
Who's just in her hey-day,
  And full of all mischief, I ween;
    So teasing! so pleasing!
    Capricious! delicious!
And you know very well whom I mean.

With an eye dark as night,
Yet than noonday more bright,
  Was ever a black eye so keen?
    It can thrill with a glance,
    With a beam can entrance,
And you know very well whom I mean.

With a stately step—such as
You'd expect in a duchess—
  And a brow might distinguish a queen,
   With a mighty proud air,
   That says "Touch me who dare,"
And you know very well whom I mean.

With a toss of the head
That strikes one dead,
  But a smile to revive one again;
   That toss so appalling!
   That smile so enthralling!
And you know very well whom I mean.

Confound her! de'il take her!—
A cruel heart-breaker—
  But hold! see that smile so serene.
   God love her! God bless her!
   May nothing distress her!
And you know very well whom I mean.

Heaven help the adorer
Who happens to bore her,
  The lover who wakens her spleen;
   But too blest for a sinner
   Is he who shall win her,
And you know very well whom I mean.
                WASHINGTON IRVING

9

PETR. Why, here's no crab; and therefore look not sour.
KATH. There is, there is.
PETR. Then show it me.
KATH. Had I a glass, I would.
PETR. What, you mean my face?
KATH. Well aim'd of such a young one.
PETR. Now, by Saint George, I am too young for you.
KATH. Yet you are wither'd.
PETR. 'Tis with cares.
KATH. I care not.
PETR. Nay, hear you, Kate. In sooth you 'scape not so.
KATH. I chafe you, if I tarry. Let me go.
PETR. No, not a whit; I find you passing gentle.
  'Twas told me you were rough and coy and sullen,
  And now I find report a very liar;
  For thou art pleasant, gamesome, passing courteous,
  But slow in speech, yet sweet as spring-time flowers.

Thou canst not frown, thou canst not look askance,
Nor bite the lip, as angry wenches will;
Nor hast thou pleasure to be cross and talk;
But thou with mildness entertain'st thy wooers,
With gentle conference, soft and affable.
Why does the world report that Kate doth limp?
O slanderous world! Kate, like the hazel-twig,
Is straight and slender, and as brown in hue
As hazel nuts and sweeter than the kernels.
O, let me see thee walk. Thou dost not halt.

KATH. Go, fool, and whom thou keep'st command.

PETR. Did ever Dian so become a grove
As Kate this chamber with her princely gait?
O, be thou Dian, and let her be Kate;
And then let Kate be chaste and Dian sportful!

KATH. Where did you study all this goodly speech?

PETR. It is extempore, from my mother-wit.

KATH. A witty mother! witless else her son.

PETR. Am I not wise?

KATH. Yes: keep you warm.

PETR. Marry, so I mean, sweet Katherine, in thy bed.
And therefore, setting all this chat aside,
Thus in plain terms. Your father hath consented
That you shall be my wife; your dowry 'greed on;
And, will you, nill you, I will marry you.
Now, Kate, I am a husband for your turn;
For, by this light, whereby I see thy beauty,
Thy beauty, that doth make me like thee well,
Thou must be married to no man but me;
For I am he am born to tame you, Kate,
And bring you from a wild Kate to a Kate
Comformable as other household Kates.

        WILLIAM SHAKESPEARE, *The Taming of the Shrew*

10

UP AT A VILLA—DOWN IN THE CITY

(As distinguished by an Italian person of quality)

Had I but plenty of money, money enough and to spare,
The house for me, no doubt, were a house in the city-square.
Ah, such a life, such a life, as one leads at the window there!

Something to see, by Bacchus, something to hear, at least!
There, the whole day long, one's life is a perfect feast;
While up at a villa one lives, I maintain it, no more than a beast.

Well, now, look at our villa! stuck like the horn of a bull
Just on a mountain-edge as bare as the creature's skull,
Save a mere shag of a bush with hardly a leaf to pull!
—I scratch my own, sometimes, to see if the hair's turned wool.

But the city, oh, the city—the square with the houses! Why?
They are stone-faced, white as a curd, there's something to take the
    eye!
Houses in four straight lines, not a single front awry!
You watch who crosses and gossips, who saunters, who hurries by:
Green blinds, as a matter of course, to draw when the sun gets high;
And the shops with fanciful signs which are painted properly.

What of a villa? Though winter be over in March by rights,
'Tis May perhaps ere the snow shall have withered well off the
    heights:
You've the brown ploughed land before, where the oxen steam and
    wheeze,
And the hills over-smoked behind by the faint gray olive-trees.

Is it better in May, I ask you? You've summer all at once;
In a day he leaps complete with a few strong April suns.
'Mid the sharp short emerald wheat, scarce risen three fingers well,
The wild tulip, at end of its tube, blows out its great red bell
Like a thin clear bubble of blood, for the children to pick and sell.

Is it ever hot in the square? There's a fountain to spout and splash!
In the shade it sings and springs; in the shine such foam-bows flash
On the horses with curling fish-tails, that prance and paddle and pash
Round the lady atop in her conch—fifty gazers do not abash,
Tho' all that she wears is some weeds round her waist in a sort of
    sash.

All the year long at the villa, nothing to see though you linger,
Except yon cypress that points like death's lean lifted forefinger.
Some think fireflies pretty, when they mix i' the corn and mingle,
Or thrid the stinking hemp till the stalks of it seem a-tingle.
Late August or early September, the stunning cicala is shrill,
And the bees keep their tiresome whine round the resinous firs on the
    hill.
Enough of the seasons,—I spare you the months of the fever and chill.

Ere you open your eyes in the city, the blessed church-bells begin:
No sooner the bells leave off, than the diligence rattles in;
You get the pick of the news, and it costs you never a pin.
By and by there's the travelling doctor gives pills, lets blood, draws
    teeth;
Or the Pulcinello-trumpet breaks up the market beneath.

At the post-office such a scene-picture—the new play, piping hot!
And a notice how, only this morning, three liberal thieves were shot.
Above it, behold the Archbishop's most fatherly of rebukes,
And beneath, with his crown and his lion, some little new law of the
    Duke's!
Or a sonnet with flowery marge, to the Reverend Don So-and-so
Who is Dante, Boccaccio, Petrarca, St. Jerome, and Cicero,
"And moreover," (the sonnet goes rhyming), "the skirts of St. Paul
    has reached,
Having preached us those six Lent-lectures more unctuous than ever
    he preached."
Noon strikes,—here sweep the procession! our lady borne smiling and
    smart
With a pink gauze gown all spangles, and seven swords stuck in her
    heart!
Bang—whang—whang, goes the drum, *tootle-te-tootle* the fife;
No keeping one's haunches still: it's the greatest pleasure in life.

But bless you, it's dear—it's dear! fowls, wine, at double the rate.
They have clapped a new tax upon salt, and what oil pays passing the
    gate
It's a horror to think of. And so, the villa for me, not the city!
Beggars can scarcely be choosers: but still—ah, the pity, the pity!
Look, two and two go the priests, then the monks with cowls and
    sandals,
And the penitents dressed in white skirts, a-holding the yellow can-
    dles.
One, he carries a flag up straight, and another a cross with handles,
And the Duke's guard brings up the rear, for the better prevention of
    scandals.
Bang—whang—whang, goes the drum, *tootle-te-tootle* the fife.
Oh, a day in the city-square, there is no such pleasure in life!

                                   Robert Browning

11

I believe we can nowhere find a better type of a perfectly free
creature than in the common house-fly. Nor free only, but brave; and
irreverent to a degree which I think no human republican could by
any philosophy exalt himself to. There is no courtesy in him; he does
not care whether it is a king or a clown whom he teases; and in every
step of his swift, mechanical march, and in every pause of his resolute
observation, there is one and the same expression of perfect egotism,
perfect independence and self-confidence, and conviction of the
world's having been made for flies. Strike at him with your hand; and
to him, the mechanical fact and external aspect of the matter is, what
to you it would be, if an acre of red clay, ten feet thick, tore itself up
from the ground in one massive field, hovered over you in the air for

a second, and came crashing down with an aim. That is the external aspect of it; the inner aspect, to his fly's mind, is of a quite natural and unimportant occurrence—one of the momentary conditions of his active life. He steps out of the way of your hand, and alights on the back of it. You cannot terrify him, nor govern him, nor persuade him, nor convince him. He has his own positive opinion on matters; not an unwise one, usually, for his own ends; and will ask no advice of yours. He has no work to do—no tyrannical instinct to obey. The earthworm has his diggings; the bee her gathering and building; the spider her cunning network; the ant her treasury and accounts. All these are comparatively slaves, or people of vulgar business. But your fly, free in the air, free in the chamber—a black incarnation of caprice —wandering, investigating, flitting, flirting, feasting at his will, with rich variety of choice in feast, from the heaped sweets of the grocer's window to those of the butcher's back-yard, and from the galled place on your cab-horse's back to the brown spot in the road, from which, as the hoof disturbs him, he rises with angry republican buzz—what freedom is like this?

JOHN RUSKIN, *The Cestus of Aglaia*, VI

12

Extreme *busyness*, whether at school or college, kirk or market, is a symptom of deficient vitality; and a faculty for idleness implies a catholic appetite and a strong sense of personal identity. There is a sort of dead-alive, hackneyed people about, who are scarcely conscious of living except in the exercise of some conventional occupation. Bring these fellows into the country, or set them aboard ship, and you will see how they pine for their desk or their study. They have no curiosity; they cannot give themselves over to random provocations; they do not take pleasure in the exercise of their faculties for its own sake; and unless Necessity lays about them with a stick, they will not even stand still. It is no good speaking to such folk: they *cannot* be idle, their nature is not generous enough; and they pass those hours in a sort of coma, which are not dedicated to furious moiling in the gold-mill. When they do not require to go to the office, when they are not hungry and have no mind to drink, the whole breathing world is a blank to them. If they have to wait an hour or so for a train, they fall into a stupid trance with their eyes open. To see them you would suppose there was nothing to look at and no one to speak with; you would imagine they were paralyzed or alienated; and yet very possibly they are hard workers in their own way, and have good eyesight for a flaw in a deed or a turn of the market. They have been to school and college, but all the time they had their eye on the medal; they have gone about in the world and mixed with clever people, but all the time they were thinking of their own affairs.

ROBERT LOUIS STEVENSON, *An Apology for Idlers*

INDEX OF NAMES

INDEX OF SELECTIONS

SUBJECT INDEX

Abandon, 39
Acting, impersonation and interpretation, 6
Allusions, 185
Announcer, voice of radio, 567
Aptitudes, in television, 599
Art:
  artfulness in, 25
  artifice in, 27
  conceals its artistry, 28
  definition of, 25
  for art's sake, 28
  interpretation as an, 3, 24
Articulation:
  improvement, 602
  in radio interpretation, 564
Articulators:
  structure of, 243
  vegetative function of, 244
Attack, forms of, 304
Author:
  character and philosophy, 47
  developmental form, 96
  literary form, 48, 87
  meaning, 136
  motivation, 76
  theme, 48, 96

Ballad, 88
  folk, 88
  literary, 89
Bodily action:
  control of, 38
  in radio interpretation, 564
  meaning through, 213
  or movement, 213
Bodily rhythm, 223, 224, 225
Breathing:
  patterns and phrasing, 169
  process, 248
  structure, 247
Broadcasting:
  control in, 559
  mike in, 559

technique in, 565
voice control in, 565

Cavalier poets, 48
Character. See Author
Choral interpretation, 510:
  director of, 523
  finding the meaning for, 522
  response in, 515; see also Response
  selection of literature for, 521
  training the ear for, 524
  values in, 514
Climax, 325
Comedy. See Voice
Commentator. See Voice
Complex tones, 253
Contrasting ideas, 152
Control:
  in interpretation, 31
  in radio interpretation, 524
  of body, 38
  of emotions, 34
  of meaning, 33
  of voice, 40
  through personality and magnetism, 36
Co-ordination:
  and economy of effort, 222
  and empathy, 217
  and rhythm, 223
  and total bodily response, 218

Director:
  in choral interpretation, 523
  in radio, 598-599
  in television, 598-599
Drama. See Voice

Ear training, 391, 477, 512, 514, 521, 524
Economy of effort. See Co-ordination
Egocentricity, in reading, 15
Elegy, 91

673